"So many times in my work as an astrologer the thought has occurred to me that if we could use the techniques of astrology for children, the world may quickly evolve into a far better place. Now a new book on this topic exists. This treatise by Gloria Star deals with innumerable aspects of astrology which address this consideration.

Gloria provides a comprehensive coverage of astrological bases geared at providing those dealing with little adults with perspective and insight. Given that these procedures are used and applied to the development of today's children, tomorrow's adults have the potential for better actualization personally, and can contribute with clarity and purpose.

This work is long awaited. Gloria's effort can be considered a major step forward in the evolution of astrology. I trust that you, too, will read these pages with a review of your own childhood projected in front of you. Thus, this book serves us adults in understanding our childhood reactions.

May I encourage you to read on . . . for yourself, for the childhood legacy of the world, and for the betterment of the planet itself."

—Philip Sedgwick
Astrologer, Author, Lecturer

"*Optimum Child* is an astrological handbook for parents which is chock-full of ways to help you nurture your child's development. Taking the viewpoint of astrology, Ms. Star reminds us that, from the moment of birth, each child must be treated as a unique and special being."

—Lauren Carlile Bradway, Ph.D.
Director, Helping Children Grow

About The Author

Gloria Star has a lifelong goal of helping others use astrology as a tool for self-awareness and positive personal growth. She has been pursuing this goal as a professional astrological counselor since 1974. Her unique approach to this ancient art includes principles and techniques drawn from many areas: gestalt psychology, psychosynthesis, psychodrama, holistic health, creative visualization, yoga, meditation and extensive metaphysical studies.

Gloria has given well-received lectures at several international astrology conferences, and regularly lectures and does workshops for astrology groups across the U.S. She is the Oklahoma Coordinator for AFAN, President of the Oklahoma Chapter of NCGR, and a member of AFA.

Gloria is the mother of two children, Taletha and Christopher. She lives in Norman, Oklahoma, where she owns and operates Astra Astrological Services. She enjoys improvising New Age music on piano, as well as singing.

To Write to the Author

We cannot guarantee that every letter written to the author can be answered, but all will be forwarded. Both the author and the publisher appreciate hearing from readers, learning of your enjoyment and benefit from this book. Llewellyn also publishes a bi-monthly news magazine with news and reviews of practical esoteric studies and articles helpful to the student, and some readers' questions and comments to the author may be answered through this magazine's columns if permission to do so is included in the original letter. The author sometimes participates in seminars and workshops, and dates and places are announced in *The Llewellyn New Times*. To write to the author, or to ask a question, write to:

Gloria Star
c/o THE LLEWELLYN NEW TIMES
P.O. Box 64383-740, St. Paul, MN 55164-0383, U.S.A.

Please enclose a self-addressed, stamped envelope for reply, or $1.00 to cover costs.

THE LLEWELLYN MODERN ASTROLOGY LIBRARY

Books for the *Leading Edge* of practical and applied astrology as we move toward the culmination of the 20th century.

This is not speculative astrology, nor astrology so esoteric as to have little practical application in meeting the needs of people in these critical times. Yet, these books go far beyond the meaning of "practicality" as seen prior to the 1980's. Our needs are spiritual as well as mundane, planetary as well as particular, evolutionary as well as progressive. Astrology grows with the times, and our times make heavy demands upon Intelligence and Wisdom.

The authors are all professional astrologers drawing from their own practice and knowledge of historical persons and events, demonstrating proof of their conclusions with the horoscopes of real people in real situations.

Modern Astrology relates the individual person in the Universe in which he/she lives, not as a passive victim of alien forces, but as an active participant in an environment expanded to the breadth *and depth* of the Cosmos. We are not alone, and our responsibilities are infinite.

The horoscope is both a measure and a guide to personal movement—seeing every act undertaken, every decision made, every event, as *time dynamic*: with effects that move through the many dimensions of space and levels of consciousness in fulfillment of Will and Purpose. Every act becomes an act of Will, for we extend our awareness to consequences reaching to the ends of time and space.

This is astrology supremely important to this unique period in human history, when Pluto transits through Scorpio, and Neptune through Capricorn, and the books in this series are intended to provide insight into the critical needs and the critical decisions that must be made.

These books, too, are "active agents," bringing to the reader knowledge which will liberate the higher forces inside each person to the end that we may fulfill that for which we were intended.

—Carl Llewellyn Weschcke

Tapes and Videos by Gloria Star

Videos

Predictions '88
The Signs of the Zodiac

Forthcoming Video

The Optimum Child

Tape Sets

Astrology Level 1 (tape set and workbook)
Astrology of the Soul
Child Guidance Through Astrology
Applied Astrology: In-depth Chart Analysis, Part I
Applied Astrology: Progressions and Transits, Part II

Llewellyn's Modern Astrology Library Series

OPTIMUM CHILD

Developing Your Child's Fullest Potential Through Astrology

Gloria Star

1987
Llewellyn Publications
St. Paul, Minnesota, 55164-0383, U.S.A.

International Standard Book Number: 0-87542-740-5
Library of Congress Catalog Number: 87-45745

First Edition, 1987
First Printing, 1987

Library of Congress Cataloging-in-Publication Data

Star, Gloria, 1948-
The optimum child.

(Llewellyn's modern astrology series)
1. Astrology and child development. I. Title.
II. Series.
BF1729.C43S7 1987 133.5'86491 87-45745
ISBN 0-87542-740-5

Cover Painting: David Egge
Horoscope Blanks and Tables: adapted from *Heaven Knows What*, Grant Lewi
Book Design: Terry Buske

Produced by Llewellyn Publications
Typography and Art property of Chester-Kent, Inc.

Published by
LLEWELLYN PUBLICATIONS
A Division of Chester-Kent, Inc.
P.O. Box 64383
St. Paul, MN 55164-0383, U.S.A.

Printed in the United States of America

Dedication

**To my children,
Taletha and Christopher**

Acknowledgements

This book has resulted from the efforts of many individuals. I extend love and gratitude to my husband, Benjamin, for his support, encouragement and meticulous editing of the manuscript. To my children, I owe much of the inspiration for this book.

There have been many teachers who have given me not only information, but guidelines to formulate my own inner understanding of this remarkable tool. To my friend and confidant Stephane, whose initial support led me to seriously explore astrology (we shared many Saturdays of study), I offer my endless gratitude. For those astrologers who have shared their knowledge and skill at astrological conferences I have had the privilege of attending over the last fifteen years, thank you. I am especially grateful to Noel Tyl, Doris Hebel, Liz Greene, Stephen Arroyo, Alan Oken, Jeff Green, Buz Myers, Philip Sedgwick and Raymond Merriman for their penetrating insights into astrology.

To the staff at Llewellyn, especially to Terry Buske and Phyllis Galde, thank you. You have made this endeavor one of joy! Special thanks are also due to Mr. Carl Llewellyn Weschcke for accepting this manuscript for publication and for encouraging me to continue writing.

I also want to express gratitude to you, my clients, students and friends who have openly shared your lives with me through your astrological charts. This sharing helps us each to grow into true wholeness. Our encounters are a constant source of joy and inspiration to me.

And to the Universal Power which unites, guides and inspires us all, thank You.

Namaste

Contents

Introduction

When we look back through history, we realize that great changes occur in new eras. The beginnings of new eras are always key times, and are usually marked by a rapid acceleration in the development of human consciousness.

This heightened awareness is helping us gain a new appreciation for our children. The children are the promise; we are the guides who help them fulfill it.

In my practice as a professional astrologer, I see a wide spectrum of individuals with diverse needs and a variety of life experiences. Yet all are seeking to find themselves. So many of my clients openly wish that they had experienced a different childhood or had more understanding parents. Underlying those wishes is a desire for self-acceptance.

Parents or teachers with greater awareness and sensitivity could certainly have provided a stronger base for many of us. Yet humanity's spiritual evolution is just now reaching the point where we are discovering significantly better ways of relating to children.

Most astrology books are intended to illumine our understanding of ourselves as adults. But our lives do not begin in adulthood: our learning and experience of life begins at the moment of our first breath.

This book approaches astrology differently. A child's needs develop *dynamically*, so our approach to astrology in childhood must encompass this dynamic development. A child whose parents, guides and teachers give him/her insights into his/her true identity will have a greater range of choices. His/her identity will be a true, creative expression of what s/he really is.

Imagine for a moment the incredible world we would live in if we could learn to live up to the optimum potentials we had as children. . . .

This book is for the child in all of us. As I was writing *Optimum Child*, I found the parts of me that were still a hurt, insecure little girl being healed. Recognizing myself and accepting my *real* needs is helping me to become a more complete woman. In all the years I have studied astrology, I am continually amazed at how much more there is to know!

If you are a new student of astrology, this book is ideal. *It assumes no prior knowledge of the subject of astrology,* and presents each topic clearly, in a straightforward manner, and with a minimum of mumbo-jumbo. You will learn all the fundamentals necessary to comprehend the basics of this fascinating subject.

If you are a parent, you will find a wealth of new insights into your child. This understanding will help you cope with your child's particular needs and demands. Study your own astrological chart as well. Remember the child you once were.

If you are a practicing astrologer, you will find *Optimum Child's* wholistic approach to interpretation an excellent way to integrate the energies in the chart. In this book, we look at the child's various levels of development and apply the astrological factors accordingly.

I was compelled to write this book by a deep sense that the world needs to help its children become who they *really* are. There are many facets of the Self which must be acknowledged. Each child has his/her own unique physical strengths and limitations, as well as a special pattern of emotional needs. We are also interested in helping the child develop the intellect in a way that will be most beneficial to him/her. Each child is also working toward a particular spiritual evolution. The horoscope is our guide to these physical, emotional, intellectual and spiritual needs.

By purposefully examining these basic levels of need in the astrological profile, we can help the child become more complete. This knowledge will enable the child to begin fulfilling his/her potentials and start on the path to truly becoming an Optimum Child.

The onset the Age of Aquarius offers us all the opportunity to move forward and upward in our growth. So many people are despairing about the future of humanity. They let their fears overshadow their dreams of a positive tomorrow. But that tomorrow is *now*. We are witnessing the birth of the children of this New Age. They will lay the foundations for a phenomenal future.

I am so hopeful for that future, and am overjoyed to be here to see it beginning. Join me in giving light, hope and love to these magnificent children. Heal yourself by nurturing these young ones. Together we *will* make a difference!

Gloria Star

Chapter One

WHY ASTROLOGY?

We all begin our lives in the same way: as small infants growing rapidly into children. At the moment we are born, we begin to express ourselves, experience our needs and interact with our environment.

This moment is precious, and, for astrologers, important. For it is at the moment of that first breath, when we become dependent upon the environment of the physical plane to sustain our lives, that we set the astrological pattern known as the horoscope. This word, which originally meant "to look at the hour," has come to refer to the circular chart used in astrology.

Mankind has used this tool for thousands of years, yet our overall understanding of its symbols continues to expand as we gain a deeper understanding of what it means to be human. In this book, we will apply the astrological symbology specifically to children. A child's expression of the Self* is not yet mature, and the astrological symbols must be interpreted with this in mind. Just as psychologists have put forth theories dealing specifically with the behavior

---

*When capitalized, "Self" (also called the Higher Self) refers to all aspects of a person, including those not evident on the physical plane. The lower-case "self" refers to the specific personality currently being projected by the Higher Self.

of children, astrologers must also redefine their usual adult focus when dealing with children.

The study of human psychology has revealed clearly defined developmental cycles and patterns of growth. Many of these are tied to physical development. In the young teen, for example, the explosion of hormones in the body creates tremendous emotional upheaval. This causes change in the child's level of awareness as the expression of the Self alters.

In astrology, we also find different energies unfolding at different ages. These are the astrological cycles, which can be clocked by the movement of the planets.

If you are new to the study of astrology, you may still have some questions about how a planet millions of miles away can have any significant effect upon your life. I struggled with this concept when I began my study of astrology, only to find that my approach to the question made it difficult to answer.

What we see in the astrological chart is a map of the heavens relative to the Earth at the time of birth. This becomes the map of our personal universe for the course of a lifetime. It is symbolic of the lessons we need to learn for the growth of our souls, the special needs we have as individuals, and indicates our potential for development.

The planets continue their revolutions around the Sun, but for a brief moment—that special moment of birth—we draw a map of the heavens relative to the time and place of birth and ask ourselves, "What does this mean? How do I fit into the scheme of the Universe? Can this chart tell me something about who I am?"

We are *not* asking, "What are the planets forcing me to do?" Rather, we are studying a symbolic pattern of the greater Universe in order to gain some insights into our own personal universe. As astrologer Isabel Hickey quoted, "The planets do not compel, they impel."

Since we can study this map of the psyche, why not study it for the child soon after birth? Why not take advantage of its information to help the child of *any* age? Most people wait until adulthood to ask themselves these crucial questions of identity. It is generally not until that time that we have sufficient consciousness to truly understand the importance of knowing who we really are.

Yet we—the parents, therapists, teachers and guides of the world's children—have a fabulous map which symbolically indicates a child's physical, mental, emotional and spiritual needs. This map can guide us in understanding the child, and help the child know him/herself better. It is important to allow a child to be who s/he really *is*, and I find astrology to be an excellent tool toward this end.

The birth chart, or natal horoscope, can give insights into the physical areas of the body which tend to be more easily stressed and which may require additional nourishment. This information has helped many of my clients with small infants to help their children grow physically stronger. We can see also how the child is likely to perceive the parents, and gain insight into the types of subconscious conditioning which would be most beneficial for him/her.

But having this wealth of information is only the beginning. Information is power, and must be used properly if it is to help instead of hurt. The parents must exercise great responsibility in using astrological information with their children so that each child's highest needs will truly be served.

Most parents I know are fine people who are genuinely interested in doing the best things they can for their children. Granted, parents have their own concerns and problems, but the ones who care find ways to direct positive energy to their children. They will avoid the ever-present temptation to bend the child completely over to their world view, rather than letting him/her experience his/her own unique way of being.

As a child you probably had secret wishes, but felt that expressing them might create difficulty with your parents. I talked with a woman recently who shared with me her deep childhood desire to be a dancer. She fondly recalled the times she would hear music in her head and dance in her back yard until she was physically exhausted.

Her parents stressed practicality above all else. The children were instructed to "obey the rules," do their homework, learn what school had to teach them and focus on "realistic expectations." Encouraged to study subjects which would provide financial security, she leaned toward a career in teaching. Her parents were supportive of this idea, because they felt it would help her be more "sensible."

She studied English literature in college and eventually became a professor. She had her first consultation with me when she was in her early forties. I mentioned that her chart indicated a love of dancing and music. With tear-glazed eyes, she asked me, "Do you think it would be okay to begin studying dance at my age?"

She has now studied dance for three years. She does not expect to become a *prima ballerina*, but simply wants to fulfill this desire she felt to be taboo in her family situation. I encourage her dancing, since I know it will aid in the opening of her creative awareness and give her a greater sense of wholeness.

What if her parents had supported this particular inclination within their young daughter? Would she be a happier, more fulfilled person now?

One thing to keep in mind when using astrology with children is that we are dealing with a process of growth. I am not an event-oriented astrologer, but see myself as a *process awareness* astrologer. We must take care to allow each child to grow into his/her unique expression of the

Self. We will, of course, condition the child according to our lifestyles and philosophical systems. But by using the chart in coordination with the changes you see in the child, you can make a world of difference. Remember that children are developing will power and can choose their responses to different situations and energies! We would do well to encourage this and learn to *listen* to the child.

There are so many different approaches to the education and rearing of children. We now seem to have more choices than ever before in guiding a child's future. But how do we know which talents to support in the child? Where can we find insights into the shy, retiring child that will tell us which talents would be more beneficially developed?

With astrology, we can more easily identify these talents. We can also intelligently choose the best type of learning system for the child. The astrological chart indicates each child's natural approach to learning and communication, thereby aiding the parent in choosing the most suitable educational system.

I have found astrology to be a wonderful application of Divine Knowledge. We gain a broadened sense of ourselves with this ancient tool, and a more objective perspective of our own identities. In using astrology to understand children, we have a tremendous opportunity to help the child learn about living in harmony with the Self and with others. This opens the child to his/her optimum potentials. And what better time is there to begin than at the beginning?

Chapter Two

RUDIMENTARY PRINCIPLES OF ASTROLOGY AND THE HOUSES

The rudimentary principles of astrology are really quite simple, yet I have always been amazed at the number of students who overlook these basic concepts in their eagerness to grasp the more complex issues. Then, when the student becomes sufficiently confused, s/he will either humbly decide to return to the basics or abandon the study of astrology altogether.

If you are well-versed in the basics of astrology, you may consider this a review. If you are just beginning to study this cosmic science, these fundamental principles will be the foundation of your understanding.

In order to make the best use of the information in this book, you must have the child's natal horoscope. The astrological birth chart, or natal horoscope, is calculated using the precise time (hour and minute), date and place of birth. Although we will not cover the mathematics involved in calculating the chart, I strongly suggest that you have an accurately calculated birth chart. If you are interested in learning the math, you will find references in the bibliography at the end of this book. You may also choose to have your chart calculated through a computer service (see the addendum for further information).

Correct birth times are necessary. Generally, a birth certificate will indicate the time of birth. If not, hospital records are often available. Mothers are not always paying attention to the clock during delivery, and may not be reliable sources of information. Being conscious of the need for accurate birth times, I was watching the clock upon the birthing of my own children, and had the time recorded immediately!

The chart itself is a circle with a variety of symbols placed within and around it. The map is circular because the circle is a perfect structure with no beginning and no end. The circle is an ancient symbol, and is often associated with the concept of the human spirit.

In Illustration 1, you will find an empty astrological chart. This chart is divided into twelve segments called *houses*, which are numbered counterclockwise from one to twelve. The houses are indicators of the different environments, persons, activities and experiences in our lives.

Mentally divide the chart in Illustration 1 into an upper and lower half. On the left you will see the *cusp*, or dividing line, of the 1st House. This house cusp is called the *Ascendant*. Directly opposite the Ascendant is the cusp of the 7th House, which is called the *Descendant*. This axis represents the *horizon*. At the top of the chart you will find the cusp of the 10th House. This cusp is called the *Midheaven*, and is often abbreviated *M.C.* for the Latin phrase *Medium Coeli*. Opposing the Midheaven is the *I.C. (Imum Coeli)*. These four house cusps are referred to as the *angles* in the astrological chart, and are sensitive points. They also denote the four points of the compass—the MC is South, the IC is North, the ASC is East, and the DSC is West. The symbols for the *planets, Sun* and *Moon* are placed within the houses. These represent the energies we experience and express in our lives. (The planets are discussed in Chapter Four.)

Energy is an extremely important concept in the study

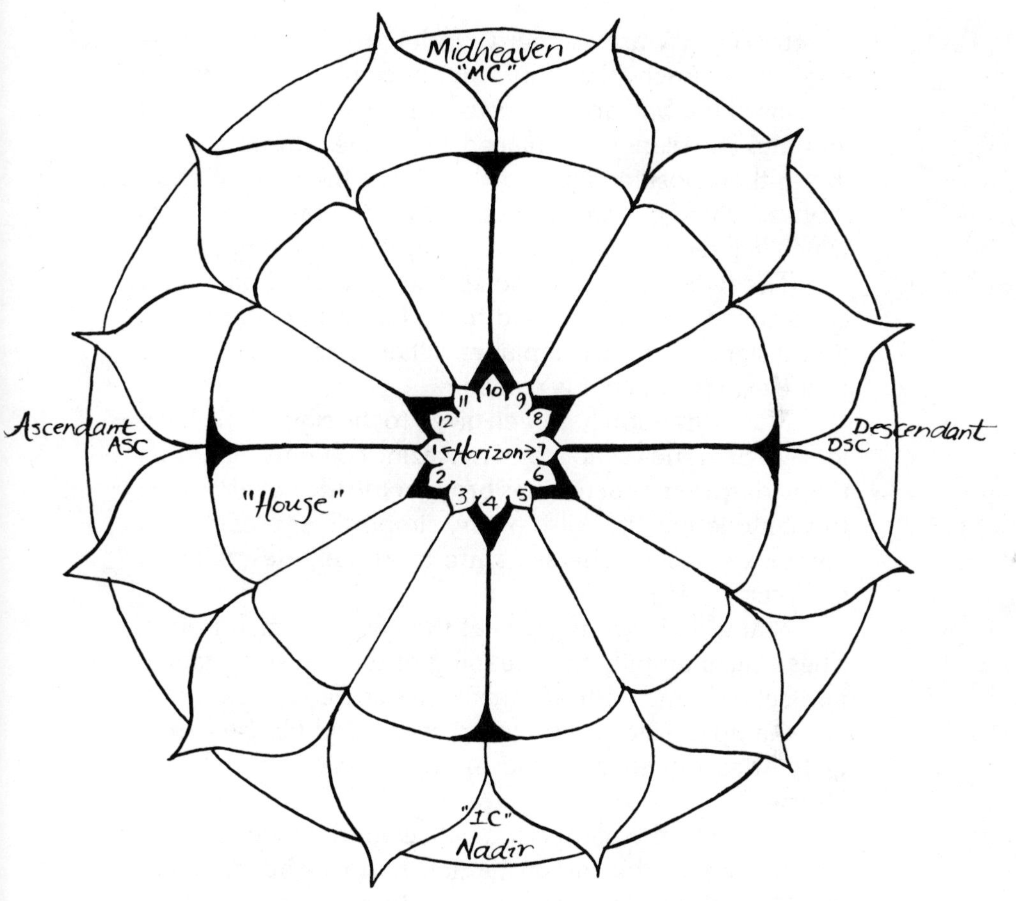

Illustration 1

of astrology. We are all energy under the direction of consciousness. Each planetary energy symbolizes different aspects of the Self and offers us insights into our personal identity. The planets are placed within the houses according to their positions in the heavens at the time of birth. Houses which contain planets indicate areas in our lives which will receive more of our attention and energy.

The twelve signs of the zodiac symbolize particular characteristics, qualities and traits. Planets appear in different signs; therefore, a planet will energize the qualities of the sign in which it is placed.

Much attention has been given to the signs, especially in "Sun Sign" newspaper and magazine columns. Although this widespread practice has brought the idea of astrology to many people, it is also a very simplistic approach to a complex subject. (The signs are more fully described in Chapter Three.)

You will also note signs at the cusps of each house. These signs amplify the meaning of the house by giving particular characteristics to that area signified by the house. For example, Aries on the cusp of the 2nd House would give Aries qualities to the energy present in the 2nd House.

Basically, the planets indicate *what* the energy is, the signs show *how* the energy manifests and the houses identify *where* the energy is expressed. Astrologers also study the interaction of the factors in the chart using geometric relationships called *aspects. Aspect patterns*, which identify themes in the birth chart, are also important.

I suggest that students learn astrology using both intellect and intuition, since both are required to fully delineate a chart. The intellectual part requires a certain amount of memory work, such as learning the basic meanings of the houses, planets and signs.

To activate the intuitive understanding, try meditating

on the astrological symbols. A good way to begin is by drawing one symbol on a piece of paper. Study the symbol; impress it in your mind. Then allow yourself to relax. Close your eyes and recall that symbol in your mind's eye. Focus only on the symbol, letting yourself get a feeling for it. Certain thoughts may come into your mind. You may also notice particular colors or special energies.

After your meditation, make some notes about your experience with the symbol. This notebook may well become one of your most valuable keys toward experiencing astrology.

Glyph	Sign	Glyph	Planet
♈	Aries	☽	Moon
♉	Taurus	☉	Sun
♊	Gemini	☿	Mercury
♋	Cancer	♀	Venus
♌	Leo	♂	Mars
♍	Virgo	♃	Jupiter
♎	Libra	♄	Saturn
♏	Scorpio	♅	Uranus
♐	Sagittarius	♆	Neptune
♑	Capricorn	♇	Pluto
♒	Aquarius		
♓	Pisces		

The Houses

The twelve houses in the astrological chart symbolize the various environments, both internal and external, in which the personality develops and expresses itself. There is a *natural zodiac* in which each of the twelve houses contains its complementary planetary and sign correspondences.

This is shown in Illustration 2. Here we see the planets and signs which "rule" the particular houses, and the traditional concepts associated with the houses.

The houses can take on different meanings when analyzing a child's chart, since a child's perspective differs dramatically from an adult's. The suggested viewpoint of the houses when dealing with children is found in Illustration 3.

1st House and the Ascendant: How I Look, My Body: My Personality. In childhood, the Ascendant and the 1st House signify the physical appearance of the child and how other people view her/him. This is basically the same meaning we find when interpreting an adult's chart. This is not surprising, since most of us have our self-image shaped by what other people tell us about ourselves. When we consider the significance of this area in the developing child, we can understand why environmental conditioning plays such an important part in the child's development of the personality self. The Ascendant's sign shows us how others will perceive the child's physical appearance and basic personality traits.

The *Aries* rising child exhibits great independence and is quite strongminded.

The *Taurus* rising child projects stubborness and stability. S/he may stay more to her/himself.

The *Gemini* rising child's sense of mischief and curiosity are his/her key traits.

The *Cancer* rising child's protectiveness and sensitivity express through his/her personality.

The *Leo* rising child's dramatic flair and personal pride are keys to his/her outward personality.

The *Virgo* rising child's meticulous manner imparts a

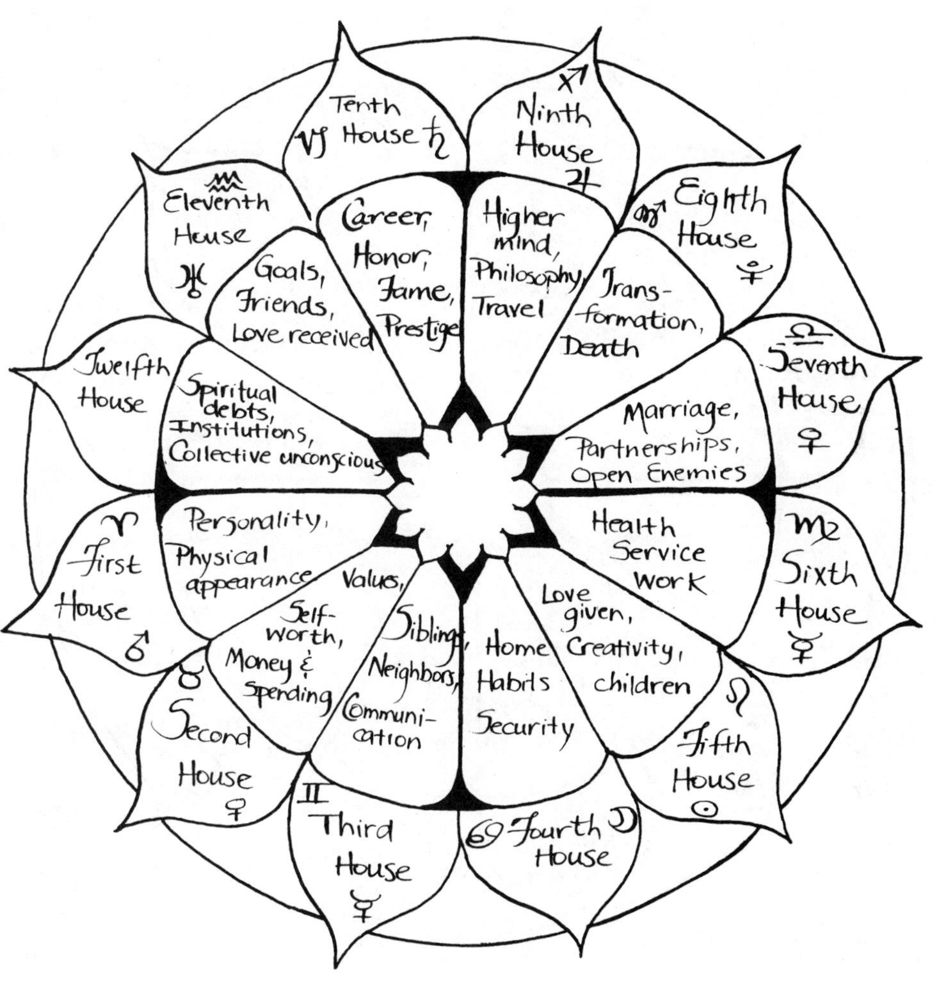

Traditional House Meanings

Illustration 2

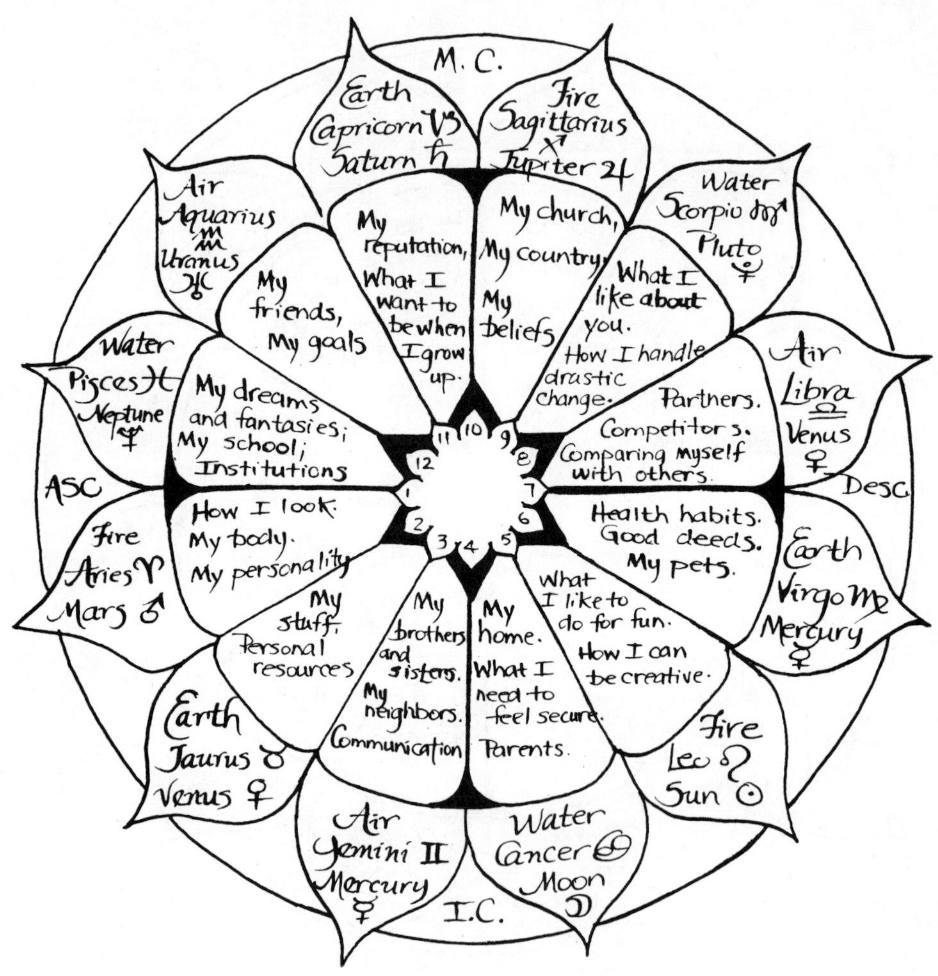

The Houses in Childhood

Illustration 3

sense of perfection to the outer self.

The *Libra* rising child shows charm, grace and consideration toward others.

The *Scorpio* rising child displays secretiveness and a sense of mystery.

The *Sagittarius* rising child's enthusiasm and free-spiritedness will shape the view others have of him/her.

The *Capricorn* rising child may show a serious nature and wry humor.

The *Aquarius* rising child may have an unusual appearance and display eccentric behavior.

The *Pisces* rising child often exhibits mystical and shy behavior.

Rising sign qualities will be further altered by the planets found in the 1st House and aspects made by the planets to the Ascendant.

I often find a strong correspondence between the rising sign of a child and the Sun, Moon or Ascending signs of the parents. This is one reason why the child displays many of the parents' traits.

2nd House: Personal Resources (My Stuff). This house deals with how the child's values are formed. Many of the child's attitudes concerning material possessions can be determined by the sign on the cusp of the 2nd House, the planet which corresponds to that sign and any planets found within the 2nd House.

The 2nd House also corresponds to the child's developing sense of self-worth. It is a natural but dangerous tendency to tie one's self-worth to the material world, especially in our society. What the child needs to learn when developing this aspect of the Self is appreciation for who and what s/he is. As parents, we can attune ourselves to the child's special qualities and fortify them through recognition and praise. This will help the child develop a greater sense of self-appreciation. "My stuff" becomes "what I am inside" instead of "what toys I have on my shelf."

3rd House: Communication, My Brothers and Sisters, My Neighbors. This area of the chart indicates how we communicate the concepts we have developed about ourselves and our world. Babies and very young children cannot really talk, so they must begin by expressing themselves non-verbally. We must realize that we communicate in many non-verbal ways. A child whose chart shows planets in the 3rd House may be constantly trying to communicate, especially if there are active personal planets like the Sun, Mercury or Mars.

We also see the child's sense of self being altered by relationships with siblings; the sign on the cusp indicates the types of relationships s/he will have with her/his brothers and sisters. For example, Mars in the 3rd House sometimes brings combativeness with siblings.

One way in which the 3rd House concepts of communication and sibling relationships operate can be seen by observing a family situation. Many communication skills are developed through interaction with brothers and sisters, since these relationships are significant on a daily basis. Older siblings may "translate" what younger children are communicating. Later, when the child becomes aware of the outside environment, neighbors come into play. These new playmates offer the child new concepts and varied opportunities for communication.

The 3rd House also deals with travel and transportation, and we can see the child's approach to travel by the sign on the cusp. The type of energy directed to traveling will be indicated by the planets in the house, or the one ruling it.

4th House: My Home, What I Need to Feel Secure. The child's personal environment is his/her first impression of the world. The 4th House tells us about the people in that environment who create a feeling of security for the child, usually either Mother or Father. Planets in this house will indicate the specific energies the child will feel from the nurturing parent.

The sign on the cusp of the Fourth House tells us what kinds of activities go on at home, and which qualities of the home environment the child identifies with. For example, the meticulous housekeeping of Virgo might be important for the child who has this sign on the cusp of the 4th House.

5th House: What I Like To Do For Fun, How I Can Be Creative. This house relates to creative self-expression. One of the best ways to encourage this is through the types of play in which a child engages. Creativity flows more easily if it is free of unnecessary inhibitions and fears.

Look to the planets in this house to find the types of energy the child will have the best time with. Uranus in the 5th House would really enjoy futuristic activities: planetariums, movies about space, and the unusual. If a child has Capricorn on the cusp of the 5th House, s/he might enjoy "working" or doing chores—something that feels constructive and purposeful.

Another concept associated with this house is giving love. Children need to learn how to give of themselves. As the child matures, s/he will learn that true creative efforts are indeed an expression of love.

6th House: Health Habits, Good Deeds, My Pets. Awareness of physical well-being is symbolized by this house. 6th House activities involve the development of good habits. The sign and planets affecting the 6th House will give clues to the child's basic well-being. They will also point to the areas which may be physically weakened and require further attention.

This is traditionally the house of service, and requires that the young child develop an awareness of other people and their needs. Children should be given opportunities to serve others by doing good deeds and favors for friends and family members.

One way to learn service is through caring for an animal friend. The child can be given the responsibilities of feeding, grooming and sharing time with his/her pet. Children who have planets in this house should definitely have their own little animal friends. With Mercury and/or Neptune placed in this house, the child is likely to have a special ability to communicate with pets.

I have always felt that pets can play a special part in a child's emotional development. Part of this development comes through performing caring service for the pet. This helps the child begin to see needs in the world outside him/herself. It also gives the child a sense that s/he is vitally connected with life.

7th House: Partners, Comparing Myself With Others, Competitors. Children with planets in this house usually like to do things with someone else most of the time. It may be difficult for these children to feel comfortable just being by themselves. They are certainly not looking for a long-term relationship or a marriage partner—they are looking for themselves through others. The other people in his/her life provide vital feedback to the child with planets in this house.

This area of development also indicates the child's approach to comparing him/herself with others: "But Ginny has orange hair, Mom!" Seeking approval from others is something we all do to feel more secure. Ultimately, however, the approval must come from within the child him/herself. This self-acceptance does not just appear from Day One—it initially requires an excellent support system in the child's personal environment.

The 7th House indicates the types of people the child will be competing against as s/he begins to be active in sports. We can use the sign on the cusp of this house to determine if the child will have a strong, positive approach to competition. The fire signs (Aries, Leo, Sagittarius) are likely to be strongest in this regard.

As the child matures, this house also deals with his/her approach to the opposite sex. When the sense of personal identity becomes muddled by the rumblings of hormones, it is often difficult to even *like* the opposite sex. I think it is interesting that pre-teen boys and girls are "open enemies," (7th House) yet later become "potential partners."

8th House: What I Like About You, How I Handle Drastic Changes. The 8th house indicates the value we place upon other people in our lives. For a child, this would be the things s/he seeks out in others. It tells us what might be a real "turn-on" or "turn-off" for the child.

This is also the area of ourselves which undergoes deep transformational changes. Planets in the 8th House indicate that a child is likely to experience drastic changes, perhaps even the deaths of significant others, during childhood. The sign on the cusp of this house indicates the child's approach to drastic change and transformations and the way he/she will deal with it.

9th House: My Church, My Country, My Beliefs. The experience of the 9th House deals with what astrologers call the "higher mind." This is an area of development which does concern the mind, but not at the basic conceptual level. These concepts are more expanded, focusing upon the overview of life a child might obtain through the teachings of his/her religion, the tenets of his/her nation, and the basic attitudes of his/her community.

During childhood, these external belief systems usually take a back seat to the child's direct experiences. As the child matures, though, s/he will have more opportunities to experience other systems of thought just by spending time with other people. I can recall my own experiences as a little girl in the Baptist church. I never questioned the teachings I was receiving, because I had no idea there was anything to question!

When I grew into my teen years, however, I had the opportunity to visit other churches with friends and began to see other approaches to worship. This was a bit shattering at first, but then it became exciting. From that time on, I was inspired to study world religions and different philosophies (still one of my passions).

We also see the 9th House as the child's approach to travel, especially to other cultures. The person who has never left her/his own culture and spent time in another can never truly understand that culture. Books, television documentaries and such cannot even begin to compare to the actual experience. The child with planets in the Ninth House will truly benefit from travel, since the Self cries out to experience other views of life.

I see this area of our lives focusing on the manner in which we integrate the world into the sense of Self. This is also the aspect of the human which needs to connect with the Divine.

10th House: My Reputation, What I Want to Be When I Grow Up. This region of self-development is not usually focused upon until the child reaches school age. At that time, interaction with others takes up most of his/her waking hours, and "reputation" and "honor" become issues the child must deal with.

As the child matures, s/he will also begin to consider what type of career might be rewarding. The primary role models are usually the parents. Secondary influences are significant others and famous people.

The child with planets in the 10th House, especially the Sun, Moon, Mercury, Venus or Mars, will devote a great deal of energy to career considerations even in the early years. The 10th House cusp, or Midheaven, is the highest point in the chart. The sign placed at the Midheaven gradually develops more and more importance as the person matures and eventually becomes "my approach to establishing my place in society." It is never too early to learn how society works or to understand the types of demands society makes before it awards "success." The sign on this house cusp tells us much about how the child may handle success.

11th House: My Friends, My Goals. Friendships are important at any age, but are especially so for the school-age child. Friends form one of the basic support systems at this time, and can dictate the standards and often the activities in which the child participates. The sign on the cusp of the 11th House tells what qualities the child seeks in a friend.

Goals are also the domain of this house. Helping a child set and master goals is important even in pre-school years. I find that parents will often set goals which are inappropriate and/or unreachable for the child. The sign on the cusp of this house indicates the types of goals which will be truly interesting to the child, and better appreciated! For example, the child with Gemini on the 11th House cusp could have a variety of goals. Because Gemini enjoys stimulation of the mind, s/he might be especially motivated if the goals involved going somewhere or doing something different.

12th House: My Dreams and Fantasies, My School, Institutions. The 12th House is the realm of the imagination: the abode of dreams, fantasies and secret desires. Here is where the "imaginary" playmates live, fairies dance and dragons hide away.

Children should be allowed to have their secret spaces. These become their inner refuge in times of distress and difficulty, and their infinite playground for just plain fun. This is the private part of the Self, where one can let go of the pressures of the outside world and float in the peaceful space of the Inner Self. Here the individual connects with the spirit of all humanity and feels the Oneness that lies beyond the illusion of separation.

The 12th House concept of "institutions" will probably apply most directly to the school the child attends. Children are generally aware of hospitals and other institutions, but usually have not spent much time inside them.

Sometimes a child born with several planets in the 12th House will have a clearer concept of what institutions are. I have a good friend, whose chart shows four planets in this house, who attended private Catholic schools until graduation. She is now part of the Sisterhood of the Catholic Church. Another client with several planets in this house had two parents who were physicians. She spent most of her first six years staying with a nurse or secretary at the hospital while Mom and Dad worked.

Basically, this house ties into the deepest recesses of our consciousness, where we connect with the One. Children with personal planets in the 12th House may feel confused about their personal identities. Sometimes these children are hard to reach. If this is the case, music can often be a good tool to bridge the gap. The younger child with planets in the 12th House may be drawn out of his/her shell through musical games and action songs. Older children may prefer to study some musical instrument, which may later become the expression of thoughts and feelings that words cannot describe.

Although these basic house meanings can be extended much further, this introduction should be sufficient to get you started. Through the houses, we gain an understanding of the *environments* of our lives—both internal and external. The persons within those environments become an active part of our sense of Self. For the child, the person and the environment might be the same thing!

The houses which contain planets have greater impact since more energy is directed into those areas. If a house does not contain a planet, we interpret the meaning of the house using the sign on the house cusp. We can further extend this to the planet which is associated with the sign on the cusp in the natural zodiac. For example, if the 5th House contains no planets, this does not mean that the child has no creative self-expression. We would look to the sign on the cusp to understand the child's approach to expressing his/her creative self. Looking further, the planet which corresponds to that sign and where it is placed will give us clues to the type of energy the child will direct into this area.

The basic concepts of astrology are the building blocks in our understanding of human nature. Since we are focusing upon children, our approach is a developmental one: we see the developing needs of the child expressed through the planets, signs and houses of the chart. None of these factors stands alone, but must be integrated within a framework of wholeness. This will offer a portrait of a complete being in succeeding stages of growth and change.

Chapter Three

THE SIGNS IN YOUTH

There are twelve signs of the zodiac. These signs embody the primary traits of the human personality. Through the signs a human being expresses special qualities which set him/her apart from others.

There is a basic organizational scheme to the signs of the zodiac relating to the four elements and the three modes. The *elements*—fire, earth, air and water—illustrate underlying factors which form the rudimentary substances in our lives. The *modes*—cardinal, fixed and mutable—are methods of expression. Each sign projects qualities of an element and a mode.

The Four Elements

Everything in our world can be described using the concepts of fire, earth, air and water. These four elements are present in our environment and within our personalities. Observing the interplay of the four elements on the physical plane can show us many fundamental truths about the human psyche.

Fire is a powerful element in our lives, warming us

when it is cold, providing us with light, and destroying things we consider useless. We have all experienced the positive qualities of fire, as well as its destructive powers.

The signs of the zodiac associated with the fiery element are *Aries, Leo* and *Sagittarius.* These three signs are active, energetic and outwardly expressive. The fiery element in children can also be felt physically (warm hugs are a pleasant trait of fiery progeny). Although each of the three fire signs will express a different level of fiery energy, there are common characteristics among them.

Psychologically, fire represents action, the outward expression of energy and a desire to be noticed. Enthusiasm and inspiration permeate the fire signs and play an important part in motivating the child. There can also be selfishness with the fiery quality. One thing to keep in mind with these children is the fact that you must tend a fire—either to keep it burning or to keep it from blazing out of control.

The element of **Earth** provides us with our sustenance on the physical plane. It is from the Earth that we receive food, materials for shelter and a foundation for our homes. This principle in astrology is signified by the signs *Taurus, Virgo* and *Capricorn.*

Earth psychologically relates to the creation of substance in our lives. Earth signs need to *apply* knowledge in order to appreciate it. There is a conservative nature in the earth signs which can even be seen in childhood. The qualities of practicality and sensibility are strongly present. Earth children often exhibit a stubborn streak.

Air is also necessary for life on the physical plane. It surrounds us, filling our lungs with the oxygen we need to survive. The lungs help us to purify the body by exhaling carbon dixoide. Air is difficult to contain, and escapes easily. It cools us, and can be harnessed to produce electrical power. Even though we cannot see air particles, we know they are there!

Children born in the air signs of *Gemini, Libra* and *Aquarius* may exhibit abstract and often elusive qualities. Psychologically, air illustrates our need to relate to one another. It is a social, relationship-oriented element, and offers a sense of diversity in our lives.

Air also represents the intellect, with all the air signs displaying a powerful mental energy. We must apply the intellect in a positive manner since the mind can be either our creator or our destroyer.

We are also surrounded by **Water** in our environment. This liquid element knows no shape of its own, but conforms to the structures around it. It provides nurturance to the earth's life forms and can be soothing, cleansing and revitalizing. Water can also bring destruction in the forms of floods and tidal waves.

Cancer, Scorpio and *Pisces* are the water signs of the zodiac, and represent the emotions and feelings in our lives. Psychologically, water signifies nurturance, emotion, receptivity, sensitivity and depth. There is a need to experience and understand things "below the surface" with the water signs. There can also be a deceptiveness associated with the watery element, since it can easily conform to whatever (or whomever) is around.

The Three Modes

The modes determine how a particular sign manifests its energy. These qualities are known as *cardinal, fixed* and *mutable*. Each sign correlates with one of three modes of action.

Cardinal energy is motivational and gets things going. Much like the ignition of an automobile, the principle of cardinality is necessary in order to get things started. Initiative, assertiveness, ambition and independence are all cardinal qualities. The cardinal signs *Aries, Cancer, Libra* and *Capricorn* all have the ability to initiate or become immediately involved in whatever events may be occurring. When exaggerated or misused, cardinality can be impatient, restless and opportunitistic.

These signs correlate with the beginnings of the four seasons: Aries, spring; Cancer, summer; Libra, fall; Capricorn, winter. There is also a desire to act without outside guidance.

Fixed signs stabilize and preserve. *Taurus, Leo, Scorpio* and *Aquarius*, the fixed signs of the zodiac, are all concerned with maintaining the status quo. There is consistency and patience in the fixed signs, but there can also be inflexibility, resistance and obsessiveness that can be rather difficult to deal with. Positive natural tendencies of the fixed signs are those of bringing inner and outer reality into oneness and the determination to complete tasks. Fixed signs correlate with the duration of the seasons.

The **Mutable** signs *Gemini, Virgo, Sagittarius* and *Pisces* are flexible and able to adapt easily. There is objectivity in the mutable signs which strengthens the ability to coordinate. The primary difficulty with mutable qualities lies in indecisive "fence-sitting." The positive natural qualities of mutability such as versatility and cooperation should receive focused attention, while the negative exaggerations involving exploitation or dissipation should be guarded against. The mutable signs correlate with the changing of the seasons.

Determining the Balance of the Elements and Modes

We can use a simple mathematical formula to fully understand how much one element influences a child's chart. Locate the signs in which the Sun, Moon, all the planets, the Ascendant and Midheaven are located. Give a value of *one* point for each planet, the Ascendant and Midheaven and *two* points each to the Sun and Moon.

After finishing this step, add together all the fire, earth, air and water signs to find the elemental balance in the chart. Use the same procedure to determine the balance of the modes by finding all the cardinal, fixed and mutable signs which are energized in the chart. Use the graph (Illustration 4) to aid you in this procedure. The example may also be helpful.

You may find one element to be extremely strong in the chart. If so, the qualities of that element will be more easily expressed by the child. For example, if air is very strong in the chart (greater than a value of five), the child's

	Cardinal	Fixed	Mutable
Fire	♈	♌	♐
Air	♎	♒	♊
Water	♋	♏	♓
Earth	♑	♉	♍

Elements and Modes

Illustration 4

focus will be more intellectual, mental and abstract. There may be one mode which is stronger than the other two. If the child's chart shows a powerful focus in cardinal signs, s/he may be a great initiator, but will need to be encouraged to finish what s/he starts!

If an element is *lacking* or has a value of one in the chart, encourage the child to express him/herself in activities which involve that element. For example, if water is lacking in the chart, encourage the child to accept and express his/her feelings more openly. Astrologer Doris Hebel suggests directing a person into activities which involve the physical element itself, such as aquariums or swimming to make up for the lacking water element. If fire is lacking, try burning candles, spending more time in the sun, and sitting in front of a fireplace. If earth is lacking, get in touch with it through gardening, standing in green grass, hugging a tree or building something out of wood. If air is lacking, the child could benefit from feeling the breeze (perhaps on the back of Mom's bike) or stimulating the mind each day by keeping a diary.

If one of the modal qualities is low or lacking, being around people who exhibit the positive aspects of those qualities might be helpful. Focusing on what the lack of this element might mean for the child would prove beneficial.

The basic concepts of the elements and modes are an excellent beginning for viewing the chart as a whole. We are trying to help the child become a whole person and a more complete expression of the Self. We must also begin to see the chart as an integrated structure rather than just isolated signs, elements, planets and houses.

The Twelve Signs in Youth

All twelve signs are present in each individual horoscope. Most charts will have more energy focused in some signs than in others. This is indicated by the placements of the Sun, Moon, planets, Ascendant, and Midheaven in the zodiac. The signs exemplify particular qualities and characteristics in our lives which will be modified as we mature. The more planets and sensitive points found in one sign, the more energy will be given to the expression of those qualities.

A child is unable to express these characteristics completely, but will gradually become a fuller expression of the Self as s/he grows. For this reason, our focus in discussing the signs is upon the early development of these qualities in childhood.

To make the best use of this section, refer to the child's chart you are studying as you read. Note the placement by sign of the Sun, Moon, each of the planets, the Ascendant and Midheaven. If you find a sign with two or more energies, these qualities will manifest more strongly. The personal planets—the Sun, Moon, Mercury, Venus, and Mars, along with the Ascendant—make up the aspects of the personality which will be the most dominant in the child's life.

Aries

It is no accident that Aries is the first sign of the zodiac. 0° of Aries is the Vernal Equinox, the new life of Spring. The qualities of Aries are fresh and alive, with a sense of new beginnings. These include leadership, assertiveness, enthusiasm and, often, impatience. Children whose charts have planets in Aries may be tremendously eager to try new things, perhaps before they have mastered the task before them! Here the fiery energy expresses itself by getting things started.

Aries shows a strong desire for freedom, a need to get

there first. Watching the children at my son's preschool get into line before lunch, I noticed two children rush immediately to the front of the line. It was not surprising for me to learn that both of these children have the Sun in Aries!

Aries often manifests in children as a high level of impatience. Planets in Aries will express more directly in an effort to waste less time and get to the point. Aries also enjoys teasing. You can even see this quality in little babies as young as nine months, already understanding how to play little teasing games with Mommy and Daddy.

This can be a physically active sign exhibiting a great deal of restlessness. When Aries is strong in an infant's chart, it is especially important for the parents to exercise the baby so s/he can sleep better. These babies will not enjoy being hemmed in by playpens!

Provide the Aries toddler with action toys. The Aries preschooler will enjoy playing ball with you or playing chase with the family pet. Elementary school age Aries enjoy playing games such as "Simon Says," or taking part in adventure scenarios such as pirates or cops and robbers. Sports is also a good outlet for an Aries child.

Aries needs to learn about the consequences of his/her actions, and parents should be alerted to this lesson. Focusing on tasks which require some follow-through will also be helpful to the child with planets in Aries. You can find toys that will teach these actions for infants and children of all ages.

Brightly colored toys are favorites of Aries babies. Aries seem to vibrate well to the color red. I've known many Aries children who love wearing fire helmets. I think this is because helmets are red and also because Aries rules the physical head. (Different signs rule different parts of the body.) Hats in general might be fun for Aries children, especially since they help the child to identify with various roles.

Aries' natural leadership abilities can be encouraged in the school-age child. Give him/her ample opportunities to interact in such activities as team sports or running for school offices. Encouraged early, the development of these abilities will instill a high level of confidence in the child.

Aries is strongly connected with will power, and you may find these children extremely strong-willed. Sometimes this results in a combative attitude, with discussions becoming arguments. The child needs to learn that it is okay for another person to have a different opinion, and that s/he need not take sides all the time. Certainly, the development of will power should be encouraged, but it needs to be balanced with an understanding of the consequences of one's actions.

Taurus

Taurus centers upon the sensual. Taurus is the fixed earth sign of the zodiac, and occurs at the time Spring is showing her finest colors. All the greens are vibrant during this time of year, and the Earth radiates life and sustenance. Taurus qualities include stability, conservatism, practicality, consistency and creativity.

Children born with planets in Taurus like to learn by experiencing in order to involve the physical senses. This allows the Taurean to integrate knowledge more completely. The Taurean child has a love for the Earth and her life forms, as well as a sense of the stability found by attaching him/herself to the things of the Earth. Babies with Taurean planets love walking in the warm Sun, touching trees, smelling flowers, and crawling in the grass. As this child grows, so can his/her appreciation for the Earth. Encourage it with activities such as indoor or outdoor gardening, working with clay, and getting in touch with the Self by touching the matter of the Earth.

Taurus is not too happy with change, and should be encouraged to participate in changes in order to understand that change does not necessarily lead to loss. I think the fear of change for so many with Taurean energy stems from the fear of losing something, and consequently losing part of the Self. Taurus tends to be possessive for this same reason—holding on means, "It's mine forever!"

This can carry over into emotional relationships and create difficulties later in life. Learning to share with friends is a necessary exercise for Taurus. A friend of mine related an experience that might help parents with children who like to hold on. She was standing in line at the supermarket behind a mother, her child and the child's grandmother. Grandmother had to leave, and the child became hysterical upon her departure. The mother held the child closely, creating a sense of calmness. Then she said, "In our lives, there are lots of comings and goings. Sometimes, we have to let someone go in order to allow something different to happen." This attitude helps in dealing with Taurus children.

Toys with varying textures and surfaces are wonderful for babies with Taurus energies. Taurus also loves to taste. Be aware that this sense can be carried too far, and could lead to a desire for too much food—at least too many "goodies!" (Chocolate is specially favored by Taureans.)

As the Taurean child grows, there will be an increased appreciation for building toys, as well as games that involve the accumulation of power. Since the lesson of gracefully letting go of things is so important for these children, games that teach cooperation and sharing is a good idea.

The Taurean child will probably enjoy saving money once s/he understands its power. S/he might appreciate piggy banks at a young age, followed by a savings account later on. Offering goods in exchange for deeds works well in motivating Taurean children. Of course, the lesson that all deeds may not result in physical repayment will be a challenging one to teach. The parents of the Taurean child are blessed if they can make him/her understand that "to give is more blessed than to receive."

Taurus has the knack of building things which last, and develops a tenacious attachment to concepts and ideas. Certain physical exercises can be a good way to attain mental or emotional resilience. The Taurus child would do well to learn yoga, tai chi or any dance movements that will encourage flexibility. Learned early, this will teach the child how to create lasting impressions and stable values while functioning from a position of flexibility.

Gemini

Gemini is the mutable air sign of the zodiac, and possesses the qualities of diversity, mental curiosity, duality, wittiness and changeability. Children whose charts show planets in Gemini are likely to be interested in many different things. There is a desire to explore something new as soon as it catches the child's attention. Gemini confers a need to experience variety and gives the ability to see many facets of an issue or idea.

In childhood, Gemini often has a sense of impish mischief. Although the young child with Gemini qualities may get into a few tight situations due to his/her endless curiosity, s/he can usually talk her/his way out of trouble or find a quick solution to extract her/himself from a jam. The rational mind seems to be activated from the very beginning.

A love of talking is often present—sometimes much to the parents' chagrin! Parents of Gemini progeny should be alerted that this child takes in every word, and is likely to repeat those words anywhere! Gemini is much like a monkey—the mimicking ability is very strong. These features are especially notable with the Gemini Moon.

Gemini characteristics in infancy seem to manifest as

early desires to experience motion and stimulation. The baby with Gemini planets or Ascendant will need a variety in her/his environments during the day if boredom is to be avoided. Often the infant will wail simply because s/he wants to go somewhere. A walk around the yard or a drive in the car may be just the thing to calm her/him.

Stories will be a favorite pastime as the child grows. There is almost always a love of books and a fascination with language. Toys that will take the child somewhere are a necessity—scooter cars for toddlers, tricycles and bicycles for older children, and eventually "a car of my own." In the future, Gemini children will most likely require their own personal space vehicles!

In learning situations, Gemini proves to be delightful and challenging. Materials need to be presented concisely and at a fairly quick pace. Since Gemini is easily distracted, a wide variety of subjects would be ideal. There is often a proclivity to abstract types of thought, such as mathematics.

Gemini children should be encouraged to present their ideas in writing. Poems and short stories are generally the favorite forms. A diary is almost a necessity for the preteen and teenager. Working on the school paper might be fun, too.

Gemini often has restless hands and requires many activities to keep them busy. The tiny child might like the wide variety of blocks, brightly colored musical keyboards or easy puzzles. As the child matures, offer him/her more complex puzzles, finger paints, pens and crayons (the variety of colors alone is often enough to draw the child) and any toy with finger keys. Toy telephones are a favorite. Later on, an erector set or advanced Lego blocks would be enticing. Building models is a good idea for that active mind and those busy hands! There may be a desire to play a musical instrument such as guitar, harp, piano or a wind instrument. Encourage these desires.

Gemini needs to learn concentration and the expansion of ideas. It is important to stress the joy of variety along with the necessity of integrating concepts. Learning to focus the mind and follow through will be very helpful to the child. The wit and cleverness of Gemini are special gifts, but there is very often a lack of tact when speaking. Teach Gemini to listen!

Cancer

Cancer, also called the Moon Child, imparts nurturance, sensitivity, protectiveness and resourcefulness. This cardinal water sign expresses very emotionally. Cancer is generally drawn to the mother, home and family. Children of this sign are often kind and caring, and usually love to be around babies and small animals.

The child with planets in Cancer must learn how to deal with his/her emotional nature in a positive way. His/her sensitivity can lead to easily hurt feelings, causing an overly protective nature to develop at a rather young age. The parents need to recognize this sensitivity and provide a stable, calm environment for the child. Excessive amounts of negative energy such as anger, loud noises or other "threatening" experiences will be difficult for the Cancerian to tolerate, and may make the child irritable.

Cancer is symbolized by the crab, whose dominant feature is its protective shell. This shield was developed to lessen its vulnerability.

Humans have their shells, too. Sometimes the child will use Mother as a shield (hiding behind her skirts is a common example). At other times, the shield is physical. Even a young child can begin developing an armor of fat. If your Cancerian is gaining too much weight, you should find out why the child is feeling vulnerable or hurt. This type of awareness early in life can help the child avoid such harsh, self-destructive patterns in adulthood.

Cancer, like the crab, moves most easily in an indirect manner. However, this behavior can manifest as manipulative and escapist if carried to extremes, resulting in confusion and mistrust on the part of everybody involved.

The Moon Child's penetrating awareness can be ripened early by encouraging the child to trust his/her feeling nature. It might be difficult to deceive such a perceptive child, so the best approach is simply to be honest at all times. Any attempt to hide the truth from a child, even when you think you are protecting him/her from hurt, may well backfire on you. Even delicate or painful situations should be explained in a thorough, reasonable manner.

I recall an adult client with both the Sun and Moon in Cancer tearfully sharing her pain about her parents' divorce when she was eleven years old. She spoke of knowing about the disharmony (of course, she could *feel* it!) long before her parents split up, but they tried to conceal their problems from her by acting as though everything was just fine. One day, her father bade her good-bye at breakfast with bags packed and trailer loaded. He never returned. Her mother would not even tell her that they were divorcing (she didn't until later), but just said, "Daddy is going away for a while." Imagine the hurt and confusion experienced by this sensitive young girl who, needless to say, has had trouble trusting in relationships throughout most of her life!

Children with Cancerian energies enjoy watching things grow. Nurturing small plants can be a joyful experience. Raising guppies or swordfish might be delightful. You can even purchase hermit crabs at pet stores or through toy catalogs!

Helping to care for younger brothers or sisters could also be pleasant, but try not to take too much advantage of this service! Remember, this child also needs to receive personal nurturance and attention. Cancerian children often enjoy working with Mother, no matter what she is doing.

The infant with Cancerian planets will probably love to be cuddled and rocked. The tactile senses are strong, and should be stimulated by toys with varying textures and temperatures. These children would really enjoy a crib aquarium hanging overhead. Music is also a particular favorite, especially singing.

As the child grows, toys which stack or fit inside one another will be fascinating. Cancerians love containers and boxes, especially pretty boxes for special things. Elementary school-age Cancerians might enjoy learning to cook, whereas the older child might like a chemistry set. Many children with planets in Cancer like sewing and crafts.

What we need to encourage in these children is a desire to share love and caring with others without feeling threatened. In learning situations, there may be a reluctance to participate if the child feels emotionally vulnerable. The approach to learning begins at home. Accepting their sensitivity and using it to bring comfort and support to the lives of others is their special gift and challenge.

Leo

The fixed fire sign of the zodiac, Leo radiates warmth, confidence and power. Leo's virtues require maturity in order to express themselves in the most positive light.

This sign occurs during the heat of summer, when everyone is enjoying the Sun, playing summertime sports and having a good time. Most Leos prefer warm climates to cool because this gives them greater access to Sol's rays. Children with the Sun, Moon, planets or sensitive points in

Leo are likely to be dramatic in self-expression, and are usually difficult to ignore! They, like the Sun, enjoy being the center of attention.

Leo often demonstrates flair and style, and tends to be rather showy. The Leo progeny needs every opportunity to express that flair, and should be encouraged to build confidence and a sense of personal power. One warning—there is often a little prince or princess complex when Leo is found rising or is energized by the personal planets.

Leo needs to learn that it is okay for others to own their own personal power, too. A family entertainment night, where everyone dances, sings, acts silly or shows off would be a good way to teach the Leo child how to share the spotlight. This would also offer him/her a special chance to shine. After a while, s/he will certainly want to direct the show, although I am certain the family will handle this situation in grand style!

If the child with Leo energies is not allowed to shine, much inner suffering will arise. Self-esteem is confused and personal power repressed. To avoid these consequences, gentle affirmations of the child's worth need to be given on a consistent basis. Most people do not have problems giving special love and attention to a small baby. "He's so cute! Look! He rolled over!" Mommy exclaims, clapping her hands. "Watch her toddling over to the puppy. Isn't she a doll?" Yet as children mature, those little victories are not met with such open enthusiasm. The Leonine nature demands recognition and approbation for its victories, and deserves to receive it. If not given, Leo will gain the attention s/he needs through less than positive actions.

Small babies with planets in Leo will enjoy time out in the Sun and strolls in the park in a carriage or backpack. There is often a fascination with animals, with a trip to the zoo being a choice option. Of course, a family cat would be a delight! Leo babies also love back rubs. My own son, with

Leo rising, has a nightly ritual of a back rub, and often asks to rub my back.

Most of these children like large toys, especially large stuffed animals. Stacking blocks and nesting blocks would encourage Leo's organizational abilities. As the child grows, save the Halloween costumes for play time. Magic kits, microphones, and any stage paraphernalia will be relished. Dancing or acting lessons would probably be pleasurable for the child.

You might find the Leo five year old in her/his room, all the stuffed toys and dolls lined up at attention while s/he gives all of them directions or recites a favorite story. Leo children love stories, especially exciting tales told or read dramatically. Encourage the child to tell his/her own stories and, later, to write them. You may have a young George Bernard Shaw on your hands!

Leo does need to learn about possessiveness, and should be encouraged to share friends as well as toys. These children sometimes have trouble coping with changes in their circle of friends. Leo likes to be the center of attention and have the controlling power with friends. Learning to use that power responsibly can be a real challenge for a young person.

Leonine pride is often difficult to handle in youth, and can be the cause of disputes. To insult a Leo is grevious indeed. Since Leo is very likely to see everyone and everything as part of him/herself, to insult a friend, parent or possession is tantamount to a personal affront. If other children are insensitive, Leo will probably set them straight.

Leo also needs to learn to appreciate the gifts and talents of others and share the limelight. This lesson can make the difference between a life of extravagant self-indulgence or an attitude of genuine philanthropy.

Virgo

The summer is drawing to a close and harvest time is at its peak when the Sun is passing through the sign of Virgo. At this time the school year begins again, people start planning their schedules more precisely and life takes on a more practical quality. The mutable earth sign of the zodiac, Virgo confers discrimination, analysis, criticism, precision and organization. Virgo has a methodical quality which is observable even in the youngest children.

Virgo is highly attuned to the physical body, and appreciates physical wellness and comfort. Slight discomforts are readily discernible by this child, who will want the homeostasis (natural balance) of the body returned as soon as possible. These babies are quick to complain about soiled diapers or sticky fingers!

One concept I have always linked to Virgo is fastidiousness. This applies especially to the physical body, but can also extend into the personal environment. Being an earthy, mutable sign, Virgo is highly sensitive. This acute sensitivity knows when something is wrong, and generally will stay uncomfortable until the situation is remedied.

Virgo prefers to know what to expect in situations in order to make the most of them. You should let the toddler and pre-schooler know each day what their schedule is likely to be. Virgo can adapt to changes (it is a mutable sign), but adapts much better with advance notice!

The young child with Virgo energies can be a great help in keeping the house clean and organized. These are the children for whom little brooms and mops were invented! Let this child know you appreciate his or her efforts, since it is very easy to take advantage of Virgo energy without saying thanks.

Even the pre-schooler would benefit from some type of reward system for jobs well done. A chart in the room listing chores or behavior appropriate for the child's age would be helpful. This can be made from construction paper or poster board, listing things such as "picking up my toys," "feeding the puppy," and "dressing myself." Colorful stars and stickers could be awarded to indicate achievement. The recognition can be its own reward, or the child could have a goal which could be achieved by accumulating a certain number of stickers. Earning fifty stickers, for example, could be rewarded by a trip to the zoo. This will give a sense of increased self-esteem to the child. Since Virgo often has problems appreciating the self, such an exercise would be extremely beneficial.

The self-esteem of children with Virgo energies is often lowered due to self-imposed expectations of perfection. These children do not enjoy doing anything less than perfectly. There may be a reluctance to share their creative projects, drawings or other work with parents, teachers or peers if it does not meet their own high standards.

I, with my Virgo Sun and Ascendant, can recall my feelings in first grade when my teacher asked us all to draw a picture of something we enjoyed doing. I set to work with my crayons and construction paper and began drawing one of my favorite activities. There was the green grass, the blue sky, the bright Sun, and, in the foreground, a clothesline. I just loved taking clothes down from the line, smelling their sun-sweetened freshness, and tumbling into the kitchen covered with sheets, towels and Daddy's big shirts.

As I drew the picture, I took great care to draw one of everything on the line. After I had completed my work of art, however, I noticed that the clothespins were bigger than Daddy's shirt. I was crushed! The teacher asked to see my picture, and I ran out of the room into the great hall outside crying.

Fortunately, I had a patient and understanding teacher. She gently coaxed me to share my drawing and was delighted. My picture was even displayed in the city children's art show. Yet there I was, humiliated in my own eyes because everything was not "perfect."

Talk with your young Virgo about his/her attitudes toward learning and doing. Let them know that you have no conditions except that they do the best they can. With Virgo, unconditional acceptance and love is more than important—it is absolutely necessary.

The infant with Virgo energies will enjoy toys that can be disassembled and/or serve more than one function. Toys requiring a high degree of manual dexterity are excellent choices. Toddlers will prefer things such as puzzles, sewing cards and books. The pre-schooler will probably be eager to read, and may also enjoy art supplies and building toys. Young children whose analytical minds are ready to blossom may be challenged by math and science, and will be fascinated by the human body.

Give Virgo opportunities to help other children. These kids are often fabulous teachers of younger brothers, sisters and neighbors. I have always thought it would be excellent to implement helping situations in the classroom. The Virgo child can be an excellent tutor to fellow students. If there is a sick friend or family member, the Virgo may act as a concerned nurse. These types of activities stimulate the need to be of service. Older children and teens should be encouraged to write and speak publicly.

Virgo's main challenge lies in the need to appreciate him/herself and others. This appreciation should have its inception in early youth, and be based on the examples set by the parents. Often, whatever Mom, Dad or school indicate to be "the right way" will be unquestioningly incorporated into his/her life. Helping the child to understand the *reasons* behind these criteria is important, since it will enable him/her to create his/her own standards as s/he matures rather than blindly following someone else's.

Libra

Libra, the cardinal air sign of the zodiac, is directed toward maintaining harmony and balance. This sense permeates the majority of Libra's qualities. The child with energies in this sign needs to experience situations in which beauty and harmony abound. There can be an aggressiveness with this sign, but it is often disguised—hence, the concept of charm arises!

Relationships are important to Libra. The omnipresent sense of balance almost always requires another person to give reflection and diversity in life. Young children with planets in Libra are likely to be very sociable, enjoying parties and other gregarious activities. The childhood tea party is a good example of a Libran activity. Even if there is not another person, the child will socialize with dolls, the family pet or stuffed animals. Yet even with this desire to relate, these children often exhibit a pronounced fickleness. This is due to the changeable nature of this airy sign.

Babies with planets in Libra are soothed by beautiful surroundings and will be delighted when someone talks to them. They will probably prefer being in a room with someone else rather than being left alone. Musical toys are favorites, as are toys which are pretty and visually interesting. Toddlers and pre-schoolers will like stories about princesses and princes, especially when they end "happily ever after." Even small Librans should be encouraged to draw, paint and develop an awareness of color. Often, talents for design show at an early age.

Balancing toys are almost a necessity. One excellent toy I remember was designed to teach math through balance. It consisted of a hanging scale from which numbers were suspended on each side. The child would hang a number on one side of the scale, then would have to balance it with the same number or two or more numbers which equaled it on the other side. The Libran concepts of balance and equality were taught very effectively. Building blocks are also good tools for learning a sense of balance.

Most Librans enjoy music, especially songs with lyrics so they can sing along! Music with beautiful harmonies is a heavenly experience for the Libran ear. Visiting art galleries and museums, attending art festivals and going to concerts would delight this child.

The Libran desire for harmony carries over into interpersonal relationships as well. Libra hates to rock the boat. S/he will use placating behavior in early childhood just to avoid unpleasantness. S/he will also have difficulty dealing with harsh words, loud mannerisms and obnoxious behavior. The refinement of this sign creates a desire for quality in all aspects of life. Distastefulness in any form can be repugnant.

One attitude children with Libran energies should develop early is to not always compare themselves with others. It is very easy for the Libran to see what s/he considers "perfection" in another person, then feel less than perfect if they are not doing exactly the same thing. If everybody else is wearing short sleeves and the Libran arrives with covered arms, s/he will feel uncomfortable and out of place. Sometimes these children have a natural sense of inferiority because they believe that someone else is better than they are.

Teach the child to appreciate the changes and growth within him/herself, using *him/herself* as the guideline. Make it clear that using another person for one's own individual standards is often dangerous and counterproductive. This is especially true in the case of external appearances. In our society today, the model of l"perfection" as projected by advertisements and the mass media is far from the reality most individuals perceive about themselves. An impressionable young child may believe that all little children have to dress or look a certain way in order to be acceptable.

Libra is continually seeking balance, and other people usually provide one side of it. This can be helpful in relationships, as it confers a considerate attitude. Learning to be considerate of others can be a positive and special focus for the child with Libra planets. A lack of consideration from others may be hurtful to these children. An open dialogue with parents can aid the child in understanding this situation more easily.

Children with Libra energies need to learn to shoulder responsibility for their own decisions and actions early in life. There can be tremendous difficulty in accepting responsibility and scapegoating may be exhibited ("The kitty ate those cookies, not me!"). Children with Libran Moons and Mercuries are notorious for their difficulty in making decisions. The decision has to be perfectly balanced to be right, and it may seem easier to not take responsibility for the decision and let someone else take care of it!

To aid these children in decision-making, try some simple exercise such as choosing clothing for the day. Once a decision is made, help the child stay with it as s/he goes about getting dressed. Sometimes parents become so frustrated with this slow decision-making process that they make all the decisions themselves in the name of efficiency. This, however, can eventually cripple the child psychologically. When the pre-schooler is getting dressed in the morning, offer a limited choice of clothes, then walk away. Allow the child to decide. Once s/he is dressed, remember to extend a hug and compliment the child on his/her choice.

Scorpio, the fixed water sign of the zodiac, presents us with the qualities of intensity, mystery, passion and resourcefulness. Because Scorpio is a water sign, there are

Scorpio

powerful emotions in play. Children with the Sun, Moon or planets in Scorpio may not show all that is brewing beneath the surface. This often creates a sense of mystery or secrecy about the child.

For the child with Scorpio energy, life is experienced at a very deep, intense level. This intensity can be frightening for a child since it penetrates the Self so completely. Another person's barely noticeable sensation could be experienced as overwhelming pain by the Scorpio.

Because the child is so sensitive, the parents and significant others need to be especially tuned in to him/her. These children probably will not tell you their feelings all the time, especially if they are hurtful ones. It is more comfortable for the child to repress the memory of the sensation and go on to something else.

Psychology has shown us some of the negative results of emotional repression: withdrawal and depression which sometimes lead to periodic explosions of extreme violence. Parents of children with the Sun, Moon, Venus or Mars in Scorpio should begin a dialogue with the child about emotions very early. This will help give the child a workable escape valve. An understanding, patient and loving parent is a true jewel for the child with Scorpio planets.

I have worked with many adults with the personal planets (Sun, Moon, Mercury, Venus or Mars) in Scorpio who have real problems with emotional relationships. This is often due to the overwhelming experience of pain when a relationship ends. Rather than easing in time, the pain just seems to penetrate more deeply into the self, creating an excruciating wound. This repressive behavior can be self-destructive.

This pattern has its roots in childhood. The child needs to learn effective ways to release pain. If there are hurt feelings, hold the child lovingly. Perhaps a massage would help. Sometimes a bath is just the thing to ease away negative feelings. If the pattern becomes repressive, it will be extremely difficult to change later on.

This intensity also has its positive channels. It is the passion of Scorpio which gives the ability to be highly creative. The progeny of this sign don't just put mental energy into a project—they tend to throw themselves completely into the creative act.

Children with personal planets in Scorpio should be encouraged to express themselves artistically or creatively. Painting and drawing can be ideal outlets. This is also a good way to release pent-up emotions—just get some finger paints, about thirty feet of paper and let it all out!

Music is also an excellent choice to complement Scorpio's sensitivity. The baby with planets in Scorpio would appreciate powerful but soothing music. Classical forms are often favored. Whether or not the child shows musical talents is not so important as exposure to this form of expression!

Toddlers would probably enjoy playing with toys in which things are hidden (the "Barrel of Monkeys" is a good example). Puzzles are also a good choice.

Scorpio children like to watch things grow. Planting a small garden indoors with your child can be a magical experience as the seed transforms itself into a flower. Since Scorpio needs to understand the process of transformation, real cocoons enclosed in transparent protective containers from which live butterflies emerge would be an excellent choice.

As the child grows, microscopes, chemistry sets or anything which will aid his/her exploration of life would be perfect. A spelunking adventure would be fabulous for the teenager; until then, family trips to caves and caverns might be enjoyable.

Scorpio's abilities often include healing, which is a positive transformational process. There is usually a fascination with the human body and the processes which can heal it. You may find that these children are interested in medicine or anatomy at a very young age. Encourage this interest since it may result in a very fine physician or healer.

One final concept relating to Scorpio is sexuality. It is extremely important that children with Scorpio planets be approached honestly about sex. An open, positive attitude is necessary for all children, but especially for those who live daily with such intensive sensitivity.

Scorpio's sexual expression is very powerful. Since Scorpio projects the qualities of transformation so intensely, the child will be especially interested in this most fundamental level of human transformation.

Small children will want to know where they came from, and this information must be presented accurately and honestly. As the child matures, the potential creation of life through sexual sharing can be discussed in a frank manner with him/her. If the parent represses his/her sexuality, the child will most certainly absorb this attitude. Given knowledge, the young person can choose to act in a responsible and mature manner when relating sexually.

Sagittarius

This mutable fire sign is the most freedom-loving sign of the zodiac. Sagittarian traits include aspiration, foresight, optimism, versatility and open-mindedness. I've often thought the song "Don't Fence Me In" was a good example of the Sagittarian theme. Sagittarian children will exemplify some of these qualities, but are likely to be a bit capricious in their behavior until they learn the importance of positive limitations.

Children with the personal planets (Sun, Moon, Mercury, Venus or Mars) in Sagittarius will exhibit a desire to learn early in life. This is stimulated by the natural need to understand as much as possible. Learning does not have to be associated with school or traditional educational systems: Sagittarians tend to be philosophical, and believe that there is much to be learned in every experience. Travel is also high on the list of favorite things to do, especially to places or events that are fun. Disneyland and Disneyworld (especially Epcot Center) are fantastic examples of Sagittarian fun.

Most children of Sagittarius will be attracted to horses, which are often associated with this sign due to their free spirit and fleet-footedness. Activities attractive to Sagittarians must provide new experiences and opportunities. These expand the personal universe and enhance the sense of personal freedom.

One aspect of this sign which can create difficulties is the ease with which distractions can occur. Focusing is sometimes a problem for these children, especially for those with the Moon or Mercury in Sagittarius. But the tendency to distraction can be positively employed. For the very small child, realize that his/her attention span will be limited and plan a series of things to do with the child. Once the child is in school doing homework, schedule breaks into his/her study times. Scheduled "distractions" sometimes make it easier for the child to focus on schoolwork. If absolute freedom is allowed with studying, though, it may never get done!

Children with Sagittarian planets often resist limitations. Playpens are frustrating for the crawler with her/his needs to explore and move about. Although it will require the parents to be more attentive, the baby would prefer the less restrictive environment of a blanket on the floor.

Once the baby begins to expand her/his horizons, s/he

can be taught limits gradually. If you want the child to respect and understand these restrictions, you will have to tell her/him why they are necessary. My daughter, with four planets in Sagittarius, nearly drove me nuts with her incessant "Why's?" beginning about age two. When I finally realized that she honestly needed to understand, I became more pliable in answering her questions. In fact, it got to the point that I would often give her the answer before she asked the question!

By appealing to reason, parents offer the child a sense of personal power and this will build a more understanding relationship with the child. Open communication will be especially helpful when dealing with the toddler who would run headlong into the street unless tethered. Use cooperation and understanding to build the fences *inside* the child and there will be less need for a leash!

Sagittarian babies and toddlers enjoy action toys, as well as toys they can take with them. Sometimes a wailing infant can be calmed by a walk around the block or a stroll in the park. I have had many parents of Sagittarian children ask me why their baby cries for long periods. This may be partly an early exercise in oration! A bigger reason may be that these children have a strong light energy, and simply resist having such a large, expanded consciousness crammed into such a tiny body!

Small children with Sagittarius' influence will enjoy walkers, since they are eager to be on the go from the very beginning. As the child gets older, s/he should be given opportunities to experience many different environments. A trip to Grandma's, a jaunt to the park, or just a change of scenery would be enjoyed.

Toys should include books and records (especially storybook tapes and records), rocking horses, pull toys and little cars. A race track will be a delight for the older Sagittarian.

The characteristic Sagittarian resistance to limitations can also extend to speech patterns ("talking a blue streak"), over-eating or over-extending the physical energy. Sagittarian children do not want to miss anything, and will probably resist scheduled bedtimes and naptimes.

The lessons the child must learn—and they are not easy ones—are learning to know the Self and developing a sense of positive limits. Personal freedom must be balanced with a true sense of personal responsibility. Teaching the Sagittarian child horsemanship in the pre-teen and early teen years would not be a bad idea. The child would learn that a horse cannot just be "ridden hard and put away wet," but must be fed, watered, groomed and loved. The physical maneuvers involved in horseback riding (especially English style) are also rigorous, requiring personal discipline along with a keen attunement to the animal. Gymnastics and track and field sports also seem especially well-suited to these children.

Most children with Sagittarian energies enjoy stories and reading, especially tales of adventure. The *Black Beauty* books are especially attractive to these children. Writing flows easily, as do the other language skills. Learning at least one foreign language is advised. Although adhering to the rules of spelling and grammar may be a problem at first, these too can be mastered.

Even the young Sagittarian may find the study of religion fascinating. The child should be taught the spiritual truths of life, since Sagittarius constantly searches for the truth.

Most children with this influence will love to play games, even in infancy. Other activities which are enjoyable involve interaction with nature. Camping, hiking and spending time outdoors in natural surroundings is important for the child influenced by Sagittarius.

There can be a wonderful generosity and optimism in

Sagittarian children, as well as a contagious sense of positivity. These children can teach us much about the Law of Abundance, since they seem to have a natural understanding of it. Their directness of speech can be a two-edged sword, although very refreshing at times. We often do not want to hear the truth. However, if there is a Sagittarian child around who thinks s/he knows the "truth" about something, be prepared to hear about it!

Capricorn

The sign of Capricorn occurs during the Winter Solstice. This cardinal earth sign has the qualities of determination, practicality, ambition, reliability and persistence. Capricorn children have a need to be respected, and truly admire adults who have earned respect. It is often said of children with Capricorn planets that they are old when they are young and young when they are old.

These children want to be in control of everything in their lives. This can be frustrating for parents with Capricorn toddlers who already want control but are not ready for it! There is an outgoing yet cautious independence in these children. My young son, who has both the Sun and Venus in Capricorn, will quietly assess a situation before he gets involved in it. At a new playground, he will slowly walk around the perimeter, observing how the other children climb up the ladders and chains, then cautiously will try one thing at a time until he feels confident. Then, however, he goes full force, running and squealing with delight as he enjoys the now familiar situation.

One way to encourage the young child with Capricorn energies is by offering him/her appropriate responsibilities for his/her age. For example, the three year old can be given the responsibility of dressing him/herself. As the child grows, his/her responsibilities can be increased, such as helping with chores around the house or feeding the family pet.

Capricorns become radiant when they receive something for their efforts. They will respond well to a "reward chart," or, once they understand the value of money, actual cash. This must be handled with care, however—a sharp Capricornian can drain Mom's cash reserves in a hurry! Self-esteem is strongly associated with physical and material results for these children. They need to feel that they are creating, building, or improving something.

Capricorn enjoys making use of available assets. These kids will definitely keep the leftovers cleared out of the refrigerator! If something is "useless," however, Capricorn wants nothing to do with it. Toys for Capricorn might include various types of building blocks, especially ones which interlock. Erector sets and other building toys are suitable. Sandboxes, digging in the dirt, working with modeling clay and other "earthy" activities would also be enjoyable.

Toys that are like Mom's or Dad's business tools such as calculators, cash registers, typewriters, tools or computers, are natural choices. At age five, my daughter, with Venus in Capricorn, would set up her toy cash register in her room on laundry day. She would "sell" her dirty clothes to me for a penny per piece. I thought that was pretty resourceful, and catered to it until she found she could make more money making potholders and selling them to the neighbors!

One challenge for the child with Capricorn energies is maintaining a positive attitude. This is absolutely necessary if the child is to express the more advantageous qualities of the sign. Because of the strong tie to the physical and material aspects of life, the child can quickly become depressed if s/he does not have some particular toy or does not get something which s/he strongly desires. The child must learn to be grateful for what s/he has, and would be blessed to understand that appreciation is the first key to abundant living.

All children of earth signs will enjoy contact with their natural elements, and Capricorn is no exception. Gardening or spending time in nature is an absolute. There will probably be a love of trees, especially those that are very large and ancient. The older Capricorn child might enjoy a tree house, especially if s/he can proudly say, "I built it myself!" Climbing is also a favorite pastime of Capricorn. Even the infant can be observed climbing, sometimes before s/he can walk! These children also love rocks and crystals.

The sense of smell is often highly developed, and small children with Capricorn planets love anything they can "scratch and sniff." Watch these children as they grow older: the first thing they may do with a new pair of shoes is smell them!

Children with Capricornian influences often have a great sense of humor. (This must be the "corn" aspect of Capricorn.) Given encouragement, these kids will offer parents and friends ample opportunities to find humor in almost any situation. Sometimes the humor centers around puns, so be ready to groan. One never knows when a Capricorn may be lurking about, ready to transform serious dialogue into his/her next play on words!

Children with Capricorn energies are often loners, or may prefer the company of older children or adults. Parents and significant adults will be observed as the models for behavior. The child will continually test and probe to see whether or not the parent is worthy of respect. Once that respect is earned, however, it will endure.

Aquarius

Aquarius introduces us to the fixed quality of air. Inventiveness and original thinking are this sign's trademark with the intellectual thrust strongly focused. Children with tiveness and original thinking are this sign's trademark with the intellectual thrust strongly focused. Children with Aquarian energies are independent, idealistic, unique and often unconventional.

Life can be an exciting challenge for the child with Aquarian influences, offering endless opportunities to find alternative ways of approaching everything. The often rebellious quality of Aquarius will not be as readily apparent in the infant, although even then the parents may be aware of an unusual detachment emanating from the baby. One mother of an Aquarian baby commented to me, "My baby seems to be out in another dimension much of the time." Perhaps he was! These babies need plenty of human contact, but they also need freedom.

Present the tiny Aquarian with unusual toys of varying shapes, sizes and textures. Toys with moving parts will encourage the child to study them to see how they work. Give the baby plenty of room to crawl about and explore. Most of these babies are friendly, and will enjoy the company of many people.

As the child of Aquarius grows, his/her sense of independence also expands. The mind is very active and inventive. Toys which can be used in inventive ways will be necessary: interlocking blocks or erector sets which may be transformed into robots, creatures from another galaxy or intergalactic radios.

There is also a fascination with technological developments. If it has buttons, knobs or dials on it, the Aquarian child will want to know what it does, how it works, and in what other ways it might possibly be used. Safeguard the stereo, the video equipment and the computer until you are ready for the child to start manipulating them! Calculators, radios, computers, synthesizers and video games are also likely targets for the Aquarian mind.

Air and space travel may hold a special fascination. Encourage these explorations, as they may be a necessary part of the child's identity. Astronomy and astrology are also natural areas of interest and study.

Geometry is often a favorite study of those with Aquarian leanings and should be encouraged in a participatory manner when the child is very young. Have the toddler walk around the perimeter of a large triangle. Find geometric shapes in daily life—the octagonal stop sign, the circular Moon, etc. Other mathematical subjects may also interest the child, especially if Mercury is in Aquarius. These should be supported and encouraged as the child is ready for them.

Aquarius is not an emotional sign, and often seems rather distant and aloof. This detachment offers the child an opportunity to understand the concept of unconditional love. S/he may be directed more to groups of people than to just one person, thereby indicating a need for several playmates. Later, larger groups of friends might be enjoyed. Becoming involved in organizations such as scouting might be worthwhile for the child. Not only would this offer her/him an opportunity to be involved with other young people, but would provide humanitarian activities in which to participate.

Aquarius needs to focus on humanity and the masses. Given a "cause," the revolutionary nature of Aquarius can be directed to facilitate needed changes within a system. Teaching the young child the advantageous methods of bringing about change is a challenge, but a necessary one. If the child cannot distinguish between the creative and destructive sides of revolution, s/he may later direct energy in ways that create difficulties.

One aspect many "grown-up" Aquarians have shared with me is that they often felt like the oddball or misfit among their peers. Feeling different can be hard for a child because s/he does not feel included.

Help the child feel comfortable with his/her uniqueness and special qualities. Encourage his/her natural inventiveness. Now that we are on the threshold of the Aquarian Age, these children are likely to lead the way into humanity's new expression on this planet. The child should be supported in his/her unique approaches to problems and in his/her concern for humanity and the planet.

Because of Aquarius' fixed nature, ideas and concepts may become rigid once they are formed. Learning to listen to others' ideas and consider them as potentially valid until proven otherwise may present a challenge. Sometimes there is a "know it all" attitude when Aquarian energies are present in the chart. This can be damaging in many ways, mostly because it creates unnecessary limitations for the child!

If this type of attitude persists, it would be wise to challenge it at every opportunity to help the child broaden his/her perspectives. Also, those with Aquarian energies must learn to trust the intuitive aspect of the Self early in life. Logic can too easily become the king for Aquarius. We certainly need logical, pragmatic thinking, but not to the exclusion of the all-important attunement to the Higher Self.

Pisces

The twelfth sign of the zodiac is the mutable water sign Pisces. Pisces represents the idealistic, intangible qualities of life—spirituality, imagination, mysticism and romanticism.

For the child with energies in this sign, life presents the challenge of staying in touch with physical plane reality while remaining attuned to the powerful inner guide. There is often a dreaminess or other-worldliness with Pisces children, as well as a sense of magic. With a heightened sensitivity to the physical, mental, emotional and spiritual levels, Pisces can experience an increased awareness of life.

The infant with energies in Pisces may be very peaceful, especially if his/her personal environment is calm and pleasant. Transcendent music is almost a necessity for these babies to help them maintain a strong sense of inner peace. If the environment is boisterous, this child will feel it more intensely than most children and may react with surprisingly strong signs of discontent.

Walks near a pond, lake or the ocean will feel wonderful to this baby. Bath time can be a special treat. Encourage an early rapport with the element of water. Pisces babies enjoy swaying movements, and might be delighted to be held or carried while Mom, Dad or a sibling dances with them. Sensations of all types are heightened. There may be a special delight when s/he finds her/his reflection in a mirror.

The toddler with energies in this sign will adore fairy tales. Stories of angels and other light beings will be mesmerizing. Aquariums may fascinate the child for long periods of time. Encourage the imagination with dressing up and games of make-believe. Since Pisces often has problems relating to physical reality, the aspects of the physical plane should be gently, but definitely, introduced. For example, the difference between a pretend bear and a real bear could be easily identified during a trip to the zoo.

Be especially sensitive to these children when allowing them to watch movies or television. Those with Pisces energies have a highly impressionable consciousness. It is too easy to allow the television to become the babysitter.

Try to spend time viewing programs with your child in order to help her/him distinguish between reality and fantasy. I am not suggesting that fantasy and imagination be repressed—in fact, they should be encouraged. But you must be a conscientious censor, since the graphic images in motion pictures and television can alter an impressionable consciousness for life.

Toys for Piscean children should encourage the imagination and creativity. Costumes, make-up and other role-playing aids will be enjoyed. Drama lessons will probably be well received by the child over age four or five.

It is easy for the child with Pisces energies to escape into an inner world to avoid interaction with others. Provide ample opportunities for the child to play with other children to balance this tendency. New situations can be a bit frightening, and should be presented to the child gradually. As the child grows, and a new activity or different situation is planned, talk with him/her about what changes are about to take place. This child has an amazing ability to adapt to new situations, but the imagination is so strong that the child may withdraw inside the self if s/he feels too afraid.

For example, if the four year old is about to begin preschool, a preview trip to the school is strongly advised. Then you can talk with the child and have him/her imagine what it would be like to be there. Generate positive, exciting feelings in this exercise. Then, when the child is dropped at preschool, it will be familiar and pleasant since s/he has already been there in reality *and* in the world of imagination.

Encourage young children with Piscean influences to share stories and fantasies with you. This encourages the sense of imagination while maintaining a connection between you and the child. By giving these children opportunities to flow into their special worlds, we encourage the positive use of their talents.

Dance is often an excellent release for the Piscean. Swimming, scuba diving or other aquatic activities would also be good outlets. There may be an interest in painting or photography—a camera would be a welcome gift. Music education might include not only dance, but voice, string instruments or synthesizers.

Growing exotic flowers or caring for tropical fish is often a favorite hobby for the young Piscean. These types of hobbies can last a lifetime.

Pisces is a channel for divine compassion. Offer these children opportunities to care for and help others. Let them know that they can make a difference. The power of their love, accompanied by the vision within them, can truly make the world a better place!

KEYWORDS: SIGNS OF THE ZODIAC

♈	ARIES	Independence, leadership, teasing, pioneering
♉	TAURUS	Stability, sensuality, conservative, consistent, creative
♊	GEMINI	Intellectual, witty, quick, curious, changeable, flighty
♋	CANCER	Sensitive, intuitive, indirect, nurturant, protective
♌	LEO	Dramatic, loyal, prideful, self-confident, courageous
♍	VIRGO	Analytical, discriminating, orderly, precise, methodical
♎	LIBRA	Peace-loving, social, charming, artistic, balancing, relating
♏	SCORPIO	Mysterious, intriguing, intense, powerful, transformational, secretive
♐	SAGITTARIUS	Understanding, philosophical, expansive, optimistic
♑	CAPRICORN	Realistic, practical, organized, cautious, determined, persistent
♒	AQUARIUS	Friendly, innovative, eccentric, inventive, unusual, humanitarian
♓	PISCES	Mystical, impressionable, imaginative, idealistic, transcendant

Table 1

Chapter Four

ENERGY: THE SUN, MOON AND PLANETS

In astrology, we concern ourselves with energy. Each human being is spiritual energy incarnate in matter. We are each a complete universe, and the power of that individual universe is directed by the Higher Self in coordination with the power of mind energy. Mind energy, which expresses as thought forms, is focused through the will power of the human being.

Learning to focus and use our individual power requires the development of personal awareness. We gain knowledge and understanding of ourselves as we mature and become more comfortable with who we are and how we function.

For the child learning to express the energies of the Self, a sense of identity has not yet formed. We must view the individual energies within the child as potentials for development. These energies are symbolized in each individual horoscope by the Sun, Moon and planets in our solar system. By understanding these symbolic concepts, we gain a deeper insight into human nature and human needs.

Developmental psychology has taught us much about

a child's various stages of growth. In the very early stages, the child is dependent upon others for physical survival. This dependency is usually focused within the child's immediate family, especially through the father and mother.

As a child matures and gradually becomes more adept in controlling bodily functions and movements, this dependency lessens somewhat. The child gains mastery over the self through a gradual process of unfoldment until, finally, s/he can demonstrate full responsibility for her/his basic survival needs. Continuing maturation gives the ability to meet other needs until a state of independence is reached and the child has "grown up."

This developmental process continues throughout life, and can be studied astrologically by observing cycles of energy called *progressions* and *transits*. Once again, we use the symbols of the Sun, Moon and planets in understanding this continual unfolding of the Self.

We must have a clear understanding of the basic meanings of the Sun, Moon and planets when applying astrology to children. Although a child will not express each of these energies completely in the early years of life, the needs and the energies are still there developing. Astrology offers a framework from which to examine the needs of a developing child, to be used with loving guidance in helping the child to fully express a sense of personal wholeness.

The Sun and Moon

The Sun and Moon are referred to as the "luminaries" or "light bodies" in the astrological chart. The Sun emanates light, while the Moon reflects it. Within the human being, the Sun is the light of the soul. It projects the individual ego, will power and sense of individuality. The Moon symbolizes the reflective nature of humanity. It is the absorbing, subconscious mind.

We also experience an understanding of ourselves through interactions with other people in our lives. For the child, the Sun and Moon are first experienced as the Father and Mother. Father illustrates the assertive sense of will power (the Sun) and Mother illustrates the receptive nurturance of the Moon.

As the child grows and externalizes the personality self, it is easy to identify parental influences. How many times have you heard someone say, "Why, she laughs just like her mother!" or, "When he said that, he looked just like his Dad!"? How often have we, as parents, had to remind ourselves of our negative habits when we observe them in our own children? The small child will not be spending time analyzing why s/he behaves in a particular manner; s/he largely just mimics what s/he sees and hears.

The Sun and Moon in the child's chart do not tell us exactly what the parents are like—they only indicate how the child *perceives* the parents. The child's perceptions of the parents will almost always be somewhat different from the parents' perceptions of themselves. Yet it is this framework of perception which determines the child's understanding of not only who the parents are, but who s/he is. We will examine these perceptions in depth in Chapter Eleven.

When we study the Sun in a child's chart, we are looking at how the sense of individuality and drive for significance might express within him/her. We can understand what might motivate a child by looking at the sign in which the Sun is placed. A child with the Sun in Leo, for example, could be motivated by recognition for his/her achievements. The father will provide the pattern the child is likely to follow for his/her idea of recognition and how to achieve it.

The sign in which the Sun is placed will also indicate which qualities the child is seeking to identify within the father. A Scorpio Sun child may easily identify with Father's repressed emotionality. But if Dad can show an acknowledgement of his emotional needs, the child may find it easier to accept the intensity of his/her own emotional nature. The qualities of Scorpio indicate a powerful ego, but one that feels vulnerable if exposed.

By studying Jungian psychology, we gain a sense of the archetypal patterns in our lives. Archetypes are models for unconscious needs which we usually project onto others in our lives. These significant others are the models we use to develop an understanding of ourselves. This projection can be identified through astrological symbology and is tremendously important in understanding the needs of the child. Parental attitudes and behavior toward the child are critical in shaping the child's emotional matrix.

The subconscious mind is symbolized by the Moon in the astrological chart. This is the matrix from which our habit patterns emerge. The archetypal projection of the Moon is Mother, who provides nurturing, comfort and security. Good keywords for the Moon are "nurturance" and "mothering." Mother is the model for the child's developing sense of how s/he will nurture and care for others, and, most importantly, how the child will nurture him/herself.

By analyzing the Sun and Moon signs in the child's chart, we observe the qualities the child needs to express through these particular energies. The energy of the Sun—will power, drive, ego, personal power—and the energy of the Moon—receptivity, nurturance, emotional security, highest needs—form the basic building blocks in understanding the child's real needs.

Too often, parents will project their own needs onto their children, thus overwhelming the child's true nature.

Although these two energies definitely show how the child perceives the parents, they indicate even more strongly who the child *really* is and what s/he needs.

In counseling parents who are divorcing, I appeal to them to allow the child to see each of them as individuals. I encourage them not to "have it out" in front of the child, or badmouth the absent parent to the child. Doing this inevitably traumatizes the child. The parents should keep any hostility they may feel toward the spouse or ex-spouse to themselves.

The Sun in the chart shows us how the child would like to be perceived, what the child needs to feel motivated toward achievement and what makes the child feel significant in the world. Characteristics identified by the signs will indicate how the child is likely to go about meeting these needs.

The Sun placed in fire signs will encourage a child to be active in expressing needs for recognition. These children may seem to "shine" more easily. The child with the earthy Sun is more grounded, and may take a practical approach to expressing the ego needs. With the Sun in water signs, a child may be more emotional about him/herself. This sensitivity creates a quieter approach to expressing will power and drive. Air sign Suns express verbally and intellectually, and tie their identities to their thoughts ("I think, therefore, I am.")

The Moon represents the subconscious mind. This aspect of ourselves operates on automatic pilot. Consider the habits in our lives. We learn how to tie our shoes when we are young, then never really have to think about it again. The subconscious mind directs the body's actions, and we can tie our shoes without "thinking."

The developing child has a very open subconscious mind, but is not just a "blank slate." Rather, this aspect of the self is most impressionable in the early years due to the dependency upon others for survival. Even small infants soon make their particular warbles and cries meaningful to the receptive parent. Observing a mother and child tells you much about their intuitive links with one another. Baby cries the cry which tells Mom, "I'm hungry!" and Mom responds by feeding him/her.

Yet Mother still has more power than Baby. Imagine the small infant, alone in the crib at night. Awakening hungry in a dark room, the baby cries. Mother awakens, arises, and touches a switch. Voila!, light magically appears! What is the baby to think of this all-powerful being who brings light into the darkness and provides warm milk for his/her nurturance? The impressions from Mommy are very important, since she provides the primary matrix for the child's habit patterns and emotional security. Mother is the Moon.

Moon energy is most significant in the first few years of life. If we can attune to the child's true needs by understanding the sign and house in which the Moon is placed, we can offer the child an optimum set of stimuli. Astrologer Noel Tyl described the Moon as the "reigning need" in the chart. This highest need must be fulfilled if the child is to achieve a sense of inner security.

Using the sign to understand the things a child needs to feel secure can be an excellent guideline for parents:

Moon in Aries will be more secure when given independence and room to move.

Moon in Taurus needs the Rock of Gibraltar, and feels best when the environment is predictable and recognizable.

Moon in Gemini needs variety and intellectual interactions with others.

Moon in Cancer feels secure when protected and cuddled.

Moon in Leo is most secure when s/he is the center of attention.

Moon in Virgo's security depends upon smoothly running circumstances. This child will feel best in a sparkling clean environment.

Moon in Libra is more secure with someone else. This energy likes to be balanced by another person.

Moon in Scorpio's security comes from a deep-level bonding with the mother, who is the archetype of the Great Mother.

Moon in Sagittarius' security is best achieved with lots of room and ample opportunity for expansion.

Moon in Capricorn's security depends upon consistency and reliability.

Moon in Aquarius needs mental stimulation and a strong mental and intuitive tie with Mother. This child also needs independence, since there is usually an intuitive sense of how to get help if needed!

Moon in Pisces needs to be one with Mother, who symbolizes Divine Love and Compassion.

The types of schedules most suited to each child can be understood through the Moon sign as well. For example, a child with the Moon in Capricorn might prefer a fairly predictable and disciplined schedule, whereas the child with the Sagittarius Moon may enjoy more time for spontaneity and games.

One way in which a child expresses Moon energy is through eating habits. The child with a fixed Moon sign is most likely to be stubborn about trying new foods, and knows exactly what s/he does and does not like. My daughter, with her Scorpio Moon, would eat only yogurt with fruit and whole grain breads from age two to three! If a child has a Gemini Moon, however, tastes may change from meal to meal.

When examining the Sun's placement by house and the sign through which its energy is directed, we gain an understanding of the child's ego self. We also see the child's perception of the assertive parent (usually the father) and the manner in which the child will exercise assertiveness.

The Moon's sign and house placement indicate the types of habits the child is most likely to develop. We gain insights into the child's perceptions of the receptive parent (usually the mother) and how the child expresses security needs. We also gain an understanding of the child's emotional expression through the Moon.

These two energies are vitally important in understanding a child. By examining them as a unit, we can see how both the inner and outer needs will be expressed.

Mercury

The planet Mercury signifies communication, inventiveness, transportation and sensory impression. It is through the vehicle of Mercury that we share our thoughts, ideas and impressions of the world.

The qualities of Mercury energy involve the translation of what is experienced inside the person to an external expression, hence the concept of communication. We communicate in many ways—through spoken or written words, gestures, body language and other expressions. We can also communicate an idea through a photograph or pictures.

The function of Mercury is to provide that communication, in whatever form. Mercury also represents the energy of transportation, which has a variety of options on the physical plane. We can transport ourselves by using the physical motion of the body (walking) or by employing a vehicle.

For the developing child, Mercurial energy brings about a series of transformations. Unable to speak in sentences or execute elaborate drawings, the tiny infant has two primary methods of expression—the voice, and generalized body movements. As the baby grows, we see several forms of Mercurial expression. Cries, gurgles and coos are transformed into sounds which are recognizable to the parents, and Baby's first words are formed. Eventually, the child learns the language of his or her world and engages in more advanced forms of communication.

The eagerness with which a child chooses to communicate verbally is indicated by the quality of the sign in which Mercury is placed. In air signs, Mercury is more readily expressive and verbal. In the earth signs, there may be a quietness of speech. A fire sign Mercury is strongly—often dramatically—expressive. Mercury in water signs is often expressed with more reticence.

Mercury offers clues to the child's sensory input. The five senses are our physical mechanisms for the observation and assimilation of the external environment. Small crawling babies are known for their tendency to put almost anything into their mouths in order to "explore" it. This inventiveness in exploring the world is the operation of the baby's Mercury.

The sign in which Mercury is placed indicates how the child approaches sensory exploration. Mercury in Aries children are likely to jump right into situations, just following the impulse to know what that thing is! The child with Mercury in Virgo might sit back and study an object before letting the senses of taste, touch and smell have their turns. The Gemini Mercury is highly curious, and may try two sensory impressions at once.

Mercury is associated with the hands and handwriting. Sign language is an effective means of communication when verbal expression is impossible. This use of the hands as the primary communication tool is another expression of Mercury.

The sign in which Mercury is placed indicates the types of things a child will enjoy doing with the hands. Mercury in Gemini is well-known for hand gestures, and may also be a good placement for writing. Mercury in Cancer might enjoy the feel of yarn, and might like creating things out of fibers and fabrics. Libran Mercury enjoys creating beauty with the hands, perhaps by painting or writing poetry. Use the basic concepts of the signs and extend them to the meaning of Mercury to understand the many ways Mercury operates for the child.

As a child grows, we see a refinement of Mercurial energy. Mercury's sign indicates the types of subjects a child enjoys learning and talking about. It is the nature of Mercurial energy to bring about improvements. By observing the child's approaches to problem solving and improving his/her environment, we are observing Mercury at work. Understanding the sign placement of Mercury will aid the parent/guide/teacher in arranging particular types of situations in which a child will feel more inventive. We also have clues to the concepts which the child will find most interesting.

Children with *Mercury in air signs* may be the most talkative, although they might not necessarily be the best listeners! These children are interested in learning about a variety of concepts. Primarily, they want to have someone with whom there can be an interchange. These children love identifying and classifying.

Children with *Mercury in fire signs* may speak without thinking (with the possible exception of Leo, who always enjoys sounding like an authority). These children are interested in ideas which can inspire them to create.

Children with *Mercury in water signs* often have their

emotions mixed up with their thoughts, and may have some difficulty separating them. There is a highly impressionable quality to the mind. These children like learning about subjects with deep meanings.

The *earthy Mercury* is interested in thinking and talking about subjects which have a practical application. "Hands-on" experience is worth a thousand words to this child.

In Homer's *Odyssey*, Mercury was the messenger of the gods. He carried messages, but did not originate them. In the astrological scheme, Mercury is also a messenger. This energy is the translator, communicator and illustrator of our thoughts.

In dealing with children, we study Mercury to find a child's easiest modes of communication. Insights into the child's areas of interest are provided through this symbology. By stimulating the child's thinking in ways s/he can identify with, we bolster the child's intellectual self-esteem. This can make learning more enticing. Through the clues Mercury offers, we can find ways to motivate the child's desire to learn and help him/her develop an understanding of this incredible world in which we live.

Venus

The planet Venus symbolizes the value systems in our lives and the manner in which we express feelings of love. Venus inspires creative efforts as well, and is the energy of artistic expression. Venus is one of the primary feminine principles in the astrological chart. Children express Venus through their experiences of love and their developing understanding of what brings pleasure and value to their lives.

The energy of Venus does not seem to be easily expressed by the very young child, but it is certainly experienced. Although children can be tender, and do display love and affection, it is not always the enduring love we consider when we think of love in the mature, intimate sense. However, the pattern for this future intimate expression is set in childhood. This is one area of the child's life which is open to development, and will definitely be colored by the child's influences and experiences. Venus is often attached to the concept of beauty, and we can certainly expose the child to things s/he will appreciate as beautiful.

The child with *Venus in air signs* loves ideas, stories, airy colors, spending time with friends and visual arts.

The *earthy Venus* is stimulated by the things of nature, and will find trees, mountains and natural surroundings beautiful.

Watery Venus is sensual, and appreciates the feeling of water, the bright colors of spring flowers, the sounds of the ocean and the embrace of the mother.

Venus in the fire signs is more showy, and enjoys things which sparkle and glitter. It loves to be active and may be enticed by candlelight or the flames of the fireplace.

Placing a child in surroundings which appeal to the Venusian nature will make creative and artistic expression easier. Ideal surroundings include not only physical structures, but compatible types of people, appealing colors, and an overall energy which is comfortable to the child.

The sign in which Venus is placed is also a good indicator of creative talents. The references in Chapter Nine will be helpful in this determination. As we develop an understanding of the interactions between planets (the aspects), we can further fine tune the expression of creative talents for the child.

Emotionally, Venus indicates the child's ability to show his/her feelings. Emotion is the outward expression of inner feelings. The sign in which Venus is placed indicates the qualities that emotional expression will take. The child with Venus in Gemini, for example, may talk about feeling a certain way while seeming quite detached from the emotion itself. The airy nature of Gemini is not comfortable with deep levels of emotions. For this reason, I suggest to parents that this child be given ample opportunity to express him/herself when confronted with emotional situations. (Of course, this encouragement is necessary for all children.) Venus in Capricorn may be a difficult placement for a child, as this sign tends to be overly structured and cautious in its qualities. A good outlet is to encourage the child's sense of humor at times when the emotions seem restricted. Capricorn love puns and corny jokes!

Venus energy is often directed to the things we value, and is expressed in the adult years by the types of material goods we desire. In the formative years, we can use the astrological indicators from Venus (its sign and house placement) to understand the kinds of things a child holds in high esteem. Sometimes we can use this revelation to offer the child a more positive reward. A child with Venus in Leo, for example, might be overly possessive of friends. S/he could be encouraged to enjoy the friend when s/he is there, then focus on a new activity when the friend chooses to leave. It should ultimately aid him/her when developing mature relationships in adult years to know that people cannot be possessed.

Mars

The energy of Mars is direct, active and assertive. Children express Mars energy through bursts of physical activity and through the basic temperament. Anger is a Martian expression, and the sign in which Mars is found will indicate how anger is expressed.

Physically, Mars expresses as the basic energy level in the individual. The *fire* signs seem to be the most physically assertive signs, conferring a powerful sense of energy and a direct expression of physical power. *Earth* signs seem to have a more moderate energy level, while the *air* signs tend to dissipate physical force. In *water* signs, Mars holds in the physical power, and indicates a good reservoir of physical strength. With water signs, however, there can be too much holding back when release would be more desirable.

In determining the types of sports or recreation a child might enjoy, use the sign in which Mars is placed for a basic guideline. (See the Table in Chapter Six.) The house placement of Mars will indicate the types of associations which might be more desirable when asserting the self. For example, group sports would be enjoyed most with Mars in the 11th House, whereas those with Mars in the 1st House might prefer individual sports such as tennis or track and field events. Combining sign and house, Mars in Pisces in the 1st House might enjoy swimming or dance as an individual athletic activity. But that same Mars in Pisces in the 7th House would prefer to dance with a partner!

Mars in Capricorn seems drawn to sports which require endurance such as marathon running. Capricorn is attracted to mountains and heights, like the goat which symbolizes it, so climbing and snow skiing are likely prospects. Finding a sport the child will enjoy is the key to aiding him/her in finding ways to generate more physical energy for him/herself.

Dealing with a child's temper is one task which most parents handle with discomfort. Anger is an emotion we all have, and which we all need to express. The key to dealing with anger is to release it in a *constructive* way whenever possible.

Children with Mars placed in water signs often have the most difficult time releasing anger; instead, they tend to repress it. Work with these children to find ways to let off steam. Perhaps getting into the element of water itself and splashing or swimming away the tension would be helpful.

Whenever a child with Mars in an air sign is angry, s/he may scream, shout and speak wounding words. Generally, Mars in air will be very open about feeling angry. Appeal to the child's need to understand this feeling by talking about what created the anger after things have cooled down a little. Discuss what the child would like to do to change the situation which led to the outburst.

Children with an earthy Mars may also hold onto anger, and can be tremendously volatile when the anger is finally released. These children are the best candidates for "working off" the anger.

The fiery Mars is open, direct and concise with anger. Once the anger is expressed, it will probably be completely released.

All children learn about the destructive side of anger after a while, but may not know how to avoid it. We can aid them by understanding the basic form the anger takes and finding creative ways to direct it. For example, the child with Mars in Leo could be encouraged to dramatize these angry feelings, becoming a lion for a while and getting in touch with the primal level of this feeling. The Mars in Virgo might be able to direct the same energy in a more precise manner, perhaps by playing drums. As the child matures, the possible ways of directing anger become more varied.

The use of physical energy begins at the moment of birth, although control of that energy is a challenge which really only comes to the fore in the early teens. At this age, the developing adolescent may find the more negative qualities of Mars surfacing. When the physical body grows stronger, assertiveness may get out of hand. Learning to control one's temperament is more difficult during these years. Fights often result. Sometimes exercises such as martial arts are helpful to the teen who has problems positively directing physical force.

Mars also represents sexual expression, which is not fully realized until the hormones begin their inevitable awakening. This new force can be confusing for the young teenager, who may often feel uncontrolled.

It is at this time that we alter our approach to ourselves and begin to assert the self in a more powerful manner. The sexual energy may be openly expressed with the Aries Mars, or more covertly expressed through Mars in Cancer. How the adolescent youth deals with Mars energy will effect his/her sexual expression in the adult years. Although much of this behavior will be learned through the adult role model, it is the basic needs of the youth which must be considered. Just because a young man has an openly assertive father doesn't mean that he needs to be openly assertive himself.

Take the example of the adolescent with Mars in Cancer. S/he will need to express her/his sexual and assertive feelings in a somewhat indirect manner. When confronted with a group of friends who are more outward and direct in their Mars expression, s/he may feel that something is wrong with her/him. There's nothing wrong, only a different approach and a less straightforward expression of energy! Cancer is sensitive, and does not blend easily with the direct, assertive quality of Mars.

By understanding Mars in a child's chart, we find clues for dealing with his/her needs for expressing physical force, temper and sexuality. The manner in which the child makes demands is seen through his/her expression of Martian energy. By focusing on the positive qualities of the sign in which Mars is placed, we can help the child deal with feelings of anger in a constructive way.

Mars energy is challenging to humans—it exudes a raw, primitive power. Fortunately, we have other aspects of the self to support and temper the development of this physical force. We must learn to confront and deal with the "beast" of the Self in order to be fully expressive. This process begins in childhood. When the child learns to accept all aspects of the Self, and learns creative ways to deal with his/her own power, there is no limit to his/her potential development.

Jupiter

The energy of Jupiter offers the individual an opportunity to expand his/her personal universe. Jupiter gives us the desire to understand the meaning of life and gain an awareness of the Universal Laws. This energy helps us pass beyond the limits of individuality and reach an understanding of Universal Truth.

Through Jupiter we achieve a sense of honor and a basic philosophy of life. Jupiter demonstrates the sense of confidence, enthusiasm and optimism which gives us the hope of a brighter day, even in difficult times.

For the child, Jupiter expresses as the desire to expand and grow. This energy definitely requires a period of maturity to realize, although it does operate at basic levels within the child.

Even the small child of four will wonder about God or universal principles as s/he contemplates the "whys" of life. Jupiter energy aids us in finding divine principles in our lives, and is often signified by a special teacher or guide. For the child, the parents are usually the first guides.

As interactions with others increase, other teachers appear.

I have always associated Jupiter with a sense of divine protection, and encourage parents to teach their children about the protective energy of Truth and Understanding. This light of truth can be illustrated through stories. The *Star Wars* theme of the dark and light sides of the Force is a good way of introducing young children to universal principles. Fairy tales and other allegorical stories have illustrated moral lessons for centuries.

I am often amazed at the level of awareness I observe in young children. Too often, parents and teachers forget the natural ability the child has to expand consciousness beyond the physical level. Given opportunities to share their understanding, children are wonderful and surprisingly insightful teachers.

Jupiter is often illustrated in the behavior of the child by the sense of "I want." The child must be taught to balance her/his long list of "I wants" with personal responsibility. Too strong a desire to expand our possessions causes us to become motivated by the materialistic aspect of Jupiter rather than by the principles of harmonious abundance.

We can appeal to the energy of Jupiter when motivating a child. Look to the house and sign position of Jupiter to find the types of things which will appeal to the child. For example, the child with Jupiter in Aquarius in the 3rd House might be easily motivated by the promise of a trip to the local planetarium with friends. This reward would appeal to the Jupiterian sense of expansion since it deals with the vastness of the solar system. Spending time with friends is important to Aquarius, and the travel this activity would provide is a perfect 3rd House activity.

Jupiter also gives indications of the child's desire to learn and increase his/her concept of the world. We can use the placement of Jupiter by sign and house to gain insights into increasing these desires within the child. When used effectively, Jupiter energy provides continuing understanding and a sense of wisdom. If not properly channeled, Jupiter can confer a sense of wanderlust and a lack of direction.

The house placement of Jupiter may also indicate what the child takes for granted. Help the child develop a sense of gratitude, especially in the area signified by Jupiter's house placement. A child with Jupiter in the 2nd House may take the material things in life for granted. By helping the child learn different values, including the management of money, the potentially difficult side of this placement can be avoided.

Generosity is a feature of Jupiter which is also significant. It is important that the child experience the true meaning of giving and sharing. There can be a fine line between generosity and wastefulness. We can be wasteful of energy in many ways, through physical, material, spiritual and emotional outlets. The house and sign in which Jupiter are placed will offer indicators of the areas in which the child needs to expand (not waste) energy. Sometimes a child does not know the difference!

Jupiter, representative of the energy of expansion, abundance, optimism, and generosity, is known as the "greater benefic" in old astrology texts. For the truly beneficial aspects of the energy to be used, the person must develop a sense of reasonable limitations. This can be enhanced or altered by other planets which support or detract from the energy of Jupiter (this will be discussed in the "Aspects" section of the book).

It is generally not until the child has developed some measure of cognitive skill that the awareness of Jupiter can be taught. Jupiter is a function of the higher mind, the part of our consciousness which can connect with the Divine. The early awareness of Jupiter deals primarily with the concepts of sharing, positive thinking, enthusiasm and hope for reward.

Saturn

The energy of Saturn is disciplined, structured and responsible. For the young child, Saturn is initially signified by the structures, limits and expectations imposed by the parents. Later, social systems such as schools and institutions take on a Saturnian role. The teachers become important disciplinarians, preparing a child for further integration into society.

Children do not like restrictions and limitations, yet the necessity of learning the positive use of limits is critical. It is truly a challenge for the parents to provide the limitations necessary for the child without inhibiting the child's creative self-expression. In the child's chart, we can see Saturn operating as the force of discipline, responsibility and structure. It provides the child with a sense of inner security.

Saturn acquaints us with the realities of existence on the physical plane. Tiny babies are concerned primarily with the basic functions of survival, but they too have Saturn in their lives. In fact, it is at this time that a child may feel the most restricted. The consciousness, which is adjusting to the reality of life in the physical form, may feel tremendously inhibited by the restrictions of physical plane existence. We need to become aware of the frustrations of the tiny infant, with his/her limited ability to express his/her wants and needs. Too often, parents are acutely aware of the limitations a child places on their lives, but forget the frustrations of the baby.

Babies learn rapidly when adjusting to their needs. One aspect of Saturn deals with daily routines and schedules, and there have been some interesting debates concerning whether or not a baby needs a definite feeding schedule or "on-demand" feedings. Even in the beginning of life on Earth, Saturn begins to set its limits!

The awareness of Saturn is another function of the developing human being which requires some maturity to understand. Saturn is symbolic of time in our lives, and deals also with our awareness of time.

Children have difficulty understanding time. When you consider that a child can base his/her perceptions of time only upon personal experience, it is no wonder that Christmas seems eons away to a child of five. A year represents one-fifth of his/her life!

Patience is a Saturnian concept, and is generally not seen in great amounts among small children. When dealing with the sense of time, children are aware of the present moment, their desires within the present moment, and very little else. As the child matures, s/he learns that some things require waiting. This aids in understanding the operation of Saturn.

Another aspect of Saturn deals with discipline. We can look to the child's house and sign placement of Saturn to understand the areas which will be most disciplined and what form the discipline will take. For example, Saturn in Leo in the 5th House may approach creativity (5th House) in a structured (Saturn) way, and could be responsive to discipline which is dramatic and consistent (Leo). Also, we can see how the child will discipline him/herself, and how much responsibility s/he will take for his/her own actions. This is further fine tuned when we examine the aspect Saturn makes with other planets in the chart.

Since Saturn represents restriction, we can view the areas where a child may feel most limited and restricted. Saturn in the 1st House may restrain the projection of the personality. Children with Saturn in the 1st House very often take on responsibilities at an early age, because of younger brothers or sisters or due to other reasons. It is important that the child be able to cope with the restraints s/he feels; otherwise a self-defeating attitude may develop.

A child truly begins to develop a sense of Saturn around age six or seven. There are cyclical patterns represented by the transit of Saturn. The transits are the positions of the planets at any given time in life compared to the pattern of the natal chart. When Saturn is making contact to the natal Saturn or to other planets by transit, the individual tends to develop a stronger sense of limitation and responsibility; this sense will be focused in the areas and energies symbolized by the planets and houses involved.

There are two basic Saturn cycles which occur at age *six to seven* and at age *thirteen to fourteen.* At the first Saturn cycle, about age seven, the child is beginning to feel very aware of the Self and of personal responsibility.

Many parents do not realize the tremendous responsibility a child feels at this age. The awareness of the world is centered strongly on the self, and the child usually feels responsible for almost anything that goes wrong. A family trauma, such as a divorce, might be interpreted by this child as being entirely his/her fault. It is crucial that the parents be aware that this age is critical in order to give much-needed support to the developing child.

About age fourteen, the second Saturn cycle occurs. By this age, the child has developed physical abilities which allow him/her to feel rather powerful, but does not yet have a complete understanding of the nature of personal responsibility. There are generally many restrictions (Saturn) placed upon the teen which s/he does not appreciate.

Some of the problems inherent in this developmental cycle can be avoided if the parent and teen can sit down together and form open lines of communication. They need to work out a system in which the teenager feels s/he is allowed adequate personal responsibility, along with some measure of freedom. The teenager will probably respond well to a balanced system of freedom and responsibility at this age, but is likely to rebel against a highly restrictive situation.

It is the function of Saturn to confer an awareness of the physical plane. Not only does it provide restriction and discipline, but it also builds the foundations and support systems which offer a sense of personal security. Many people place security exclusively in the realm of material form, such as financial and material security. This is only one level of security, and one which is never totally reliable!

The most reliable level of security is the *inner* sense of security. This comes from learning to attune to the universal principles which teach us harmony within life. Granted, attaining a measure of material security aids in a sense of personal security, but it is not sufficient unto itself.

Saturn also symbolizes guilt and fear. Because of the restrictive nature of this energy, our response to it often comes through these negative reactions. Certainly, caution is a worthwhile form of Saturnine energy, but too often children are taught overwhelming fear. If allowed to be paralyzed by fear, the child cannot react in creative ways when dealing with obstacles in life.

Guilt's paralyzing effect makes it a close cousin to fear. Guilt usually results when a child is reprimanded for disobeying the "rules." Understanding that certain behavior is irresponsible or inappropriate need not produce feelings of extreme guilt in the child.

For the developing child, the archetype of Saturn is played through the parents, often most strongly through the father. The way in which Father gives the child messages of consistency, reliability, personal responsibility and caution will determine a pattern which the child will probably follow for the remainder of his/her life. The sign, house placement and aspects of Saturn in the chart tell us much about the child's developing need for security and structure in life. Structure and inhibition are two separate concepts, but often become confused in the formative years.

Consider the analogy of building a house. A strong, level foundation is laid, then the framework is built. Saturn provides the foundation and framework in the life of the child. In order to have a level foundation and a solid frame of reference in life, the child needs to receive consistent messages from the parents. Saturn represents this need for consistency, reliability and dependability. Without a clear sense of Saturn, the child has no real reference points for the developing self. In later chapters, we will explore aspects of Saturn and the ways in which this structure can be built or undermined.

Uranus

Uranus symbolizes supercharged energy. It provides us with a sense of the rare, eccentric and unique aspects of life. Through Uranus, we gain an awareness of Universal Brotherhood—the common ground of humanity.

This energy operates at a level of intuitive awareness, and confers a "knowingness." It is this aspect of life that psychologists are describing when they speak of the "other" side of the brain. This right-brain functioning is not logical, but is the aspect of the Self which attunes to a higher level of awareness.

Until the discovery of Uranus, Saturn was accepted as the boundary of our solar system. The planets beyond the bounds of Saturn—Uranus, Neptune and Pluto—are called the *outer planets* in astrology. We enter the realm beyond the personal self once we pass the boundary of Saturn. These transpersonal planets operate at the level of expanded awareness in the individual, and require a directed approach in order to be fully utilized. In childhood, Uranus is experienced as the strange, exceptional and ingenious.

Children with Uranus placed in an angular house (1st, 4th, 7th or 10th) may feel out of step with their peers. They may complain that they just don't fit in.

If this is the case, assure the child that his/her uniqueness is simply different. I will never forget the new sense of confidence I felt in my early teens when I read Thoreau and realized that it was okay to be different! We are so geared to become like everyone else and be a good clone (the workings of Saturn)! It feels secure to have a group, a belief or an ideal which is "acceptable."

Uranus is the unique—the part of us that is exceptional and *not* like everybody else. Uranus gifts us with special intuitive talents which enable us to attune to a Universal Mind. When strongly placed in the chart, the individual can become a "way shower," or spiritual teacher. Dealing with this can be difficult and confusing for a child who is struggling to maintain a sense of personal identity in the face of continual change. Uranus is another energy which may require some time to develop and appreciate fully.

The house in which Uranus is placed will indicate the aspect of the self which will be most unique. A child with Uranus in Libra in the 5th House may have outstanding talents in expressing artistry (5th House) through painting or other art forms (Libra). (Of course, we would analyze other aspects and planets to completely decipher the creative potential, although Uranus is a good indicator of special genius.) The ease of flow of the talents suggested by Uranus can be determined by the aspects Uranus makes to the personal planets (Sun, Moon, Mercury, Venus and Mars) in the chart.

Uranus energy is sometimes unmanageable until the individual knows how to flow with it. Flowing with this uniquely charged aspect of the Self requires a strong sense of self. Therefore, the parents and supportive others in the life will do well to offer unconditional support of the child's creative genius until the child can provide that support for him/herself. The independent nature of Uranus is also one aspect of the Self which requires some maturity to handle. However, babies with powerful Uranian vibrations seem independent even in the crawling stages!

Directed in an irresponsible manner, Uranus is disruptive and destructively revolutionary. This energy can bring about radical and revolutionary change within the individual, as well as offering him/her the ability to bring about changes within society as a whole. "Freedom" and "individuality" are the watchwords of Uranus.

To truly express these aspects of life, one must have a greater understanding of the reasons for change and accept the responsibility that accompanies personal freedom. These lessons are not easy ones for the young child or adolescent. Parents, guides and teachers can give the child opportunities to express personal individuality and uniqueness while also demonstrating the necessity of understanding the demands of society. (This can be a rather tricky proposal, since most adults do not understand how to do this either!)

Neptune

The illusory, mystical and other worldly aspects of life are symbolized by the planet Neptune. Neptune's vibrations have a sensitizing effect. This sensitivity has its effects on all aspects of life—physical, mental, emotional and spiritual.

Neptune is Divine Compassion. Through this energy, we can attune ourselves to the principles of Universal

Love. Neptune can also operate as the deceiver, and bring disappointments when the deceptions and delusions are revealed. It is hard to determine from the chart alone how the child will use any of these energies. Neptune, like an elusive, mystical butterfly, requires special development to be used in its highest form.

Neptune moves very slowly through the zodiac, and its sign placement has a generational effect. During the passage of Neptune in Libra, from 1942 to 1956, the "Flower Children" were born. At this writing, Neptune is in Capricorn, where it will remain through 1998. Understanding the sign placement of Neptune will give some clues to the beliefs of the generation in which a child is born.

Neptune tells us about the things we worship and the concepts we hold sacred. The Flower Children hold the idea of love and peace as sacred—a very Libran attitude. Those born with Neptune in Capricorn are more likely to hold the Capricornian concepts of determination, consistency and material success as sacred. There could be a very conservative quality in these children. They will understand the need to appreciate and care for the things of the Earth if they want to keep them.

The house placement of Neptune indicates the areas which are especially sensitized, and in which a more refined aspect of the self operates. For example, Neptune in the 3rd House brings an intuitive and mystical quality to communication. There may be a special intuitive link with the siblings. Neptune in the 6th House often brings a heightened intuitive sensitivity to animals.

The imagination is the realm of Neptune. We all know that children have wonderful imaginations. This is because they are more easily attuned to the inner realms of consciousness—the rational mind has not yet dominated the imagination.

In order to maintain imaginative creativity, the child can be taught ways to distinguish between physical reality and the alternate reality of the inner planes. In the past, parents and society have given strong messages that the special inner world is inferior to the "real" world. They were mistaken, however—reality has many levels of expression!

Neptune energy is intangible. The illusions created on the movie screen are Neptunian, but create a powerful impression on the conscious and subconscious mind. Does this mean that this impact is not real? As we understand the mutiple facets of human consciousness, we begin to tap into the realm of Neptune.

The world of dreams is also Neptunian. If you tell a child that a dream is not real, you shatter a level of the child's awareness. But explaining intangibles is difficult, so for centuries parents have been throwing up their hands and telling children, "It's not real! It's only a dream." Yes, it is a dream, but on its own level it is quite real. (The film *Dreamscape* took an interesting look at this question.)

What we have to explain to the child is that the horrifying beast in a nightmare is only a fear inside him/herself. We can show the child ways to banish these beasts.

My children have shared their dreams with me since they were very young. If a child wakes up frightened from a nightmare, physical caresses and a soothing voice will help bring him/her into a different level of reality. Tell the child that s/he is okay and give her/him some special comfort. Talk about making friends with the growling dog or sending light to the yucky monsters. I was so delighted when my three year old awakened one morning to tell me, "The monsters were after me, but I just threw pink flowers on them and then they were my friends."

The child must learn when imagination is and isn't appropriate. Imagination can be encouraged through art, storytelling, music or dramatic performance. I think children are naturally attuned to Neptunian vibrations even more than the coarser physical plane vibrations. We should encourage the child to maintain this attunement while gradually developing a greater awareness of the physical plane. By accepting this need in the child, we encourage the link with the Higher Self through creative expression while balancing it with an understanding of physical principles. By doing so, we avoid the tyranny of rational thought over intuition and imagination. This encourages the evolution of a more complete, balanced person.

Pluto

Pluto is the extremist of the zodiac, and operates at a very deep, intense level. The energy of this planet is normally inaccessible to the human consciousness. With attention to development of the inner realms and the awakening of the intuitive Self, Pluto is more readily expressive. The energies of Pluto take some time to manifest, but act as a powerful catalyst for transformation and regeneration when they do emerge.

Pluto represents the *evolutionary energy* of the zodiac.* Evolution occurs at all levels of life—physical, emotional, mental and spiritual. For the child, directed awareness of this energy is very difficult, since the personal self must be developed before this aspect can awaken. Although the energy of Pluto may be felt during the childhood years, it is not usually directed consciously at this time.

Pluto symbolizes the primordial essence of man. This energy flows from the Great Mother (the feminine principle of Divine Power) and is responsible for the radical changes brought about by birth and death. As human consciousness has matured, we have come to realize that

---

*See Jeff Green's *Pluto: Evolutionary Journey of The Soul* (Llewellyn).

these transformations take place more frequently in our lives than we thought. We experience many deaths and rebirths as we grow spiritually and psychologically. Often, the energy of Pluto is the stimulus for drastic changes in individuals when they move away from one level of functioning and into a radically new one.

In childhood, Pluto is felt as a compulsive, sometimes overwhelming force. Pluto is a generational planet, moving very slowly through the zodiac. Therefore, the placement by sign tells more about the transformational influence Pluto will have on that particular *generation* than it will about the changes in the individual.

However, when interpreting the child's astrological chart, the house placement indicates the *personal* expression of this energy. The house in which Pluto is placed will be the area of life in which the most drastic changes and transformations will take place. To further understand the workings of Pluto, we examine the aspects between Pluto and the other planetary energies. (This will be more critically examined in the following sections of this book.)

Pluto was discovered at the same time human beings learned to split the atom. This discovery coincided with the beginning of the Atomic Age, a period in human evolu tion in which we have developed the power to annihilate all life on the planet. Such is the power of Pluto to bring about change at the deepest levels of existence.

In the life of a child, Plutonian energy is experienced through changes in both the external and internal environments. Even children must often cope with death in their lives. If we can teach the child the truths of life, death and transformation, s/he can accept this aspect of deep, inner change more readily.

One good way to acquaint the child with Plutonian concepts without creating fear is through the metamorphic story of a tadpole changing into a frog. The child can be concepts without creating fear is through the metamorphic story of a tadpole changing into a frog. The child can be shown this miraculous transformation, and see the gradual development of one body structure into another. Watching another dramatically changing life cycle—egg to hatching to chick to bird—is also a good lesson.

We have other transformational processes to share with children. We can plant seeds together. We can have rituals at the time of death which are celebrations of change, yet which still allow the release of personal grief. Often, an opportunity to deal with death presents itself when a family pet dies. To hide these things from a child is damaging. Children have a remarkable way of understanding truth if it is just straightforwardly presented to them! Parents so often shield their children from truth because they fear their own pain. Love and understanding heal pain much more quickly than repression and fear.

Because of the deep level of Plutonian energy, many people fear it. Here truly lies the beast in the underworld, the dragon within the Self. Sometimes that dragon is placed in the child's inner consciousness through the fears of the parents. This can manifest as repressive and obsessive behavior. I know many adults who are dealing with the removal of these old dragons, often in painful ways. Perhaps we can implant more positive images in the minds of our children and teach them ways to banish these overwhelming fears.

Pluto is the darkness from which light emerges. To avoid the dark places within the Self is to avoid the ability to truly open to the Light! The child can be taught a sense of his/her own power in very positive terms, without experiencing the fear of annihilation.

Working on continual self-improvement promotes positive self-transformation. This can be encouraged even in early childhood. Where there are shadowy fears, illuminate them with the light of understanding. Where there is dark despair, carry the bright torch of hope. Now, more than at any other time in history, we must equip our children with these powerful tools. They are the ones who must use the evolutionary energy of Pluto to determine the fate of all humanity—to avert the possible destruction of the Earth by creating a planetary awareness of the deeper meaning of life.

Retrograde Planets

Because we calculate the astrological chart based upon the positions of the planets relative to the Earth, we often encounter a phenemenon called *retrogradation*. Retrogradation means to move backward, and planets in retrograde do in fact appear to be moving backward. (Of course, a planet does not *really* back up, but it does give that illusion from our viewpoint here on Earth.) When a planet is in apparent retrograde motion, we note it in the chart by the symbol " ℞ ."

We encounter this phenemenon frequently in our everyday lives. Have you ever been passing another automobile and experienced the sensation that the other car was going backward? This illusion is especially notable when two cars are passing on a curve.

When planets are in retrograde motion, the faster planet (the one closest to the Sun) is passing a slower planet in its orbit. A typical chart contains two retrograde planets.

The Sun is never retrograde because we are in orbit around it, and the Moon likewise does not retrograde in its orbit around Earth.

When a planet is in apparent retrograde motion, its energy seems to turn inward before it externalizes. This

KEYWORDS: THE PLANETS

☉ SUN	Individuality, ego, will power, drive, vitality, the Father
☽ MOON	Receptivity, nurturance, emotional security, highest needs, subconscious, the Mother
☿ MERCURY	Communication, senses, ideas, humor, inventiveness, intellect, transportation
♀ VENUS	Love, values, emotions, aesthetics, harmony, beauty, artistry
♂ MARS	Physical energy, assertiveness, temperament, strength
♃ JUPITER	Confidence, generosity, enthusiasm, optimism, prosperity consciousness, understanding
♄ SATURN	Discipline, control, structure, responsibility, karma, crystallization
♅ URANUS	Independence, originality, intuition, uniqueness, sense of humanity and brotherhood
♆ NEPTUNE	Idealism, imagination, illusion, escape, sensitivity, universality, beliefs, spirituality
♇ PLUTO	Transformation, regeneration, power, extremism, concentration, evolution

Table 2

can be a useful quality in personal development, since it allows a deeper level of introspection regarding the essence of the energy. Sometimes, however, there is a sense of frustration when retrogrades are present.

Mercury Retrograde. Mercury retrogrades about three times each year. When it is retrograde in the natal chart, the reasoning and thinking processes are more sensitive. There may be more deliberation in decision making. Parents and teachers may feel that a child takes too long to answer questions. Extra patience on their part will encourage the child to communicate.

Sometimes those with Mercury retrograde at birth find that it is easier to write than talk. Rather than impeding the ability to communicate, this placement often enhances the ability to express ideas through the written word. Many notable writers have been born with Mercury retrograde, including Norman Mailer, Anne Frank, Isak Dinesen, and Henry Miller.

The child with Mercury retrograde at birth needs to learn to trust his/her ability to express thoughts and ideas, and should be given plenty of opportunities to communicate. This chart placement often leads to some ingenious ideas and concepts. Letter writing may be a favorite pastime, and diaries can be helpful in objectifying thoughts.

Venus Retrograde. Since Venus is the expression of emotion, an involution of this energy adds intensity to the feeling nature. There is sometimes a reticence in expressing affection. Retrograde Venus can be challenging for the female teen since she may mistrust her own sense of femininity.

Values can be on the unusual side, with an attraction to unique art forms. Artistic expression (through music, painting, acting, poetry, etc.) is often a positive approach in dealing with Venus retrograde. (Songwriter Carole King and actress Sally Field both have Venus retrograde.) Encourage the child with Venus retrograde to reaffirm his/her self-worth. As a parent, give strong messages to establish positive self-esteem within the child.

Mars Retrograde. The outgoing, assertive, competitive energy of Mars is often frustrated when retrograde. When this planet retrogrades, the physical energy is often slowed. Self-confidence may seem blocked, and needs to be boosted by establishing a firm sense of personal strength.

Physical assertiveness is not always easy when Mars retrogrades, but there can be great success when the individual learns to thoroughly visualize an action before physically performing it. Affirmations which increase personal confidence will prove helpful in achieving a sense of positive direction. Actor Jack Nicholson and tennis champ Billie Jean King were born with Mars retrograde.

Jupiter Retrograde. There can be a strengthening of personal faith with Jupiter retrograde, because ideals and philosophical beliefs are developed within the self. These ideals and morals may run counter to those of society at large. Writers William Butler Yeats (who wrote extensively about mystical philosophical concepts) and Upton Sinclair were both born with Jupiter retrograde. The expansive energy of Jupiter is positively enhanced when retrograde, because the inner search for truth is strongly empowered.

Saturn Retrograde. Trusting inner security is a primary lesson for the child born with Saturn retrograde. Saturn provides structure, direction and discipline, and teaches us about our priorities. Having this planet in retrograde sometimes makes it difficult to learn these lessons at first.

As astrologer Noel Tyl suggests in his book *The Horo-*

scope as Identity, Saturn retrograde may indicate problems relating to the parent who provides this structure in the early years. With our changing society, we are seeing Saturn's structuring influence being expressed through both the male and female parents. (However, most children still perceive the father as the primary Saturnian influence.) Very often this parent is inaccessible to the child, either because s/he is absent, constantly working, or emotionally distant. The child must learn to go within and achieve his/her own sense of structure, direction and personal discipline.

Questions about security can be paramount. Affirmations which confer a sense of confidence, achievement and personal strength can be powerful tools. These children can be remarkably self-disciplined and focused once this sense of self-doubt is overcome. Pianist Van Cliburn, actor Sean Connery, dancer/actress Leslie Caron and singer Dionne Warwick were all born with Saturn retrograde.

Uranus Retrograde. The sense of uniqueness and individuality exemplified by the energy of Uranus is strongly accentuated in retrograde. There is a powerful urge to break free of all forms of restriction and achieve true personal freedom. The knowledge that external freedom can only come when inner freedom exists is inborn with these individuals.

Many individuals born with Uranus retrograde have achieved positive recognition for their special talents. Some examples are Sir Winston Churchill, Johnny Carson, Katherine Hepburn and Anne Morrow Lindberg. Children born with Uranus retrograde will need acknowledgement of their uniqueness, especially if Uranus retrograde is placed in the angular houses (1st, 4th, 7th or 10th).

Neptune Retrograde. Neptune's energy draws us into the inner self where we dream, visualize, imagine and escape.

When Neptune retrogrades, this introspective energy is even more deeply sensitized. There can be a strong desire to escape the ordinary world and its pressures.

The positive use of creative imagination is absolutely essential in this situation. These children also need to learn very early in their lives the difference between physical plane reality (what we usually think of as "real") and imagination or illusion. Imagination should certainly be encouraged, but in ways that are constructive to the child's growth.

Neptune's house placement will indicate the area in which the child needs a creative escape and how s/he can be effective in using the imagination. Farrah Fawcett, Yoko Ono, and Ralph Waldo Emerson were all born with Neptune retrograde at birth.

Pluto Retrograde. Pluto spends about half of each year in retrograde motion. In dealing with Pluto retrograde, parents can help the child understand his/her sense of personal power in relationship to other people and situations. The child may feel somewhat mistrustful of this life process and needs to develop a trust of him/herself. Developing honesty is quite helpful in this regard.

Planetary retrogrades help the child develop an inner awareness of the energy involved. Often, there is also a counterpoint between how the child will use the energy and how society expects the energy to be utilized. This can be positively useful or disruptive, depending on how the energy is channeled. The planets which seem to be positively intensified by retrogradation are Jupiter and Uranus, with Mars and Saturn being the most frustrated by retrogradation.

Chapter Five

PLANETARY ASPECTS

Planetary aspects in astrology are the geometric relationships between the planets and sensitive points to one another. Aspects modify the basic meaning of the planets.

A simple example of a planetary aspect is the cycle of the Moon. We can see the Moon's aspect to the Sun from the amount of light it is reflecting. The "dark of the Moon" is the time the Moon begins its cycle. At this time the Sun and Moon are said to be in *conjunction* with one another. We then observe the Moon becoming apparently larger in the sky, with the crescent changing to the quarter Moon. This illustrates the *square* aspect between the Moon and Sun. At the time of the Full Moon, the Moon is in *opposition* to the Sun, making a 180 degree aspect to it. When the Moon begins to wane, or decrease in light, other aspects between the Moon and Sun are seen. Astrologers measure these aspects in terms of degrees of the zodiac, giving several of the degree correlations names and meanings.

Understanding the basic meanings of the planets, signs and houses allows us to integrate various factors in the chart. Aspects are the next step in this process of integration. Blending the concepts of planets, signs and houses together gives us a general overview. Adding the aspects, however, gives us a much more detailed and meaningful view of the person.

These relationships between planets are tremendously important in comprehending the whole person. Different aspects have particular meanings, and can significantly alter the basic surge of a planetary energy. Some aspects create harmony, while others create tension.

The simplest aspect to find is called the *conjunction*. The conjunction is the zero degree aspect, with the two planets in conjunction appearing adjacent to one another in the chart. It is rare that two or more planets are exactly the same degree and minute. In our example, we find two planets in conjunction which are three degrees from each other. This allowance is called the "orb." (A list of aspects, their degrees and suggested orbs is found in Table Three.)

The conjunction is a powerful aspect, uniting two planetary energies so that they empower each other. A conjunction of the Sun and Mars will unite the active, assertive energy of Mars with the vitality and will power of the Sun. This adds a positive assertiveness, a sense of impatience and an increased drive to the personality. When delineating the conjunction aspect, using the keywords "unites" or "is united with" will help you in determining the basic meaning of the aspect.

Aspects can be qualified as *harmonious* and *flowing*, or as *dynamic* and *tension-producing*. Two planetary energies which are supporting one another through a flowing aspect would be easier to handle than two planetary energies which form a dynamic, tension-producing relationship. The aspects, their basic meanings and their state of harmony or tension, is noted in Table Four.

The conjunction is the only aspect which, in itself, is neither harmonious or dynamic—its quality is determined by the nature of the two interacting planets. A conjunction of two personal planets will often be harmonious. Conjunctions of personal and outer planets may create a bit more distress, however, since these involve integration of the outer and inner self. Saturn conjunctions often bring frustrations and delays. I have found that most aspects between the personal planets and Saturn will reflect the restrictive nature of Saturn, regardless of the aspect. More information on aspects will be found in the following chapters.

The Major Aspects

Conjunction

The conjunction has been discussed above. To find the conjunctions in a chart, look for planets which are adjacent to each other.

Two planets can be conjunct even if they are not in the same sign. There are thirty degrees in each sign of the zodiac. Once we reach 29 degrees 59 minutes of Aries, we move to zero degrees zero minutes of Taurus. If we have the Sun at 28 degrees Aries and Venus at 2 degrees Taurus, the Sun and Venus are conjunct within an orb of 4 degrees. These two energies are united in their expression, with the vitality of the Sun giving power to the artistic nature of Venus. This aspect would be one indicator of an artistically expressive individual. Conjunctions are aspects of *focus* and *unity*.

Opposition

It is also easy to spot oppositions in the astrological chart. An opposition aspect is 180 degrees. Oppositions represent the principles of *polarity* and *duality*. This opposition/polarity principle is also illustrated in the natural

Conjunction Aspect
"0°"

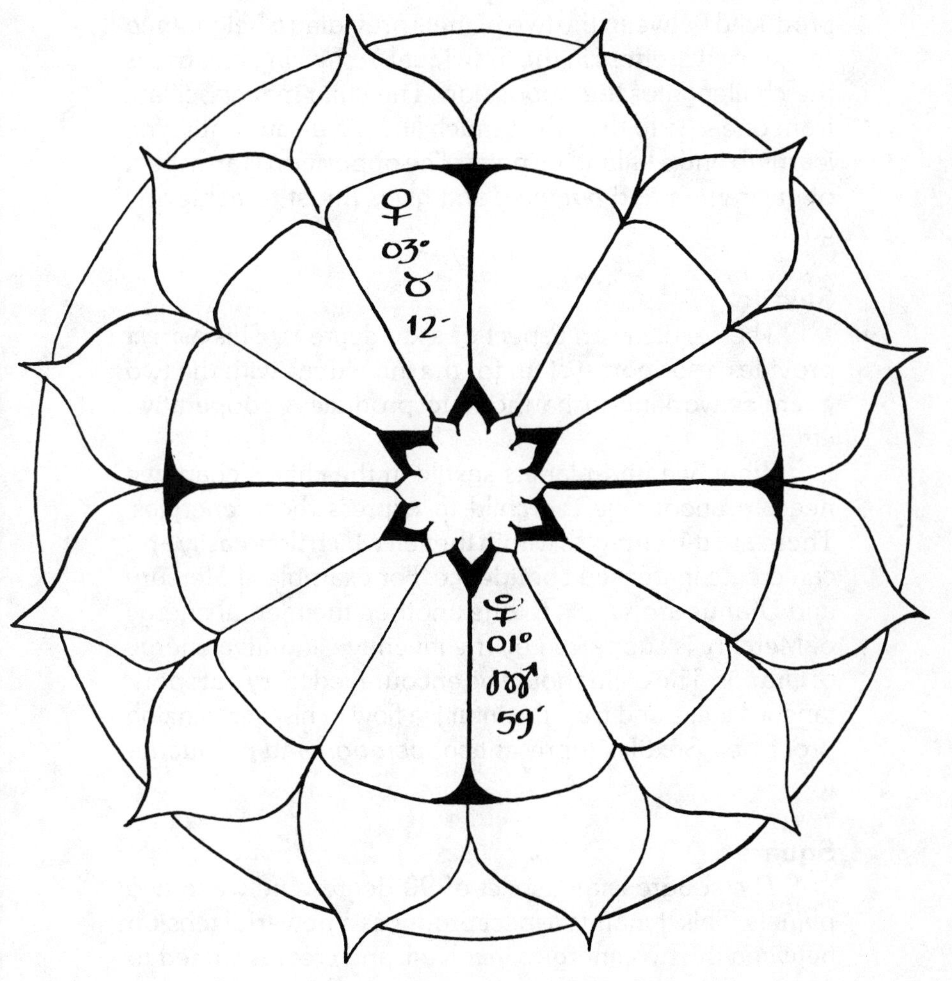

Opposition Aspect
"180°"

progression of the zodiac, with each sign having its polar opposite (see Table 5). This aspect is dynamic, with the tension produced between the two planets providing a heightened sense of awareness in the individual. Achieving balance is the challenge of the opposition. The child may vascillate from one side to the other, much like a see-saw, until s/he learns to find a balancing point. The opposition is an aspect of *awareness* and *balance*, and gives thrust to achieving goals.

Sextile

The sextile is an aspect of sixty degrees. This aspect provides a support system for the individual, with the two energies working in harmony to produce a cooperative effort.

When we find planets sextile in the child's chart, we need to encourage the child to express those energies. These are the energies within the self which flow easily and can create increased confidence. For example, if Mercury and Uranus are sextile to one another, the mental energy of Mercury is supported by the inventive, intuitive energy of Uranus. The child should be encouraged to try out spontaneous ideas and trust the intuitive flow in his/her thinking processes. Sextiles represent *cooperation* and *productivity*.

Square

The square is an aspect of 90 degrees between two planets. This dynamic aspect produces a powerful tension between the two energies involved, and creates a need to resolve it. It is difficult to ignore energies which are squaring one another—the tension can sometimes be explosive!

Squares drive the individual to improve the parts of him/herself signified by the planets involved, thus stimulating growth in the individual.

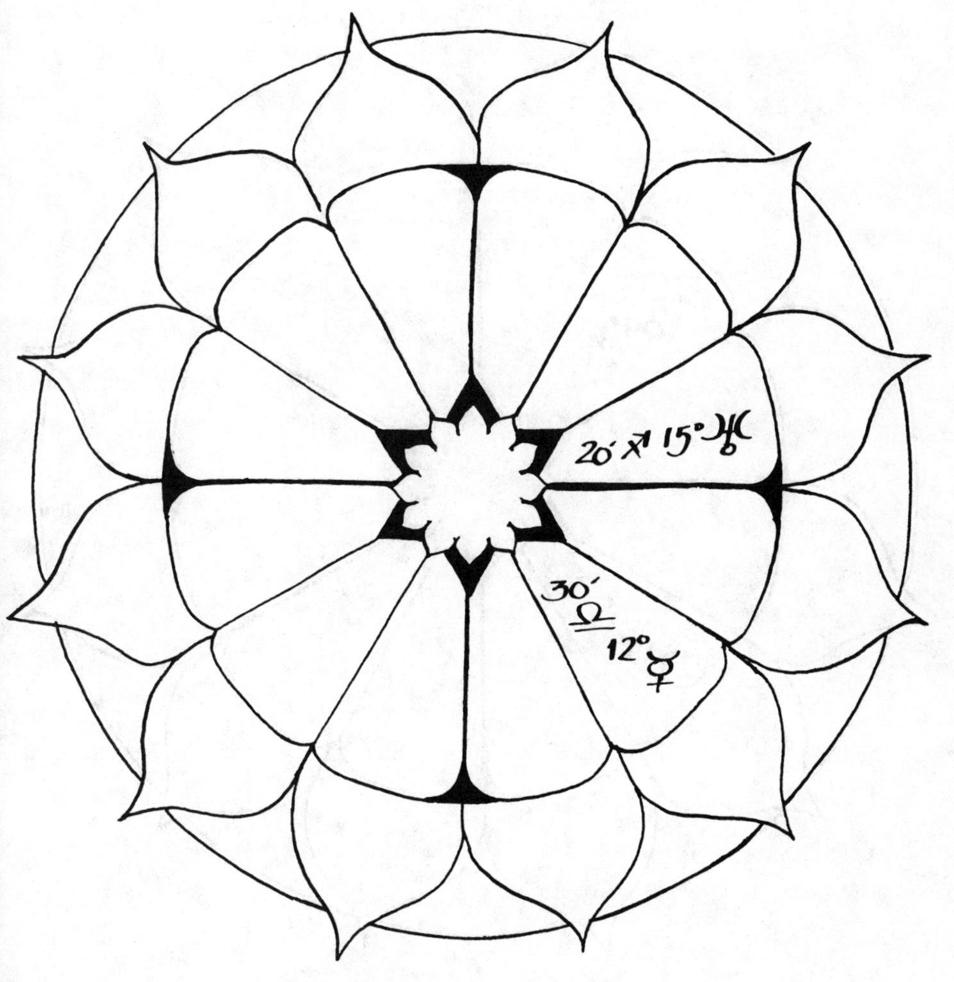

Sextile Aspect
“60°”

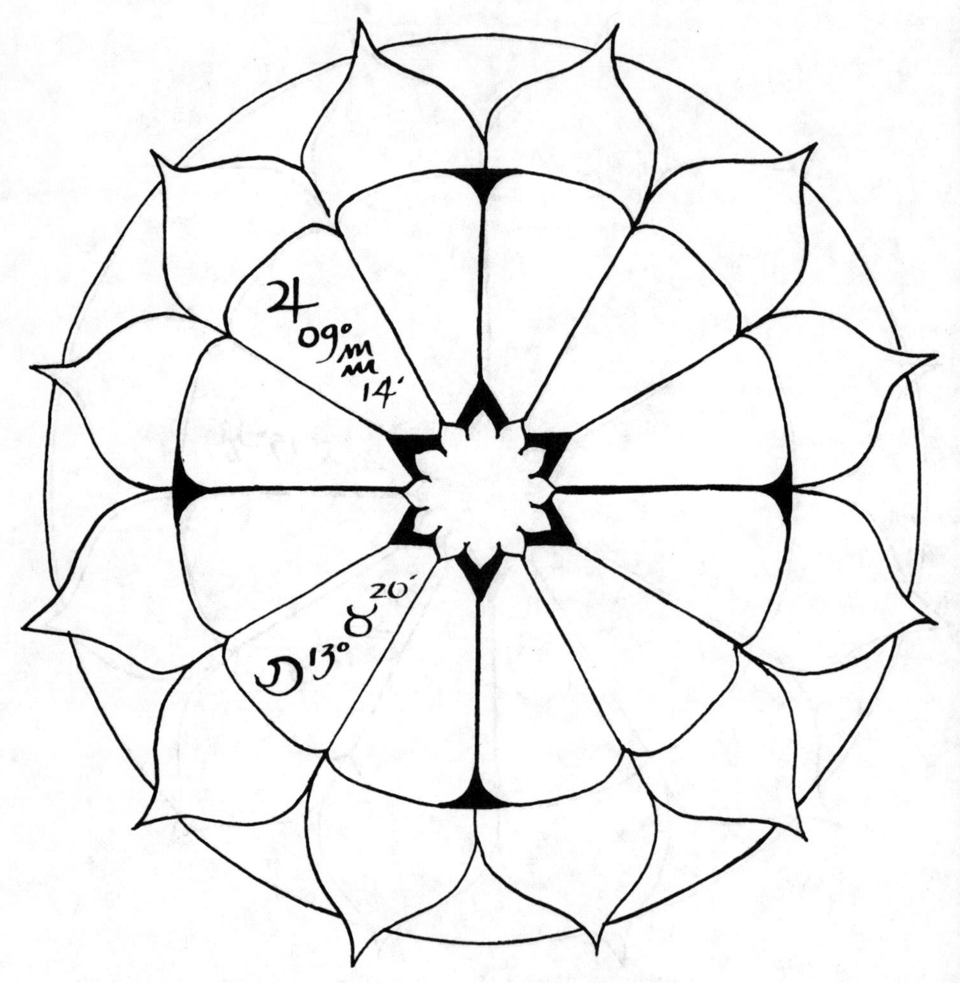

Square Aspect
"90°"

Planets which are squaring one another offer very powerful opportunities for growth within the child. For example, a child with the Moon squaring Jupiter (see example) will need to overcome tendencies to overindulge the self and overextend him/herself emotionally. Once this is learned, s/he will have a better sense of her/his boundaries in personal relationships. *Tension* and *frustration* are the keynotes of the square.

Trine

Planets which trine one another are 120 degrees apart and flow harmoniously together. The ease with which these energies support one another gives increased confidence to the child, although the gifts of the planets involved may be taken for granted too easily. In order to create opportunities through the trine, the child must learn how to apply him/herself and make the most of situations. Trines are special gifts which must be used to be appreciated. This is the aspect of *ease* and *opportunity*.

The Minor Aspects

The so-called "minor" aspects are a bit more difficult to locate in the chart. I use a smaller orb of influence in these aspects, since the angles are not as strong as the angles of the "major" aspects. Although these angles are less prominent, the aspects still have a notable effect.

Semisextile

The semisextile is an aspect of 30 degrees. Here the planets represent qualities which are dissimilar, but which naturally flow into one another in the natural progression of the zodiac. This is an aspect of continuity and flow which works like steps moving us from one level to the next. Two planets in semisextile represent *rapport* and *continuity*.

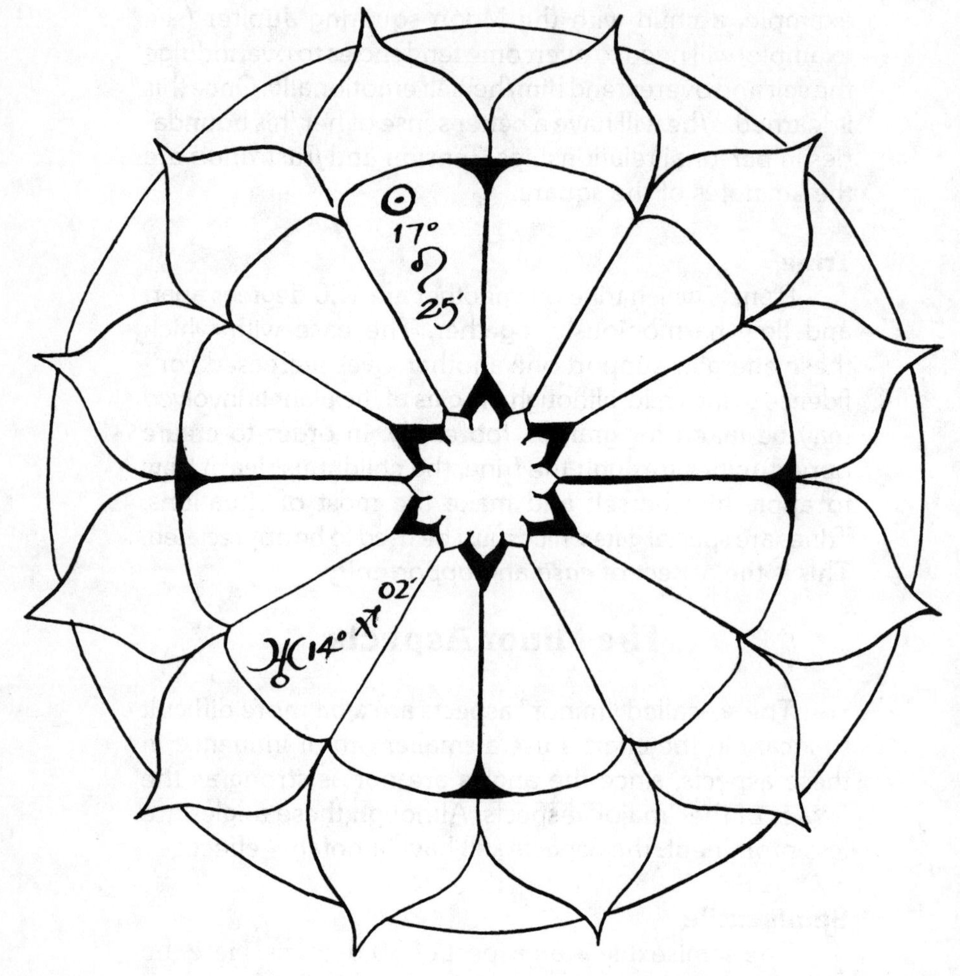

Trine Aspect
"120°"

Glyph	Aspect	Degree	Degree of Orb
☌	Conjunction	0	7
⚺	Semisextile	30	2
∠	Semisquare	45	2
⚹	Sextile	60	5
☆	Quintile	72	1
□	Square	90	7
△	Trine	120	7
⚼	Sesquiquad	135	2
⚻	Inconjunct	150	2
☍	Opposition	180	7

Table 3

Harmonious Aspects	**Basic Meanings**
Semisextile	Continuity, Rapport
Sextile	Cooperation, Productivity
Quintile	Potential, Talent
Trine	Ease, Opportunity
Dynamic Aspects	**Basic Meanings**
Semisquare	Irritation, Contrast
Square	Tension, Frustration
Sesquiquad	Disruption, Aggravation
Inconjunct	Adjustment, Reorientation
Opposition	Challenge, Separation
Conjunction	Focus, unity

Table 4

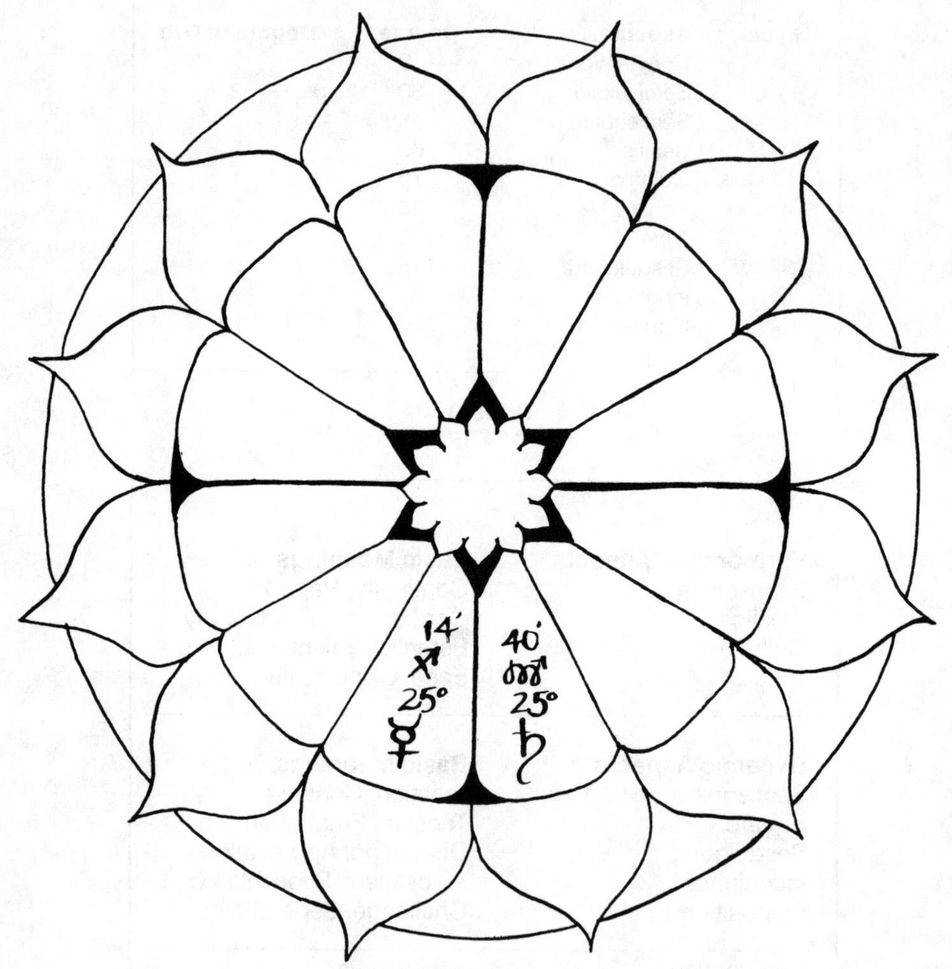

Semisextile Aspect
"30°"

Semisquare

The 45 degree aspect is called the semisquare, which is an aspect of friction and irritation. A good analogy for the semisquare is the discomfort one might feel when wearing heavy wool against bare skin in the summertime.

To work with the semisquare energies, one must learn how to appropriately apply the energies involved. If a child has Mars and Uranus semisquare to one another (see example), s/he might be stimulated to act rashly or take dangerous risks. The quick-acting nature of Uranus could be helpful in some applications, but the child must learn the proper times and places to do his/her daring deeds. (S/he should skateboard on a quiet sidewalk during the day rather than a busy street at night, for example.) Keywords for the semisquare are *irritation* and *contrast*.

Quintiles

Quintiles are aspects of 72 degrees, and represent a child's special talents and potentials. These talents generally require maturity and inner balance to be developed with any consistency. Planets which are quintile one another are automatically fine-tuned.

Sesquiquad

Sesquiquad aspects are 135 degrees apart, and are disruptive and aggravating. Planets which are sesquiquad are like a pinch, and are sometimes difficult to resolve. These planetary energies disrupt the status quo, and can undermine personal security if the disruptive energy is not consciously replaced by more positive and harmonious action.

Inconjunct

Inconjunct aspects are found between planets which are 150 degrees apart. (This aspect is also called a *quin-*

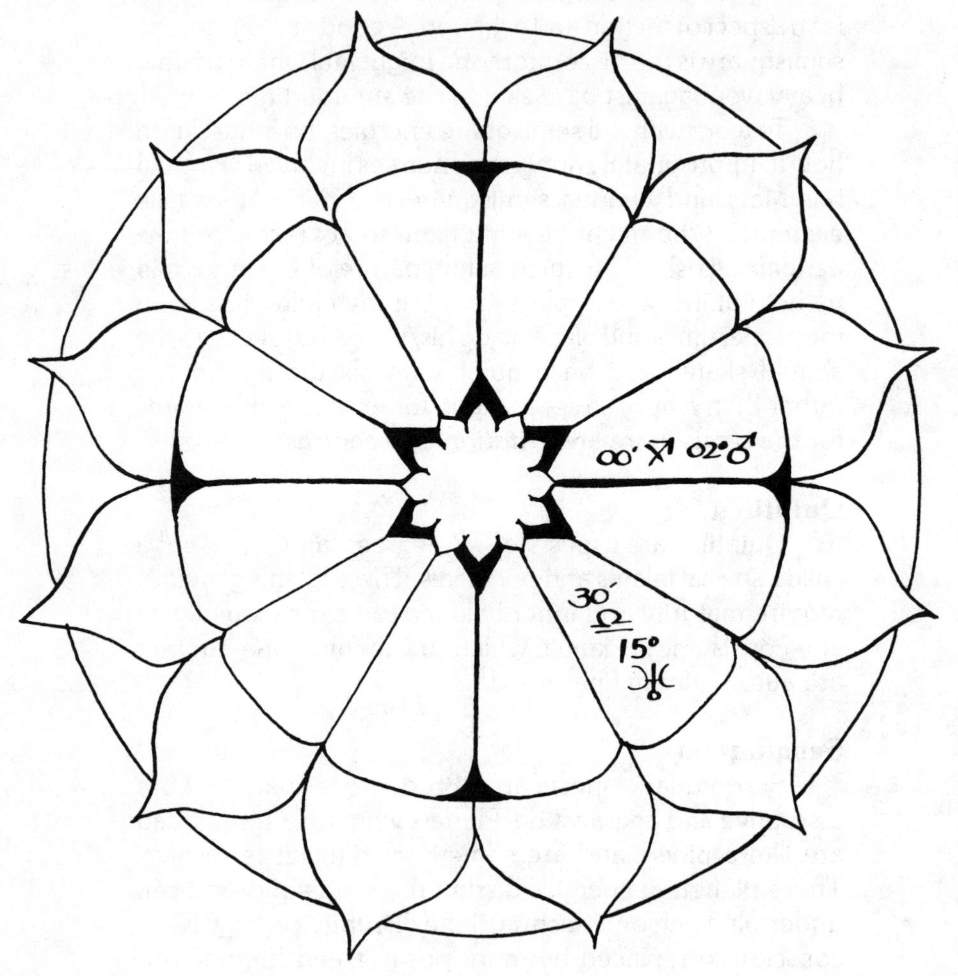

Semisquare Aspect
"45°"

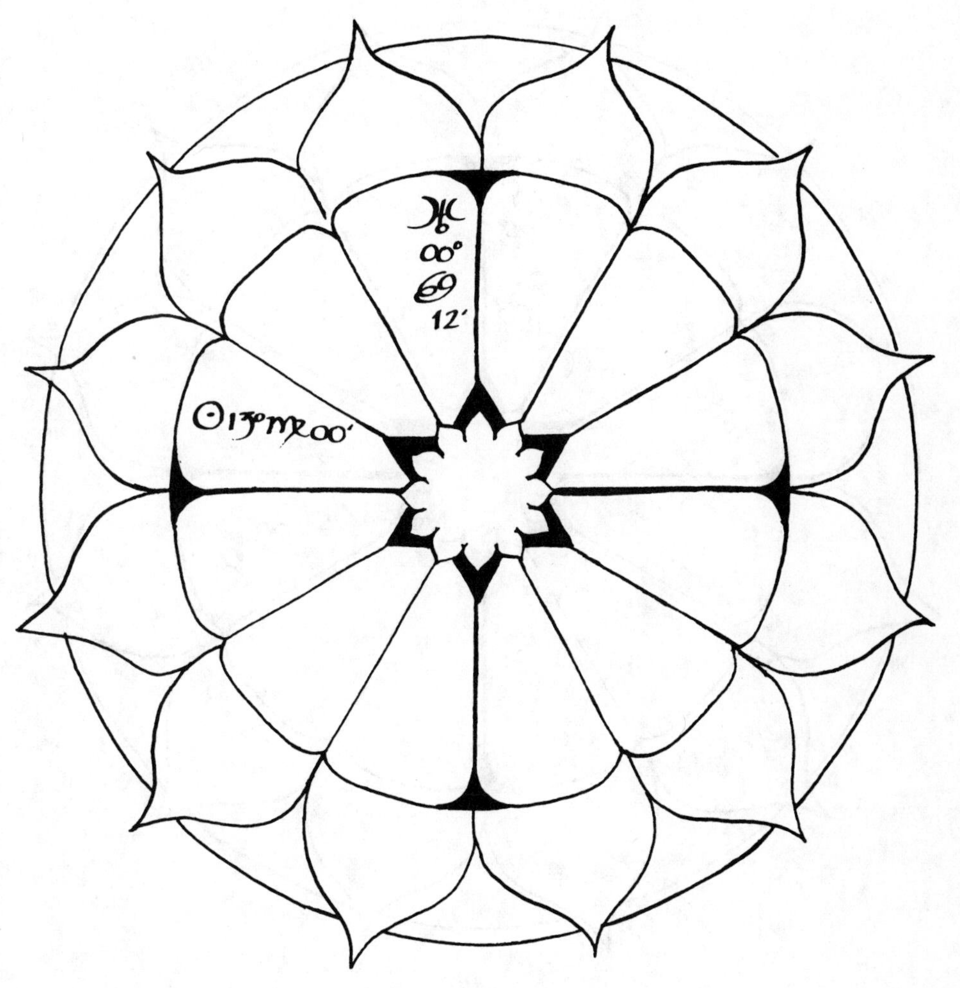

Quintile Aspect
"72°"

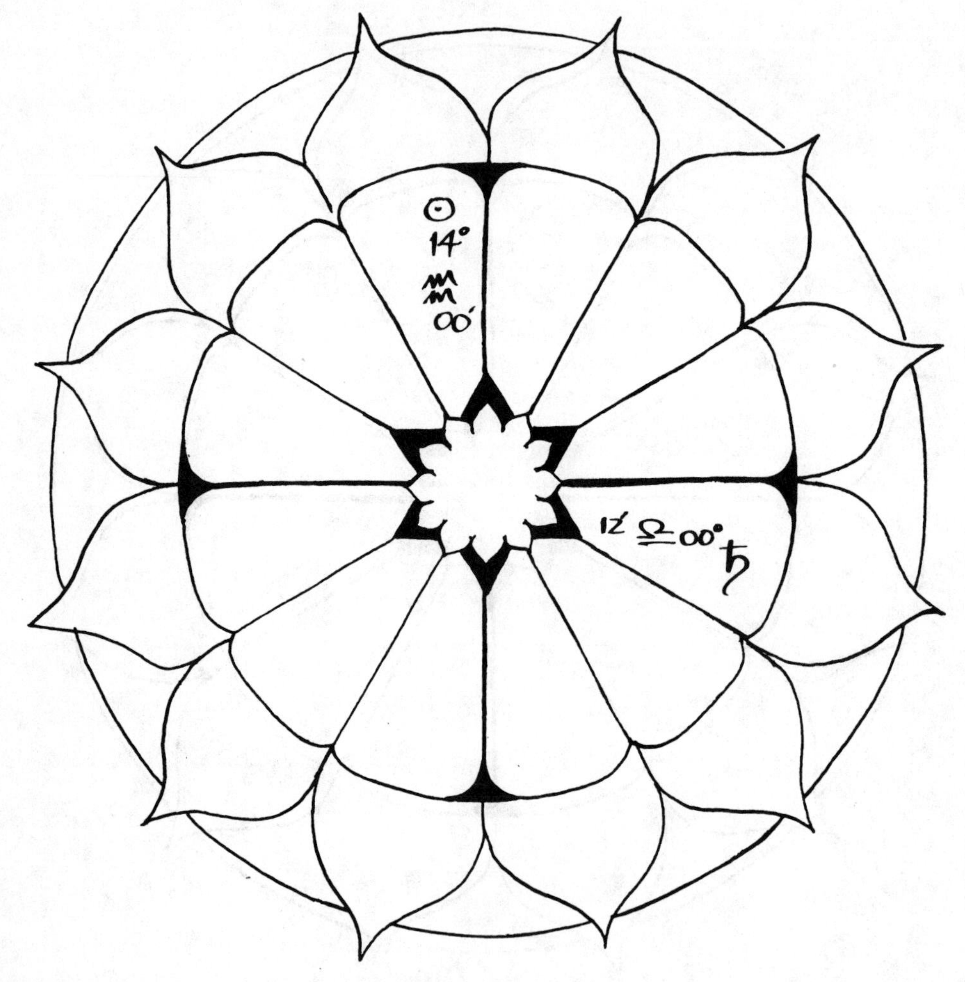

Sesquiquad Aspect
"135°"

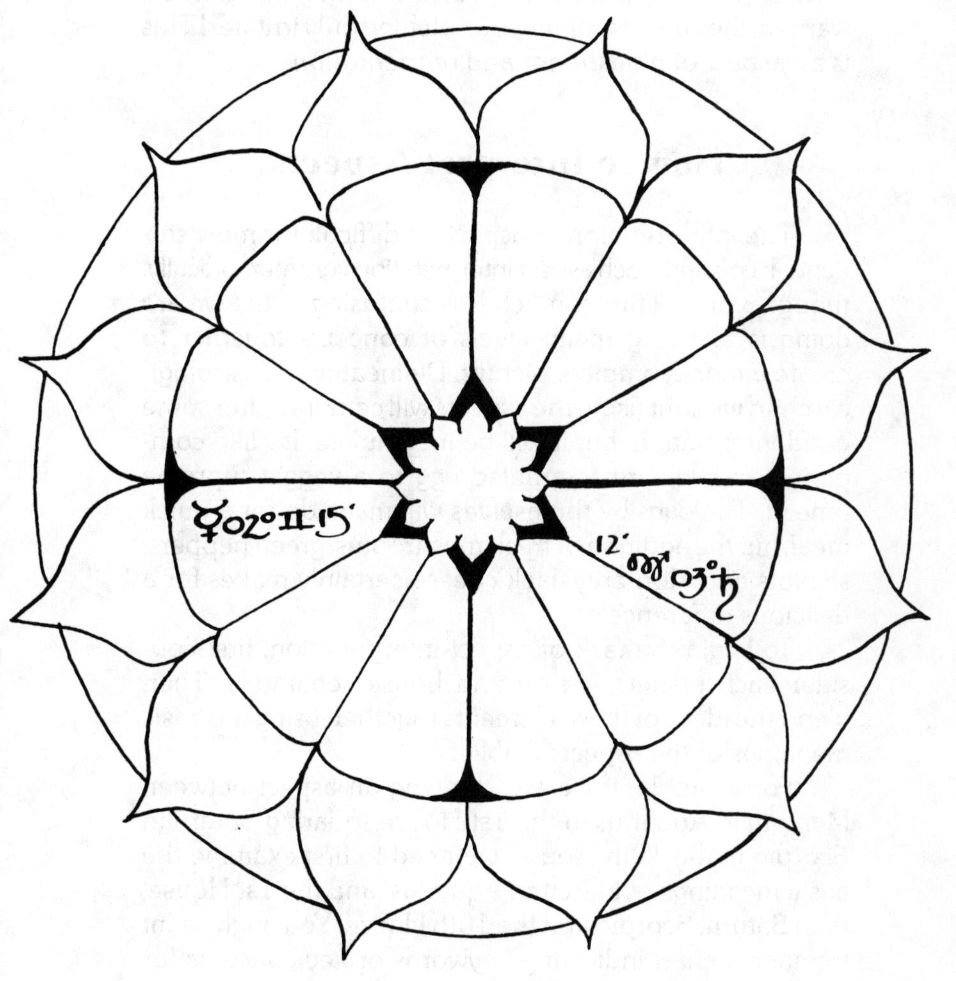

Inconjunct Aspect
"150°"

cunx.) Inconjuncts are like itching, requiring that the individual make adjustments to deal with the energies. Be warned, though—sometimes scratching only irritates! This is an aspect of *adjustment* and *reorientation*.

How to Interpret Aspects

The interpretation of aspects is difficult for most students. If you approach aspect interpretation very methodically, though, you will find it much less confusing. What we are doing is blending many levels of concepts together to create a more complete picture. Delineating an astrological chart without using the aspects will certainly offer some good information, but it will be incomplete. It's like comparing an ordinary scrambled egg to a veggie supreme omelet. The eggs by themselves will make do for a quick meal, but the addition of fresh mushrooms, green peppers, shallots and Monterey Jack cheese certainly makes for a delicious difference!

To begin the task of aspect interpretation, first consider each planet, its sign and house separately. Then blend the ideas of these elements together, using the basic meanings of the aspects (Table 5).

For example, if we are studying an aspect between Mercury in Aquarius in the 1st House squaring Saturn in Scorpio in the 10th House, we need to first examine the basic meanings of Mercury, Aquarius, and the 1st House, then Saturn, Scorpio and the 10th House. You might want to make a chart indicating keywords or key concepts for each of these factors. (See Table 6).

Mercury, the energy of communication, is expressed in an *inventive, unusual, independent or eccentric manner* (Aquarius) and is directed through the 1st House (*personality, how other people see me*). This child might

OPPOSING SIGNS

Aries	Libra
Taurus	Scorpio
Gemini	Sagittarius
Cancer	Capricorn
Leo	Aquarius
Virgo	Pisces

Table 5

Blending Concepts

Mercury	**Aquarius**	**1st House**
Communication	Inventive	Personality
	Unusual	How others see me
	Eccentric	
	Inventive	

In aspect to:

Saturn	**Scorpio**	**10th House**
Structure	Intense	My Reputation
Discipline	Powerful	Father/Mother
		What I Want to Do...

Table 6

need to express himself as an independent thinker. However, there is conflict because of the square from Saturn (*restriction, structure, or security needs*) which might inhibit this free and independent communication or expression.

How might this be limited? Look to the sign and house in which Saturn is found. The sign Scorpio, which is *intense, powerful and charismatic*, is found in the 10th House. For a child, the 10th House and Saturn often reflect the Father. Perhaps there is a powerful and intense father (Saturn in Scorpio in the 10th House) who expects a more structured (Saturn) type of thinking (Mercury) from the child. The 10th House also deals with *reputation and honor* in one's life. The child may fear (Saturn) a loss (Saturn) of reputation (10th House) if he speaks his mind and shares his independent or eccentric ideas.

All these interpretations result from a very simple process of using key concepts and keywords. You might find it helpful in your study of astrology to memorize a few key concepts about each planet, sign and house. This will help you to become more independent of books when interpreting charts.

Chart Patterns

Closely related to planetary aspects is the study of patterns within the personality. Four major patterns are helpful in delineating the child's chart, although there are also many others. These are the *Stellium*, the *Grand Trine*, the *T-Square* and the *Grand Cross.*

The Stellium

The Stellium or Satellium consists of three or more planets which are all conjunct one another (see illustration).

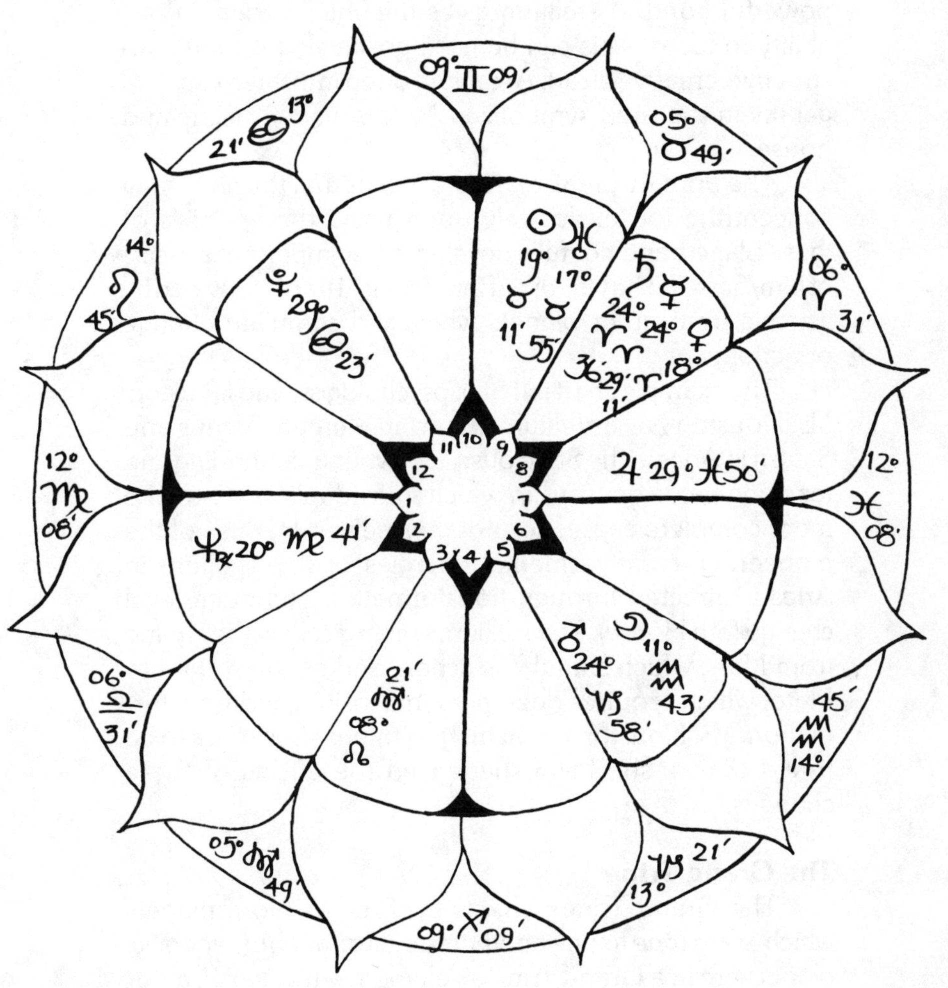

Stellium
(8th House)

These energies are concentrated, and unite to form a powerful bond. A stellium gives the child a tremendous ability to focus. This can be used positively through constructive, creative effort. A stellium often indicates a special genius in the area symbolized by the planets, signs and house.

The primary pitfall of the stellium is that the child may concentrate too exclusively upon using the energies of these planets and not fully develop other important aspects of him/herself. The way out of this potential trap is provided by aspects from other planets which will stimulate change or action.

The example chart is that of psychologist Jean Houston. Ms. Houston has a stellium involving Mercury, Venus and Saturn in Aries in the 8th House. Her writing, counseling and teaching focus on ways in which individuals can become more complete expressions of themselves. Her use of the pioneering, creative mental energies of this stellium in Aries is directed through transformation and deep-level change (8th House). The stellium is energized by the square from Mars, which stimulates action, and by the square to Pluto, which requires deep personal insight and transformation. Ms. Houston is teaching us things she *knows* to be true, because she has experienced the effects of these changes.

The Grand Trine

The Grand Trine consists of three or more planets which are in trine to one another (see illustration). Generally, planets are in a Grand Trine by element—fire, earth, air or water. The Grand Trine is a circuit of energy which continually flows through an individual's life. This pattern seems to give a sense of "divine protection" to the person so blessed. However, like the trine it represents, it can be easily taken for granted.

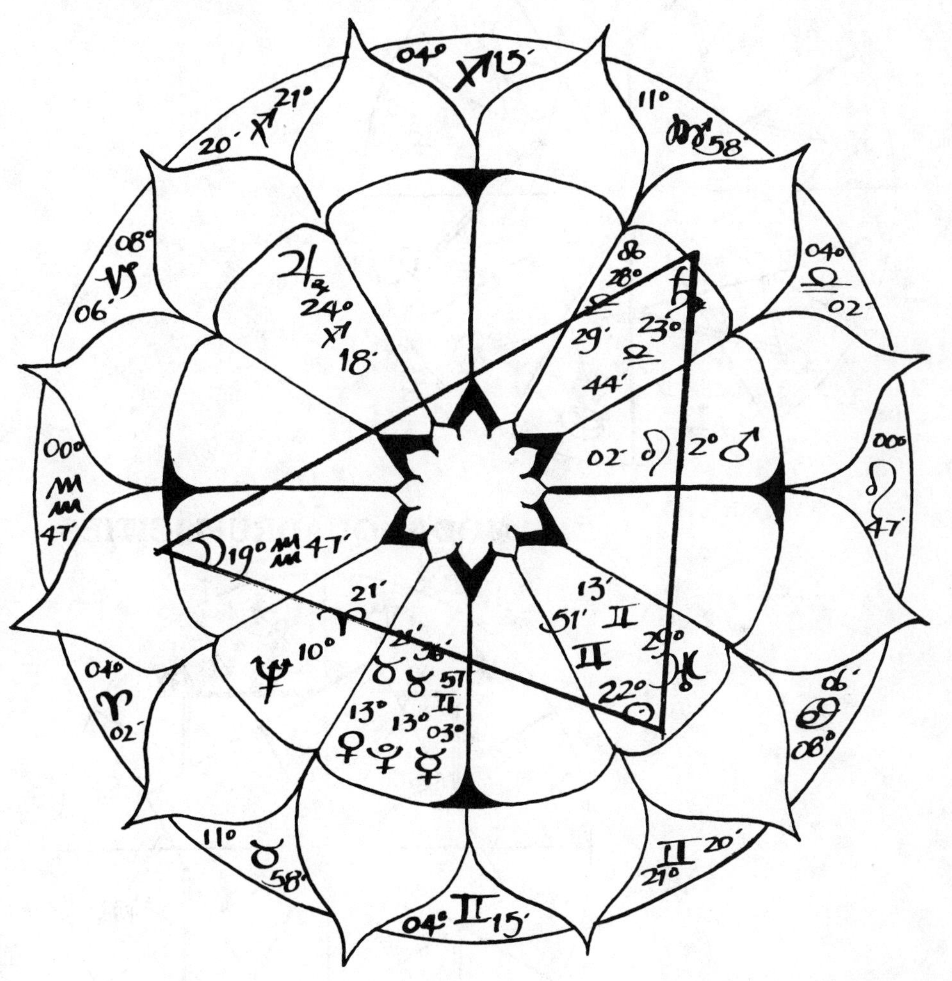

Grand Trine (Air)

ELEMENTAL TRIPLICITIES

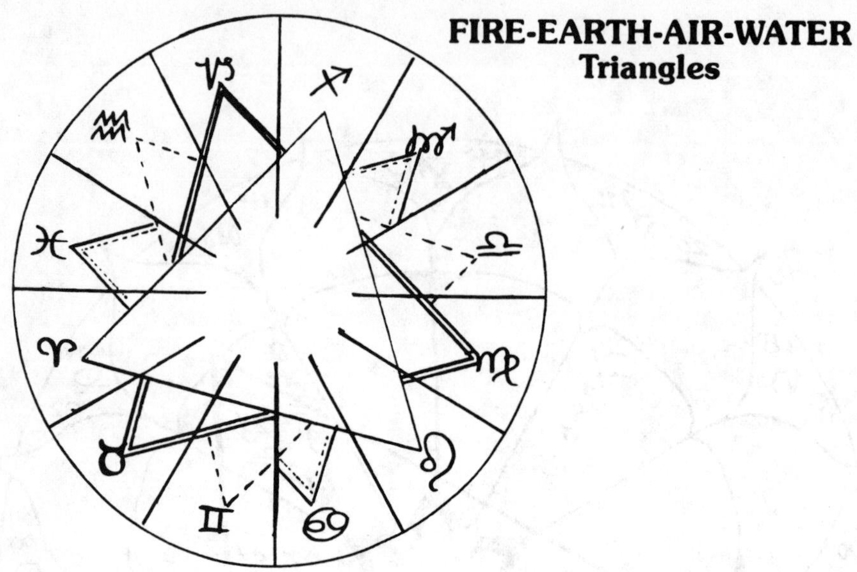

FIRE-EARTH-AIR-WATER
Triangles

MODAL QUADRUPLICITIES

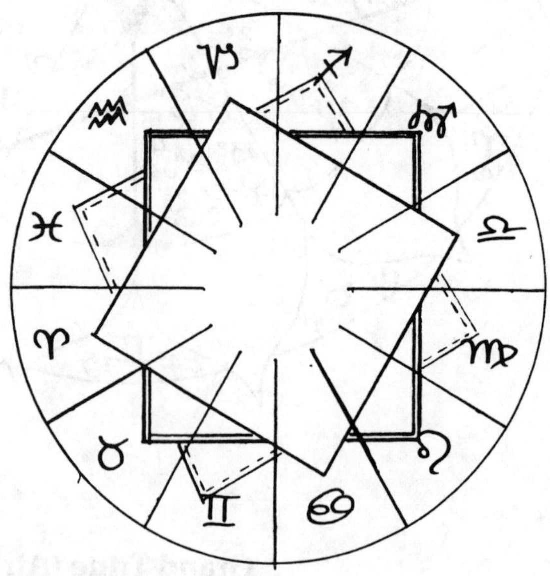

CARDINAL-FIXED-MUTABLE
Squares & Opposites

Once developed by the child, this powerful circuit of energy will confer a strength and resilience which will be tremendously helpful throughout his/her life. To interpret this pattern, consider the key concepts of the element involved to basically support the planets in their signs and houses. Grand Trines in air have a powerful mental/intellectual thrust; in water, an emotional support; in fire, an inspirational focus; and in earth, a practical, sensible approach.

To help the child use this pattern of energy most effectively, encourage activities which will help the child appreciate this special flow. With the Air Grand Trine, s/he can develop her/his intellectual abilities by applying mental energy to creative projects. The child will also benefit from learning to listen to others and their ideas.

The Water Grand Trine sometimes brings a sense of emotional containment to the child. S/he can benefit from learning how to give of him/herself and by developing consideration of others' feelings.

With the Fire Grand Trine, a child can sometimes overwhelm others with his/her dramatic intensity. Directing this fiery energy into philosophical studies and becoming aware of Universal Laws will help him/her to become a more efficient instrument for the Higher Self as s/he matures.

The Earth Grand Trine gives the child a keen sense of practicality. S/he should be encouraged to build things. There may also be a special sense of how to deal with money. The child can benefit by learning how to balance this strong sense of materiality with an appreciation for life's deeper, nontangible values.

The T-Square

The T-Square aspect involves three or more planets, the Ascendant or Midheaven, which are in square to one

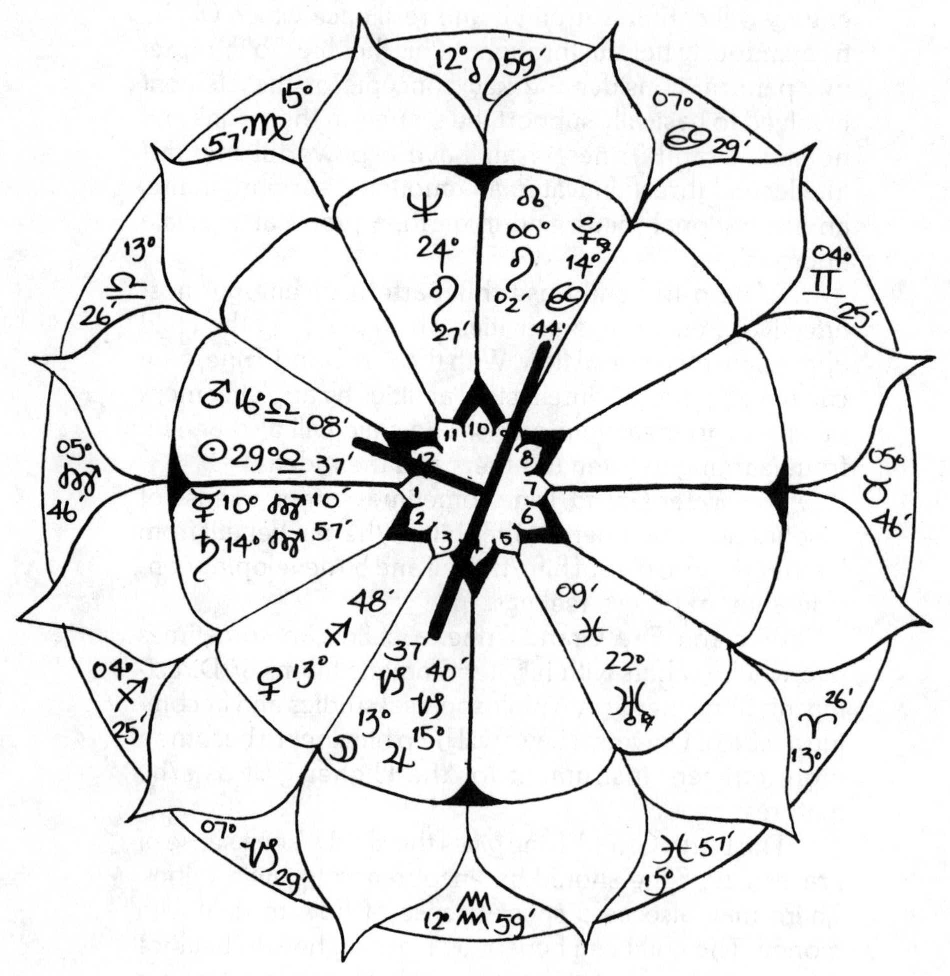

T-Square Cardinal

another. This pattern is made up of two squares and an opposition (see illustration). The planets are usually in the same mode (cardinal, fixed or mutable). With the T-Square, we see a focus of energy which is continually tense and often frustrating.

By understanding these underlying frustrations in the child, we can offer her/him support and help find creative ways to release them. Consider the T-Square as a perpetual motion machine. As long as continual growth and positive awareness accompanies the energies involved, the child will continuously move forward in his/her development. If fear, guilt, or too much anxiety accompany the child's approach to life, the T-Square can prove to be the source of much personal aggravation and frustration.

Look to the house opposite the open arm of the T-Square (see illustration) to find creative ways to focus the energy and resolve much of the tension. In our example, the 6th House is the open arm of the T-Square, because it is opposite Mars which is squared by the Moon and Pluto. By encouraging the child to develop good habits, the tension of the T-Square will be positively ventilated.

The Grand Cross

The Grand Cross involves four or more planets or the Ascendant or Midheaven which are in opposition and square to one another (see illustration). This pattern creates continual stress. Children who have Grand Crosses need to learn positive ways to relax and relieve tension. These children are motivated to build, achieve and succeed, but the obstacles to their goals may sometimes seem insurmountable. Much support is needed from the parents and family to give the child a true sense of purpose in directing these energies. Learning to accept both victory and defeat is paramount.

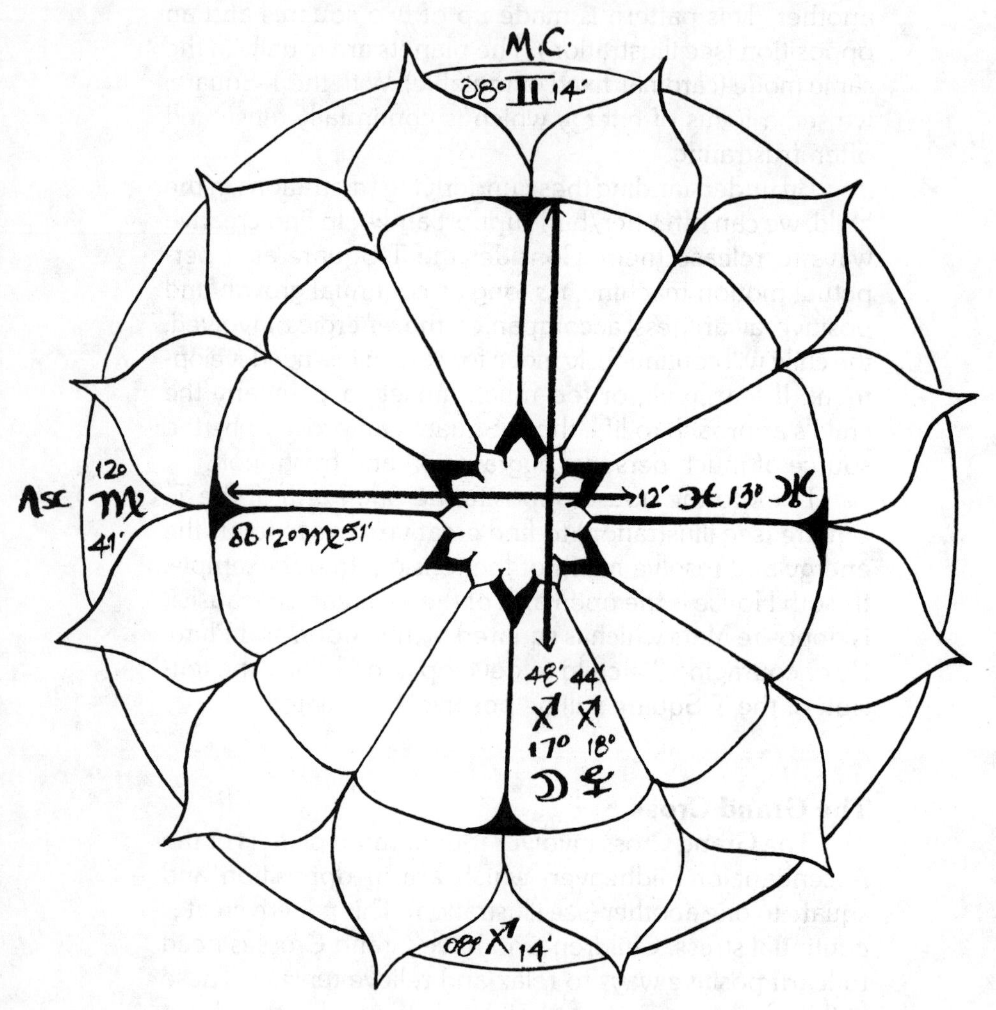

Asc-MC-Neptune-Moon-Pluto

Through the application of aspects and chart patterns, we gain deeper insights into the child's astrological chart. In the chapters which follow, we will integrate the concepts of planets, signs and houses in approaching the child's physical, mental, emotional and spiritual needs.

It is of primary importance that we remember to use these astrological insights into childhood responsibly. Each child is born with special gifts and special lessons to learn. As parents, teachers and guides of children, we have the task of aiding the child's discovery of the Self through love and understanding.

Chapter Six

PHYSICAL NEEDS

The human being must develop four types of bodies—physical, emotional, mental and spiritual. We mature within these frameworks, and must learn to integrate and balance the needs of each body.

The growing awareness that all of these bodies coexist within each of us has revived interest in holistic approaches to health. "Holistic" implies harmony between the functions and needs of all the parts. True physical well-being involves harmony between the physical, emotional, mental and spiritual aspects of the Self, making wholeness and wellness very closely linked!

In approaching the physical needs of the child, therefore, we must keep in mind that this aspect is just one part of a greater whole. One way to study physical health and fitness while maintaining a holistic perspective is through medical astrology. Please realize that we are not attempting to "diagnose" or "prescribe," just offering suggestions to aid in balancing and harmonizing the body, mind and spirit.

Each of the planets, signs and houses has a correlation to the physical body. The two houses which relate most directly to physical strength are the 1st and 6th, although all the houses have some impact upon the reasons behind physical wellness or "dis-ease." The signs correlate with particular parts of the body, whereas the planets symbolize how these parts are likely to be affected. The following information encompasses some of the simpler approaches to determining a child's physical needs, and covers certain aspects of well-being I find extremely important in the developing child.

Planetary Energies and the Physical Body

Correlating the planetary energies to the child's physical needs provides us with some fascinating information. Each planetary energy most strongly influences a particular part of the physical body.

The Sun

Physically, the Sun represents the child's basic energy level. It is through Sun energy that *prana,* or life force, flows, creating vitality in the human body. By maintaining a balanced diet based upon whole, natural foods, we offer this vitality continued renewal. Filling the body with dietary pollutants such as artificial colors, flavors and preservatives can rob it of its physical vitality.

We can also enhance physical vitality by directly absorbing the rays of the Sun (in moderation, of course!). We are responsible for maintaining a smoothly running physical vehicle. Ignoring fundamental physical needs will diminish the child's capacity to endure the stresses of life.

The Moon

Moon energy corresponds to the basic body cycles and regulates bodily fluids. Eating habits are also a function of the Moon. The Moon is our emotional link to physical health, and represents our basic security needs.

It is impossible for a child to be healthy if s/he does not have her/his primary emotional needs fulfilled. When the emotions are imbalanced, the bodily cycles are also out of balance. The body also has a difficult time fully assimilating the nutrients from food if a child eats while under extreme stress or is emotionally upset at mealtime.

Repressed emotions such as anger, fear, guilt, jealousy and low self-esteem can also cause physical problems. Medicine is increasingly recognizing the link between physical and emotional well-being. Aspects from the Moon to other planets will indicate the different ways in which the emotional needs are affected. With the Moon aspecting Mars, the child's increased impatience may make it hard for him/her to express anger positively—especially if the aspect is dynamic. Aspects between the Moon and Saturn frustrate or limit emotional expression, often through feelings of inadequacy or guilt. (This will be further discussed in Chapter Seven, "Emotional Needs.")

For the girl entering puberty, understanding and coping with the menstrual cycle can initially present problems. Learning about this cycle not only helps the young woman intellectually, but brings a more stable emotional approach to menstruation and the changing hormonal cycle.

If the chart shows aspects between the Moon and Saturn, she may have negative feelings about this cyclical process. With Uranus aspecting the Moon, her menstrual cycle may be erratic, and there may be symptoms of premenstrual syndrome (PMS). Increasing Vitamin B6, Vitamin E, calcium and magnesium may be helpful.

Mercury

Mercury corresponds to the nervous pathways in the body, the system within the human which links impulses and responses. Children who have several aspects to Mercury from other planets may experience tremendous amounts of mental and nervous energy, and could have difficulty resting or slowing down.

There is an association between Mercury and the thyroid gland, which regulates the metabolic rate. When the thyroid is functioning improperly, the metabolism will be either too slow or too fast. The thyroid, seated in the throat, correlates to the throat chakra of the body. This chakra, or energy center, regulates the mental functioning. When harmony exists between the Divine Flow and personality self, intuitive and logical thought flow in a balanced manner. But if the logical thought processes begin to overrule the intuition, an imbalance in this chakra will result and can create a corresponding imbalance in thyroid functioning. This is often a problem when Mercury is in dynamic aspect to Uranus or Pluto.

Nutritionally supporting the thyroid can prove helpful in balancing thyroid function. Adding kelp and dulse (seaweeds) to the diet will nourish the thyroid gland with the iodine, minerals and vitamins needed for its proper functioning without overloading the body with salt. These can be used directly on foods as seasoning or taken in tablet form as supplements.

Thiamine deficiency is also implicated with Mercury aspecting the outer planets. Some good-tasting fresh sources of thiamine are green vegetables, coconut, pineapple, almonds, peanuts, wheat germ and nutritional yeast.

In balancing the psychological and physical indicators of poor thyroid functioning, parents can teach children how to positively direct their thoughts. Needless worry can be replaced by creative story-telling or writing. Allowing intuitive thoughts to guide and direct his/her life is one of the greatest lessons a child can learn. It is especially important to the child whose chart indicates Mercury stress, since the intellect will usually try to overpower the intuition.

Venus

Venus denotes the types of food a child will like, especially his/her taste for sweets. It also rules the veins of the body, and can indicate possible blood disease and imbalances. Venus is also associated with the kidneys and the throat due to its correspondence with the signs Libra and Taurus.

I have seen children with Venus in dynamic aspect to Saturn who will eat when they do not feel loved. If this type of behavior continues, a structure (Saturn) of fat may result, creating even more overwhelming problems with self-esteem.

Venus also corresponds to the blood sugar. Aspects from the outer planets to Venus are very often indicators of potential blood sugar problems. This is especially notable when difficult aspects from Saturn, Uranus, Neptune and Pluto to Venus are present. The behavioral problems associated with low blood sugar are unpleasant: irritability, hyperactivity or lethargy (sometimes they alternate!), and lack of mental clarity. A parent may think the child is just being difficult, when s/he is really suffering from a bio-chemical imbalance!

Balancing the blood sugar can sometimes be accomplished through dietary changes alone. Encourage the child to eat small, frequent, nutritionally rich meals. Avoid refined carbohydrates (sugar, white flour, etc.) and processed foods. Adding fresh fruits, nuts and freshly prepared raw juices is helpful. Supplementing the diet with Vitamin B6 and GTF Chromium can be helpful. Take care when using supplements, however, as you can create new imbalances if you are not properly guided!

Mars

Mars energizes the physical body and the vitality of the Sun. It is through Mars that the child expresses physical assertiveness. The adrenal glands and muscles are also associated with Mars, as is the assimilation of many minerals such as iron, phosphorus, chlorine, selenium and sodium.

Mars is associated with body temperature. Inflammation is a Martian process, and a child whose chart has a strongly aspected Mars may respond to physical stress with increased body temperatures. This is one indicator that the body is fighting back and regenerating itself. The approach of always bringing down body temperature when a child is ill may ultimately do him/her more harm than good. If the child is extremely uncomfortable, catnip or chamomile baths are often helpful. Of course, very high fevers should never go unchecked, but we must realize that sometimes fever is a good sign!

Children whose charts show dynamic aspects between Mars and Uranus may often be involved in accidents, since they tend to take risks more! The child with Mars-Saturn aspects may have a low level of physical energy, and should be encouraged to devote some time to physical activity in order to raise energy levels.

To develop a continual reserve of energy, the child needs positive outlets for physical activity. Some kinds of physical recreation which will appeal to the child can be determined by the placement of Mars by sign in the chart (Refer to Table 7 for more information.)

The house placement of Mars indicates the types of environment and people a child will enjoy interacting with while participating in sports. I have noticed that children who have Mars placed near the angles of the chart need to express their physical strength to others. A four-year old boy with Mars opposing his Ascendant and Aries at the Midheaven recently approached me, flexing his muscles. "I'm strong!" he exclaimed. His mother tells me that he will try to lift almost anything. She is having difficulty explaining to him that while he can certainly grow up and have great strength, he will probably not be twelve feet tall or be able to lift a house with one hand!

Jupiter

Jupiter is the largest planet in our solar system and corresponds to the liver, the largest organ in the human body. I had learned in anatomy class that the liver was large, but I found out just how massive it is when I was in nursing school. During my surgical clerkship, I had the good fortune to scrub for several cholecystectomies (removal of the gallbladder). The gallbladder is just beneath the liver, and someone has to hold the liver up and out of the way to expose it to the surgeon's scalpel.

One morning, I was the one chosen to retract the liver. After holding this organ with a surgical instrument for about twenty minutes, the muscles in my arm were pleading for a rest. Then, when the surgeon told me I would have to hold it for several minutes more, I thought *I* would collapse. Since that time, I have had a healthy respect for this king-sized organ!

Jupiter is also related to the breakdown of fats and carbohydrates in the body. The liver acts as the body's detoxifying agent. This breakdown of toxic materials also warms the blood, generating most of the body's heat. Children who have dynamic aspects between Jupiter and Saturn could have a sluggishly functioning liver. They will probably be more sensitive to food additives and other chemicals, since the liver may not break these substances down rapidly enough.

Aspects from Jupiter to other planets may also indicate overindulgence. Children with Venus-Jupiter aspects are notorius for their love of sweets, and Moon-Jupiter aspects are likely indicators of overeating in general. The natural expansiveness of Jupiter needs to be directed outside the self through adventure, generosity and good humor.

The child who compulsively overeats is probably not even aware of this habit, since overeating is often an unconscious act.

Help the child become conscious of what, when and where s/he is eating. Avoid rewarding these children with goodies like chocolate bars, cake or ice cream—they will associate the need for reward with negative, self-indulgent behavior. Try rewarding the child with a trip to the zoo, the wild animal park or some other outing that provides learning, fun and sharing.

Saturn

Saturn correlates to the framework of the body: the bones, skin, teeth and nails. It also correlates to collagen, the "glue" which holds our cells together.

Harmonious aspects between Saturn and Venus generally indicate beautiful, healthy skin, whereas dynamic aspects could indicate skin problems such as eczema, acne, excessive dryness or psoriasis. Adding Vitamins C and E to the diet is helpful when these aspects are present.

Saturn also rules calcium and its absorption in the body. We all know the importance of calcium in the formation of healthy bones and teeth in children. Children with insufficient calcium in the diet suffer from rickets and often have poorly formed teeth. Another factor in calcium absorption is adequate amounts of Vitamin D.

Sun-Saturn aspects in the chart may indicate lowered physical vitality, since Saturn has an inhibiting effect when in dynamic relationship to the Sun. The flowing aspects generally bring a controlled, cautious approach to health. The immune system can be aided by increasing Vitamins A and D in the diet. These occur naturally in fish liver oil.

Uranus

Uranus corresponds to the nerve impulses of the body.

Contacts from Uranus to other planets can indicate an erratically functioning nervous system, especially in times of extreme stress.

The child whose chart shows a powerfully aspected Uranus, or Uranus conjuncting an angle (ASC, MC, etc.) may display erratic behavior. Mars-Uranus aspects often go hand in hand with hyperactivity, but this should be manageable with proper diet. There have also been direct correlations between hyperactivity and some food additives.

Uranus sometimes has the effect of creating reversals of energy. Children with aspects between Uranus and the Sun, Moon or ASC sometimes have a reversed response to medication. Observe this child carefully when administering *any* type of medication. If at all possible, try the least intrusive methods of caring for illnesses first!

Neptune

Neptune sometimes makes it difficult to assess the child's physical vitality. Children who have Neptune conjunct the Ascendant or in the 1st House may be difficult to diagnose, because they often present misleading symptoms.

Neptune in aspect to any planet will sensitize that planet. For this reason, children who have aspects from Neptune to the personal planets are likely to be extremely sensitive to drugs and alcohol. They should be given smaller than normal dosages of medication since they could experience an extreme reaction or sensitivity to any given drug.

I have seen many correlations between Moon-Neptune and Sun-Neptune dynamic aspects and allergies in the child. The Moon-Neptune aspects seem to be more indicative of food allergies, while Sun-Neptune aspects correspond more to environmental allergies. Sometimes children may have allergies and not present common allergic symptoms such as asthma or hives. Instead, there may be heightened irritability, lethargy, headaches, hyperactivity or other symptoms.

Parents might be aided by keeping a journal of foods the child eats and any resulting symptoms (e.g. drinking or eating milk products may give the child headaches). If a correlation seems to be established, the suspected food might be eliminated from the diet for a while. These types of studies are time-consuming, but can ultimately result in a more harmonious and healthful situation.

Pluto

Pluto corresponds to the endocrine glands and cell regeneration in the body. Plutonian energy functions at the deepest level of consciousness, and is also indicative of deep emotional needs. Aspects from any planet to Pluto may indicate a possible breakdown of the body system ruled by that planet due to psychological distress.

For example, Sun-Pluto aspects are sometimes found when an individual develops problems with the heart, which is ruled by the Sun. Sometimes this is simply the body reacting to the individual pushing beyond his/her limits for too long. Teaching the child to recognize the need for rest and relaxation can be important for his/her long-term vitality. Adequate nourishment is, of course, necessary. Inclusion of Vitamin E as a dietary supplement might also be considered.

The Signs and the Body

The twelve signs of the zodiac correspond to the body parts. If a child has several planets in one sign, that particular system of the body may be easily stressed. Some of the correspondences are noted below.

Aries rules the face, the cranium, and the arteries and veins of the head and neck.

Taurus rules the neck and its vertebrae along with the musculature, veins and arteries in this area. The throat is also ruled by Taurus.

Gemini rules the shoulders, arms, hands and lungs as well as the musculature, veins and arteries of these areas.

Cancer rules the stomach, breasts, chest, and diaphragm as well as the musculature, arteries and veins in these areas.

Leo rules the heart, the lower back and the muscles, veins and arteries of these body parts.

Virgo corresponds to the pancreas, spleen, intestinal tract and the muscles, veins and arteries of the upper abdominal area.

Libra rules the kidneys (renal glands), lumbar vertebrae, and the veins, arteries and muscles which support these areas.

Scorpio rules the reproductive organs, the colon, and the pelvic bones as well as the muscles, veins and arteries which supply them.

Sagittarius rules the thighs, the sciatic nerve, the saphenous vein (the largest vein of the body), the coccyx, ilium, femur and sacrum, as well as the muscles, veins and arteries associated with these areas.

Capricorn rules the knees and their ligaments, the gallbladder, the iliac artery and the popliteal vein.

Aquarius rules the ankles, the tibia and fibula, the calves, blood circulation, and the spinal cord.

Pisces rules the feet, the lymphatic system, and the body's mucus level.

MARS IN THE SIGNS: RECREATION and SPORTS*	
ARIES	Running (especially sprints), martial arts, baseball, tennis, fencing, free calisthenics (gymnastics), acrobatics, acrobatic skiing, athletic dancing, tap dancing
TAURUS	Weightlifting, tai chi, ballroom dancing, discus throwing, pummel horse (gymnastics), football (especially defense positions), table tennis, snorkeling, golf
GEMINI	Handball, racquetball, juggling, jump rope, parallel and uneven parallel bars (gymnastics), badminton, tennis, basketball, bicycling, skateboarding, hang-gliding, wind-surfing, fencing, pole-vaulting
CANCER	Swimming, surfing, water skiing, scuba diving, tai kwan do karate, golf, fishing, boating, snorkeling, folk dancing, belly dancing
LEO	Gymnastics, distance running, rodeo, high-diving, surfing, golf, captain and/or quarterback of football team
VIRGO	Racquetball, handball, table tennis, tennis, scuba-diving, aerobic dancing, yoga, gymnastics, English riding, figure skating, baseball
LIBRA	Ballroom dancing, yoga, tai chi, ice dancing, balance beam (gymnastics), juggling, ballet dancing.
SCORPIO	Swimming, diving, most gymnastic events, deep sea scuba diving, high jumping, hatha yoga, endurance sports, aerobics, body contact sports
SAGITTARIUS	Archery, horseback riding (especially jumping) javelin throwing, high jumping, broad jumping, hiking, soccer
CAPRICORN	Snow skiing, mountain climbing, rock climbing, hiking, running (especially marathons), figure skating, endurance sports, tai chi
AQUARIUS	Figure skating, roller skating, hang gliding, skateboarding, symnastics, basketball, volleyball, baseball, relay races, parachuting, skydiving.
PISCES	Swimming, snorkeling, deep sea diving, dancing, English riding, fishing, ice dancing

* These activities are intended as suggestions and should not be considered as limiting factors.

Table 7

The 1st and 6th Houses

The 1st and 6th Houses are the two houses which are primarily related to physical health.

The 1st House corresponds to the physical body itself. The sign on the Ascendant indicates the basic qualities of physical health. Any planets placed in the 1st House will also affect physical strength. The energies which strengthen the physical body are the Sun, Mars, Venus and Jupiter. The energies of the Moon, Saturn, Neptune and Pluto often have a detrimental effect on overall physical health.

The Moon can tie the child's state of health to his/her emotional stability. Saturn's influence often leads to excessive levels of physical stress. The child will need to learn holistic relaxation methods such as biofeedback in order to compensate for this contact. Neptune sensitizes the physical body, and can be indicative of allergic reactions or sensitivity in general. Pluto sometimes has an undermining effect on the physical body. If Pluto forms dynamic aspects with other planets, it can indicate potentially self-destructive health problems. These will generally be related to repressed emotional factors.

The 6th House's correlation to health has much to do with the child's health and hygiene habits. A child with planetary energies in this house will pay more attention to health. Developing responsibility for physical well-being will be more crucial for the child with an energized 6th House.

In evaluating the overall health of the child, first consider the Sun, Moon and Ascendant with their signs and aspects. Then locate those planets which have the greatest number of aspects. The areas occupied or ruled by these planets may require special attention. The sign most influenced also should be noted, and will serve as an indicator of the child's special needs.

The best thing we can do for our children's health is to offer them the highest quality foods, a positive attitude about their bodies and physical well-being, and abundant love and attention. Helping the child develop a balanced lifestyle is a primary responsibility for the parents. The examples and lessons in childhood form the primary framework for habits later in life. To alter a negative habit requires focused attention and great effort. A child whose personal habits are conducive to good health, however, will have more time and energy for other pursuits as s/he matures.

Chapter Seven

THE EMOTIONAL NEEDS OF THE CHILD

Each planet in the chart indicates a level of need, and many of the planetary energies have a profound correlation to emotional development. In the earliest years, a child's emotional security is determined by the relationship his/her mother and father. Interactions with siblings or grandparents can also be a factor, although relating beyond the immediate family is usually rare. The child is open to influences by these individuals, and will project her/himself upon them.

In analyzing astrological symbols to understand the developing child's emotional needs, we must also become aware of some of the basic psychological mechanisms operating in his/her life. The child will be ready to unfold varying aspects of the Self at different ages. In the very early months, a baby is struggling to figure out his/her new body and learn how it works. S/he is also familiarizing her/himself with the external environment and the people within it. We must consider the different phases of development in relation to the astrological symbology if we are to successfully apply astrology to children.

The Personal Planets

The Sun, Moon and personal planets (Mercury, Venus and Mars) symbolize the aspects of the personality which are most readily discernible. The Sun, which determines the sense of Self, may not seem to be manifesting externally in the infant. However, the physical expression of the Sun—basic vitality—is strongly manifested. A limited expression of Sun energy seems to emerge in the pre-school years, although the true awareness of the Self will not be complete for many years to come.

Lunar energy encompasses subconscious motivations and the basic instinctual and habitual responses. This level of expression begins to manifest from the moment of birth, since the baby does have a strong inner awareness of what is happening. Our exploration of the emotional needs, then, should begin with the Moon, the indicator of early psychological development.

The Moon

Most of our emotional responses are made without forethought—we simply react to a situation without thinking. These responses are based upon prior experiences in similar situations.

For the developing child, the emotional response patterns may be strongly influenced by the primary caretaker, usually Mother. Although the child does have his/her own particular needs, it is difficult for a tiny infant to tell Mommy, "I like that color," or "Play more of that music," or "I really feel good when you rub my feet." Mommy will know these things if she opens her intuitive mind, however, since she will be tuning in to the child's subconscious nature.

The child's highest needs will be symbolized by the Moon's sign and house placement. These needs remain with the child throughout life. The ease or difficulty with which the true needs will be realized can be further delineated by examining the aspects from the Moon to the other planets. The sign placement of the Moon is the basic guideline in determining the child's highest needs. This fundamental emotional framework is further altered by house placement and aspects from the Moon to other energies in the chart.

Moon in Aries needs to be independent, and will probably be very direct in expressing all desires. The baby with an Aries Moon is likely to be tremendously impatient. Activity is highly important. As the baby grows, s/he will be more and more active, and is likely to explore anything and everything.

The small child retains this impatience, and may express it with bursts of temper. As s/he matures, the child will find that by becoming mentally inventive instead of throwing temper tantrums, s/he will not have to wait so long for things to happen. Here, we have a strong sense of creativity. This child needs to be noticed, and needs to lead.

Moon in Taurus can be very stubborn, and likes to know what to expect in all situations. The small child with a Taurus Moon will probably not enjoy sudden changes of environment, an alteration in diet, or any unexpected change which has not been previously introduced.

There is often a loving placidity about these children, especially in the early years. The child's parents will appreciate his/her patience. This child needs to build a strong security base, but must watch becoming too emotionally attached to people, places and things.

Moon in Gemini enjoys diversity, and may be easily distracted in the very early months. There will be a wide variety of interests and quickly changing moods. As the child grows, s/he may be uncomfortable with highly charged emotional situations unless they can be explained rationally or expressed verbally.

The highest need here revolves around diversity and continual mental activity. Consistency may equal boredom for the Gemini Moon. These children need to move about, and should be provided with all sorts of little transportation toys. They feel a tremendous need to communicate thoughts, which tends to spur early communication skills.

Moon in Cancer is emotionally sensitive, with a strong attachment to the mother, home and family. These babies do not want to see Mother go anywhere without them. Apron strings were invented for the Cancer Moon!

As these children grow, they may feel a strong need to nurture others. They should have plenty of "babies" in the form of dolls, pets, plants and, if possible, smaller children. Their need for nurturance and protection is primary.

Moon in Leo craves attention, and will employ highly dramatic means to get it if necessary. Sign this child up for acting lessons as soon as possible so s/he can get lots of attention by performing on the stage! Leo likes to be in the center of whatever is happening, and children with a Leo Moon demonstrate this even more so than the Leo Sun. The highest need revolves around being that center.

There is sometimes an almost royal luxuriousness and laziness with the Leo Moon. The Leo Moon child also exudes a special warm radiance which is difficult to resist.

The proper use of this charismatic power is part of the lesson Leo has to learn.

Moon in Virgo needs to feel appreciated. There is sometimes a sense of not measuring up, since these children expect themselves and everyone else to be perfect. Of course, these standards for perfection are likely to come from the way Mom did it!

These children will have very strong preferences, but those preferences can be changed through reasoning. They feel the need to do something for someone else, and the Virgo Moon child should be given every opportunity to help other people. S/he has a tremendous curiosity about how things work, especially the workings of the body. These are the children you are likely to find playing "doctor" with the kid next door.

Moon in Libra needs to feel peaceful, and wants to feel that they are equal to (or better than) everyone else. Because of this need, these children sometimes spend too much time comparing themselves with others rather than setting goals for their own personal development. Sometimes they feel a sense of inferiority, since the need for perfection and balance in all things is very strong. Emotions tend to vascillate in an attempt to maintain balance.

Consistency in the external environment is important. These children need to relate to someone else, and will feel more secure when they have companions. Refinement is required even in childhood.

Moon in Scorpio is deeply sensitive, and has powerful, intense emotions. Because of this, it is often difficult for this child to openly express his/her feelings. Parents must learn to observe subtle changes in the child in order to understand what is troubling her/him. Scorpio Moon needs to have some secrets, and should be allowed plenty of privacy—a "secret treasure box" would be perfect.

In infancy, the Scorpio Moon child is tremendously sensitive, even to subtle stimulation. The parents should be alerted to this sensitivity, and should frequently offer the baby soothing, comforting caresses. These children need to learn that the deep feelings they experience are okay. If not, they may develop an emotional coldness in order to hide or repress their natural sensitivity.

Moon in Sagittarius craves the freedom to move about and explore the world. Even small babies with this Moon placement are eager to venture out into the world. The Sagittarius Moon also loves to play games, tell stories and learn new things. This need to expand may include overindulgence at the dinner table as well! An urge to know the truth will stimulate this child to ask many questions.

Moon in Capricorn prefers to control the emotions. The emotional nature is keenly felt, but may be difficult to express. This child needs to feel responsible and respected, and will enjoy the company of mature individuals.

A wry sense of humor may be noticeable, even in childhood. Capricorn Moon children need structure in their lives, and appreciate a carefully scheduled lifestyle. Lax attitudes and irresponsibility from adults will undermine his/her sense of security. Consistency of behavior is needed.

Moon in Aquarius prefers to stay away from emotional expression, and may seem rather detached. Children with this Moon placement often develop strong ties to their friends. It is important that this child finds a way to feel unique and special. If that uniqueness is not appreciated, the child may become even more emotionally detached from those in his/her personal environment.

A life which is too severely structured may engender a rebellious streak in this child. However, his/her inventiveness should be channeled in constructive directions. This child may actually *need* to travel in outer space, via airplanes and other "spacecraft."

Moon in Pisces is very emotionally sensitive, and can easily absorb the moods of others in the environment. This child needs to blend with others and feel a bonding with the significant people in his/her life. There is also a need to escape from ordinary reality into a world of fantasy and imagination. A primary challenge is to integrate the inner and outer environments. The highest need is to feel a peaceful tranquility.

These Moon sign interpretations are basic guidelines which use key concepts of the Moon and the signs. Additional information on the basic security needs of the child is obtained by using the house placement of the Moon. The child with a 10th House Moon, for example, needs recognition and feels the need to achieve. The type of achievement is determined by the qualities of the Moon sign.

Use the house placement to determine the areas which are most important to the child's sense of personal security. The house placement will also show which kinds of people and situations may significantly effect his/her sense of security.

The Moon energy is further altered by aspects to other planets.

Moon and Mercury

The Moon contacting Mercury harmoniously will aid the child in communicating his/her needs. Conversely, the

Moon in dynamic aspect to Mercury is likely to create difficulty in separating the emotions from rational concepts. The child's need to communicate is heightened, giving a thrust to this aspect of development. Interactions with others become an important focus.

Moon and Venus

The Moon and Venus bring the need for relationships and artistic expression into focus. With flowing aspects, artistic expression may emerge easily. If the aspect is dynamic, there can be an increased sense of vulnerability if the child is asked to perform or share his/her artistic talents in public. Supportive parents and teachers can help him/her in overcoming reticence and shyness.

In relationships, Moon-Venus aspects also bring increased emotional vulnerability. The child may be afraid to risk leaving one situation and going on to another. This is the "having my cake and eating it too" aspect. Emotional manipulation of others can result.

Regardless of the nature of the aspect, Moon-Venus contacts bring a sweetness to the personality. This sweetness is usually less negatively manipulative with the flowing aspects than with the dynamic ones.

Moon and Mars

Moon to Mars is a stressful aspect which brings impatience and, often, a strong sense of inner turmoil. All Moon-Mars aspects seem to be emotionally manipulative, with the dynamic aspects indicating a more devious use of the energy. This is the aspect my friend Stephane calls, "Let's you and him fight!"—an actual *need* for some sort of conflict. It is as though crisis propels the individual into action.

During childhood, these crises will probably revolve around the child's circle of friends, although you may also observe attempted manipulation of Mom and Dad. Generally, these children operate well in crisis situations—they're on home turf!

Moon and Jupiter

Moon-Jupiter contacts create a sense of optimism. The pitfalls of these contacts, especially in the dynamic aspects, involve having great expectations of the self and of others. Carly Simon's 1970's hit song "Anticipation" captures the feeling of Moon-Jupiter rather well: "Anticipation is making me late. It's keepin' me waitin'."

By continually projecting one's hopes into the future, it is difficult to be happy with situations in the present. This lesson is reluctantly learned in childhood. This is the "I want it NOW!" syndrome.

Another facet of Moon-Jupiter deals with overindulgence. These children may have difficulty knowing when to quit, especially at mealtime.

Moon and Saturn

Moon-Saturn aspects indicate inner frustrations and difficulty expressing the emotions. Even the flowing aspects may have a strong measure of emotional control. The need for consistency, structure and reliability is paramount with these children.

With a Moon-Saturn aspect, the child's need for nurturance may be so overwhelming that s/he seems depressed and melancholy much of the time. This can be alleviated somewhat by offering the child a sense of responsibility and purpose. Ignoring the signs of depression can create a block which will be difficult to overcome in the adult years.

The dynamic aspect between the Moon and Saturn brings a sense of insecurity, giving the child an especially strong need for approval from the parents. The parents should be encouraged to offer special positive input to the child. Sometimes a parent is simply unable to give much energy to the child, due to a divorce, strong commitments to work, or other situations involving absence or limitation.

When this is the case, the child has a special need for a stable emotional base. The expression of feelings may be inhibited. Positive methods of dealing with fear and anxiety should be taught early. The fearfulness s/he experiences is often due to feeling too alone and alienated from much-needed support.

Moon and Uranus

Moon aspecting Uranus brings a powerful need for independent thought and action. Rapidly shifting emotions are likely. Rebelliousness is also quite probable with the dynamic aspects. A sense of emotional insecurity could come from a feeling that mother is inconsistent and changes too rapidly. (This may be the actual situation, or just the child's perception of it.)

The child with Moon-Uranus aspects will require a strong measure of independence. S/he will definitely feel different from most of his/her friends. These feelings can bring a sense of alienation if they are not dealt with positively.

Moon and Neptune

Moon-Neptune aspects bring real emotional responses to imaginary situations. The consciousness is tremendously impressionable, and external stimuli should be screened for excessive harshness or too many negative vibrations. Vibrations are quite real to these psychically sensitive children. They can *feel* when something is wrong; it is impossible to hide feelings from them.

These children need to integrate their inner world with the outer reality. If the parents are continually telling the child, "It's only your imagination," the child will not only begin to mistrust his/her inner feelings, but will also tend to trust the parents less. The child may be flowing easily into an altered level of awareness and just not know how to deal with it. The parents need to exhibit special sensitivity when dealing with this child.

Moon and Pluto

The child with Moon-Pluto aspects is emotionally intense, and may feel that his/her emotions overtake him/her too readily. With dynamic aspects , the Moon-Pluto child may repress emotions too easily, and can be too open to extreme feelings or fear.

Many of my adult clients who have difficult Moon-Pluto aspects have shared extremely painful situations with me. The message they often received from the parents was, "Don't be," or "Don't feel." Many actually began to feel that being alive was somehow wrong, and several of them often wondered exactly why they had to remain among the living!

Yet the life force is tremendously powerful with this aspect. The real fear may come from having a strong, magnetic power and not understanding how to use it. There is sometimes a denial of personal needs with Moon-Pluto aspects. This can result in a feeling of extreme loss of contact with the sensitive and receptive parts of the self.

These children need to develop their own personal power and feel okay about having it. They need to be given permission not only to have their feelings, but to express them freely.

The Sun

The energy of the Sun is tied to emotional security and

the sense of Self. The individuality of the Sun energy begins to emerge once the child has developed enough mastery over basic bodily functions that s/he can start paying more attention to the outside world. The Sun is a major factor in determining, "Who am I?" This radiance of Self really becomes focused once the child is relating to others on a more frequent basis, especially in the school years.

Although the full power of the Sun energy does not mature until the early adult years, its formative stages begin in childhood. The sign in which the Sun is found gives clues to the qualities the child will focus upon in developing a self-image. House placement tells us where the child needs special recognition. Aspects to other planets will further define the areas having and lacking support in the development of self-image. The more difficult aspects involve contacts from the Sun to Saturn and the outer planets Uranus, Neptune and Pluto.

Sun and Jupiter

When the Sun and Jupiter are in contact, the child may have an exaggerated sense of self-importance. This is especially true with the dynamic aspects. Sometimes the child is overindulged by the parents (usually the father). These children often feel that the parents expect a great deal from them. With the flowing aspects, these expectations may be more easily integrated.

Sometimes, the child may experience difficulty simply accepting her/himself as s/he really is. These are the children who excel at "truth-stretching." If the child is applauded for her/his honest efforts, the need to stretch her/his own importance will not be so great. When the child learns to honestly accept him/herself, it is easier for him/her to assess his/her limitations as well as realize the ultimate possibilities for growth and expansion.

Sometimes, because limitations are hard to assess, the

child cannot learn to say "No" and will over-obligate him/herself. This can result in damage to his/her self-esteem if all those obligations cannot be met.

Sun and Saturn

Sun-Saturn aspects may inhibit the exercise of will power and self-projection. The child with dynamic aspects from the Sun to Saturn may sense that s/he is somehow inadequate. This feeling of inferiority can be altered by positive reinforcement from the parents toward the child's achievements.

The need for approval is powerful with Sun-Saturn contacts. The flowing aspects may bring a sense of support from the parental structure, while the dynamic aspects give the child a sense that the parents are somehow disappointed in him/her. Self-criticism is often too exaggerated with the difficult aspects.

Learning to accept personal responsibility and being rewarded for this achievement will greatly aid this child. This can begin in the preschool years. Also, Sun-Saturn dynamic aspects indicate a need for the child to have an especially secure relationship with Father. If the father is absent or inaccessible, the child needs some other grounding male influence.

Sun and Uranus

Sun-Uranus aspects provide the child with unique qualities. With the flowing aspects, this uniqueness is more readily accepted by the child and by society. The dynamic aspects, however, are a different story! With these aspects, the child may often feel like a fifth wheel, out of place in the world.

Helping the child appreciate her/his uniqueness is paramount when Sun-Uranus aspects are present. Sometimes a desire to rebel against authority or be different from

Dad will spur the child to create disruptions in his/her environment. These children need to learn how to use their unique qualities to inspire *positive* changes in the world around them. Freedom always entails responsibility—a lesson which may be a challenge for the Sun-Uranus child to learn.

Sun and Neptune

Sun-Neptune aspects in the chart confer a mystical quality to the child. These children often have difficulty being noticed and may feel invisible, especially if the aspects are the conjunction, square or opposition. It is hard for anyone with Sun-Neptune aspects to see themselves clearly, and this can be especially confusing for a child. Those with flowing aspects may appreciate feedback from the world about their self-image, whereas the child with dynamic aspects from the Sun to Neptune may resist such information—the *illusion* may be too comfortable a reality.

Attunement to subtle vibrational levels is easy for these children, and this extreme sensitivity can create problems. Losing the self to external masks may also be a challenge for these children—it may be easier for them to play roles than to find the Self. Learning music, dramatic arts, or dance might help the child positively channel this energy so that the sense of self becomes more easily identified.

It is very important with these children for the adult to clearly distinguish between what is real and what is imaginary. Movies, television and other forms of entertainment should be carefully screened, or at least shared with the child so that feedback from the physical plane will be immediately available.

Sun and Pluto

Sun-Pluto aspects are among the most difficult in

childhood, since the child must deal with power issues from the beginning. With the flowing, harmonious aspects, the power of the self may be more easily acceptable. But with the dynamic aspects, his/her power is likely to either be undermined or felt as some monstrous beast.

The child with Sun-Pluto aspects will be attracted to the superhero—the ordinary human who transforms him/herself into a superpowered being. Learning that s/he is also superpowered is hard for these youngsters. With the dynamic aspects, the child may feel continually stripped of his/her power. Family situations such as the separation from or loss of a parent can further enhance these feelings. The relationship with the father is especially critical in this case, since the child may actually perceive him as an adversary.

This child must be given ample opportunities to express personal power, but without becoming overbearing. I have talked with many mothers of children with Sun-Pluto aspects who often have trouble saying "No" to their child. The child must learn that there is a right and wrong use of personal power. Otherwise, the pattern of overbearing behavior and the extreme desire to control others could become intense in the adult years. If the child is continually struggling to have power over someone else, the real issue is probably that the child does not feel s/he has permission simply to "Be," or to exercise any real control in her/his life.

Dynamic aspects between the Sun and Pluto sometimes create a self-destructive energy within the child. The child with Sun-Pluto aspects is in touch with the Source, and can feel this Higher Power strongly.

In the early years, this feeling is projected onto the parents. The child does this in order to identify it and find a frame of reference for it. With the dynamic aspects, the child may feel threatened by this powerful energy, especially if the environment is not supportive of the child's need to integrate his personal power with that of the Higher Self. The child may feel that if s/he cannot be more than human, s/he has no reason to exist. What s/he needs to learn is that s/he *is* more than just a personality, and that this personality is connected with a Higher Source.

The self-destructive nature of the dynamic Sun-Pluto aspects often results from an inability to deal with defeats. Things which may appear small to adults (like problems with grades in school) may feel overwhelming to the child. The child wants to feel worthy of his/her own power, and part of that worth is determined by the quality of the child's performance in the external world. If the child can learn to use self-improvement techniques, this aspect may be handled more easily.

Self-improvement during childhood involves activities that allow the child to see that s/he is getting better. Learning to set goals and objectives that are within the grasp of the child is extremely important. These children should not be degraded. If they are, they will just fight back harder, and perhaps get themselves into situations which are personally toxic. The parents, teachers and guides of these children need to find ways to allow the child to continually assess his/her own worth without becoming ruthless or harsh with him/herself or others.

Aspects Between Sun and Moon

Now that we have a clearer understanding of the basic emotional needs indicated by the Sun and Moon, we need to examine how these energies work together in the chart. The external, assertive Sun aspecting the receptive, subconscious Moon is a primary determining factor in a child's emotional security. The Sun represents the masculine side of the self, while the Moon is the feminine side. Aspects between the Moon and Sun in the chart indicate a significant need for the child to deal with these primary elements of the personality. The child whose chart does not indicate a Sun-Moon aspect may not need to focus on these dynamics so intensely.

Moon-Sun conjunctions indicate a union of the conscious and subconscious aspects of the self. This child may perceive the parents as a powerful unit in his/her life. Usually, this aspect brings an easy integration of the emotional needs and the ego-self. The masculine and feminine aspects of the self seem to be well balanced in this child.

When the Moon and Sun are in dynamic aspect (e.g. square or opposition) to one another, there is a conflict between the subconscious needs and the external self. The child may feel pressured to act in a way s/he does not feel good about. Usually, this pressure results from wanting something s/he does not really need.

Sometimes the Moon-Sun dynamic aspects indicate difficulty in the relationship between the mother and father. If this is present in the external environment, the child will definitely have difficulty integrating the masculine and feminine aspects of him/herself. One part of the self will suffer in favor of the other.

Many women who have these friction-producing aspects have difficulty feeling "feminine." The drive to achieve or to exercise will power can overcome the inner receptive needs of the self. When dealing with young children who have this aspect, we need to give positive feedback about both the feeling nature and the assertive part of the Self.

When the flowing aspects (i.e., sextile and trine) between Moon and Sun are present, there may be an easier connection between the feminine and masculine parts of the Self. These children still need a good external support system, but are more emotionally stable. They are likely to feel a sense of integrated indentity much more readily.

Mercury

Mercury is not traditionally considered an emotional energy. However, Mercury's role in the expression of feelings is highly important. Mercury is the articulation of feelings, and influences how we communicate them.

Most human beings are more comfortable if they can talk about their emotional experiences to someone special. A child needs to feel that s/he can talk about anything with her/his parents, and that it is okay to share feelings and ideas. When a child is not given opportunities to communicate her/his emotional needs, s/he will have problems communicating almost anything else! Mercury's function in our lives is to link internal processes to the external world, and one of the most important inner processes is the experience of emotion.

Another way Mercury plays a part in the emotional life of the child is through the child's ability to distinguish between a *feeling* and a *thought*. Children who have Mercury placed in water signs tend to think with their feelings! Aspects from Mercury to the Moon and Venus are also indicators of the entanglement of thought and feeling. These aspects bring the sensitive, feeling part of the Self in contact with the rational, cognitive part.

With the conjunction and the dynamic aspects between Mercury and the Moon or Venus, the child may become emotionally upset if s/he is not understood intellectually. If an error in judgement is made, the emotional self may become upset. Certainly, these aspects will give a special sensitivity to the child in her/his abilities to "feel" another person's thoughts, but there can be some confusion tied in with these energies.

When the Sun and Mercury are conjunct at birth, the child may be especially sensitive if someone criticizes or challenges his/her ideas. This is because the ego self (Sun) and the communicative abilities (Mercury) are united. It is difficult for the child to separate communication of thoughts and ideas from the ego or sense of Self.

This can add a tremendous force to the child's mental energy, but it can also be a problem if s/he does not learn to distinguish between her/his ideas and her/his identity. In classroom situations, this could create a problem when the child makes a mistake. The child may feel that the intellectual error reflects badly upon him/her and feel less self-esteem. S/he needs to be thought of as intelligent.

Sun-Mercury conjunctions can have a positive impact if the child learns to channel this need to have his/her ideas recognized. Such mediums as public speaking, debate or creative writing would all be good outlets.

Another way in which Mercury can create emotional problems is seen with Mercury-Jupiter contacts. Here, the child tends to stretch the truth. The expansive quality of Jupiter adds just a few more inches to the size of that fish! This is usually more marked with the dynamic aspects between Mercury and Jupiter. There may be a feeling from the child that the plain reality of a situation is not enough.

To positively deal with this, encourage the child to tell or write stories, both fiction and non-fiction. Offer positive feedback and deal honestly with the child about what is true and what is not.

When Mercury and Saturn are together in dynamic aspect, the child may worry excessively. Saturn can have a burdening effect upon the mind energy. These children can benefit from learning how to focus upon positive thoughts.

The child with dynamic aspects between Mercury and Uranus may sense that s/he thinks differently from most of her/his friends. Sometimes these unusual thoughts can be alienating. S/he may have the impression that s/he is "weird."

If parents can teach the child how to use these original thoughts creatively, s/he will have more confidence in her/his creative ideas. Reinforcing trust of the intuitive mind is also helpful to these children.

When Mercury and Neptune are united, especially in dynamic aspect, a child may tell lies. This can definitely have emotional repercussions! A child who is taught the ability to distinguish between fact and fiction will be better able to deal with these types of aspects.

Parents can listen attentively to the tall tales, appreciating the child's imaginings, but need to encourage the child to tell the truth when relating actual events! Parents also need to be aware that the cute little "stories" told at age five, if left uncorrected, can give the child the impression that s/he can lie without being caught. This could lead to sociopathic behavior later on.

With Mercury and Pluto in conjunction or dynamic aspect, thoughts and ideas have a compelling sense of urgency. The child may be secretive with his/her thoughts in order to seem mysterious or enigmatic. This is helpful when solving mysteries or doing scientific research, but it can make honest emotional communication difficult. Parents and friends may often be met with silence if the child simply does not want to communicate. If there is communication, it can be irritatingly manipulative.

The child will be greatly helped if parents can work with him/her to understand that sharing ideas and feelings can enhance his/her command of a situation. The Mercury-Pluto child may be intellectually ruthless toward the self, and can feel assaulted if the ideas or thoughts s/he expresses are criticized. Accepting changes in attitudes and ideas is absolutely necessary for these children.

Venus

A child feels a greater sense of worth when s/he is given love and appreciation. The energy of Venus involves the expression of what we value, what we love and who is important in our lives.

Another aspect of Venusian energy is Self-love. By allowing ourselves to love another person, we are fulfilling a personal need within ourselves. Small children are notoriously selfish, and usually have to be taught to share their energy, their possessions and their time. Much of the child's behavior will, of course, be conditioned by the parents and society. Each child, however, will have his/her own particular needs in the expression of love.

Artistic expression is another Venusian manifestation, and is a wonderful way of sharing and opening a part of the inner self to the world outside. Children have creative needs which should be allowed to blossom.

Observing children's behavior, one will note that crawling babies and very young toddlers are reluctant to share. They tend to play by themselves and rarely interact with other babies (even though they may enjoy being near them). These babies are slowly unfolding their identity, which is still rather amorphous. They are likely to believe, "My toy is part of me."

Venusian expression seems to be easier for the child after about age four, when the child may really want to give something to another person. But children are more fully involved in the Venusian stage of development during the teen years, when "falling in love" becomes a reality. But, regardless of the child's age, s/he needs to feel love from others.

Venus is also one of the most sexually expressive energies of the chart. Children begin to deal with sexuality very early in life, although it awakens more powerfully when the hormones become active during puberty. Venus is one of the archetypes of feminine energy in the individual. Its sign and house placement, along with its aspects, will indicate how comfortable the child is with the feminine aspects of the Self.

The sign placement of Venus offers insights into the way a child wants to love and be loved. Its placement by house will tell us what the child appreciates, the type of environment in which a child feels most creative, and the directions in which love energy is likely to flow. Venus in the Eleventh House, for example, is strongly attached to relationships with friends—much love is given and received through friendships.

Aspects from Venus to other planets are indicators not only of the expression of love, but also how the self-worth is affected.

Venus and Jupiter

Venus-Jupiter aspects often confer a sense of generosity and a very strong need to relate to others. The expectations of others may be a problem, and the child will benefit by practicing the art of unconditional love.

Venus and Saturn

Venus-Saturn aspects inhibit the expression of love. Even the flowing aspects are restrictive (Saturn being Saturn), and the dynamic aspects are harder still to deal with.

Dynamic aspects between Venus and Saturn can be indicators of low self-esteem in the child. The child may feel that s/he must do certain things, or do things in a particular way, to be loved. These self-imposed restrictions on receiving love can be tremendously detrimental to the child's ability to openly express feelings of love.

Sometimes there is fear associated with love when these aspects are present—the fear that the love may not be there, or the fear that love will cause pain. The parents can help the child by becoming sensitive to the barriers the child builds against intimacy. Developing a trust in his/her own feelings is hard for this child. Once the sexual self begins to develop, it is important for the child with Venus-Saturn contacts to be able to cope with these feelings without fear and guilt.

Venus and Uranus

Venus aspects to Uranus can bring the need for a highly unusual form of love. This love is definitely in need of unconditional acceptance. The need for free emotional expression is powerful, since spontaneous emotion is a definite reality. These kids are often the champions of the underdog. Parents may wonder why Samantha brings home the weirdest kids in the school—it's because she can relate to them!

Children with Venus-Uranus aspects may enjoy group associations, team activities, and things they can do with others. However, there is also a need to stand out in the crowd. You may find the child with Venus-Uranus aspects beginning a new fashion revolution or setting trends. The need is to be different, and to let others know that being different is fantastic!

Venus and Neptune

Venus-Neptune aspects can confer a tremendous emotional sensitivity to the child. The emotional expression is linked with divine love, offering the child an opportunity to be a vehicle for divine compassion. The creative energies are extraordinarily sensitive, with a strong attraction to music, dance and other flowing art forms.

Because there is such a powerful sensitivity, these children can easily be hurt by the insensitivity of others. Emotional expression may be difficult because this aspect, with its elusive feelings, sometimes makes it hard for the child to know exactly how s/he feels.

Because of this, the child may be too easily influenced by others, especially with the dynamic aspects. Venus-Neptune *is* unconditional love. Forgiveness and compassion are easily understood and expressed, especially with the flowing aspects. Give this child an opportunity to help others.

Venus and Pluto

Intense, powerful emotional expression is the key to Venus-Pluto energy. Attachment is a real problem with Venus-Pluto, because once love feelings are there, they are deeply ingrained. With the flowing aspects, the ability to transform and continually alter the sense of self-worth is present. Growth and change are seen as part of life's natural course of events. Positive self-transformation is relatively easy to develop.

However, with the dynamic aspects between Venus and Pluto, the child may sense that love is self-destructive. A strong association between love and pain may be present. We know that Neptune sensitizes. Pluto *deepens*, and opens us up to the most vulnerable parts of ourselves.

When Venus and Pluto interact dynamically, opening up to the depths of emotion may hurt. Vulnerability can be guarded against to such an extent that the child can shut him/herself away from love entirely.

To change this, the parents, guides and teachers of these children must patiently show him/her how to outwardly express feelings. Art and other creative activities can be good tools. It must be understood that the art is not being judged. However, the child is likely to feel mistrustful of others, and must learn to trust his/her own feelings before others can be trusted.

When sexual feelings begin to be aroused, the child needs to have an outlet for their expression without guilt. Sometimes teens with Venus-Pluto contacts will begin to have sexual feelings and then feel so guilty that they cannot deal with them. If the young person can learn that this is just another part of the Self emerging, the guilt will be less overwhelming.

The parents can help by being supportive, empathizing with and talking about these "weird new feelings." What a difference this will make for the teenager or child! This aspect, when positively developed, confers upon the individual the ability to heal through love.

Mars

The emotional energy of Mars expresses through assertiveness, anger, strength and sexuality. For the small child, angry feelings will be one of the early introductions to Martian force. We all have feelings of anger, and must learn to express them without being self-destructive. Parents need to allow the child to have his/her angry feelings.

Positive assertiveness is also directed through Martian thrust. This masculine energy is sometimes difficult for female children to embrace, but they must accept and direct it too!

The sign and house placements of Mars will indicate the areas in which the child needs to be assertive and show how the assertiveness will be directed. Mars in water signs is often a difficult expression, especially the frustratingly indirect flow of Mars in Cancer. The child with Mars in an air sign may dissipate the energy too rapidly by shouting angry words. When dealing with anger, the child with Mars in a fire sign will be the most direct, while those with Mars in earth or water signs tend to repress angry feelings.

The key to Mars energy is that it needs to be *released* or *transmuted*. Children may have difficulty transmuting energy, though, since this requires inner awareness.

When a child becomes angry, s/he can learn to direct the anger in nondestructive ways. Parents can provide an outlet such as a punching ball or pillows on the bed so that the child has a physical release when necessary. The child needs to learn that anger is normal, but destruction through anger will create problems. *To punish a child for express ing anger will only cause the child to repress angry feelings and become even more destructive!* The task at hand is to teach the child that the negative expressions of anger directed at others will result in pain, whereas diffusing the anger non-destructively will open a doorway to change.

Mars and Saturn

Mars aspects to Saturn are likely to restrict the feelings of anger, causing the child to feel trapped inside his/her anger. This inhibited energy may then be released in cruel ways. The harmonious aspects between Mars and Saturn often aid in the constructive use of assertive energy.

The dynamic aspects will often inhibit the expression of anger, which can create physical and emotional difficulty. Sometimes these children have parents who inhibit their self-assertiveness, which tends to create anger toward the parents. This is self-destructive and will block an easy flow of understanding between parent and child.

Sexual assertiveness is often uncomfortable for these children, since there is frequently a restrictive attitude toward sexual expression from the parents. Healthy caution is one thing, but guilt about the feelings of sexuality is damaging to the young person. The teenager with difficult Mars-Saturn aspects is especially susceptible to these feelings.

Teaching him/her that sexual feelings are a normal part of growing up will alleviate much of this turmoil. Replacing guilt with an awareness of the possible consequences of his/her sexual actions will give the young person a choice. The ability to make choices strengthens his/her sense of personal power, whereas guilt feelings will simply be frustrating.

Mars and Uranus

Mars-Uranus is usually quick tempered. Any aspect between these two planets confers a need to generate lots of excitement. The child should be given ample opportunity to express him/herself freely, but could benefit from the lessons of positive caution as well. These children may be fascinated with high-risk activities such as skydiving or ski jumping, and should be encouraged to explore these activities *after* adequate instruction!

The dynamic aspects often bring an explosive temper, especially when the child feels s/he has been too inhibited! Sexual interests may develop early. These impulsive young people may act first, then think about consequences later.

Learning to consider the results of her/his actions will give this child a sense of personal confidence. S/he must learn that responsibility goes hand in hand with freedom. Part of that responsibility comes from understanding that every action has a consequence.

Mars and Neptune

Mars-Neptune aspects dissipate anger. With the dynamic aspects, the child may have angry feelings, but will have difficulty finding an outlet for them. Anger is not an easy emotion with Mars-Neptune contacts because it can cause so much confusion. Teenage males with dynamic Mars-Neptune contacts often overcompensate for assertiveness by becoming the super-athlete or the model male. Surrender is frustrating to these children. Teenage girls often over-idealize the "macho" male image, or may have problems dealing with boys in a realistic manner.

Because a realistic assessment of others is blocked by idealism, the child may either feel powerless or victimized. This can lead to escapist forms of behavior.

Sometimes, these children feel a profound need to rescue others from painful situations—they can identify with the pain! This can create a trap for the child, however, who may develop a tendency to be drawn into addictive behavior patterns. Certainly helping others is admirable, but the other person must learn how to help him/herself. Most children do not have the objectivity to understand this, and will simply identify with the other person.

Teaching the child to cope with feelings of despair by using his/her natural talent of visualizing a more positive reality can help. Encourage the child to bring this vision into action, to see that the hope for a better tomorrow is valid. Children with Mars-Neptune aspects are often rather charismatic, and can be a positive influence in the lives of others.

Mars and Pluto

Mars-Pluto is likely to have a strong sense of personal power. A sense of omnipotence may be present, even in young children. With the harmonious aspects, the child is likely to have a magnetic personality. S/he can express anger creatively through sports or other activities. The child with dynamic aspects between Mars and Pluto may feel powerless because s/he has a powerful father or others who usurp her/his personal power. Anger is likely to be repressed by difficult Mars-Pluto contracts, causing it to work against the child. Negative self-concepts and improper use of personal power can result.

These children must be given permission to express their power and their anger. They need to learn that ventilating angry feelings when they surface is better than letting them build up and then explode like a volcano!

Positive expressions of personal power can come by supporting the child's need to influence or bring change into the lives of others. Help the child target ways in which s/he could help someone else—perhaps helping an ailing friend or relative. Teens can volunteer to work in hospitals or veterinary clinics and be part of healing work.

These children need to see transformation in action. This happens around us all the time, especially in situations in which a person is becoming whole following an illness. S/he needs to change things, and can be shown ways to bring about positive change in the world. Working on projects to improve or renovate the house or yard is also a helpful way to teach these lessons.

The child with Mars-Pluto may be most drawn to sexual experimentation. Sometimes, when the harsh aspects are present, the early experiences of sexual sharing are traumatic. The key issues revolve around the acceptance and positive directions of personal power, and learning not to allow others to absorb or steal that power from them.

Jupiter, Saturn and the Outer Planets in Emotional Expression

The personal planets form the foundation of a child's emotional sense of self. Aspects from Jupiter, Saturn and the outer planets will either strengthen or weaken this emotional profile.

Each of the planets typifies an expression of need.

Jupiter represents the need for confidence and optimism; Saturn, the need for structure and discipline; Uranus, the need to feel special; Neptune, the need to reach inside the Self; and Pluto, the need to express power.

As we have seen in the preceding material, these planets can have a powerful influence in the child's emerging personality. The individual often senses the operation of the outer planets as "circumstances beyond my control," at least until a significant level of self-understanding has been achieved. Children may feel especially powerless in their early years, but, with encouragement from aware parents, can begin to harmonize more readily with themselves and their true needs.

Jupiter

Jupiter inspires growth through conferring a sense of hope and confidence. For the child, Jupiter is the bright promise of tomorrow. The sign in which Jupiter is placed will indicate the dominant theme which emerges in the child's overall philosophy of life. The house placement of Jupiter will indicate where the child feels a sense of openness and enthusiasm.

Jupiter indicates our attitudes toward generosity and sharing as well. If a child believes that sharing will in some way diminish what s/he has, s/he will be reluctant to do it. The parents can teach the child that sharing is a constant flowing cycle—the more we give, the more we receive. This is the Law of Abundance. Before it is recognized spiritually, it must be experienced emotionally!

Self-indulgence can be a negative form of Jupiterian need, and will surface when the child feels a lack of confidence. Aware parents can be alerted to this type of behavior and help the child avoid negative patterns of indulgent behavior.

Saturn, Restriction and Discipline

The structured, restrictive energy of Saturn is uncomfortable to many adults. This energy often feels binding during the childhood years, thus creating a sense of lack or loss. A child's conditioning toward Saturnian energy will be directly related to how the adults in his/her life express it. Parents need to provide a sound and consistent framework that feels trustworthy to the child. If the adult has problems dealing with positive restraints and responsibility, the child is also likely to have difficulties!

As parents, we are learning more profound approaches to dealing with our children. When I am counseling adults, I often see problems which are direct results of the difficult aspects between the personal energies and Saturn. Feelings of loss, rejection and undue restriction are common.

In dealing with children whose charts indicate harsh Saturn contacts, I am working directly with the child's Saturn element: the parents. If the child is of school age, we can usually see some of the self-critical elements of these contacts already surfacing.

One mother told me that her young teenage daughter, through her continual need for "perfect structures" in her life, projected a wall between the two of them. She related situations in which her daughter would deny her own abilities. The mother would feel compelled to point out how her daughter was limiting herself. The daughter would then withdraw and create even stronger barriers between her mother and herself.

I suggested that this mother focus upon her daughter's *strengths* for a while. The two of them also began a yoga class together, something the mother had previously criticized. This sharing provided a link for them. Now the daughter is opening up more to her mother, asking for ways to improve some of her negative attitudes.

We should not blame the parents when we see difficult

Saturn aspects. Rather, the parents need to be encouraged to project as much unconditional love and understanding as possible toward their child. It is, after all, the child's chart we are examining.

What we do see with many Saturn aspects, however, is the child's own sense of limitation, frustration or loss. This is often projected upon the parents, society or teachers. In the adult years, the projection is the government, the boss and so on. Children must learn to deal with the *realities* of life. This is the primary symbol of Saturn—the necessities of life, the real world.

This real world does not have to be negative, but can provide a secure and powerful base of operations. The difference comes when the child develops an attitude of positive abundance—the energy of Jupiter. If there is an antidote to Saturn, it's Jupiter! However, all factors must work in balance with one another. Saturn requires balance in order to be useful.

If this need for structure and discipline within the self is not developed by the child, it will generally be provided by the external environment in the form of denials and limited opportunities. This need for balance is one of the reason why Saturn's placement in Libra (where it is considered to be exalted) is a natural plus. The energy itself is continually seeking that balance.

Astrologers have recently developed a positive respect for Saturn energy, but we still understand its restrictive influence in our lives. If we are to live on a more harmonious plane, each individual must recognize the need for personal responsibility. This is a positive use of Saturn. These responses begin in childhood, and are conditioned by the parents.

Saturn is often described as the "shadow of the self." That shadow does not have to be feared, only recognized. In helping a child deal with his/her feelings of fear, guilt or jealousy, we are nurturing a positive attitude toward Saturn. Often, the fear is just a reflex. Sometimes, by working with a child's negative feelings, the parents can begin to deal openly with theirs. This kind of family healing is wonderful to watch.

Ultimately, the structures Saturn provides are within the Self. They are not houses or bank accounts or even parents. The real structure is a reliance upon our own inner strength and the willingness to take responsibility for every action, thought and feeling we have. To begin learning this in childhood will build a tremendous foundation of personal trust in one's own abilities. It will help the child to become a more complete expression of the Self.

Uranus, Neptune and Pluto

These planets move very slowly and remain in a sign for long periods of time. Generally, personal awareness of these energies is not illustrated in early childhood. In fact, there is a generational influence suggested by the sign in which these planets are placed.

We see the child coping with these planetary energies through their contacts to the personal planets (as described earlier). However, the house placement of these planets will indicate where within the Self the child experiences these higher needs. For example, if Uranus is placed in the 5th House, the child will need to express a unique (Uranus) creativity (5th House). Unusual art forms, innovative music and inventive games will be part of the child's needs. The need to feel special is strong for every child, and Uranus' house placement will give you ideas of how to encourage the child to develop that sense of uniqueness.

Neptune's need to reach inside the self and Pluto's need to express power can be interpreted by studying the house placements of these planets as well. Recognize, however, that the child may not exhibit a personal awareness of these energies as part of the self until s/he reaches maturity.

The Ascendant in Emotional Expression

The Ascendant is a highly sensitive point in the chart. This is the mask we wear before the world. Sometimes that mask is easily removed; at other times, the mask becomes the Self.

Understanding how we project ourselves to the world aids in personal integration. A child begins developing this mask through observing, feeling and experiencing the reactions of others to him/herself. The sign on the Ascendant and the planets in the 1st House give indicators about this part of the personality projection.

Using the key concepts for the qualities of the sign, you can determine how the child will project him/herself to the world. If Leo is rising, the child will project a proud, dramatic and powerful image of the Self. With Pisces rising, s/he would project a more tranquil, mystical image. The planets conjuncting the Ascendant, whether in the 12th or 1st House, will further alter this projection.

The Sun conjunct the Ascendant gives a "sunny" disposition. These children tend to be highly noticeable, and like to shine above the crowd.

The Moon conjunct the Ascendant adds a receptive quality to the personality. The child may feel self-protective. His/her emotions are more noticeable.

Mercury on the Ascendant connects the personality to the intellect. The child may be very talkative and communicative. The mental abilities will provide part of the "mask" for this child, and will be a sensitive area of the self.

Venus on the Ascendant can bring physical beauty. This planet may create a need within the child to present the most beautiful image possible. This is a two-edged sword, because the child may feel a need to be "perfectly" beautiful. If his/her beauty does not meet these exacting standards, the child could feel insecure.

Mars on the Ascendant confers a need to project strength and energy. These children will often be highly energetic. Assertiveness is a key factor in personality projection, and physical activity is a must.

Jupiter on the Ascendant projects a sense of confidence, optimism and enthusiasm. However, it can also exaggerate the personality. Sometimes over-indulgence is noticeable, causing the body to expand. Here is the image of the jolly fat person. Which part of the image is the mask?

Saturn on the Ascendant projects seriousness. The child may seem to be more responsible and mature than his/her years might indicate. Taking things too seriously can be a problem. This child often wants to project an adult image.

Uranus on the Ascendant indicates the need to be different. These children might be trend setters. Their mask is the desire to be unique.

Neptune on the Ascendant is the actor. These children can be like chameleons, changing their personalities to fit their environment. They also can project a mystical beauty.

Pluto on the Ascendant projects a powerful vibration. This mask is often very heavy for the child. These children go through tremendous personality changes during life, although they sometimes happen gradually. Reactions to the child can be extreme. Generally, these children know where they stand with others.

Planets in the First House will have similar effects to planets conjuncting the Ascendant. Planets which aspect the Ascendant (by trine, square, etc.) will further alter the personality projection.

The Child's Emotional Profile

We have examined the astrological energies as they specifically relate to a child's emotional needs. The first six years of a child's life are ruled by the energy of the Moon, the primary emotional need. During these years, a child will receive thousands of messages about who s/he is, and will be matching those messages to her/his needs. These are critical years, when the strengths and weaknesses indicated by the planetary profile are most impressionable.

The child who is strongly supported emotionally by parents and family may find it easier to balance some of the difficult factors of the personality. If the support and understanding are not present, these factors seem to loom larger for the child.

One way to begin understanding the child's basic needs is to blend together the meanings of the Sun, Moon and Ascendant. These three factors indicate the child's fundamental personality needs. Next, examine the personal planets along with their signs, houses and aspects. You may find a theme emerging in the chart which indicates the child's primary weaknesses and strengths.

For example, if the chart shows several aspects from Saturn to the Sun, Moon and personal planets, the child will need to work through his/her fears and guilt feelings. Learning that mental attitudes can make the difference in happiness or sorrow is critical.

If Uranus is heavily aspected, the child will need to appreciate his/her uniqueness and learn to channel it in a productive manner. Balancing intuitive and rational thinking is necessary.

Should the chart contain several aspects between Neptune and the personal energies, the child may have difficulty relating to the "real world." Encouraging her/him to develop creative talents will help integrate his/her personality profile.

The child with strong Plutonian influences needs to accept his/her intensity. Learning to channel personal power could create conflicts with others until s/he feels a strong measure of self-worth.

Through patience, love and understanding, we can guide the children on our planet to a more complete expression of themselves. This truly offers hope for a brighter tomorrow as we step through the doorway into the Aquarian Age.

Chapter Eight

INTELLECTUAL NEEDS

One of the most fascinating aspects of child development is the child's mental unfoldment. There are many factors involved in intellect—the ability to conceptualize, the communication of concepts and thoughts, memory, creative ideas, the application of rational thought, judicial thinking, decision-making, speculative thought and more.

The intellect carries us beyond emotion into a more objective frame of reference. A child is not initially an intellectual creature, although a few prodigious children seem to have high capacities for intellectual development. These are the ones you find orating memorized Shakespearean soliloquies at age four while other children are just beginning to speak coherent sentences!

Most parents want their child to have an excellent mind, since we live in an age when the intellect is highly prized. But sometimes this focus on the development of a powerful intellect overpowers other needs a child may have. In order to be whole, the child must achieve a balance between the mental, emotional, physical and spiritual parts of the Self—only then can the power of the intellect be used to its utmost. Otherwise, the mental capacities are likely to be misdirected in order to compensate for underdevelopment in some other area.

Through astrology, we can determine many facets of the flowering mental energy. We become acquainted with a basic spiritual law: "What you think, you become." Astrological factors which have strong intellectual connotations are the Moon, Mercury, Jupiter, Saturn and Uranus. The houses with strong intellectual focus are Houses 3, 9, and 11. Air is the element of the intellect, with fire providing inspiration.

The Moon and Mercury

A small baby begins to explore her/his personal environment through the five senses, which are interpreted through the energy of Mercury. When the baby sees Mother's familiar face, his/her mind sends signals of recognition. These senses are also used in learning. The concept of "hot" is too often learned by being burned. The sense of taste is one of the first senses a baby uses to learn—almost everything goes into his/her mouth!

As a child grows, environmental exploration becomes more refined. No longer does s/he put everything into her/his mouth—s/he can now begin to identify objects by their shapes, colors and textures. The mind gains the ability to integrate information. The placements of the Moon and Mercury by sign are strong indicators of how the child perceives his/her environment.

The Moon signifies our thought patterns, with her sign and aspects symbolizing their basic nature. The Moon in air signs is likely to generate abstract thinking. In earth signs, the thoughts are focused on the physical plane. In water signs, they are impressionable and may even be "photographic." And in fire signs, the thoughts are highly active and creative.

Through the Moon, we experience the uniqueness of our lives, then hold those experiences in the subconscious vaults of the mind. Aspects from the Moon to the other planets alters the basic flow of the thought patterns. Saturn disciplines the thinking, while Uranus electrifies and sometimes scatters it. Mercury shows us how the child communicates these thought patterns.

Mercury's sign, house and aspects are primary indicators of the intellect's outward expression. Mercury's developmental cycle occurs from age seven to thirteen. During this cycle of growth, a child focuses on understanding him/herself and the world in which s/he lives. Language is mastered; communication skills are refined. During these years, the child will project the qualities of Mercurial energy more strongly.

The child with Mercury in Aries may be very direct in communication and highly creative mentally. His/her basic approach may be to get the facts, then go on to something new.

With Mercury in Taurus, the child may be reticent to communicate until s/he has "the facts." S/he will want to be certain before speaking or committing him/herself to an idea. These are children who observe, then speak.

Mercury in Gemini is quick, witty and easily distracted. These trivia gatherers like to learn a little about a lot. I think of Mercury in Gemini as the "butterfly mind."

Cancerian Mercury may have a photographic memory, and is often indirect in communication. These children are mentally protective, and are likely to hold back information until they are certain that it is safe to speak.

Mercury in Leo wants to speak with authority and presence, and is usually interested in discussing something s/he already knows about. The mind becomes easily attached to concepts and ideas. This child may be difficult to persuade once s/he has made up his/her mind!

With a Virgo Mercury, the child tends to analyze situations before communicating anything and feels the need to speak clearly, distinctly and "properly." Mercury in Virgo sometimes has a mental "fence-sitting" posture, since the child definitely wants to be right.

Mercury in Libra communicates beautifully, with flowing images and word-pictures. S/he may be highly indecisive, and often asks the opinions of others or seeks out an authoritative source before making commitments.

With Mercury in Scorpio, the child will usually probe deeply into subjects and will communicate only when necessary. His/her mind is fascinated by the mysterious.

The child with Mercury in Sagittarius likes to speak profound truths (as s/he sees them) and is often interested in learning things which have moral messages. There is an adventurous quality to the mind and distractions can be a problem.

Capricorn Mercury is disciplined and focused. The child's communication is likely to be concerned with things which have practical value. These children often have "common sense" in abundance.

The Aquarian Mercury is blessed with an original and abstract mind, and will prefer learning things which can benefit humanity. This child will find communication by electronic means fascinating, and his/her ideas will be rather unusual. One thing you may often hear from the child with Mercury in Aquarius is, "I know . . . ." This "know-it-all" attitude can become very irritating at almost any age!

The Pisces Mercury is imaginative, impressionable and usually quiet. These children will often just answer "Yes" or "No" rather than elaborating on ideas so they can get back into their own personal world more quickly.

These basic ideas about Mercury in the signs should give you a concept of how different children communicate their mental energies. A child will talk about things which interest him/her. The signs of the Moon and Mercury indicate some of these interests, but the planetary aspects and house positions of these energies tell us even more.

Sun and Mercury

Because Mercury is so close to the Sun in its orbit, the only major aspect possible between these two bodies is the conjunction. When the Sun and Mercury are conjunct in the chart, generally the child will have strong ties between the ego self and the intellect. This can give a powerful boost to the mental energy. Powerful oratorical abilities may be present. Words are expressed dramatically and with authority.

There can be difficulties with this aspect, however, since the child may have problems accepting others's ideas. Teaching him/her how to listen effectively will prove highly beneficial. Criticism of the child's ideas may make him/her defensive. In classroom situations, this can create a difficult situation for the teacher. Parents can help the child by teaching him/her that differences of opinion do not mean that his/her ideas are not okay.

Moon and Mercury

Harmonious aspects between the Moon and Mercury in the chart will indicate an easy flow with the perceptive, intuitive self and the ability to relate thoughts that are easily understood. Communicating and learning blend easily and harmoniously. Listening is a large part of learning, and harmonious aspects between the Moon and Mercury often enhance listening abilities. This child is aware of the need to relate to both the inside and outside worlds. The feeling nature supports the thinking nature. Changes in the subconscious habit patterns might be easy to bring about, which can facilitate learning about new subjects.

Dynamic aspects beteween the child's Moon and Mercury are likely to indicate perceptual problems, since the emotions tend to get in the way of the thinking process. It may be difficult for the child to share his/her innermost thoughts without losing something in the translation; hence, a feeling of being "misunderstood" may arise. Parents need to offer increased support to the child in any new learning situations. These aspects are also likely to create reluctance in learning new subjects. Problems could result if the child changes schools or teachers.

Mercury and Venus

When these two planets contact one another, the child will be drawn to the artistic expression of ideas. The only possible major aspects are the conjunction and sextile. Even the dynamic (the semi-square) aspect will enhance the child's artistic abilities, but there may be some frustration in achieving his/her desired result.

The child often enjoys listening to or reading poetry or prose. Creative writing should be encouraged at an early age by playing story-telling games with the child. Once in school, s/he may be especially interested in studying literature.

Developing a genteel manner of speech will be easy for the child with the sextile between Mercury and Venus. In fact, coarse speech may be offensive to this child! S/he may also give special attention to his/her handwriting, which could turn out to be quite beautiful.

Mercury and Mars

When Mercury and Mars contact one another, the intellect is strongly energized. There is a certain degree of impatience, even with the flowing aspects. Ideas and concepts have to be presented in a concise manner if the child's attention is to be maintained!

When Mercury conjuncts Mars in the chart, the mental curiosity is sharpened. The child wants to learn, explore and experience, and may have trouble with directions like "Wait a minute!" Sometimes s/he will argue just to keep the mind moving. This argumentative attitude can be quite irritating until the parents realize that the child is simply exercising her/his mind. For him/her, an argument is better than no conversation at all! These children usually love to tease.

With flowing aspects between Mercury and Mars, there may often be a pioneering attitude. The child is eager to explore new ideas and concepts, and learns quickly.

The dynamic aspects between Mercury and Mars promote tremendous mental activity, sometimes hyperactivity. These children have difficulty sitting still and focusing for long periods. If the parents can understand the child's need to be continually active, they can cope more effectively with him/her. Encouraging physical activity offers the child an opportunity to burn off some of this mental energy. This child may have difficulty developing good study habits, but they are absolutely necessary.

Mercury and Jupiter

Aspects between Mercury and Jupiter influence the child's intellectual maturation. Jupiter helps us to assimilate information. Although much of Jupiter's influence is in the social realms of culture and religion, it is also the process by which we integrate larger concepts. The concept of "sharing," for example, cannot really be understood as an abstract idea: the child must personally experience how his/her society views it. Even a child with a sharp mind will be severely limited in attaining a sense of personal identity if s/he cannot appropriately integrate his/her thoughts into society.

Jupiter brings expansion of the mind. With harmonious aspects between Mercury and Jupiter, the child feels confident and comfortable with his/her mental and communicative abilities. S/he will constantly seek to learn and understand.

The dynamic aspects between these two planets will still create the need to expand personal knowledge, but it is likely to be motivated by the feeling that "I don't know enough." This attitude or feeling of inferiority can create a situation in which the child is continually "enhancing" everything s/he says. Learning to accept any type of personal mediocrity may be very difficult for this child. Mercury-Jupiter dynamics can also bring many distractions to the thoughts, since the child may try to learn a little about everything rather than focusing on a limited number of interests.

Mercury and Saturn

With Mercury aspecting Saturn, mental concentration is enhanced. The harmonious aspects confer a strong sense of mental discipline and a sharp, reliable memory. The thought processes are more readily accessible and tend to center around areas that are practical and sensible.

With dynamic aspects between Mercury and Saturn, the child may not trust his/her mental abilities. S/he may feel a sense of severe mental limitation, even if that limitation is not actually present! Sometimes the child may be reluctant to speak or share information for fear that what s/he says may be inadequate, wrong or otherwise incomplete.

Father is likely to play a powerful role, and could be considered omniscient by the child. He may also seem to have strong expectations of the child's intellectual performance. These children may sometimes feel that his/her thoughts and ideas are met with undue criticism. The type of criticism the child receives will largely determine how much s/he trusts her/his intellectual abilities.

Whatever the child's inherent intellectual ability, it can be enhanced by the cultivation of positive mental attitudes. Criticism is likely to feel too harsh to the child with Mercury-Saturn discordant aspects, even if it comes as an opportunity to learn. Learning through experience, however, is probably the most appropriate method for him/her.

Mercury and Uranus

Mercury-Uranus aspects confer brilliance and an ingenious quality to the intellect. Inventiveness is a dominant trait of these aspects. With flowing aspects, the intuition enhances the mental abilities, inspiring and guiding original thought. The dynamic aspects confer the same qualities, but on a more erratic basis.

The child will be easily stimulated mentally, but may have some problems focusing the mind (scattering of the thoughts is a problem even with the harmonious aspects). Step-by-step rational thought is not easy for the child with Mercury-Uranus aspects. The mind assimilates data so quickly that the child may not be aware of all the steps involved—s/he just has the answer! When asked to explain the reasons behind his/her thinking, these children may be stumped. Learning mathematical theorems in their later school years will be helpful to them, although not always enjoyed!

Mercury and Neptune

Mercury-Neptune aspects enhance the use of creative imagery and imagination. Neptune adds a permeable, highly impressionable quality to the mind. With harmonious aspects between Mercury and Neptune, the intuition is highly developed. The mind is tremendously sensitive, and can easily attune itself to inner levels of thought. These children may have "imaginary playmates"—non-physical beings who are only "imaginary" to those who can't see them.

Once the child begins to relate to others frequently, the ability to link his/her thoughts with others may be very powerful. These are the kids who can "psych" the teacher in classroom situations and know exactly what to expect on examinations. (It's no problem when you can tune into the teacher's thoughts!)

With dynamic aspects between Mercury and Neptune, the child may spend too much time within him/herself and/or may have great trouble sharing ideas and information coherently. S/he may be able to reach out more easily by developing a less structured, more artistic form of communication.

I also see impressionable, easily influenced children with dynamic Mercury-Neptune aspects who feel that they don't have a mind of their own. Spending time in an earthy, natural environment is often helpful in grounding this child's mental energies. Playing instrumentals or singing vocal music can help these children to express their original concepts.

Mercury and Pluto

Mercury-Pluto indicates mental intensity. The mind probes persistently below the surface, seeking to find the secrets hidden there. With flowing aspects between Mercury and Pluto, the drive to do empirical scientific research may be strong. There is a strong drive to find the root cause, to understand the ultimate "who, what, where, when, how and why." There is a forceful, concentrated learning ability.

With the dynamic aspect, the mental concentration can become compulsive and dogmatic. These children are not light thinkers! Any Mercury-Pluto aspect confers great depth of thought and persistent mental energy.

House Placement

The house placement of Mercury indicates the aspects of life and personal development which the child may find most interesting. A child with two or more planets in houses 3 or 9 will feel a stronger motivation to develop the intellect, regardless of which planetary energies are there. If Saturn is present, there will be a need to learn in order to feel secure. Saturn may also bring a reticence in the approach to learning if placed in the 3rd or 9th house.

We use the placement of Mercury in the house to determine a child's intellectual interests. A child with Mercury in Scorpio in the 6th House, for example, will be fascinated by human anatomy and physiology. Use the house placement to determine a good study environment for the school-age child. Children with Mercury in the 12th House may prefer a private, closed room for study, whereas the child with Mercury in the 7th House might prefer to study with a best buddy.

Approaches to Learning

Education is a primary feature of childhood, and parents now have more choices in the education of their children. They can choose open classrooms, Montessori methods, Waldorf schools and more. Some parents are even teaching their babies to read before they are two years old!

Some children will be better suited to one learning experience, while others will learn more easily in a different situation. Looking at the energies of the Moon, Mercury, Jupiter and Saturn will tell us which approach would be best suited for a particular child.

Moon Speed

The Moon's speed in the chart fundamentally affects

the child's approach to learning. The Moon moves at variable speeds in her rotation around the Earth. If you have a computer-calculated chart, the speed of the Moon is probably indicated. If you calculated your own chart, you found the Moon's speed before you could determine the exact place ment by degree and sign of the zodiac.

Astrologer Marc Edmund Jones first introduced me to the idea of Moon speed as a variable in learning. He suggested that speeds above thirteen degrees ten minutes (13:10) should be considered as fast, whereas speed below this demarcation would be considered slow. The individual with a fast Moon seems to be eager to confront the experiences of life. These children are the ones who may jump into new situations, often spontaneously.

With the slower Moon speeds (less than 13:10), the child may be somewhat reluctant to approach new situations. These children tend to be observers who only enter into new situations after a period of cautious consideration.

Moon speeds which are extremely fast (above fourteen-and-a-half degrees—14:30) seem to be associated with steel-trap minds, and suggest the ability to learn quickly and retain practically forever.

By blending the needs of the Moon, Mercury, Saturn and Jupiter in the chart, we can determine some excellent approaches to a child's education. The child with Saturn positively contacted by the Moon and/or Mercury would probably do well in open classroom situations, since self-discipline would be easier expressed. The child with Mercury-Uranus aspects might enjoy some structure, but would not want to be held back by slower students. These children might do well in accelerated classes which allow the child to move at his/her own pace while still receiving adequate supervision and guidance from his/her teachers.

If a child shows a great deal of fear about learning

(harsh aspects from Saturn or Pluto to the Moon and/or Mercury), the parents would do well to arrange loving, non-judgmental guidance for the child. This might be easily accomplished through a counselor or aide who works with learning problems. Many learning problems have their roots in *emotional*, not intellectual, difficulties. Some learn ing problems may also have their roots in physical disturbances.

Parents often judge the child by his/her performance in school. Even preschool children can feel pressured by the parents to perform. ("Say your ABC's." "Can you count to 100?")

Encouragement and testing are two different things. Small children do not like to be tested—life is enough of a test for them! They do enjoy learning, but need to be encouraged to learn at their own pace. Finding that pace is one of the primary tasks of parents and teachers. Allowing the child to feel comfortable with his/her strengths and limitations is important in aiding the optimum development of the child's intellectual needs.

Chapter Nine

CREATIVE SELF-EXPRESSION AND TALENTS

Most parents want their children to develop some sort of "special" talent. For the parents, this usually means a sizable outlay of cash for the necessary instruction. For the child, it means discipline, time and energy.

Most people find it difficult to determine exactly which creative talents their child possesses, especially when s/he offers no overt signals. Under these circumstances, it is easiest for the parents to push the child toward the creative directions most attractive to them personally. They may not even consider whether or not the child has any real talent in these areas.

The child's astrological profile, however, is an excellent guide to his/her special interests and abilities. Using this informative tool can help eliminate an extended "talent search" by the parents. It can help offer a child several alternatives which will not only provide creative outlets, but enhance her/his psychological strengths as well.

I studied piano as a young girl. The studio was one of the most respected in our city, and the program was unrelentingly rigorous. Our teacher, a grande dame in her sixties, was very demanding. To attend a lesson unprepared was to be met with a reprimand, no lesson and a harsh phone call to Mother or Dad. In our music theory classes, my fellow students and I shared horror stories of what happened "the time I forgot a Bach Invention halfway through."

Most of my compatriots were not really excited about studying music—it was just "something Mom and Dad wanted me to do." I remember one young boy, about age ten, who said he really wanted to study ballet. His dad "freaked," however, and said that if he was going to have anything moving to the music, it would be his fingers! This example illustrates how easy it is for parents to limit their children's natural development without even intending to.

If we are to give our children the opportunity to become whole, powerful beings, then creative self-expression must be a free-flowing part of their personal power. Through the astrological chart, we gain a sense of the child's needs at many levels. We can understand the basic qualities which make up the personality, and can better guide the child in the blossoming of his/her creative potential.

Creativity involves attunement to the inner realm through *imagination* and *intuition*. A child's fantasies must be expressed through her/his natural abilities, whether they are manifested through the voice, the hands, the entire body or other means. Most people, when asked about their own creativity, think that they don't have any! They think of "creative people" as artists, musicians, actors, or others who make their living in the fine arts.

But creativity can take many forms outside this narrow definition. The key is tuning in to the imagination, then expressing it physically. Creativity requires receptivity to our Higher Selves and the surrender of our physical vehicles to our particular creative flow. This brings a completeness which balances the body, mind and spirit.

A child needs energy to execute her/his talents, the

discipline to learn the necessary skills and, hopefully, some type of reward for his/her accomplishments. Developing the creative flow helps us to reach for the best within ourselves. This instills confidence, personal power and inner strength.

The primary areas to examine in determining creative talents are the 5th House, any planets in this house, and the sign on the 5th House cusp. Venus, her sign, house placement and aspects will also be indicative of the child's particular artistry. Mars shows the type of energy the child has to execute these talents. Saturn adds discipline and focus to the creative efforts. Uranus, Neptune and Pluto give the inner awareness necessary for the tasks.

All of the planetary energies are involved in the creative process. The factors noted above, however, are the best indicators of creative artistry within the individual.

The Sun

The Sun, which is the Divine Spark, gives us the drive to create. It gives the ego its unique creative identity.

The Moon

The Moon's receptivity is also part of the creative flow. It is through the conscious conditioning of the subconscious processes that we connect ourselves with the Higher Self.

The Moon also indicates the thought forms of the individual. Study the sign in which the Moon is placed to understand where the child is when s/he goes inside her/himself.

Mercury

Mercury is involved in the creation of ideas and the communication of creative concepts. If Mercury is placed on the angles of the chart, the child will be likely to communicate his/her creative ideas to others.

If Mercury and Jupiter are in aspect to each other, the child may be interested in journalism. Inspirational writing could also be a good creative outlet.

Connections to the transpersonal planets give Mercury's energy a link to the collective unconscious. This may confer an ability to attune to the masses. If writing skills are developed by the child who has Mercury contacting the outer planets, s/he could become a translator of people's unconscious needs. These types of skills are necessary for the creative writer. This attunement is also helpful if the individual is interested in mass media or advertising.

Linked by aspect to Uranus, Mercury translates intuitive impulses into rational thought. This is the "original thinker," the inventive mind. These children may be drawn to creative areas of television, radio or other electronic media.

Aspecting Neptune, Mercury's creativity is more transcendent. Poetry and prose are likely creative expressions. Acting is also a strong possibility.

With Mercury aspecting Pluto, the mind probes deeply. Creativity could involve transformational thought, introspection and regeneration. Mystery writing, science fiction and psychological dramas could probably prove intriguing for this child.

Jupiter

Jupiter instills confidence in the Self. The child with strong, supportive Jupiter aspects will instinctively want to share his/her creative expression with the world. There is a natural enthusiasm which can be quite contagious!

Jupiter strengthens the child most when found in flowing aspects to the Sun, Moon and Venus. The child will probably trust in a Higher Power to provide for his/her needs.

CREATIVE FOCUS: VENUS IN THE SIGNS

ARIES	Jewelry making, designing hats, hairdressing, glass-blowing and glass work, metal etching, ceramics, woodburning, public speaking, drums, athletic dancing.
TAURUS	Singing and music, painting and drawing, flower gardening, confectionmaking, jewelrymaking, clay sculpting, pottery.
GEMINI	Writing, making models, puppetry, computer games (creating original games), caricature drawing, debate and oratory, broadcasting, violin, guitar, prestidigitation (magic tricks), wind instruments.
CANCER	Cooking, gardening, water colors, jewelrymaking (especially with silver), pottery, dollmaking, singing, water ballet, photography, knitting and sewing.
LEO	Acting, circus performing, movie-making, jewelry-making (especially with gold), directing, persuasive speaking, creating games.
VIRGO	Writing, public speaking, sewing, sculpting, drafting, piano, anatomical drawing, fine-line drawing and etching, calligraphy, making models and miniatures, crafts, percussion instruments.
LIBRA	Acting, painting and drawing, making confections, fashion design, flower arranging, musical ability, poetry writing.
SCORPIO	Magic acts, dancing, painting, writing, gardening (esp. growing bulb flowers), piano, mystery writing, underwater photography, guitar, bass guitar, cello.
SAGITTARIUS	Writing and journalism, dancing, animal training (esp. horses), broadcasting, public speaking, promoting others.
CAPRICORN	Classical music, music composition, wood-working, gardening, comedy, cartooning, ice sculpting, ice-skating and ice-dancing, pottery, sculpting, crafts, creations with crystals.
AQUARIUS	Music composition, astrology, synthesized music, ice-skating, computer programming, anything to do with television and radio, innovative art forms, painting.
PISCES	Dance, ballet, acting, singing, painting, photography, swimming, harp, guitar and "etheric" instruments, mime, makeup and costume design, ventriloquism, animation, visionary art.

Table 8

The 5th House

The 5th House is called "the house of creative self-expression." It is below the horizon, which indicates that it involves internalized energy. The 5th House is also the area of the chart which signifies the giving of love, which can be expressed through creative activities.

The polar opposite of the 5th House, the 11th House, tells us about receiving love. It balances the 5th House by bringing in feedback from the outside world. This is the house of friends, who applaud us when we succeed, encourage us when we are down, and inspire us to continue.

Another aspect of the 5th House is play. Creativity flows most easily and is most beneficial when the child is doing something s/he really loves to do. Through the creative process, the child opens to greater self-love. This increases the child's sense of personal worth and gives more power to the creative efforts.

When examining the 5th House to understand the underlying creative expression of the child, first look to the sign on the house cusp. Consider the qualities of that sign. Aquarius, for example, is inventive, futuristic, and avant garde. These qualities would permeate the creative self.

Then we study the planets in the 5th House, along with their signs and aspects. If there are no planets there, look to the planet which rules the sign on the cusp. Find that planet in the chart, along with its house, sign, and aspects. This indicates the child's underlying theme in creative expression.

In the chart of Wolfgang Amadeus Mozart, the 5th House contains the Sun, Mercury and Saturn in Aquarius. His sense of individuality (Sun) was strongly tied to creative expression in a unique and original form (Aquarius).

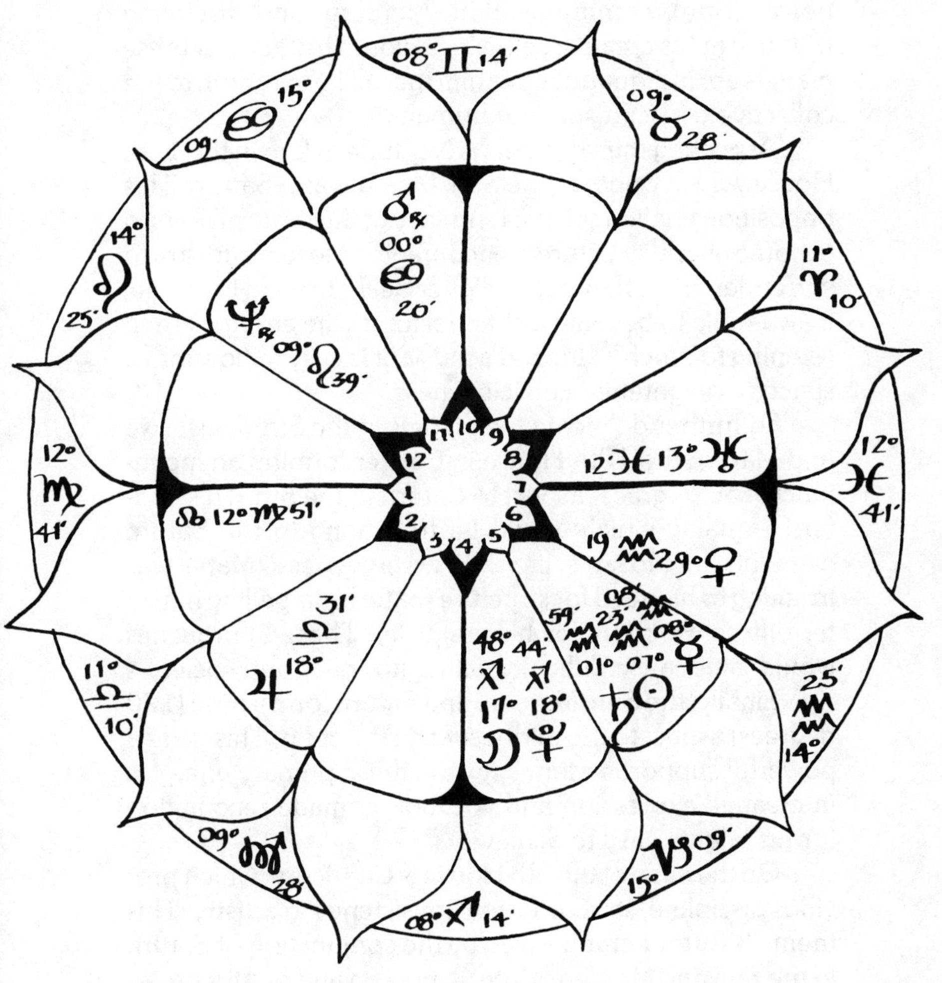

Wolfgang Amadeus Mozart
January 27, 1756
8:00 P.M. LMT
Salzburg, Austria

The planets in this house are all conjunct, uniting will power (Sun), communication (Mercury) and discipline (Saturn) in his creative self-expression. The fact that these planets are in Aquarius gave him the ability to tune in to the collective consciousness of humanity.

Aspecting these planets is Neptune in Leo in the 11th House, which opposes the Sun, Mercury and Saturn. This opposition challenged the tendency of the three planets to become overly structured, encouraging Mozart's artistry to surrender to the flow of his Higher Self. Through Neptune, he was able to become a channel for divine energy. When listening to much of Mozart's music, it is easy to flow into a space of heightened consciousness.

To further delineate the planets in the 5th House, we find Mars in the 10th House in Cancer forming an inconjunct (150 degrees) aspect to Saturn in the 5th. This confers a quality which would be frustrating to the Saturn elements in Mozart's life. His assertiveness (Mars) was irritating to his need for structure (Saturn), impelling him to try different outlets for his creativity. These approaches would later cause difficulty with authorities and society.

Finally, the Sun, Mercury and Saturn form a trine (120 degrees) aspect to the Midheaven in the chart. This gives a powerful support system between these primary energies in creative expression and vocation. It made recognition for his talents easy to achieve.

On the cusp of the 5th House is Capricorn, which provides discipline, structure, and consistency to artistry. This theme is further emphasized by the conjunction of Saturn to the Sun and Mercury. Both Capricorn and Saturn prefer to do things perfectly, and Mozart was known to have produced entire musical scores written note perfect on the first draft!

In our next example, we find a chart which contains *no*

planets in the 5th House. This does not infer that this individual was not creatively expressive, though! Scorpio is on the cusp of this house, adding transformation and intensity to the creative flow.

The planet which corresponds to Scorpio is Pluto, which is found in the 12th House in Cancer. This indicates a strong attunement to the collective unconscious, an ability to reach people in the deepest recesses of themselves. Her energy could also bring about transformational change in others.

Pluto's aspects are numerous. First, Pluto conjuncts the Ascendant in Cancer, and widely conjuncts Venus in the 1st House. Also, Pluto trines Uranus in Pisces in the 10th House, as well as the Midheaven. Finally, Pluto is square Jupiter in Libra in the 4th House. Not only is the intensity of emotional expression strong, but the essence of the Self-projection (1st House) as "the artist" (Venus) is enhanced.

With the T-Square between Mercury in Cancer, Saturn in Libra and the Moon at 29 degrees Sagittarius, there is frustration expressing the highest needs. But this is overcome by the willingness to take a chance on asserting her uniqueness, illustrated by a second T-Square between the Sun, Mars and Uranus.

The personality expression (Ascendant), vocation (Midheaven), and basic security system (IC) are all involved in a need to be creatively expressive. The powerful, vital energy with which these needs are expressed is enhanced by the Sun, Mars, Uranus T-Square.

This is the chart of Judy Garland, who played the role of Dorothy in *The Wizard of Oz.* In this role, she carried the consciousness of humanity into a magically transformed world. She later portrayed the sterotypical "All-American Girl" in a series of roles, creating a model followed by an entire generation.

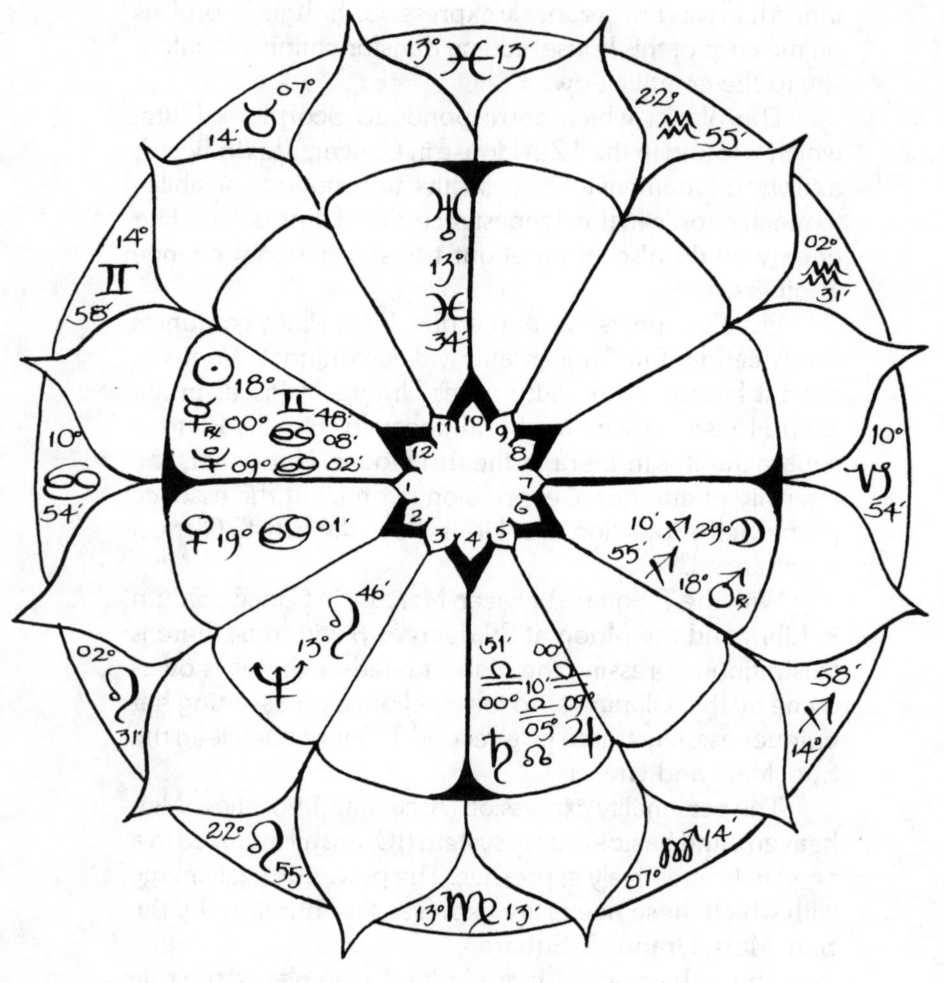

Judy Garland
June 10, 1922
6:00 A.M.
Grand Rapids, Minnesota

Venus

Venus, the expression of artistry, is also important in a creative context. This is the energy which allows us to experience and express our feelings. Venus also represents beauty, a quality which lies within each of us and which we all need to feel and express.

The sign in which Venus is placed offers input concerning the artistic gifts of the child. Venus in Leo is artistically dramatic and bold. Venus in Pisces is sensitive, flowing, musical and transcendent. Venus in Capricorn flows in a more structured manner, with classical art forms often preferred. In Table 8, the correspondence of the sign Venus occupies to the child's artistic learnings are noted. These are only intended as basic guidelines to the analysis of creative artistry.

We also look to the planets which contact Venus by aspect. These tell us about the support the Venusian energy receives or the obstacles which it may encounter.

Sun and Venus

The only major aspect is the conjunction. With the Sun conjunct Venus, the sense of self is expressed with grace and charm in a refined, artistic manner. With this dynamic aspect, the child may at times be less than certain of his/her creative potential.

The Sun gives a dramatic power to the artistic expression, while Venus makes beauty an important part of the self-concept. Even minor aspects between the Sun and Venus may indicate an interest in performing, with the dynamic vitality of the Sun boosting the artistic energy of Venus. This would be helpful in acting, public speaking or modeling.

Moon and Venus

Venus aspected by the Moon involves a deep need to be creative. The child should be offered ample creative projects, even at a young age. If the aspect between the Moon and Venus is flowing, it will be easy for the child to express her/himself creatively. The dynamic aspects can create difficulties, however. S/he may feel insecure about her/himself and allow this feeling of inferiority to block creative expression.

Encouragement from the parents will help this child be more free with her/his creative flow. The conflict created by the dynamic aspect can in itself be the impetus for the child to explore creative outlets, if only to release some of the tension s/he feels inside! These aspects often confer talents in the more emotional art forms, especially music.

Mercury and Venus

Mercury contacting Venus adds to the communicative nature of the creative flow. There may be talents in writing or speaking. Poetry and prose can be easy expressions, especially with the sextiles between Mercury and Venus.

Look to the elemental nature of the planets. If they are in air signs, writing beautiful words which communicate the idea of love may be easy. In fire signs, inspirational writing is more expressive. If there are different elements, blend those concepts. Encourage writing in all forms when these aspects are present.

The child's handwriting may be artistic, with art forms such as calligraphy being appealing. Mercury is connected to the hands, so the hands themselves may be instruments of artistic expression. Crafts and needlework are often enjoyed.

The speaking voice is often melodic. Encourage the child to read aloud to you. Later on, s/he might enjoy giving poetry readings or competing in speech contests in school.

Venus and Mars

Venus-Mars contacts give an assertive, direct quality to the creative flow. Drums and percussion instruments are strong expressions of Venus-Mars contacts. Athletic dancing might be enjoyable. More athletic forms of Venusian expression such as tap dancing, break dancing, or gymnastic events could provide good outlets for the planetary energy.

With dynamic aspects between Venus and Mars, a child may feel some inner frustration in expressing creativity. These children can be aided by learning graceful, flowing body movements. This could help them develop a positive outlet for energy which sometimes comes in uncontrolled bursts. Otherwise s/he may feel like a "klutz," with physical awkwardness involving them in embarrassing situations.

Venus and Jupiter

Venus-Jupiter aspects confer confidence, especially when they are harmonious. These children often attract the support of others in their artistic expression. They may be easily inspired by a teacher or other mentor. Usually they love to travel and read; writing may be a strong talent, and so may public speaking.

These children are also positive supporters of others. This is a helpful connection to find in the chart of a cheerleader!

Venus and Saturn

Venus-Saturn contacts bring discipline and structure to artistic expression. The flowing aspects can develop powerful abilities to discipline artistic efforts, thereby perfecting the skills necessary to become outstanding.

Dynamic aspects between Venus and Saturn may make the child too critical of his/her own efforts, thus restricting the creative flow and causing feelings of frustration. Creative talents may be overly structured and the spontaneity is lost or diluted.

The child may show special talents in the classical art forms with the harmonious aspects. There is also a strong sense of the business end of the arts.

Venus and Uranus

Venus-Uranus aspects add a unique flavor to artistry. Tastes will be unusual, futuristic, and sometimes strange! The "untried" is fascinating. Applications of technological innovations to art may be a strong tendency (e.g. synthesized music, electronic art). These children can be creatively innovative, and are sometimes prodigious in their artistic expression.

One factor which can be frustrating with Venus-Uranus contacts is an inability to focus and concentrate. Spontaneous inspiration may distract the child from completing the artistic project at hand. A young boy comes to mind who has Venus inconjunct Uranus in his chart. By age fifteen, he had "studied" (I use the term loosely!) piano, harp, oboe, violin, flute and guitar. His mother, who described her son's room as "the attic of the local music store," was becoming rather upset—he had just requested a synthesizer for Christmas!

The synthesizer seemed like the optimum choice, however, since it can produce an endless variety of sounds. I encouraged her to buy it. Two years later, he was still working with electronic instruments, and was adapting his violin to run through his synthesizer! This was a perfect use of Venus inconjunct Uranus.

Venus and Neptune

Venus-Neptune aspects bring sensitivity, mysticism, and vision to the creative expression. Venus-Neptune aspects are often most easily expressed through music, although painting, acting and dance are also excellent outlets for this energy. With contacts between Venus and Neptune, the child can apply creative visualization very effectively. If the aspects are flowing, these visualizations will be even more easily realized.

These connections are strong indicators of dramatic talents. There can be an outstanding ability to project a beautiful image. This lends itself to modeling or other situations in which a photogenic appearance is important.

The dynamic aspects between Venus and Neptune indicate a need to express the inner self creatively, yet something always seems to be lost in the translation. It may be difficult for parents or others to relate to what the child is trying to express artistically. With training, this confusing outflow can be more easily clarified.

The sensitive refinement of Venus-Neptune is usually attracted to transcendant qualities in visual art and in music. These children are visionary artists.

Venus and Pluto

Venus-Pluto contacts bring intensity, power and passion to artistic expression. There is a sensuality which could be expressed through painting (especially through the use of heavier mediums such as acrylics and oils). Transforming stone into statue is an excellent outlet for Venus-Pluto.

These children can also create something new from something old. I have a client with a Venus-Pluto conjunct whose passion is collecting old lace, which she uses in her original clothing designs.

Sometimes these children can inspire transformational change in others through their use of artistic expression. With dynamic aspects between Venus and Pluto, the child must learn how to express intensity without alienating her/his audience.

With these basic ideas, we begin to see the primary factors which determine a child's creative abilities. Venus' placement by house tells us much about the child's creative artistry. With Venus in the 1st House, the child will want to present a beautiful image to the world. The manner of dress, action and speaking are likely to be refined. Venus in the 10th House may want to develop an artistic career, or at least have some public exposure of his/her artistic talents.

Mars

Mars indicates the type of energy the child uses to execute his/her talents. Mars in Virgo, for example, may be an excellent percussionist—the physical energy can be directed in precise ways with the hands. Mars in Virgo could also direct physical energy through meticulous hand movements in activities such as line drawings, hand-carved art, and needlework.

We also look to Mars to understand the child's basic physical energy level. If a child is interested in becoming a dancer, but has Mars squaring Saturn and opposing Neptune, s/he may not have enough physical energy to endure the rigorous regimen of a dancer. Extreme supportive measures would have to be taken such as increased rest, heightened nutrition and extensive training and conditioning.

Mars also indicates the ability to assert the self. The child who wants to perform in public would benefit from a strongly placed Mars, or from positive aspects between Mars and other planets in the chart.

Saturn Aspects

Aspects from personal planets to Saturn indicate the child's approach to discipline. The need for discipline in developing creative artistry is paramount. Without focus, there is little achievement or improvement in the quality of artistic output.

Some children simply resist discipline. To offset this negativity, parents might try a motivational reward system. This sort of positive reinforcement brings more powerful gains than negative reinforcement.

To determine which types of rewards would appeal to the child, study the 2nd and 10th houses, the Moon and Venus. Rewarding the child with things which help him/her feel more secure (Moon) will benefit him/her and help him/her accept the need for discipline. The types of activities your child finds pleasurable will be shown by the sign placement of Venus (e.g., Venus in Pisces might enjoy an afternoon movie as a reward for her/his guitar practice). These reward systems will add self-worth and confidence.

Saturn does not have to bring limitations and restrictions—it can also bring concentration, focus and crystallization. The child whose chart indicates strong Saturn aspects may be the best candidate for some type of classical artistic expression, since s/he will appreciate form and structure.

The types of support the child needs will also be indicated by Saturn in the chart, with the flowing aspects indicating the most harmonious support system. When dynamic aspects are present, the child may feel too pressured by the parents or others to be more than s/he really is. Parents need to be careful of their expectations of their children when these types of aspects are present.

Generally, children are not particularly interested in

artistic expression until they reach school age, although creativity and the imaginative flow should be stimulated at early ages. Encourage the child to sing, dance, paint, draw, act silly, tell stories, make funny faces—whatever it takes to let him/her know that you enjoy his/her spontaneous creativity. Parents and teachers can gain some insights into the most powerful talents the child may have, or at least into the talents the child is ready to develop.

Through analyzing the needs and potential talents symbolized by the 5th House, Venus, Mars and the other planets, we can determine positive creative directions for the child and encourage him/her to explore and express these aspects of the self. Whether or not a child will become a professional artist or musician is not the issue here. We are addressing each child's need to do something that feels creative and special to him/her. You may be raising, teaching, or counseling a future Picasso, Pavarotti or Michael Jackson, but it does not matter if the child is exceptionally talented—what s/he needs to feel is that there is something s/he he does especially well, in her/his own special way. This will build confidence, a feeling of personal worth and the potential for a tremendously abundant future.

Chapter Ten

THE SPIRITUAL NEEDS OF THE CHILD

As a child matures, his/her awareness expands. The developing child's world grows even more complex as s/he tries to balance the physical, emotional, intellectual and spiritual aspects of life. By focusing on this balance during the childhood years, the child will acquire greater personal power. Maintaining balance and harmony between these need systems is a constant challenge requiring different areas of emphasis at different ages.

We do not generally think in terms of a child's spiritual awareness, since the "higher mind" functions are not fully developed until later in life. But children *do* have spiritual needs, and these needs are emphasized at different times along with the physical, emotional and intellectual needs.

Webster defines *spiritual* as "of, relating to, or consisting of spirit: incorporeal; concerned with religious values." My own concept of "spiritual" involves an attunement to the inner needs as directed by a Higher Source, as well as an awareness of the connection between the Higher and lower parts of the Self. To be spiritually aware is to *know* the presence of the Divine. Intuition, which is knowledge received directly from the Higher Self, is a function of this connection between the spirit of wo/man (the individual) and the spirit of the One.

Children have a need to evolve spiritually, to *know* that they are connected with a power beyond themselves. This divine presence exists within the child, but is not always easy to identify.

The energies in the astrological chart which are generally considered to have "spiritual" connotation are Jupiter and the outer planets: Uranus, Neptune and Pluto. For me, however, the entire symbology of the chart is spiritual, since it indicates the needs that must be actualized in order for a person to become whole. By becoming one with the needs of the soul, we grow spiritually. If we are separated from any of our need levels—physical, mental, emotional or spiritual—we cannot become whole.

Imbalance occurs when the whole spectrum of human needs is not considered. For example, the act of eating a meal does not simply entail the assimilation of food. It is a process of enhancing development on all levels, since physical hunger interferes with the ability to be filled emotionally, mentally and spiritually. The same is true of spiritual hunger—if it is not filled, there will be something out of balance in the other need levels.

As we acquire a greater understanding of the need for integration and wholeness in our lives, we can see how to apply it in childhood. Children wonder about the changes in their lives. What causes them? Why do they happen? Explanations, of course, must be given at a level the child can comprehend. Even at age four, my son was recently concerned with identifying God: "What is God, Mommy? Where is God? How did God make the tomatoes on our table?"

Rather than simplistically answering "God can do anything because that's the way it is," I told him that God works inside us when we plant the tomato seeds. We tend the growing plants, work in harmony with the Earth, Sun and water, and help the plants to grow healthy and strong.

The conversation really got interesting when he asked, "Well, if God is everywhere, does that mean that if we eat tomatoes we are eating God?" So now Mom has to find a way of explaining the parts of the Whole!

When parents are confronted with a child's spiritual questions, they are confronted with questions they must also answer for themselves. We begin to see the beautiful interaction between teaching and learning. If we are to apply spiritual principles to astrology, then we must develop a personal awareness of these principles on a spiritual level.

Spirituality Today Versus Yesterday

We are in the midst of powerful changes in human evolution. Personal and spiritual awareness have undergone tremendous changes in the last fifty years. Family structures are radically different, with the extended family now almost a thing of the past in our society. There has been an alteration in the roles women play in society, with more options available to women for their creative outlets. On a global level, we now face the possibility of the destruction of the very planet which sustains our lives.

Every change which occurs in the external environment is symbolic of changes in humankind's inner environment. If we watch the changes in the world around us, within our society and within our families and relationships, we can see that the inner or spiritual needs of individuals are also taking a different focus.

In my study of history, I have found far-reaching changes in societal structures. We live today in a *patrilinear* society, a male-dominated culture. This is neither good nor bad, but is simply the current state of affairs. In the past there have been many matrilinear societies, in which the women were the ruling force.

With the increased focus upon Christianity, the principles of the Divine are strongly correlated with a male energy. God is considered a masculine principle. Even Eastern religions consider the male to be more spiritually advanced, with the result that women hold very limited power in these societies.

In Western society, the Feminist Movement is breaking up some of these views. This is symbolic of changes going on within each of us. We are feeling an increasing need to reach a balance within ourselves, to allow the receptive aspect of our natures to blossom more fully.

As psychology probes more deeply into human nature, we are understanding more and more the importance of allowing a child to grow into him/herself and fulfill his/her needs. We are realizing the damage which can be done if parents inhibit this natural development. More parents are now concerned with allowing their children to exercise their full potentials.

Parental roles are changing in our society. More women are working outside the home. Fathers are beginning to be more open and loving with their children. Women are becoming more assertive of their needs. With all these changes in family roles, the child's position is also evolving. In the past, a child was not given as much credibility, and approval was gained only by meeting his/her parents' sometimes rigid standards. Today it is becoming more important that the child be true to his/her *own* unique standards.

If we look to society as an indicator of humankind's spiritual evolution, we can observe the changing place of the Church in society. The primary role of the Church has been to teach "right" living, offering guidelines for proper, moral behavior. God has been portrayed as the Divine Judge. Children have looked to these teachings as the fundamental principles for living.

But as society changes, so must the role of the Church if it is to maintain any validity in the evolutionary process. At a time when fathers were stern family leaders, God was seen as stern and often angry. But now the idea of a God of Love is becoming more powerful, and fathers in our society are becoming freer to love and be loving. This is one example of how spiritual needs dictate change in a society.

Now that individuals are seeking to know themselves and become whole beings, the concept of God is reaching a more universal definition. As children experience the changes within their parents, they also experience a new definition of their own inner needs. Just as relationships between men and women are evolving, so is the relationship between wo/man and God evolving. We are seeking to find a Oneness, a connection with the Divine.

I have met many people who, without realization, have sought to find their parents through some spiritual path. Many of the "seekers" I have encountered have had difficult relationships with their parents, and often did not have one parent present in their lives. With these needs lacking in the family, the logical place to seek them is through a spiritual path.

There is a danger, though, in transferring an emotional need to a spiritual one. Certainly, an individual can find ways to balance the self by seeking spiritual truths, but there can also be pitfalls. I have watched many young people transfer an emotional lack onto a spiritual teacher or minister. The tacher becomes the child's missing father; the spiritual counselor becomes Mother as the child tries to fill the gaping emotional void in his/her life.

The child whose parents are self-aware individuals is truly blessed. As we evolve spiritually, we will find children seeking spiritual answers from a more balanced and secure perspective. This gives the parents a challenging but rewarding responsibility: they must not only attend to their own needs for growth, but must also remain attentive to the child's deeper needs. I am seeing this type of relationship forming now in many families. Just as the structure of the family has evolved in the past, so it continues to change now.

Spiritual Principles Illustrated by the Planets

Each planet illustrates different spiritual principles.

The **Sun** is the divine spark in the human, the nurtured seed which blossoms into the will power of the Self.

The **Moon** principle is the soul which receives input from the Divine Source.

Mercury connects the human with the Divine through the mind. It illustrates the spiritual law, "What you think, you become."

Venus is the principle of love—not just a physical or emotional connection with another person, but a spiritual bonding.

Mars is the principle of physical power, which is necessary for the human instrument to express the spiritual self.

Jupiter is the hunger to understand the Divine presence, and is the application of the Law of Abundance. Through Jupiter we gain wisdom.

Saturn is the Law of Karma, illustrating, "What you sow, so shall you reap." Through Saturn we mature.

Uranus is the principle of intuition, the connection from the Mind of the One to the mind of the individual. Through Uranus, we know.

Neptune represents Divine Compassion, the surrender

of the ego to the greater needs of the whole and the guidance of the Higher Self. Through Neptune we attune to vibration.

Pluto eliminates the extraneous and brings transformation into our lives. Through Pluto, we are able to transmute difficulty into creative change.

Astrological charts for children give us *possibilities*, showing us potentials which can be developed but which are not yet realized. Without self-awareness, the whole person is not complete. The process of developing self-awareness lasts one's entire lifetime, beginning with the moment of the first breath (perhaps even while in the womb).

In aiding the child's spiritual maturation, we must feed the physical, mental and emotional needs. I think the spiritual knowledge children need most is how to uncover the truths of life. Although tempting, it is dangerous to look at an astrological chart and judge a particular child to be a "highly evolved spiritual being." Nor should the opposite be assumed about a child who has difficulty adjusting to the physical plane because of emotional blocks and unresolved anger. S/he needs to sort these out before the spiritual awareness can be significantly opened.

A child may have a special connection with the higher realms of consciousness in the very early years, but cannot explain or express this connection to the outside world. As parents and teachers, we must give the child permission to have this awareness and acknowledge that it is okay. I have spoken with many children who tell me about their contacts with beings on other levels. They describe them as angels, fairies or whatever words fit with their understanding. Even tiny children, about age two, will tell me about the light they see when they close their eyes or the lights around another person. This is one level of spiritual awareness.

One thing we can do to help the child develop a stronger spiritual constitution is to use affirmations. Parents unknowingly give their children affirmations all the time: "You are such a brat!" or, "You are an angel."

Either concept can be difficult for the child. The child may not even know what a "brat" is, but the parent's attitude and tone of voice will certainly provide a strong hint! If the child believes him/herself to be a brat, s/he will work to become the personification of one.

The child whose mother calls him/her an "angel," may also face considerable confusion. "Well, if I am an angel," the child may think, "then everything I do is okay!" If we, as parents, will really listen to the way we speak to our children, we will begin to realize that we are, indeed, programming the child's consciousness.

Affirmations are positive ways to program a child's subconscious mind. Through the use of positive affirmations, we can help the child build a stronger connection with the Higher Self. Specific energy blockages indicated by planetary aspects in the chart can be transmuted to a more creative and positive expression by altering the child's attitude about how this energy operates within him/her. When considering the planetary aspects, we should find ways to work *with* these energies instead of against them!

With very small children, affirmations are most easily used in simple songs or chants. Use any tune you enjoy. Children usually don't care if you have a beautiful voice, they just like to sing along. Why not have your child singing, "I am the light and I am shining," instead of the latest Coca-Cola commercial?

When she was about three years old, my daughter would sing about what she saw around her. She sang lyrics such as "The birds are flying in the blue sky. I like the way they fly. I feel like a bird." Sometimes, when she would be feeling low, I would suggest to her that we make up a song about something especially lovely. This changed the focus of her mind energy and lifted her mood. This is an example of affirmations in action!

As the child matures, affirmations can be part of a morning or evening ritual. Your child may want to invent some of his/her own special affirmations. It is fun to share in this experience, and it offers the child a positive approach to making creative change in his/her life.

Connections between personal energies and the outer planets seem to heighten spiritual sensitivity. But these same energies can also create havoc in the child's psychological make-up because they are not easy to rationally understand. It is these factors which can benefit the most by the use of positive affirmations and creative visualizations.

Saturn Aspects

Saturn is a feminine planet and is the ruler of the sign Capricorn, yet we usually perceive Saturn as the Father. If we consider Saturn as the primary structure upon which our security is built, we can conceive of this energy as working through many levels of a child's experience. Not only is Saturn energy felt through parental structures, but through the basic foundations of society. Many of these foundations have their origins in religious teachings, since Saturn has a rather moral connotation. These morals are tied to the idea, "If you do something wrong, you will have to pay the price."

Saturn represents the Law of Karma, which enforces life's natural balance. When a child is taught to be personally responsible for her/his actions, s/he is learning how to properly deal with Saturn energy. Through this type of understanding, a child learns why s/he should behave in a particular manner.

If Saturn is aspecting a personal planet in the chart,

the child will be forced to confront this particular aspect of him/herself realistically and honestly. This does not mean negatively. However, we humans have difficulty with concepts such as "realistic" and "honest"! The limitation a child may feel through Saturn is usually present because the child needs to deal with a particular aspect of him/herself honestly. A child who has Venus squaring Saturn, for example, may feel that expressing love is a frightening proposition. S/he may perceive God as rather demanding, giving love only if s/he is "perfect." These children must learn to become more giving in order to receive, a spiritual lesson learned through an emotional release.

The child with challenging Saturn aspects in the chart will all too often resist the necessary confrontations in his/her life rather than working through them. The parents need to give these children ample opportunities to appreciate themselves and their particular gifts. It may be too easy to focus upon what the child does *not* have, rather than helping him/her see what s/he does have.

Affirmations: "I love to give to others."
"I deserve love."

Uranus Aspects

A child with contacts between Uranus and the personal planets may be very original or eccentric. S/he may seem to march to the beat of her/his own drum all the time. This is also true of children who have Uranus near the angles of the chart. These children need to learn how to trust the intuitive insights in their lives. They can benefit from exercises for quieting the mind, especially once the child is about five years of age.

Creative channels of expression must remain open for these children. Even with dynamic aspects between the personal planets and Uranus, the disruptive nature of the energy does not have to be the overriding influence if the child can learn to handle it.

The energy of Uranus is one aspect of the intuitive link between the human mind and the higher Mind. When a child has increased Uranian energy, illustrated through Uranus' placement on the angles of the chart or in contact with the personal planets, s/he has a need to balance the rational and intuitive mind. Intuitive insights are usually powerful! These children may feel guided to do things their rational minds do not understand. With patient guidance from parents and teachers, the child can learn to trust these impulses. It is through this source that the child opens to original concepts and ideas.

Affirmation: "I am special, I am me!"
"I listen to the voice inside me
for guidance."
"I want to know the truth."

Neptune Aspects

With Neptune contacts, a child is drawn into the inner realms more easily. When personal planets are contacting Neptune, or when Neptune is near the Ascendant in the chart, the child may seem rather removed much of the time. Focusing on artistic expression is often helpful to these children in bringing spiritual awareness into the personal realm.

The difficulty with Neptune and personal planet contacts lies in the desire to escape. The child has a special attunement to Divine Love, and desires to bask in this radiance. There may be special attunements which the child does not understand, and which should be met by the parents with understanding and acceptance. To tell a child that something s/he perceives is wrong just because the parents don't see it that way is damaging to the child.

However, these children do need to learn how to balance physical plane reality with inner awareness. The spiritual need is to see the pure and perfect in each person and in all life. This can lead to over-idealization, since the need for that perception may be so great as to overwhelm reality.

Neptune's realm is beyond "normal" reality. Children seem more easily connected to these parts of the self in the early years. But as the rational mind begins its development, they seem to lose much or all of this attunement. It is difficult to maintain a balance when Neptune energies are strong. It is easy for the child to spend hours daydreaming in a world of inner visions. Rather than discourage this, we need to aid the child in focusing his/her visions and finding ways to direct them.

The process of creative visualization is a product of Neptunian energy. To do this, we create a desirable concept—a wish or a hope—within the mind. By focusing mental energy in this manner, we can crystallize this hope for ourselves and create a more positive reality.

The trick with creative visualization is learning what our real needs are. We must realize what our strengths and limitations may be in achieving what we desire from our lives. A child does not accept as many limitations as an adult—these are usually learned! However, a child can be encouraged to use the energy of his/her hopes and dreams to make his/her life more the way s/he wants it to be. What the child has to learn is how to balance his/her personal wants with personal responsibility. Do you recall the Disney song, "When You Wish Upon a Star?" This song has been a favorite among children for decades. It encourages a child to dream his/her dreams and make wishes, because they *can* come true. This song itself can be an affirmation for the child!

As parents and teachers, we need to aid the child with

Neptunian vision to direct these wishes toward achieving peace and harmony on our planet. These children have the gifts necessary to help this process come to fruition.

> *Affirmation:* "My guardian angel is my good friend."
> "I can make my dreams come true."
> "I am love."

Pluto Aspects

With personal planets contacting Pluto, the spiritual needs evolve around continual transformation. This can be most difficult for a child, who needs consistency and stability in order to feel comfortable. Drastic and sometimes difficult losses may accompany these contacts. These children must learn early about positive self-transformation, and must learn to appreciate themselves for who and what they are, and to understand the limitations confronting themselves and others.

This child may feel especially attuned to the power of the Source, but will probably not understand how to use this power. These aspects require a great deal of maturity to manifest in their most positive light. The *Star Wars* films are wonderful examples of the use of Plutonian energy. Each child will be confronted with his/her own power very early in life, but may not know how to direct it. Whether or not the child becomes a healer or a destroyer is strongly dependent upon how s/he deals with Plutonian energy.

We are, as a society, also confronted with this task. Nuclear power, which harnesses the physical properties of plutonium, can destroy our planet. We must realize that we have power equal to the splitting of the plutonian atom within us. This power comes from our connection with the

Source of Life. Once again, the symbology of the external environment illustrates what we are learning at the level of spiritual awareness.

Affirmation: "I am the Light and I am shining!"
"My power comes from my Higher Self."

The Houses

Houses 4, 8, 9 and 12 have a more "spiritual" focus in our lives. Planets in these houses will spur the child to seek answers about the deeper meanings of life.

A child who has a powerful *4th House* focus will need to develop a sense of rootedness, and will probably approach spirituality in an emotional manner. The parents will most likely be viewed as spiritual teachers.

With an *8th House* focus, children are concerned with the mysterious and hidden aspects of life. Children with several planets in the 8th House may often be confronted with death. They will be forced to integrate an understanding of death and transformation into their consciousness rather early.

The *9th House* focus gives a child a desire to understand the workings of spiritual laws. These children might enjoy the interactions they will have in religious activities at churches, temples, synagogues, ashrams and other places of worship and spiritual growth.

A child with a *12th House* focus may be deeply drawn into the Self. These children need time for privacy and reflection. This child will also need to understand transpersonal human needs, and loves to feel that s/he can make a difference in the lives of other people.

Basically, the maturation of spiritual need is independent upon fulfillment of the other needs in childhood. Children seek to find the truth, and will initially trust that what the parents present to them is Truth. Hopefully, with mankind's increasing spiritual awareness, parents will present the Truth to their children more openly than in the past. When children come to parents with questions about "otherworldly" experiences, dreams, images, and illusions, the parent's response will condition the child's sense of this aspect of life. Offering the child permission to have these contacts and share them with the parents can make an important difference in his/her developing spiritual awareness.

Whether or not the parents offer permission, every human being must come in contact with the spiritual realm at some point. Some will be comfortable immersing themselves in this aspect of life, others will not. If a child is encouraged to question and explore these dimensions of life, his/her spiritual foundation will better prepare him/her to deal with the varied situations s/he will encounter in adulthood.

Chapter Eleven

THE CHILD'S PERCEPTION OF THE PARENTS

The child's perception of the parents can be seen through his/her astrological chart. These perceptions are an important factor in the child's responses to the parents.

Our personal Universe is perceived from within. If we are feeling balanced, centered and happy, the world looks bright. Other people seem helpful and supportive. But if we suffer from emotional trauma, physical setbacks or other problems, our perceptions become clouded. The world can seem dark and cold, and other people may seem hostile and unfriendly.

This is especially true for children. When a child feels physically or emotionally low, his/her behavior and responsiveness suffer. In relationships with others, children and adults alike will project their feelings and perceptions onto other people.

We have within ourselves many parts of the whole. At a very basic level, we have a feminine, receptive side *(anima)* and a masculine, assertive side (*animus*). For small children, these inner parts are difficult to perceive. They develop an understanding of themselves only through identification with significant others in their lives.

This anima/animus concept was presented by Carl Jung, and has helped to clarify a great deal about how human relationships work. The feminine side of the child will initially identify with Mother, while the masculine side will relate to Father. Therefore, when studying a child's astrological chart, we can delineate the feminine perceptions through the Moon (Mother) and Venus (women), and the masculine perceptions through the Sun and Saturn (Father) and Mars (men).

The child needs to experience him/herself through projecting his/her needs within his/her personal environment. There are particular things a child needs from the parents in order to attain a stronger sense of his/her own identity.

The Sun, which is the primary masculine energy in the chart, is the sense of self. This sense of individuality may be strongly tied to the initial relationship with the father and, later, to interactions with other significant male figures. The Sun powerfully affects the child's perceptions of Father; if the father is supportive and consistent, the child may feel that his/her own individuality is reliable and strong.

Mother often takes on the role of primary parent of a child. In this case, the projection of Father (Sun) energy may fall upon Mother, or may be transferred to other significant males. This idea will be explored in more depth as we examine aspects later in this chapter.

What the child perceives about the father comes from within. I have observed this when counseling families with several children. In one family, each child has the same Sun sign. All these children described the father in very similar terms. But in another family with four children, aged several years apart, the children's Sun signs were different. They each described their father quite differently.

The need for inner security is strongly associated with the Moon, which is the projection of the Mother. Through the Moon, we find our sense of emotional fulfillment and the primary feminine aspects of the self. Relationships with the Mother and female figures are signified by the Moon. The specific type of nurturance a child needs is determined by the sign and house placement of the Moon. This need is then projected upon the Mother.

Fathers are often the nurturant parent for a child. If this is the case, Moon energies will be projected upon the Father.

The other personal planets also reflect what a child needs from the parents.

Mercury illustrates communication needs, the types of learning experiences best suited for the child, and the mental expression of the Self.

Venus, the expression of artistry and love, is also a feminine aspect of the Self. It is experienced through the manner in which the child feels love and expresses her/his sense of beauty.

Physical self-expression is signified by *Mars,* which also indicates the types of physical activity a child would like to share with the parents. Mars is one of the masculine principles in the chart.

Through *Jupiter* the child learns his/her philosophical and moral attitudes. These are first taught by the parents, then by society.

Saturn indicates the child's response to and need for discipline, structure and consistency. Saturn is also a factor associated with Father, since the male parent has traditionally taken the role of disciplinarian and primary force behind the structure of the family. Now that family structures are changing, however, many mothers are providing the Saturnine influence.

The outer planets *Uranus, Neptune* and *Pluto* are experienced at a deeper psychological level. These energies are involved with levels of awareness beyond the personality. Most children have little sense of these transpersonal energies unless they contact the personal planets, Jupiter or Saturn. Thus, if the parents do not personify these higher principles, the child will not perceive them as readily until s/he has established a sense of Self outside the realm of parental influence.

The Child's Perceptions of Mother Through the Moon

The sign in which the Moon is placed will offer insights into how the child perceives the mother. It makes no difference whether the mother sees herself in this light or not—the child holds these particulars perceptions of her because s/he is projecting his/her own inner needs for security onto her. As a child matures into adulthood, these perceptions determine how that individual will play the nurturant/mothering role.

Moon in Aries may perceive Mother as highly independent and strong-minded.

Moon in Taurus may perceive Mother as stable, conservative, possessive and earthy.

Moon in Gemini perceives Mother as mentally active, talkative, changeable and sometimes hard to pin down.

Moon in Cancer perceives Mother as nurturant, protective and sometimes smothering.

Moon in Leo perceives Mother as powerful, strong-willed, and rather queenly.

Moon in Virgo sees Mother as fastidious and tidy, always concerned with his/her health and proper behavior. The way Mom does it is perfect!

Moon in Libra sees Mother as interested in personal appearance and constantly interacting with someone. The Libra Moon child's mother may seem especially pretty to the child, symbolizing the ideal of true beauty.

Moon in Scorpio may see Mom as quietly powerful, insightful, and sometimes ominous. Mother is usually viewed as highly spiritual, the projection of the Divine Goddess.

Moon in Sagittarius perceives Mother as the teacher of spiritual truth. Mother may also seem very independent and sometimes unreliable.

Moon in Capricorn sees Mother as having a strict set of rules for behavior. Mother represents control, organization, determination and persistence.

Moon in Aquarius may find Mother hard to reach and very unusual. Mom seems free spirited, innovative and highly mental.

Moon in Pisces perceives Mother as personifying an ideal. Mom may be like an angel to the child, with a calming, mystical quality. Mom may also be difficult to figure out, since she does not always seem real.

The Moon sign is the underlying theme of the child's feminine self, which is projected upon the mother. Aspects from other planets to the Moon will alter these perceptions. With the softer, harmonious aspects, the child may handle the psychological traumas of his/her early life easily and with more support. Otherwise, the impact of emotionally difficult situations is usually dealt with only after the child is an adult in the throes of self-analysis.

Moon and Mercury

The Moon aspecting Mercury will open lines of communication between Mother and child. The child will perceive Mother as communicative. If the aspect is dynamic, the communication may often take the form of disagreements later on!

Moon and Venus

Moon to Venus gives a sharing of artistic support between Mother and child. Beauty and Mother may be synonymous to this child. The difficult aspects may find the mother vicariously attempting to live her artistic fantasies through the child.

Moon and Mars

When the Moon and Mars are connected in the child's chart, the child may see Mother as assertive, a woman ready to stand up for her own rights and beliefs. When dynamic aspects occur, the child's feelings of anger are often projected upon Mother. Sometimes these children have a basically angry temperament, and need positive directions for that anger through the mother's example. If Mother has difficulty expressing anger, then the child will feel a strong inner frustration with his/her own angry feelings.

Moon and Jupiter

Moon to Jupiter finds the mother who may encourage the child to expand and grow—perhaps a bit *too* much. ("Now, eat everything on your plate!") This expansion also involves the child's moral sense, which is modeled after Mother's.

Moon and Saturn

Moon to Saturn often brings a sense of separation or alienation from the mother. I have often seen these aspects in the charts of first children whose mothers were just learning about the responsibilities and restrictions that motherhood brings. These children often feel that they have to grow up too soon and take on major responsibilities earlier than their peers.

It is highly important that the mother not make the child feel that s/he must be "perfect." She must allow him/her to have his/her virtues and shortcomings. These children may feel that the mother is not providing his/her fundamental needs, and may seek a substitute for the nurturant quality s/he feel is lacking. Sometimes, with difficult aspects, the child perceives Mother to be tremendously judgemental. S/he may feel guilty if s/he cannot meet the high standards Mother seems to require of her/him.

Moon and Uranus

Moon-Uranus children see Mother as unique. This uniqueness may be a plus for the child, or s/he may think that "My mom is weird." With dynamic aspects, the child often feels that the mother is too inconsistent in providing nurturance, protection and support. One day, Mom may be balanced and approachable; the next day, she may seem to be unreachable. There may also be inconsistent messages from Mom about the child's independence.

The mother must make an effort to deal with the child consistently. Mom is viewed as being intuitive, and how the mother uses this intuitive flow will have a great effect upon the child's future use of his/her intuitive perceptions. As the child reaches school age, her/his mother may seem to be radically different from the other moms. If Mother has been secure in her sense of individuality, the child will not find this to be a problem. If Mom has been bizarre in her actions and disrespectful of herself, the child may have difficulty dealing with her/his feelings about her.

Moon and Neptune

Moon to Neptune perceives the mother as being rather vague, psychic, or difficult to reach. Mom may seem to be "out in the ozone" much of the time, or may be interested in spiritual aspects of life which the child has difficulty perceiving. With flowing aspects, this perception may be easily integrated and accepted.

Mother must personify a perfect ideal. If Mother fails in this, the child may be sorely disappointed and have difficulty relating to her/his feminine self and other women later in life.

Mother may also be the perpetrator of a false illusion for the child. Sometimes the mother is an alcoholic or projects other escapist tendencies. Often the child has difficulty identifying with Mother at all, and may believe that s/he was really left on the doorstep by a mysterious stranger.

Moon and Pluto

With the Moon aspecting Pluto, the child may think Mom has eyes in the back of her head. Mom is powerful, absorbing, and perceived as "all-knowing." The child could sense that Mother holds the power of life and death. This can be a strong negative if the aspect is difficult and not confronted maturely.

Mother may seem highly judgemental. She may also be expected to be "Superwoman"—able to cook dinner while leaping tall buildings with a single bound. This projection originates from the deep levels of the psyche, where the child feels that s/he must be more than human.

In some cases, Mother is so powerful that the child feels consumed by her and loses all sense of self. The child's emotions will be intense and often painful, and can easily be repressed. Mother may be experienced as heavy and emotionally intense, and may overwhelm the child with her own emotionality.

Mother can aid the child by striving to maintain open communications with him/her. She needs to give the child opportunities to exercise and own his/her own power, beginning in the early years. If mother usurps the child's sense of personal power, the child will experience difficulty later in life in achieving personal fulfillment and emotional openness. If Mom radiates messages of "Don't feel" to the child, some serious problems can develop. Sometimes this occurs with Moon-Pluto contacts. The child believes that "Something's wrong with me because I feel this way," or, "If I tell Mom about this, she'll have my head on a platter."

The Child's Perception of Father

The child's perceptions of the father are strongly symbolized by the energy of the Sun in the astrological chart. Aspects from Jupiter, Saturn and the outer planets will reflect particular alterations in the child's perceptions of Father. And, of course, the sign qualities will reflect the specific characteristics involved in these perceptions.

Sun and Jupiter

With Sun-Jupiter contacts, Father is the great provider, sometimes giving many material things to compensate for lost time. Father may be seen as optimistic or enthusiastic. Sometimes, with dynamic aspects between the Sun and Jupiter, the child feels great expectations from Father. If this is the case, a child may continually "expand" the truth of his/her accomplishments in order to gain acceptance and praise from him.

Sun and Saturn

Sun-Saturn contacts are notorious in astrology for creating a difficult relationship between Father and child. The restrictive, inhibiting and separative influence of Saturn colliding with the dynamic will power of the Sun does not generally make for compatibility and harmony!

The child may feel that Dad is just not there for him/her. Dad may be unavailable physically because of death, divorce, or a demanding job—whatever the reasons, the child feels Dad's absence keenly. Consequently, the child may overract by feeling that Dad is too critical or demanding. If the father is not present, the child may feel that s/he was abandoned. This can lead to intense feelings of guilt: "I was so bad that I made Daddy go away."

These types of feelings can lead to inhibited self-expression in the child, ultimately producing a less balanced adult. This can result in a mistrust of all men and authority figures. These children need loving, patient and accepting guidance from the father and other significant males in his/her life.

Sun and Uranus

Sun-Uranus contacts can produce perceptions of an exceptional father. They can also cause the child to see the father as too aloof and lead to feelings that Dad is unreliable or undependable. Dad may be rather eccentric. Sometimes, the child sees the father as a mold so unique that s/he could never fit into it. S/he sees the father as beyond the limitations and structures of society, offering the child a different viewpoint of life from the "norm." When given an opportunity to prove his/her own uniqueness to Father, the child will feel less isolated from the whole of society.

Sun and Neptune

Sun-Neptune contacts are especially difficult in childhood, since the evasive nature of Neptune makes it difficult for the child to see the "real" father. Dad can be over-idealized; he may even have disappeared. I have often seen dynamic Sun-Neptune aspects in children whose fathers left when they were tiny. These aspects are also common in the charts of children of alcoholic or drug-dependent fathers, and may also be felt by the child with the Sun in the 12th House.

Even the easier aspects are apt to create energies through which the child sees only an illusion of Father. This can produce problems in seeing the Self for the child, since the role model is viewed through rose-colored glasses. The child may also expect the father to be rather saintly, and can be disappointed when s/he finds that this is not the case. These aspects call for honest relationships between parent and child.

Sun and Pluto

Sun-Pluto contacts are similar to Moon-Pluto perceptions. The child may perceive Dad as a superhero. You know the type: on the outside he looks like a regular guy, but inside he transforms into Superman. The child is likely to view Father as all-knowing, all-powerful and omniscient. This can block the child's ability to assert his/her own personal power.

With Sun-Pluto contacts, especially the dynamic aspects, the child may perceive Father as being ruthless. Sometimes these images are not even projected by the father to the child. They can come about through the child's fantasies and the impressions s/he has gleaned through observing life.

It is very easy for the child with Sun-Pluto contacts to sense that Dad does not want him/her to exist. Fathers of these children need to continually remind the child that s/he is genuinely loved and appreciated.

Saturn and Father

Another concept children have about the father can be analyzed by examining Saturn in the chart. Saturn brings structure, form and solidity. Saturn energy feels judgmental and limiting much of the time, especially in childhood. Many children are anything but delighted at the prospect of being "responsible"—that's what adults are supposed to be, not kids!

The placement of Saturn not only symbolizes the physical father, but also authority in society. Father is usually the model who teaches the child the lessons of authority. The sign and house placement of Saturn in the chart, along with its aspects, indicates the child's responses to discipline, responsibility and structure. In these areas, the influence of the father is likely to be very strong.

Although we cannot always determine how the parents

view themselves, we can gain insights into how the child views the parents. This viewpoint can aid parents by helping them understand the child's personal needs in relation to their own. Parents tend to reflect a child back at him/herself, and some children will have more difficulty than others in accepting these reflections. Children will also project certain qualities and attitudes upon the parents.

This process of mirroring can go back and forth indefinitely until the parents start offering the child opportunities to see the reflection of his/her own true self. As conscious interaction occurs more and more between parents and children, more powerful transformational changes can be made in the child's life. By doing this, we can begin to bridge the gaps between parent and child.

Chapter Twelve

DEVELOPMENTAL CRISES IN CHILDHOOD

One of the outstanding features of astrology is the study of cycles, which are analyzed using the basic natal chart as a blueprint. At certain times, which are indicated by the cyclical transits and progressions to the natal chart, different aspects of the Self will be emphasized. This process of basic human development is logical and easily mapped.

When a child does not meet these established criteria for development, parents often become concerned and look for the underlying causes of slowed or accelerated development. There are often interesting correlations in the chart for these alterations. Specific astrological cycles can be helpful to parents and counselors of children in understanding psychological, social and creative development.

Moon Cycles

One of the first cycles I ask parents to be aware of are the natural cycles of the Moon. Small babies seem to be especially fretful and sensitive during the three days around a Full Moon. This is especially true of babies born at the time of the Full Moon (when the Sun and Moon are in opposition in the chart). The child's emotional sensitivity is often increased at this time. Although I have not completed a "scientific" study of this concept, I have talked with hundreds of mothers whose experiences have confirmed this. As the baby grows, this sensitivity seems to decrease somewhat.

Another period of increased sensitivity occurs when the Moon returns to the sign it was in at birth. During these two to three days each month, the child may be very emotionally expressive, and is likely to cling to Mother. A baby is more reluctant to let Mommy out of his/her sight.

Once a child is able to communicate, this can be a good period to have discussions with him/her about his/her feelings; s/he will be able to express feelings more freely during this time. If there have been hurts or disappointments, they may be easier to understand fully and examine during this cycle.

The time when the Moon is traveling through the child's 12th House by transit is another significant period. The 12th House transit of the Moon pulls the child more deeply inside him/herself. Small babies are sometimes more physically vulnerable at this time, and should be guarded against excessive exposure to any environmental extremes (e.g. very cold or hot temperatures). Young children may be somewhat apprehensive, and may have very vivid dreams during this two-to-four-day transiting period. Parents who are aware of this can more easily deal with the child's fears, which may well be imaginary. Teens may withdraw more readily during this time, and may seem hard to reach. It is important for parents to realize that their children may need this period for reflection and privacy.

Over the course of the cycle of the Moon, every planet

is contacted and each house in the chart is sensitized. As planets are contacted by the Moon, their energies become more focused in relation to the child's needs. This is a very simple cycle to observe, even for a novice. A current astrological calendar or ephemeris will indicate the daily placement of the Moon by sign.

The Progressed Moon

The progressed Moon is calculated using precise mathematical formulas. These calculations should be made by a professional astrologer or astrological computing service in order to be fully useful. Once you have the progressions calculated, you can use the Secondary Progressed motion of the Moon to determine important periods of change in the child's life. The Secondary Progressed Moon (based upon the "day-for-a-year" formula) indicates when aspects in the child's life will be emotionally heightened. (See the bibliography for more information about Secondary Progressions.)

If the Moon at birth falls in the early degrees of a sign (e.g. two degrees Aries), it will be about two and one-half years before the progressed Moon changes signs (moving into Taurus). This transition would mark one of the first significant changes in the child's emotional security base. If the Moon at birth is in the middle degrees of a sign (e.g. fifteen degrees Aries), the Progressed Moon would move into the next sign (Taurus) about the age of eighteen months.

What I have observed in these early changes of the Moon by sign is a different emotional focus in the child's life. Sometimes the family may move, forcing the child to adapt to new surroundings. At other times there may be changes in the family such as a divorce, new siblings, marriages, or Mom's return to work outside the home.

The external event is not as important as the fact that the child is experiencing a new emotional level of him/

herself. At first this new level of experience is likely to feel strange, confusing or otherwise disconcerting. The child needs additional support and understanding from the parents at this time. If s/he does not receive added care and concern from the parents during these transitions, a gradual undermining of her/his emotional security is likely to result.

As the progressed Moon continues its motion through the chart, different aspects of the Self will be activated. It takes 27 to 29 years for the progressed Moon to travel completely around the chart and return to its natal position. This process of maturing is slow, deliberate and repetitive. It allows the child to learn early that change can be made without negative results, and that it is the only way s/he can constantly develop her/his different levels of needs.

The child's understanding of this will help the parents to be more effective in dealing with change as well. By being aware of when these progressed Moon changes are occurring, the parents and guides of the child can be ready to help him/her over these new emotional hurdles.

Saturn and Uranus Cycles

Saturn represents the process of time itself. At this point in human evolution, we conceive of time as linear—involving past, present, and future. This is a rather simple system, and easy for the logical mind to grasp. But there are also other conceptualizations of time, one of which is cyclical. These time cycles mark periods of review, giving us opportunities for increased awareness of ourselves and our purpose. Saturn and Uranus cycles are two such markers which indicate significant periods of growth.

The transits of Saturn to the natal chart mark periods of increased responsibility, more focused awareness and, usually, increased limitations. Saturn's cycle takes about 28 years from the time of birth until it cycles, by transit, back to its natal position. The precise length of this cycle varies from person to person, and must be calculated. The maturational processes a person undergoes during this first Saturn cycle are the basis for his/her responses throughout the rest of his/her life.

Uranus is the awakener, offering new possibilities by breaking up the structures Saturn so carefully builds. Uranus embodies the process of personal freedom, and its cycles mark this unfolding.

The first major contact of Saturn to its natal position occurs at age six or seven. Astrologically speaking, this is the time Saturn first squares its natal position by transit. Physically, the child is losing the baby teeth and developing permanent teeth (Saturn rules teeth). In our society, this is the time the child enters public school and is no longer under the primary tutelage of the parents. Society begins shaping the child more directly. S/he must respond more readily to discipline and structure or suffer the consequences. Peer pressure begins to develop.

Another factor which is of marked importance at this age deals with the psyche. This child feels responsible for *everything*. Parents may not realize the far-reaching impact these types of feelings have for the child. If the parents divorce at this time, the child may feel responsible for the divorce, responsible for the care of the custodial parent, and responsible for the resulting turmoil and unhappiness. S/he may never say a word, but may internalize these feelings of guilt. Whatever changes are occurring in the outside world may well be "my fault" or "my glory," depending upon the circumstances. Parents and teachers who are aware of this process can help the child by making it clear that s/he may not have been the cause.

The child can be given additional responsibilities during this first Saturn square, but also needs to receive rewards or recognition for fulfilling them. This aids in the child's approach to meeting new challenges and taking on new tasks. At this time, Uranus usually forms a semi-sextile (thirty degree) aspect to its natal position, moving the child's awareness into a new concept of freedom. Parents can begin to teach the lessons of harmonizing freedom and responsibility at this age. Additionally, the child's perceptions of the world are increased during this cycle.

The second major contact Saturn makes to its natal position in the chart is the opposition about age fourteen. This is the period of puberty: the hormones are awakening, the physical body is once again growing rapidly, and the child is becoming an adolescent. At this age, Uranus forms a sextile (sixty degree) aspect to its natal position.

The task at age fourteen is to balance personal responsibility (Saturn) with freedom (Uranus). This is also a marked "identity crisis" as the child begins to see him/herself as markedly different from his/her parents. The confrontation indicated by the opposition often leads to open conflict with the parents and with authority in general.

But the opposition, depicted by a straight line, is also a bridge, indicating that this is the time to close the gap between parent and child. Parents can focus on the special and unique aspects of the child emphasized by the Uranus sextile and allow him/her increased freedom as s/he accepts increased responsibility. If the parental and/or societal structure is too rigid during this cycle, the child's rebellion is likely to be pronounced.

The last major contacts of Saturn and Uranus to the natal planets during "childhood" are at age twenty-one. At this age Saturn is once again making a square to its natal position; the child is leaving another nest. In our society, this is the age of "legal adulthood." Uranus is also contacting natal Uranus by square about age twenty-one.

Major life changes are prompting the young adult to become his/her own person, build his/her own foundations and test his/her wings. Many young adults complete their college educations about this time, and must begin to relate to the "real world." The "real world" at age seven was still protective. At this age, it sometimes feels adversarial.

Jupiter Cycles

Jupiter typifies expansion, optimism, and increased confidence. It takes Jupiter about twelve years to return to its natal position by transit. During the course of Jupiter's transit through the chart, the child gains an expanded awareness of the planetary energies and environments (houses) indicated by the exact natal placement of Jupiter. Jupiter's contacts to its natal position represent crucial periods.

The first square from Jupiter to its natal position occurs about age three. This phase coincides with open interaction with other children. A wider exploration of the personal environment ensues, with the child heading off toward new horizons at the first opportunity.

The young child is also challenged to expand the mind. S/he wants to hear stories, communicates more readily and is generally a bit rebellious. This rebelliousness may be partially due to a need to go beyond established limits; Jupiter contacts often tempt us to push these limits until they break! If this cycle coincides with the progressed Moon changing signs, the rebellion may be even more marked. Tethering the child may not be the best answer, but it is understandable why many parents choose to find some reasonable method of restricting a child's movement during this active phase.

Jupiter opposes its natal position about age six. This coincides with the first Saturn square and the Uranus semi-sextile. Fortunately, Jupiter reinforces a need for expansion and stimulates an eagerness to learn. Saturn is there to keep some positive boundaries.

At this age the mind is ripe for more abstract forms of learning such as mathematics and reading. Prior to this, such abstract concepts might have infringed upon the creative, imaginative processes. The very young child (under six) especially needs to keep the creative flow open, since s/he seems to respond to life in a "right-brain" manner.

The next Jupiter square occurs at age nine. Many children begin to look a little chunky at this age. Once again, the child is raring to get beyond his/her limitations. S/he may be a bit snippy and seem "too big for his/her britches." This period can be most effectively used if the child can be given ample challenges for the mind and be urged to develop a willingness to give in exchange for what s/he wants to receive.

During the first Jupiter return, at age twelve, the child becomes more confident. Mental functioning is strong, and his/her communicative abilities are nearing an adult level. At this age the child is usually a joy, and begins to seek companionship from the parents. This is a wonderful time to travel, study and learn with a child.

The next periods of Jupiter squares, oppositions and conjunctions occur at roughly ages fifteen (square), eighteen (opposition), twenty-one (square) and twenty-four (conjunction). Correlating the Jupiterian concept of needing to go beyond limits with the Saturn and Uranus cycles gives us a clearer understanding of the developing child.

Other Planetary Transits

By following the transits of planets to the child's natal

chart, parents can more readily understand the frustrations and the growth confronting the him/her. Transits from Mars are easily marked in the early years of development, indicating times when physical energy and temper run high.

When Mars makes dynamic contacts to the Sun, Moon, Mercury, or Mars, the child will seem more volatile. If Mars is making a dynamic aspect by transit to Saturn, the child may feel excessively frustrated and seem harder to handle. With dynamic transits from Mars to Uranus, the child may act boisterous and tend to take too many risks. Noting these particular times can help parents when planning special activities with a child. If you are planning a trip to Grandma's house during the time Mars is opposing the child's Uranus, Grandma may wonder how you ever deal with such a rambunctious child—and she'll probably be glad to see you leave!

I also encourage parents to watch Mars transits for times when children seem more accident prone. Especially challenging are the dynamic aspects when Mars transits natal Mars, Saturn, Uranus and Pluto. When Mars transits natal Mars, the child feels the need to test his/her strength and courage, and may instigate squabbles with friends or push him/herself too far, too fast. Mars contacting Saturn may bring a clash with a resistant force, and the child should be guarded against exceeding his/her limitations.

Mars-Uranus periods mark times when the child is willing to take dangerous risks (jumping off the house to see how it feels to land). With dynamic aspects between Mars and Neptune, the child is often "spaced out" and may not pay enough attention to potential dangers. Mars-Pluto dynamic transits sometimes bring him/her into contact with circumstances beyond his/her control which could result in accidents.

To understand these transits, use the key concepts of

the planetary energies involved. During transits of Mercury, the child shows interest in communicating and sharing ideas. Venus transits are times when artistic energies can be more easily encouraged.

When working with a child's chart, remember that the expression of the energy is still maturing. The child's response to the energy will depend heavily upon the type of support received from the parents and family.

The Continuing Process of Human Development

Our development does not end with childhood. We continue to grow, change, meet challenges and gain more self-awareness each day of our lives. But it is the delicate beginnings of childhood which will often determine how we will act and react as adults. The Universe gives us many opportunities to find ourselves. If we fall short during one challenge, we will certainly have other opportunities!

In my career as a professional astrological counselor, I encourage my clients to focus upon the tasks before them and develop at whatever level their experience and awareness allow. The beginnings of wholeness are rooted in our childhood. This sense of wholeness is a continual process, filled with joy, wisdom and an ever-increasing understanding of ourselves and the Universe in which we live. Self-acceptance increases and self-awareness becomes more refined.

As you grow and prosper in your life through interactions with the young children on our planet, seek to recover the Optimum Child within yourself. Heal that child by loving, teaching and growing with your own children. Through love and understanding, we can become whole and powerful beings together.

APPENDIX

Optimum Child is written for a wide audience. For those of you who are new to astrology, we have included tables in the Appendix which will help you determine planetary placements.

Throughout the latter half of the book, many references are made to the planetary aspects in the astrological chart. The Tables will help you locate many of them. This will facilitate your use of the information in the text. Enjoy!

All of the chart information is done in the Koch House system. The source is Lois Rodden. If you would like your chart done by computer, please send $5.00 to Llewellyn's Personal Services, P.O. Box 64383-740, St. Paul, MN 55164. Be sure to include your birth date, year, exact time and place. Include the county as well as the city and state. Indicate if you want your chart done in the Koch system or in the Placidus system. It will be done in Placidus unless stated otherwise. The author prefers using the Koch system in her work.

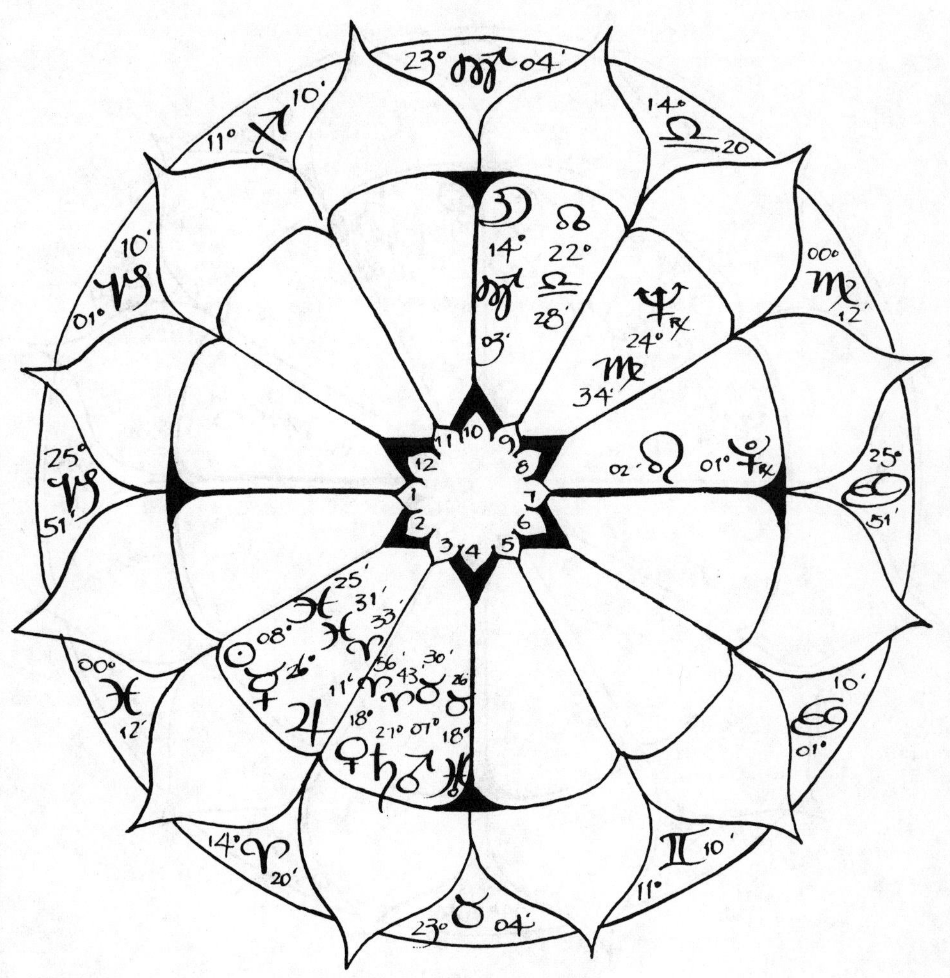

Mario Andretti

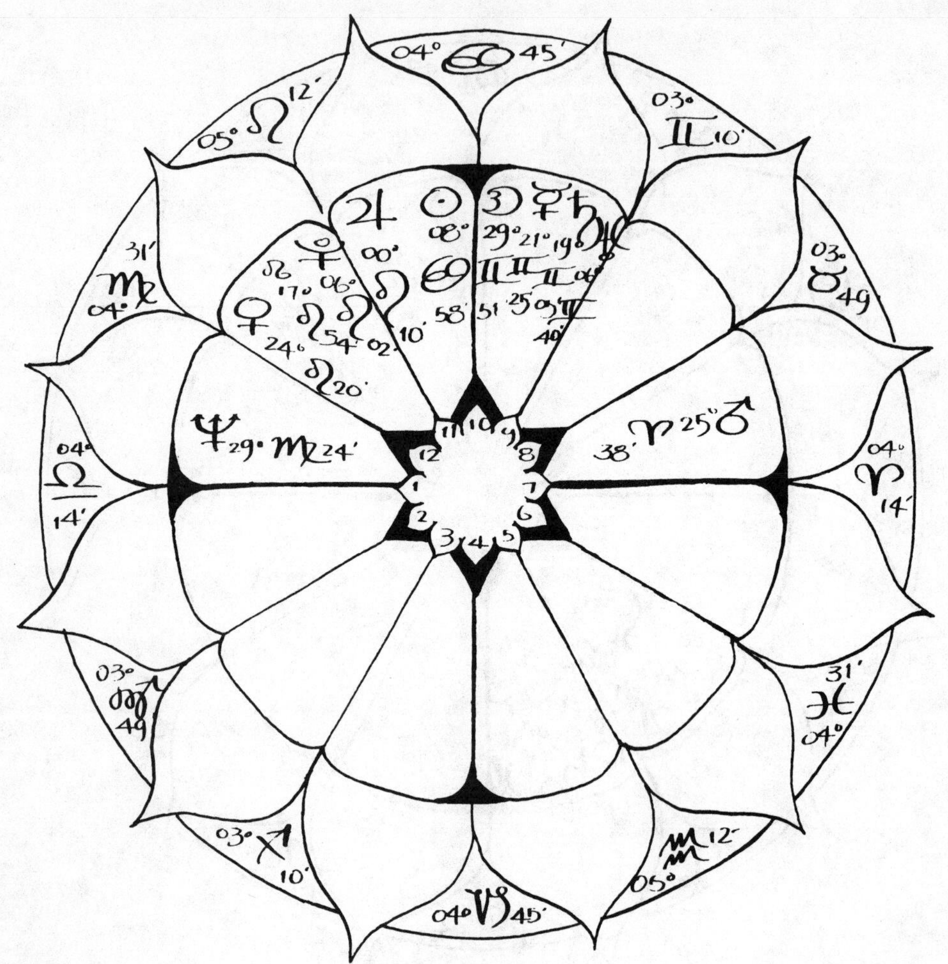

Arthur Ashe

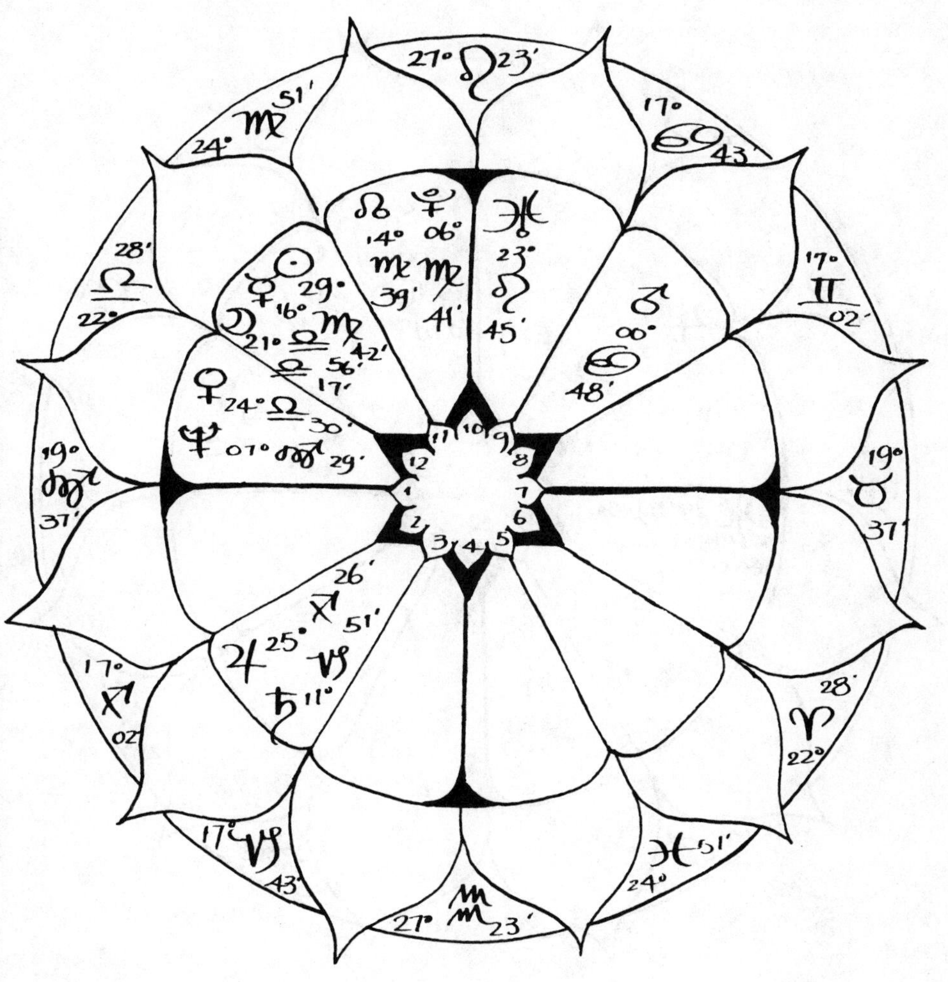

Tai Babilonia

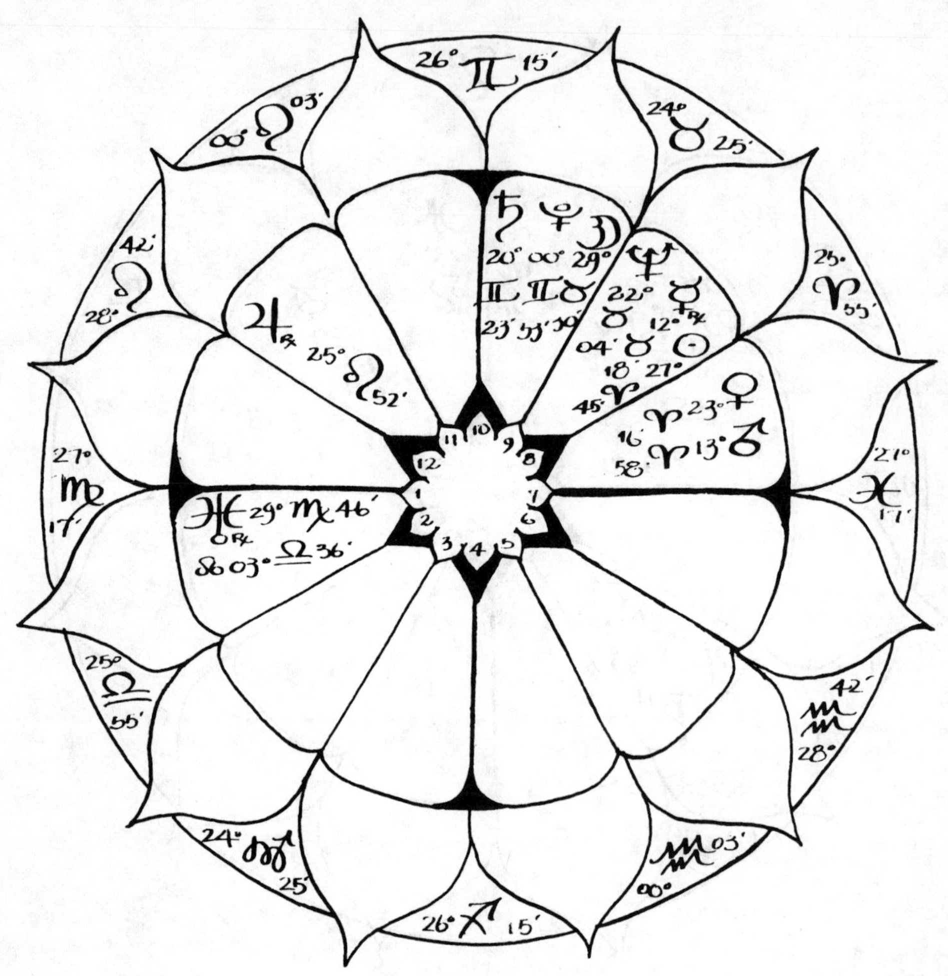

**Karen Blixen
(Isak Dinesen)**

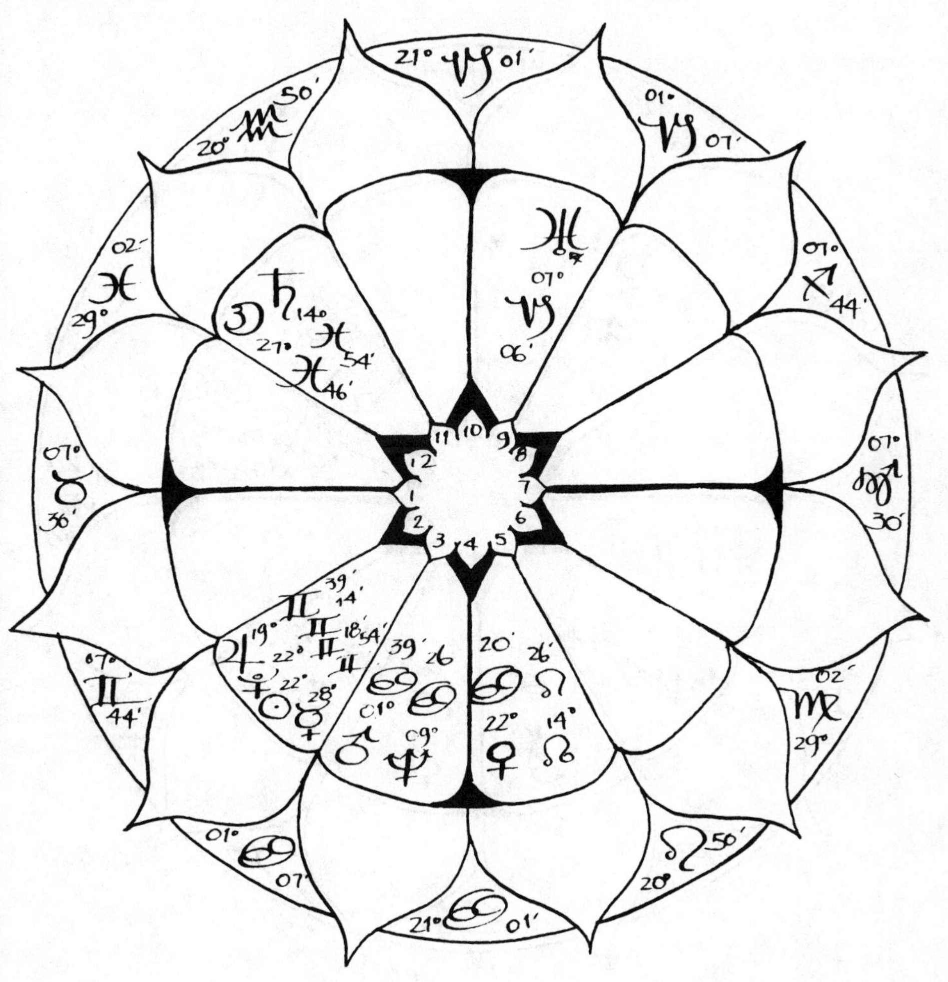

Margaret Bourke White

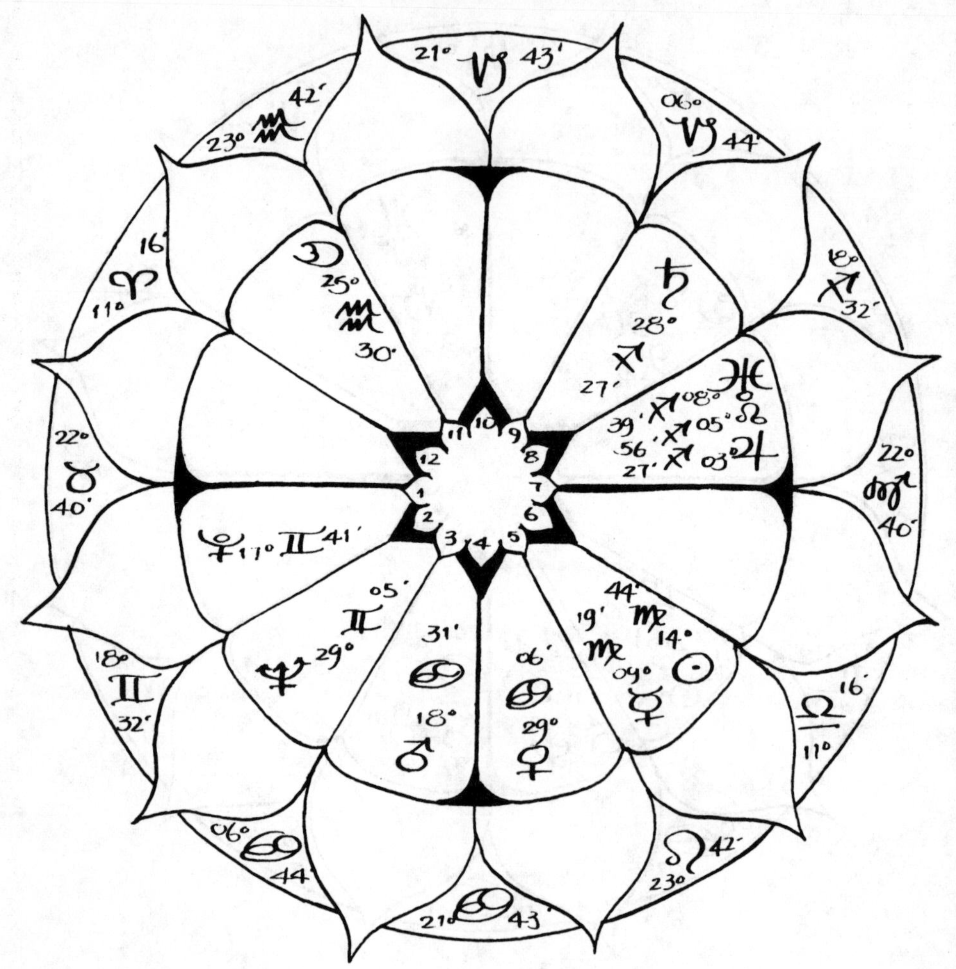

Taylor Caldwell

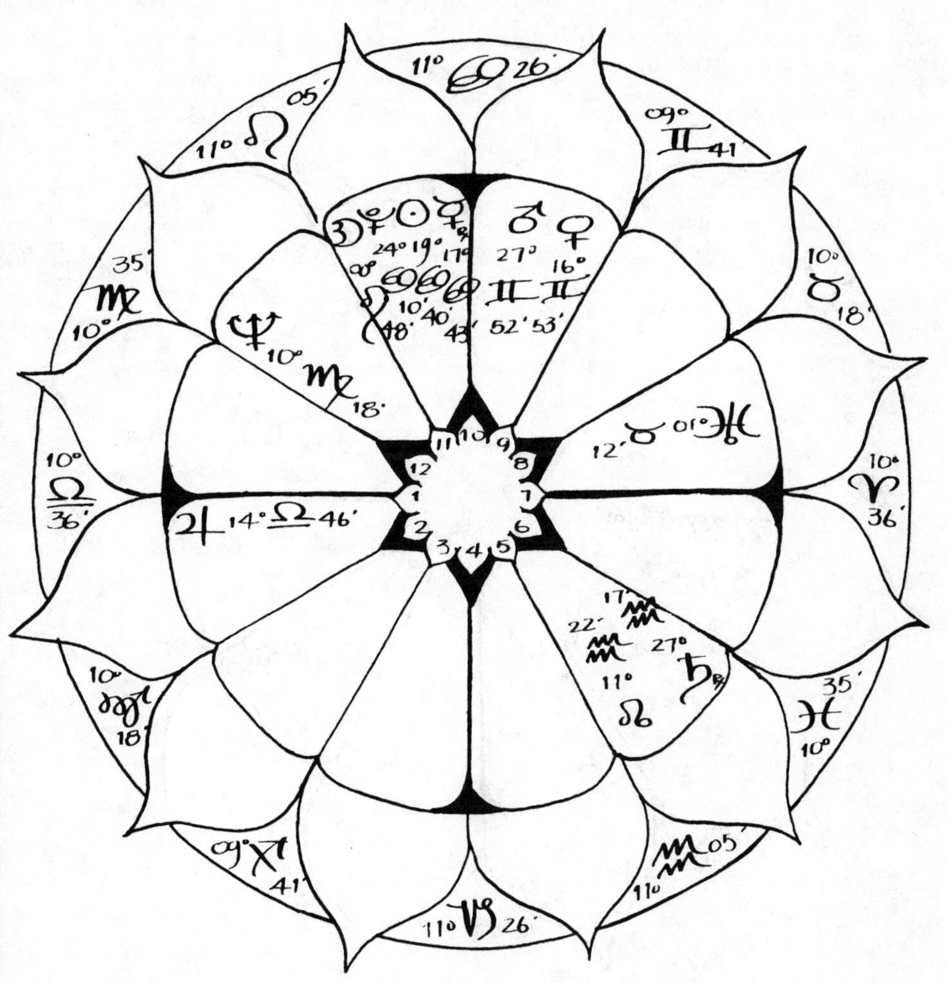

Van Cliburn

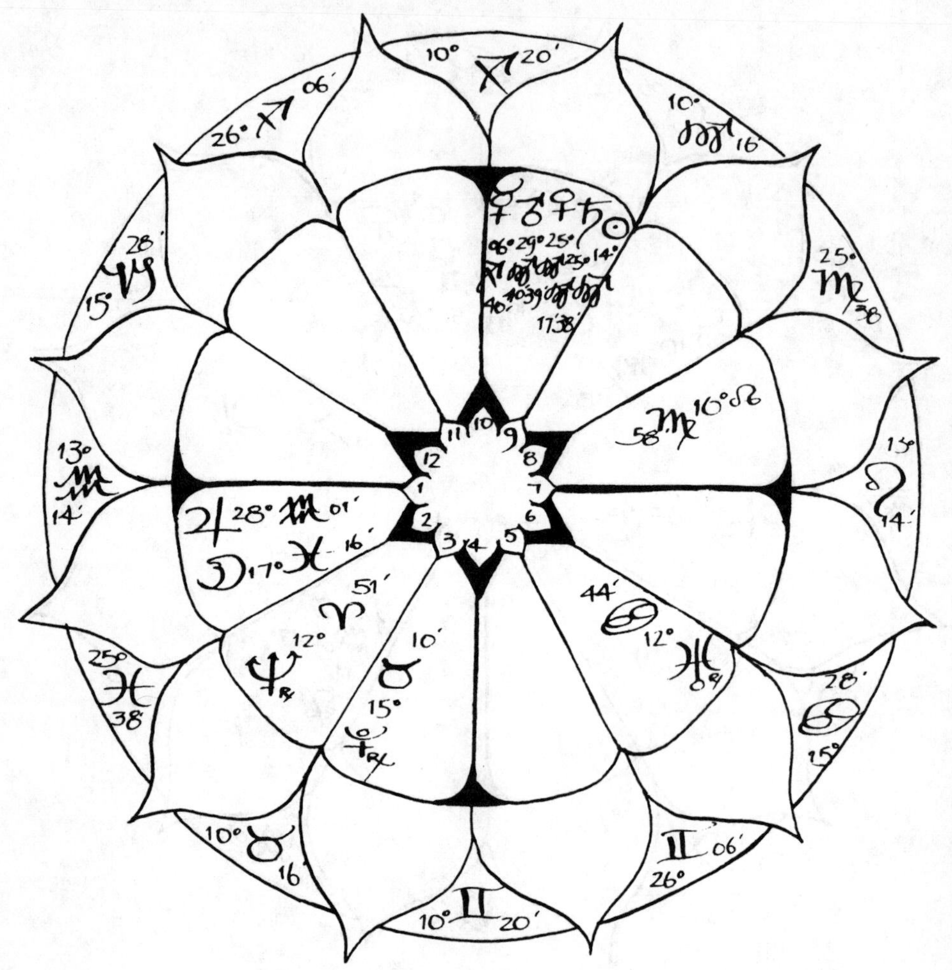

Madame Marie Curie

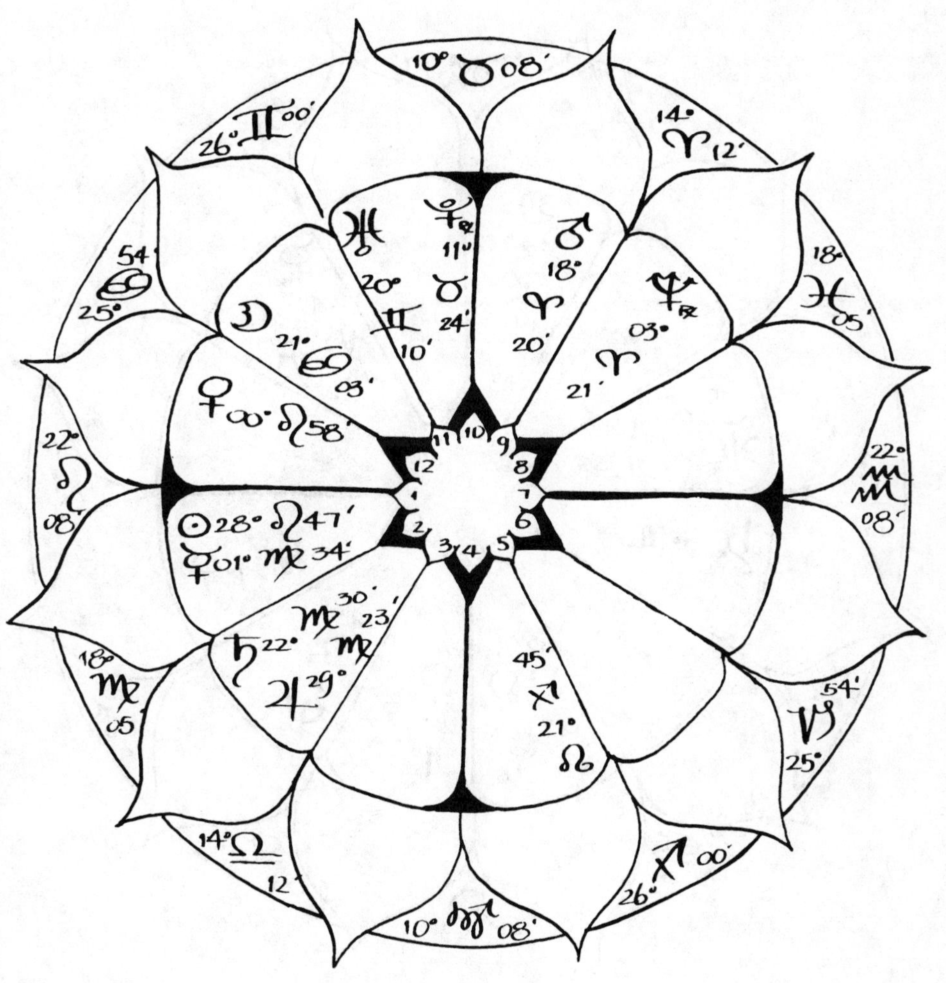

Claude Debussy

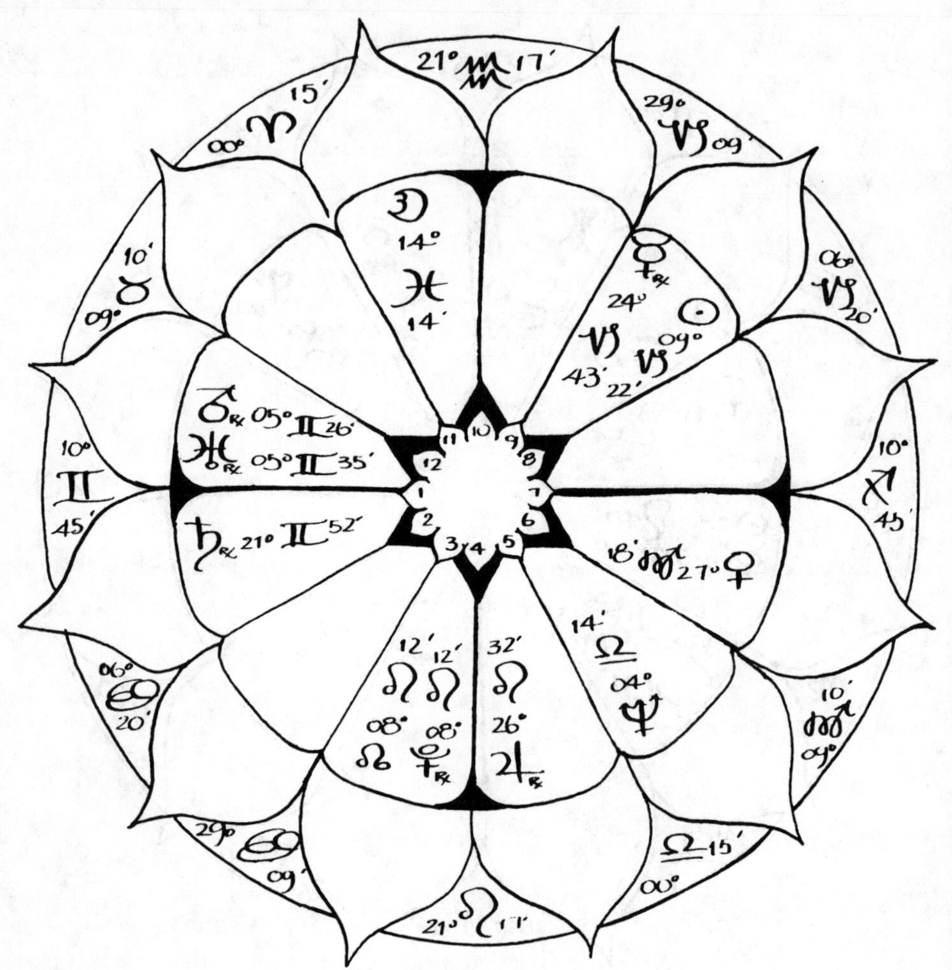

John Denver

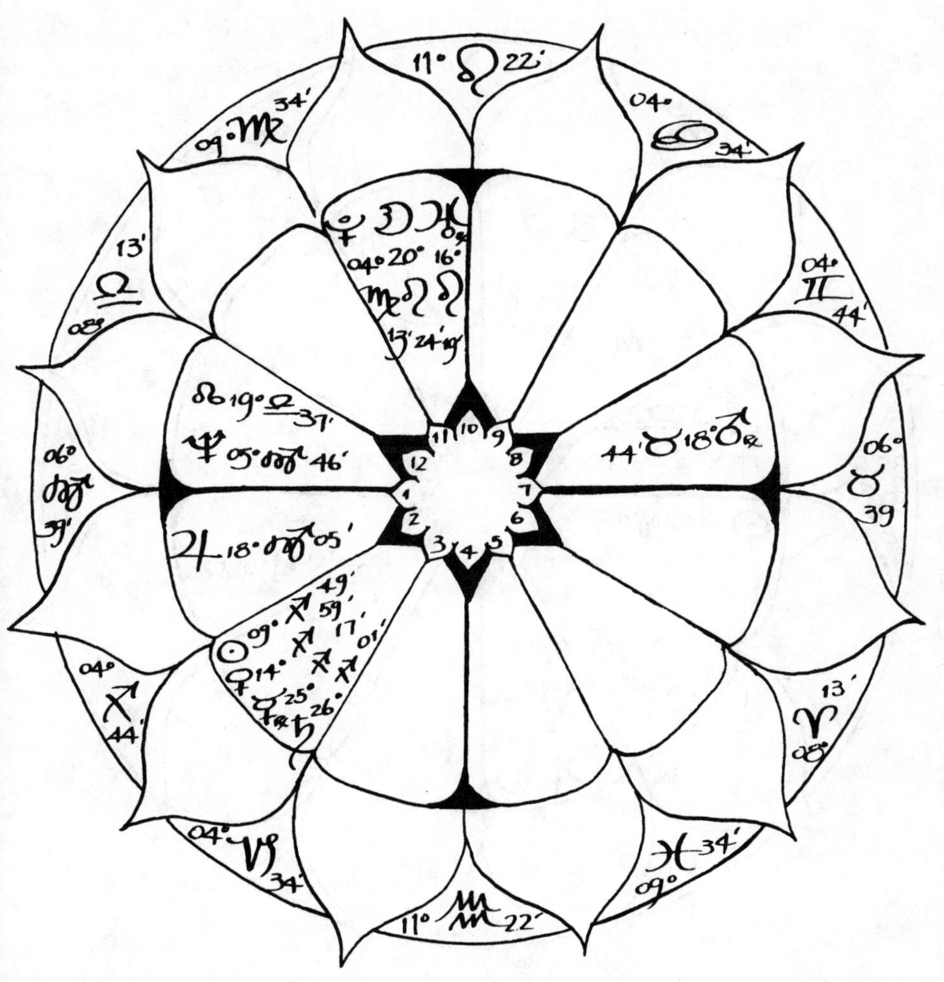

Randy Gardner

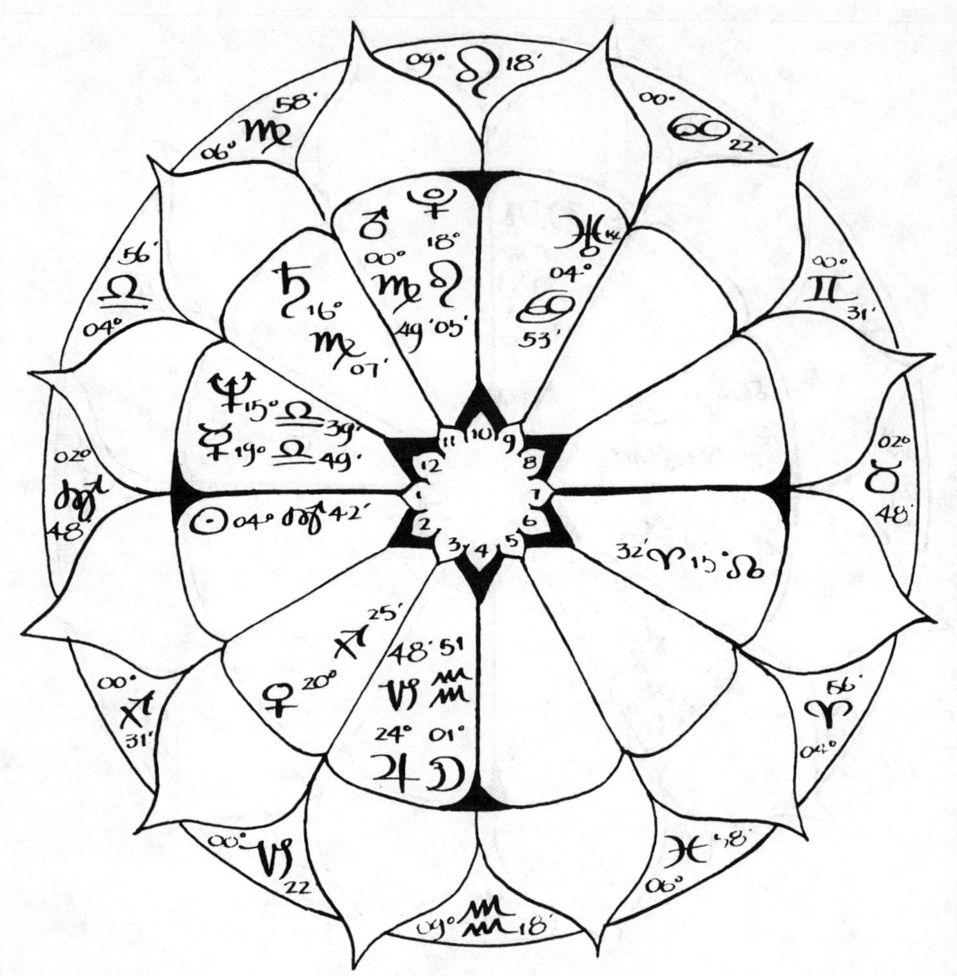

Bruce Jenner

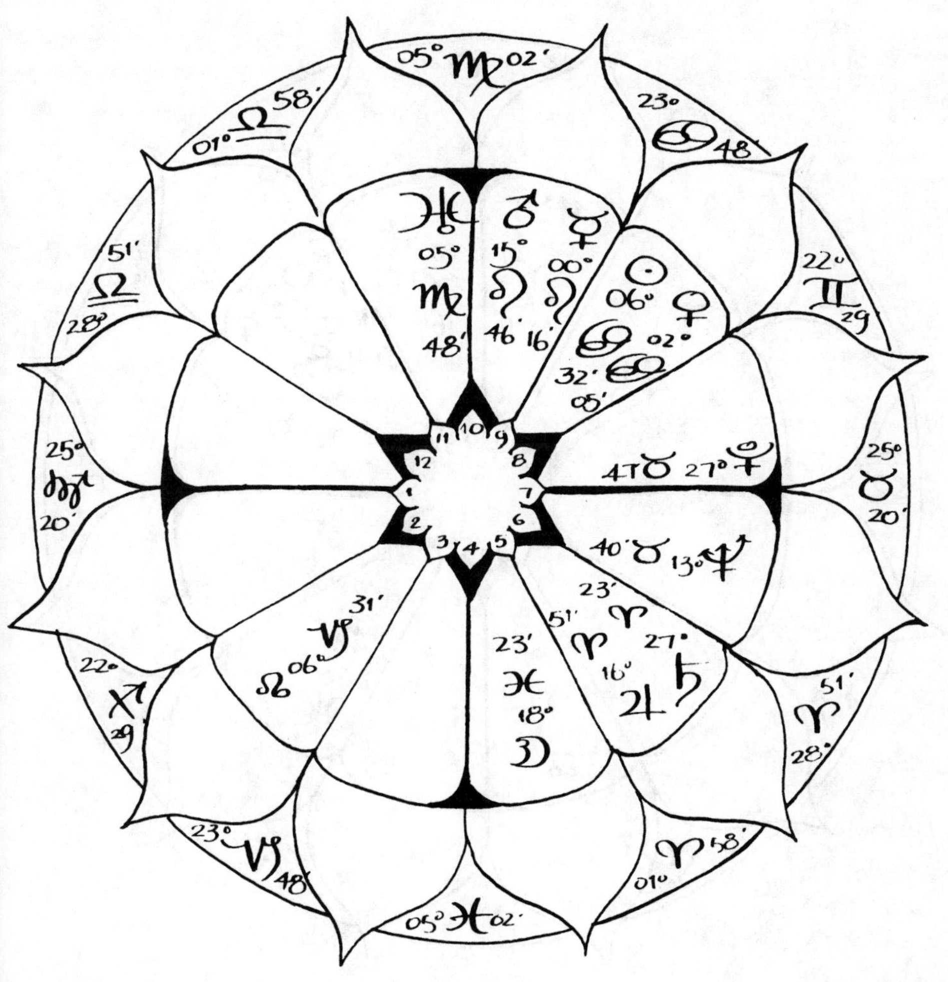

Helen Keller

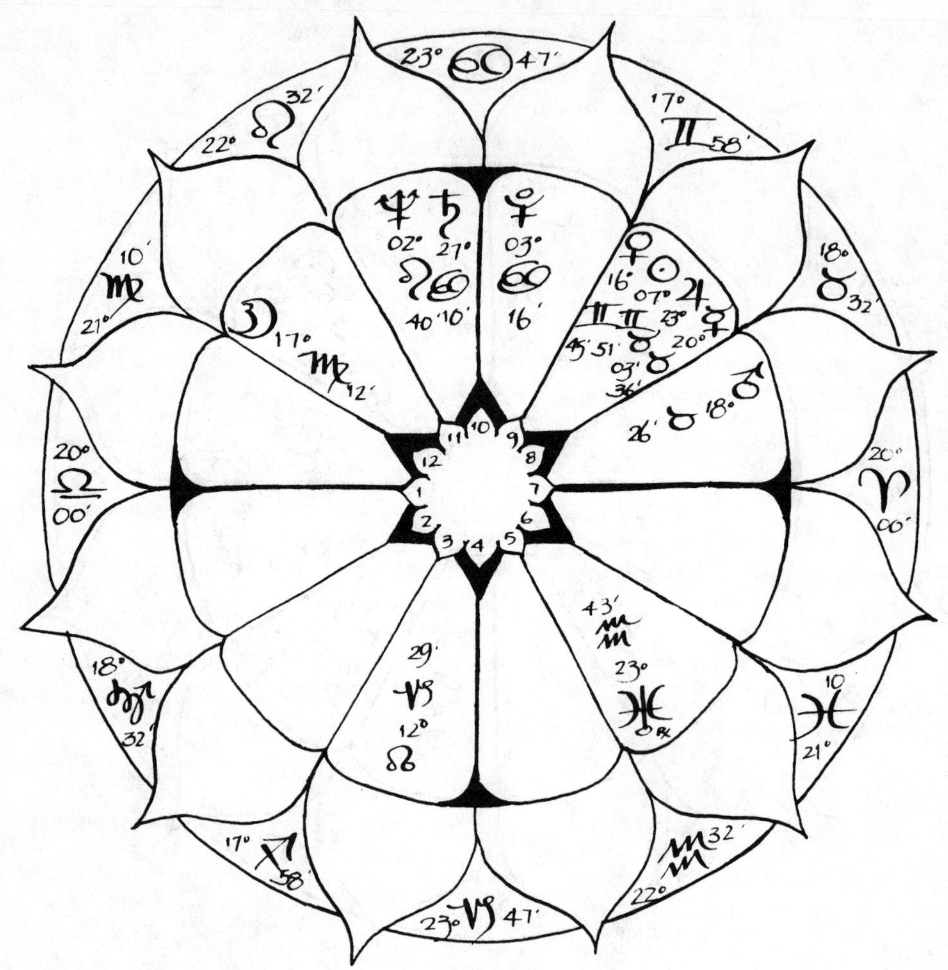

John F. Kennedy

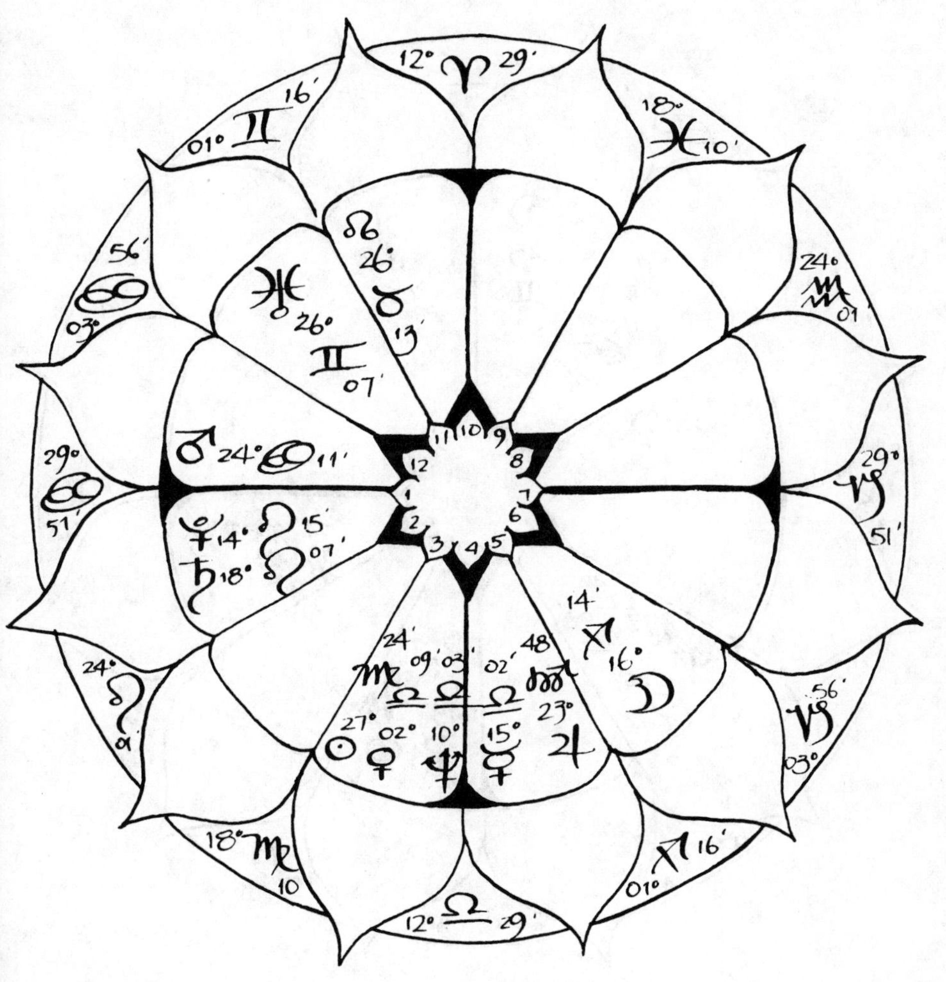

Stephen King

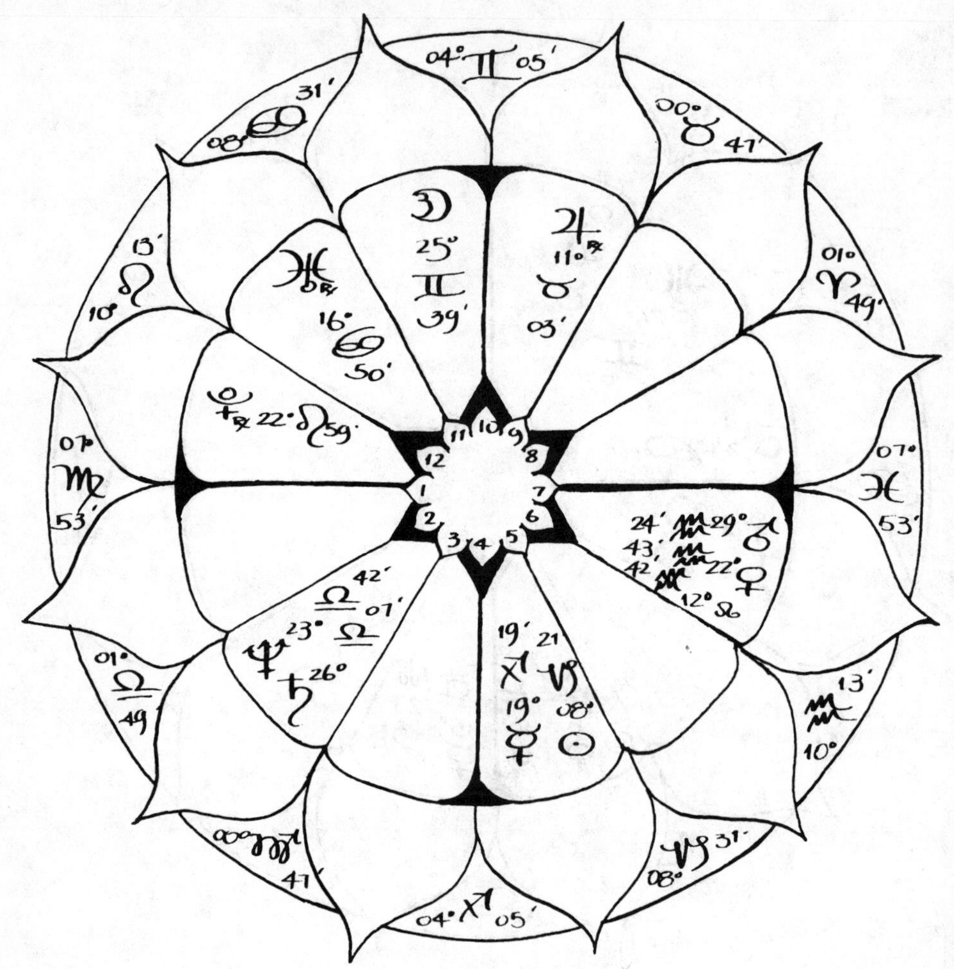

Gelsey Kirkland

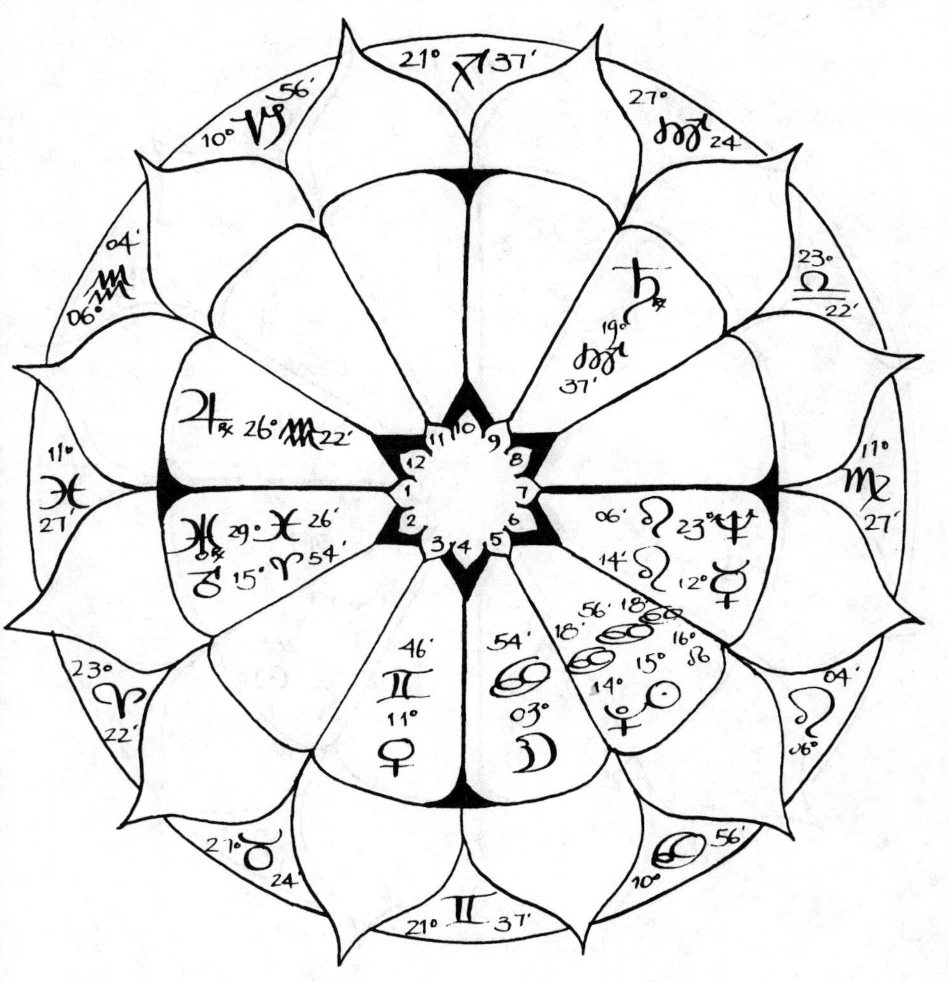

Elisabeth Kubler Ross

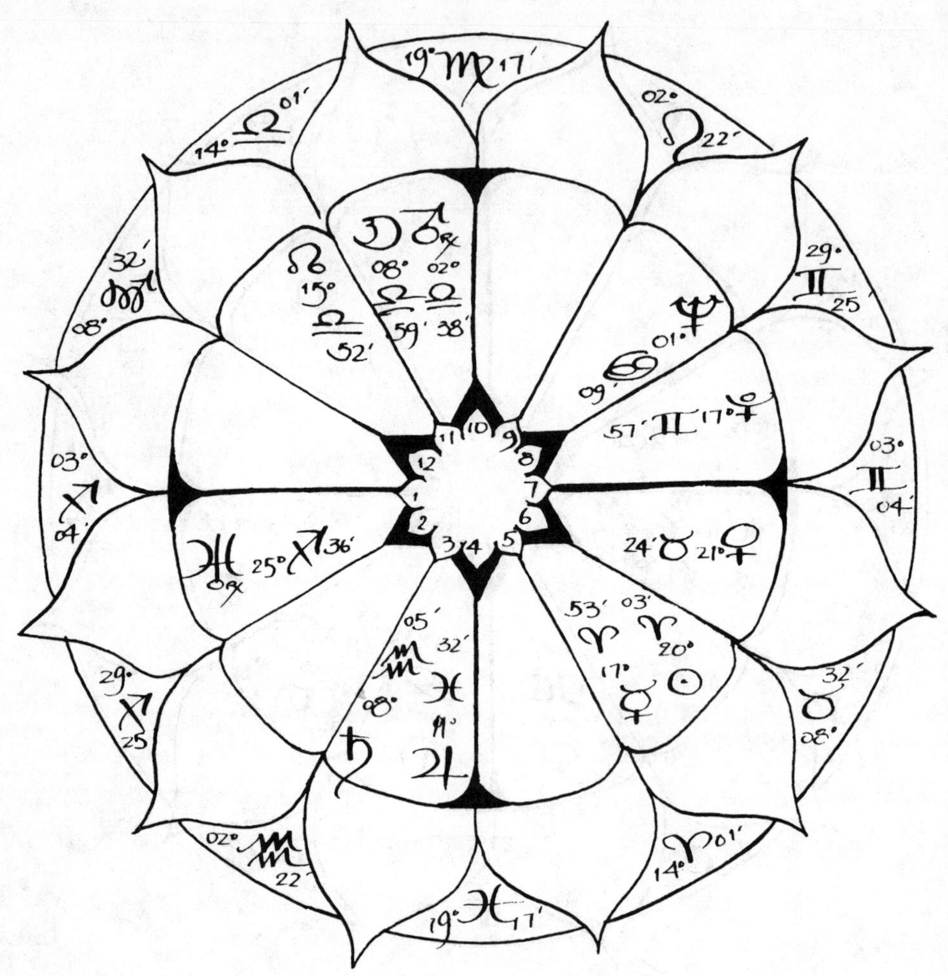

Clare Booth Luce

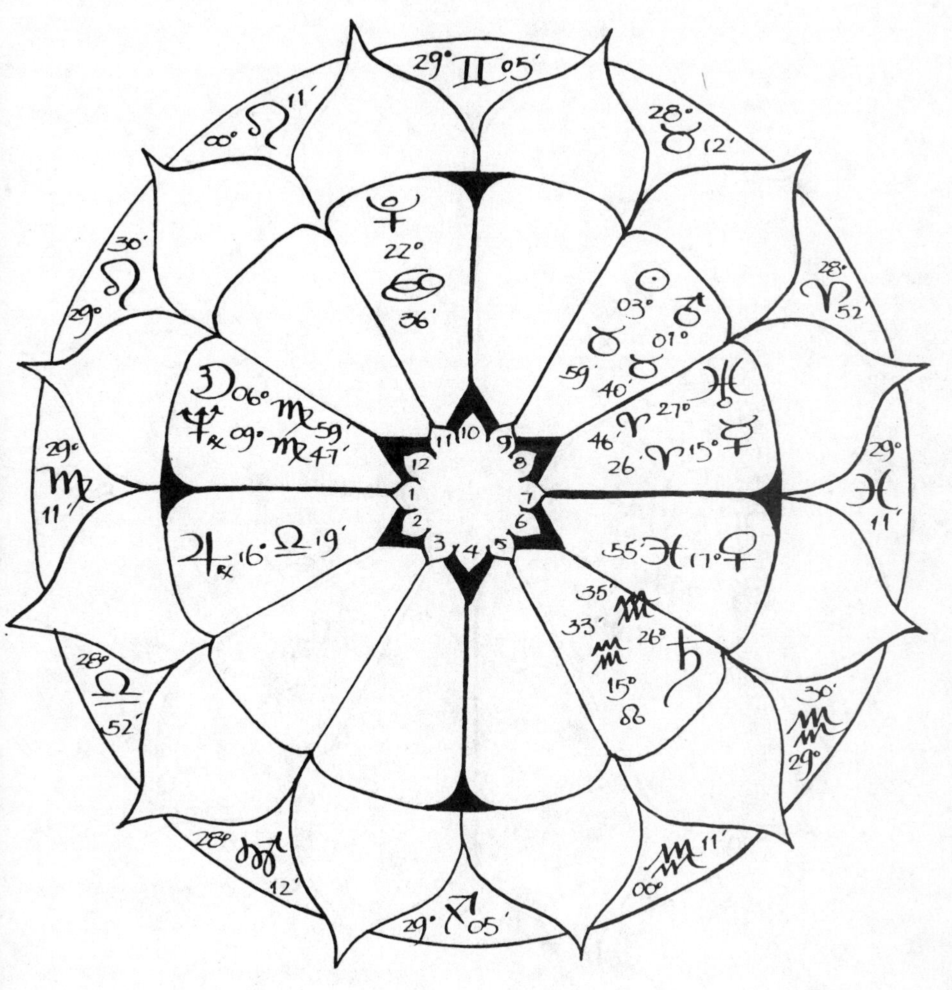

Shirley MacLaine

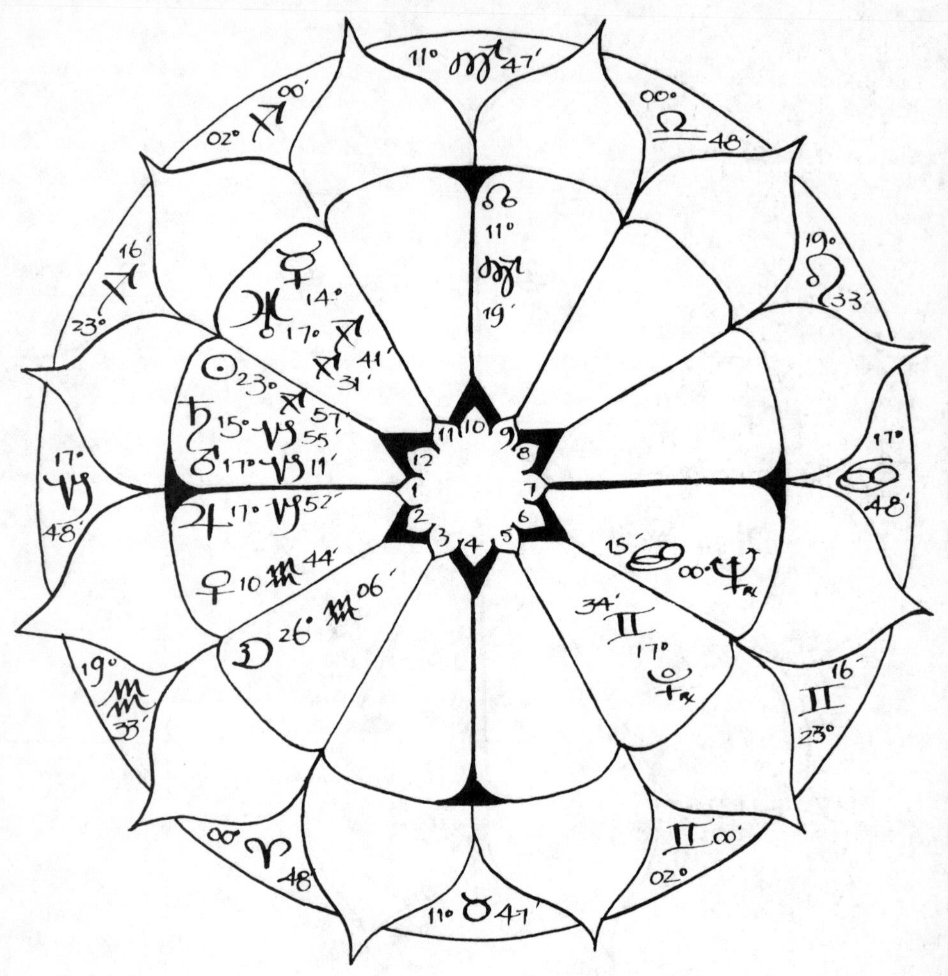

Margaret Mead

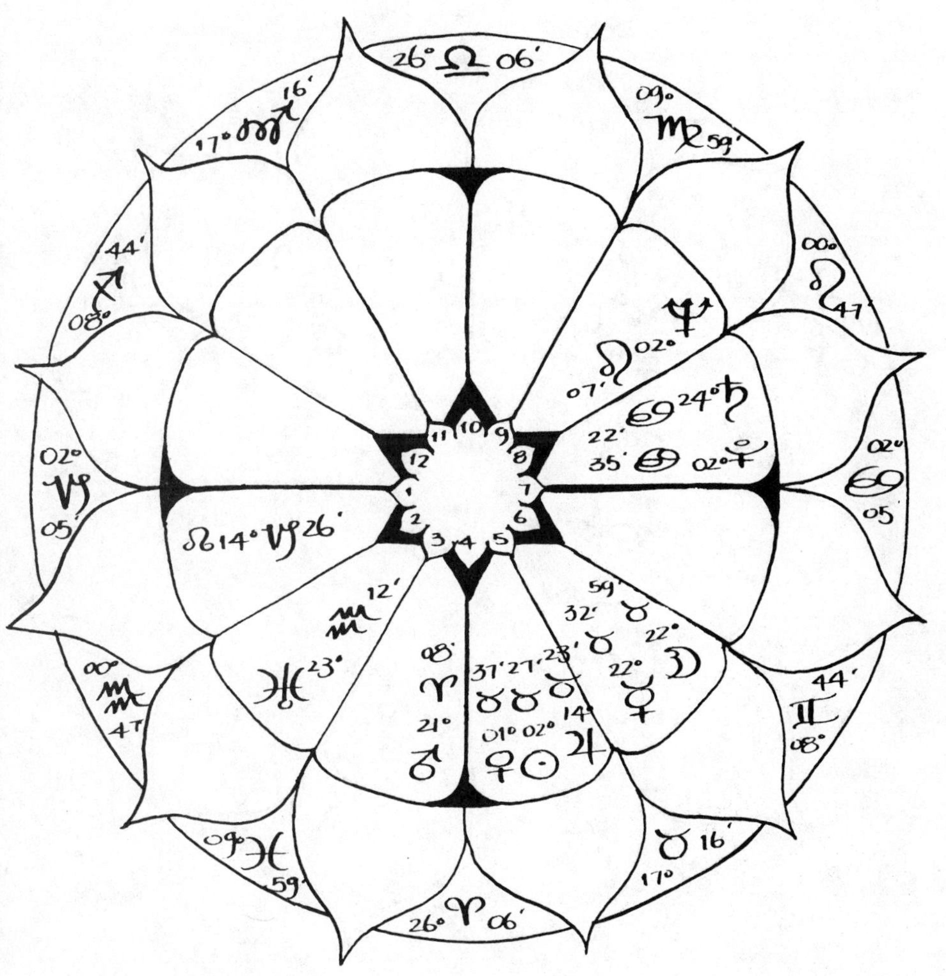

Yehudi Menuhin

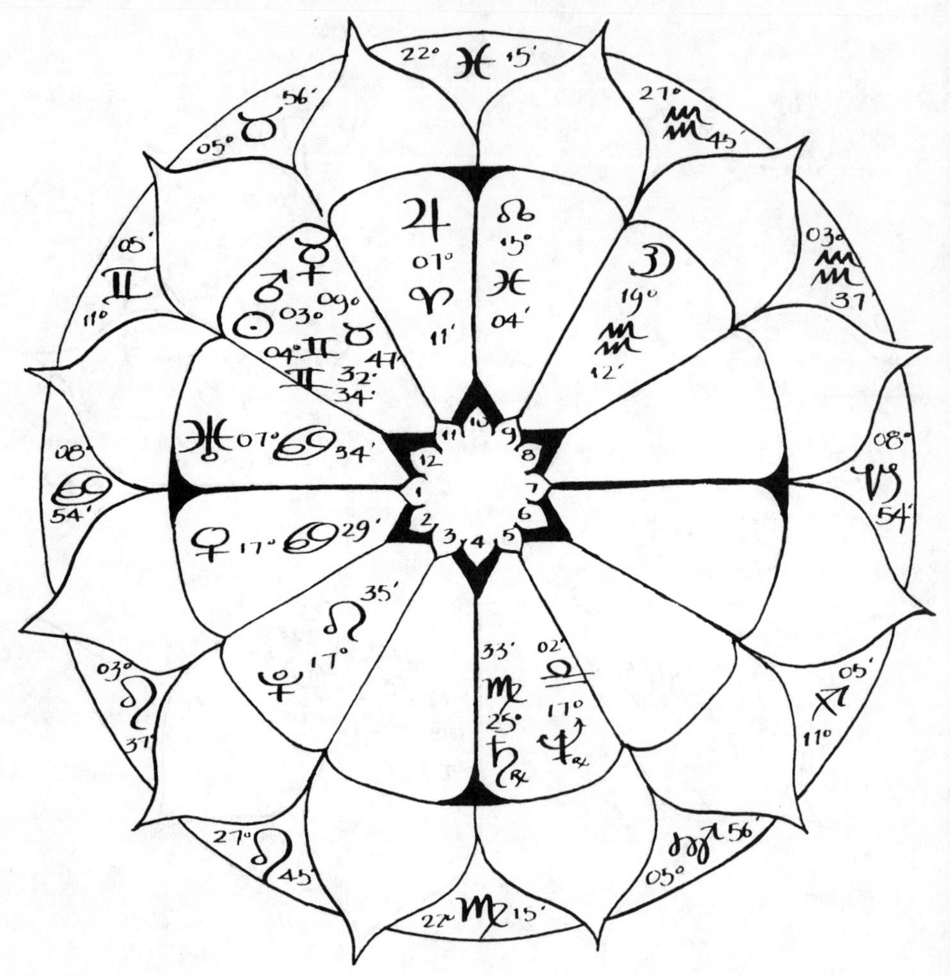

Sally Ride

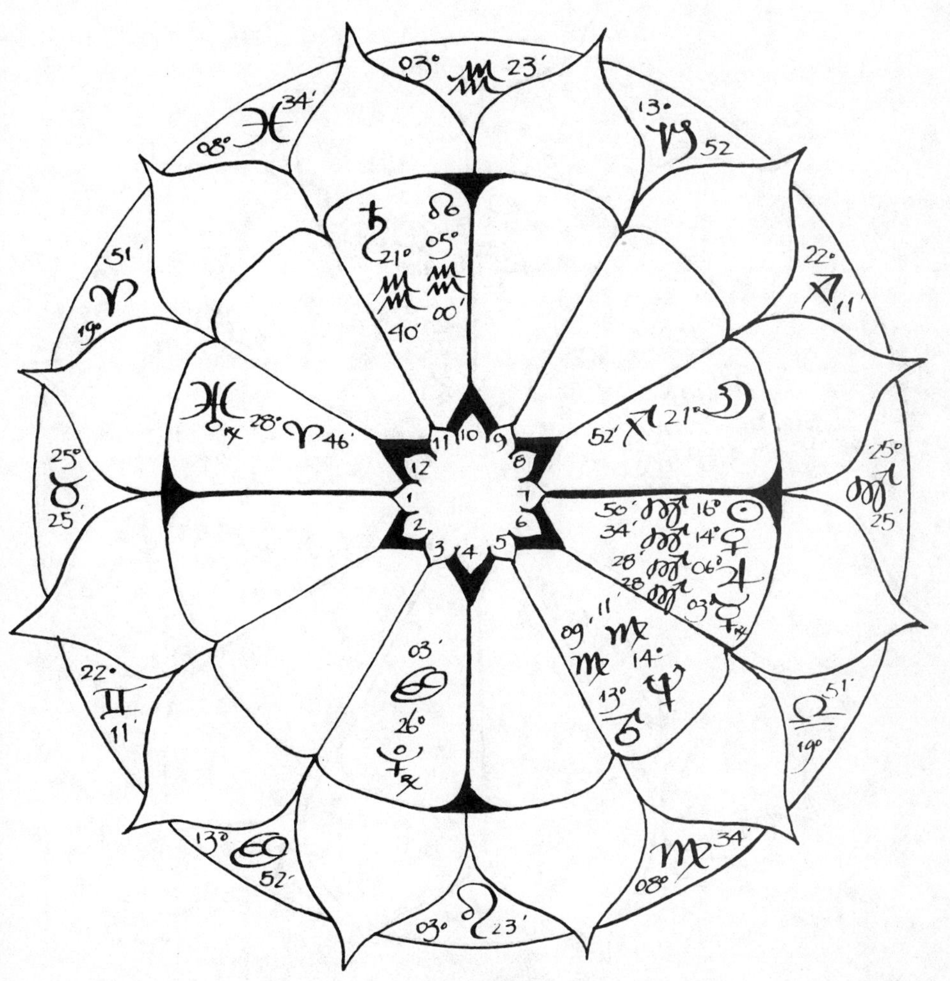

Carl Sagan

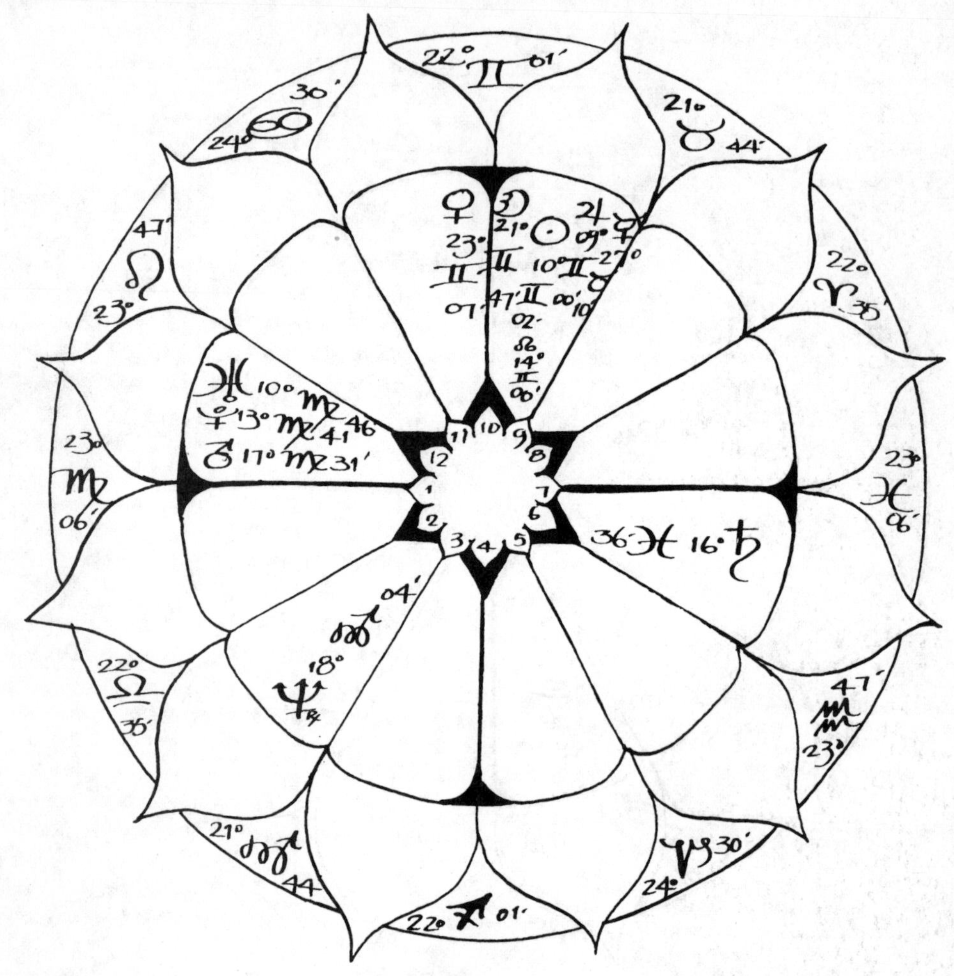

Brooke Shields

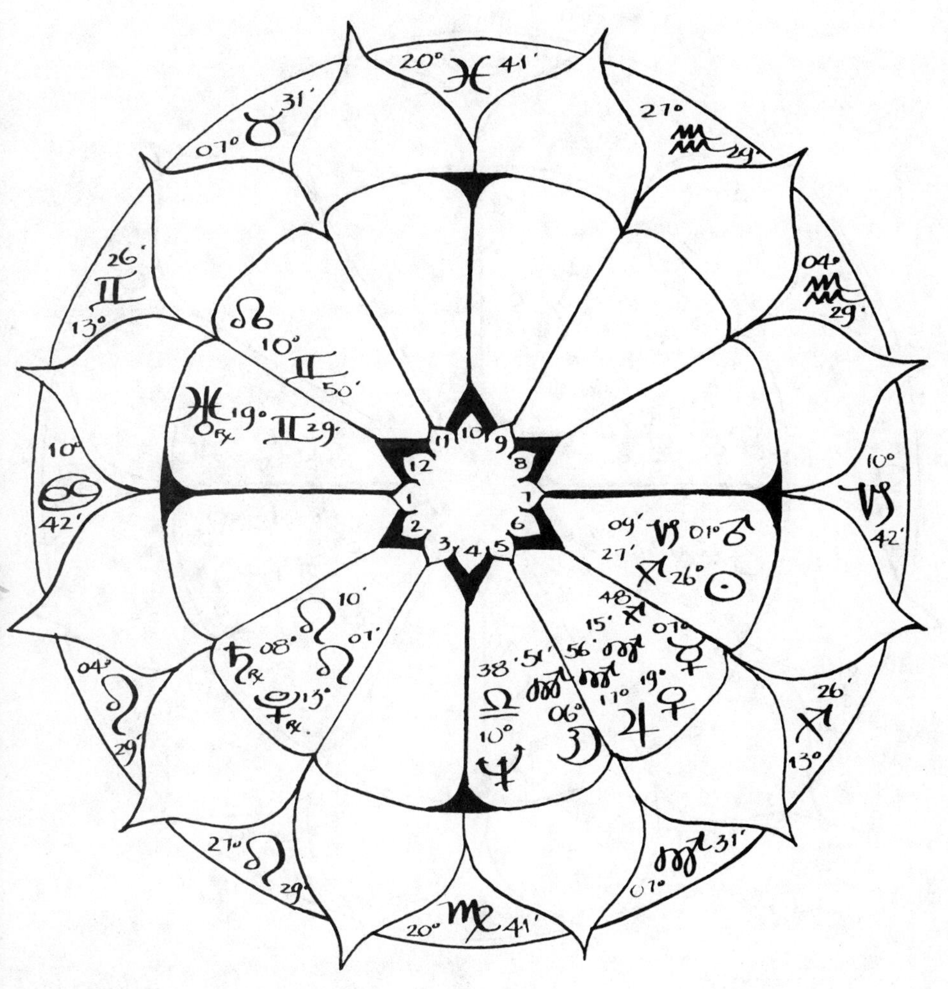

Steven Spielberg

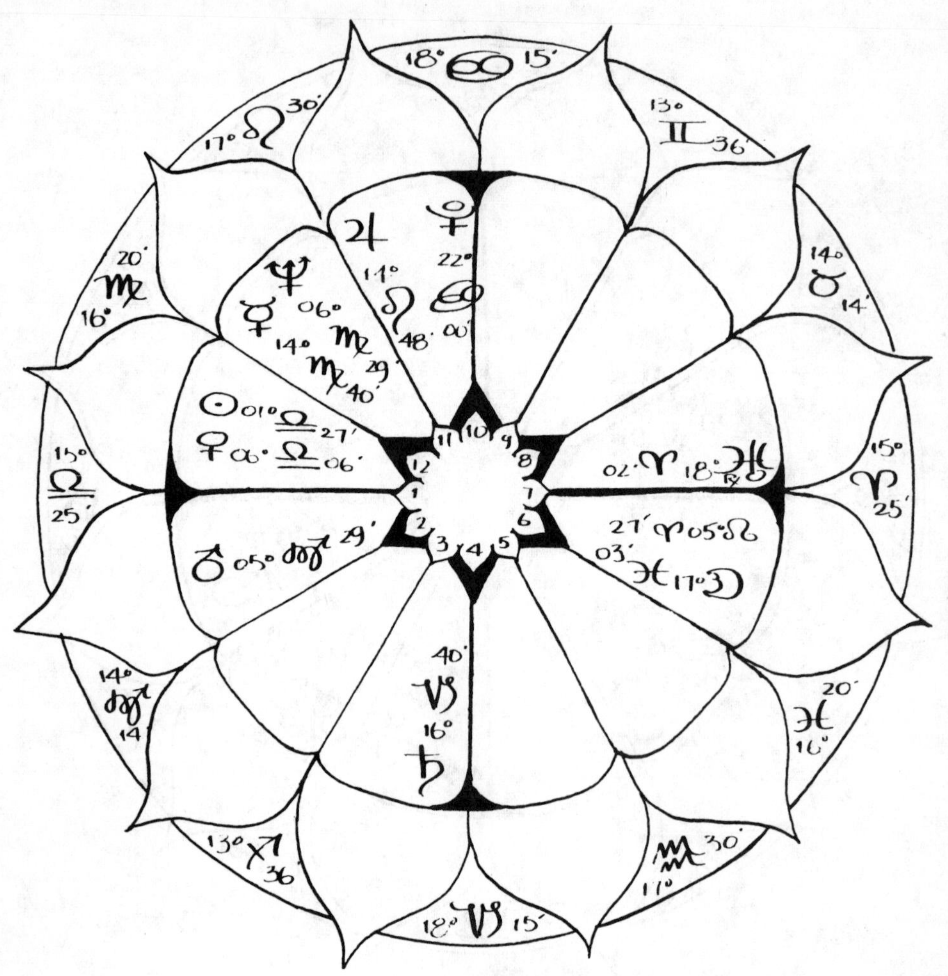

Barbara Walters

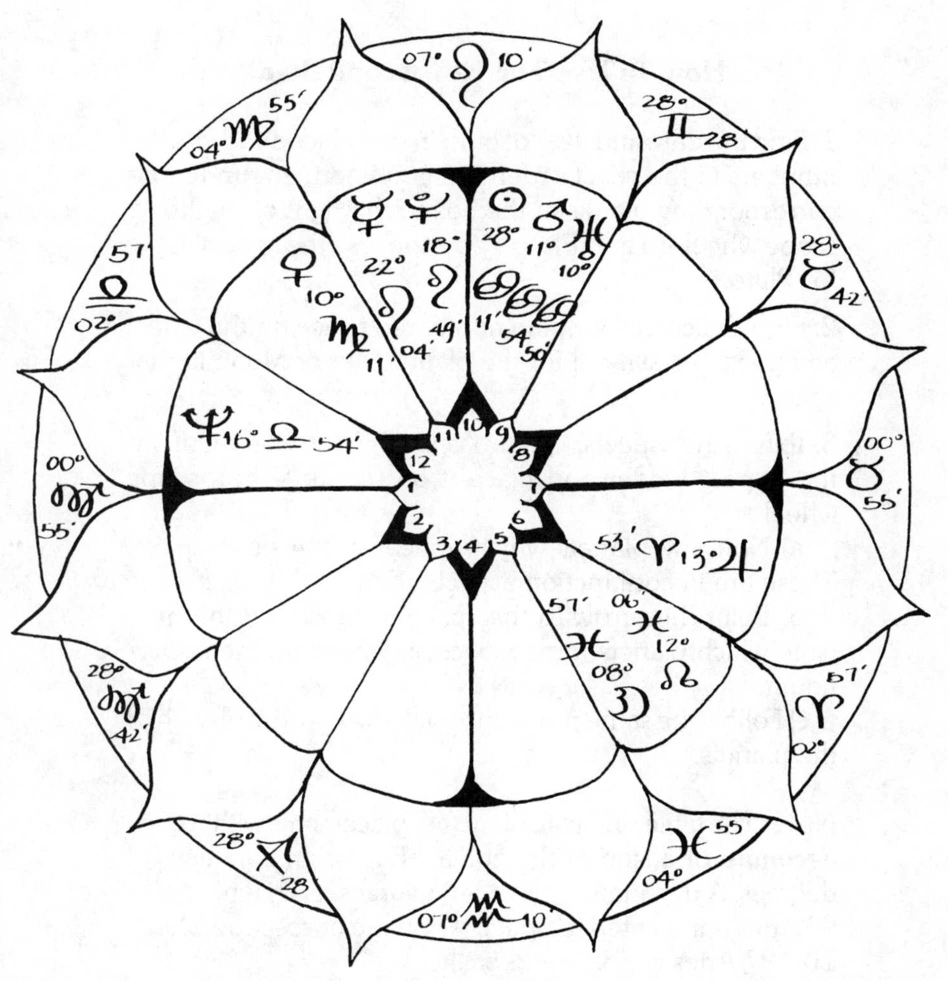

Robin Williams

How To Use The Horoscope Blank

1. Find the date and year of birth in the tables and write the numbers in the exact order that you find them under the corresponding blanks in the box to the right of the horoscope wheel. To find Pluto's position, use the special table for Pluto.

2. Find the corresponding numbered space on the wheel and place the symbol for the planet, Sun or Moon in that space.

3. To find the aspects, use the Aspect Finder wheel. Cut out the Aspect Finder and place it on the large horoscope wheel.

a) Note the planets which appear in the same space. These are in conjunction aspect.

b) Point the arrow to the space occupied by the Sun. Note which planets form aspects indicated on the Aspect finder.

c) Follow the same procedure with the Moon and each of the planets.

Note: The tables indicate planetary placements within each *decanate* of a sign of the zodiac. Each sign contains 30 degrees. A decanate is ⅓, or ten degrees, of a sign. (e.g. 0-9° Aries is indicated in Space #1 on the horoscope wheel, 10-19° Aries is Space #2, etc.).

The results of this procedure will give you a *roughly* calculated chart, not a precise one such as you can obtain through a professional astrological service. Once you have the chart calculated based upon the precise time, date and place of birth, you may even find the faster moving planets in different signs. We use this form as a *simplified* method to calculate the birth chart and introduce you to an easy way to find aspects!

Here you will find the positions of Pluto listed with the date it entered a particular space on the Horoscope Blank and the date it left that numbered space. These numbered spaces are also called decanates. You will use these numbers for Pluto in the box on the Horoscope Blank as well as for placing Pluto in the chart.

PLUTO THROUGH THE DECANATES

ENTER	EXIT	DECANATE Space No.	ENTER	EXIT	DECANATE Space No.
01/01/1890	07/06/1893	7	07/04/1952	10/19/1956	15
07/07/1893	11/14/1893	8	10/20/1956	01/14/1957	16
11/15/1893	05/21/1894	7	01/15/1957	08/18/1957	15
05/16/1894	07/17/1903	8	08/19/1957	04/10/1958	16
07/18/1903	11/25/1903	9	04/11/1958	06/09/1958	15
11/26/1903	06/02/1904	8	06/10/1958	09/05/1962	16
06/03/1904	01/21/1905	9	09/06/1962	04/06/1963	17
01/22/1905	04/14/1905	8	04/07/1963	07/02/1963	16
04/15/1905	09/09/1912	9	07/03/1963	11/03/1966	17
09/10/1912	10/19/1912	10	11/04/1966	02/11/1967	18
10/20/1912	07/08/1913	9	02/12/1967	08/31/1967	17
07/09/1913	12/27/1913	10	09/01/1967	10/04/1971	18
12/28/1913	05/25/1914	9	10/05/1971	04/16/1972	19
05/26/1914	09/21/1921	10	04/17/1972	07/29/1972	18
09/22/1921	10/28/1921	11	07/30/1972	10/24/1975	19
10/29/1921	07/18/1922	10	10/25/1975	04/11/1976	20
07/19/1922	01/08/1923	11	04/12/1976	08/20/1976	19
01/09/1923	06/02/1923	10	08/21/1976	11/03/1979	20
06/03/1923	08/13/1930	11	11/04/1979	04/23/1979	21
08/14/1930	12/31/1930	12	04/24/1980	08/28/1980	20
01/01/1931	06/26/1931	11	08/29/1980	11/04/1983	21
06/27/1931	03/18/1932	12	11/05/1983	05/17/1984	22
03/19/1932	04/16/1932	11	05/18/1984	08/27/1984	21
04/17/1932	10/07/1937	12	08/28/1984	11/04/1987	22
10/08/1937	11/24/1937	13	11/05/1987	06/19/1988	23
11/25/1937	08/02/1938	12	06/20/1988	08/16/1988	22
08/03/1938	02/06/1939	13	08/17/1988	01/15/1991	23
02/07/1939	06/13/1939	12	01/16/1991	03/30/1991	24
06/14/1939	10/06/1944	13	03/31/1991	11/04/1991	23
10/07/1944	12/15/1944	14	11/05/1991	01/15/1995	24
12/16/1944	08/06/1945	13	01/16/1995	04/20/1995	25
08/07/1945	02/27/1946	14	04/21/1995	11/09/1995	24
02/28/1946	06/11/1946	13	11/10/1995	01/29/1999	25
06/12/1946	08/28/1951	14	01/30/1999	04/26/1999	26
08/29/1951	02/23/1952	15	04/27/1999	11/22/1999	25
02/24/1952	07/03/1952	14	11/23/1999	12/31/1999	26

	JAN	FEB	MAR	APR	MAY	JUNE	JULY	AUG	SEPT	OCT	NOV	DEC
1	29 26 26 26 18 5 34 17 23	32 31 30 30 18 5 34 17 23	35 32 35 33 18 6 34 17 23	2 36 3 1 17 6 35 17 23	5 4 2 5 16 7 35 17 23	8 9 6 9 17 7 35 17 23	10 13 12 13 19 8 35 17 23	13 18 16 16 20 9 35 17 23	16 23 15 20 22 9 35 17 23	19 27 20 23 24 10 35 17 23	22 31 24 27 27 10 35 17 23	25 34 26 30 29 9 35 17 24
2	29 28 26 26 18 5 34 17 23	32 32 30 30 18 5 34 17 23	35 33 35 34 18 6 34 17 23	2 2 3 1 17 6 35 17 23	5 5 2 5 16 7 35 17 23	8 11 6 9 17 7 35 17 23	10 14 13 13 19 8 35 17 23	13 20 16 16 20 9 35 17 23	16 24 15 20 22 9 35 17 23	19 28 20 23 24 10 35 17 23	22 32 24 27 27 10 35 17 23	25 35 26 30 29 9 35 17 24
3	29 29 26 26 18 5 34 17 23	32 33 30 30 18 5 34 17 23	35 34 35 34 18 6 34 17 23	2 3 3 2 17 6 35 17 23	5 7 2 5 16 7 35 17 23	8 12 7 9 17 7 35 17 23	11 16 13 13 19 8 35 17 23	14 21 16 17 20 9 35 17 23	17 26 15 20 22 9 35 17 23	19 29 20 23 24 10 35 17 23	23 33 25 27 27 10 35 17 23	26 1 26 30 29 9 35 17 24
4	29 30 27 26 18 5 34 17 23	32 35 31 30 18 5 34 17 23	35 36 36 34 18 6 34 17 23	2 4 3 2 17 6 35 17 23	5 8 2 5 16 7 35 17 23	8 13 7 9 17 7 35 17 23	11 17 13 13 19 8 35 17 23	14 22 15 17 20 9 35 17 23	17 27 15 20 22 9 35 17 23	20 30 20 23 24 10 35 17 23	23 35 25 27 27 10 35 17 23	26 2 25 30 29 9 35 17 24
5	29 31 27 26 18 5 34 17 23	32 36 31 30 18 5 34 17 23	35 1 36 34 18 6 34 17 23	2 6 3 2 17 6 35 17 23	5 10 2 6 17 7 35 17 23	8 15 7 9 17 7 35 17 23	11 19 13 13 19 8 35 17 23	14 24 15 17 21 9 35 17 23	17 28 15 20 23 9 35 17 23	20 31 20 23 25 10 35 17 23	23 36 25 27 27 10 35 17 23	26 3 25 30 29 9 35 17 24
6	29 32 27 27 18 5 34 17 23	29 1 31 31 18 5 34 17 23	35 2 36 34 18 6 34 17 23	2 7 3 2 16 6 35 17 23	5 11 2 6 17 7 35 17 23	8 16 7 9 17 8 35 17 23	11 20 13 13 19 8 35 17 23	14 25 15 17 21 9 35 17 23	17 29 15 21 23 9 35 17 23	20 33 20 23 25 10 35 17 23	23 1 25 28 27 10 35 17 23	26 4 25 30 29 9 35 17 24
7	29 34 27 27 18 5 34 17 23	32 2 31 31 18 5 34 17 23	35 2 36 34 17 6 34 17 23	2 9 2 2 16 6 35 17 23	5 12 2 6 17 7 35 17 23	8 18 8 10 17 8 35 17 23	11 21 13 13 19 8 35 17 23	14 26 15 17 21 9 35 17 23	17 31 15 21 23 9 35 17 23	20 34 21 23 25 10 35 17 23	23 2 25 28 27 10 35 17 23	26 6 25 30 29 9 35 17 24
8	29 35 27 27 18 5 34 17 23	32 4 31 31 18 5 34 17 23	35 5 36 34 17 6 34 17 23	2 10 2 2 16 6 35 17 23	5 14 3 6 17 7 35 17 23	8 19 8 9 18 8 35 17 23	11 23 13 13 19 8 35 17 23	14 27 15 17 21 9 35 17 23	17 32 15 21 23 9 35 17 23	20 35 21 23 25 10 35 17 23	23 4 25 28 27 10 35 17 23	26 7 25 31 29 9 35 17 24
9	29 36 27 27 18 5 34 17 23	33 5 31 31 18 5 34 17 23	35 6 36 34 17 6 34 17 23	2 11 2 2 16 6 35 17 23	5 15 3 6 17 7 35 17 23	8 20 8 9 18 8 35 17 23	11 24 14 13 19 8 35 17 23	14 28 15 17 21 9 35 17 23	17 33 16 21 23 9 35 17 23	20 36 21 23 25 10 35 17 23	23 5 25 28 27 10 35 17 23	26 9 25 31 29 9 35 17 24
10	29 1 27 27 18 5 34 17 23	33 6 32 31 18 5 34 17 23	35 7 1 35 17 6 34 17 23	2 13 2 2 16 6 35 17 23	5 17 3 6 17 7 35 17 23	8 22 8 9 18 8 35 17 23	11 25 14 14 19 8 35 17 23	14 30 15 17 21 9 35 17 23	17 34 16 21 23 9 35 17 23	20 1 21 25 25 10 35 17 23	23 6 25 28 27 10 35 17 23	26 10 25 31 29 9 35 17 24
11	30 3 27 27 18 5 34 17 23	33 8 32 31 18 5 34 17 23	36 9 1 35 17 6 34 17 23	3 14 2 3 16 6 35 17 23	6 18 3 6 17 7 35 17 23	8 23 8 9 18 8 35 17 23	11 26 14 14 19 8 35 17 23	14 31 15 17 21 9 35 17 23	17 35 16 21 23 9 35 17 23	20 3 21 25 25 10 35 17 23	23 8 26 28 27 10 35 17 23	26 11 25 31 30 9 35 17 24
12	30 4 27 27 18 5 34 17 23	33 9 32 31 18 5 34 17 23	36 10 1 35 17 6 34 17 23	3 16 2 3 16 6 35 17 23	6 19 3 6 17 7 35 17 23	9 24 9 10 18 8 35 17 23	11 28 14 14 19 8 35 17 23	14 32 15 18 21 9 35 17 23	17 1 16 21 23 9 35 17 23	20 4 21 25 25 10 35 17 23	23 9 26 28 27 10 35 17 23	26 13 25 31 30 9 35 17 24
13	30 5 27 28 18 5 34 17 23	33 11 32 31 18 5 34 17 24	36 12 1 35 17 6 34 17 23	3 17 2 3 16 6 35 17 23	6 21 3 7 17 7 35 17 23	9 25 9 10 18 8 35 17 23	12 29 14 14 19 8 35 17 23	15 33 15 18 21 9 35 17 23	17 2 16 21 23 9 35 17 23	20 5 22 25 25 10 35 17 23	24 10 26 28 27 10 35 17 23	27 14 25 31 30 9 35 17 24
14	30 7 28 28 18 5 34 17 23	33 12 32 32 18 5 34 17 24	36 13 1 35 17 6 34 17 23	3 18 2 3 16 6 35 17 23	6 22 3 7 17 7 35 17 23	9 27 9 10 18 8 35 17 23	12 30 14 14 19 8 35 17 23	15 34 15 18 21 9 35 17 23	18 3 16 22 23 9 35 17 23	21 7 22 25 25 10 35 17 23	24 12 26 28 28 10 35 17 23	27 16 25 31 30 9 35 17 24
15	30 8 28 28 18 5 34 17 23	33 14 32 32 18 5 34 17 24	36 15 2 35 17 6 34 17 23	3 20 2 3 16 6 35 17 23	6 23 3 7 17 7 35 17 23	9 28 9 11 18 8 35 17 23	12 31 14 14 19 8 35 17 23	15 36 15 18 21 9 35 17 23	18 4 17 22 23 9 35 17 23	21 8 22 25 25 10 35 17 23	24 13 26 28 28 10 35 17 23	27 17 25 31 30 9 35 17 24
16	30 10 28 28 18 5 34 17 23	33 15 33 32 18 5 34 17 24	36 16 2 35 17 6 34 17 23	3 21 2 3 16 6 35 17 23	6 25 4 7 17 7 35 17 23	9 29 9 11 18 8 35 17 23	12 32 14 14 19 8 35 17 23	15 1 15 18 21 9 35 17 23	18 6 17 22 23 9 35 17 23	21 9 22 25 25 10 35 17 23	24 15 26 29 28 10 35 17 23	27 19 25 31 30 9 35 17 24
17	30 11 28 28 18 5 34 17 23	33 17 33 32 18 5 34 17 24	36 17 2 35 17 6 34 17 23	3 22 2 3 16 6 35 17 23	6 26 4 7 17 7 35 17 23	9 30 10 11 18 8 35 17 23	12 34 15 14 19 8 35 17 23	15 2 15 18 21 9 35 17 23	18 7 17 22 23 9 35 17 23	21 11 22 25 25 10 35 17 23	24 16 26 29 28 10 35 17 23	27 20 25 31 30 9 35 17 24
18	30 13 28 28 18 5 34 17 23	33 18 33 32 18 5 34 17 24	36 19 2 36 17 6 34 17 23	3 24 2 3 16 6 35 17 23	6 27 4 7 17 7 35 17 23	9 31 10 11 18 8 35 17 23	12 35 15 15 20 8 35 17 23	15 3 15 18 21 9 35 17 23	18 8 17 22 23 9 35 17 23	21 12 22 25 25 10 35 17 23	24 18 26 29 28 9 35 17 23	27 21 25 31 30 9 35 17 24
19	30 14 28 28 18 5 34 17 23	34 20 33 32 18 5 34 17 24	36 20 2 36 17 6 35 17 23	3 25 2 4 16 6 35 17 23	6 28 4 7 17 7 35 17 23	9 33 10 11 18 8 35 17 23	12 36 15 15 20 8 35 17 23	15 5 15 18 21 9 35 17 23	18 10 17 22 23 9 35 17 23	21 14 22 26 26 10 35 17 23	24 19 26 29 28 9 35 17 23	27 23 25 31 30 9 35 17 24
20	30 16 28 28 18 5 34 17 23	34 21 33 32 18 5 34 17 24	36 22 2 36 17 6 35 17 23	3 26 2 4 16 6 35 17 23	6 29 4 7 17 7 35 17 23	9 34 10 11 18 8 35 17 23	12 1 15 15 20 9 35 17 23	15 6 14 19 21 9 35 17 23	18 11 18 22 24 9 35 17 23	21 16 23 26 26 10 35 17 23	24 20 26 29 28 9 35 17 24	27 24 25 31 30 9 35 17 24
21	31 17 29 29 18 5 34 17 23	34 22 33 32 18 5 34 17 24	1 23 2 36 17 6 35 17 23	4 27 2 4 16 6 35 17 23	6 31 4 7 17 7 35 17 23	9 35 11 11 18 8 35 17 23	12 2 15 15 20 9 35 17 23	15 7 14 19 22 9 35 17 23	18 13 18 22 24 9 35 17 23	21 17 23 26 26 10 35 17 23	24 22 26 29 28 9 35 17 24	27 25 25 31 30 9 35 17 24
22	31 19 29 29 18 5 34 17 23	34 23 34 33 18 5 34 17 24	1 24 2 36 17 6 35 17 23	4 29 2 4 16 6 35 17 23	7 32 4 8 17 7 35 17 23	10 36 11 11 18 8 35 17 23	12 4 15 15 20 9 35 17 23	15 9 14 19 22 9 35 17 23	18 14 18 22 24 10 35 17 23	21 18 23 26 26 10 35 17 23	24 23 26 29 28 9 35 17 24	27 26 25 31 30 9 35 17 24
23	31 20 29 29 18 5 34 17 23	34 25 34 33 18 5 34 17 24	1 25 3 36 17 6 35 17 23	4 30 2 4 16 7 35 17 23	7 33 5 8 17 7 35 17 23	10 2 11 12 18 8 35 17 23	12 5 15 15 20 9 35 17 23	15 10 14 19 22 9 35 17 23	18 16 18 23 24 10 35 17 23	21 19 23 26 26 10 35 17 23	25 24 26 29 28 9 35 17 24	28 28 25 32 30 9 35 17 24
24	31 21 29 29 18 5 34 17 23	34 26 34 33 18 5 34 17 24	1 27 3 36 17 6 35 17 23	4 31 2 4 16 7 35 17 23	7 34 5 8 17 7 35 17 23	10 3 11 12 18 8 35 17 23	13 6 15 15 20 9 35 17 23	16 12 14 19 22 9 35 17 23	19 17 18 23 24 10 35 17 23	22 21 23 26 26 10 35 17 23	25 26 26 29 28 9 35 17 24	28 29 26 32 31 9 35 17 24
25	31 23 29 29 18 5 34 17 23	34 27 34 33 18 5 34 17 24	1 28 3 36 17 6 35 17 23	4 32 2 4 16 7 35 17 23	7 35 5 8 17 7 35 17 23	10 4 11 12 18 8 35 17 23	13 8 15 15 20 9 35 17 23	16 13 14 19 22 9 35 17 23	19 18 18 23 24 10 35 17 23	22 22 23 26 26 10 35 17 23	25 27 26 29 28 9 35 17 24	28 30 26 32 31 9 35 17 24
26	31 24 29 29 18 5 34 17 23	34 28 34 33 18 5 34 17 24	1 29 3 1 17 6 35 17 23	4 33 2 4 16 7 35 17 23	7 1 5 8 17 7 35 17 23	10 6 12 12 18 8 35 17 23	13 9 15 16 20 9 35 17 23	16 15 14 19 22 9 35 17 23	19 20 19 23 24 10 35 17 23	22 24 23 26 26 10 35 17 23	25 28 26 30 28 9 35 17 24	28 31 26 32 31 9 35 17 24
27	31 25 29 29 18 5 34 17 23	34 29 35 33 18 5 34 17 24	1 30 3 1 17 6 35 17 23	4 35 2 5 16 7 35 17 23	7 2 5 8 17 7 35 17 23	10 7 12 12 18 8 35 17 23	13 11 15 16 20 9 35 17 23	16 16 14 19 22 9 35 17 23	19 21 19 23 24 10 35 17 23	22 25 24 26 26 10 35 17 23	25 29 26 30 28 9 35 17 24	28 33 26 32 31 9 35 17 24
28	31 26 30 29 18 5 34 17 23	34 31 35 33 18 5 34 17 24	1 31 3 1 17 6 35 17 23	4 36 2 5 16 7 35 17 23	7 3 6 8 17 7 35 17 23	10 8 12 12 18 8 35 17 23	13 12 15 16 20 9 35 17 23	16 18 14 20 22 9 35 17 23	19 23 19 23 24 10 35 17 23	22 26 24 27 26 10 35 17 23	25 31 26 30 29 9 35 17 24	28 34 26 32 31 9 35 17 24
29	31 27 30 30 18 5 34 17 23	**1965**	1 33 3 1 17 6 35 17 23	4 1 2 5 16 7 35 17 23	7 5 6 8 17 7 35 17 23	10 10 12 12 18 8 35 17 23	13 14 15 16 20 9 35 17 23	16 19 14 20 22 9 35 17 23	19 24 19 23 24 10 35 17 23	22 27 24 27 26 10 35 17 23	25 32 26 30 29 9 35 17 24	28 35 26 32 31 9 35 17 24
30	31 29 30 30 18 5 34 17 23		1 34 3 1 11 6 35 17 23	4 3 2 5 16 7 35 17 23	7 6 6 9 17 7 35 17 23	10 11 12 12 19 8 35 17 23	13 15 15 16 20 9 35 17 23	16 21 14 20 22 9 35 17 23	19 25 19 23 24 10 35 17 23	22 29 24 27 26 10 35 17 23	25 33 26 30 29 9 35 17 24	28 36 26 32 31 9 35 17 24
31	32 30 30 30 18 5 34 17 23		2 35 3 1 17 6 35 17 23		7 8 6 9 17 7 35 17 23		13 17 15 16 20 9 35 17 24	16 22 14 20 22 9 35 17 23		22 30 24 27 26 10 35 17 23		28 1 26 32 31 9 35 17 24

	JAN	FEB	MAR	APR	MAY	JUNE	JULY	AUG	SEPT	OCT	NOV	DEC
1	28 3 27 32 31 9 35 17 24	32 7 31 31 34 9 35 17 24	34 8 36 31 36 9 35 17 24	2 13 36 33 2 9 36 17 24	5 17 2 36 4 9 36 17 24	8 23 8 4 7 10 36 17 24	10 26 13 7 9 11 36 17 23	13 31 13 11 11 11 36 17 23	16 35 15 15 13 12 36 17 23	19 3 21 18 15 13 36 18 24	22 7 25 22 17 13 36 18 24	25 11 23 26 18 13 36 18 24
2	29 4 27 32 31 9 35 17 24	32 9 31 31 34 9 35 17 24	35 10 36 31 36 9 35 17 24	2 15 36 33 2 9 36 17 24	5 19 2 36 5 9 36 17 24	8 24 8 4 7 10 36 17 24	10 28 13 7 9 11 36 17 23	13 32 13 11 11 11 36 17 23	16 1 16 15 13 12 36 17 23	19 4 21 18 15 13 36 18 24	22 9 25 22 17 13 36 18 24	25 12 23 26 18 13 36 18 24
3	29 5 27 32 31 9 35 17 24	32 10 32 31 34 9 35 17 24	35 11 36 31 36 9 35 17 24	2 16 36 33 2 9 36 17 24	5 20 2 36 5 9 36 17 24	8 25 9 4 7 10 36 17 24	11 29 13 7 9 11 36 17 23	14 33 13 11 11 11 36 17 23	17 2 16 15 13 12 36 17 23	19 5 21 18 15 13 36 18 24	23 10 25 23 17 13 36 18 24	26 14 24 26 18 13 36 18 24
4	29 6 27 32 31 9 35 17 24	32 12 32 31 34 9 35 17 24	35 12 1 31 36 9 35 17 24	2 18 36 33 2 9 36 17 24	5 22 3 36 5 9 36 17 24	8 27 9 4 7 10 36 17 24	11 30 13 7 9 11 36 17 23	14 34 13 11 11 11 36 17 23	17 3 16 15 13 12 36 17 23	20 6 21 19 15 13 36 18 24	23 11 25 23 17 13 36 18 24	26 15 24 26 18 13 36 18 24
5	29 8 27 32 32 9 35 17 24	32 13 32 31 34 9 35 17 24	35 14 1 31 36 9 35 17 24	2 19 36 33 3 9 36 17 24	5 23 3 36 5 9 36 17 24	8 28 9 4 7 10 36 17 24	11 31 13 8 9 11 36 17 23	14 35 13 11 11 11 36 17 23	17 4 16 15 13 12 36 17 23	20 8 21 19 15 13 36 18 24	23 13 25 23 17 13 36 18 24	26 16 24 26 19 13 36 18 24
6	29 9 27 32 32 9 35 17 24	32 15 32 31 34 9 35 17 24	35 15 1 31 36 9 35 17 24	2 21 36 33 3 9 36 17 24	5 24 3 1 5 10 36 17 24	8 29 9 4 7 10 36 17 24	11 32 13 8 9 11 36 17 23	14 1 13 11 11 12 36 17 23	17 5 16 15 13 12 36 17 23	20 9 22 19 15 13 36 18 24	23 14 25 23 17 13 36 18 24	26 18 24 27 19 13 36 18 24
7	29 11 27 32 32 9 35 17 24	32 16 32 30 34 9 35 17 24	35 17 1 31 36 9 35 17 24	2 22 36 34 3 9 36 17 24	5 26 3 1 5 10 36 17 24	8 30 9 4 7 10 36 17 24	11 34 13 8 9 11 36 17 23	14 2 13 11 11 12 36 17 23	17 7 17 15 13 12 36 17 23	20 10 22 19 15 13 36 18 24	23 15 25 23 17 13 36 18 24	26 19 24 27 19 13 36 18 24
8	29 12 28 32 32 9 35 17 24	32 18 33 30 34 9 35 17 24	35 19 1 31 36 9 35 17 24	2 24 36 34 3 9 36 17 24	5 27 3 1 5 10 36 17 24	8 32 10 4 7 10 36 17 24	11 35 13 8 9 11 36 17 23	14 3 13 12 11 12 36 17 23	17 8 17 15 13 12 36 17 23	20 11 22 19 15 13 36 18 24	23 17 25 23 17 13 36 18 24	26 21 24 27 19 13 36 18 24
9	29 14 28 32 32 9 35 17 24	32 19 33 30 34 9 35 17 24	35 20 1 31 36 9 35 17 24	2 25 36 34 3 9 36 17 24	5 28 3 1 5 10 36 17 24	8 33 10 4 7 10 36 17 24	11 36 14 8 9 11 36 17 23	14 4 13 12 11 12 36 17 23	17 9 17 16 13 12 36 17 23	20 13 22 19 15 13 36 18 24	23 18 25 23 17 13 36 18 24	26 22 24 27 19 13 36 18 24
10	29 15 28 32 32 9 35 17 24	33 21 33 30 34 9 35 17 24	35 21 1 31 1 9 35 17 24	2 26 36 34 3 9 36 17 24	5 30 4 1 5 10 36 17 24	8 34 10 5 7 10 36 17 24	11 1 14 8 9 11 36 17 23	14 6 13 12 11 12 36 17 23	17 11 17 16 13 12 36 17 23	20 14 22 19 15 13 36 18 24	23 20 25 23 17 13 36 18 24	26 23 24 27 19 13 36 18 24
11	30 17 28 32 32 9 35 17 24	33 22 33 30 34 9 35 17 24	35 23 1 31 1 9 35 17 24	3 28 36 34 3 9 36 17 24	5 31 4 1 5 10 36 17 24	8 35 10 5 7 10 36 17 24	11 2 14 8 9 11 36 17 23	14 7 13 12 12 12 36 17 23	17 12 17 16 14 12 36 17 23	20 16 22 19 15 13 36 18 24	23 21 25 23 17 13 361 8 24	26 25 24 27 19 13 36 18 24
12	30 18 28 32 32 9 35 17 24	33 23 33 30 35 9 35 17 24	36 24 1 31 1 9 36 17 24	3 29 36 34 3 9 36 17 24	6 32 4 1 5 10 36 17 24	9 36 10 5 7 10 36 17 24	11 4 14 8 10 11 36 17 23	14 8 13 12 12 12 36 17 23	17 13 18 16 14 12 36 17 23	20 17 22 20 15 13 36 18 24	23 23 25 23 17 13 36 18 24	26 26 25 27 19 13 36 18 24
13	30 20 28 32 32 9 35 17 24	33 25 33 30 35 9 35 17 24	36 26 1 31 1 9 36 17 24	3 30 36 34 3 9 36 17 24	6 33 4 1 5 10 36 17 24	9 2 10 5 8 10 36 17 24	12 5 14 8 10 11 36 17 23	14 10 13 12 12 12 36 17 23	17 15 18 16 14 12 36 18 23	20 19 23 20 16 13 36 18 24	24 24 25 24 17 13 36 18 24	27 28 25 27 19 13 36 18 24
14	30 21 28 32 32 9 35 17 24	33 26 34 30 35 9 35 17 24	36 27 1 31 1 9 36 17 24	3 31 36 34 3 9 36 17 24	6 34 4 1 5 10 36 17 24	9 3 11 5 8 10 36 17 23	12 6 14 9 10 11 36 17 23	15 11 13 12 13 12 36 17 23	18 16 18 16 14 12 36 18 23	21 20 23 20 16 13 36 18 24	24 25 24 24 17 13 36 18 24	27 28 25 27 19 13 36 18 24
15	30 22 29 32 32 9 35 17 24	33 27 34 30 35 9 35 17 24	36 28 1 32 1 9 36 17 24	3 32 36 34 3 9 36 17 24	6 36 4 2 6 10 36 17 24	9 4 11 5 8 10 36 17 23	12 8 14 9 10 11 36 17 23	15 13 13 12 13 12 36 17 23	18 18 18 16 14 12 36 18 23	21 22 23 20 16 13 36 18 24	24 27 24 24 17 13 36 18 24	27 30 25 28 19 13 36 18 24
16	30 24 29 32 32 9 35 17 24	33 28 34 30 35 9 35 17 24	36 29 1 32 1 9 36 17 24	3 34 36 34 3 9 36 17 24	6 1 5 2 6 10 36 17 24	9 5 11 5 8 10 36 17 23	12 9 14 9 10 11 36 17 23	15 14 13 13 13 12 36 17 23	18 19 18 16 14 12 36 18 23	21 23 23 20 16 13 36 18 24	24 28 24 24 18 13 36 18 24	27 32 25 28 19 13 36 18 24
17	30 25 29 32 32 9 35 17 24	33 30 34 30 35 9 35 17 24	36 30 1 32 1 9 36 17 24	3 35 36 35 3 9 36 17 24	6 2 5 2 6 10 36 17 24	9 7 11 5 8 10 36 17 23	12 10 14 9 10 11 36 17 23	15 16 13 13 13 12 36 17 23	18 21 18 16 14 12 36 18 23	21 25 23 20 16 13 36 18 24	24 29 24 24 18 13 36 18 24	27 33 25 28 19 13 36 18 24
18	30 26 29 32 33 9 35 17 24	33 31 34 30 35 9 35 17 24	36 32 1 32 1 9 36 17 24	3 36 1 35 4 9 36 17 24	6 3 5 2 6 10 36 17 24	9 8 11 6 8 10 36 17 23	12 12 14 9 10 11 36 17 23	15 17 13 13 13 12 36 17 23	18 22 19 17 14 12 36 18 24	21 26 23 20 16 13 36 18 24	24 31 24 24 18 13 36 18 24	27 34 25 28 19 13 36 18 24
19	30 27 29 32 33 9 35 17 24	33 32 35 30 35 9 35 17 24	36 33 1 32 1 9 36 17 24	3 1 1 35 4 9 36 17 24	6 5 5 2 6 10 36 17 24	9 9 11 6 8 10 36 17 23	12 13 14 9 10 11 36 17 23	15 19 13 13 13 12 36 17 23	18 24 19 17 14 12 36 18 24	21 27 23 20 16 13 36 18 24	24 32 24 24 18 13 36 18 24	27 35 26 28 19 13 36 18 24
20	30 29 29 31 33 9 35 17 24	34 33 35 30 35 9 35 17 24	36 34 1 32 1 9 36 17 24	3 2 1 35 4 9 36 17 24	6 6 5 2 6 10 36 17 24	9 11 12 6 8 10 36 17 23	12 15 14 9 10 11 36 17 23	15 20 13 13 13 12 36 17 23	18 25 19 17 14 12 36 18 24	21 29 23 21 16 13 36 18 24	24 33 24 24 18 13 36 18 24	27 36 26 28 19 13 36 18 24
21	31 30 30 31 33 9 35 17 24	34 34 35 30 35 9 35 17 24	36 35 1 32 1 9 36 17 24	4 4 1 35 4 9 36 17 24	6 7 6 2 6 10 36 17 24	9 12 12 6 8 10 36 17 23	12 16 13 9 10 11 36 17 23	15 22 13 13 13 12 36 17 23	18 27 19 17 14 12 36 18 24	21 30 24 21 16 13 36 18 24	24 34 23 25 18 13 36 18 24	27 2 26 28 19 13 36 18 24
22	31 31 30 31 33 9 35 17 24	34 35 35 30 35 9 35 17 24	1 36 1 32 1 9 36 17 24	4 5 1 35 4 9 36 17 24	7 9 6 2 6 10 36 17 24	10 14 12 6 8 11 36 17 23	12 18 13 10 10 11 36 17 23	15 23 14 13 13 12 36 17 23	18 28 19 17 14 12 36 18 24	21 31 24 21 16 13 36 18 24	24 36 23 25 18 13 36 18 24	27 3 26 29 19 13 36 18 24
23	31 32 30 31 33 9 35 17 24	34 1 35 30 35 9 35 17 24	1 2 36 32 2 9 36 17 24	4 6 1 35 4 9 36 17 24	7 10 6 2 6 10 36 17 24	10 15 12 6 8 11 36 17 23	12 19 13 10 10 11 36 17 23	15 24 14 13 13 12 36 17 23	18 29 19 17 14 12 36 18 24	21 32 24 21 16 13 36 18 24	25 1 23 25 18 13 36 18 24	28 4 26 29 19 13 36 18 24
24	31 33 30 31 33 9 35 17 24	34 2 35 30 35 9 35 17 24	1 3 36 32 2 9 35 17 24	4 8 1 35 4 9 36 17 24	7 11 6 3 6 10 36 17 24	10 17 12 6 8 11 36 17 23	13 21 13 10 10 11 36 17 23	16 26 14 14 13 12 36 17 23	19 30 20 17 14 12 36 18 24	22 34 24 21 16 13 36 18 24	25 2 23 25 18 13 36 18 24	28 5 26 29 20 13 36 18 24
25	31 35 30 31 33 9 35 17 24	34 3 36 30 36 9 35 17 24	1 4 36 32 2 9 36 17 24	4 9 1 35 4 9 36 17 24	7 13 7 3 6 10 36 17 24	10 18 12 6 8 11 36 17 23	13 22 13 10 10 11 36 17 23	16 27 14 14 13 12 36 17 23	19 32 20 17 14 12 36 18 24	22 35 24 21 16 13 35 18 24	25 3 23 25 18 13 36 18 24	28 6 26 29 20 13 36 18 24
26	31 36 30 31 33 9 35 17 24	34 4 36 31 36 9 35 17 24	1 5 36 32 2 9 36 17 24	4 10 1 36 4 9 36 17 24	7 14 7 3 6 10 36 17 24	10 19 12 6 8 11 36 17 23	13 23 13 10 10 11 36 17 23	16 28 14 14 13 12 36 17 23	19 33 20 18 14 12 36 18 24	22 36 24 21 16 13 36 18 24	25 4 23 25 18 13 36 18 24	28 8 27 29 20 13 36 18 24
27	31 1 30 31 33 9 35 17 24	34 6 36 31 36 9 35 17 24	1 7 36 32 2 9 36 17 24	4 12 2 36 4 9 36 17 24	7 16 7 3 6 10 36 17 24	10 21 13 7 9 11 36 17 23	13 25 13 10 11 11 36 17 23	16 29 14 14 13 12 36 17 23	19 34 20 18 15 12 36 18 24	22 1 24 21 16 13 36 18 24	25 6 23 25 18 13 36 18 24	28 9 27 29 20 13 36 18 24
28	31 2 31 31 33 9 35 17 24	34 7 36 31 36 9 35 17 24	1 8 36 33 2 9 35 17 24	4 13 2 36 4 9 35 17 24	7 17 7 3 6 10 36 17 24	10 22 13 7 9 11 36 17 23	13 26 13 10 11 11 36 17 23	16 31 15 14 13 12 36 17 23	19 35 20 18 15 13 36 18 24	22 2 24 22 16 13 36 18 24	25 7 23 25 18 13 36 18 24	28 10 27 29 20 13 36 18 24
29	31 3 31 31 33 9 35 17 24		1 9 36 33 2 9 35 17 24	4 14 2 36 4 9 35 17 24	7 18 7 3 7 10 36 17 24	10 24 13 7 9 11 36 17 23	13 27 13 10 11 11 36 17 23	16 32 15 14 13 12 36 17 23	19 36 20 18 15 13 36 18 24	22 4 24 22 16 13 36 18 24	25 8 23 26 18 13 36 18 24	28 12 27 29 20 13 36 18 24
30	31 5 31 31 33 9 35 17 24	1966	1 11 36 33 2 9 35 17 24	4 16 2 36 4 9 36 17 24	7 20 8 3 7 10 36 17 24	10 25 13 7 9 10 36 17 23	13 28 13 10 11 11 36 17 23	16 33 15 14 13 12 36 17 23	19 1 21 18 18 13 36 18 24	22 5 24 22 17 13 36 18 24	25 10 23 26 18 13 36 18 24	28 13 27 30 20 13 36 18 24
31	32 6 31 31 34 9 35 17 24		1 12 36 33 2 9 36 17 24		7 21 8 3 7 10 36 17 24		13 30 13 11 11 11 36 17 23	16 34 15 14 13 12 36 17 23		22 6 25 22 17 13 36 18 24		28 15 27 30 20 13 36 18 24

	JAN	FEB	MAR	APR	MAY	JUNE	JULY	AUG	SEPT	OCT	NOV	DEC
1	28 16 27 30 20 13 36 18 24	32 21 33 34 21 12 36 18 24	34 22 35 1 22 12 36 18 24	2 27 35 5 21 12 1 18 24	4 31 3 8 20 12 1 18 24	7 36 10 12 20 13 2 18 24	10 3 12 15 21 13 2 18 24	13 7 11 17 22 14 2 18 24	16 12 17 16 24 15 2 18 24	19 15 22 15 26 15 1 18 24	22 21 22 18 28 16 1 18 24	25 24 24 21 30 16 1 18 24
2	29 17 28 30 20 13 36 18 24	32 23 33 34 21 12 36 18 24	35 24 35 1 22 12 36 18 24	2 29 35 5 21 12 1 18 24	5 32 4 9 20 12 1 18 24	8 1 10 12 20 13 2 18 24	10 4 12 15 21 13 2 18 24	13 8 11 17 22 14 2 18 24	16 13 17 16 24 15 2 18 24	19 17 22 16 16 15 1 18 24	22 22 22 18 28 16 1 18 24	25 26 24 21 31 16 1 18 24
3	29 19 28 30 20 13 36 18 24	32 24 33 34 21 12 36 18 24	35 25 35 1 22 12 36 18 24	2 30 35 5 21 12 1 18 24	5 33 4 9 20 12 1 18 24	8 2 10 12 20 13 2 18 24	11 5 12 15 21 13 2 18 24	13 10 12 17 22 14 2 18 24	16 14 17 16 24 15 2 18 24	19 18 22 16 26 15 1 18 24	22 24 22 18 28 16 1 18 24	26 27 24 21 31 16 1 18 24
4	29 20 28 30 20 13 36 18 24	32 26 33 34 21 12 36 18 24	35 27 35 1 22 12 1 18 24	2 31 35 5 21 12 1 18 24	5 35 4 9 20 12 1 18 24	8 3 10 12 20 13 2 18 24	11 6 11 15 21 13 2 18 24	14 11 12 17 22 14 2 18 24	17 16 18 16 24 15 2 18 24	20 20 22 16 26 15 1 18 24	23 25 22 18 28 16 1 18 24	26 29 24 21 31 16 1 18 24
5	29 22 28 30 20 13 36 18 24	32 27 33 34 21 12 36 18 24	35 28 35 2 22 12 1 18 24	2 33 35 5 21 12 1 18 24	5 36 4 9 20 12 1 18 24	8 4 10 12 20 13 2 18 24	11 7 11 15 21 13 2 18 24	14 12 12 17 22 14 2 18 24	17 17 18 16 24 15 2 18 24	20 21 22 16 26 15 1 18 24	23 27 22 18 28 16 1 18 24	26 30 24 21 31 16 1 18 24
6	29 23 28 30 20 13 36 18 24	32 28 33 34 21 12 36 18 24	35 29 35 2 22 12 1 18 24	2 34 35 5 21 12 1 18 24	5 1 4 9 20 12 1 18 24	8 5 10 12 20 13 2 18 24	11 9 11 15 21 13 2 18 24	14 14 12 17 22 14 2 18 24	17 19 18 16 24 15 2 18 24	20 23 22 16 26 15 1 18 24	23 28 22 18 29 16 1 18 24	26 32 25 21 31 16 1 18 24
7	29 24 28 31 20 13 36 18 24	32 29 34 34 21 12 36 18 24	35 30 34 2 22 12 1 18 24	2 35 35 6 21 12 1 18 24	5 2 5 9 20 12 1 18 24	8 7 10 13 20 13 2 18 24	11 10 11 15 21 13 2 18 24	14 15 12 17 22 14 2 18 24	17 20 18 16 24 15 2 18 24	20 24 22 16 26 15 1 18 24	23 29 22 18 29 16 1 18 24	26 33 25 21 31 16 1 18 24
8	29 26 29 31 20 13 36 18 24	32 31 34 35 21 12 36 18 24	35 32 34 2 22 12 1 18 24	2 36 36 6 21 12 1 18 24	5 3 5 9 20 12 1 18 24	8 8 11 13 20 13 2 18 24	11 11 11 15 21 13 2 18 24	14 16 12 17 22 14 2 18 24	17 22 18 16 24 15 2 18 24	20 26 22 16 26 15 1 18 24	23 31 22 18 29 16 1 18 24	26 34 25 22 31 16 1 18 24
9	29 27 29 31 20 13 26 18 24	32 32 34 35 21 12 36 18 24	35 33 34 2 22 12 1 18 24	2 1 36 6 21 12 1 18 24	5 5 5 9 20 12 1 18 24	8 9 11 13 20 13 2 18 24	11 13 11 16 21 13 2 18 24	14 18 13 17 23 14 2 18 24	17 23 18 16 24 15 2 18 24	20 27 23 16 26 15 1 18 24	23 32 22 18 29 16 1 18 24	26 35 25 22 31 16 1 18 24
10	29 28 29 31 20 13 36 18 24	33 33 34 35 21 12 36 18 24	35 34 34 2 22 12 1 18 24	2 3 36 6 21 12 1 18 24	5 6 5 9 20 12 1 18 24	8 10 11 13 20 13 2 18 24	11 14 11 16 21 13 2 18 24	14 19 13 17 23 14 2 18 24	17 25 19 15 24 15 2 18 24	20 28 23 16 27 15 1 18 24	23 33 22 19 29 16 1 18 24	26 1 25 22 31 16 1 18 24
11	30 30 29 31 20 13 36 18 24	33 34 34 35 21 12 36 18 24	35 35 34 2 22 12 36 18 24	3 4 36 6 21 12 1 18 24	5 7 5 10 20 12 1 18 24	8 11 11 13 20 13 2 1 18 24	11 15 11 16 21 13 2 18 24	14 21 13 17 23 14 2 18 24	17 26 19 15 25 15 2 18 24	20 30 23 16 27 15 1 18 24	23 35 22 19 29 16 1 18 24	26 2 25 22 31 16 1 18 24
12	30 31 29 31 20 13 36 18 24	33 36 34 35 21 12 36 18 24	36 36 34 2 22 12 1 18 24	3 5 36 6 21 12 1 18 24	6 8 6 10 20 12 1 18 24	9 13 11 13 20 13 2 18 24	11 17 11 16 21 13 2 18 24	14 22 13 17 23 14 2 18 24	17 27 19 15 25 15 2 18 24	20 31 23 16 27 15 1 18 24	23 36 22 19 29 16 1 18 24	26 3 25 22 31 16 1 18 24
13	30 32 29 31 20 13 36 18 24	33 1 35 35 22 12 36 18 24	36 1 34 3 22 12 1 18 24	3 6 36 6 21 12 1 18 24	6 9 6 10 20 12 1 18 24	9 14 11 13 20 13 2 18 24	11 18 11 16 21 13 2 18 24	14 24 13 17 23 14 2 18 24	17 29 19 15 25 15 2 18 24	20 32 23 16 27 15 1 18 24	23 1 22 19 29 16 1 18 24	27 4 26 22 31 16 1 18 24
14	30-34 30 31 20 13 36 18 24	33 2 35 35 22 12 36 18 24	36 3 34 3 22 12 1 18 24	3 7 36 6 21 12 1 18 24	6 11 6 10 20 12 1 18 24	9 16 11 13 20 13 2 18 24	12 20 11 16 21 13 2 18 24	15 25 13 17 23 14 2 18 24	18 30 19 15 25 15 2 18 24	20 34 23 16 27 15 1 18 24	24 2 22 19 29 16 1 18 24	27 5 26 22 31 16 1 18 24
15	30 35 30 32 21 13 36 18 24	33 3 35 35 22 12 36 18 24	36 4 34 3 22 12 1 18 24	3 9 1 7 21 12 1 18 24	6 12 6 10 20 12 1 18 24	9 17 11 13 20 13 2 18 24	12 21 11 16 21 14 2 18 24	15 26 14 17 23 14 2 18 24	18 31 19 15 25 15 2 18 24	21 35 23 16 27 15 1 18 24	24 3 22 19 29 16 1 18 24	27 7 26 22 32 16 1 18 24
16	30 36 30 32 21 13 36 18 24	33 4 35 36 22 12 36 18 23	36 5 34 3 22 12 1 18 24	3 10 1 7 21 12 1 18 24	6 13 6 10 20 12 1 18 24	9 19 11 13 20 13 2 18 24	12 23 11 16 21 14 2 18 24	15 28 14 17 23 14 2 18 24	18 33 20 15 25 15 2 18 24	21 36 23 16 27 15 1 18 24	24 4 22 19 29 16 1 18 24	27 8 26 22 32 16 1 18 24
17	30 1 30 32 21 12 36 18 24	33 6 35 36 22 12 36 18 24	36 6 34 3 22 12 36 18 24	3 11 1 7 21 12 1 18 24	6 15 7 10 20 12 1 18 24	9 20 11 14 20 13 2 18 24	12 24 11 16 21 14 2 18 24	15 29 14 17 23 14 2 18 24	18 34 20 15 25 15 2 18 24	21 1 23 16 27 15 1 18 24	24 6 22 19 29 16 1 18 24	27 9 26 23 32 16 1 18 24
18	30 2 30 32 21 12 36 18 24	33 7 35 36 22 12 36 18 24	36 8 34 3 22 12 1 18 24	3 12 1 7 21 12 1 18 24	6 16 7 10 20 12 1 18 24	9 21 11 14 20 13 2 18 24	12 25 11 16 21 14 2 18 24	15 30 14 17 23 14 2 18 24	18 35 20 15 25 15 2 18 24	21 2 23 16 27 15 1 18 24	24 7 22 19 29 16 1 18 24	27 10 26 23 32 16 1 18 24
19	30 4 30 32 21 12 36 18 24	33 8 35 36 22 12 36 18 24	36 9 34 3 22 12 1 18 24	3 14 1 7 21 12 1 18 24	6 18 7 10 20 12 1 18 24	9 23 11 14 20 13 2 18 24	12 27 11 16 21 14 2 18 24	15 32 14 17 23 14 2 18 24	18 36 20 15 25 15 2 18 24	21 4 23 17 27 15 1 18 24	24 8 22 19 30 16 1 18 24	27 11 27 23 32 16 1 18 24
20	30 5 31 32 21 12 36 18 24	34 9 35 36 22 12 36 18 24	36 10 34 3 22 12 1 18 24	3 15 1 7 21 12 1 18 24	6 19 7 11 20 12 1 18 24	9 24 12 14 20 13 2 18 24	12 28 11 16 22 14 2 18 24	15 33 15 17 23 14 2 18 24	18 2 20 15 25 15 2 18 24	21 5 23 17 27 16 1 18 24	24 9 22 20 30 16 1 18 24	27 13 27 23 32 16 1 18 24
21	31 6 31 32 21 12 36 18 24	34 11 35 36 22 12 36 18 24	36 11 34 4 22 12 1 18 24	4 17 2 7 21 12 1 18 24	6 20 8 11 20 12 1 18 24	9 26 12 14 20 13 2 18 24	12 29 11 16 22 14 2 18 24	15 34 15 17 23 14 2 18 24	18 3 20 15 25 15 1 18 24	21 6 23 17 27 16 1 18 24	24 11 22 20 30 16 1 18 24	27 14 27 23 32 16 1 18 24
22	31 7 31 32 21 12 36 18 24	34 12 35 36 22 12 36 18 24	1 13 34 4 22 12 1 18 24	4 18 2 7 21 12 1 18 24	7 22 8 11 20 13 2 18 24	9 27 12 14 20 14 2 18 24	12 31 11 16 22 14 2 18 24	15 35 15 16 23 14 2 18 24	18 4 20 15 25 15 1 18 24	21 7 23 17 27 16 1 18 24	24 12 23 20 30 16 1 18 24	27 15 27 23 32 16 1 18 24
23	31 9 31 33 21 12 36 18 24	34 13 35 36 22 12 36 18 24	1 14 34 4 22 12 1 18 24	4 20 2 8 21 12 1 18 24	7 23 8 11 20 12 1 18 24	10 29 12 14 20 13 2 18 24	12 32 11 16 22 14 2 18 24	15 1 15 16 23 14 2 18 24	18 5 21 15 25 15 1 18 24	21 8 23 17 27 16 1 18 24	24 13 23 20 30 16 1 18 24	28 17 27 23 32 16 1 18 24
24	31 10 31 33 21 12 36 18 24	34 15 35 1 22 12 36 18 24	1 16 34 4 22 12 1 18 24	4 21 2 8 21 12 1 18 24	7 25 8 11 20 13 1 18 24	10 30 12 14 20 13 2 18 24	13 33 11 16 22 14 2 18 24	16 2 15 16 23 14 2 18 24	19 6 21 15 25 15 1 18 24	21 10 23 17 28 16 1 18 24	25 14 23 20 30 16 1 18 24	28 18 27 23 32 16 1 18 24
25	31 11 31 33 21 12 36 18 24	34 16 35 1 22 12 36 18 24	1 17 34 4 22 12 1 18 24	4 23 2 8 21 12 1 18 24	7 26 8 11 20 13 1 18 24	10 31 12 14 21 13 2 18 24	13 34 11 17 22 14 2 18 24	16 3 16 16 23 14 2 18 24	19 7 21 15 26 15 1 18 24	22 11 23 17 28 16 1 18 24	25 16 23 20 30 16 1 18 24	28 19 28 24 32 16 1 18 24
26	31 13 32 33 21 12 36 18 24	34 18 35 1 22 12 36 18 24	1 19 34 4 22 12 1 18 24	4 24 2 8 20 12 1 18 24	7 28 9 11 20 13 1 18 24	10 33 12 14 21 13 2 18 24	13 35 11 17 22 14 2 18 24	16 4 16 16 24 14 2 18 24	19 9 21 15 26 15 1 18 24	22 12 23 17 28 16 1 18 24	25 17 23 20 30 16 1 18 24	28 21 28 24 32 16 1 18 24
27	31 14 32 33 21 12 36 18 24	34 19 35 1 22 12 36 18 24	1 20 34 4 22 12 1 18 24	4 26 3 8 20 12 1 18 24	7 29 9 11 20 13 1 18 24	10 34 12 14 21 13 2 18 24	13 1 11 17 22 14 2 18 24	16 5 16 16 24 14 2 18 24	19 10 21 15 26 15 1 18 24	22 13 23 17 28 16 1 18 24	25 18 23 20 30 16 1 18 24	28 22 28 24 32 16 1 18 24
28	31 16 32 33 21 12 36 18 24	34 21 35 1 22 12 36 18 24	1 22 34 4 22 12 1 18 24	4 27 3 8 20 12 1 18 24	7 31 9 11 20 13 1 18 24	10 35 12 15 21 13 2 18 24	13 2 11 17 22 14 2 18 24	16 7 16 16 24 14 2 18 24	19 11 21 15 26 15 1 18 24	22 15 23 17 28 16 1 18 24	25 20 23 20 30 16 1 18 24	28 24 24 24 33 16 1 18 24
29	31 17 32 33 21 12 36 18 24	1967	1 23 34 5 22 12 1 18 24	4 28 3 8 20 12 1 18 24	7 32 9 12 20 13 1 18 24	10 36 12 15 21 13 2 18 24	13 3 11 17 22 14 2 18 24	16 8 16 16 24 14 2 18 24	19 13 21 15 26 15 1 18 24	22 16 23 17 28 16 1 18 24	25 21 24 21 30 16 1 18 24	28 25 28 24 33 16 1 18 24
30	31 19 32 33 21 12 36 18 24		1 25 35 5 22 12 1 18 24	4 30 3 8 20 12 1 18 24	7 33 9 12 20 13 1 18 24	10 1 12 15 21 13 2 18 24	13 5 11 17 22 14 2 18 24	16 9 17 16 24 14 2 18 24	19 14 21 15 26 15 1 18 24	22 18 23 17 28 16 1 18 24	25 23 24 21 30 16 1 18 24	28 27 28 24 33 16 1 18 24
31	32 20 32 34 21 12 36 18 24		1 26 35 5 22 12 1 18 24		7 34 9 12 20 13 2 18 24		13 6 11 17 22 14 2 18 24	16 10 17 16 24 15 2 18 24		22 19 23 18 28 16 1 18 24		28 28 28 24 33 16 1 18 24

	JAN	FEB	MAR	APR	MAY	JUNE	JULY	AUG	SEPT	OCT	NOV	DEC
1	28 30 29 24 33 16 1 18 24	32 34 33 28 35 16 1 18 24	35 1 32 32 1 15 2 18 24	2 5 36 36 4 15 2 18 24	5 8 5 3 6 15 2 18 24	8 13 10 7 8 15 3 18 24	10 16 9 11 10 16 3 18 24	13 21 13 15 12 16 3 18 24	16 27 18 18 14 17 3 18 24	19 31 22 22 16 18 3 19 24	22 36 21 26 18 18 3 19 24	25 3 25 29 20 18 2 19 24
2	29 31 29 25 33 16 1 18 24	32 36 34 28 35 16 1 18 24	35 2 32 32 2 15 2 18 24	2 6 36 36 4 15 2 18 24	5 9 5 3 6 15 2 18 24	8 14 10 7 8 15 3 18 24	11 18 9 11 10 16 3 18 24	13 23 13 15 12 16 3 18 24	16 28 19 18 14 17 3 18 24	19 32 22 22 16 18 3 19 24	22 1 21 26 18 18 3 19 24	25 4 25 30 20 18 2 19 24
3	29 32 29 25 33 16 1 18 24	32 1 34 28 35 16 1 18 24	35 3 32 32 2 15 2 18 24	2 7 36 36 4 15 2 18 24	5 11 6 3 6 15 2 18 24	8 15 10 7 8 15 3 18 24	11 19 9 11 10 16 3 18 24	14 24 13 15 12 16 3 18 24	17 30 19 19 14 17 3 18 24	19 33 22 22 16 18 3 19 24	23 2 21 26 18 18 3 19 24	26 5 25 30 20 18 2 19 24
4	29 34 29 25 33 16 1 18 24	32 2 34 29 35 16 1 18 24	35 4 32 32 2 15 2 18 24	2 9 36 36 4 15 2 18 24	5 12 6 4 6 15 2 18 24	8 17 10 7 8 15 3 18 24	11 20 9 11 10 16 3 18 24	14 26 13 15 12 16 3 18 24	17 31 19 19 14 17 3 18 24	20 35 22 22 16 18 3 19 24	23 3 21 26 18 18 3 19 24	26 7 26 30 20 18 2 19 24
5	29 35 29 25 33 16 1 18 24	32 3 34 29 36 16 1 18 24	35 5 32 32 2 15 2 18 24	2 10 36 36 4 15 2 18 24	5 13 6 4 6 15 2 18 24	8 18 10 8 8 15 3 18 24	11 22 9 11 10 16 3 18 24	14 27 13 15 12 16 3 18 24	17 32 19 19 14 17 3 18 24	20 36 22 23 16 18 3 19 24	23 5 21 26 18 18 3 19 24	26 8 26 30 20 18 2 19 24
6	29 36 29 25 33 16 1 18 24	32 5 34 29 36 16 1 18 24	35 7 32 32 2 15 2 18 24	2 11 36 36 4 15 2 18 24	5 14 6 4 6 15 2 18 24	8 19 10 8 8 15 3 18 24	11 23 9 11 10 16 3 18 24	14 29 14 15 13 16 3 18 24	17 34 19 19 15 17 3 18 24	20 1 22 23 16 18 3 19 24	23 6 21 26 18 18 3 19 24	26 9 26 30 20 18 2 19 24
7	29 1 30 25 33 16 1 18 24	32 6 34 29 36 16 1 18 24	35 8 32 32 2 15 2 18 24	2 12 36 36 4 15 2 18 24	5 16 7 4 6 15 2 18 24	8 21 10 8 9 15 3 18 24	11 25 9 11 11 16 3 18 24	14 30 14 15 13 16 3 18 24	17 35 19 19 15 17 3 18 24	20 2 22 23 16 18 3 19 24	23 7 21 27 18 18 3 19 24	26 10 26 30 20 18 2 19 24
8	29 3 30 25 33 16 1 18 24	32 7 34 29 36 16 1 18 24	35 9 33 33 2 15 2 18 24	2 13 1 36 4 15 2 18 24	5 17 7 4 6 15 2 18 24	8 22 10 8 9 15 3 18 24	11 26 9 12 11 16 3 18 24	14 31 14 15 13 16 3 18 24	17 36 19 19 15 17 3 18 24	20 4 21 23 17 18 3 19 24	23 8 21 27 18 18 3 19 24	26 11 26 30 20 18 2 19 24
9	29 4 30 25 33 16 1 18 24	32 8 34 29 36 16 1 18 24	35 10 33 33 2 15 2 18 24	2 15 1 1 4 15 2 18 24	5 18 7 4 7 15 2 18 24	8 24 10 8 9 15 3 18 24	11 28 9 12 11 16 3 18 24	14 33 14 16 13 16 3 18 24	17 2 20 19 15 17 3 18 24	20 5 21 23 17 18 3 19 24	23 9 22 27 18 18 3 19 24	26 13 26 30 20 18 2 19 24
10	29 5 30 25 34 16 1 18 24	33 9 34 29 36 16 1 18 24	35 11 33 33 2 15 2 18 24	3 16 1 1 4 15 2 18 24	5 20 7 4 7 15 2 18 24	8 25 10 8 9 15 3 18 24	11 29 9 12 11 16 3 18 24	14 34 15 16 13 16 3 18 24	17 3 20 19 15 17 3 18 24	20 6 21 23 17 18 3 19 24	23 11 22 27 19 18 3 19 24	26 14 26 31 20 18 2 19 24
11	29 6 30 26 34 16 1 18 24	33 11 34 29 36 16 1 18 24	36 13 33 33 2 15 2 18 24	3 18 1 1 5 15 2 18 24	6 21 7 4 7 15 2 18 24	9 27 10 8 9 15 3 18 24	11 31 9 12 11 16 3 18 24	14 36 15 16 13 17 3 18 24	17 4 20 20 15 17 3 18 24	20 7 21 23 17 18 3 19 24	23 12 22 27 19 18 3 19 24	26 15 27 31 20 18 2 19 24
12	30 7 30 26 34 16 1 18 24	33 12 33 29 36 16 1 18 24	36 14 33 33 2 15 2 18 24	3 19 1 1 5 15 2 18 24	6 23 7 5 7 15 2 18 24	9 28 10 8 9 15 3 18 24	11 32 9 12 11 16 3 18 24	14 1 15 16 13 17 3 18 24	17 5 20 20 15 17 3 18 24	20 8 21 23 17 18 3 19 24	23 13 22 27 19 18 3 19 24	27 16 27 31 20 18 2 19 24
13	30 9 31 26 34 16 1 18 24	33 13 33 30 36 16 1 18 24	36 15 33 33 2 15 2 18 24	3 21 2 1 5 15 2 18 24	6 24 8 5 7 15 2 18 24	9 30 10 9 9 15 3 18 24	12 33 9 12 11 16 3 18 24	15 2 15 16 13 17 3 18 24	18 7 20 20 15 17 3 18 24	20 10 21 23 17 18 3 19 24	24 14 22 27 19 18 2 19 24	27 18 27 31 21 18 2 19 24
14	30 10 31 26 34 16 1 18 24	33 15 33 30 36 16 1 18 24	36 17 33 33 2 15 2 18 24	3 22 2 1 5 15 2 18 24	6 26 8 5 7 15 3 18 24	9 31 9 9 9 15 3 18 24	12 35 10 12 11 16 3 18 24	15 3 15 16 13 17 3 18 24	18 8 20 20 15 17 3 18 24	21 11 19 24 17 18 3 19 24	24 15 22 27 19 18 2 19 24	27 19 27 31 21 18 2 19 24
15	30 11 31 26 34 16 1 18 24	33 16 33 30 36 16 1 18 24	36 18 33 33 3 15 2 18 24	3 24 2 1 5 15 2 18 24	6 27 8 5 7 15 3 18 24	9 33 9 9 9 15 3 18 24	12 36 10 12 11 16 3 18 24	15 5 15 16 13 17 3 18 24	18 9 20 20 15 17 3 18 24	21 12 19 24 17 18 3 19 24	24 17 23 28 19 18 2 19 24	27 20 27 31 21 18 2 19 24
16	30 12 31 26 34 16 1 18 24	33 17 33 20 26 16 1 18 24	36 20 33 34 3 15 2 18 24	3 25 2 1 5 15 2 18 24	6 29 8 5 7 15 3 18 24	9 34 9 9 9 16 3 18 24	12 1 10 13 11 16 3 18 24	15 6 16 16 13 17 3 18 24	18 10 20 20 15 17 3 18 24	21 13 19 24 17 18 3 19 24	24 18 23 28 19 18 2 19 24	27 22 27 31 21 18 2 19 24
17	30 14 31 26 34 16 1 18 24	33 19 33 20 26 16 1 18 24	36 21 33 34 3 15 2 18 24	3 27 2 1 5 15 2 18 24	6 30 8 5 7 15 3 18 24	9 35 9 9 9 16 3 18 24	12 3 10 13 11 16 3 18 24	15 7 16 16 13 17 3 18 24	18 11 21 20 15 17 3 18 24	21 15 19 24 17 18 3 19 24	24 19 23 28 19 18 2 19 24	27 23 28 31 21 18 2 19 24
18	30 15 31 26 34 16 1 18 24	33 20 33 30 1 16 1 18 24	36 23 34 34 3 15 2 18 24	3 28 3 2 5 15 2 18 24	6 32 8 5 7 15 3 18 24	9 36 9 9 9 16 3 18 24	12 4 10 13 11 16 3 18 24	15 8 16 17 13 17 3 18 24	18 13 21 20 15 17 3 18 24	21 16 20 24 17 18 3 19 24	24 21 23 28 19 18 2 19 24	27 25 28 31 21 18 2 19 24
19	30 16 32 27 34 16 1 18 24	33 22 33 30 1 16 1 18 24	36 24 34 34 3 15 2 18 24	3 29 3 2 5 15 2 18 24	6 33 8 5 7 15 3 18 24	9 2 9 9 9 16 3 18 24	12 5 10 13 11 16 3 18 24	15 9 16 17 13 17 3 18 24	18 14 21 21 15 17 3 18 24	21 17 20 24 17 18 3 19 24	24 22 23 28 19 18 2 19 24	27 26 28 32 21 18 2 19 24
20	30 18 32 27 34 16 1 18 24	34 23 33 30 1 16 1 18 24	36 26 34 34 3 15 2 18 24	3 31 3 2 5 15 2 18 24	6 34 9 6 7 15 3 18 24	9 3 9 9 9 16 3 18 24	12 6 10 13 11 16 3 18 24	15 10 16 17 13 17 3 18 24	18 15 21 21 15 17 3 18 24	21 19 20 24 17 18 3 19 24	24 24 23 28 19 18 2 19 24	27 28 28 32 21 18 2 19 24
21	31 19 32 27 34 16 1 18 24	34 24 33 31 1 16 2 18 24	1 27 34 34 3 15 2 18 24	4 32 3 2 5 15 2 18 24	6 36 9 6 7 15 3 18 24	9 4 9 9 9 16 3 18 24	12 7 11 13 11 16 3 18 24	15 12 17 17 13 17 3 18 24	18 16 21 21 15 17 3 15 24	21 20 20 24 17 18 3 19 24	24 25 23 28 19 18 2 19 24	27 29 28 32 21 18 2 19 24
22	31 21 32 27 34 16 1 18 24	34 26 32 31 1 16 2 18 24	1 28 34 34 3 15 2 18 24	4 33 3 2 5 15 2 18 24	7 1 9 6 7 15 3 18 24	10 5 9 10 10 16 3 18 24	12 8 11 13 12 16 3 18 24	15 13 17 17 14 17 3 18 24	18 18 21 21 16 17 3 18 24	21 21 20 25 17 18 3 19 24	24 27 24 28 19 18 2 19 24	28 31 28 32 21 18 2 19 24
23	31 22 32 27 35 16 1 18 24	34 27 32 31 1 16 2 18 24	1 30 34 34 3 15 2 18 24	4 35 4 2 5 15 2 18 24	7 2 9 6 8 15 3 18 24	10 6 9 10 10 16 3 18 24	13 10 11 13 12 16 3 18 24	15 14 17 17 14 17 3 18 24	19 19 21 21 16 17 3 18 24	21 23 20 25 17 18 3 19 24	25 28 24 28 19 18 2 19 24	28 32 29 32 21 18 2 19 24
24	31 23 32 27 35 16 1 18 24	34 29 32 31 1 16 2 18 24	1 31 34 35 3 15 2 18 24	4 36 4 2 5 15 2 18 24	7 3 9 6 8 15 3 18 24	10 8 9 10 10 16 3 18 24	13 11 11 14 12 16 3 18 24	16 16 17 17 14 17 3 18 24	19 21 21 21 16 17 3 18 24	22 24 20 25 18 18 3 19 24	25 30 24 29 19 18 2 19 24	28 34 29 32 21 18 2 19 24
25	31 25 33 27 35 16 1 18 24	34 30 32 31 1 16 2 18 24	1 32 34 35 3 15 2 18 24	4 1 4 2 6 15 2 18 24	7 4 9 6 8 15 3 18 24	10 9 9 10 10 16 3 18 24	13 12 11 14 12 16 3 18 24	16 17 17 17 14 17 3 18 24	19 22 21 21 16 17 3 18 24	22 26 20 25 18 18 3 19 24	25 31 24 29 19 18 2 19 24	28 35 29 32 21 18 2 19 24
26	31 26 33 27 35 16 1 18 24	34 31 32 31 1 16 2 18 24	1 34 35 35 3 15 2 18 24	4 2 4 3 6 115 2 18 24	7 6 9 6 8 15 3 18 24	10 10 9 10 10 16 3 18 24	13 13 11 14 12 16 3 18 24	16 18 17 18 14 17 3 18 24	19 24 21 21 16 18 3 18 24	22 27 20 25 18 18 3 19 24	25 33 24 29 20 18 2 19 24	28 36 29 32 31 18 2 19 24
27	31 28 33 28 35 16 1 18 24	34 33 32 31 1 16 2 18 24	1 35 35 35 3 15 2 18 24	4 3 4 3 6 15 2 18 24	7 7 9 6 8 15 3 18 24	10 11 9 10 10 16 3 18 24	13 15 12 14 12 16 3 18 24	16 20 18 18 14 17 3 18 24	19 25 21 22 16 18 3 18 24	22 29 20 25 18 18 3 19 24	25 34 24 29 20 18 2 19 24	28 2 29 32 21 18 2 19 24
28	31 29 33 28 35 16 1 18 24	34 34 32 31 1 15 2 18 24	1 36 35 35 4 15 2 18 24	4 5 5 3 6 15 2 18 24	7 8 9 7 8 15 3 18 24	10 12 9 10 10 16 3 18 24	13 16 12 14 12 16 3 18 24	16 21 18 18 14 17 3 18 24	19 26 21 22 16 18 3 18 24	22 30 20 25 18 18 3 19 24	25 35 25 29 20 18 2 19 24	28 3 29 33 21 18 2 19 24
29	31 30 33 28 35 16 1 18 24	34 35 32 32 1 15 2 18 24	1 1 35 35 4 15 2 18 24	4 6 5 3 6 15 2 18 24	7 9 9 7 8 15 3 18 24	10 14 9 10 10 16 3 18 24	13 17 12 14 12 16 3 18 24	16 22 18 18 14 17 3 18 24	19 28 22 22 16 18 3 19 24	22 32 20 25 18 18 3 19 24	25 1 25 29 20 18 2 19 24	28 4 29 33 21 18 2 19 24
30	31 32 33 28 35 16 1 18 24	**1968**	1 3 35 35 4 15 2 18 24	4 7 5 3 6 15 2 18 24	7 10 10 7 8 15 3 19 24	10 15 9 11 10 16 3 18 24	13 19 12 14 12 16 3 18 24	16 24 18 18 14 17 3 18 24	19 29 22 22 16 18 3 19 24	22 33 20 26 18 18 3 19 24	25 2 25 29 20 18 2 19 24	28 5 30 33 22 18 2 19 24
31	32 33 33 28 35 16 1 18 24		2 4 35 35 4 15 2 18 24		7 12 10 7 8 15 3 19 24		13 20 12 14 12 16 3 18 24	16 25 18 18 14 17 3 18 24		22 34 20 26 18 18 3 19 24		28 6 30 33 22 18 2 19 24

	JAN	FEB	MAR	APR	MAY	JUNE
1	29 8 30 33 22 19 2 19 24	32 12 31 36 23 19 3 19 24	35 13 32 3 25 19 3 19 24	2 17 1 3 26 18 3 19 24	5 21 7 2 26 18 4 19 24	8 26 7 3 25 18 4 18 24
2	29 9 30 33 22 19 2 19 24	32 13 31 36 23 19 3 19 24	35 14 32 3 25 19 3 19 24	2 19 1 3 26 18 3 19 24	5 22 7 2 26 18 4 19 24	8 28 7 3 25 18 4 18 24
3	29 10 30 33 22 19 2 19 24	32 14 31 1 23 19 3 19 24	35 15 32 3 25 19 3 19 24	2 20 1 3 26 18 4 19 24	5 24 7 2 26 18 4 19 24	8 29 7 3 25 18 4 18 24
4	29 11 30 33 22 19 2 19 24	32 16 31 1 23 19 3 19 24	35 17 32 3 25 19 3 19 24	2 21 1 3 26 18 3 19 24	5 25 7 2 26 18 4 19 24	8 31 7 3 25 18 4 18 24
5	29 12 31 34 22 19 2 19 24	32 17 31 1 24 19 3 19 24	35 18 32 3 25 19 3 19 24	2 23 2 3 26 18 3 19 24	5 27 7 2 26 18 4 19 24	8 32 7 3 25 18 4 18 24
6	29 14 31 34 22 19 2 19 24	32 18 31 1 24 19 3 19 24	35 19 31 3 25 19 3 19 24	2 14 2 3 26 18 3 19 24	5 28 7 2 26 18 4 19 24	8 34 7 3 25 18 4 18 24
7	29 15 31 34 22 19 2 19 24	32 20 31 1 24 19 3 19 24	35 21 33 3 25 19 3 19 24	2 26 2 2 26 18 3 19 24	5 30 7 2 26 18 4 19 24	8 35 7 4 25 18 4 18 24
8	29 16 31 34 22 19 2 19 24	32 21 31 1 24 19 3 19 24	35 22 33 3 25 19 3 19 24	2 27 2 2 26 18 3 19 24	5 31 7 2 26 18 4 19 24	8 36 7 4 25 18 4 18 24
9	29 17 31 34 22 19 2 19 24	33 22 31 1 24 19 3 19 24	35 23 33 3 25 19 3 19 24	2 29 2 2 26 18 3 19 24	5 33 7 2 26 18 4 19 24	8 2 7 4 25 18 4 18 24
10	29 19 31 34 22 19 2 19 24	33 24 31 1 24 19 3 19 24	35 25 33 3 25 19 3 19 24	2 30 3 2 26 18 3 19 24	5 34 7 2 26 18 4 19 24	8 3 7 4 25 18 4 18 24
11	30 20 31 34 22 19 2 19 24	33 25 31 1 24 19 3 19 24	36 26 33 3 25 19 3 19 24	3 31 3 2 26 18 3 19 24	6 35 8 2 26 18 4 19 24	8 4 7 4 25 18 4 18 24
12	30 21 32 34 22 19 2 19 24	33 26 31 1 24 19 3 19 24	36 28 33 3 25 19 3 19 24	3 33 3 2 26 18 3 19 24	6 1 8 2 26 18 4 19 24	9 5 7 4 25 18 4 18 24
13	30 23 32 34 22 19 2 19 24	33 28 31 1 24 19 3 19 24	36 29 34 3 25 19 3 19 24	3 34 3 2 26 18 3 18 24	6 2 8 2 26 18 4 19 24	9 7 7 4 25 18 4 18 24
14	30 24 32 35 22 19 2 19 24	33 29 31 2 24 19 3 19 24	36 30 34 3 25 19 3 19 24	3 36 3 2 26 18 3 19 24	6 3 8 2 26 18 4 19 24	9 8 7 4 25 18 4 18 24
15	30 25 32 35 22 19 2 19 24	33 31 31 2 24 19 3 19 24	36 32 34 3 25 19 3 19 24	3 1 4 2 26 18 3 19 24	6 4 8 2 26 18 4 19 24	9 9 7 4 25 18 4 18 24
16	30 27 32 35 22 19 2 19 24	33 32 31 2 24 19 3 19 24	36 33 34 3 25 19 3 19 24	3 2 4 2 26 18 3 19 24	6 6 8 2 26 18 4 19 24	9 10 7 4 25 18 4 18 24
17	30 28 32 35 23 19 2 19 24	33 34 31 2 24 19 3 19 24	36 35 34 3 25 19 3 19 24	3 3 4 2 26 18 3 19 24	6 7 8 2 26 18 4 19 24	9 11 7 4 25 18 4 18 24
18	30 30 32 35 23 19 2 19 24	33 35 31 2 24 19 3 19 24	36 36 34 3 25 19 3 19 24	3 5 4 2 26 18 3 19 24	6 8 8 2 26 18 4 19 24	9 12 7 5 25 18 4 18 24
19	30 31 32 35 23 19 2 19 24	34 1 31 2 24 19 3 19 24	36 1 34 3 25 19 3 19 24	3 6 4 2 26 18 3 19 24	6 9 8 2 26 18 4 19 24	9 14 7 5 25 18 4 18 24
20	30 33 32 35 23 19 2 19 24	34 2 31 2 24 19 3 19 24	36 3 35 3 25 19 3 19 24	3 7 5 2 26 18 3 19 24	6 10 8 2 26 18 4 19 24	9 15 7 5 25 18 4 18 24
21	31 34 32 35 23 19 2 19 24	34 3 31 2 24 19 3 19 24	1 4 35 3 25 19 3 19 24	4 8 5 2 26 18 3 19 24	6 12 8 2 26 18 4 18 24	9 16 7 5 25 18 4 18 24
22	31 36 32 35 23 19 2 19 24	34 4 31 2 24 19 3 19 24	1 5 35 3 25 19 3 19 24	4 10 5 2 26 18 3 19 24	7 13 8 2 26 18 4 18 24	10 17 7 5 25 18 4 18 24
23	31 1 32 35 23 19 2 19 24	34 6 31 2 24 19 3 19 24	1 6 35 3 26 19 3 19 24	4 11 5 2 26 18 3 19 24	7 14 8 2 26 18 4 18 24	10 19 7 5 25 18 4 18 24
24	31 2 32 36 23 19 2 19 24	34 7 31 2 24 19 3 19 24	1 8 35 3 26 19 3 19 24	4 12 5 2 26 18 3 19 24	7 15 8 2 26 18 4 18 24	10 20 8 5 25 18 4 18 24
25	31 4 32 36 23 19 2 19 24	34 8 31 2 24 19 3 19 24	1 9 36 3 26 19 3 19 24	4 13 6 2 26 18 3 19 24	7 16 8 3 26 18 4 18 24	10 21 8 5 25 18 4 19 24
26	31 5 32 36 23 19 2 19 24	34 9 32 2 25 19 3 19 24	1 10 36 3 26 19 3 19 24	4 14 6 2 26 18 3 19 24	7 18 7 3 26 18 4 18 24	10 23 8 5 25 18 4 19 24
27	31 6 32 36 23 19 2 19 24	34 10 32 3 25 19 3 19 24	1 11 36 3 26 19 3 19 24	4 16 6 2 26 18 3 19 24	7 19 7 3 26 18 4 18 24	10 24 8 5 25 18 4 19 24
28	31 7 32 36 23 19 2 19 24	34 12 32 3 25 19 3 19 24	1 12 36 3 26 19 3 19 24	4 16 6 2 26 18 3 19 24	7 20 7 3 26 18 4 18 24	10 25 8 6 25 18 4 19 24
29	31 8 31 36 23 19 3 19 24		1 14 36 3 26 19 3 19 24	4 17 6 2 26 18 3 19 24	7 22 7 3 26 18 4 18 24	10 27 8 6 25 18 4 19 24
30	31 10 31 36 23 19 3 19 24	1969	1 15 36 3 26 19 3 19 24	4 18 6 2 26 18 3 19 24	7 23 7 3 26 18 4 18 24	10 29 8 6 25 18 4 19 24
31	32 11 31 36 23 19 3 19 24		2 16 1 3 26 19 3 19 24		7 25 7 3 26 18 4 18 24	

	JULY	AUG	SEPT	OCT	NOV	DEC
1	10 30 8 6 25 18 4 19 24	13 35 14 9 25 19 4 19 24	16 4 19 13 26 19 4 19 24	19 8 19 16 28 20 4 19 24	22 12 21 20 30 21 4 19 24	25 15 26 24 32 21 4 19 24
2	10 32 8 6 25 18 4 19 24	13 1 15 9 25 19 4 19 24	16 5 19 13 26 19 4 19 24	19 9 19 17 28 20 4 19 24	22 13 22 20 30 21 4 19 24	25 16 26 24 32 21 4 19 24
3	11 33 9 6 25 18 4 19 24	14 2 15 9 25 19 4 19 24	17 7 19 13 26 19 4 19 24	19 10 19 17 28 20 4 19 24	23 14 22 21 30 21 4 19 24	26 18 26 24 33 21 4 19 24
4	11 34 9 6 25 18 4 19 24	14 3 15 10 25 19 4 19 24	17 8 19 13 26 19 4 19 24	20 11 19 17 28 20 4 19 24	23 15 22 21 30 21 4 19 24	26 19 27 24 33 21 4 19 24
5	11 36 9 6 25 18 4 19 24	14 5 15 10 25 19 4 19 24	17 9 19 13 27 19 4 19 24	20 12 19 17 28 20 4 19 24	23 17 22 21 31 21 4 19 24	26 20 27 25 33 21 4 19 24
6	11 1 9 6 25 18 4 19 24	14 6 15 10 25 19 4 19 24	17 10 20 13 27 19 4 19 24	20 14 19 17 28 20 4 19 24	23 18 22 21 31 21 4 19 24	26 21 27 25 33 21 4 19 24
7	11 3 9 7 25 18 4 19 24	14 7 15 10 25 19 4 19 24	17 12 20 14 27 19 4 19 24	20 15 19 17 29 20 4 19 24	23 19 22 21 31 21 4 19 24	26 23 27 25 33 21 4 19 24
8	11 4 9 7 25 18 4 19 24	14 8 16 10 25 19 4 19 24	17 13 20 14 27 19 4 19 24	20 16 18 17 29 20 4 19 24	23 21 23 21 31 21 4 19 24	26 24 27 25 33 21 4 19 24
9	11 5 10 7 25 18 4 19 24	14 10 16 10 25 19 4 19 24	17 14 20 14 27 19 4 19 24	20 17 18 17 29 20 4 19 24	23 22 23 21 31 21 4 19 24	26 26 28 25 33 21 4 19 24
10	11 6 10 7 25 18 4 19 24	14 11 16 10 25 19 4 19 24	17 15 20 14 27 20 4 19 24	20 18 19 18 29 20 4 19 24	23 23 23 21 31 21 4 19 24	26 27 28 25 33 21 4 19 24
11	11 7 10 7 25 18 4 19 24	14 12 16 10 25 19 4 19 24	17 16 20 14 27 20 4 19 24	20 20 19 18 29 20 4 19 24	23 25 23 22 31 21 4 19 24	26 29 28 25 33 21 4 19 24
12	11 9 10 7 25 18 4 19 24	14 13 16 11 25 19 4 19 24	17 18 29 14 27 20 4 19 24	20 21 19 18 29 20 4 19 24	23 26 23 22 31 21 4 19 24	26 30 28 25 33 21 4 19 24
13	12 10 10 7 25 18 4 19 24	15 14 16 11 25 19 4 19 24	18 19 20 14 27 20 4 19 24	20 22 19 18 29 20 4 19 24	24 28 23 22 31 21 4 19 24	27 32 28 26 33 21 4 19 24
14	12 11 11 7 25 18 4 19 24	15 15 17 11 25 19 4 19 24	18 20 20 14 27 20 4 19 24	21 24 19 18 29 20 4 19 24	24 29 24 22 31 21 4 19 24	27 33 28 26 33 21 4 19 24
15	12 12 11 7 25 18 4 19 24	15 17 17 11 26 19 4 19 24	18 21 20 15 27 20 4 19 24	21 25 19 18 29 20 4 19 24	24 31 24 22 31 21 4 19 24	27 34 28 26 33 21 4 19 24
16	12 13 11 7 25 19 4 19 24	15 18 17 11 26 19 4 19 24	18 23 20 15 27 20 4 19 24	21 27 19 18 29 20 4 19 24	24 32 24 22 31 21 4 19 24	27 36 28 26 34 21 4 19 24
17	12 15 11 8 25 19 4 19 24	15 19 17 11 26 19 4 19 24	18 24 20 15 27 20 4 19 24	21 28 19 18 29 20 4 19 24	24 33 24 22 31 21 4 19 24	27 1 29 26 34 22 4 19 24
18	12 16 11 8 25 19 4 19 24	15 20 17 11 26 19 4 19 24	18 26 20 15 27 20 4 19 24	21 29 19 18 29 20 4 19 24	24 35 24 22 31 21 4 19 24	27 2 29 26 34 22 4 19 24
19	12 17 12 8 25 19 4 19 24	15 22 17 11 26 19 4 19 24	18 27 20 15 27 20 4 19 24	21 31 19 19 29 20 4 19 24	24 36 24 23 32 21 4 19 24	27 4 29 26 34 22 4 19 24
20	12 18 12 8 25 19 4 19 24	15 23 18 11 26 19 4 19 24	18 30 20 15 27 20 4 19 24	21 32 19 19 29 20 4 19 24	24 1 24 23 32 21 4 19 24	27 5 29 26 34 22 4 19 24
21	12 19 12 8 25 19 4 19 24	15 24 18 12 26 19 4 19 24	18 30 20 15 27 20 4 19 24	21 34 20 19 29 20 4 19 24	24 3 25 23 32 21 4 19 24	27 6 29 27 34 22 4 19 24
22	12 21 12 8 25 19 4 19 24	15 26 18 12 26 19 4 19 24	18 31 20 15 28 20 4 19 24	21 35 20 19 30 20 4 19 24	24 4 25 23 32 21 4 19 24	27 8 29 27 34 22 4 19 24
23	12 22 13 8 25 19 4 19 24	15 27 18 12 26 19 4 19 24	18 33 20 15 28 20 4 19 23	21 36 20 19 30 20 4 19 24	25 5 25 23 32 21 4 19 24	28 9 29 27 34 22 4 19 24
24	13 23 13 8 25 19 4 19 24	16 29 18 12 26 19 4 19 24	19 34 20 16 28 20 4 19 24	22 2 20 19 30 20 4 19 24	25 7 25 23 32 21 4 19 24	28 10 30 27 34 22 4 19 24
25	13 25 13 8 25 19 4 19 24	16 30 18 12 26 19 4 19 24	19 36 20 16 28 20 4 19 24	22 3 20 19 30 20 4 20 24	25 8 25 23 32 21 4 19 24	28 11 30 27 34 22 4 19 24
26	13 26 13 9 25 19 4 19 24	16 32 18 12 26 19 4 19 24	19 1 19 16 28 20 4 19 24	22 5 20 20 30 20 4 19 24	25 9 25 23 32 21 4 19 24	28 12 20 27 34 22 4 19 24
27	13 28 13 9 25 19 4 19 24	16 33 18 12 26 19 4 19 24	19 2 19 16 28 20 4 19 24	22 6 21 20 30 21 4 19 24	25 10 26 24 32 21 4 19 24	28 14 30 27 34 22 4 19 24
28	13 29 14 9 25 19 4 19 24	16 35 19 12 26 19 4 19 24	19 4 19 16 28 20 4 19 24	22 7 21 20 30 21 4 19 24	25 12 26 24 32 21 4 19 24	28 15 30 27 34 22 4 19 24
29	13 31 14 9 25 19 4 19 24	16 36 19 16 26 19 4 19 24	19 5 19 16 28 20 4 19 24	22 8 21 20 30 21 4 19 24	25 13 26 24 32 21 4 19 24	28 16 30 28 34 22 4 19 24
30	13 32 14 9 25 19 4 19 24	16 2 19 13 26 19 4 19 24	19 6 19 16 28 20 4 19 24	22 10 21 20 30 21 4 19 24	25 14 26 24 32 21 4 19 24	28 17 30 28 35 22 4 19 24
31	13 34 14 9 25 19 4 19 24	16 3 19 13 26 19 4 19 24		22 11 21 20 30 21 4 19 24		28 18 30 28 35 22 4 19 24

	JAN	FEB	MAR	APR	MAY	JUNE	JULY	AUG	SEPT	OCT	NOV	DEC
1	29 20 30 28 35 22 4 19 24	32 24 29 32 1 22 4 19 25	34 25 33 35 3 22 4 19 25	2 31 2 3 5 22 4 19 25	5 35 6 7 7 21 5 19 25	8 4 5 11 9 21 5 19 24	10 7 10 14 11 21 5 19 24	13 12 16 18 13 21 6 19 24	16 16 18 21 17 22 6 19 24	19 20 17 23 17 22 6 19 24	22 24 23 24 19 23 6 20 24	25 28 27 22 21 24 5 20 25
2	29 21 30 28 35 22 4 19 24	32 26 29 32 1 22 4 19 25	35 27 33 35 3 22 4 19 25	2 32 3 3 5 22 4 19 25	5 36 6 7 7 21 5 19 25	8 5 5 11 9 21 5 19 24	10 9 10 14 11 21 5 19 24	13 13 16 18 13 21 6 19 24	16 18 18 21 15 22 6 19 24	19 21 18 23 17 22 6 19 24	22 26 23 24 19 23 5 20 24	25 29 27 22 21 24 5 20 25
3	29 22 30 28 35 22 4 19 24	32 27 29 32 1 22 4 19 24	35 28 33 35 3 22 4 19 25	2 34 3 3 5 22 4 19 25	5 1 6 7 7 21 5 19 25	8 6 5 11 10 21 5 19 24	11 10 10 14 12 21 5 19 24	14 14 16 18 14 21 6 19 24	17 19 18 21 15 22 6 19 24	19 22 18 23 17 22 6 19 24	23 27 23 24 19 23 5 20 24	26 31 27 22 21 24 5 20 25
4	29 24 30 28 35 22 4 19 24	32 29 29 32 1 22 4 19 25	35 30 33 36 3 22 4 19 25	2 35 3 4 5 22 4 19 25	5 3 6 7 8 21 5 19 24	8 8 5 11 10 21 5 19 24	11 11 10 15 12 21 5 19 24	14 16 16 18 14 21 6 19 24	17 20 18 21 16 22 6 19 24	20 23 18 24 17 22 6 19 24	23 28 23 24 19 23 5 20 24	26 32 28 22 21 24 5 20 25
5	29 25 30 28 35 22 4 19 24	32 30 30 32 1 22 4 19 25	35 31 33 36 3 22 4 19 25	2 36 3 4 6 22 4 19 25	5 4 6 7 8 21 5 19 24	8 9 5 11 10 21 5 19 24	11 12 11 15 12 21 5 19 24	14 17 16 18 14 21 6 19 24	17 21 18 24 16 22 6 19 24	20 25 18 24 18 22 6 19 24	23 30 23 24 19 23 5 20 24	26 34 28 23 21 24 5 20 25
6	29 26 30 29 35 22 4 19 25	32 32 30 32 1 22 4 19 25	35 33 34 36 3 22 4 19 25	2 2 3 4 6 22 4 19 25	5 5 6 7 8 21 5 19 24	8 10 6 11 10 21 5 19 24	11 13 11 15 12 21 5 19 24	14 18 16 18 14 21 6 19 24	17 22 18 21 16 22 6 19 24	20 26 18 24 18 22 6 19 24	23 31 23 24 20 23 5 20 24	26 35 28 23 21 24 5 20 25
7	29 28 30 29 35 22 4 19 25	32 33 30 33 1 22 4 19 25	35 34 34 36 3 22 4 19 25	2 3 4 4 6 22 4 19 25	5 7 5 8 8 21 5 19 24	8 11 6 11 10 21 5 19 24	11 15 11 15 12 21 5 19 24	14 19 16 18 14 21 6 19 24	17 24 18 21 16 22 6 19 24	20 27 18 24 18 22 6 19 24	23 33 24 23 20 23 5 20 25	26 36 28 23 22 24 5 20 25
8	29 29 30 29 35 22 4 19 25	32 35 30 33 2 22 4 19 25	35 36 34 36 4 22 4 19 25	2 5 4 4 6 22 4 19 25	5 8 5 8 8 21 5 19 24	8 13 6 11 10 21 5 19 24	11 16 11 15 12 21 5 19 24	14 20 17 18 14 21 6 19 24	17 25 18 22 16 22 6 19 24	20 29 19 24 18 22 6 19 24	23 34 24 23 20 23 5 20 25	26 2 28 23 22 24 5 20 25
9	29 31 30 29 35 22 4 19 25	32 36 30 33 2 22 4 19 25	35 1 34 36 4 22 4 19 25	2 6 4 4 6 22 4 19 25	5 9 5 8 8 21 5 19 24	8 14 6 12 10 21 5 19 24	11 17 11 15 12 21 5 19 24	14 22 17 19 14 21 6 19 24	17 26 18 22 16 22 6 19 24	20 30 19 24 18 22 6 19 24	23 35 24 23 20 23 5 20 25	26 3 28 23 22 24 5 20 25
10	29 32 30 29 35 22 4 19 25	33 2 30 33 2 22 4 19 25	35 2 34 36 4 22 4 19 25	2 7 4 4 6 22 4 19 25	5 11 5 8 8 21 5 19 24	8 15 6 12 10 21 5 19 24	11 18 12 15 12 21 5 19 24	15 23 17 19 14 21 6 19 24	17 28 18 22 16 22 6 19 24	20 31 19 24 18 22 6 19 24	23 1 24 23 20 23 5 20 25	26 5 28 23 22 24 5 20 25
11	30 34 30 29 35 22 4 19 25	33 3 30 33 2 22 4 19 25	36 4 34 1 4 22 4 19 25	3 9 4 4 6 22 4 19 25	5 12 5 8 8 21 5 19 24	8 16 6 12 10 21 5 19 24	11 19 12 15 12 21 6 19 24	15 24 17 19 14 21 6 19 24	17 29 18 22 16 22 6 19 24	20 33 19 24 18 23 6 19 24	23 2 24 23 20 23 5 20 25	26 6 28 23 22 24 5 20 25
12	30 35 30 29 36 22 4 19 25	33 4 30 33 2 22 4 19 25	36 5 35 1 4 22 4 19 25	3 10 4 5 6 22 4 19 25	6 13 5 8 8 21 5 19 24	9 17 6 12 10 21 5 19 24	11 21 12 15 12 21 6 19 24	15 25 17 19 14 21 6 19 24	17 31 18 22 16 22 6 19 24	20 34 19 24 18 23 6 19 24	23 4 24 23 20 23 5 20 25	26 7 28 23 22 24 5 20 25
13	30 1 30 29 36 22 4 19 25	33 6 30 33 2 22 4 19 25	36 7 35 1 4 22 4 19 25	3 11 5 5 6 22 4 19 25	6 14 5 8 8 21 5 19 24	9 19 6 12 10 21 5 19 24	12 22 12 16 12 21 6 19 24	15 27 17 19 14 21 6 19 24	17 32 17 22 16 22 6 19 24	20 36 19 24 18 23 6 19 24	24 5 24 23 20 23 5 20 25	27 9 28 23 22 24 5 20 25
14	30 2 30 30 36 22 4 19 25	33 7 31 33 2 22 4 19 25	36 9 35 1 4 22 4 19 25	3 12 5 5 6 22 4 19 25	6 15 5 8 8 21 5 19 24	9 20 7 12 10 21 5 19 24	12 23 12 16 12 21 6 19 24	15 28 17 19 14 21 6 19 24	18 34 17 22 16 22 6 19 24	21 1 20 24 18 23 6 19 24	24 7 25 23 20 23 5 20 25	27 10 28 23 22 24 5 20 25
15	30 3 30 30 36 22 4 19 25	33 8 31 34 2 22 4 19 25	36 10 35 1 4 22 4 19 25	3 13 5 5 6 22 4 19 25	6 17 5 9 8 21 5 19 24	9 21 7 12 10 21 5 19 24	12 25 13 16 12 21 6 19 24	15 30 17 19 14 21 6 19 24	18 35 17 22 16 22 6 19 24	21 3 20 24 18 23 6 19 24	24 8 25 23 20 23 5 20 25	27 11 28 23 22 24 5 20 25
16	30 5 29 30 36 22 4 19 25	33 9 31 34 2 22 4 19 25	36 11 35 1 4 22 4 19 25	3 15 5 5 6 22 4 19 25	6 18 5 9 8 21 5 19 24	9 22 7 12 10 21 5 19 24	12 26 12 16 12 21 6 19 24	15 31 18 19 14 22 6 19 24	18 1 17 22 16 22 6 19 24	21 4 20 24 18 23 6 20 24	24 9 25 23 20 23 5 20 25	27 13 28 23 22 25 5 20 25
17	30 6 29 30 36 22 4 19 25	33 11 31 34 2 22 4 19 25	36 12 35 1 4 22 4 19 25	3 16 5 5 6 22 5 19 25	6 19 5 9 8 21 5 19 24	9 24 7 13 10 21 5 19 24	12 27 13 16 12 21 6 19 24	15 33 18 19 14 22 6 19 24	18 2 17 22 16 22 6 19 24	21 6 20 24 18 23 6 20 24	24 10 25 23 20 23 5 20 25	27 14 28 23 22 24 5 20 25
18	30 7 29 30 36 22 4 19 25	33 12 31 34 2 22 4 19 25	36 14 36 1 4 22 4 19 25	3 17 5 9 8 22 5 19 25	6 20 5 9 8 21 5 19 24	9 25 7 13 11 21 5 19 24	12 29 13 16 12 21 6 19 24	15 34 18 20 14 22 6 19 24	18 3 17 22 16 22 6 19 24	21 7 20 24 18 23 6 20 24	24 12 25 23 20 23 5 20 25	27 15 28 23 22 24 5 20 25
19	30 8 29 30 36 22 4 19 25	33 13 31 34 2 22 4 19 25	36 15 36 2 4 22 4 19 25	3 18 5 5 7 22 5 19 25	6 22 5 9 9 21 5 19 24	9 27 7 13 11 21 5 19 24	12 30 13 16 13 21 6 19 24	15 36 18 20 15 22 6 19 24	18 5 17 23 17 22 6 19 24	21 8 20 24 18 23 6 20 24	24 13 25 23 20 23 5 20 25	27 16 28 23 22 24 5 20 25
20	30 10 29 30 36 22 4 19 25	34 14 31 34 2 22 4 19 25	36 16 36 2 4 22 4 19 25	3 19 5 6 7 22 5 19 25	6 23 5 9 9 21 5 19 24	9 28 8 13 11 21 5 19 24	12 32 14 16 13 21 6 19 24	15 1 18 20 15 22 6 19 24	18 6 17 23 17 22 6 19 24	21 10 21 24 18 23 6 20 24	24 14 26 23 20 23 5 20 25	27 17 28 23 22 24 5 20 25
21	31 11 29 30 36 22 4 19 25	34 15 32 34 2 22 4 19 25	36 17 36 2 4 22 4 19 25	4 21 5 6 7 22 5 19 25	6 24 5 9 9 21 5 19 24	9 29 8 13 11 21 5 19 24	12 33 14 16 13 21 6 19 24	15 3 18 20 15 22 6 19 24	18 8 17 23 17 22 6 19 24	21 11 21 24 19 23 6 20 24	24 15 26 23 21 23 5 20 25	27 18 28 23 22 24 5 20 25
22	31 12 29 31 36 22 4 19 25	34 17 32 34 3 22 4 19 25	1 18 36 2 5 22 4 19 25	4 22 6 6 7 22 5 19 25	7 26 5 9 9 21 5 19 24	10 31 8 13 11 21 5 19 24	12 35 14 17 13 21 6 19 24	15 4 18 20 15 22 6 19 24	18 9 17 23 17 22 6 19 24	21 12 21 24 19 23 6 20 24	24 17 26 23 21 23 5 20 25	27 20 28 23 22 24 5 20 25
23	31 13 29 31 36 22 4 19 25	34 18 32 35 3 22 4 19 25	1 20 1 2 5 22 4 19 25	4 23 6 6 7 22 5 19 25	7 27 5 10 9 21 5 19 24	10 32 8 13 11 21 5 19 24	12 36 14 17 13 21 6 19 24	15 5 18 20 15 22 6 19 24	18 10 17 23 17 22 6 19 24	21 13 21 24 19 23 6 20 24	25 18 26 23 21 23 5 20 25	28 21 28 23 23 24 5 20 25
24	31 14 29 31 36 22 4 19 25	34 19 32 35 3 22 4 19 25	1 21 1 2 5 22 4 19 25	4 25 6 6 7 22 5 19 25	7 29 5 10 9 21 5 19 24	10 34 8 13 11 21 5 19 24	13 2 14 17 13 21 6 19 24	16 7 18 20 15 22 6 19 24	19 11 17 23 17 22 6 19 24	22 15 21 24 19 23 6 20 24	25 19 26 23 21 23 5 20 25	28 22 28 23 23 24 5 20 25
25	31 16 29 31 1 22 4 19 25	34 20 32 35 3 22 4 19 25	1 22 1 2 5 22 4 19 25	4 26 6 6 7 22 5 19 25	7 30 5 10 9 21 5 19 24	10 35 8 13 11 21 5 19 24	13 3 14 17 13 21 6 19 24	16 8 18 20 15 22 6 19 24	19 13 17 23 17 22 6 19 24	22 16 21 24 19 23 6 20 24	25 20 26 23 21 23 5 20 25	28 23 28 23 23 24 5 20 25
26	31 17 29 31 1 22 4 19 25	34 21 32 35 3 22 4 19 25	1 23 1 2 5 22 4 19 25	4 27 6 6 7 22 5 19 25	7 31 5 10 9 21 5 19 24	10 1 9 14 11 21 5 19 24	13 4 15 17 13 21 6 19 24	16 9 18 20 15 22 6 19 24	19 14 17 23 17 22 6 19 24	22 17 22 24 19 23 6 20 24	25 21 26 23 21 24 5 20 25	28 25 27 24 23 24 5 20 25
27	31 18 29 31 1 22 4 19 25	34 23 32 35 3 22 4 19 25	1 25 1 3 5 22 4 19 25	4 29 6 6 7 22 5 19 25	7 33 5 10 9 21 5 19 24	10 2 9 14 11 21 5 19 24	13 6 15 17 13 21 6 19 24	16 10 18 20 15 22 6 19 24	19 15 17 23 17 22 6 19 24	22 18 22 24 19 23 6 20 24	25 23 27 23 21 24 5 20 25	28 26 27 24 23 24 5 20 25
28	31 19 29 31 1 22 4 19 25	34 24 33 35 3 22 4 19 25	1 26 2 3 5 22 4 19 25	4 30 6 7 7 22 5 19 25	7 34 5 10 9 21 5 19 24	10 3 9 14 11 21 5 19 24	13 7 15 17 13 21 6 19 24	16 12 18 21 15 22 6 19 24	19 16 17 23 17 22 6 19 24	22 19 22 24 19 23 6 20 24	25 24 27 22 21 24 5 20 25	28 27 27 24 23 24 5 20 25
29	31 20 29 31 1 22 4 19 25		1 27 2 3 5 22 4 19 25	4 32 6 7 7 22 5 19 25	7 36 5 10 9 21 5 19 24	10 5 9 14 11 21 5 19 24	13 8 15 17 13 21 6 19 24	16 13 18 21 15 22 6 19 24	19 17 17 23 17 22 6 19 24	22 21 22 24 19 23 6 20 24	25 25 27 22 21 24 5 20 25	28 29 27 24 23 24 5 20 25
30	31 22 29 32 1 22 4 19 25	1970	1 28 2 3 5 22 4 19 25	4 33 6 7 7 22 5 19 25	7 1 5 10 9 21 5 19 24	10 6 9 14 11 21 5 19 24	13 10 15 17 13 21 6 19 24	16 14 18 21 15 22 6 19 24	19 18 17 23 17 22 6 19 24	22 22 22 24 19 23 6 20 24	25 26 27 22 21 24 5 20 25	28 30 27 24 23 24 5 20 25
31	32 23 29 32 1 22 4 19 25		1 29 2 3 5 22 4 19 25		7 2 5 10 9 21 5 19 24		13 11 15 18 13 21 6 19 24	16 15 18 21 15 22 6 19 24		22 23 22 24 19 23 6 20 24		28 32 27 24 23 24 5 20 25

	JAN	FEB	MAR	APR	MAY	JUNE	JULY	AUG	SEPT	OCT	NOV	DEC
1	28 33 28 24 23 / 24 5 20 25	32 2 29 27 25 / 25 5 20 25	34 3 34 30 27 / 25 5 20 25	1 8 3 34 29 / 25 5 20 25	4 12 3 1 30 / 25 6 19 25	7 16 5 5 32 / 24 6 19 25	10 20 11 9 33 / 24 7 19 24	13 24 16 12 32 / 24 7 19 24	16 29 15 16 32 / 24 7 20 24	19 32 19 20 32 / 25 7 20 24	22 2 24 24 33 / 25 7 20 25	25 5 27 28 35 / 26 7 20 25
2	28 35 27 24 23 / 24 5 20 25	32 4 30 27 25 / 25 5 20 25	34 5 34 30 27 / 25 5 20 25	2 10 3 34 29 / 25 5 20 25	4 13 3 1 30 / 25 6 19 25	7 18 5 5 32 / 24 6 19 25	10 21 12 9 33 / 24 7 19 24	13 25 16 13 32 / 24 7 19 24	16 30 15 16 32 / 24 7 20 24	19 34 19 20 32 / 25 7 20 24	22 3 24 24 33 / 25 7 20 25	25 7 27 28 35 / 26 7 20 25
3	29 36 27 24 23 / 24 5 20 25	32 5 30 27 25 / 25 5 20 25	35 6 34 30 27 / 25 5 20 25	2 11 4 34 29 / 25 5 20 25	5 14 3 2 30 / 25 6 19 25	8 19 6 5 32 / 24 6 19 25	10 22 12 9 33 / 24 7 19 24	13 26 16 13 32 / 24 7 19 24	16 31 15 17 32 / 24 7 20 24	19 35 19 20 32 / 25 7 20 25	22 5 24 24 33 / 25 7 20 25	25 8 27 28 35 / 26 7 20 25
4	29 1 27 24 23 / 24 5 20 25	32 7 30 27 25 / 25 5 20 25	35 8 34 30 27 / 25 5 20 25	2 12 4 34 29 / 25 5 20 25	5 16 3 2 30 / 25 6 19 25	8 20 6 5 32 / 24 6 19 25	11 23 12 9 33 / 24 7 19 24	13 28 16 13 32 / 24 7 19 24	16 32 15 17 32 / 24 7 20 24	19 1 19 20 32 / 25 7 20 25	22 6 24 24 33 / 25 7 20 25	26 10 27 28 35 / 26 7 20 25
5	29 3 27 24 23 / 24 5 20 25	32 8 30 27 25 / 25 5 20 25	35 9 35 31 27 / 25 5 20 25	2 14 4 34 29 / 25 5 20 25	5 17 3 2 30 / 25 6 19 25	8 21 6 6 32 / 24 6 19 25	11 24 12 9 33 / 24 7 19 24	14 29 16 13 32 / 24 7 19 24	17 34 15 17 32 / 24 7 20 24	20 2 19 21 32 / 25 7 20 25	23 8 24 24 33 / 25 7 20 25	26 11 27 28 35 / 26 7 20 25
6	29 4 27 24 23 / 24 5 20 25	32 9 30 27 25 / 25 5 20 25	35 10 35 31 27 / 25 5 20 25	2 15 4 34 29 / 25 5 20 25	5 18 3 2 31 / 25 6 19 25	8 22 6 6 32 / 24 6 19 25	11 26 12 9 33 / 24 7 19 24	14 31 16 13 32 / 24 7 19 24	17 36 15 17 32 / 24 7 20 24	20 4 19 21 32 / 25 7 20 25	23 9 24 25 33 / 25 7 20 25	26 12 27 28 35 / 26 7 20 25
7	29 6 27 24 23 / 24 5 20 25	32 10 30 28 25 / 25 5 20 25	35 11 35 31 27 / 25 5 20 25	2 16 4 34 29 / 25 5 20 25	5 19 3 2 31 / 25 6 19 25	8 24 6 6 32 / 24 6 19 25	11 27 13 9 33 / 24 7 19 24	14 32 16 13 32 / 24 7 19 24	17 1 15 17 32 / 24 7 20 24	20 5 20 21 32 / 25 7 20 25	23 10 25 25 33 / 25 7 20 25	26 14 27 28 35 / 26 7 20 25
8	29 7 27 24 23 / 24 5 20 25	32 12 30 28 25 / 25 5 20 25	35 13 25 31 27 / 25 5 20 25	2 17 4 35 29 / 25 6 20 25	5 20 3 2 31 / 25 6 19 25	8 25 7 6 32 / 24 6 19 25	11 28 13 10 33 / 24 7 19 24	14 33 16 13 32 / 24 7 19 24	17 2 15 17 32 / 24 7 20 24	20 7 20 21 32 / 25 7 20 25	23 11 25 25 33 / 25 7 20 25	26 15 27 29 35 / 26 7 20 25
9	29 8 27 25 24 / 24 5 20 25	32 13 31 28 25 / 25 5 20 25	35 14 35 31 27 / 25 5 20 25	2 18 4 35 29 / 25 6 20 25	5 21 3 2 31 / 25 6 19 25	8 26 7 6 32 / 24 6 19 25	11 30 13 10 33 / 24 7 19 24	14 35 16 13 32 / 24 7 19 24	17 4 15 17 32 / 24 7 20 24	20 8 20 21 32 / 25 7 20 25	23 13 25 25 34 / 25 7 20 25	26 16 27 29 35 / 26 7 20 25
10	29 9 27 25 24 / 24 5 20 25	32 14 31 28 26 / 25 5 20 25	35 15 36 31 27 / 25 5 20 25	2 19 4 35 29 / 25 6 20 25	5 23 3 2 31 / 25 6 19 25	8 27 7 6 32 / 24 6 19 25	11 31 13 10 33 / 24 7 19 24	14 36 16 14 32 / 24 7 19 24	17 6 15 17 32 / 24 7 20 24	20 10 20 21 32 / 25 7 20 25	23 14 25 25 34 / 25 7 20 25	26 17 27 29 35 / 26 7 20 25
11	29 11 27 25 24 / 24 5 20 25	33 15 31 28 26 / 25 5 20 25	35 16 36 31 27 / 25 5 20 25	2 21 4 35 29 / 25 6 20 25	5 24 3 2 31 / 25 6 19 25	8 29 7 6 32 / 24 6 19 25	11 33 13 10 33 / 24 7 19 24	14 2 16 14 32 / 24 7 19 24	17 7 15 18 32 / 24 7 20 24	20 11 20 21 32 / 25 7 20 25	23 15 25 25 34 / 25 7 20 25	26 19 27 29 35 / 26 7 20 25
12	30 12 27 25 24 / 24 5 20 25	33 16 31 28 26 / 25 5 20 25	35 17 36 31 27 / 25 5 20 25	3 22 4 35 29 / 25 6 20 25	5 25 3 3 31 / 25 6 19 25	8 30 7 6 32 / 24 6 19 25	11 34 13 10 33 / 24 7 19 24	14 3 16 14 32 / 24 7 19 24	17 9 15 18 32 / 24 7 20 24	20 12 20 21 32 / 25 7 20 25	23 17 25 25 34 / 26 7 20 25	26 20 27 29 35 / 26 7 20 25
13	30 13 27 25 24 / 24 5 20 25	33 18 31 28 26 / 25 5 20 25	36 19 36 31 27 / 25 5 20 25	3 23 4 35 29 / 25 6 20 25	6 27 3 3 31 / 25 6 19 25	9 32 8 6 32 / 24 6 19 25	11 35 14 10 33 / 24 7 19 24	14 5 16 14 32 / 24 7 19 24	17 10 16 18 32 / 24 7 20 24	20 13 21 22 32 / 25 7 20 25	23 18 25 25 34 / 26 7 20 25	26 21 26 29 36 / 26 7 20 25
14	30 14 27 25 24 / 24 5 20 25	33 19 31 28 26 / 25 5 20 25	36 20 36 32 27 / 25 5 20 25	3 24 4 35 29 / 25 6 20 25	6 28 3 3 31 / 25 6 19 25	9 33 8 7 32 / 24 6 19 25	11 1 14 10 33 / 24 7 19 24	14 6 16 14 32 / 24 7 19 24	17 11 16 18 32 / 24 7 20 24	20 15 21 22 32 / 25 7 20 25	23 19 25 26 34 / 26 7 20 25	27 22 26 29 36 / 26 7 20 25
15	30 16 27 25 24 / 24 5 20 25	33 20 31 28 26 / 25 5 20 25	36 21 1 32 28 / 25 5 20 25	3 26 4 35 29 / 25 6 19 25	6 29 3 3 31 / 25 6 19 25	9 34 8 7 32 / 24 6 19 25	12 2 14 10 33 / 24 7 19 24	15 8 16 14 32 / 24 7 19 24	18 12 16 18 32 / 24 7 20 24	20 16 21 22 32 / 25 7 20 25	24 20 26 26 34 / 26 7 20 25	27 23 26 29 36 / 26 7 20 25
16	30 17 28 25 24 / 24 5 20 25	33 21 32 29 26 / 25 5 20 25	36 22 1 32 28 / 25 5 20 25	3 27 4 35 29 / 25 6 19 25	6 30 3 3 31 / 25 6 19 25	9 36 8 7 32 / 24 6 19 25	12 4 14 11 33 / 24 7 19 24	15 9 16 14 32 / 24 7 19 24	18 14 16 18 32 / 24 7 20 24	21 17 21 22 32 / 25 7 20 25	24 21 26 26 34 / 26 7 20 25	27 25 26 29 36 / 26 7 20 25
17	30 18 28 25 24 / 24 5 20 25	33 22 32 29 26 / 25 5 20 25	36 23 1 32 28 / 25 5 20 25	3 28 4 36 29 / 25 6 19 25	6 32 3 3 31 / 25 6 19 25	9 1 8 7 32 / 24 6 19 25	12 5 14 11 33 / 24 7 19 24	15 10 16 14 32 / 24 7 19 24	18 15 16 18 32 / 24 7 20 24	21 18 21 22 32 / 25 7 20 25	24 23 26 26 34 / 26 7 20 25	27 26 26 30 36 / 26 7 20 25
18	30 19 28 25 24 / 24 5 20 25	33 24 32 29 26 / 25 5 20 25	36 25 1 32 28 / 25 5 20 25	3 29 3 36 30 / 25 6 19 25	6 33 3 3 31 / 25 6 19 25	9 3 9 7 32 / 24 6 19 25	12 6 14 11 33 / 24 7 19 24	15 11 16 15 32 / 24 7 20 24	18 16 16 18 32 / 24 7 20 24	21 19 21 22 32 / 25 7 20 25	24 24 26 26 34 / 26 7 20 25	27 27 26 30 36 / 26 7 20 25
19	30 20 28 26 24 / 24 5 20 25	33 25 32 29 26 / 25 5 20 25	36 26 1 32 28 / 25 5 20 25	3 31 3 36 30 / 25 6 19 25	6 35 4 3 31 / 25 6 19 25	9 4 9 7 32 / 24 6 19 25	12 8 14 11 33 / 24 7 19 24	15 13 16 15 32 / 24 7 20 24	18 17 16 19 32 / 25 7 20 24	21 21 22 22 33 / 25 7 20 25	24 25 26 26 34 / 26 7 20 25	27 28 26 30 36 / 26 7 20 25
20	30 22 28 26 24 / 24 5 20 25	33 26 32 29 26 / 25 5 20 25	36 27 2 32 28 / 25 5 20 25	3 32 3 36 30 / 25 6 19 25	6 36 4 4 31 / 25 6 19 25	9 5 9 7 32 / 24 6 19 25	12 9 15 11 33 / 24 7 19 24	15 14 16 15 32 / 24 7 20 24	18 18 17 19 32 / 25 7 20 24	21 22 22 22 33 / 25 7 20 25	24 26 26 26 34 / 26 7 20 25	27 29 26 30 36 / 26 7 20 25
21	30 23 28 26 24 / 25 5 20 25	34 28 32 29 26 / 25 5 20 25	36 28 2 32 28 / 25 5 20 25	3 34 3 36 30 / 25 6 19 25	6 2 4 4 31 / 25 6 19 25	9 7 9 7 32 / 24 6 19 24	12 11 15 11 33 / 24 7 19 24	15 15 16 15 32 / 24 7 20 24	18 20 17 19 32 / 25 7 20 24	21 23 22 23 33 / 25 7 20 25	24 28 26 26 34 / 26 7 20 25	27 31 26 30 36 / 26 7 20 25
22	31 24 28 26 24 / 25 5 20 25	34 29 33 29 26 / 25 5 20 25	36 30 2 33 28 / 25 5 20 25	4 35 3 36 30 / 25 6 19 25	6 3 4 4 31 / 25 6 19 25	9 8 9 8 32 / 24 6 19 24	12 12 15 11 33 / 24 7 19 24	15 16 16 15 32 / 24 7 20 24	18 21 17 19 32 / 25 7 20 24	21 24 22 23 33 / 25 7 20 25	24 29 26 27 34 / 26 7 20 25	27 32 26 30 36 / 26 7 20 25
23	31 25 28 26 24 / 25 5 20 25	34 30 33 29 26 / 25 5 20 25	1 31 2 33 28 / 25 5 20 25	4 1 3 36 30 / 25 6 19 25	7 4 4 4 31 / 25 6 19 25	9 10 10 8 32 / 24 6 19 24	12 13 15 11 33 / 24 7 19 24	15 18 16 15 32 / 24 7 20 24	18 22 17 19 32 / 25 7 20 24	21 25 22 23 33 / 25 7 20 25	24 30 27 27 34 / 26 7 20 25	27 34 26 30 36 / 26 6 20 25
24	31 27 28 26 24 / 25 5 20 25	34 32 33 29 26 / 25 5 20 25	1 33 2 33 28 / 25 5 20 25	4 2 3 36 30 / 25 6 19 25	7 6 4 4 31 / 25 6 19 25	10 11 10 8 32 / 24 6 19 24	12 14 15 11 32 / 24 7 19 24	15 19 16 15 32 / 24 7 20 24	18 23 17 19 32 / 25 7 20 24	21 27 22 23 33 / 25 7 20 25	25 31 27 27 34 / 26 7 20 25	28 35 26 30 36 / 26 6 20 25
25	31 28 28 26 25 / 25 5 20 25	34 33 33 30 26 / 25 5 20 25	1 34 2 33 28 / 25 5 20 25	4 4 3 1 30 / 25 6 19 25	7 7 4 4 31 / 25 6 19 25	10 12 10 8 32 / 24 6 19 24	13 16 15 12 32 / 24 7 19 24	16 20 16 15 32 / 24 7 20 24	19 24 17 19 32 / 25 7 20 24	21 28 23 23 33 / 25 7 20 25	25 33 27 27 34 / 26 7 20 25	28 1 26 31 36 / 26 6 20 25
26	31 30 29 26 25 / 25 5 20 25	34 35 33 30 27 / 25 5 20 25	1 36 3 33 28 / 25 5 20 25	4 5 3 1 30 / 25 6 19 25	7 9 4 4 31 / 25 6 19 25	10 13 10 8 32 / 24 6 19 24	13 17 15 12 32 / 24 7 19 24	16 21 16 16 32 / 24 7 20 24	19 26 18 19 32 / 25 7 20 24	22 29 23 23 33 / 25 7 20 25	25 34 27 27 34 / 26 7 20 25	28 2 26 31 36 / 27 6 20 25
27	31 31 29 26 25 / 25 5 20 25	34 36 34 30 27 / 25 5 20 25	1 1 3 33 28 / 25 5 20 25	4 7 3 1 30 / 25 6 19 25	7 10 5 4 32 / 25 6 19 25	10 15 11 8 32 / 24 6 19 24	13 18 15 12 32 / 24 7 19 24	16 22 16 16 32 / 24 7 20 24	19 27 18 20 32 / 25 7 20 24	22 30 23 23 33 / 25 7 20 25	25 36 27 27 35 / 26 7 20 25	28 3 26 31 36 / 27 6 20 25
28	31 33 29 26 25 / 25 5 20 25	34 2 34 30 27 / 25 5 20 25	1 3 3 33 28 / 25 5 20 25	4 8 3 1 30 / 25 6 19 25	7 11 5 5 32 / 25 6 19 25	10 16 11 8 32 / 24 7 19 24	13 19 16 12 32 / 24 7 19 24	16 24 16 16 32 / 24 7 20 24	19 28 18 20 32 / 25 7 20 24	22 32 23 23 33 / 25 7 20 25	25 1 27 27 35 / 26 7 20 25	28 5 26 31 36 / 27 6 20 25
29	31 34 29 27 25 / 25 5 20 25	1971	1 4 3 33 28 / 25 5 20 25	4 9 3 1 30 / 25 6 19 25	7 13 5 5 32 / 24 6 19 25	10 17 11 8 33 / 24 7 19 24	13 20 16 12 32 / 24 7 19 24	16 25 15 16 32 / 24 7 20 24	19 29 18 20 32 / 25 7 20 24	22 33 23 24 33 / 25 7 20 25	25 2 27 27 35 / 26 7 20 25	28 6 26 31 36 / 27 6 20 25
30	31 36 29 27 25 / 25 5 20 25		1 6 3 33 28 / 25 5 20 25	4 11 3 1 30 / 25 6 19 25	7 14 5 5 32 / 24 6 19 25	10 18 11 9 33 / 24 7 19 24	13 22 16 12 32 / 24 7 19 24	16 26 15 16 32 / 24 7 20 24	19 30 18 20 32 / 25 7 20 24	22 35 23 24 33 / 25 7 20 25	25 4 27 28 35 / 26 7 20 25	28 8 26 31 36 / 27 6 20 25
31	31 1 29 27 25 / 25 5 20 25		1 7 3 34 29 / 25 5 20 25		7 15 5 5 32 / 24 6 19 25		13 23 16 12 32 / 24 7 19 24	16 27 15 16 32 / 24 7 20 24		22 36 23 24 33 / 25 7 20 25		28 9 26 31 36 / 27 6 20 25

	JAN	FEB	MAR	APR	MAY	JUNE	JULY	AUG	SEPT	OCT	NOV	DEC
1	28 11 26 31 1 27 6 20 25	32 15 30 35 3 27 6 20 25	34 17 36 3 5 28 6 20 25	2 22 1 6 7 28 7 20 25	4 25 2 9 9 28 7 20 25	7 30 7 10 11 28 7 20 25	10 33 13 8 13 28 8 20 25	13 3 14 9 15 27 8 20 25	16 8 15 12 16 27 8 20 25	19 12 20 15 18 27 8 20 25	22 17 25 19 20 28 8 20 25	25 20 24 22 22 28 8 21 25
2	28 12 26 32 1 27 6 20 25	32 17 31 35 3 27 6 20 25	35 19 36 3 5 28 6 20 25	2 23 1 6 7 28 7 20 25	5 26 2 9 9 28 7 20 25	8 31 7 10 11 28 7 20 25	10 35 13 8 13 28 8 20 25	13 4 14 9 15 27 8 20 25	16 9 15 12 17 27 8 20 25	19 13 20 15 19 27 8 20 25	22 18 25 19 20 28 8 20 25	25 21 24 22 22 29 8 21 25
3	29 13 26 32 1 27 6 20 25	32 18 31 36 3 27 6 20 25	35 20 36 3 5 28 6 20 25	2 24 1 6 7 28 7 20 25	5 28 2 9 9 28 7 20 25	8 32 7 10 11 28 7 20 25	11 36 13 8 13 28 8 20 25	13 5 14 9 15 27 8 20 25	16 11 15 12 17 27 8 20 25	19 14 20 15 19 27 8 20 25	22 19 25 19 21 28 8 20 25	25 22 24 22 23 29 8 21 25
4	29 15 27 32 1 27 6 20 25	32 19 31 36 3 27 6 20 25	35 21 36 3 5 28 6 20 25	2 25 1 6 7 28 7 20 25	5 29 2 9 9 28 7 20 25	8 34 8 10 11 28 7 20 25	11 1 13 8 13 28 8 20 25	14 7 14 9 15 27 8 20 25	17 12 15 12 17 27 8 20 25	19 16 21 15 19 27 8 20 25	23 20 25 19 21 28 8 20 25	26 24 24 23 23 29 8 21 25
5	29 16 27 32 1 27 6 20 25	32 20 31 36 3 27 6 20 25	35 22 36 3 5 28 6 20 25	2 27 1 7 7 28 7 20 25	5 30 2 9 9 28 7 20 25	8 35 8 10 11 28 7 20 25	11 3 13 8 13 28 8 20 25	14 8 14 9 15 27 8 20 25	17 13 15 12 17 27 8 20 25	20 17 21 15 19 27 8 20 25	23 22 25 19 21 28 8 20 25	26 25 24 23 23 29 8 21 25
6	29 17 27 32 1 27 6 20 25	32 21 31 36 3 27 6 20 25	35 23 36 3 5 28 6 20 25	2 28 1 7 7 28 7 20 25	5 31 2 9 9 28 7 20 25	8 36 8 10 11 28 7 20 25	11 4 13 8 13 28 8 20 25	14 10 14 9 15 27 8 20 25	17 15 15 12 17 27 8 20 25	20 18 21 15 19 28 8 20 25	23 23 25 19 21 28 8 20 25	26 26 24 23 23 29 8 21 25
7	29 18 27 32 1 27 6 20 25	32 23 31 36 3 27 6 20 25	35 25 1 3 5 28 6 20 25	2 29 1 7 7 28 7 20 25	5 33 3 9 9 28 7 20 25	8 2 8 10 11 28 7 20 25	11 5 13 8 13 28 8 20 25	14 11 14 9 15 27 8 20 25	17 16 16 12 17 27 8 20 25	20 19 21 16 19 28 8 20 25	23 24 25 19 21 28 8 20 25	26 27 24 23 23 29 8 21 25
8	29 19 27 32 1 27 6 20 25	32 24 32 36 3 27 6 20 25	35 26 1 3 5 28 6 20 25	2 30 1 7 7 28 7 20 25	5 34 3 9 9 28 7 20 25	8 3 9 10 11 28 7 20 25	11 7 14 8 13 28 8 20 25	14 12 14 10 15 27 8 20 25	17 17 16 12 17 27 8 20 25	20 21 21 16 19 28 8 20 25	23 25 25 19 21 28 8 20 25	26 28 24 23 23 29 8 21 25
9	29 20 27 32 1 27 6 20 25	32 25 32 36 3 27 6 20 25	35 27 1 4 5 28 6 20 25	2 32 1 7 7 28 7 20 25	5 35 3 9 9 28 7 20 25	8 5 9 10 11 28 8 20 25	11 8 14 8 13 28 8 20 25	14 14 14 10 15 27 8 20 25	17 19 16 13 17 27 8 20 25	20 22 21 16 19 28 8 20 25	23 26 25 19 21 28 8 20 25	26 30 24 23 23 29 8 21 25
10	29 22 27 33 1 27 6 20 25	32 26 32 36 3 27 6 20 25	35 28 1 4 5 28 6 20 25	2 33 1 7 7 28 7 20 25	5 1 3 9 9 28 7 20 25	8 6 9 9 11 28 8 20 25	11 10 14 8 13 28 8 20 25	14 15 14 10 15 27 8 20 25	17 20 16 13 17 27 8 20 25	20 23 21 16 19 28 8 20 25	23 27 25 20 21 28 8 20 25	26 31 24 23 23 29 8 21 25
11	29 23 27 33 1 27 6 20 25	33 28 32 36 3 27 6 20 25	35 30 1 4 5 28 7 20 25	3 35 1 7 7 28 7 20 25	5 2 3 9 9 28 7 20 25	8 8 9 9 11 28 8 20 25	11 12 14 8 13 28 8 20 25	14 16 14 10 15 27 8 20 25	17 21 16 13 17 27 8 20 25	20 24 22 16 19 28 8 20 25	23 29 25 20 21 28 8 20 25	26 32 24 23 23 29 8 21 25
12	29 24 27 33 1 27 6 20 25	33 29 32 1 3 27 6 20 25	36 31 1 4 5 28 7 20 25	3 36 1 7 7 28 7 20 25	6 4 3 9 9 28 7 20 25	9 9 9 9 11 28 8 20 25	11 13 14 8 13 28 8 20 25	14 18 14 10 15 27 8 20 25	17 22 17 13 17 27 8 20 25	20 25 22 16 19 28 8 20 25	23 30 26 20 21 28 8 20 25	26 33 24 24 23 29 8 21 25
13	30 25 28 33 2 27 6 20 25	33 30 32 1 4 28 6 20 25	36 32 1 4 5 28 7 20 25	3 1 1 7 7 28 7 20 25	6 5 3 10 9 28 7 20 25	9 11 10 9 11 28 8 20 25	11 14 14 8 13 28 8 20 25	14 19 14 10 15 27 8 20 25	17 23 17 13 17 27 8 20 25	20 27 22 16 19 28 8 20 25	23 31 26 20 21 28 8 20 25	27 35 24 24 23 29 8 21 25
14	30 26 28 33 2 27 6 20 25	33 32 33 1 4 38 6 20 25	36 34 2 4 6 28 7 20 25	3 3 1 7 8 28 7 20 25	6 7 4 10 9 28 7 20 25	9 12 10 9 11 28 8 20 25	12 16 14 8 13 28 8 20 25	15 20 14 10 15 27 8 20 25	18 25 17 13 17 27 8 20 25	20 28 22 16 19 28 8 20 25	24 33 26 20 21 28 8 20 25	27 36 24 24 23 29 8 21 25
15	30 28 28 33 2 27 6 20 25	33 33 33 1 4 28 6 20 25	36 35 2 4 6 28 7 20 25	3 5 1 7 8 28 7 20 25	6 8 4 10 10 28 7 20 25	9 13 10 9 12 28 8 20 25	12 17 14 8 13 27 8 20 25	15 21 13 10 15 27 8 20 25	18 26 17 13 17 27 8 20 25	21 29 22 17 19 28 8 20 25	24 34 26 20 21 28 8 20 25	27 1 25 24 24 29 8 21 25
16	30 29 28 33 2 27 6 20 25	33 34 33 1 4 28 6 20 25	36 1 2 4 6 28 7 20 25	3 6 1 8 8 28 7 20 25	6 10 4 10 10 28 7 20 25	9 15 10 9 12 28 8 20 25	12 18 14 8 13 27 8 20 25	15 23 13 10 15 27 8 20 25	18 27 17 13 17 27 8 20 25	21 30 22 17 19 28 8 20 25	24 35 26 20 21 28 8 20 25	27 3 25 24 24 29 8 21 25
17	30 31 28 33 2 27 6 20 25	33 36 33 1 4 28 6 20 25	36 2 2 5 6 28 7 20 25	3 8 1 8 8 28 7 20 25	6 11 4 10 10 28 7 20 25	9 16 11 9 12 28 8 20 25	12 19 14 8 14 27 8 20 25	15 24 13 10 16 27 8 20 25	18 28 18 13 18 27 8 20 25	21 31 23 17 19 28 8 20 25	24 36 26 20 21 28 8 20 25	27 4 25 24 24 29 8 21 25
18	30 32 28 34 2 27 6 20 25	33 1 33 1 4 28 6 20 25	36 4 2 5 6 28 7 20 25	3 9 1 8 8 28 7 20 25	6 13 4 10 10 28 7 20 25	9 17 11 9 12 28 8 20 25	12 21 14 8 14 27 8 20 25	15 25 13 10 16 27 8 20 25	18 29 18 13 18 27 8 20 25	21 33 23 17 20 28 8 20 25	24 2 26 21 22 28 8 20 25	27 6 25 24 24 29 8 21 25
19	30 33 28 34 2 27 6 20 25	33 3 33 1 4 28 6 20 25	36 5 2 5 6 28 7 20 25	3 10 1 8 8 28 7 20 25	6 14 4 10 10 28 7 20 25	9 19 11 9 12 28 8 20 25	12 22 14 8 14 27 8 20 25	15 26 13 10 16 27 8 20 25	18 31 18 14 18 27 8 20 25	21 34 23 17 20 28 8 20 25	24 3 26 21 22 28 8 21 25	27 7 25 24 24 29 8 21 25
20	30 35 29 34 2 27 6 20 25	33 4 34 2 4 28 6 20 25	36 7 2 5 6 28 7 20 25	3 11 1 8 8 28 7 20 25	6 15 5 10 10 28 7 20 25	9 20 11 9 12 28 8 20 25	12 23 15 8 14 27 8 20 25	15 27 13 11 16 27 8 20 25	18 32 18 14 18 27 8 20 25	21 36 23 17 20 28 8 20 25	24 5 26 21 22 28 8 21 25	27 9 25 25 24 29 8 21 25
21	30 36 29 34 2 27 6 20 25	34 6 34 2 4 28 6 20 25	36 8 2 5 6 28 7 20 25	3 13 1 8 8 28 7 20 25	6 16 5 10 10 28 7 20 25	9 21 11 9 12 28 8 20 25	12 24 15 8 14 27 8 20 25	15 29 14 11 16 27 8 20 25	18 33 18 14 18 27 8 20 25	21 1 23 17 20 28 8 20 25	24 6 25 21 22 28 8 21 25	27 10 25 25 24 29 8 21 25
22	31 2 29 34 2 27 6 20 25	34 7 34 2 4 28 6 20 25	1 9 2 5 6 28 7 20 25	4 14 1 8 8 28 7 20 25	7 18 5 10 10 28 7 20 25	9 22 11 9 12 28 8 20 25	12 25 15 9 14 27 8 20 25	15 30 14 11 16 27 8 20 25	18 35 18 14 18 27 8 20 25	21 2 23 17 20 28 8 20 25	24 8 25 21 22 28 8 21 25	27 12 25 25 24 29 8 21 25
23	31 3 29 34 2 27 6 20 25	34 8 34 2 4 28 6 20 25	1 11 2 5 6 28 7 20 25	4 16 1 8 8 28 7 20 25	7 19 5 10 10 28 7 20 25	10 23 11 9 12 28 8 20 25	12 27 15 9 14 27 8 20 25	15 31 14 11 16 27 8 20 25	18 36 19 14 18 27 8 20 25	21 4 23 17 20 28 8 20 25	24 9 25 21 22 28 8 21 25	28 13 26 25 24 29 8 21 25
24	31 5 29 34 2 27 6 20 25	34 10 34 2 4 28 6 20 25	1 12 2 5 6 28 7 20 25	4 17 1 8 8 28 7 20 25	7 20 5 10 10 28 7 20 25	10 25 12 9 12 28 8 20 25	13 28 15 9 14 27 8 20 25	15 33 14 11 16 27 8 20 25	19 2 19 14 18 27 8 20 25	21 6 24 18 20 28 8 20 25	25 11 25 21 22 28 8 21 25	28 14 26 25 24 29 8 21 25
25	31 6 29 34 2 27 6 20 25	34 11 35 2 4 28 6 20 25	1 13 2 5 6 28 7 20 25	4 18 1 8 8 28 7 20 25	7 21 6 10 10 28 7 20 25	10 26 12 9 12 28 8 20 25	13 29 15 9 14 27 8 20 25	16 34 14 11 16 27 8 20 25	19 3 19 14 18 27 8 20 25	22 7 24 18 20 28 8 20 25	25 12 25 21 22 28 8 21 25	28 16 26 25 24 29 8 21 25
26	31 7 29 35 2 27 6 20 25	34 12 35 2 4 28 6 20 25	1 15 2 5 6 28 7 20 25	4 19 1 8 8 28 7 20 25	7 22 6 10 10 28 7 20 25	10 27 12 8 12 28 8 20 25	13 30 15 9 14 27 8 20 25	16 35 14 11 16 27 8 20 25	19 5 19 14 18 27 8 20 25	22 9 24 18 20 28 8 20 25	25 14 25 22 22 28 8 21 25	28 17 26 25 24 29 8 21 25
27	31 9 30 35 2 27 6 20 25	34 14 35 2 4 28 6 20 25	1 16 2 6 6 28 7 20 25	4 20 1 8 8 28 7 20 25	7 24 6 10 10 28 7 20 25	10 28 12 8 12 28 8 20 25	13 32 15 9 14 27 8 20 25	16 1 14 11 16 27 8 20 25	19 6 19 14 18 27 8 20 25	22 10 24 18 20 28 8 20 25	25 15 25 22 22 28 8 21 25	28 18 26 25 24 29 8 21 25
28	31 10 30 35 3 27 6 20 25	34 15 35 2 5 28 6 20 25	1 17 2 6 6 28 7 20 25	4 22 1 9 8 28 7 20 25	7 25 6 10 10 28 7 20 25	10 29 12 8 12 28 8 20 25	13 33 15 9 14 27 8 20 25	16 2 14 11 16 27 8 20 25	19 8 20 15 18 27 8 20 25	22 11 24 18 20 28 8 20 25	25 16 25 22 22 28 8 21 25	28 20 26 26 24 29 8 21 25
29	31 11 30 35 3 27 6 20 25	34 16 35 3 5 28 6 20 25	1 18 2 6 7 28 7 20 25	4 23 2 9 9 28 7 20 25	7 26 6 10 10 28 7 20 25	10 31 12 8 12 28 8 20 25	13 34 15 9 14 27 8 20 25	16 4 14 11 16 27 8 20 25	19 9 20 15 18 27 8 20 25	22 13 24 18 20 28 8 20 25	25 18 25 22 22 28 8 21 25	28 21 26 26 24 29 8 21 25
30	31 13 30 35 3 27 6 20 25	1972	1 20 2 6 7 28 7 20 25	4 24 2 9 9 28 7 20 25	7 27 7 10 11 28 7 20 25	10 32 13 8 12 28 8 20 25	13 36 15 9 14 27 8 20 25	16 5 14 11 16 27 8 20 25	19 10 20 15 18 27 8 20 25	22 14 24 18 20 28 8 20 25	25 19 24 22 22 28 8 21 25	28 22 27 26 24 29 8 21 25
31	31 14 30 35 3 27 6 20 25		1 21 2 6 7 28 7 20 25		7 29 7 10 11 28 7 20 25		13 1 14 9 14 27 8 20 25	16 6 14 12 16 27 8 20 25		22 15 24 18 20 28 8 20 25		28 23 27 26 24 29 8 21 25

	JAN	FEB	MAR	APR	MAY	JUNE	JULY	AUG	SEPT	OCT	NOV	DEC
1	28 24 27 26 24 29 8 21 25	32 29 32 30 27 30 8 21 25	34 30 36 33 29 31 8 21 25	2 34 35 1 31 31 8 21 25	5 2 2 5 33 31 8 20 25	7 7 9 9 35 32 9 20 25	10 11 13 12 1 31 9 20 25	13 16 12 16 3 31 9 20 25	16 21 16 20 4 31 10 20 25	19 24 21 23 4 31 10 21 25	22 29 24 27 3 31 10 21 25	25 32 23 30 3 31 10 21 25
2	29 26 27 26 25 29 8 21 25	32 30 32 30 27 30 8 21 25	35 31 36 34 29 31 8 21 25	2 36 35 1 31 31 8 21 25	5 3 3 5 33 31 8 20 25	8 9 9 9 35 32 9 20 25	10 13 13 13 1 31 9 20 25	13 17 12 16 3 31 9 20 25	16 22 16 20 4 31 10 20 25	19 25 21 24 4 31 10 21 25	22 30 24 27 3 31 10 21 25	25 33 23 30 3 31 10 21 25
3	29 27 27 26 25 29 8 21 25	32 31 32 30 27 30 8 21 25	35 32 36 34 29 31 8 21 25	2 1 35 2 31 31 8 21 25	5 5 3 5 33 31 8 20 25	8 10 9 9 35 32 9 20 25	10 14 13 13 1 31 9 20 25	13 19 12 16 3 31 9 20 25	16 24 17 20 4 31 10 20 25	19 26 21 24 4 31 10 21 25	22 31 24 27 3 31 10 21 25	25 34 24 30 3 31 10 21 25
4	29 28 27 26 25 29 8 21 25	32 33 32 30 27 30 8 21 25	35 33 36 34 29 31 8 21 25	2 2 35 2 31 31 8 21 25	5 6 3 5 33 32 8 20 25	8 12 9 9 35 32 9 20 25	11 15 13 13 1 31 9 20 25	14 20 12 17 3 31 9 20 25	17 25 17 20 4 31 10 20 25	19 28 22 24 4 31 10 21 25	23 32 24 27 3 31 10 21 25	26 36 24 30 3 31 10 21 25
5	29 29 27 27 25 29 8 21 25	32 34 33 30 27 30 8 21 25	35 35 36 34 29 31 8 21 25	2 4 35 2 31 31 8 21 25	5 8 3 5 33 32 8 20 25	8 13 10 9 35 32 9 20 25	11 17 13 13 1 31 9 20 25	14 22 12 17 3 31 9 20 25	17 26 17 20 4 31 10 20 25	20 29 22 24 4 31 10 21 25	23 34 24 27 3 31 10 21 25	26 1 24 30 3 31 10 21 25
6	29 30 28 27 25 29 8 21 25	32 35 33 31 27 30 8 21 25	35 36 36 34 29 31 8 21 25	2 5 35 2 31 31 8 21 25	5 9 3 6 33 32 8 20 25	8 14 10 9 35 32 9 20 25	11 18 13 13 1 31 9 20 25	14 23 12 17 3 31 9 20 25	17 27 17 21 4 31 10 21 25	20 30 22 24 4 31 10 21 25	23 35 24 27 3 31 10 21 25	26 2 24 30 3 31 10 21 25
7	29 32 28 27 25 29 8 21 25	32 1 33 31 27 30 8 21 25	35 2 36 34 29 31 8 21 25	2 7 35 2 31 31 8 21 25	5 11 4 6 33 32 8 20 25	8 16 10 10 35 32 9 20 25	11 19 13 13 1 31 9 20 25	14 24 12 17 3 31 9 20 25	17 28 17 21 4 31 10 21 25	20 32 22 24 4 31 10 21 25	23 36 24 28 3 31 10 21 25	26 4 24 30 3 31 10 21 25
8	29 33 28 27 25 29 8 21 25	32 2 33 31 27 30 8 21 25	35 3 36 34 29 31 8 21 25	2 8 35 2 31 31 8 21 25	5 12 4 6 33 32 8 20 25	8 17 10 10 36 32 9 20 25	11 21 13 13 1 31 9 20 25	14 25 12 17 3 31 9 20 25	17 30 17 21 4 31 10 21 25	20 33 22 24 4 31 10 21 25	23 2 23 28 3 31 10 21 25	26 5 24 30 3 31 10 21 25
9	29 34 28 27 25 29 8 21 25	32 3 33 31 27 30 8 21 25	35 4 36 34 29 31 8 21 25	2 10 36 2 31 31 8 21 25	5 14 4 6 33 32 8 20 25	8 19 10 10 36 32 9 20 25	11 22 13 13 2 31 9 20 25	14 26 12 17 3 31 9 20 25	17 31 18 21 4 31 10 21 25	20 34 22 24 4 31 10 21 25	23 3 23 28 3 31 10 21 25	26 7 24 30 3 31 10 21 25
10	29 36 28 27 25 29 8 21 25	33 5 33 31 27 30 8 21 25	35 6 36 35 29 31 8 21 25	2 11 36 2 31 31 8 21 25	5 15 4 6 34 32 8 20 25	8 20 10 10 36 32 9 20 25	11 23 13 14 2 31 9 20 25	14 28 12 17 3 31 9 20 25	17 32 18 21 4 31 10 21 25	20 35 22 24 4 31 10 21 25	23 4 23 28 3 31 10 21 25	26 8 25 31 3 31 10 21 25
11	29 1 28 27 25 29 8 21 25	33 6 34 31 27 30 8 21 25	35 7 36 35 29 31 8 21 25	2 13 36 3 31 31 8 21 25	5 16 4 6 34 32 8 20 25	8 21 11 10 36 32 9 20 25	11 24 13 14 2 31 9 20 25	14 29 12 17 3 31 9 20 25	17 33 18 21 4 31 10 21 25	20 1 22 25 4 31 10 21 25	23 6 23 28 3 31 10 21 25	26 10 25 31 3 31 10 21 25
12	30 2 29 27 25 29 8 21 25	33 8 34 31 27 30 8 21 25	36 9 36 35 29 31 8 21 25	3 14 36 3 32 31 8 21 25	6 18 5 6 34 32 8 20 25	8 22 11 10 36 32 9 20 25	11 26 13 14 2 31 9 20 25	14 30 12 18 3 31 10 20 25	17 35 18 21 4 31 10 21 25	20 2 23 25 4 31 10 21 25	23 7 23 28 3 31 10 21 25	26 11 25 31 3 31 10 21 25
13	30 4 29 28 25 29 8 21 25	33 9 34 31 27 30 8 21 25	36 10 36 35 29 31 8 21 25	3 15 36 3 32 31 8 20 25	6 19 5 6 34 32 8 20 25	9 23 11 10 36 32 9 20 25	11 27 13 14 2 31 9 20 25	14 31 13 18 3 31 10 20 25	17 36 18 21 4 31 10 21 25	20 3 23 25 4 31 10 21 25	23 9 23 28 3 31 10 21 25	26 13 25 31 3 31 10 21 25
14	30 5 29 28 25 29 8 21 25	33 10 34 32 28 30 8 21 25	36 11 36 35 29 31 8 21 25	3 17 36 3 32 31 8 20 25	6 20 5 7 34 32 8 20 25	9 25 11 10 36 32 9 20 25	12 28 13 14 2 31 9 20 25	15 32 13 18 3 31 10 20 25	18 1 18 21 4 31 10 21 25	20 5 23 25 4 31 10 21 25	24 10 23 28 3 31 10 21 25	27 14 25 31 3 31 10 21 25
15	30 7 29 28 25 30 8 21 25	33 11 34 32 28 30 8 21 25	36 13 36 35 30 31 8 21 25	3 18 36 3 32 31 8 20 25	6 21 5 7 34 32 8 20 25	9 26 11 11 36 32 9 20 25	12 29 12 14 2 31 9 20 25	15 34 13 18 4 31 10 20 25	18 3 19 22 4 31 10 21 25	21 6 23 25 4 31 10 21 25	24 12 23 28 3 31 10 21 25	27 15 25 31 3 31 10 21 25
16	30 8 29 28 26 30 8 21 25	33 13 35 32 28 30 8 21 25	36 14 35 35 30 31 8 21 25	3 19 36 3 32 31 8 20 25	6 23 5 7 34 32 8 20 25	9 27 11 11 36 32 9 20 25	12 30 12 14 2 31 9 20 25	15 35 13 18 4 31 10 20 25	18 4 19 22 4 31 10 21 25	21 8 23 25 4 31 10 21 25	24 13 23 28 3 31 10 21 25	27 17 25 31 3 32 10 21 25
17	30 9 29 28 26 30 8 21 25	33 14 35 32 28 30 8 21 25	36 16 35 35 30 31 8 21 25	3 20 36 3 32 31 8 20 25	6 24 6 7 34 32 8 20 25	9 28 11 11 36 32 9 20 25	12 31 12 14 2 31 9 20 25	15 36 13 18 4 31 10 20 25	18 5 19 22 4 31 10 21 25	21 9 23 25 4 31 10 21 25	24 14 23 29 3 31 10 21 25	27 18 26 31 3 32 10 21 25
18	30 11 29 28 26 30 8 21 25	33 16 35 32 28 30 8 21 25	36 17 35 36 30 31 8 21 25	3 22 1 3 32 31 8 20 25	6 25 6 7 34 32 8 20 25	9 29 12 11 36 32 9 20 25	12 33 12 15 2 31 9 20 25	15 2 13 18 4 31 10 20 25	18 7 19 22 4 31 10 21 25	21 11 23 25 4 31 10 21 25	24 16 23 29 3 31 10 21 25	27 20 26 31 3 32 10 21 25
19	30 12 30 28 26 30 8 21 25	33 17 35 32 28 30 8 21 25	36 18 35 36 30 31 8 21 25	3 23 1 4 32 31 8 20 25	6 26 6 7 34 32 8 20 25	9 31 12 11 36 32 9 20 25	12 34 12 15 2 31 9 20 25	15 3 14 19 4 31 10 20 25	18 8 19 22 4 31 10 21 25	21 12 23 25 4 31 10 21 25	24 17 23 29 3 31 10 21 25	27 21 26 31 3 32 10 21 25
20	30 14 30 28 26 30 8 21 25	34 19 35 32 28 30 8 21 25	36 20 35 36 30 31 8 21 25	3 24 1 4 32 31 8 20 25	6 27 6 7 34 32 8 20 25	9 32 12 11 36 32 9 20 25	12 35 12 15 2 31 9 20 25	15 4 14 19 4 31 10 20 25	18 10 20 22 4 31 10 21 25	21 13 23 26 4 31 10 21 25	24 19 23 29 3 31 10 21 25	27 22 26 31 3 32 10 21 25
21	30 15 30 29 26 30 8 21 25	34 20 35 32 28 30 8 21 25	36 21 35 36 30 31 8 21 25	3 25 1 4 32 31 8 20 25	6 29 6 7 34 32 8 20 25	9 33 12 11 36 32 9 20 25	12 1 12 15 2 31 9 20 25	15 6 14 19 4 31 10 20 25	18 11 20 22 4 31 10 21 25	21 15 24 26 4 31 10 21 25	24 20 23 29 3 31 10 21 25	27 23 26 31 3 32 10 21 25
22	31 17 30 29 26 30 8 21 25	34 21 35 33 28 30 8 21 25	1 22 35 36 30 31 8 21 25	4 26 1 4 32 31 8 20 25	6 30 7 8 34 32 8 20 25	9 34 12 11 36 32 9 20 25	12 2 12 15 2 31 9 20 25	15 7 14 19 4 31 10 20 25	18 12 20 22 4 31 10 21 25	21 16 24 26 4 31 10 21 25	24 21 23 29 3 31 10 21 25	27 25 26 31 3 32 10 21 25
23	31 18 30 29 26 30 8 21 25	34 22 36 33 28 30 8 21 25	1 23 35 36 30 31 8 21 25	4 28 1 4 32 31 8 20 25	7 31 7 8 34 32 9 20 25	10 35 12 12 1 32 9 20 25	12 3 12 15 2 31 9 20 25	15 8 14 19 4 31 10 20 25	18 14 20 23 4 31 10 21 25	21 18 24 26 4 31 10 21 25	24 22 23 29 3 31 10 21 25	28 26 27 31 3 32 10 21 25
24	31 19 30 29 26 30 8 21 25	34 24 36 33 28 30 8 21 25	1 24 35 36 30 31 8 21 25	4 29 1 4 32 31 8 20 25	7 32 7 8 35 32 9 20 25	10 1 12 12 1 32 9 20 25	12 5 12 15 2 31 9 20 25	15 10 14 19 4 31 10 20 25	18 15 20 23 4 31 10 21 25	21 19 24 26 4 31 10 21 25	25 24 23 29 3 31 10 21 25	28 27 27 31 3 32 10 21 25
25	31 20 31 29 26 30 8 21 25	34 25 36 33 28 30 8 21 25	1 26 35 36 30 31 8 21 25	4 30 2 4 32 31 8 20 25	7 33 7 8 35 32 9 20 25	10 2 12 12 1 32 9 20 25	13 6 12 15 2 31 9 20 25	16 11 15 19 4 31 10 20 25	19 17 20 23 4 31 10 21 25	22 20 24 26 4 31 10 21 25	25 25 23 29 3 31 10 21 25	28 28 27 31 3 32 10 21 25
26	31 22 31 29 26 30 8 21 25	34 26 36 33 28 30 8 21 25	1 27 35 1 30 31 8 21 25	4 31 2 4 33 31 8 20 25	7 35 8 8 35 32 9 20 25	10 4 12 12 1 32 9 20 25	13 7 12 16 3 31 9 20 25	16 13 15 19 4 31 10 20 25	19 18 20 23 4 31 10 21 25	22 21 24 26 4 31 10 21 25	25 26 23 29 3 31 10 21 25	28 29 27 31 3 32 10 21 25
27	31 23 31 29 26 30 8 21 25	34 27 36 33 28 30 8 21 25	1 28 35 1 30 31 8 21 25	4 32 2 5 33 31 8 20 25	7 36 8 8 35 32 9 20 25	10 5 12 12 1 32 9 20 25	13 9 12 16 3 31 9 20 25	16 14 15 19 4 31 10 20 25	19 19 21 23 4 31 10 21 25	22 23 24 26 3 31 10 21 25	25 27 23 29 3 31 10 21 25	28 30 27 31 3 32 9 21 25
28	31 24 31 29 26 30 8 21 25	34 28 36 33 29 30 8 21 25	1 29 35 1 30 31 8 21 25	4 34 2 5 33 31 8 20 25	7 1 8 8 35 32 9 20 25	10 7 12 12 1 31 9 20 25	13 10 12 16 3 31 9 20 25	16 16 15 19 4 31 10 20 25	19 21 21 23 4 31 10 21 25	22 24 24 26 3 31 10 21 25	25 28 23 30 3 31 10 21 25	28 32 27 31 4 32 9 21 25
29	31 25 31 30 26 30 8 21 25	1973	1 30 35 1 31 31 8 21 25	4 35 2 5 33 31 8 20 25	7 3 8 8 35 32 9 20 25	10 8 13 12 1 31 9 20 25	13 12 12 16 3 31 9 20 25	16 17 15 20 4 31 10 20 25	19 22 21 23 4 31 10 21 25	22 25 24 27 3 31 10 21 25	25 30 23 30 3 31 10 21 25	28 33 27 31 4 32 9 21 25
30	31 26 32 30 26 30 8 21 25		1 32 35 1 31 31 8 21 25	4 36 2 5 33 31 8 20 25	7 4 8 9 35 32 9 20 25	10 10 13 12 1 31 9 20 25	13 13 12 16 3 31 9 20 25	16 18 16 20 4 31 10 20 25	19 23 21 23 4 31 10 21 25	22 26 24 27 3 31 10 21 25	25 31 23 30 3 31 10 21 25	28 34 28 32 4 32 9 21 25
31	31 28 32 30 27 30 8 21 25		1 33 35 1 31 31 8 21 25		7 6 9 9 35 32 9 20 25		13 14 12 16 3 31 9 20 25	16 20 16 20 4 31 10 20 25		22 28 24 27 3 31 10 21 25		28 35 28 32 4 32 9 21 25

	JAN	FEB	MAR	APR	MAY	JUNE	JULY	AUG	SEPT	OCT	NOV	DEC
1	28 1 28 32 4 32 9 21 25	32 5 33 30 5 33 9 21 25	34 6 34 30 6 33 9 21 25	1 12 35 33 8 34 9 21 25	4 16 4 36 10 35 10 21 25	7 21 10 3 12 35 10 21 25	10 24 10 7 14 35 10 21 25	13 29 12 11 16 35 11 21 25	16 33 18 14 18 35 11 21 25	19 1 22 18 20 34 11 21 25	22 5 21 22 22 34 11 21 25	25 9 24 26 24 34 11 21 25
2	29 2 28 32 4 32 9 21 25	32 7 33 30 5 33 9 21 25	35 8 33 30 7 33 9 21 25	2 13 35 33 8 34 9 21 25	5 17 4 36 10 35 10 21 25	8 22 10 4 12 35 10 21 25	10 26 10 7 14 35 10 21 25	13 30 12 11 16 35 11 21 25	16 35 18 15 18 35 11 21 25	19 2 22 18 20 34 11 21 25	22 7 21 22 22 34 11 21 25	25 10 24 26 24 34 11 21 25
3	29 3 28 32 4 32 9 21 25	32 8 33 30 5 33 9 21 25	35 9 33 31 7 33 9 21 25	2 15 35 33 8 34 9 21 25	5 18 4 36 10 35 10 21 25	8 23 10 4 12 35 10 21 25	10 27 10 7 14 35 10 21 25	13 31 12 11 16 35 11 21 25	16 36 18 15 18 35 11 21 25	19 3 22 18 20 34 11 21 25	22 8 21 22 22 34 11 21 25	25 12 25 26 24 34 11 21 25
4	29 5 28 32 4 32 9 21 25	32 10 34 30 5 33 9 21 25	35 11 33 31 7 33 9 21 25	2 16 35 33 8 34 9 21 25	5 20 5 36 10 35 10 21 25	8 25 10 4 12 35 10 21 25	11 28 10 7 14 35 10 21 25	14 32 12 11 16 35 11 21 25	17 1 18 15 18 35 11 21 25	20 4 22 19 20 34 11 21 25	23 9 21 22 22 34 11 21 25	26 13 25 26 24 34 11 21 25
5	29 6 29 32 4 32 9 21 25	32 11 34 30 5 33 9 21 25	35 12 33 31 7 33 9 21 25	2 17 35 33 8 34 9 21 25	5 21 5 36 10 35 10 21 25	8 26 10 4 12 35 10 21 25	11 29 10 7 14 35 10 21 25	14 34 12 11 16 35 11 21 25	17 2 18 15 18 35 11 21 25	20 6 22 19 20 34 11 21 25	23 11 21 23 22 34 11 21 25	26 15 25 26 24 34 11 21 25
6	29 7 29 32 4 32 9 21 25	32 13 34 30 5 33 9 21 25	35 14 33 31 7 33 9 21 25	2 19 36 33 9 34 9 21 25	5 22 5 1 10 35 10 21 25	8 27 10 4 12 35 10 21 25	11 30 10 7 14 35 10 21 25	14 35 12 11 16 35 11 21 25	17 3 18 15 18 35 11 21 25	20 7 22 19 20 34 11 21 25	23 12 21 23 22 34 11 21 25	26 16 25 26 24 34 11 21 25
7	29 9 29 32 4 32 9 21 25	32 14 34 30 5 33 9 21 25	35 15 33 31 7 33 9 21 25	2 20 36 33 9 34 9 21 25	5 24 5 1 10 35 10 21 25	8 28 10 4 12 35 10 21 25	11 32 10 7 14 35 10 21 25	14 36 13 11 16 35 11 21 25	17 5 19 15 18 35 11 21 25	20 8 22 19 20 34 11 21 25	23 14 21 23 22 34 11 21 25	26 18 25 27 24 34 11 21 25
8	29 10 29 31 4 32 9 21 25	32 16 34 30 5 33 9 21 25	35 17 33 31 7 33 9 21 25	2 22 36 34 9 34 9 21 25	5 25 5 1 10 35 10 21 25	8 30 10 4 12 35 10 21 25	11 33 10 8 14 35 10 21 25	14 1 13 12 16 35 11 21 25	17 6 19 15 18 35 11 21 25	20 10 22 19 20 34 11 21 25	23 15 21 23 22 34 11 21 25	26 19 25 27 24 34 11 21 25
9	29 12 29 31 4 32 9 21 25	32 17 34 30 5 33 9 21 25	35 18 33 31 7 33 9 21 25	2 23 36 34 9 34 9 21 25	5 27 6 1 11 35 10 21 25	8 31 10 4 12 35 10 21 25	11 34 10 8 14 35 10 21 25	14 2 13 12 16 35 11 21 25	17 7 19 15 18 35 11 21 25	20 11 22 19 20 34 11 21 25	23 17 21 23 22 34 11 21 25	26 20 25 27 24 34 11 21 25
10	29 13 29 31 4 32 9 21 25	32 19 34 30 5 33 9 21 25	35 19 33 31 7 33 9 21 25	2 24 36 34 9 34 9 21 25	5 28 6 1 11 35 10 21 25	8 32 10 5 12 35 10 21 25	11 35 10 8 14 35 10 21 25	14 4 13 12 16 35 11 21 25	17 9 19 16 18 35 11 21 25	20 13 22 19 20 34 11 21 25	23 18 21 23 22 34 11 21 25	26 22 26 27 24 34 11 21 25
11	29 15 30 31 4 32 9 21 25	33 20 34 30 6 33 9 21 25	35 21 33 31 7 33 9 21 25	2 25 36 34 9 34 9 21 25	5 29 6 1 11 35 10 21 25	8 33 11 5 13 35 10 21 25	11 36 10 8 14 35 10 21 25	14 5 14 12 16 35 11 21 25	17 10 19 16 18 35 11 21 25	20 14 22 19 20 34 11 21 25	23 19 21 23 22 34 11 21 25	26 23 26 27 24 34 11 22 25
12	30 16 30 31 4 32 9 21 25	33 21 34 30 6 33 9 21 25	36 22 33 31 7 33 9 21 25	3 27 36 34 9 34 9 21 25	5 30 6 1 11 35 10 21 25	8 34 11 5 13 35 10 21 25	11 2 10 8 14 35 10 21 25	14 6 14 12 16 35 11 21 25	17 12 19 16 18 35 11 21 25	20 15 22 20 20 34 11 21 25	23 21 21 23 22 34 11 21 25	26 24 26 27 24 34 11 22 25
13	30 18 30 31 4 32 9 21 25	33 23 35 30 6 33 9 21 25	36 23 33 31 7 34 9 21 25	3 28 1 34 9 34 9 21 25	6 31 7 1 11 35 10 21 25	9 35 11 5 13 35 10 21 25	11 3 10 8 14 35 10 21 25	14 8 14 12 16 35 11 21 25	17 13 19 16 18 35 11 21 25	20 17 22 20 20 34 11 21 25	23 22 22 24 22 34 11 21 25	26 26 26 27 25 34 11 22 25
14	30 19 30 31 4 32 9 21 25	33 24 35 30 6 33 9 21 25	36 25 33 31 7 34 9 21 25	3 29 1 34 9 34 9 21 25	6 32 7 1 11 35 10 21 25	9 1 11 5 13 35 10 21 25	12 4 10 9 15 35 10 21 25	14 9 14 12 16 35 11 21 25	17 15 20 16 18 35 11 21 25	20 18 22 20 20 34 11 21 25	24 23 22 24 23 34 11 21 25	27 27 26 27 25 34 11 22 25
15	30 20 30 31 4 32 9 21 25	33 25 35 30 6 33 9 21 25	36 26 33 31 7 34 9 21 25	3 30 1 34 9 34 9 21 25	6 33 7 2 11 35 10 21 25	9 2 11 5 13 35 10 21 25	12 5 10 9 15 35 10 21 25	15 11 14 12 17 35 11 21 25	18 16 20 16 19 35 11 21 25	21 20 22 20 21 34 11 21 25	24 25 22 24 23 34 11 21 25	27 28 26 28 25 34 11 22 25
16	30 22 30 31 4 32 9 21 25	33 26 35 30 6 33 9 21 25	36 27 33 31 7 34 9 21 25	3 31 1 34 9 34 9 21 25	6 35 7 2 11 35 10 21 25	9 3 11 5 13 35 10 21 25	12 7 10 9 15 35 10 21 25	15 12 15 13 17 35 11 21 25	18 18 20 16 19 35 11 21 25	21 21 22 20 21 34 11 21 25	24 26 22 24 23 34 11 21 25	27 29 27 28 25 34 11 22 25
17	30 23 31 31 4 32 9 21 25	33 27 35 30 6 33 9 21 25	36 28 33 32 7 34 9 21 25	3 33 1 34 9 34 9 21 25	6 36 7 2 11 35 10 21 25	9 5 11 5 13 35 10 21 25	12 8 10 9 15 35 10 21 25	15 14 15 13 17 35 11 21 25	18 19 20 16 19 35 11 21 25	21 23 22 20 21 34 11 21 25	24 27 22 24 23 34 11 21 25	27 31 27 28 25 35 11 22 25
18	30 24 31 31 4 32 9 21 25	33 29 35 30 6 33 9 21 25	36 29 33 32 7 34 9 21 25	3 34 1 35 9 34 9 21 25	6 1 8 2 11 35 10 21 25	9 6 11 5 13 35 10 21 25	12 10 10 9 15 35 10 21 25	15 15 15 13 17 35 11 21 25	18 20 20 17 19 35 11 21 25	21 24 22 20 21 34 11 21 25	24 29 22 24 23 34 11 21 25	27 32 27 28 25 35 11 22 25
19	30 25 31 31 4 32 9 21 25	33 30 34 30 6 33 9 21 25	36 31 33 32 8 34 9 21 25	3 35 2 35 9 34 9 21 25	6 2 8 2 11 35 10 21 25	9 7 11 6 13 35 10 21 25	12 11 10 9 15 35 10 21 25	15 17 15 13 17 35 11 21 25	18 22 20 17 19 35 11 21 25	21 25 22 20 21 34 11 21 25	24 30 22 24 23 34 11 21 25	27 33 27 28 25 35 11 22 25
20	30 27 31 31 4 32 9 21 25	33 31 34 30 6 33 9 21 25	36 32 34 32 8 34 9 21 25	3 36 2 35 9 34 9 21 25	6 4 8 2 11 35 10 21 25	9 9 11 6 13 35 10 21 25	12 13 10 9 15 35 10 21 25	15 18 15 13 17 35 11 21 25	18 23 20 17 19 35 11 21 25	21 27 22 21 21 34 11 21 25	24 31 23 24 23 34 11 21 25	27 34 27 28 25 35 11 22 25
21	30 28 31 31 4 32 9 21 25	34 32 34 30 6 33 9 21 25	36 33 34 32 8 34 9 21 25	3 2 2 35 9 34 9 21 25	6 5 8 2 11 35 10 21 25	9 10 11 6 13 35 10 21 25	12 14 10 9 15 35 10 21 25	15 20 16 13 17 35 11 21 25	18 25 21 17 19 34 11 21 25	21 28 22 21 21 34 11 21 25	24 32 23 25 23 34 11 21 25	27 35 27 28 25 35 11 22 25
22	31 29 31 31 5 32 9 21 25	34 33 34 30 6 33 9 21 25	36 34 34 32 8 34 9 21 25	4 3 2 35 9 34 9 21 25	6 7 8 2 11 35 10 21 25	9 12 11 6 13 35 10 21 25	12 16 10 9 15 35 11 21 25	15 21 16 13 17 35 11 21 25	18 26 21 17 19 34 11 21 25	21 29 22 21 21 34 11 21 25	24 33 23 25 23 34 11 21 25	27 1 27 28 25 35 11 22 25
23	31 30 32 31 5 32 9 21 25	34 35 34 30 6 33 9 21 25	1 36 34 32 8 34 9 21 25	4 4 2 35 10 34 9 21 25	7 8 8 2 11 35 10 21 25	10 13 11 6 13 35 10 21 25	12 17 10 10 15 35 11 21 25	15 22 16 13 17 35 11 21 25	18 27 21 17 19 34 11 21 25	21 30 22 21 21 34 11 21 25	24 35 23 25 23 34 11 21 25	27 2 28 29 25 35 11 22 25
24	31 31 32 31 5 32 9 21 25	34 36 34 30 6 33 9 21 25	1 1 34 32 8 34 9 21 25	4 6 3 35 10 34 9 21 25	7 10 9 3 11 35 10 21 25	10 15 11 6 13 35 10 21 25	12 19 10 10 15 35 11 21 25	15 24 16 14 17 35 11 21 25	18 28 21 17 19 34 11 21 25	21 31 22 21 21 34 11 21 25	25 36 23 25 23 34 11 21 25	28 3 28 29 25 35 11 22 25
25	31 32 32 31 5 32 9 21 25	34 1 34 30 6 33 9 21 25	1 2 34 32 8 34 9 21 25	4 7 3 35 10 34 9 21 25	7 11 9 3 11 35 10 21 25	10 16 11 6 13 35 10 21 25	13 20 11 10 15 35 11 21 25	16 25 16 14 17 35 11 21 25	19 29 21 17 19 34 11 21 25	22 33 22 21 21 34 11 21 25	25 1 23 25 23 34 11 21 25	28 4 28 29 25 35 11 22 25
26	31 34 32 31 5 32 9 21 25	34 2 34 30 6 33 9 21 25	1 3 34 32 8 34 9 21 25	4 9 3 35 10 34 9 21 25	7 12 9 3 12 35 10 21 25	10 18 11 6 13 35 10 21 25	13 21 11 10 15 35 11 21 25	16 26 16 14 17 35 11 21 25	19 31 21 18 19 34 11 21 25	22 34 22 21 21 34 11 21 25	25 2 23 25 23 34 11 21 25	28 6 28 29 25 35 11 22 25
27	31 35 32 31 5 32 9 21 25	34 4 34 30 6 33 9 21 25	1 5 34 32 8 34 9 21 25	4 10 3 36 10 34 9 21 25	7 14 9 3 12 35 10 21 25	10 19 10 7 14 35 10 21 25	13 23 11 10 15 35 11 21 25	16 27 17 14 17 35 11 21 25	19 32 21 18 19 34 11 21 25	22 35 21 21 21 34 11 21 25	25 4 24 25 23 34 11 21 25	28 7 28 29 26 35 11 22 25
28	31 36 32 31 5 32 9 21 25	34 5 34 30 6 33 9 21 25	1 6 34 32 8 34 9 21 25	4 11 3 36 10 34 9 21 25	7 15 9 3 12 35 10 21 25	10 20 10 7 14 35 10 21 25	13 24 11 10 15 35 11 21 25	16 29 17 14 17 35 11 21 25	19 33 21 18 19 34 11 21 25	22 36 21 22 21 34 11 21 25	25 5 24 25 23 34 11 21 25	28 8 28 29 26 35 11 22 25
29	31 1 33 31 5 32 9 21 25	1974	1 8 34 33 8 34 9 21 25	4 13 4 36 10 34 9 21 25	7 17 9 3 12 35 10 21 25	10 22 10 7 14 35 10 21 25	13 25 11 10 15 35 11 21 25	16 30 17 14 17 35 11 21 25	19 34 22 18 19 34 11 21 25	22 1 21 22 21 34 11 21 25	25 6 24 26 24 34 11 21 25	28 10 29 29 26 35 11 22 25
30	31 3 33 30 5 33 9 21 25		1 9 35 33 8 34 9 21 25	4 14 4 36 10 35 10 21 25	7 18 9 3 12 35 10 21 25	10 23 10 7 14 35 10 21 25	13 26 11 10 16 35 11 21 25	16 31 17 14 18 35 11 21 25	19 35 22 18 20 34 11 21 25	22 3 21 22 22 34 11 21 25	25 8 24 26 24 34 11 21 25	28 11 29 29 26 35 11 22 25
31	31 4 33 30 5 33 9 21 25		1 10 35 33 8 34 9 21 25		7 19 10 3 12 35 10 21 25		13 28 11 11 16 35 11 21 25	16 32 17 14 18 35 11 21 25		22 4 21 22 22 34 11 21 25		28 13 29 30 26 35 11 22 25

	JAN	FEB	MAR	APR	MAY	JUNE	JULY	AUG	SEPT	OCT	NOV	DEC
1	28 14 29 30 26 35 11 22 25	32 20 33 34 28 35 11 22 26	34 21 32 1 30 36 11 22 26	1 26 36 5 33 1 11 22 26	4 29 6 8 35 1 11 21 26	7 33 9 12 1 2 11 21 25	10 36 8 15 3 3 11 21 25	13 5 13 17 6 3 12 21 25	16 10 19 15 7 3 12 21 25	19 13 21 15 9 3 13 22 25	22 19 21 18 10 2 13 22 25	25 23 25 21 9 2 13 22 26
2	28 16 29 30 26 35 11 22 25	32 21 33 34 28 35 11 22 26	34 22 32 1 30 36 11 22 26	2 27 36 5 33 1 11 22 26	4 30 6 9 35 1 11 21 26	7 35 9 12 1 2 11 21 25	10 2 8 15 3 3 11 21 25	13 6 13 17 6 3 12 21 25	16 11 19 15 7 3 12 21 25	19 14 21 15 9 3 13 22 25	22 20 21 18 10 2 13 22 25	25 24 26 21 9 2 13 22 26
3	29 17 29 30 26 35 11 22 25	32 22 33 34 28 35 11 22 26	35 23 32 1 30 36 11 22 26	2 28 36 5 33 1 11 22 26	5 31 6 9 35 1 11 21 26	8 36 9 12 1 2 11 21 25	10 3 8 15 3 3 11 21 25	13 7 14 17 6 3 12 21 25	16 12 19 15 8 3 12 21 25	19 16 21 15 9 3 13 22 25	22 22 21 18 10 2 13 22 25	25 25 26 21 9 2 13 22 26
4	29 19 30 30 26 35 11 22 25	32 24 33 34 28 35 11 22 26	35 25 32 1 30 36 11 22 26	2 29 36 5 33 1 11 22 26	5 33 6 9 35 1 11 21 26	8 1 9 12 1 2 11 21 25	11 4 8 15 4 3 12 21 25	14 9 14 17 6 3 12 21 25	16 14 19 15 8 3 12 21 25	19 18 20 15 9 2 13 22 25	22 23 21 18 10 2 13 22 25	26 27 26 21 9 2 13 22 26
5	29 20 30 30 26 35 11 22 25	32 25 33 34 28 35 11 22 26	35 26 32 2 31 36 11 22 26	2 31 36 5 33 1 11 22 26	5 34 6 9 35 2 11 21 26	8 2 9 12 1 2 11 21 25	11 5 9 15 4 3 12 21 25	14 10 14 17 6 3 12 21 25	17 15 19 15 8 3 12 21 25	20 19 20 15 9 2 13 22 25	23 25 21 18 10 2 13 22 25	26 28 26 21 9 2 13 22 26
6	29 21 30 30 26 35 11 22 25	32 26 32 34 29 35 11 22 26	35 27 32 2 31 36 11 22 26	2 32 1 5 33 1 11 22 26	5 35 7 9 35 2 11 21 26	8 3 9 12 2 2 11 21 25	11 7 9 15 4 3 12 21 25	14 12 14 17 6 3 12 21 25	17 17 19 15 8 3 12 21 25	20 21 20 15 9 2 13 22 25	23 26 21 18 10 2 13 22 25	26 29 26 21 9 2 13 22 26
7	29 23 30 30 26 35 11 22 25	32 28 32 34 29 35 11 22 26	35 28 32 2 31 36 11 22 26	2 33 1 6 33 1 11 22 26	5 36 7 9 35 2 11 21 26	8 5 8 12 2 2 11 21 25	11 8 9 15 4 3 12 21 25	14 13 14 17 6 3 12 21 25	17 18 19 15 8 3 12 21 25	20 22 20 16 9 2 13 22 25	23 27 22 18 10 2 13 22 25	26 31 26 21 9 2 13 22 26
8	29 24 30 31 26 35 11 22 25	32 29 32 34 29 35 11 22 26	35 30 32 2 31 36 11 22 26	2 34 1 6 33 1 11 22 26	5 1 7 9 35 2 11 21 26	8 6 8 13 2 2 11 21 25	11 9 9 15 4 3 12 21 25	14 14 15 17 6 3 12 21 25	17 20 19 15 8 3 12 21 25	20 24 20 16 9 2 13 22 25	23 29 22 18 10 2 13 22 25	26 32 26 22 9 2 13 22 26
9	29 25 30 31 26 35 11 22 25	32 30 32 35 29 36 11 22 26	35 31 32 2 31 36 11 22 26	2 35 1 6 33 1 11 21 26	5 3 7 9 35 2 11 21 26	8 7 8 13 2 2 11 21 25	11 11 9 15 4 3 12 21 25	14 16 15 17 6 3 12 21 25	17 21 20 15 8 3 12 21 25	20 25 20 16 9 2 13 22 25	23 30 22 18 10 2 13 22 25	26 33 27 22 9 2 13 22 26
10	29 27 31 31 27 35 11 22 25	32 31 32 35 29 36 11 22 26	35 32 33 2 31 36 11 22 26	2 36 1 6 33 1 11 21 26	5 4 7 9 36 2 11 21 26	8 9 8 13 2 2 11 21 25	11 12 9 15 4 3 12 21 25	14 17 15 17 6 3 12 21 25	17 23 20 15 8 3 12 21 25	20 27 20 16 9 2 13 22 25	23 31 22 18 10 2 13 22 25	26 34 27 22 9 2 13 22 26
11	29 28 31 31 27 35 11 22 25	33 32 32 35 29 36 11 22 26	35 33 33 2 31 36 11 22 26	2 2 2 6 33 1 11 21 26	5 5 7 10 36 2 11 21 26	8 10 8 13 2 2 11 21 25	11 14 9 16 4 3 12 21 25	14 19 15 17 6 3 12 21 25	17 24 20 15 8 3 12 21 25	20 28 20 16 9 2 13 22 25	23 32 22 19 10 2 13 22 25	26 36 27 22 9 2 13 22 26
12	30 29 31 31 27 35 11 22 25	33 34 32 35 29 36 11 22 26	35 34 33 2 31 36 11 22 26	3 3 2 6 33 1 11 21 26	5 6 8 10 36 2 11 21 25	8 11 8 13 2 2 11 21 25	11 15 9 16 4 3 12 21 25	14 21 15 17 6 3 12 21 25	17 26 20 15 8 3 12 21 25	20 29 20 16 9 2 13 22 25	23 34 22 19 10 2 13 22 25	26 1 27 22 9 2 13 22 26
13	30 30 31 31 27 35 11 22 25	33 35 32 35 29 36 11 22 26	36 36 33 3 31 36 11 22 26	3 4 2 6 33 1 11 21 26	6 8 8 10 36 2 11 21 25	9 13 8 13 2 2 11 21 25	11 17 9 16 4 3 12 21 25	14 22 16 16 6 3 12 21 25	17 27 20 15 8 3 12 21 25	20 30 20 16 9 2 13 22 25	23 35 22 19 10 2 13 22 25	26 2 27 22 9 2 13 22 26
14	30 31 31 31 27 35 11 22 25	33 36 32 35 29 36 11 22 26	36 1 33 3 31 36 11 22 26	3 5 2 6 34 1 11 21 26	6 9 8 10 36 2 11 21 25	9 14 8 13 2 2 11 21 25	11 18 10 16 4 3 12 21 25	14 23 16 16 6 3 12 21 25	17 28 20 15 8 3 12 21 25	20 32 19 16 9 2 13 22 25	23 36 23 19 10 2 13 22 25	27 3 27 22 9 2 13 22 26
15	30 33 31 31 27 35 11 22 25	33 1 32 35 29 36 11 22 26	36 2 33 3 31 36 11 22 26	3 7 2 7 34 1 11 21 26	6 10 8 10 36 2 11 21 25	9 16 8 13 2 2 11 21 25	12 20 10 16 4 3 12 21 25	15 25 16 16 6 3 12 21 25	18 29 20 15 8 3 12 21 25	21 33 19 16 9 2 13 22 25	24 1 23 19 10 2 13 22 25	27 4 28 22 9 2 13 22 26
16	30 34 32 32 27 35 11 22 25	33 2 31 35 29 36 11 22 26	36 3 33 3 31 36 11 22 26	3 8 3 7 34 1 11 21 26	6 12 8 10 36 2 11 21 25	9 17 8 13 2 2 11 21 25	12 21 10 16 4 3 12 21 25	15 26 16 16 6 3 12 21 25	18 31 20 15 8 3 12 21 25	21 34 19 16 9 2 13 22 25	24 2 23 19 10 2 13 22 25	27 6 28 23 9 2 13 22 26
17	30 35 32 32 27 35 11 22 25	33 3 31 36 29 36 11 22 26	36 4 33 3 31 36 11 22 26	3 9 3 7 34 1 11 21 26	6 13 8 10 36 2 11 21 25	9 18 8 13 2 2 11 21 25	12 22 10 16 5 3 12 21 25	15 27 16 16 7 3 12 21 25	18 32 20 15 8 3 12 21 25	21 35 19 16 9 2 13 22 25	24 4 23 19 10 2 13 22 25	27 7 28 23 9 2 13 22 26
18	30 36 32 32 27 35 11 22 25	33 5 31 36 29 36 11 22 26	36 6 34 3 32 36 11 22 26	3 11 3 7 34 1 11 21 26	6 14 8 10 36 2 11 21 25	9 21 8 14 2 2 11 21 25	12 23 10 16 5 3 12 21 25	15 29 16 16 7 3 12 21 25	18 33 20 15 8 3 12 21 25	21 36 19 16 9 2 13 22 25	24 5 23 19 10 2 13 22 25	27 8 28 23 9 2 13 22 26
19	30 1 32 32 27 35 11 22 26	33 6 31 36 29 36 11 22 26	36 7 34 3 32 36 11 22 26	3 12 3 7 34 1 11 21 26	6 16 8 10 36 2 11 21 25	9 22 8 14 3 2 11 21 25	12 25 11 16 5 3 12 21 25	15 30 17 16 7 3 12 21 25	18 34 21 15 8 3 12 21 25	21 2 19 16 9 2 13 22 25	24 6 23 19 10 2 13 22 25	27 10 28 23 9 2 13 22 26
20	30 3 32 32 27 35 11 22 26	33 7 31 36 30 36 11 22 26	36 8 34 3 32 36 11 22 26	3 13 3 7 34 1 11 21 26	6 17 8 11 36 2 11 21 25	9 23 8 14 3 2 11 21 25	12 26 11 16 5 3 12 21 25	15 31 17 16 7 3 12 21 25	18 36 21 15 8 3 12 21 25	21 3 19 16 9 2 13 22 25	24 7 24 19 10 2 13 22 25	27 11 28 23 9 2 13 22 26
21	30 4 32 32 27 35 11 22 26	34 9 31 36 30 36 11 22 26	36 10 34 4 32 36 11 22 26	3 15 4 7 34 1 11 21 26	6 19 8 11 36 2 11 21 25	9 24 8 14 3 2 11 21 25	12 28 11 16 5 3 12 21 25	15 32 17 16 7 3 12 21 25	18 1 21 15 8 3 12 21 25	21 4 19 17 9 2 13 22 25	24 9 24 20 10 2 13 22 26	27 12 28 23 8 2 13 22 26
22	31 5 32 32 27 35 11 22 26	34 10 31 36 30 36 11 22 26	36 11 34 4 32 36 11 22 26	4 16 4 7 34 1 11 21 26	6 20 8 11 36 2 11 21 25	9 25 8 14 3 2 11 21 25	12 29 11 16 5 3 12 21 25	15 33 17 16 7 3 12 21 25	18 2 21 15 9 3 12 21 25	21 5 19 17 10 2 13 22 25	24 10 24 20 9 2 13 22 26	27 14 29 23 8 2 13 22 26
23	31 6 32 32 27 35 11 22 26	34 11 31 36 30 36 11 22 26	1 12 34 4 32 1 11 22 26	4 18 4 7 34 1 11 21 26	7 22 9 11 1 2 11 21 25	9 27 8 14 3 2 11 21 25	12 30 11 16 5 3 12 21 25	15 35 17 16 7 3 12 21 25	18 3 21 15 9 3 12 21 25	21 6 19 17 10 2 13 22 25	24 11 24 20 9 2 13 22 26	27 15 29 23 8 2 13 22 26
24	31 8 33 33 28 35 11 22 26	34 13 31 36 30 36 11 22 26	1 14 34 4 32 1 11 22 26	4 19 4 8 34 1 11 21 26	7 23 9 11 1 2 11 21 25	10 28 8 14 3 2 11 21 25	12 31 11 16 5 3 12 21 25	15 36 17 16 7 3 12 21 25	18 4 21 15 9 3 12 21 25	21 8 20 17 10 2 13 22 25	25 13 24 20 9 2 13 22 26	28 16 29 23 8 2 13 22 26
25	31 9 33 33 28 35 11 22 26	34 14 31 1 30 36 11 22 26	1 15 35 4 32 1 11 22 26	4 21 5 8 34 1 11 21 26	7 24 9 11 1 2 11 21 25	10 29 8 14 3 2 11 21 25	13 33 12 16 5 3 12 21 25	16 1 18 16 7 3 12 21 25	19 5 21 15 9 3 12 21 25	21 9 20 17 10 2 13 22 25	25 14 24 20 9 2 13 22 26	28 18 29 24 8 2 13 22 26
26	31 11 33 33 28 35 11 22 26	34 16 32 1 30 36 11 22 26	1 17 35 4 32 1 11 22 26	4 22 5 8 34 1 11 21 26	7 26 9 11 1 2 11 21 25	10 30 8 14 3 2 11 21 25	13 34 12 16 5 3 12 21 25	16 2 18 16 7 3 12 21 25	19 7 21 15 9 3 12 21 25	22 10 20 17 10 2 13 22 25	25 15 25 20 9 2 13 22 26	28 19 29 24 8 2 13 22 26
27	31 12 33 33 28 35 11 22 26	34 18 32 1 30 36 11 22 26	1 18 35 4 32 1 11 22 26	4 24 5 8 35 1 11 21 26	7 27 9 11 1 2 11 21 25	10 32 8 14 3 3 11 21 25	13 35 12 16 5 3 12 21 25	16 3 18 16 7 3 12 21 25	19 8 21 15 9 3 12 22 25	22 12 20 17 10 2 13 22 25	25 17 25 20 9 2 13 22 26	28 21 29 24 8 2 13 22 26
28	31 14 33 33 28 35 11 22 26	34 19 32 1 30 36 11 22 26	1 19 35 4 32 1 11 22 26	4 25 5 8 35 1 11 21 26	7 28 9 11 1 2 11 21 25	10 33 8 14 3 3 11 21 25	13 36 12 16 5 3 12 21 25	16 5 18 16 7 3 12 21 25	19 9 21 15 9 3 12 22 25	22 13 20 17 10 2 13 22 25	25 18 25 20 9 2 13 22 26	28 22 30 24 8 2 13 22 26
29	31 15 33 33 28 35 11 22 26		1 21 35 5 32 1 11 22 26	4 26 5 8 35 1 11 21 26	7 30 9 12 1 2 11 21 25	10 34 8 15 3 3 11 21 25	13 1 13 16 5 3 12 21 25	16 6 18 16 7 3 12 21 25	19 11 21 15 9 3 13 22 25	22 14 20 17 10 2 13 22 25	25 20 25 20 9 2 13 22 26	28 23 30 24 8 2 13 22 26
30	31 17 33 33 28 35 11 22 26	1975	1 23 35 5 32 1 11 22 26	4 28 6 8 35 1 11 21 26	7 31 9 12 1 2 11 21 25	10 35 8 15 3 3 11 21 25	13 3 13 16 5 3 12 21 25	16 7 18 16 7 3 12 21 25	19 12 21 15 9 3 13 22 25	22 16 20 17 10 2 13 22 25	25 21 25 21 9 2 13 22 26	28 25 30 24 8 2 13 22 26
31	31 18 33 33 28 35 11 22 26		1 24 36 5 33 1 11 22 26		7 32 9 12 1 2 11 21 25		13 4 13 17 5 3 12 21 25	16 8 18 16 7 3 12 21 25		22 17 20 17 10 2 13 22 25		28 26 30 24 8 2 13 22 26

	JAN	FEB	MAR	APR	MAY	JUNE
1	28 28 30 24 8 2 13 22 26	32 32 30 28 8 2 12 22 26	34 34 32 32 9 3 12 22 26	2 3 1 35 10 4 12 22 26	4 6 7 3 12 4 12 22 26	7 11 6 7 13 5 12 22 26
2	28 29 30 24 8 2 12 22 26	32 34 30 28 8 2 12 22 26	35 36 32 32 9 3 12 22 26	2 4 2 36 10 4 12 22 26	5 7 7 3 12 4 12 22 26	8 12 6 7 13 5 12 22 26
3	29 30 30 25 8 2 12 22 26	32 35 30 28 8 2 12 22 26	35 1 32 32 9 3 12 22 26	2 5 2 36 10 4 12 22 26	5 9 7 3 12 4 12 22 26	8 13 6 7 13 5 12 22 26
4	29 32 31 25 8 2 12 22 26	32 36 30 28 8 2 12 22 26	35 2 33 32 9 3 12 22 26	2 7 2 36 10 4 12 22 26	5 10 7 4 12 4 12 22 26	8 14 6 7 14 5 12 22 26
5	29 33 31 25 8 2 12 22 26	32 1 30 29 8 2 12 22 26	35 3 33 32 9 3 12 22 26	2 8 2 36 10 4 12 22 26	5 11 7 4 12 4 12 22 26	8 16 6 7 14 5 12 22 26
6	29 34 31 25 8 2 12 22 26	32 2 30 29 8 2 12 22 26	35 4 33 32 9 3 12 22 26	2 9 2 36 10 4 12 22 26	5 13 7 4 12 4 12 22 26	8 18 6 8 14 5 12 22 26
7	29 35 31 25 8 2 12 22 26	32 4 30 29 8 2 12 22 26	35 6 33 32 9 3 12 22 26	2 10 3 36 10 4 12 22 26	5 14 7 4 12 4 12 22 26	8 19 6 8 14 5 12 22 26
8	29 36 31 25 8 2 12 22 26	32 5 30 29 8 2 12 22 26	35 7 33 33 9 3 12 22 26	2 11 3 36 10 4 12 22 26	5 15 7 4 12 4 12 22 26	8 20 6 8 14 5 12 22 26
9	29 2 31 25 8 2 12 22 26	32 6 30 29 8 2 12 22 26	35 8 33 33 9 3 12 22 26	2 13 3 36 10 4 12 22 26	5 17 7 4 12 4 12 22 26	8 22 6 8 14 5 12 22 26
10	29 3 31 25 8 2 12 22 26	32 7 30 29 8 2 12 22 26	35 9 33 33 9 3 12 22 26	2 14 3 1 10 4 12 22 26	5 18 7 4 12 4 12 22 26	8 23 6 8 14 5 12 22 26
11	29 4 31 26 8 2 12 22 26	33 8 30 29 8 2 12 22 26	35 11 34 33 9 3 12 22 26	3 16 4 1 11 4 12 22 26	5 19 7 4 12 4 12 22 26	8 25 6 8 14 5 12 22 26
12	29 5 31 26 8 2 12 22 26	33 10 30 29 8 2 12 22 26	36 12 34 33 9 3 12 22 26	3 17 4 1 11 4 12 22 26	6 20 7 5 12 5 12 22 26	9 26 6 8 14 5 12 22 26
13	30 6 31 26 8 2 12 22 26	33 11 30 30 8 3 12 22 26	36 13 34 33 9 3 12 22 26	3 19 4 1 11 4 12 22 26	6 22 7 5 12 5 12 22 26	9 28 6 8 14 5 12 22 26
14	30 8 31 26 8 2 12 22 26	33 13 30 30 8 3 12 22 26	36 15 34 33 9 3 12 22 26	3 20 4 1 11 4 12 22 26	6 23 7 5 12 5 12 22 26	9 29 6 9 14 5 12 22 26
15	30 9 31 26 8 2 12 22 26	33 14 30 30 8 3 12 22 26	36 16 34 33 9 3 12 22 26	3 22 4 1 11 4 12 22 26	6 25 7 5 12 5 12 22 26	9 31 7 9 14 5 13 22 26
16	30 10 31 26 8 2 12 22 26	33 15 30 30 8 3 12 22 26	36 18 34 34 9 3 12 22 26	3 23 4 1 11 4 12 22 26	6 26 7 5 12 5 12 22 26	9 32 7 9 14 5 13 22 26
17	30 12 31 26 8 2 12 22 26	33 17 31 30 8 3 12 22 26	36 19 35 34 9 3 12 22 26	3 25 5 1 11 4 12 22 26	6 28 7 5 12 5 12 22 26	9 33 7 9 14 5 13 22 26
18	30 13 31 26 8 2 12 22 26	33 19 31 30 8 3 12 22 26	36 21 35 34 9 3 12 22 26	3 26 5 2 11 4 12 22 26	6 30 7 5 12 5 12 22 26	9 34 7 9 14 5 13 22 26
19	30 15 31 27 8 2 12 22 26	33 20 31 30 8 3 12 22 26	36 22 35 34 9 3 12 22 26	3 28 5 2 11 4 12 22 26	6 31 6 5 13 5 12 22 26	9 36 7 9 14 5 13 22 26
20	30 16 31 27 8 2 12 22 26	33 21 31 30 8 3 12 22 26	36 23 35 34 9 3 12 22 26	3 29 5 2 11 4 12 22 26	6 32 6 6 13 5 12 22 26	9 1 7 9 14 5 13 22 26
21	30 17 31 27 8 2 12 22 26	34 23 31 31 8 3 12 22 26	36 25 35 34 10 3 12 22 26	4 30 5 2 11 4 12 22 26	6 34 6 6 13 5 12 22 26	9 2 7 9 14 5 13 22 26
22	31 19 31 27 8 2 12 22 26	34 24 31 31 8 3 12 22 26	1 26 36 34 10 3 12 22 26	4 31 5 2 11 4 12 22 26	7 35 6 6 13 5 12 22 26	9 3 7 10 15 5 13 22 26
23	31 20 31 27 8 2 12 22 26	34 26 31 31 8 3 12 22 26	1 28 36 34 10 3 12 22 26	4 33 6 2 11 4 12 22 26	7 36 6 6 13 5 12 22 26	10 4 7 10 15 5 13 22 26
24	31 22 31 27 8 2 12 22 26	34 27 31 31 8 3 12 22 26	1 29 36 35 10 3 12 22 26	4 34 6 2 11 4 12 22 26	7 1 6 6 13 5 12 22 26	10 6 8 10 15 5 13 22 26
25	31 23 30 27 8 2 12 22 26	34 28 31 31 9 3 12 22 26	1 31 36 35 10 3 12 22 26	4 35 6 2 11 4 12 22 26	7 3 6 6 13 5 12 22 26	10 7 8 10 15 5 13 22 26
26	31 25 30 27 8 2 12 22 26	34 30 32 31 9 3 12 22 26	1 32 36 35 10 3 12 22 26	4 36 6 3 11 4 12 22 26	7 4 6 6 13 5 12 22 26	10 8 8 10 15 6 13 22 26
27	31 26 30 27 8 2 12 22 26	34 31 32 31 9 3 12 22 26	1 33 36 35 10 3 12 22 26	4 1 6 3 11 4 12 22 26	7 5 6 6 13 5 12 22 26	10 9 8 10 15 6 13 22 26
28	31 27 30 28 8 2 12 22 26	34 32 32 31 9 3 12 22 26	1 34 1 35 10 3 12 22 26	4 3 6 3 11 4 12 22 26	7 6 6 7 13 5 12 22 26	10 11 8 10 15 6 13 22 26
29	31 29 30 28 8 2 12 22 26	34 33 32 32 9 3 12 22 26	1 35 1 35 10 3 12 22 26	4 4 6 3 11 4 12 22 26	7 7 6 7 13 5 12 22 26	10 12 8 10 15 6 13 22 26
30	31 30 30 28 8 2 12 22 26	**1976**	1 36 1 35 10 3 12 22 26	4 5 6 3 11 4 12 22 26	7 8 6 7 13 5 12 22 26	10 13 9 11 15 6 13 22 26
31	31 31 30 28 8 2 12 22 26		1 1 1 35 10 4 12 22 26		7 10 6 7 13 5 12 22 26	

	JULY	AUG	SEPT	OCT	NOV	DEC
1	10 14 9 11 15 6 13 22 26	13 20 15 14 17 6 13 22 26	16 25 19 18 19 6 13 22 26	19 29 18 22 21 7 14 22 26	22 34 22 26 23 6 14 22 26	25 1 27 29 25 6 14 22 26
2	10 16 9 11 15 6 13 22 26	13 21 15 15 17 6 13 22 26	16 26 19 18 19 6 13 22 26	19 30 18 22 21 6 14 22 26	22 35 22 26 23 6 14 22 26	25 2 27 30 25 6 14 22 26
3	11 17 9 11 15 6 13 22 26	13 23 15 15 17 6 13 22 26	16 28 19 19 19 6 13 22 26	19 31 18 22 21 6 14 22 26	22 36 22 26 23 6 14 22 26	25 4 27 30 25 6 14 22 26
4	11 19 9 11 15 6 13 22 26	14 24 15 15 17 6 13 22 26	17 29 19 19 19 6 14 22 26	19 33 18 22 21 6 14 22 26	23 1 22 26 23 6 14 22 26	26 5 27 30 25 6 14 22 26
5	11 20 9 11 15 6 13 22 26	14 25 16 15 17 6 13 22 26	17 31 19 19 19 6 14 22 26	20 34 18 22 21 6 14 22 26	23 3 23 26 23 6 14 22 26	26 6 27 30 25 6 14 22 26
6	11 21 10 11 15 6 13 22 26	14 27 16 15 17 6 13 22 26	17 32 19 19 19 6 14 22 26	20 35 18 23 21 6 14 22 26	23 4 23 26 23 6 14 22 26	26 7 27 30 25 6 14 22 26
7	11 23 10 11 15 6 13 22 26	14 28 16 15 17 6 13 22 26	17 33 19 19 19 6 14 22 26	20 1 18 23 21 6 14 22 26	23 5 23 27 23 6 14 22 26	26 8 27 30 26 6 14 22 26
8	11 24 10 12 15 6 13 22 26	14 30 16 15 17 6 13 22 26	17 34 19 19 19 6 14 22 26	20 2 18 23 21 6 14 22 26	23 6 23 27 23 6 14 22 26	26 9 28 30 26 6 14 22 26
9	11 26 10 12 16 6 13 22 26	14 31 16 16 17 6 13 22 26	17 36 19 19 19 7 14 22 26	20 3 18 23 21 6 14 22 26	23 7 23 27 24 6 14 22 26	26 11 28 30 26 6 14 22 26
10	11 27 11 12 16 6 13 22 26	14 32 16 16 17 6 13 22 26	17 1 19 19 19 7 14 22 26	20 4 18 23 21 6 14 22 26	23 9 23 27 24 6 14 22 26	26 12 28 30 26 6 14 22 26
11	11 29 11 12 16 6 13 22 26	14 34 17 16 18 6 13 22 26	17 2 19 20 20 7 14 22 26	20 5 18 23 22 6 14 22 26	23 10 24 27 24 6 14 22 26	26 13 28 31 26 6 14 22 26
12	11 30 11 12 16 6 13 22 26	14 35 17 16 18 6 13 22 26	17 3 19 20 20 7 14 22 26	20 6 19 23 22 6 14 22 26	23 11 24 27 24 6 14 22 26	26 14 28 31 26 6 14 22 26
13	11 31 11 12 16 6 13 22 26	14 36 17 16 18 6 13 22 26	17 4 19 20 20 7 14 22 26	20 8 19 24 22 6 14 22 26	23 12 24 27 24 6 14 22 26	27 16 28 31 26 6 14 22 26
14	12 33 11 12 16 6 13 22 26	15 1 17 16 18 6 13 22 26	18 6 19 20 20 7 14 22 26	20 9 19 24 22 6 14 22 26	24 13 24 27 24 6 14 22 26	27 17 28 31 26 6 14 22 26
15	12 34 12 12 16 6 13 22 26	15 2 17 16 18 6 13 22 26	18 7 19 20 20 7 14 22 26	21 10 19 24 22 6 14 22 26	24 15 24 27 24 6 14 22 26	27 19 29 31 26 6 14 22 26
16	12 35 12 13 16 6 13 22 26	15 4 17 16 18 6 13 22 26	18 8 19 20 20 7 14 22 26	21 11 19 24 22 6 14 22 26	24 16 24 28 24 6 14 22 26	27 20 29 31 26 6 14 22 26
17	12 36 12 13 16 6 13 22 26	15 5 17 16 18 6 13 22 26	18 9 19 20 20 7 14 22 26	21 13 19 24 22 6 14 22 26	24 17 24 28 24 6 14 22 26	27 21 29 31 26 6 14 22 26
18	12 2 12 13 16 6 13 22 26	15 6 18 17 18 6 13 22 26	18 10 19 20 20 7 14 22 26	21 14 20 24 22 6 14 22 26	24 19 25 28 24 6 14 22 26	27 23 29 31 26 6 14 22 26
19	12 3 12 13 16 6 13 22 26	15 7 18 17 18 6 13 22 26	18 12 19 21 20 7 14 22 26	21 15 20 24 22 6 14 22 26	24 20 25 28 24 6 14 22 26	27 24 29 32 26 6 14 22 26
20	12 4 13 13 16 6 13 22 26	15 8 18 17 18 6 13 22 26	18 13 19 21 20 7 14 22 26	21 17 20 24 22 6 14 22 26	24 22 25 28 24 6 14 22 26	27 26 29 32 27 6 14 22 26
21	12 5 13 13 16 6 13 22 26	15 10 18 17 18 6 13 22 26	18 14 18 21 20 7 14 22 26	21 18 20 24 22 6 14 22 26	24 23 25 28 24 6 14 22 26	27 27 29 32 27 6 14 22 26
22	12 6 13 13 16 6 13 22 26	15 11 18 17 18 6 13 22 26	18 16 18 21 20 7 14 22 26	21 20 20 25 22 6 14 22 26	24 25 25 28 24 6 14 22 26	27 29 29 32 27 6 14 22 26
23	12 8 13 13 16 6 13 22 26	15 12 18 17 18 6 13 22 26	18 17 18 21 20 7 14 22 26	21 21 20 25 22 6 14 22 26	24 26 25 28 25 6 14 22 26	28 30 30 32 27 6 14 22 26
24	13 9 13 14 16 6 13 22 26	15 14 18 17 18 6 13 22 26	19 19 18 21 20 7 14 22 26	21 23 21 25 22 6 14 22 26	25 28 26 29 25 6 14 22 26	28 32 30 32 27 6 14 22 26
25	13 10 14 14 17 6 13 22 26	16 15 18 17 18 6 13 22 26	19 20 18 21 20 7 14 22 26	22 24 21 25 23 6 14 22 26	25 30 26 29 25 6 14 22 26	28 33 30 32 27 6 14 22 26
26	13 11 14 14 17 6 13 22 26	16 16 18 18 19 6 13 22 26	19 22 18 21 21 7 14 22 26	22 26 21 25 23 6 14 22 26	25 31 26 29 25 6 14 22 26	28 34 30 32 27 6 14 22 26
27	13 13 14 14 17 6 13 22 26	16 18 19 18 19 6 13 22 26	19 23 18 22 21 7 14 22 26	22 27 21 25 23 6 14 22 26	25 32 26 29 25 6 14 22 26	28 35 30 32 27 6 14 22 26
28	13 14 14 14 17 6 13 22 26	16 19 19 18 19 6 13 22 26	19 25 18 22 21 7 14 22 26	22 28 21 25 23 6 14 22 26	25 33 26 29 25 6 14 22 26	28 1 30 33 27 6 14 22 26
29	13 16 14 14 17 6 13 22 26	16 21 19 18 19 6 13 22 26	19 26 18 22 21 7 14 22 26	22 30 21 25 23 6 14 22 26	25 35 26 29 25 6 14 22 26	28 2 30 33 27 6 14 22 26
30	13 17 15 14 17 6 13 22 26	16 22 19 18 19 6 13 22 26	19 28 18 22 21 7 14 22 26	22 31 22 26 23 6 14 22 26	25 36 26 29 25 6 14 22 26	28 3 30 33 27 6 14 22 26
31	13 18 15 14 17 6 13 22 26	16 24 19 18 19 6 13 22 26		22 32 22 26 23 6 14 22 26		28 4 30 33 27 6 14 22 26

	JAN	FEB	MAR	APR	MAY	JUNE	JULY	AUG	SEPT	OCT	NOV	DEC
1	28 5 30 33 27 6 14 22 26	32 10 29 36 30 6 14 23 26	34 11 33 2 32 6 14 23 26	2 15 3 2 34 6 13 22 26	4 19 4 1 1 7 13 22 26	7 24 5 3 3 8 14 22 26	10 28 10 6 5 8 14 22 26	13 33 16 9 7 9 14 22 26	16 2 17 13 9 10 15 22 26	19 5 18 16 11 10 15 22 26	22 10 23 20 13 10 15 23 26	25 13 27 24 13 10 15 23 26
2	29 7 29 33 27 6 14 22 26	32 11 29 36 30 6 14 23 26	35 12 33 2 32 6 14 23 26	2 17 3 2 34 6 13 22 26	5 20 4 1 1 7 13 22 26	8 26 5 3 3 8 14 22 26	10 30 11 6 5 8 14 22 26	13 35 16 9 7 9 14 22 26	16 3 17 13 9 10 15 22 26	19 7 18 17 11 10 15 22 26	22 11 23 20 13 10 15 23 26	25 14 27 24 13 10 15 23 26
3	29 8 29 33 28 6 14 22 26	32 12 29 36 30 6 14 23 26	35 13 34 3 32 6 14 23 26	2 18 3 2 34 6 13 22 26	5 22 4 1 1 7 13 22 26	8 27 5 3 3 8 14 22 26	10 31 11 6 5 8 14 22 26	13 36 16 9 8 9 14 22 26	16 4 17 13 9 10 15 22 26	19 8 18 17 11 10 15 22 26	22 12 23 21 13 10 15 23 26	25 16 28 24 13 10 15 23 26
4	29 9 29 33 28 6 14 23 26	32 14 29 1 30 6 14 23 26	35 15 34 3 32 6 14 23 26	2 20 4 2 35 6 13 22 26	5 23 4 1 1 7 13 22 26	8 29 5 3 3 8 14 22 26	11 33 11 6 5 8 14 22 26	14 1 16 10 8 9 14 22 26	17 5 17 13 9 10 15 22 26	19 9 18 17 11 10 15 22 26	23 13 24 21 13 10 15 23 26	26 17 28 24 14 10 15 23 26
5	29 10 29 33 28 6 14 23 26	32 15 30 1 30 6 14 23 26	35 16 34 3 32 6 14 23 26	2 21 4 2 35 6 13 22 26	5 25 4 1 1 7 13 22 26	8 30 6 3 3 8 14 22 26	11 34 11 6 6 8 14 22 26	14 3 16 10 8 9 14 22 26	17 7 17 13 9 10 15 22 26	20 10 19 17 11 10 15 22 26	23 15 24 21 13 10 15 23 26	26 18 28 25 14 10 15 23 26
6	29 12 29 34 28 6 14 23 26	32 16 30 1 30 6 14 23 26	35 17 34 3 32 6 14 23 26	2 23 4 2 35 7 13 22 26	5 26 4 1 1 7 13 22 26	8 32 6 3 3 8 14 22 26	11 35 11 6 6 8 14 22 26	14 4 16 10 8 9 14 22 26	17 8 17 13 9 10 15 22 26	20 11 19 17 11 10 15 22 26	23 16 24 21 13 10 15 23 26	26 19 28 25 14 10 15 23 26
7	29 13 29 34 28 6 14 23 26	32 17 30 1 30 6 14 23 26	35 19 34 3 32 6 14 23 26	2 24 4 2 35 7 13 22 26	5 28 4 1 1 7 13 22 26	8 33 6 3 3 8 14 22 26	11 1 11 6 6 9 14 22 26	14 5 17 10 8 9 14 22 26	17 9 16 14 9 10 15 22 26	20 13 19 17 11 10 15 22 26	23 17 24 21 13 10 15 23 26	26 21 28 25 14 10 15 23 26
8	29 14 29 34 28 6 14 23 26	32 19 30 1 30 6 14 23 26	35 20 34 3 32 6 13 23 26	2 25 4 2 35 7 13 22 26	5 29 4 1 1 7 13 22 26	8 34 6 4 4 8 14 22 26	11 2 12 7 6 9 14 22 26	14 6 17 10 8 9 14 22 26	17 11 16 14 9 10 15 22 26	20 14 19 17 12 10 15 22 26	23 19 24 21 13 10 15 23 26	26 22 28 25 14 10 15 23 26
9	29 16 29 34 28 6 14 23 26	32 21 30 1 30 6 14 23 26	35 22 35 3 33 6 13 23 26	2 27 4 2 35 7 13 22 26	5 31 4 1 1 7 13 22 26	8 35 6 4 4 8 14 22 26	11 3 12 7 6 9 14 22 26	14 7 17 10 8 9 14 22 26	17 12 16 14 9 10 15 22 26	20 15 19 17 12 10 15 22 26	23 20 24 21 13 10 15 23 26	26 24 28 25 14 10 15 23 26
10	29 17 28 34 28 6 14 23 26	33 22 30 1 30 6 14 23 26	35 23 35 3 33 6 13 23 26	2 28 4 2 35 7 13 22 26	5 32 4 2 1 7 13 22 26	8 1 6 4 4 8 14 22 26	11 4 12 7 6 9 14 22 26	14 9 17 10 8 9 14 22 26	17 13 16 14 10 10 15 22 26	20 16 19 18 12 10 15 22 26	23 21 24 21 13 10 15 23 26	26 25 28 25 14 10 15 23 26
11	29 18 28 34 28 6 14 23 26	33 23 30 1 31 6 14 23 26	35 25 35 3 33 6 13 23 26	2 29 4 2 35 7 13 22 26	5 34 4 2 1 7 13 22 26	8 2 6 4 4 8 14 22 26	11 5 12 7 6 9 14 22 26	14 10 17 10 8 9 14 22 26	17 14 16 14 10 10 15 22 26	20 18 20 18 12 10 15 22 26	23 23 25 22 13 10 15 23 26	26 27 28 25 14 10 15 23 26
12	30 19 28 34 28 6 14 23 26	33 25 31 1 31 6 14 23 26	36 26 35 3 33 6 13 23 26	3 31 5 2 35 7 13 22 26	6 35 4 2 2 7 13 22 26	8 3 7 4 4 8 14 22 26	11 7 13 7 6 9 14 22 26	14 11 17 10 8 9 14 22 26	17 16 16 14 10 10 15 22 26	20 19 20 18 12 10 15 22 26	23 24 25 22 13 10 15 23 26	26 28 28 25 14 10 15 23 26
13	30 21 28 34 28 6 14 23 26	33 26 31 1 31 6 14 23 26	36 27 35 3 33 6 13 23 26	3 32 5 2 35 7 13 22 26	6 36 4 2 2 7 13 22 26	9 4 7 4 4 8 14 22 26	11 8 13 7 6 9 14 22 26	14 12 17 11 8 9 14 22 26	17 17 16 14 10 10 15 22 26	20 21 20 18 12 10 15 22 26	23 26 25 22 13 10 15 23 26	26 30 28 26 14 10 15 23 26
14	30 22 28 34 28 6 14 23 26	33 28 31 1 31 6 14 23 26	36 29 36 3 33 6 13 23 26	3 34 5 2 35 7 13 22 26	6 1 4 2 2 7 13 22 26	9 6 7 4 4 8 14 22 26	12 9 13 7 6 9 14 22 26	15 13 17 11 8 9 14 22 26	18 18 16 14 10 10 15 22 26	20 22 20 18 12 10 15 22 26	24 27 25 22 13 10 15 23 26	27 31 28 26 14 10 15 23 26
15	30 24 28 35 28 6 14 23 26	33 29 31 2 31 6 14 23 26	36 30 36 3 33 6 13 23 26	3 35 5 2 35 7 13 22 26	6 2 4 2 2 7 13 22 26	9 7 7 4 4 8 14 22 26	12 10 13 7 6 9 14 22 26	15 15 17 11 8 9 14 22 26	18 20 16 14 10 10 15 22 26	21 23 20 18 12 10 15 22 26	24 29 25 22 13 10 15 23 26	27 33 28 26 14 10 15 23 26
16	30 25 28 35 29 6 14 23 26	33 31 31 2 31 6 14 23 26	36 31 36 3 33 6 13 23 26	3 36 5 1 35 7 13 22 26	6 4 4 2 2 7 14 22 26	9 8 7 4 4 8 14 22 26	12 11 14 7 6 9 14 22 26	15 16 17 11 8 9 14 22 26	18 21 16 15 10 10 15 22 26	21 25 20 18 12 10 15 22 26	24 30 25 22 13 10 15 23 26	27 34 28 26 14 10 15 23 26
17	30 27 28 35 29 6 14 23 26	33 32 31 2 31 6 14 23 26	36 33 36 3 33 6 13 23 26	3 1 5 1 36 7 13 22 26	6 5 4 2 2 7 14 22 26	9 9 7 4 4 8 14 22 26	12 13 14 8 6 9 14 22 26	15 17 17 11 8 9 14 22 26	18 22 16 15 10 10 15 22 26	21 26 21 18 12 10 15 22 26	24 31 25 22 13 10 15 23 26	27 35 28 26 14 10 15 23 26
18	30 28 28 35 29 6 14 23 26	33 33 31 2 31 6 14 23 26	36 34 36 3 33 6 13 23 26	3 3 5 1 36 7 13 22 26	6 6 4 2 2 7 14 22 26	9 10 8 4 4 8 14 22 26	12 14 14 8 6 9 14 22 26	15 19 17 11 9 9 15 22 26	18 24 16 15 10 10 15 22 26	21 28 21 19 12 10 15 23 26	24 33 26 22 13 10 15 23 26	27 1 28 26 14 10 15 23 26
19	30 29 28 35 29 6 14 23 26	33 34 32 2 31 6 14 23 26	36 35 1 3 33 6 13 23 26	3 4 5 1 36 7 13 22 26	6 7 4 2 2 7 14 22 26	9 12 8 5 4 8 14 22 26	12 15 14 8 6 9 14 22 26	15 20 17 11 9 9 15 22 26	18 25 16 15 10 10 15 22 26	21 29 21 19 12 10 15 23 26	24 34 26 23 13 10 15 23 26	27 2 28 26 14 10 15 23 26
20	30 31 28 35 29 6 14 23 26	34 35 32 2 31 6 14 23 26	36 1 1 3 33 6 13 23 26	3 5 5 1 36 7 13 22 26	6 8 4 2 2 7 14 22 26	9 13 8 5 4 8 14 22 26	12 16 14 8 7 9 14 22 26	15 22 17 11 9 9 15 22 26	18 27 16 15 11 10 15 22 26	21 31 21 19 12 10 15 23 26	24 36 26 23 13 10 15 23 26	27 3 28 26 14 10 15 23 26
21	30 32 28 35 29 6 14 23 26	34 1 32 2 31 6 14 23 26	36 2 1 3 33 6 13 23 26	3 6 5 1 36 7 13 22 26	6 10 4 2 2 7 14 22 26	9 14 8 5 4 8 14 22 26	12 18 14 8 7 9 14 22 26	15 23 17 12 9 9 15 22 26	18 28 16 15 11 10 15 22 26	21 32 21 19 12 10 15 23 26	24 1 26 23 13 10 15 23 26	27 4 28 27 14 10 15 23 26
22	31 34 28 35 29 6 14 23 26	34 2 32 2 31 6 14 23 26	1 3 1 3 34 6 13 23 26	4 7 5 1 36 7 13 22 26	6 11 4 2 2 7 14 22 26	9 15 8 5 5 8 14 22 26	12 19 14 8 7 9 14 22 26	15 24 17 12 9 9 15 22 26	18 30 17 15 11 10 15 22 26	21 33 22 19 12 10 15 23 26	24 3 26 23 13 10 15 23 26	27 6 27 27 13 10 15 23 26
23	31 35 28 35 29 6 14 23 26	34 4 32 2 31 6 14 23 26	1 4 1 3 34 6 13 23 26	4 9 5 1 36 7 13 22 26	7 12 4 2 2 7 14 22 26	10 17 9 5 5 8 14 22 26	12 20 15 8 7 9 14 22 26	15 26 17 12 9 9 15 22 26	18 31 17 15 11 10 15 22 26	21 35 22 19 12 10 15 23 26	24 4 26 23 13 10 15 23 26	28 7 27 27 13 10 15 23 26
24	31 36 28 35 29 6 14 23 26	34 5 32 2 32 6 14 23 26	1 5 2 3 34 6 13 23 26	4 10 5 1 36 7 13 22 26	7 13 4 2 2 8 14 22 26	10 18 9 5 5 8 14 22 26	12 22 15 8 7 9 14 22 26	15 27 17 12 9 9 15 22 26	18 32 17 16 11 10 15 22 26	21 36 22 19 12 10 15 23 26	25 5 26 23 13 10 15 23 26	28 8 27 27 13 9 15 23 26
25	31 1 28 36 29 6 14 23 26	34 6 33 2 32 6 14 23 26	1 7 2 3 34 6 13 23 26	4 11 5 1 36 7 13 22 26	7 14 4 2 2 8 14 22 26	10 19 9 5 5 8 14 22 26	13 23 15 8 7 9 14 22 26	16 29 17 12 9 9 15 22 26	19 34 17 16 11 10 15 22 26	22 1 22 19 12 10 15 23 26	25 6 27 23 13 10 15 23 26	28 9 27 27 13 9 15 23 26
26	31 3 29 36 29 6 14 23 26	34 7 33 2 32 6 14 23 26	1 8 2 3 34 6 13 23 26	4 12 5 1 36 7 13 22 26	7 16 4 2 3 8 14 22 26	10 21 9 5 5 8 14 22 26	13 25 15 9 7 9 14 22 26	16 30 17 12 9 9 15 22 26	19 35 17 16 11 10 15 22 26	22 3 22 20 12 10 15 23 26	25 7 27 23 13 10 15 23 26	28 10 27 27 13 9 15 23 26
27	31 4 29 36 29 6 14 23 26	34 8 33 2 32 6 14 23 26	1 9 2 3 34 6 13 23 26	4 14 5 1 36 7 13 22 26	7 17 4 3 3 8 14 22 26	10 22 9 5 5 8 14 22 26	13 26 15 9 7 9 14 22 26	16 31 17 12 9 10 15 22 26	19 36 17 16 11 10 15 22 26	22 4 22 20 12 10 15 23 26	25 8 27 24 13 10 15 23 26	28 12 27 27 13 9 15 23 26
28	31 5 29 36 29 6 14 23 26	34 9 33 2 32 6 14 23 26	1 10 2 3 34 6 13 23 26	4 15 5 1 36 7 13 22 26	7 18 5 3 3 8 14 22 26	10 24 10 5 5 8 14 22 26	13 28 15 9 7 9 14 22 26	16 33 17 12 9 10 15 22 26	19 2 17 16 11 10 15 22 26	22 5 22 20 12 10 15 23 26	25 10 27 24 13 10 15 23 26	28 13 27 27 13 9 15 23 26
29	31 6 29 36 30 6 14 23 26	1977	1 11 3 3 34 6 13 23 26	4 16 5 1 1 7 13 22 26	7 20 5 3 3 8 14 22 26	10 25 10 5 5 8 14 22 26	13 29 15 9 7 9 14 22 26	16 34 17 12 9 10 15 22 26	19 3 18 16 11 10 15 22 26	22 6 23 20 12 10 15 23 26	25 11 27 24 13 10 15 23 26	28 14 27 28 13 9 15 23 26
30	31 7 29 36 30 6 14 23 26		1 13 3 2 34 6 13 23 26	4 18 4 1 1 7 13 22 26	7 21 5 3 3 8 14 22 26	10 26 10 6 5 8 14 22 26	13 31 16 9 7 9 14 22 26	16 35 17 13 9 10 15 22 26	19 4 18 16 11 10 15 22 26	22 7 23 20 13 10 15 23 26	25 12 27 24 13 10 15 23 26	28 15 27 28 13 9 15 23 26
31	32 9 29 36 30 6 14 23 26		1 14 3 2 34 6 13 22 26		7 23 5 3 3 8 14 22 26		13 32 16 9 7 9 14 22 26	16 1 17 13 9 10 15 22 26		22 9 23 20 13 10 15 23 26		28 16 27 28 13 9 15 23 26

	JAN	FEB	MAR	APR	MAY	JUNE	JULY	AUG	SEPT	OCT	NOV	DEC
1	28 18 27 28 13 9 15 23 26	32 23 30 32 12 9 15 23 26	34 24 35 35 12 9 15 23 26	1 29 3 3 12 9 15 23 26	4 33 2 7 13 10 15 23 26	7 2 6 11 15 10 15 23 26	10 5 12 14 16 11 15 23 26	13 10 16 18 18 12 15 23 26	16 14 15 21 20 12 16 23 26	19 17 19 23 22 13 16 23 26	22 22 24 23 24 13 17 23 26	25 26 26 22 27 13 17 23 26
2	29 19 27 28 13 9 15 23 26	32 24 30 32 12 9 15 23 26	35 25 35 35 12 9 15 23 26	1 30 3 3 12 9 15 23 26	5 34 2 7 13 10 15 23 26	8 3 6 11 15 10 15 23 26	10 7 12 14 16 11 15 23 26	13 11 16 18 18 12 15 23 26	16 16 15 21 20 12 16 23 26	19 19 19 23 22 13 16 23 26	22 24 24 23 24 13 17 23 26	25 28 26 22 27 13 17 23 26
3	29 20 27 28 13 9 15 23 26	32 25 30 32 12 9 15 23 26	35 26 35 36 12 9 15 23 26	2 32 3 3 12 9 15 23 26	5 36 2 7 13 10 15 23 26	8 4 6 11 15 10 15 23 26	10 8 12 14 17 11 15 23 26	13 12 16 18 18 12 15 23 26	16 17 15 21 20 12 16 23 26	19 20 20 23 22 13 16 23 26	23 25 24 23 24 13 17 23 26	25 29 26 22 27 13 17 23 26
4	29 22 27 28 13 9 15 23 26	32 27 30 32 12 9 15 23 26	35 28 35 36 12 9 15 23 26	2 33 3 4 12 9 15 23 26	5 1 2 7 13 10 15 23 26	8 6 6 11 15 10 15 23 26	11 9 13 14 17 11 15 23 26	14 13 16 18 18 12 16 23 26	17 18 15 21 20 12 16 23 26	20 22 20 23 22 13 16 23 26	23 27 24 23 25 13 17 23 26	26 31 26 22 27 13 17 23 26
5	29 23 27 28 13 9 15 23 26	32 28 30 32 12 9 15 23 26	35 29 35 36 12 9 15 23 26	2 35 3 4 12 9 15 23 26	5 2 2 7 13 10 15 23 26	8 7 7 11 15 10 15 23 26	11 10 13 15 17 11 15 23 26	14 14 16 18 18 12 16 23 26	17 19 15 21 20 12 16 23 26	20 23 20 23 22 13 16 23 26	23 28 25 23 25 13 17 23 26	26 32 26 22 27 13 17 23 26
6	29 25 27 29 13 9 15 23 26	32 29 31 32 12 9 15 23 26	35 31 36 36 12 9 15 23 26	2 36 3 4 12 9 15 23 26	5 4 2 7 13 10 15 23 26	8 8 7 11 15 10 15 23 26	11 11 13 15 17 11 15 23 26	14 16 16 18 19 12 16 23 26	17 21 15 21 20 12 16 23 26	20 24 20 23 22 13 16 23 26	23 30 25 23 25 13 17 23 26	26 34 26 22 27 13 17 23 26
7	29 26 27 29 13 9 15 23 26	32 31 31 33 12 9 15 23 26	35 32 36 36 12 9 15 23 26	2 1 3 4 12 9 15 23 26	5 5 2 8 13 10 15 23 26	8 9 7 11 15 10 15 23 26	11 13 13 15 17 11 15 23 26	14 17 16 18 19 12 16 23 26	17 22 15 21 21 12 16 23 26	20 26 20 23 23 13 16 23 26	23 31 25 23 25 13 17 23 26	26 35 26 22 27 13 17 23 26
8	29 28 27 29 13 9 15 23 26	32 33 31 33 12 9 15 23 26	35 34 36 36 12 9 15 23 26	2 3 3 4 12 9 15 23 26	5 6 2 8 14 10 15 23 26	8 11 7 11 15 10 15 23 26	11 14 13 15 17 11 15 23 26	14 18 16 18 19 12 16 23 26	17 23 15 21 21 12 16 23 26	20 27 20 23 23 13 16 23 26	23 32 25 23 25 13 17 23 26	26 36 25 22 27 13 17 23 26
9	29 29 27 29 13 9 15 23 26	32 34 31 33 12 9 15 23 26	35 35 36 36 12 9 15 23 26	2 4 3 4 12 9 15 23 26	5 7 3 8 14 10 15 23 26	8 12 8 12 15 10 15 23 26	11 15 13 15 17 11 15 23 26	14 20 16 18 19 12 16 23 26	17 25 15 22 21 12 16 23 26	20 28 21 24 23 13 16 23 26	23 34 25 23 25 13 17 23 26	26 2 25 22 27 13 17 23 26
10	29 31 27 29 13 9 15 23 26	32 36 31 33 12 9 15 23 26	35 1 36 36 12 9 15 23 26	2 5 3 4 12 9 15 23 26	5 8 3 8 14 10 15 23 26	8 13 8 12 15 11 15 23 26	11 16 14 15 17 11 15 23 26	14 21 16 19 19 12 16 23 26	17 26 15 22 21 12 16 23 26	20 30 21 24 23 13 16 23 26	23 35 25 23 25 13 17 23 26	26 3 25 22 27 13 17 23 26
11	29 32 27 29 13 9 15 23 26	33 1 31 33 12 9 15 23 26	35 2 36 1 12 9 15 23 26	2 7 3 4 12 9 15 23 26	5 10 3 8 14 10 15 23 26	8 14 8 12 15 11 15 23 26	11 17 14 15 17 11 15 23 26	14 22 16 19 19 12 16 23 26	17 27 16 22 21 12 16 23 26	20 31 21 24 23 13 16 23 26	23 1 25 23 25 13 17 23 26	26 4 25 22 27 13 17 23 26
12	30 34 27 29 13 9 15 23 26	33 2 32 33 12 9 15 23 26	36 3 1 1 12 9 15 23 26	3 8 3 5 12 9 15 23 26	5 11 3 8 14 10 15 23 26	8 15 8 12 15 11 15 23 26	11 19 14 15 17 11 15 23 26	14 23 15 19 19 12 16 23 26	17 29 16 22 21 13 16 23 26	20 32 21 24 23 13 16 23 26	23 2 26 23 25 13 17 23 26	26 5 25 22 27 13 17 23 26
13	30 35 27 29 13 9 15 23 26	33 4 32 33 12 9 15 23 26	36 4 1 1 12 9 15 23 26	3 9 2 5 12 9 15 23 26	6 12 3 8 14 10 15 23 26	9 16 8 12 15 11 15 23 26	11 20 14 16 17 11 15 23 26	14 25 15 19 19 12 16 23 26	17 30 16 22 21 13 16 23 26	20 34 21 24 23 13 16 23 26	23 3 26 23 25 13 17 23 26	26 7 25 23 27 13 17 23 26
14	30 36 27 30 13 9 15 23 26	33 5 32 33 12 9 15 23 26	36 6 1 1 12 9 15 23 26	3 10 2 5 13 9 15 23 26	6 13 3 8 14 10 15 23 26	9 18 9 12 15 11 15 23 26	12 21 14 16 17 11 15 23 26	14 26 15 19 19 12 16 23 26	17 32 16 22 21 13 16 23 26	20 35 21 24 23 13 16 23 26	24 5 26 23 25 13 17 23 26	27 8 25 23 27 13 17 23 26
15	30 2 28 30 13 9 15 23 26	33 6 32 34 12 9 15 23 26	36 7 1 1 12 9 15 23 26	3 11 2 5 13 9 15 23 26	6 14 3 9 14 10 15 23 26	9 19 9 12 15 11 15 23 26	12 23 14 16 17 11 15 23 26	15 28 15 19 19 12 16 23 26	18 33 16 22 21 13 16 23 26	21 1 22 24 23 13 16 23 26	24 6 26 23 25 13 17 23 26	27 9 25 23 28 13 17 23 26
16	30 3 28 30 13 9 15 23 26	33 7 32 34 12 9 15 23 26	36 8 1 1 12 9 15 23 26	3 13 2 5 13 9 15 23 26	6 16 3 9 14 10 15 23 26	9 20 9 12 16 11 15 23 26	12 24 14 16 17 11 15 23 26	15 29 15 19 19 12 16 23 26	18 35 16 22 21 13 16 23 26	21 2 22 24 23 13 16 23 26	24 7 26 22 25 13 17 23 26	27 10 25 23 28 13 17 23 26
17	30 4 28 30 13 9 15 23 26	33 8 32 34 12 9 15 23 26	36 9 2 1 12 9 15 23 26	3 14 2 5 13 9 15 23 26	6 17 3 9 14 10 15 23 26	9 22 9 12 16 11 15 23 26	12 25 14 16 17 11 15 23 26	15 31 15 19 19 12 16 23 26	18 36 17 22 21 13 16 23 26	21 4 22 24 23 13 16 23 26	24 8 26 22 25 13 17 23 26	27 12 25 23 28 13 17 23 26
18	30 5 28 30 13 9 15 23 26	33 10 33 34 12 9 15 23 26	36 10 2 1 12 9 15 23 26	3 15 2 5 13 9 15 23 26	6 18 4 9 14 10 15 23 26	9 23 9 13 16 11 15 23 26	12 27 15 16 17 11 15 23 26	15 32 15 19 19 12 16 23 26	18 1 17 22 21 13 16 23 26	21 5 22 24 23 13 16 23 26	24 10 26 22 26 13 17 23 26	27 13 25 23 28 13 17 23 26
19	30 7 28 30 13 9 15 23 26	33 11 33 34 12 9 15 23 26	36 12 2 2 12 9 15 23 26	3 16 2 5 13 10 15 23 26	6 19 4 9 14 10 15 23 26	9 25 10 13 16 11 15 23 26	12 28 15 16 17 11 15 23 26	15 34 15 20 19 12 16 23 26	18 3 17 22 21 13 16 23 26	21 6 22 24 23 13 16 23 26	24 11 26 22 26 13 17 23 26	27 14 25 23 28 13 17 23 26
20	30 8 28 30 13 9 15 23 26	33 12 33 34 12 9 15 23 26	36 13 2 2 12 9 15 23 26	3 17 2 6 13 10 15 23 26	6 21 4 9 14 10 15 23 26	9 26 10 13 16 11 15 23 26	12 30 15 16 17 11 15 23 26	15 35 15 20 19 12 16 23 26	18 4 17 22 21 13 16 23 26	21 8 22 24 23 13 16 23 26	24 12 26 22 26 13 17 23 26	27 15 25 23 28 13 17 23 26
21	30 9 28 30 13 9 15 23 26	34 13 33 34 12 9 15 23 26	36 14 2 2 12 9 15 23 26	3 19 2 6 13 10 15 23 26	6 22 4 9 14 10 15 23 26	9 28 10 13 16 11 15 23 26	12 31 15 16 18 11 15 23 26	15 1 15 20 19 12 16 23 26	18 5 17 23 21 13 16 23 26	21 9 23 24 24 13 16 23 26	24 13 26 22 26 13 17 23 26	27 16 25 23 28 13 17 23 26
22	31 10 28 31 13 9 15 23 26	34 14 33 34 12 9 15 23 26	1 15 2 2 12 9 15 23 26	4 20 2 6 13 10 15 23 26	6 23 4 9 14 10 15 23 26	9 29 10 13 16 11 15 23 26	12 33 15 17 18 11 15 23 26	15 2 15 20 20 12 16 23 26	18 7 18 23 22 13 16 23 26	21 10 23 24 24 13 16 23 26	24 14 26 22 26 13 17 23 26	27 18 25 23 28 13 17 23 26
23	31 11 29 31 13 9 15 23 26	34 16 33 35 12 9 15 23 26	1 17 2 2 12 9 15 23 26	4 22 2 6 13 10 15 23 26	7 25 4 10 14 10 15 23 26	10 31 11 13 16 11 15 23 26	12 34 15 17 18 11 15 23 26	15 3 15 20 20 12 16 23 26	18 8 18 23 22 13 16 23 26	21 11 23 24 24 13 16 23 26	24 16 27 22 26 13 17 23 26	27 19 25 23 28 13 17 23 26
24	31 12 29 31 12 9 15 23 26	34 17 34 35 12 9 15 23 26	1 18 3 2 12 9 15 23 26	4 23 2 6 13 10 15 23 26	7 26 4 10 14 10 15 23 26	10 32 11 13 16 11 15 23 26	12 35 15 17 18 11 15 23 26	15 5 15 20 20 12 16 23 26	18 9 18 23 22 13 16 23 26	21 12 23 24 24 13 16 23 26	25 17 27 22 26 13 17 23 26	28 20 25 23 28 13 17 23 26
25	31 14 29 31 12 9 15 23 26	34 18 34 35 12 9 15 23 26	1 19 3 2 12 9 15 23 26	4 24 2 6 13 10 15 23 26	7 28 5 10 14 10 15 23 26	10 34 11 13 16 11 15 23 26	13 1 15 17 18 12 15 23 26	16 6 15 20 20 12 16 23 26	19 10 18 23 22 13 16 23 26	22 14 23 24 24 13 16 23 26	25 18 27 22 26 13 17 23 26	28 21 25 23 28 13 17 23 26
26	31 15 29 31 12 9 15 23 26	34 20 34 35 12 9 15 23 26	1 21 3 2 12 9 15 23 26	4 26 2 6 13 10 15 23 26	7 30 5 10 14 10 15 23 26	10 35 11 14 16 11 15 23 26	13 3 15 17 18 12 15 23 26	16 7 14 20 20 12 16 23 26	19 12 18 23 22 13 16 23 26	22 15 23 24 24 13 16 23 26	25 19 27 22 26 13 17 23 26	28 23 26 23 28 13 17 23 26
27	31 16 29 31 12 9 15 23 26	34 21 34 35 12 9 15 23 26	1 22 3 3 12 9 15 23 26	4 27 2 6 13 10 15 23 26	7 31 5 10 14 10 15 23 26	10 36 11 14 16 11 15 23 26	13 4 15 17 18 12 15 23 26	16 8 14 20 20 12 16 23 26	19 13 18 23 22 13 16 23 26	22 16 23 24 24 13 16 23 26	25 20 27 22 26 13 17 23 26	28 24 26 23 28 13 17 23 26
28	31 17 29 31 12 9 15 23 26	34 22 34 35 12 9 15 23 26	1 23 3 3 12 9 15 23 26	4 29 2 6 13 10 15 23 26	7 33 5 10 14 10 15 23 26	10 2 12 14 16 11 15 23 26	13 5 15 17 18 12 15 23 26	16 10 14 20 20 12 16 23 26	19 14 19 23 22 13 16 23 26	22 17 24 23 24 13 17 23 26	25 22 27 22 26 13 17 23 26	28 25 26 24 29 13 17 23 26
29	31 19 29 31 12 9 15 23 26		1 25 3 3 12 9 15 23 26	4 30 2 7 13 10 15 23 26	7 34 5 10 15 10 15 23 26	10 3 12 14 16 11 15 23 26	13 6 16 17 18 12 15 23 26	16 11 14 21 20 12 16 23 26	19 15 19 23 22 13 16 23 26	22 19 24 23 24 13 17 23 26	25 23 26 22 26 13 17 23 26	28 26 26 24 29 13 17 23 26
30	31 20 30 32 12 9 15 23 26		1 26 3 3 12 9 15 23 26	4 31 2 7 13 10 15 23 26	7 35 6 10 15 10 15 23 26	10 4 12 14 16 11 15 23 26	13 8 16 17 18 12 15 23 26	16 12 14 21 20 12 16 23 26	19 16 19 23 22 13 16 23 26	22 20 24 23 24 13 17 23 26	25 24 26 22 26 13 17 23 26	28 28 26 24 29 13 17 23 26
31	31 21 30 32 12 9 15 23 26	1978	1 28 3 3 12 9 15 23 26		7 1 6 10 15 10 15 23 26		13 9 16 18 18 12 15 23 26	16 13 14 21 20 12 16 23 26		22 21 24 23 24 13 17 23 26		28 29 26 24 29 13 17 23 26

	JAN	FEB	MAR	APR	MAY	JUNE	JULY	AUG	SEPT	OCT	NOV	DEC
1	28 31 26 24 29 13 17 23 26	32 1 31 27 31 13 17 23 26	34 2 36 30 33 12 16 23 26	1 7 36 34 36 12 16 23 26	4 10 2 1 2 12 16 23 26	7 14 8 5 5 13 16 23 26	10 17 13 9 7 13 16 23 26	13 22 13 13 9 14 17 23 26	16 27 15 16 11 15 17 23 26	19 31 20 20 13 15 17 23 26	22 36 25 24 14 16 18 23 26	25 4 24 28 16 16 18 24 26
2	28 32 26 24 29 13 17 23 26	32 2 31 27 31 13 17 23 26	34 3 36 30 34 12 16 23 26	2 8 36 34 36 12 16 23 26	5 11 2 1 2 13 16 23 26	7 16 8 5 5 13 16 23 26	10 19 13 9 7 13 16 23 26	13 23 13 13 9 14 17 23 26	16 28 15 17 11 15 17 23 26	19 32 21 20 13 15 17 23 26	22 1 25 24 15 16 18 23 26	25 5 24 28 16 16 18 24 26
3	29 34 27 24 29 13 17 23 26	32 4 31 27 31 13 17 23 26	35 4 36 30 34 12 16 23 26	2 9 36 34 36 12 16 23 26	5 12 2 2 2 13 16 23 26	8 17 8 5 5 13 16 23 26	10 20 13 9 7 14 16 23 26	13 25 13 13 9 14 17 23 26	16 29 15 17 11 15 17 23 26	19 33 21 20 13 15 17 23 26	22 3 25 24 15 16 18 23 26	25 7 24 28 16 16 18 24 26
4	29 36 27 24 29 13 17 23 26	32 5 31 27 32 13 17 23 26	35 6 36 30 34 12 16 23 26	2 10 36 34 36 12 16 23 26	5 13 2 2 2 13 16 23 26	8 18 8 5 5 13 16 23 26	11 21 13 9 7 14 16 23 26	14 26 13 13 9 14 17 23 26	16 31 16 17 11 15 17 23 26	19 35 21 21 13 15 17 23 26	22 4 25 24 15 16 18 23 26	26 8 24 28 16 16 18 24 26
5	29 1 27 24 29 13 17 23 26	32 6 32 27 32 13 17 23 26	35 7 1 31 34 12 16 23 26	2 12 36 34 36 12 16 23 26	5 15 2 2 3 13 16 23 26	8 19 9 6 5 13 16 23 26	11 22 13 9 7 14 16 23 26	14 27 13 13 9 14 17 23 26	17 33 16 17 11 15 17 23 26	20 36 21 21 13 16 17 23 26	23 5 25 24 15 16 18 23 26	26 9 24 28 16 16 18 24 26
6	29 3 27 24 29 13 17 23 26	32 7 32 27 32 13 17 23 26	35 8 1 31 34 12 16 23 26	2 13 36 34 36 12 16 23 26	5 16 3 2 3 13 16 23 26	8 20 9 6 5 13 16 23 26	11 24 13 9 7 14 16 23 26	14 29 13 13 9 14 17 23 26	17 34 16 17 11 15 17 23 26	20 2 21 21 13 16 17 23 26	23 7 25 25 15 16 18 23 26	26 10 24 28 16 16 18 24 26
7	29 4 27 24 29 13 17 23 26	32 9 32 28 32 13 17 23 26	35 10 1 31 34 12 16 23 26	2 14 36 34 36 12 16 23 26	5 17 3 2 3 13 16 23 26	8 22 9 6 5 13 16 23 26	11 25 13 9 7 14 16 23 26	14 30 13 13 9 14 17 23 26	17 36 16 17 11 15 17 23 26	20 3 21 21 13 16 17 23 26	23 8 25 25 15 16 18 23 26	26 12 24 28 16 16 18 24 26
8	29 5 27 24 29 13 17 23 26	32 10 32 28 32 13 17 23 26	35 11 1 31 34 12 16 23 26	2 15 36 35 36 12 16 23 26	5 18 3 2 3 13 16 23 26	8 23 9 6 5 13 16 23 26	11 26 13 10 7 14 16 23 26	14 32 13 13 9 14 17 23 26	17 1 16 17 11 15 17 23 26	20 5 22 21 13 16 17 23 26	23 10 25 25 15 16 18 23 26	26 13 24 29 16 16 18 24 26
9	29 7 27 25 29 13 17 23 26	32 11 32 28 32 13 17 23 26	35 12 1 31 34 12 16 23 26	2 16 36 35 1 12 16 23 26	5 19 3 2 3 13 16 23 26	8 24 9 6 5 13 16 23 26	11 28 14 10 7 14 16 23 26	14 33 13 14 9 14 17 23 26	17 3 17 17 11 15 17 23 26	20 6 22 21 13 16 17 23 26	23 11 25 25 15 16 18 23 26	26 14 24 29 16 16 18 24 26
10	29 8 28 25 30 13 17 23 26	32 12 33 28 32 13 17 23 26	35 13 1 31 34 12 16 23 26	2 17 36 35 1 12 16 23 26	5 21 3 2 3 13 16 23 26	8 26 10 6 5 13 16 23 26	11 29 14 10 7 14 16 23 26	14 35 13 14 9 14 17 23 26	17 4 17 17 11 15 17 23 26	20 8 22 21 13 16 17 23 26	23 12 25 25 15 16 18 24 26	26 16 24 29 16 16 18 24 26
11	29 9 28 25 30 13 17 23 26	33 13 33 28 32 13 17 23 26	35 14 1 31 34 12 16 23 26	2 19 36 35 1 12 16 23 26	5 22 3 3 3 13 16 23 26	8 27 10 6 5 13 16 23 26	11 31 14 10 7 14 16 23 26	14 36 13 14 10 14 17 23 26	17 5 17 18 12 15 17 23 26	20 9 22 21 13 16 17 23 26	23 13 25 25 15 16 18 24 26	26 17 24 29 16 16 18 24 26
12	30 10 28 25 30 13 17 23 26	33 15 33 28 32 13 17 23 26	35 16 1 31 34 12 16 23 26	3 20 36 35 1 12 16 23 26	5 23 4 3 3 13 16 23 26	8 28 10 6 5 13 16 23 26	11 32 14 10 8 14 16 23 26	14 2 13 14 10 14 17 23 26	17 7 17 18 12 15 17 23 26	20 10 22 21 13 16 18 23 26	23 15 25 25 15 16 18 24 26	26 18 24 29 16 16 18 24 26
13	30 11 28 25 30 13 17 23 26	33 16 33 28 32 13 17 23 26	36 17 1 31 34 12 16 23 26	3 21 36 35 1 12 16 23 26	6 25 4 3 3 13 16 23 26	9 30 10 7 5 13 16 23 26	11 34 14 10 8 14 16 23 26	14 3 13 14 10 14 17 23 26	17 8 17 18 12 15 17 23 26	20 11 22 22 13 16 18 23 26	23 16 25 25 15 16 18 24 26	26 19 24 29 16 16 18 24 26
14	30 13 28 25 30 13 17 23 26	33 17 33 28 32 13 17 23 26	36 18 1 32 35 12 16 23 26	3 22 36 35 1 12 16 23 26	6 26 4 3 3 13 16 23 26	9 31 10 7 6 13 16 23 26	11 35 14 10 8 14 16 23 26	14 4 13 14 10 14 17 23 26	17 9 18 18 12 15 17 23 26	20 13 22 22 14 16 18 23 26	24 17 25 26 15 16 18 24 26	27 20 25 29 16 16 18 24 26
15	30 14 28 25 30 13 17 23 26	33 18 33 28 32 13 17 23 26	36 19 1 32 35 12 16 23 26	3 24 36 35 1 12 16 23 26	6 28 4 3 3 13 16 23 26	9 32 11 7 6 13 16 23 26	12 1 14 11 8 14 16 23 26	15 5 13 14 10 14 17 23 26	18 11 18 18 12 15 17 23 26	21 14 23 22 14 16 18 23 26	24 18 25 26 15 16 18 24 26	27 21 25 29 16 16 18 24 26
16	30 15 28 25 30 13 17 23 26	33 19 34 29 32 13 17 23 26	36 20 1 32 35 12 16 23 26	3 25 36 36 1 12 16 23 26	6 29 4 3 3 13 16 23 26	9 34 11 7 6 13 16 23 26	12 2 14 11 8 14 16 23 26	15 7 13 14 10 14 17 23 26	18 12 18 18 12 15 17 23 26	21 15 23 22 14 16 18 23 26	24 19 25 26 15 16 18 24 26	27 23 25 30 16 16 18 24 26
17	30 16 29 25 30 13 17 23 26	33 21 34 29 33 13 17 23 26	36 22 1 32 35 12 16 23 26	3 26 36 36 1 12 16 23 26	6 30 4 3 3 13 16 23 26	9 36 11 7 6 13 16 23 26	12 4 14 11 8 14 16 23 26	15 8 13 15 10 14 17 23 26	18 13 18 18 12 15 17 23 26	21 16 23 22 14 16 18 23 26	24 21 25 26 15 16 18 24 26	27 24 25 30 16 16 18 24 26
18	30 17 29 25 30 13 17 23 26	33 22 34 29 33 13 17 23 26	36 23 1 32 35 12 16 23 26	3 28 36 36 1 12 16 23 26	6 32 5 3 4 13 16 23 26	9 1 11 7 6 13 16 23 26	12 5 14 11 8 14 16 23 26	15 10 13 15 10 15 17 23 26	18 14 18 18 12 15 17 23 26	21 17 23 22 14 16 18 23 26	24 22 24 26 15 16 18 24 26	27 25 25 30 16 16 18 24 26
19	30 19 29 26 30 13 17 23 26	33 23 34 29 33 12 17 23 26	36 24 1 32 35 12 16 23 26	3 29 1 36 1 12 16 23 26	6 33 5 4 4 13 16 23 26	9 2 11 7 6 13 16 23 26	12 6 14 11 8 14 16 23 26	15 11 13 15 10 15 17 23 26	18 15 18 19 12 15 17 23 26	21 19 23 22 14 16 18 23 26	24 23 24 26 15 16 18 24 26	27 27 25 30 16 16 18 24 26
20	30 20 29 26 30 13 17 23 26	33 25 34 29 33 12 17 23 26	36 25 1 32 35 12 16 23 26	3 31 1 36 1 12 16 23 26	6 35 5 4 4 13 16 23 26	9 4 11 7 6 13 16 23 26	12 7 14 11 8 14 17 23 26	15 12 13 15 10 15 17 23 26	18 17 19 19 12 15 17 23 26	21 20 23 22 14 16 18 23 26	24 25 24 26 15 16 18 24 26	27 28 25 30 17 16 18 24 26
21	30 21 29 26 30 13 17 23 26	34 26 35 29 33 12 17 23 26	36 27 1 32 35 12 16 23 26	3 32 1 36 1 12 16 23 26	6 36 5 4 4 13 16 23 26	9 5 11 8 6 13 16 23 26	12 9 14 11 8 14 17 23 26	15 13 13 15 10 15 17 23 26	18 18 19 19 12 15 17 23 26	21 21 23 23 14 16 18 23 26	24 26 24 26 15 16 18 24 26	27 29 26 30 17 16 18 24 26
22	31 22 29 26 31 13 17 23 26	34 27 35 29 33 12 17 23 26	36 28 1 33 35 12 16 23 26	4 34 1 36 2 12 16 23 26	6 1 5 4 4 13 16 23 26	9 7 12 8 6 13 16 23 26	12 10 14 11 8 14 17 23 26	15 14 13 15 10 15 17 23 26	18 19 19 19 12 15 17 23 26	21 22 23 23 14 16 18 23 26	24 27 24 27 15 16 18 24 26	27 31 26 30 17 16 18 24 26
23	31 23 30 26 31 13 17 23 26	34 29 35 29 33 12 17 23 26	1 29 1 33 35 12 16 23 26	4 35 1 36 2 12 16 23 26	7 3 6 4 4 13 16 23 26	9 8 12 8 6 13 16 23 26	12 11 14 11 8 14 17 23 26	15 16 14 15 10 15 17 23 26	18 20 19 19 12 15 17 23 26	21 23 24 23 14 16 18 23 26	24 28 24 27 16 16 18 24 26	27 32 26 30 17 16 18 24 26
24	31 25 30 26 31 13 17 23 26	34 30 35 30 33 12 17 23 26	1 31 1 33 35 12 16 23 26	4 36 1 1 2 12 16 23 26	7 4 6 4 4 13 16 23 26	10 9 12 8 6 13 16 23 26	12 12 14 12 8 14 17 23 26	15 17 14 15 10 15 17 23 26	18 21 19 19 12 15 17 23 26	21 25 24 23 14 16 18 23 26	25 30 24 27 16 16 18 24 26	28 34 26 31 17 16 18 24 26
25	31 26 30 26 31 13 17 23 26	34 32 35 30 33 12 16 23 26	1 32 1 33 35 12 16 23 26	4 2 1 1 2 12 16 23 26	7 5 6 4 4 13 16 23 26	10 10 12 8 6 13 16 23 26	13 14 14 12 8 14 17 23 26	16 18 14 16 10 15 17 23 26	19 23 19 19 12 15 17 23 26	21 26 24 23 14 16 18 23 26	25 31 24 27 16 16 18 24 26	28 35 26 31 17 16 18 24 26
26	31 28 30 26 31 13 17 23 26	34 33 35 30 33 12 16 23 26	1 34 1 33 35 12 16 23 26	4 3 1 1 2 12 16 23 26	7 7 6 4 4 13 16 23 26	10 11 12 8 6 13 16 23 26	13 15 14 12 8 14 17 23 26	16 19 14 16 11 15 17 23 26	19 24 20 19 12 15 17 23 26	22 27 24 23 14 16 18 23 26	25 33 24 27 16 16 18 24 26	28 1 26 31 17 16 18 24 26
27	31 29 30 26 31 13 17 23 26	34 35 36 30 33 12 16 23 26	1 35 1 33 36 12 16 23 26	4 5 1 1 2 12 16 23 26	7 8 6 4 4 13 16 23 26	10 13 12 8 6 13 16 23 26	13 16 14 12 9 14 17 23 26	16 20 14 16 11 15 17 23 26	19 25 20 20 13 15 17 23 26	22 29 24 23 14 16 18 23 26	25 34 24 27 16 16 18 24 26	28 2 26 31 17 16 18 24 26
28	31 31 30 26 31 13 17 23 26	34 36 36 30 33 12 16 23 26	1 1 36 33 36 12 16 23 26	4 6 1 1 2 12 16 23 26	7 10 7 5 4 13 16 23 26	10 14 12 8 7 13 16 23 26	13 17 13 12 9 14 17 23 26	16 22 14 16 11 15 17 23 26	19 26 20 20 13 15 17 23 26	22 30 24 23 14 16 18 23 26	25 35 24 27 16 16 18 24 26	28 3 27 31 17 16 18 24 26
29	31 32 30 27 31 13 17 23 26	1979	1 2 36 33 36 12 16 23 26	4 7 2 1 2 12 16 23 26	7 11 7 5 4 13 16 23 26	10 15 13 9 7 13 16 23 26	13 18 13 12 9 14 17 23 26	16 23 14 16 11 15 17 23 26	19 28 20 20 13 15 17 23 26	22 31 24 24 14 16 18 23 26	25 1 24 27 16 16 18 24 26	28 5 27 31 17 16 18 24 26
30	31 34 31 27 31 13 17 23 26		1 4 36 34 36 12 16 23 26	4 9 2 1 2 12 16 23 26	7 12 7 5 4 13 16 23 26	10 16 13 9 7 13 16 23 26	13 19 13 12 9 14 17 23 26	16 24 15 16 11 15 17 23 26	19 29 20 20 13 15 17 23 26	22 32 24 24 14 16 18 23 26	25 2 24 28 16 16 18 24 26	28 6 27 31 17 16 18 24 26
31	31 35 31 27 31 13 17 23 26		1 5 36 34 36 12 16 23 26		7 13 7 5 5 13 16 23 26		13 21 13 12 9 14 17 23 26	16 25 15 16 11 15 17 23 26		22 34 24 24 14 16 18 23 26		28 7 27 31 17 16 18 24 26

	JAN	FEB	MAR	APR	MAY	JUNE	JULY	AUG	SEPT	OCT	NOV	DEC
1	28 9 27 32 17 16 18 24 26	32 13 32 35 17 16 18 24 27	34 16 35 3 16 16 18 24 27	2 20 35 6 15 16 18 24 27	4 23 3 9 15 16 18 24 27	7 28 9 10 16 16 18 24 27	10 32 12 8 18 16 18 24 27	13 1 11 9 20 17 18 24 26	16 6 17 12 22 17 18 24 26	19 10 22 15 24 18 19 24 26	22 15 23 19 26 18 19 24 26	25 18 24 22 28 19 19 24 27
2	28 10 27 32 17 16 18 24 26	32 15 32 35 17 16 18 24 27	35 17 35 3 16 16 18 24 27	2 21 35 6 15 16 18 24 27	5 25 3 9 15 16 18 24 27	8 29 10 10 16 16 18 24 27	10 33 12 8 18 16 18 24 27	13 2 11 9 20 17 18 24 26	16 8 17 12 22 17 18 24 26	19 11 22 15 24 18 19 24 26	22 16 23 19 26 19 19 24 26	25 19 24 22 28 19 19 24 27
3	29 11 28 32 17 16 18 24 27	32 16 33 36 17 16 18 24 27	35 18 35 3 16 16 18 24 27	2 22 35 6 15 16 18 24 27	5 26 4 9 15 16 18 24 27	8 31 10 9 16 16 18 24 27	11 34 12 8 18 16 18 24 27	13 4 12 9 20 17 18 24 26	16 9 17 12 22 17 18 24 26	19 13 22 15 24 18 19 24 26	22 17 23 19 26 19 19 24 26	25 20 24 23 28 19 19 24 27
4	29 13 28 32 17 16 18 24 27	32 17 33 36 17 16 18 24 27	35 19 35 3 16 16 18 24 27	2 24 35 6 15 16 18 24 27	5 27 4 9 15 16 18 24 27	8 32 10 9 17 16 18 24 27	11 36 12 8 18 16 18 24 27	14 5 12 9 20 17 18 24 26	17 10 17 12 22 17 18 24 26	19 14 22 15 24 18 19 24 26	23 18 22 19 26 19 19 24 26	26 22 24 23 28 19 19 24 27
5	29 14 28 32 17 16 18 24 27	32 18 33 36 17 16 18 24 27	35 20 35 3 16 16 18 24 27	2 25 35 7 15 16 18 24 27	5 28 4 9 15 16 18 24 27	8 33 10 9 17 16 18 24 27	11 1 12 8 18 16 18 24 27	14 7 12 9 20 17 18 24 26	17 12 18 12 22 17 18 24 26	20 15 22 15 24 18 19 24 26	23 20 22 19 26 19 19 24 27	26 23 24 23 28 19 19 24 27
6	29 15 28 32 17 16 18 24 27	32 19 33 36 17 16 18 24 27	35 22 35 3 16 16 18 24 27	2 26 35 7 15 16 18 24 27	5 30 4 9 15 16 18 24 27	8 35 10 9 17 16 18 24 27	11 3 12 8 18 16 18 24 27	14 8 12 9 20 17 18 24 26	17 13 18 12 22 17 18 24 26	20 16 22 16 24 18 19 24 26	23 21 22 19 26 19 19 24 27	26 24 24 23 28 19 19 24 27
7	29 16 28 32 17 16 18 24 27	32 21 33 36 17 16 18 24 27	35 23 35 3 16 16 18 24 27	2 27 35 7 15 16 18 24 27	5 31 4 9 15 16 18 24 27	8 36 10 9 17 16 18 24 27	11 4 12 8 18 16 18 24 27	14 9 12 9 20 17 18 24 26	17 14 18 12 22 17 18 24 26	20 17 22 16 24 18 19 24 26	23 22 22 19 26 19 19 24 27	26 25 25 23 29 19 19 24 27
8	29 17 28 32 17 16 18 24 27	32 22 34 36 17 16 18 24 27	35 24 35 4 16 16 18 24 27	2 29 36 7 15 16 18 24 27	5 32 5 9 16 16 18 24 27	8 2 10 9 17 16 18 24 27	11 6 12 8 18 16 18 24 27	14 11 12 10 20 17 18 24 26	17 15 18 12 22 17 18 24 26	20 19 22 16 24 18 19 24 26	23 23 22 19 26 19 19 24 27	26 26 25 23 29 19 19 24 27
9	29 19 28 33 17 16 18 24 27	32 23 34 36 17 16 18 24 27	35 25 35 4 15 16 18 24 27	2 30 36 7 15 16 18 24 27	5 34 5 9 16 16 18 24 27	8 3 11 9 17 16 18 24 27	11 7 12 8 18 16 18 24 27	14 12 12 10 20 17 18 24 26	17 17 18 13 22 17 18 24 26	20 20 22 16 24 18 19 24 26	23 24 22 20 26 19 19 24 27	26 28 25 23 29 19 19 24 27
10	29 20 29 33 17 16 18 24 27	32 24 34 36 17 16 18 24 27	35 26 35 4 15 16 18 24 27	2 31 36 7 15 16 18 24 27	5 35 5 10 16 16 18 24 27	8 5 11 9 17 16 18 24 27	11 8 11 8 18 16 18 24 27	14 13 13 10 20 17 18 24 26	17 18 18 13 22 17 18 24 26	20 21 23 16 24 18 19 24 26	23 26 22 20 26 19 19 24 27	26 29 25 23 29 19 19 24 27
11	29 21 29 33 17 16 18 24 27	33 26 34 1 17 16 18 24 27	35 28 35 4 15 16 18 24 27	3 33 36 7 15 16 18 24 27	5 1 5 10 16 16 18 24 27	8 6 11 9 17 16 18 24 27	11 10 11 8 18 16 18 24 27	14 14 13 10 20 17 18 24 26	17 19 19 13 22 17 18 24 26	20 22 23 16 24 18 19 24 26	23 27 22 20 27 19 19 24 27	26 30 25 23 29 19 19 24 27
12	29 22 29 33 17 16 18 24 27	33 27 34 1 16 16 18 24 27	36 29 34 4 15 16 18 24 27	3 34 36 7 15 16 18 24 27	6 2 5 10 16 16 18 24 27	9 7 11 9 17 16 18 24 27	11 11 11 8 18 16 18 24 27	14 16 13 10 20 17 18 24 26	17 20 19 13 22 17 18 24 26	20 23 23 16 24 18 19 24 26	23 28 22 20 27 19 19 24 27	26 32 25 24 29 19 19 24 27
13	30 23 29 33 17 16 18 24 27	33 28 34 1 16 16 18 24 27	36 31 34 4 15 16 18 24 27	3 36 36 7 15 16 18 24 27	6 4 6 10 16 16 18 24 27	9 9 11 9 17 16 18 24 27	11 12 11 8 19 16 18 24 27	14 17 13 10 20 17 18 24 26	17 21 19 13 22 17 18 24 26	20 25 23 16 24 18 19 24 26	23 29 22 20 27 19 19 24 27	27 33 26 24 29 19 19 24 27
14	30 25 29 33 17 16 18 24 27	33 30 35 1 16 16 18 24 27	36 32 34 4 15 16 18 24 27	3 1 36 7 15 16 18 24 27	6 5 6 10 16 16 18 24 27	9 10 11 9 17 16 18 24 27	12 14 11 8 19 16 18 24 27	15 18 13 10 20 17 18 24 26	18 23 19 13 22 17 18 24 26	20 26 23 16 25 18 19 24 26	24 31 22 20 27 19 19 24 27	27 34 26 24 29 19 19 24 27
15	30 26 29 33 17 16 18 24 27	33 31 35 1 16 16 18 24 27	36 33 34 4 15 16 18 24 27	3 3 36 7 15 16 18 24 27	6 7 6 10 16 16 18 24 27	9 12 11 9 17 16 18 24 27	12 15 11 8 19 16 18 24 27	15 19 13 10 20 17 18 24 26	18 24 19 13 23 18 18 24 26	21 27 23 17 25 18 19 24 26	24 32 22 20 27 19 19 24 27	27 36 26 24 29 19 19 24 27
16	30 28 30 33 17 16 18 24 27	33 33 35 1 16 16 18 24 27	36 35 34 4 15 16 18 24 27	3 4 1 8 15 16 18 24 27	6 8 6 10 16 16 18 24 27	9 13 11 9 17 16 18 24 27	12 16 11 8 19 16 18 24 27	15 20 14 10 21 17 18 24 26	18 25 19 13 23 18 18 24 26	21 28 23 17 25 18 19 24 26	24 33 22 20 27 19 19 24 27	27 1 26 24 29 19 19 24 27
17	30 29 30 34 17 16 18 24 27	33 34 35 1 16 16 18 24 27	36 36 34 5 15 16 18 24 27	3 6 1 8 15 16 18 24 27	6 9 6 10 16 16 18 24 27	9 14 11 9 17 16 18 24 27	12 17 11 8 19 16 18 24 27	15 22 14 10 21 17 18 24 26	18 26 20 13 23 18 18 24 26	21 30 23 17 25 18 19 24 26	24 35 22 21 27 19 19 24 27	27 2 26 24 29 19 19 24 27
18	30 30 30 34 17 16 18 24 27	33 35 35 1 16 16 18 24 27	36 2 34 5 15 16 18 24 27	3 7 1 8 15 16 18 24 27	6 11 7 10 16 16 18 24 27	9 15 12 9 17 16 18 24 27	12 19 11 8 19 16 18 24 27	15 23 14 10 21 17 18 24 26	18 28 20 13 23 18 18 24 26	21 31 23 17 25 18 19 24 26	24 36 22 21 27 19 19 24 27	27 4 26 24 29 19 19 24 27
19	30 32 30 34 17 16 18 24 27	33 1 35 1 16 16 18 24 27	36 3 34 5 15 16 18 24 27	3 9 1 8 15 16 18 24 27	6 12 7 10 16 16 18 24 27	9 17 12 9 17 16 18 24 27	12 20 11 8 19 16 18 24 27	15 24 14 10 21 17 18 24 26	18 29 20 14 23 18 18 24 26	21 32 23 17 25 18 19 24 26	24 1 22 21 27 19 19 24 27	27 5 26 24 29 19 19 24 27
20	30 33 30 34 17 16 18 24 27	33 3 35 2 16 16 18 24 27	36 5 34 5 15 16 18 24 27	3 10 1 8 15 16 18 24 27	6 13 7 10 16 16 18 24 27	9 18 12 9 17 16 18 24 27	12 21 11 8 19 16 18 24 27	15 25 14 11 21 17 18 24 26	18 30 20 14 23 18 18 24 26	21 34 23 17 25 18 19 24 26	24 3 22 21 27 19 19 24 27	27 7 27 25 30 19 19 24 27
21	30 35 30 34 17 16 18 24 27	34 4 35 2 16 16 18 24 27	36 6 34 5 15 16 18 24 27	4 11 1 8 15 16 18 24 27	6 15 7 10 16 16 18 24 27	9 19 12 8 17 16 18 24 27	12 22 11 8 19 16 18 24 27	15 27 15 11 21 17 18 24 26	18 31 20 14 23 18 18 24 26	21 35 23 17 25 18 19 24 26	24 4 22 21 27 19 19 24 27	27 8 27 25 30 19 19 24 27
22	31 36 31 34 17 16 18 24 27	34 5 35 2 16 16 18 24 27	1 8 34 5 15 16 18 24 27	4 13 2 8 15 16 18 24 27	7 16 8 10 16 16 18 24 27	9 20 12 8 17 16 18 24 27	12 23 11 8 19 16 18 24 27	15 28 15 11 21 17 18 24 26	18 32 20 14 23 18 18 24 26	21 1 23 17 25 18 19 24 26	24 5 22 21 27 19 19 24 27	27 10 27 25 30 19 19 24 27
23	31 2 31 34 17 16 18 24 27	34 7 35 2 16 16 18 24 27	1 9 34 5 15 16 18 24 27	4 14 2 8 15 16 18 24 27	7 17 8 10 16 16 18 24 27	10 21 12 8 17 16 18 24 27	12 25 11 8 19 16 18 24 27	15 29 15 11 21 17 18 24 26	18 34 20 14 23 18 18 24 26	21 2 23 18 25 18 19 24 26	24 7 23 21 27 19 19 24 27	28 11 27 25 30 19 19 24 27
24	31 3 31 34 17 16 18 24 27	34 8 36 2 16 16 18 24 27	1 10 34 5 15 16 18 24 27	4 15 2 8 15 16 18 24 27	7 18 8 10 16 16 18 24 27	10 22 12 8 18 16 18 24 27	13 26 11 8 19 16 18 24 27	15 31 15 11 21 17 18 24 26	19 36 21 14 23 18 18 24 26	21 4 23 18 25 18 19 24 26	25 8 23 21 28 19 19 24 27	28 13 27 25 30 19 19 24 27
25	31 4 31 34 17 16 18 24 27	34 9 36 2 16 16 18 24 27	1 12 34 5 15 16 18 24 27	4 16 2 8 15 16 18 24 27	7 19 8 10 16 16 18 24 27	10 24 12 8 18 16 18 24 27	13 27 11 9 19 16 18 24 26	16 32 15 11 21 17 18 24 26	19 1 21 14 23 18 18 24 26	22 5 23 18 25 18 19 24 26	25 10 23 22 28 19 19 24 27	28 14 27 25 30 19 19 24 27
26	31 5 31 35 17 16 18 24 27	34 11 36 2 16 16 18 24 27	1 13 34 5 15 16 18 24 27	4 17 2 8 15 16 18 24 27	7 20 8 10 16 16 18 24 27	10 25 12 8 18 16 18 24 27	13 28 11 9 19 16 18 24 26	16 34 16 11 21 17 18 24 26	19 2 21 14 23 18 18 24 26	22 7 23 18 25 18 19 24 26	25 12 23 22 28 19 19 24 27	28 15 28 25 30 19 19 24 27
27	31 7 31 35 17 16 18 24 27	34 12 36 2 16 16 18 24 27	1 14 34 6 15 16 18 24 27	4 19 2 8 15 16 18 24 27	7 22 9 10 16 16 18 24 27	10 26 12 8 18 16 18 24 27	13 30 11 9 19 16 18 24 26	16 35 16 11 21 17 18 24 26	19 4 21 14 23 18 18 24 26	22 8 23 18 25 18 19 24 26	25 13 23 22 28 19 19 24 27	28 16 28 25 30 19 19 24 27
28	31 8 32 35 17 16 18 24 27	34 13 36 3 16 16 18 24 27	1 15 34 6 15 16 18 24 27	4 20 3 9 15 16 18 24 27	7 23 9 10 16 16 18 24 27	10 28 12 8 18 16 18 24 27	13 31 11 9 19 16 18 24 26	16 1 16 11 21 17 18 24 26	19 5 21 15 23 18 18 24 26	22 10 23 18 26 18 19 24 26	25 14 23 22 28 19 19 24 27	28 17 28 26 30 19 19 24 27
29	31 10 32 35 17 16 18 24 27	34 14 35 3 16 16 18 24 27	1 16 35 6 15 16 18 24 27	4 21 3 9 15 16 18 24 27	7 24 9 10 16 16 18 24 27	10 29 12 8 18 16 18 24 27	13 33 11 9 20 17 18 24 26	16 2 16 11 21 17 18 24 26	19 7 21 15 23 18 18 24 26	22 11 23 18 26 18 19 24 26	25 16 23 22 28 19 19 24 27	28 19 28 26 30 19 19 24 27
30	31 11 32 35 17 16 18 24 27	**1980**	1 18 35 6 15 16 18 24 27	4 22 3 9 15 16 18 24 27	7 25 9 10 16 16 18 24 27	10 30 12 8 18 16 18 24 27	13 34 11 9 20 17 18 24 26	16 4 17 12 21 17 18 24 26	19 8 21 15 24 18 19 24 26	22 12 23 18 26 18 19 24 26	25 17 24 22 28 19 19 24 27	28 20 28 26 30 19 19 24 27
31	31 12 32 35 17 16 18 24 27		1 19 35 6 15 16 18 24 27		7 27 9 10 16 16 18 24 27		13 35 11 9 20 17 18 24 26	16 5 17 12 22 17 18 24 26		22 14 23 18 26 18 19 24 26		28 21 28 26 30 19 19 24 27

	JAN	FEB	MAR	APR	MAY	JUNE	JULY	AUG	SEPT	OCT	NOV	DEC
1	29 23 29 26 31 19 19 24 27	32 27 34 30 33 20 19 24 27	35 28 32 34 35 19 19 25 27	2 32 35 1 2 19 19 24 27	5 36 5 5 4 19 19 24 27	8 5 10 9 6 19 19 24 27	10 9 9 13 8 19 19 24 27	13 14 12 16 10 19 19 24 27	16 19 18 20 12 20 19 24 27	19 22 22 24 14 20 20 24 27	22 27 21 27 16 21 20 24 27	25 30 25 30 18 22 20 25 27
2	29 24 29 26 31 19 19 24 27	32 28 34 30 33 20 19 24 27	35 29 32 34 35 19 19 25 27	2 34 35 2 2 19 19 24 27	5 2 5 5 4 19 19 24 27	8 7 10 9 6 19 19 24 27	11 11 9 13 8 19 19 24 27	13 16 13 17 10 19 19 24 27	16 20 18 20 12 20 19 24 27	19 24 22 24 14 20 20 24 27	22 28 21 27 16 21 20 24 27	25 31 25 30 18 22 20 25 27
3	29 25 29 26 31 19 19 24 27	32 30 34 30 33 20 19 24 27	35 30 33 34 35 19 19 25 27	2 35 36 2 2 19 19 24 27	5 3 5 5 4 19 19 24 27	8 8 10 9 6 19 19 24 27	11 12 9 13 8 19 19 24 27	14 17 13 17 11 19 19 24 27	17 22 19 20 13 20 19 24 27	19 25 22 24 14 20 20 24 27	23 29 21 27 16 21 20 24 27	26 33 25 30 18 22 20 25 27
4	29 26 29 27 31 19 19 24 27	32 31 34 30 33 20 19 24 27	35 32 33 34 35 19 19 25 27	2 1 36 2 2 19 19 24 27	5 5 6 6 4 19 19 24 27	8 10 10 9 6 19 19 24 27	11 14 9 13 9 19 19 24 27	14 18 13 17 11 19 19 24 27	17 23 19 20 13 20 19 24 27	20 26 22 24 14 20 20 24 27	23 30 21 27 16 21 20 24 27	26 34 25 30 18 22 20 25 27
5	29 27 29 27 31 19 19 24 27	32 32 34 31 33 20 19 24 27	35 33 33 34 36 19 19 25 27	2 2 36 2 2 19 19 24 27	5 6 6 6 4 19 19 24 27	8 11 10 9 6 19 19 24 27	11 15 9 13 9 19 19 24 27	14 20 13 17 11 19 19 24 27	17 24 19 21 13 20 19 24 27	20 27 22 24 15 20 20 24 27	23 32 21 27 16 21 20 24 27	26 35 25 30 18 22 20 25 27
6	29 29 29 27 31 19 19 24 27	32 34 34 31 33 20 19 24 27	35 34 33 34 36 19 19 25 27	2 4 36 2 2 19 19 24 27	5 8 6 6 4 19 19 24 27	8 13 10 10 7 19 19 24 27	11 16 9 13 9 19 19 24 27	14 21 13 17 11 19 19 24 27	17 25 19 21 13 20 19 24 27	20 28 22 24 15 20 20 24 27	23 33 21 28 16 21 20 24 27	26 1 26 30 18 22 20 25 27
7	29 30 30 27 31 19 19 24 27	32 35 34 31 34 20 19 24 27	35 36 33 34 36 19 19 25 27	2 5 36 2 2 19 19 24 27	5 9 6 6 4 19 19 24 27	8 14 10 10 7 19 19 24 27	11 18 9 13 9 19 19 24 27	14 22 14 17 11 19 19 24 27	17 26 19 21 13 20 19 24 27	20 30 22 24 15 20 20 24 27	23 34 21 28 16 21 20 24 27	26 2 26 30 18 22 20 25 27
8	29 31 30 27 31 19 19 24 27	32 36 34 31 34 20 19 24 27	35 1 33 34 36 19 19 25 27	2 7 36 2 2 19 19 24 27	5 11 6 6 4 19 19 24 27	8 15 10 10 7 19 19 24 27	11 19 9 13 9 19 19 24 27	14 23 14 17 11 19 19 24 27	17 28 19 21 13 20 19 24 27	20 31 22 24 15 20 20 24 27	23 36 21 28 17 21 20 24 27	26 3 26 30 18 22 20 25 27
9	29 33 30 27 31 19 19 24 27	33 2 34 31 34 20 19 24 27	35 3 33 35 36 19 19 25 27	2 8 1 2 2 19 19 24 27	5 12 7 6 5 19 19 24 27	8 17 10 10 7 19 19 24 27	11 20 9 14 9 19 19 24 27	14 24 14 17 11 19 19 24 27	17 29 19 21 13 20 19 24 27	20 32 22 25 15 20 20 24 27	23 1 21 28 17 21 20 24 27	26 5 26 31 18 22 20 25 27
10	29 34 30 27 31 20 19 24 27	33 3 34 31 34 19 19 24 27	35 4 33 35 36 19 19 25 27	3 10 1 3 2 19 19 24 27	5 13 7 6 5 19 19 24 27	8 18 10 10 7 19 19 24 27	11 21 9 14 9 19 19 24 27	14 26 14 17 11 19 19 24 27	17 30 20 21 13 20 19 24 27	20 33 22 25 15 20 20 24 27	23 3 22 28 17 21 20 24 27	26 6 26 31 18 22 20 25 27
11	30 35 30 27 31 20 19 24 27	33 5 34 31 34 19 19 24 27	36 6 33 35 36 19 19 25 27	3 11 1 3 2 19 19 24 27	6 15 7 6 5 19 19 24 27	8 19 10 10 7 19 19 24 27	11 22 9 14 9 19 19 24 27	14 27 14 18 11 19 19 24 27	17 31 20 21 13 20 19 24 27	20 35 22 25 15 20 20 24 27	23 4 22 28 17 21 20 24 27	26 8 27 31 18 22 21 25 27
12	30 1 30 28 31 20 19 24 27	33 6 34 31 34 19 19 24 27	36 7 33 35 36 19 19 25 27	3 12 1 3 2 19 19 24 27	6 16 7 7 5 19 19 24 27	9 20 10 10 7 19 19 24 27	11 24 9 14 9 19 19 24 27	14 28 15 18 11 19 19 24 27	17 33 20 21 13 20 19 24 27	20 36 22 25 15 21 20 24 27	23 6 22 28 17 21 20 24 27	26 9 27 31 18 22 21 25 27
13	30 2 31 28 32 20 19 24 27	33 8 34 32 34 19 19 24 27	36 9 33 35 36 19 19 25 17	3 14 1 3 3 19 19 24 27	6 17 7 7 5 19 19 24 27	9 22 10 10 7 19 19 24 27	12 25 10 14 9 19 19 24 27	15 29 15 18 11 19 19 24 27	18 34 20 22 13 20 20 24 27	20 2 22 25 15 21 20 24 27	24 7 22 28 17 21 20 24 27	27 11 27 31 18 22 21 25 27
14	30 4 31 28 32 20 19 24 27	33 9 34 32 34 19 19 24 27	36 10 33 35 36 19 19 25 27	3 15 1 3 3 19 19 24 27	6 18 8 7 5 19 19 24 17	9 23 10 11 7 19 19 24 27	12 26 10 14 9 19 19 24 27	15 31 15 18 11 19 19 24 27	18 35 20 22 13 20 20 24 27	21 3 22 25 15 21 20 24 27	24 9 22 28 17 21 20 24 27	27 12 27 31 18 22 21 25 27
15	30 5 31 28 32 20 19 24 27	33 10 34 32 34 19 19 24 27	36 11 33 35 36 19 19 25 27	3 16 2 3 3 19 19 24 27	6 20 8 7 5 19 19 24 27	9 24 10 11 7 19 19 24 27	12 27 10 14 9 19 19 24 27	15 32 15 18 11 19 19 24 27	18 1 20 22 13 20 20 24 27	21 5 21 25 15 21 20 24 27	24 10 22 28 17 21 20 24 27	27 13 27 31 18 22 21 25 27
16	30 6 31 28 32 20 19 24 27	33 12 34 32 34 19 19 24 27	36 13 33 35 36 19 19 25 27	3 17 2 3 3 19 19 24 27	6 21 8 7 5 19 19 24 27	9 25 10 11 7 19 19 24 27	12 28 10 14 9 19 19 24 27	15 33 15 18 11 19 19 24 27	18 2 20 22 13 20 20 24 27	21 6 21 25 15 21 20 24 27	24 12 22 29 17 21 20 24 27	27 15 27 31 18 22 21 25 27
17	30 8 31 28 32 20 19 24 27	33 13 33 32 34 19 19 24 27	36 14 33 36 36 19 19 25 27	3 19 2 3 3 19 19 24 27	6 22 8 7 5 19 19 24 27	9 26 10 11 7 19 19 24 27	12 30 10 15 9 19 19 24 27	15 35 16 18 11 19 19 24 27	18 4 20 22 13 20 20 24 27	21 8 21 25 15 21 20 24 27	24 13 23 29 17 21 20 25 27	27 17 27 31 19 22 21 25 27
18	30 9 31 28 32 20 19 24 27	33 14 33 32 34 19 19 25 27	36 15 33 36 1 19 19 25 27	3 20 2 4 3 19 19 24 27	6 23 8 7 5 19 19 24 27	9 28 10 11 7 19 19 24 27	12 31 10 15 9 19 19 24 27	15 36 16 18 12 19 19 24 27	18 5 21 22 14 20 20 24 27	21 9 21 26 15 21 20 24 27	24 14 23 29 17 21 20 25 27	27 18 28 31 19 22 21 25 27
19	30 11 32 28 32 20 19 24 27	34 16 33 32 34 19 19 25 27	36 16 34 36 1 19 19 25 27	3 21 2 4 3 19 19 24 27	6 24 8 7 5 19 19 24 27	9 29 10 11 7 19 19 24 27	12 32 10 15 10 19 19 24 27	15 1 16 19 12 19 19 24 27	18 7 21 22 14 20 20 24 27	21 10 21 26 15 21 20 24 27	24 16 23 29 17 21 20 25 27	27 19 28 31 19 22 21 25 27
20	30 12 32 29 32 20 19 24 27	34 17 33 32 35 19 19 25 27	36 18 34 36 1 19 19 25 27	3 22 3 4 3 19 19 24 27	6 25 9 8 5 19 19 24 27	9 30 10 11 8 19 19 24 27	12 34 10 15 10 19 19 24 27	15 3 16 19 12 19 19 24 27	18 8 21 22 14 20 20 24 27	21 12 21 26 15 21 20 24 27	24 18 23 29 17 21 20 25 27	27 20 28 31 19 22 21 25 27
21	31 13 32 29 32 20 19 24 27	34 18 33 33 35 19 19 25 27	1 19 34 36 1 19 19 24 27	4 23 3 4 3 19 19 24 27	6 27 9 8 5 19 19 24 27	9 31 10 11 8 19 19 24 27	12 35 10 15 10 19 19 24 27	15 4 16 19 12 19 19 24 27	18 10 21 22 14 20 20 24 27	21 13 21 26 15 21 20 24 27	24 18 23 29 17 21 20 25 27	27 22 28 31 19 22 21 25 27
22	31 15 32 29 32 20 19 24 27	34 19 33 33 35 19 19 25 27	1 20 34 36 1 19 19 24 27	4 25 3 4 3 19 19 24 27	7 28 9 8 5 19 19 24 27	10 33 10 12 8 19 19 24 27	12 36 11 15 10 19 19 24 27	15 6 17 19 12 19 19 24 27	18 11 21 23 14 20 20 24 27	21 15 21 26 16 21 20 24 27	24 19 23 29 17 21 20 25 27	28 23 28 31 19 22 21 25 27
23	31 16 32 29 32 20 19 24 27	34 21 33 33 35 19 19 25 27	1 21 34 36 1 19 19 24 27	4 26 3 4 3 19 19 24 27	7 29 9 8 6 19 19 24 27	10 34 9 12 8 19 19 24 27	13 2 11 15 10 19 19 24 27	15 7 17 19 12 19 19 24 27	18 12 21 23 14 20 20 24 27	21 16 21 26 16 21 20 24 27	25 21 24 29 17 21 20 25 27	28 24 28 31 19 22 21 25 27
24	31 17 32 29 32 20 19 24 27	34 22 33 33 35 19 19 25 27	1 22 34 36 1 19 19 24 27	4 27 3 4 3 19 19 24 27	7 30 9 8 6 19 19 24 27	10 35 9 12 8 19 19 24 27	13 3 11 15 10 19 19 24 27	16 8 17 19 12 20 19 24 27	19 14 21 23 14 20 20 24 27	22 17 20 26 16 21 20 24 27	25 22 24 29 17 21 20 25 27	28 25 28 31 19 22 21 25 27
25	31 19 33 29 32 20 19 24 27	34 23 33 33 35 19 19 25 27	1 24 34 1 1 19 19 24 27	4 28 4 4 3 19 19 24 27	7 32 9 8 6 19 19 24 27	10 1 9 12 8 19 19 24 27	13 4 11 16 10 19 19 24 27	16 10 17 19 12 20 19 24 27	19 15 21 23 14 20 20 24 27	22 18 20 26 16 21 20 24 27	25 23 24 29 17 21 20 25 27	28 26 29 31 19 22 21 25 27
26	31 20 33 29 33 20 19 24 27	34 24 32 33 35 19 19 25 27	1 25 34 1 1 19 19 24 27	4 29 4 5 4 19 19 24 27	7 33 9 8 6 19 19 24 27	10 2 9 12 8 19 19 24 27	13 6 11 16 10 19 19 24 27	16 11 17 19 12 20 19 24 27	19 16 21 23 14 20 20 24 27	22 20 20 26 16 21 20 24 27	25 24 24 29 18 21 20 25 27	28 27 29 31 19 22 21 25 27
27	31 21 33 29 33 20 19 24 27	34 25 32 33 35 19 19 25 27	1 26 35 1 1 19 19 24 27	4 31 4 5 4 19 19 24 27	7 34 9 8 6 19 19 24 27	10 3 9 12 8 19 19 24 27	13 7 11 16 10 19 19 24 27	16 13 17 20 12 20 19 24 27	19 18 21 23 14 20 20 24 27	22 21 20 26 16 21 20 24 27	25 25 24 30 18 21 20 25 27	28 29 29 31 19 22 21 25 27
28	31 22 33 30 33 20 19 24 27	34 26 32 33 35 19 19 25 27	1 27 35 1 1 19 19 24 27	4 32 4 5 4 19 19 24 27	7 36 9 8 6 19 19 24 27	10 5 9 12 8 19 19 24 27	13 9 12 16 10 19 19 24 27	16 14 18 20 12 20 19 24 27	19 19 22 23 14 20 20 24 27	22 22 20 27 16 21 20 24 27	25 27 24 30 18 22 20 25 27	28 30 29 31 19 22 21 25 27
29	31 23 33 30 33 20 19 24 27		1 29 35 1 1 19 19 24 27	4 33 5 5 4 19 19 24 27	7 1 10 9 6 19 19 24 27	10 6 9 12 8 19 19 24 27	13 10 12 16 10 19 19 24 27	16 15 18 20 12 20 19 24 27	19 20 22 23 14 20 20 24 27	22 23 20 27 16 21 20 24 27	25 28 25 30 18 22 20 25 27	28 31 29 31 19 22 21 25 27
30	32 24 33 30 33 20 19 24 27		1 30 35 1 1 19 19 24 27	4 35 5 5 4 19 19 24 27	7 2 10 9 6 19 19 24 27	10 8 9 13 8 19 19 24 27	13 12 12 16 10 19 19 24 27	16 17 18 20 12 20 19 24 27	19 21 22 23 14 20 20 24 27	22 25 20 27 16 21 20 24 27	25 29 25 30 18 22 20 25 27	28 32 29 31 19 22 21 25 27
31	32 26 33 30 33 20 19 24 27	1981	2 31 35 1 2 19 19 24 27		7 4 10 9 6 19 19 24 27		13 13 12 16 10 19 19 24 27	16 18 18 20 12 20 19 24 27		22 26 20 27 16 21 20 24 27		28 34 30 31 19 22 21 25 27

	JAN	FEB	MAR	APR	MAY	JUNE	JULY	AUG	SEPT	OCT	NOV	DEC
1	29 35 30 31 19 22 21 25 27	32 4 31 30 20 22 21 25 27	35 5 32 30 20 23 21 25 27	2 10 1 33 20 22 20 25 27	5 14 6 36 19 22 20 25 27	8 19 8 4 19 22 20 25 27	11 23 8 7 20 22 20 25 27	13 27 14 11 21 22 20 25 27	16 31 19 15 23 22 20 25 27	19 34 19 18 25 23 21 25 27	22 4 21 22 28 23 21 25 27	25 7 26 26 30 24 22 25 27
2	29 36 30 31 19 22 21 25 27	32 5 31 30 20 22 21 25 27	35 6 32 30 20 23 21 25 27	2 12 1 33 19 22 20 25 27	5 16 7 36 19 22 20 25 27	8 20 8 4 19 22 20 25 27	11 24 8 7 20 22 20 25 27	13 28 14 11 21 22 20 25 27	16 33 19 15 23 22 20 25 27	19 35 19 18 25 23 21 25 27	22 5 21 22 28 23 21 25 27	25 9 26 26 30 24 22 25 27
3	29 1 30 31 19 22 21 25 27	32 7 31 30 20 22 21 25 27	35 8 32 31 20 23 21 25 27	2 13 1 33 19 22 20 25 27	5 17 7 36 19 22 20 25 27	8 22 8 4 19 22 20 25 27	11 25 8 7 20 22 20 25 27	14 29 14 11 21 22 20 25 27	17 34 19 15 23 22 20 25 27	19 1 19 19 25 23 21 25 27	23 6 21 22 28 23 21 25 27	26 10 26 26 30 24 22 25 27
4	29 3 30 31 19 22 21 25 27	32 8 31 30 20 22 21 25 27	35 9 32 31 20 23 21 25 27	2 14 1 33 19 22 20 25 27	5 18 7 36 19 22 20 25 27	8 23 7 4 19 22 20 25 27	11 26 9 8 20 22 20 25 27	14 31 15 11 22 22 20 25 27	17 35 19 15 23 22 21 25 27	20 3 19 19 25 23 21 25 27	23 8 22 23 28 23 21 25 27	26 12 26 26 30 24 22 25 27
5	29 4 30 31 19 22 21 25 27	32 10 31 30 20 22 21 25 27	35 11 32 31 20 23 21 25 27	2 16 1 33 19 22 20 25 27	5 19 7 1 19 22 20 25 27	8 24 7 4 19 22 20 25 27	11 27 9 8 20 22 20 25 27	14 32 15 11 22 22 20 25 27	17 36 20 15 23 22 21 25 27	20 4 19 19 26 23 21 25 27	23 9 22 23 28 23 21 25 27	26 13 27 27 30 24 22 25 27
6	29 6 31 31 19 22 21 25 27	32 11 31 30 20 22 21 25 27	35 12 32 31 20 23 21 25 27	2 17 1 33 19 22 20 25 27	5 21 7 1 19 22 20 25 27	8 25 7 4 19 22 20 25 27	11 29 9 8 20 22 20 25 27	14 33 15 11 22 22 20 25 27	17 2 20 15 24 22 21 25 27	20 6 19 19 26 23 21 25 27	23 11 22 23 28 23 21 25 27	26 15 27 27 30 24 22 25 27
7	29 7 31 31 19 22 21 25 27	32 13 31 30 20 22 21 25 27	35 13 33 31 20 23 21 25 27	2 18 2 34 19 22 20 25 27	5 22 7 1 19 22 20 25 27	8 26 7 4 19 22 20 25 27	11 30 9 8 20 22 20 25 27	14 34 15 12 22 22 20 25 27	17 3 20 15 24 22 21 25 27	20 7 19 19 26 23 21 25 27	23 12 22 23 28 23 21 25 27	26 16 27 27 30 24 22 25 27
8	29 9 31 31 19 22 21 25 27	32 14 31 30 20 22 21 25 27	35 15 33 31 20 23 21 25 27	2 20 2 34 29 22 20 25 27	5 23 7 1 19 22 20 25 27	8 28 7 4 19 22 20 25 27	11 31 9 8 20 22 20 25 27	14 36 15 12 22 22 20 25 27	17 4 20 16 24 22 21 25 27	20 8 19 19 26 23 21 25 27	23 14 22 23 28 23 21 25 27	26 17 27 27 30 24 22 25 27
9	29 10 31 31 20 22 21 25 27	32 15 31 30 20 22 21 25 27	35 16 33 31 20 23 21 25 27	2 21 2 34 19 22 20 25 27	5 24 7 1 19 22 20 25 27	8 29 7 5 19 22 20 25 27	11 32 9 8 20 22 20 25 27	14 1 16 12 22 22 20 25 27	17 6 20 16 24 22 21 25 27	20 10 19 19 26 23 21 25 27	23 15 22 23 28 23 21 25 27	26 19 27 27 30 24 22 25 27
10	29 12 31 31 20 22 21 25 27	33 17 31 30 20 23 21 25 27	35 18 33 31 20 23 21 25 27	2 22 2 34 19 22 20 25 27	5 26 8 1 19 22 20 25 27	8 30 7 5 19 22 20 25 27	11 33 10 8 20 22 25 25 27	14 2 16 12 22 22 20 25 27	17 7 20 16 24 22 21 25 27	20 11 19 19 26 23 21 25 27	23 16 23 23 29 24 21 25 27	26 20 27 27 31 24 22 25 27
11	30 13 31 31 20 22 21 25 27	33 18 31 30 20 23 21 25 27	36 19 33 31 20 22 21 25 27	3 24 2 34 19 22 20 25 27	5 27 8 1 19 22 20 25 27	8 31 7 5 19 22 20 25 27	11 35 10 8 20 22 20 25 27	14 3 16 12 22 22 20 25 27	17 9 20 16 24 22 21 25 27	20 13 19 20 26 23 21 25 27	23 18 23 24 29 24 21 25 27	26 21 28 27 31 24 22 25 27
12	30 15 31 31 20 22 21 25 27	33 19 31 30 20 23 21 25 27	36 20 33 31 20 22 21 25 27	3 25 3 34 19 22 20 25 27	6 28 8 1 19 22 20 25 27	9 32 7 5 19 22 20 25 27	11 36 10 8 20 22 20 25 27	14 4 16 12 22 22 20 25 27	17 10 20 16 24 22 21 25 27	20 14 19 20 26 23 21 25 27	23 19 23 24 29 24 21 25 27	26 23 28 27 31 24 22 25 27
13	30 16 32 31 20 22 21 25 27	33 21 31 30 20 23 21 25 27	36 21 33 31 20 22 21 25 27	3 26 3 34 19 22 20 25 27	6 29 8 1 19 22 20 25 27	9 34 7 5 19 22 20 25 27	12 1 10 9 20 22 20 25 27	14 6 16 12 22 22 20 25 27	17 11 20 16 24 22 21 25 27	20 15 19 20 26 23 21 25 27	24 20 23 24 29 24 21 25 27	27 24 28 28 31 24 22 25 27
14	30 17 32 31 20 22 21 25 27	33 22 31 30 20 23 21 25 27	36 23 34 31 20 22 21 25 27	3 27 3 34 19 22 20 25 27	6 30 8 2 19 22 20 25 27	9 35 7 5 19 22 20 25 27	12 2 10 9 20 22 20 25 27	15 8 16 12 22 22 20 25 27	18 13 20 16 24 22 21 25 27	21 17 19 20 26 23 21 25 27	24 22 23 24 29 24 21 25 27	27 25 28 28 31 24 22 25 27
15	30 19 32 31 20 22 21 25 27	33 23 31 30 20 23 21 25 27	36 24 34 31 20 22 21 25 27	3 28 3 34 19 22 20 25 27	6 32 8 2 19 22 20 25 27	9 36 7 5 19 22 20 25 27	12 4 11 9 20 22 20 25 27	15 9 17 13 22 22 20 25 27	18 14 20 16 24 22 21 25 27	21 18 19 20 26 23 21 25 27	24 23 23 24 29 24 21 25 27	27 26 28 28 31 24 22 25 27
16	30 20 32 31 20 22 21 25 27	33 24 31 30 20 23 21 25 27	36 25 34 31 20 22 21 25 27	3 29 4 34 19 22 20 25 27	6 33 8 2 19 22 20 25 27	9 1 7 5 19 22 20 25 27	12 5 11 9 21 22 20 25 27	15 10 17 13 22 22 20 25 27	18 16 20 17 24 22 21 25 27	21 19 19 20 26 23 21 25 27	24 24 24 24 29 24 21 25 27	27 28 28 28 31 24 22 25 27
17	30 21 32 31 20 22 21 25 27	33 25 31 30 20 23 21 25 27	36 26 34 32 20 22 21 25 27	3 31 4 35 19 22 20 25 27	6 34 8 2 19 22 20 25 27	9 3 7 5 19 22 20 25 27	12 7 11 9 21 22 20 25 27	15 12 17 13 22 22 20 25 27	18 17 20 17 24 22 21 25 27	21 21 19 20 26 23 21 25 27	24 25 24 24 29 24 21 25 27	27 29 28 28 31 24 22 25 27
18	30 22 32 31 20 22 21 25 27	33 27 31 30 20 23 21 25 27	36 28 34 32 20 22 21 25 27	3 32 4 35 19 22 20 25 27	6 35 8 2 19 22 20 25 27	9 4 7 6 19 22 20 25 27	12 8 11 9 21 22 20 25 27	15 13 17 13 22 22 20 25 27	18 19 20 17 24 22 21 25 27	21 22 19 20 26 23 21 25 27	24 27 24 24 29 24 21 25 27	27 30 29 28 31 24 22 25 27
19	30 24 32 31 20 22 21 25 27	34 28 31 30 20 23 21 25 27	36 29 34 32 20 22 21 25 27	3 33 4 35 19 22 20 25 27	6 1 8 2 19 22 20 25 27	9 6 7 6 19 22 20 25 27	12 10 11 9 21 22 20 25 27	15 15 17 13 22 22 20 25 27	18 20 20 17 24 22 21 25 27	21 23 19 21 27 23 21 25 27	24 28 24 25 29 24 21 25 27	27 31 29 28 31 24 22 25 27
20	30 25 32 31 20 22 21 25 27	34 29 31 30 20 23 21 25 27	36 30 34 32 20 22 21 25 27	3 34 4 35 19 22 20 25 27	6 2 8 2 19 22 20 25 27	9 7 7 6 19 22 20 25 27	12 11 12 9 21 22 20 25 27	15 16 17 13 22 22 20 25 27	18 21 20 17 24 22 21 25 27	21 25 19 21 27 23 21 25 27	24 29 24 25 29 24 21 25 27	27 32 29 28 31 24 22 25 27
21	31 26 32 31 20 22 21 25 27	34 30 31 30 20 23 21 25 27	1 31 35 32 20 22 21 25 27	4 36 5 35 19 22 20 25 27	6 3 8 2 19 22 20 25 27	9 9 7 6 19 22 20 25 27	12 13 12 10 21 22 20 25 27	15 18 18 13 23 22 20 25 27	18 23 20 17 25 22 21 25 27	21 26 19 21 27 23 21 25 27	24 30 24 25 29 24 21 25 27	27 33 29 28 31 24 22 25 27
22	31 27 32 31 20 22 21 25 27	34 31 31 30 20 23 21 25 27	1 32 35 32 20 22 21 25 27	4 1 5 35 19 22 20 25 27	7 5 8 2 19 22 20 25 27	10 10 7 6 19 22 20 25 27	12 14 12 10 21 22 20 25 27	15 19 18 13 23 22 20 25 27	18 24 20 17 25 22 21 25 27	21 27 20 21 27 23 21 25 27	24 31 24 25 29 24 21 25 27	27 35 29 29 31 24 22 25 27
23	31 28 32 31 20 22 21 25 27	34 33 31 30 20 23 21 25 27	1 34 35 32 20 22 21 25 27	4 3 5 35 19 22 20 25 27	7 6 8 3 19 22 20 25 27	10 12 7 6 19 22 20 25 27	12 16 12 10 21 22 20 25 27	15 21 18 14 23 22 20 25 27	18 25 20 17 25 23 21 25 27	21 28 20 21 27 23 21 25 27	25 33 25 25 29 24 21 25 27	28 36 29 29 32 24 22 25 27
24	31 30 32 30 20 22 21 25 27	34 34 31 30 20 23 21 25 27	1 35 35 32 20 22 21 25 27	4 4 5 35 19 22 20 25 27	7 8 8 3 19 22 20 25 27	10 13 8 6 20 22 20 25 27	13 17 12 10 21 22 20 25 27	16 22 18 14 23 22 20 25 27	19 26 20 17 25 23 21 25 27	22 29 20 21 27 23 21 25 27	25 34 25 25 29 24 21 25 27	28 1 29 29 32 24 22 25 27
25	31 31 32 30 20 22 21 25 27	34 35 31 30 20 23 21 25 27	1 36 35 32 20 22 21 25 27	4 6 5 35 19 22 20 25 27	7 9 8 3 19 22 20 25 27	10 15 8 6 20 22 20 25 27	13 18 13 10 21 22 20 25 27	16 23 18 14 23 22 20 25 27	19 27 20 18 25 23 21 25 27	22 31 20 21 17 23 21 25 27	25 35 25 25 29 24 21 25 27	28 2 30 29 32 24 22 25 27
26	31 32 32 30 20 22 21 25 27	34 1 32 30 20 23 21 25 27	1 2 35 32 20 22 20 25 27	4 7 6 36 19 22 20 25 27	7 11 8 3 19 22 20 25 27	10 16 8 7 20 22 20 25 27	13 20 13 10 21 22 20 25 27	16 24 18 14 23 22 20 25 27	19 29 20 18 25 23 21 25 27	22 32 20 21 27 23 21 25 27	25 36 25 25 29 24 21 25 27	28 4 30 29 32 24 22 25 27
27	31 33 32 30 20 22 21 25 27	34 2 32 30 20 23 21 25 27	1 3 36 32 20 22 20 25 27	4 8 6 36 19 22 20 25 27	7 12 8 3 19 22 20 25 27	10 17 8 7 20 22 20 25 27	13 21 13 10 21 22 20 25 27	16 25 18 14 23 22 20 25 27	19 30 20 18 25 23 21 25 27	22 33 20 22 27 23 21 25 27	25 2 25 26 29 24 21 25 27	28 5 30 29 32 25 22 25 27
28	31 35 32 30 20 22 21 25 27	34 4 32 30 20 23 21 25 27	1 5 36 33 20 22 20 25 27	4 10 6 36 19 22 20 25 27	7 13 8 3 19 22 20 25 27	10 19 8 7 20 22 20 25 27	13 22 13 10 21 22 20 25 27	16 27 18 14 23 22 20 25 27	19 31 20 18 25 23 21 25 27	22 34 21 22 27 23 21 25 27	25 3 26 26 30 24 21 25 27	28 7 30 29 32 25 22 25 27
29	31 36 32 30 20 22 21 25 27		1 6 36 33 20 22 20 25 27	4 11 6 36 19 22 20 26 27	7 15 8 3 19 22 20 25 27	10 20 8 7 20 22 20 25 27	13 23 13 11 21 22 20 25 27	16 28 19 14 23 22 20 25 27	19 32 20 18 25 23 21 25 27	22 36 21 22 27 23 21 25 27	25 4 26 26 30 24 21 25 27	28 8 30 30 32 25 22 25 27
30	31 1 32 30 20 22 21 25 27	1982	1 7 36 33 20 22 20 25 27	4 13 6 36 19 22 20 25 27	7 16 8 3 19 22 20 25 27	10 21 8 7 20 22 20 25 27	13 25 14 11 21 22 20 25 27	16 29 19 14 23 22 20 25 27	19 33 20 18 25 23 21 25 27	22 1 21 22 27 23 21 25 27	25 6 26 26 30 24 22 25 27	28 10 30 30 32 25 22 25 27
31	32 3 32 30 20 22 21 25 27		1 9 36 33 20 22 20 25 27		7 18 8 4 19 22 20 25 27		13 26 14 11 21 22 20 25 27	16 30 19 15 23 22 20 25 27		22 2 21 22 27 23 21 25 27		28 11 30 30 32 25 22 25 27

	JAN	FEB	MAR	APR	MAY	JUNE	JULY	AUG	SEPT	OCT	NOV	DEC
1	29 13 30 30 32 25 22 25 27	32 18 29 34 35 25 22 25 27	34 19 33 1 1 25 22 25 27	2 24 2 5 3 26 22 25 27	5 27 6 9 5 25 22 25 27	7 32 5 12 8 25 21 25 27	10 35 9 15 10 25 21 25 27	13 3 15 16 12 25 21 25 27	16 8 19 15 14 25 22 25 27	19 12 17 15 16 25 22 25 27	22 17 22 18 17 26 22 25 27	25 21 27 21 19 26 23 25 27
2	29 14 31 30 32 25 22 25 27	32 19 29 34 35 25 22 25 27	35 20 33 1 1 25 22 25 27	2 25 2 5 3 26 22 25 27	5 28 6 9 5 25 22 25 27	8 33 5 12 8 25 21 25 27	10 36 10 15 10 25 21 25 27	13 4 16 16 12 25 21 25 27	16 9 19 15 14 25 22 25 27	19 13 18 15 16 25 22 25 27	22 19 23 18 18 26 22 25 27	25 22 27 21 19 26 23 25 27
3	29 16 31 30 32 25 22 25 27	32 21 29 34 35 25 22 25 27	35 22 33 1 1 25 22 25 27	2 26 3 5 3 26 22 25 27	5 29 6 9 6 25 22 25 27	8 34 5 12 8 25 21 25 27	11 1 10 15 10 25 21 25 27	14 6 16 16 12 25 21 25 27	16 11 19 15 14 25 22 25 27	19 15 18 15 16 25 22 25 27	22 20 23 18 18 26 22 25 27	26 24 27 21 19 26 23 25 27
4	29 17 31 30 32 25 22 25 27	32 22 29 34 35 25 22 25 27	35 23 33 2 1 26 22 25 27	2 27 3 5 3 26 22 25 27	5 31 6 9 6 25 22 25 27	8 35 5 12 8 25 21 25 27	11 2 10 15 10 25 21 25 27	14 7 16 16 12 25 21 25 27	17 12 19 15 14 25 22 25 27	20 16 18 15 16 25 22 25 27	23 21 23 18 18 26 22 25 27	26 25 27 21 19 26 23 25 27
5	29 18 31 30 32 25 22 25 27	32 23 30 34 35 25 22 25 27	35 24 33 2 1 26 22 25 27	2 29 3 5 3 26 22 25 27	5 32 6 9 6 25 22 25 27	8 36 5 12 8 25 21 25 27	11 3 10 15 10 25 21 25 27	14 8 16 16 12 25 21 25 27	17 14 19 15 14 25 22 25 27	20 18 18 15 16 25 22 25 27	23 22 23 18 18 26 22 25 27	26 26 28 21 19 26 23 25 27
6	29 20 31 31 33 25 22 25 27	32 25 30 34 35 25 22 25 27	35 25 33 2 1 26 22 25 27	2 30 3 6 4 26 22 25 27	5 33 6 9 6 25 22 25 27	8 1 6 12 8 25 21 25 27	11 5 10 15 10 25 21 25 27	14 10 16 16 12 25 21 25 27	17 15 19 15 14 25 22 25 27	20 19 18 16 16 25 22 25 27	23 24 23 18 18 26 22 25 27	26 28 28 21 20 27 23 25 27
7	29 21 31 31 33 25 22 25 27	32 26 30 35 35 25 22 25 27	35 27 34 2 1 26 22 25 27	2 31 3 6 4 26 22 25 27	5 34 6 9 6 25 21 25 27	8 3 6 13 8 25 21 25 27	11 6 11 15 10 25 21 25 27	14 11 16 16 12 25 21 25 27	17 17 18 15 14 25 22 25 27	20 21 18 16 16 25 22 25 27	23 25 23 18 18 26 22 25 27	26 29 28 22 20 27 23 25 27
8	29 22 31 31 33 25 22 25 27	32 27 30 35 35 25 22 25 27	35 28 34 2 1 26 22 25 27	2 32 4 6 4 26 22 26 27	5 35 6 9 6 25 21 25 27	8 4 6 13 8 25 21 25 27	11 8 11 15 10 25 21 25 27	14 13 16 16 12 25 21 25 27	17 18 18 15 14 25 22 25 27	20 22 18 16 16 25 22 25 27	23 27 24 18 18 26 22 25 27	26 30 28 22 20 27 23 25 27
9	29 24 31 31 33 25 22 25 27	32 28 30 35 35 25 22 25 27	35 29 34 2 1 26 22 25 27	2 33 4 6 4 26 22 25 27	5 1 6 9 6 25 21 25 27	8 5 6 13 8 25 21 25 27	11 9 11 15 10 25 21 25 27	14 14 17 16 12 25 21 25 27	17 20 18 15 14 25 22 25 27	20 23 19 16 16 25 22 25 27	23 28 24 18 18 26 22 25 27	26 31 28 22 20 27 23 25 27
10	29 25 31 31 33 25 22 25 27	33 29 30 35 35 25 22 25 27	35 30 34 2 1 26 22 25 27	2 35 4 6 4 26 22 25 27	5 2 6 10 6 25 21 25 27	8 7 6 13 8 25 21 25 27	11 10 11 15 10 25 21 25 27	14 16 17 16 12 25 21 25 27	17 21 18 15 14 25 22 25 27	20 25 19 16 16 25 22 25 27	23 29 24 19 18 26 22 25 27	26 32 28 22 20 27 23 25 27
11	30 26 31 31 33 25 22 25 27	33 30 30 35 35 25 22 25 27	35 31 34 2 1 26 22 25 27	3 36 4 6 4 26 22 25 27	5 3 6 10 6 25 21 25 27	8 8 6 13 8 25 21 25 27	11 12 11 16 10 25 21 25 27	14 17 17 16 12 25 21 25 27	17 23 18 15 14 25 22 25 27	20 26 19 16 16 25 22 25 27	23 30 24 19 18 26 22 25 27	26 34 28 22 20 27 23 25 27
12	30 27 31 31 33 25 22 25 27	33 32 30 35 35 25 22 25 27	36 33 34 3 2 26 22 25 27	3 1 4 6 4 26 22 25 27	6 5 6 10 6 25 21 25 27	9 10 6 13 8 25 21 25 27	11 14 12 16 10 25 21 25 27	14 19 17 16 12 25 21 25 27	17 24 18 15 14 25 22 25 27	20 27 19 16 16 25 22 25 27	23 32 24 19 18 26 22 25 27	26 35 28 22 20 27 23 25 27
13	30 28 30 31 33 25 22 25 27	33 33 30 35 36 25 22 25 27	36 34 34 3 2 26 22 25 27	3 2 4 6 4 26 22 25 27	6 6 6 10 6 25 21 25 27	9 11 6 13 8 25 21 25 27	12 15 12 16 10 25 21 25 27	14 20 17 16 12 25 21 25 27	17 25 18 15 14 25 22 25 27	20 28 19 16 16 25 22 25 27	24 33 24 19 18 26 22 25 27	27 36 29 22 20 27 23 25 27
14	30 30 30 32 33 25 22 25 27	33 34 30 35 36 25 22 25 27	36 35 35 3 2 26 22 25 27	3 4 5 7 4 26 22 25 27	6 7 6 10 6 25 21 25 27	9 13 6 13 8 25 21 25 27	12 17 12 16 10 25 21 25 27	15 22 17 16 13 25 21 25 27	18 26 18 15 14 25 22 25 27	21 30 19 16 16 25 22 25 27	24 34 24 19 18 26 22 25 27	27 1 19 22 20 27 23 26 27
15	30 31 30 32 33 25 22 25 27	33 35 31 36 36 25 22 25 27	36 36 35 3 2 26 22 25 27	3 5 5 7 4 26 22 25 27	6 9 6 10 6 25 21 25 27	9 14 7 13 9 25 21 25 27	12 18 12 16 11 25 21 25 27	15 23 17 16 13 25 21 25 27	18 28 18 15 15 25 22 25 27	21 31 20 16 16 25 22 25 27	24 35 25 19 18 26 22 25 27	27 2 29 22 20 27 23 26 27
16	30 32 30 32 33 25 22 25 27	33 1 31 36 36 25 22 25 27	36 1 35 3 2 26 22 25 27	3 6 5 7 4 26 22 25 27	6 10 5 10 6 25 21 25 27	9 16 7 13 9 25 21 25 27	12 19 13 16 11 25 21 25 27	15 24 17 16 13 25 21 25 27	18 29 18 15 15 25 22 25 27	21 32 20 16 16 25 22 25 27	24 36 25 19 18 26 22 25 27	27 4 29 23 20 27 23 26 27
17	30 33 30 32 33 25 22 25 27	33 2 31 36 36 25 22 25 27	36 3 35 3 2 26 22 25 27	3 8 5 7 4 26 22 25 27	6 12 5 10 7 25 21 25 27	9 17 7 14 9 25 21 25 27	12 21 13 16 11 25 21 25 27	15 26 18 16 13 25 21 25 27	18 30 17 15 15 25 22 25 27	21 33 20 16 17 25 22 25 27	24 2 25 19 18 26 22 25 27	27 5 29 23 20 27 23 26 27
18	30 34 30 32 34 25 22 25 27	33 3 31 36 36 25 22 25 27	36 4 35 3 2 26 22 25 27	3 9 5 7 4 26 22 25 27	6 13 5 10 7 25 21 25 27	9 18 7 14 9 25 21 25 27	12 22 13 16 11 25 21 25 27	15 27 18 16 13 25 21 25 27	18 31 17 15 15 25 22 25 27	21 34 20 16 17 25 22 25 27	24 3 25 19 18 26 22 25 27	27 6 29 23 20 27 23 26 27
19	30 36 30 32 34 25 22 25 27	33 4 31 36 36 25 22 25 27	36 5 36 3 2 26 22 25 27	3 11 5 7 4 26 22 25 27	6 14 5 11 7 25 21 25 27	9 20 7 14 9 25 21 25 27	12 23 13 16 11 25 21 25 27	15 28 18 16 13 25 21 25 27	18 32 17 15 15 25 22 25 27	21 36 20 16 17 25 22 25 27	24 4 25 20 19 26 22 25 27	27 8 29 23 20 27 23 26 27
20	30 1 30 32 34 25 22 25 27	34 6 31 36 36 25 22 25 27	36 7 36 4 2 26 22 25 27	3 12 5 7 5 26 22 25 27	6 16 5 11 7 25 21 25 27	9 21 7 14 9 25 21 25 27	12 25 13 16 11 25 21 25 27	15 29 18 16 13 25 21 25 27	18 34 17 15 15 25 22 25 27	21 1 20 17 17 26 22 25 27	24 6 25 20 19 26 22 25 27	27 9 29 23 20 27 23 26 27
21	31 2 29 32 34 25 22 25 27	34 7 31 36 36 25 22 25 27	36 8 36 4 2 26 22 25 27	4 13 6 7 5 26 22 25 27	6 17 5 11 7 25 21 25 27	9 22 7 14 9 25 21 25 27	12 26 14 16 11 25 21 25 27	15 30 18 16 13 25 21 25 27	18 35 17 15 15 25 22 25 27	21 2 21 17 17 26 22 25 27	24 7 26 20 19 26 22 25 27	27 11 29 23 20 27 23 26 27
22	31 3 29 33 34 25 22 25 27	34 8 31 36 36 25 22 25 27	1 9 36 4 2 26 22 25 27	4 15 6 7 5 25 22 25 27	7 19 5 11 7 25 21 25 27	10 24 8 14 9 25 21 25 27	12 27 14 16 11 25 21 25 27	15 32 18 16 13 25 21 25 27	18 36 17 15 15 25 22 25 27	21 3 21 17 17 26 22 25 27	24 8 26 20 19 26 22 25 27	27 12 29 23 20 27 23 26 27
23	31 5 29 33 34 25 22 25 27	34 10 32 1 36 25 22 25 27	1 11 36 4 2 26 22 25 27	4 16 6 8 5 25 22 25 27	7 20 5 11 7 25 21 25 27	10 25 8 14 9 25 21 25 27	12 28 14 16 11 25 21 25 27	15 33 18 16 13 25 21 25 27	18 1 17 15 15 25 22 25 27	21 5 21 17 17 26 22 25 27	24 10 26 20 19 26 22 25 27	28 13 29 23 20 27 23 26 27
24	31 6 29 33 34 25 22 25 27	34 11 32 1 36 25 22 25 27	1 12 1 4 3 26 22 25 27	4 18 6 8 5 25 22 25 27	7 21 5 11 7 25 21 25 27	10 26 8 14 9 25 21 25 27	13 29 14 16 11 25 21 25 27	16 34 18 16 13 25 21 25 27	19 2 17 15 15 25 22 25 27	22 6 21 17 17 26 22 25 27	24 11 26 20 19 26 23 25 27	28 15 29 24 21 27 23 26 27
25	31 7 29 33 34 25 22 25 27	34 13 32 1 1 25 22 25 27	1 14 1 4 3 26 22 25 27	4 19 6 8 5 25 22 25 27	7 23 5 11 7 25 21 25 27	10 27 8 14 9 25 21 25 27	13 31 14 16 11 25 21 25 27	16 35 18 16 13 25 22 25 27	19 4 17 15 15 25 22 25 27	22 7 21 17 17 26 22 25 27	25 12 26 20 19 26 23 25 27	28 16 29 24 21 27 23 26 27
26	31 9 29 33 34 25 22 25 27	34 14 32 1 1 25 22 25 27	1 15 1 4 3 26 22 25 27	4 20 6 8 5 25 22 25 27	7 24 5 11 7 25 21 25 27	10 29 8 14 9 25 21 25 27	13 32 14 16 11 25 21 25 27	16 36 18 16 13 25 22 25 27	19 5 17 15 15 25 22 25 27	22 9 21 17 17 26 22 25 27	25 14 26 20 19 26 23 25 27	28 18 29 24 21 27 23 26 27
27	31 10 29 33 34 25 22 25 27	34 16 32 1 1 25 22 25 27	1 17 1 4 3 26 22 25 27	4 22 6 8 5 25 22 25 27	7 25 5 11 7 25 21 25 27	10 30 9 14 9 25 21 25 27	13 33 15 16 11 25 21 25 27	16 2 18 16 13 25 22 25 27	19 6 17 15 15 25 22 25 27	22 10 22 17 17 26 22 25 27	25 15 26 20 19 26 23 25 27	28 19 29 24 21 27 23 26 27
28	31 12 29 33 34 25 22 25 27	34 17 32 1 1 25 22 25 27	1 18 1 5 3 26 22 25 27	4 23 6 8 5 25 22 25 27	7 27 5 12 7 25 21 25 27	10 31 9 15 9 25 21 25 27	13 34 15 16 11 25 21 25 27	16 3 18 15 13 25 22 25 27	19 8 17 15 15 25 22 25 27	22 11 22 17 17 26 22 25 27	25 17 27 21 19 26 23 25 27	28 21 29 24 21 27 23 26 27
29	31 13 29 33 34 25 22 25 27	1983	1 20 2 5 3 26 22 25 27	4 24 6 8 5 25 22 25 27	7 28 5 12 7 25 21 25 27	10 32 9 15 9 25 21 25 27	13 35 15 16 11 25 21 25 27	16 4 18 15 13 25 22 25 27	19 9 17 15 15 25 22 25 27	22 13 22 17 17 26 22 25 27	25 18 27 21 19 26 23 25 27	28 22 29 24 21 27 23 26 27
30	31 15 29 34 34 25 22 25 27		1 21 2 5 3 26 22 25 27	4 26 6 8 5 25 22 25 27	7 29 5 12 7 25 21 25 27	10 33 9 15 10 25 21 25 27	13 1 15 16 12 25 21 25 27	16 5 19 15 14 25 22 25 27	19 10 17 15 16 25 22 25 27	22 14 22 17 17 26 22 25 27	25 20 27 21 19 26 23 25 27	28 23 29 24 21 27 23 26 27
31	32 16 29 34 35 25 22 25 27		1 22 2 5 3 26 22 25 27		7 30 5 12 7 25 21 25 27		13 2 15 16 12 25 21 25 27	16 7 19 15 14 25 22 25 27		22 16 22 18 17 26 22 25 27		28 25 28 24 21 27 23 26 27

	JAN	FEB	MAR	APR	MAY	JUNE	JULY	AUG	SEPT	OCT	NOV	DEC
1	28 26 28 24 21 27 23 26 27	32 31 29 28 23 28 23 26 28	35 33 34 32 24 28 23 26 28	2 1 4 36 24 29 23 26 28	5 4 3 3 24 29 23 26 28	8 9 5 7 23 29 23 26 28	10 13 11 11 23 28 22 26 27	13 18 16 15 24 28 22 25 27	16 24 16 18 25 28 23 25 27	19 27 19 22 27 28 23 26 27	22 32 24 26 29 28 23 26 27	25 35 27 30 32 29 24 26 28
2	29 27 28 25 21 27 23 26 27	32 32 30 28 23 28 23 26 28	35 34 34 32 24 28 23 26 28	2 2 4 36 24 29 23 26 28	5 6 3 3 24 29 23 26 28	8 11 6 7 23 29 23 26 28	11 14 12 11 23 28 22 26 27	13 20 16 15 24 28 23 25 27	16 25 16 19 25 28 23 25 27	19 29 19 22 27 28 23 26 27	22 33 24 26 29 28 23 26 27	25 36 28 30 32 29 24 26 28
3	29 28 28 25 21 27 23 26 27	32 33 30 29 23 28 23 26 28	35 35 34 32 24 28 23 26 28	2 4 4 36 24 29 23 26 28	5 7 3 4 24 29 23 26 28	8 12 6 7 23 29 23 26 28	11 16 12 11 23 28 22 26 27	14 21 16 15 24 28 23 25 27	17 26 16 19 25 28 23 25 27	19 30 19 22 27 28 23 26 27	23 34 24 26 30 28 23 26 27	26 2 28 30 32 29 24 26 28
4	29 30 28 25 21 27 23 26 27	32 34 30 29 23 28 23 26 28	35 36 34 32 24 28 23 26 28	2 5 4 36 24 29 23 26 28	5 8 3 4 24 29 23 26 28	8 13 6 8 23 29 23 26 28	11 17 12 11 23 28 22 26 27	14 23 16 15 24 28 23 25 27	17 28 16 19 25 28 23 25 27	20 31 19 23 27 28 23 26 27	23 35 24 26 30 28 23 26 27	26 3 28 30 32 29 24 26 28
5	29 31 28 25 21 27 23 26 27	32 35 30 29 23 28 23 26 28	35 1 35 32 24 28 23 26 28	2 6 4 36 24 29 23 26 28	5 10 3 4 24 29 23 26 28	8 15 6 8 23 29 23 26 28	11 19 12 11 23 28 22 26 27	14 24 16 15 24 28 23 25 27	17 29 16 19 25 28 23 25 27	20 32 19 23 27 28 23 26 27	23 1 24 26 30 28 23 26 27	26 4 28 30 32 29 24 26 28
6	29 32 28 25 21 27 23 26 27	32 36 30 29 23 28 23 26 28	35 3 35 32 24 28 23 26 28	2 7 4 36 24 29 23 26 28	5 11 3 4 24 29 23 26 28	8 16 6 8 23 29 23 26 28	11 20 12 11 23 28 22 26 27	14 25 17 15 24 28 23 25 27	17 30 16 19 26 28 23 25 27	20 33 19 23 28 28 23 26 27	23 2 24 27 30 28 23 26 27	26 5 28 30 32 29 24 26 28
7	29 33 28 25 21 27 23 26 27	32 2 30 29 23 28 23 26 28	35 4 35 33 24 28 23 26 28	2 9 4 36 24 29 23 26 28	5 12 3 4 24 29 23 26 28	8 18 6 8 23 29 23 26 28	11 21 13 12 23 28 22 26 27	14 27 17 15 24 28 23 25 27	17 31 16 19 26 28 23 25 27	20 35 20 23 28 28 23 26 27	23 3 25 27 30 28 23 26 27	26 6 28 30 32 29 24 26 28
8	29 34 28 25 21 27 23 26 27	32 3 30 29 23 28 23 26 28	35 5 35 33 24 28 23 26 28	2 10 4 1 24 29 23 26 28	5 13 3 4 24 29 23 26 28	8 19 7 8 23 29 23 26 28	11 23 13 12 23 28 22 26 27	14 28 17 16 24 28 23 25 27	17 33 16 19 24 28 23 25 27	20 36 20 23 28 28 23 26 27	23 4 25 27 30 29 23 26 27	26 8 27 30 32 29 24 26 28
9	29 36 28 25 21 27 23 26 27	32 4 30 29 23 28 23 26 28	35 6 35 33 24 28 23 26 28	2 11 4 1 24 29 23 26 28	5 15 3 4 24 29 23 26 28	8 20 7 8 23 29 23 26 28	11 24 13 12 23 28 22 26 27	14 29 17 16 24 28 23 25 27	17 34 16 19 26 28 23 25 27	20 1 20 23 28 28 23 26 27	23 5 25 27 30 29 23 26 27	26 9 27 30 32 29 24 26 28
10	29 1 28 26 21 27 23 26 27	33 5 31 29 23 28 23 26 28	35 8 36 33 24 28 23 26 28	3 13 4 1 24 29 23 26 28	5 16 3 4 24 29 23 26 28	8 22 7 8 23 29 23 26 28	11 26 13 12 23 28 22 26 27	14 30 17 16 24 28 23 25 27	17 35 16 20 26 28 23 25 27	20 2 20 23 28 28 23 26 27	23 7 25 27 30 29 23 26 27	26 10 27 31 32 29 24 26 28
11	29 2 28 26 21 27 23 26 27	33 7 31 29 23 28 23 26 28	36 9 36 33 24 28 23 26 28	3 14 4 1 24 29 23 26 28	6 18 3 5 24 29 23 26 28	9 23 7 8 23 29 23 26 28	11 27 13 12 23 28 22 26 27	14 32 17 16 24 28 23 25 27	17 36 16 20 26 28 23 25 27	20 3 20 23 28 28 23 26 27	23 8 25 27 30 29 23 26 27	26 11 27 31 32 29 24 26 28
12	30 3 28 26 22 27 23 26 27	33 8 31 30 23 28 23 26 28	36 10 36 33 24 28 23 26 28	3 15 4 1 24 29 23 26 28	6 19 3 5 24 29 23 26 28	9 24 7 9 23 29 23 26 28	11 28 13 12 23 28 22 26 27	14 33 17 16 24 28 23 25 27	17 1 16 20 26 28 23 25 27	20 5 20 23 28 28 23 26 27	23 9 25 27 30 29 23 26 27	27 13 27 31 32 29 24 26 28
13	30 5 28 26 22 27 23 26 27	33 9 31 30 23 28 23 26 28	36 12 36 33 24 28 23 26 28	3 17 4 1 24 29 23 26 28	6 21 3 5 24 29 23 26 28	9 25 8 9 23 29 23 26 28	12 29 14 12 23 28 22 26 27	15 34 17 16 24 28 23 25 27	18 2 16 20 26 28 23 25 27	20 6 21 24 28 28 23 26 27	24 10 25 27 30 29 23 26 27	27 14 27 31 33 29 24 26 28
14	30 6 28 26 22 27 23 26 27	33 11 31 30 23 28 23 26 28	36 13 36 33 24 28 23 26 28	3 18 4 1 24 29 23 26 28	6 22 3 5 23 29 23 26 28	9 26 8 9 23 29 23 26 28	12 31 14 12 23 28 22 26 27	15 35 17 16 24 28 23 25 27	18 4 16 20 26 28 23 25 27	21 7 21 24 28 28 23 26 27	24 12 26 28 30 29 23 26 27	27 16 27 31 33 29 24 26 28
15	30 7 28 26 22 27 23 26 27	33 12 31 30 23 28 23 26 28	36 15 1 34 24 28 23 26 28	3 20 4 1 24 29 23 26 28	6 24 3 5 23 29 23 26 28	9 29 8 9 23 28 23 26 28	12 32 14 13 23 28 22 26 27	15 36 17 16 24 28 23 25 27	18 5 16 20 26 28 23 25 27	21 8 21 24 28 28 23 26 27	24 13 26 28 30 29 23 26 27	27 17 27 31 33 29 24 26 28
16	30 9 28 26 22 27 23 26 27	33 14 32 30 23 28 23 26 28	36 16 1 34 24 28 23 26 28	3 21 4 2 24 29 23 26 28	6 25 3 5 23 29 23 26 29	9 30 8 9 23 28 23 26 28	12 33 14 13 23 28 22 25 27	15 2 17 17 24 28 23 25 27	18 6 16 20 26 28 23 25 27	21 9 21 24 28 28 23 26 27	24 15 26 28 31 29 23 26 27	27 18 27 31 33 29 24 26 28
17	30 10 28 26 22 27 23 26 27	33 15 32 30 23 28 23 26 28	36 18 1 34 24 29 23 26 28	3 23 4 2 24 29 23 26 28	6 26 4 5 23 29 23 26 28	9 31 8 9 23 28 23 26 28	12 34 14 13 23 28 22 25 27	15 3 17 17 24 28 23 25 27	18 7 16 20 26 28 23 25 27	21 11 21 24 28 28 23 26 27	24 16 26 28 31 29 23 26 27	27 20 26 31 33 29 24 26 28
18	30 11 28 27 22 27 23 26 27	33 17 32 30 23 28 23 26 28	36 19 1 34 24 29 23 26 28	3 24 4 2 24 29 23 26 28	6 28 4 5 23 29 23 26 28	9 32 9 9 23 28 23 26 28	12 36 14 13 23 28 22 25 27	15 4 17 17 25 28 23 25 27	18 9 16 21 26 28 23 25 27	21 12 21 24 28 28 23 26 27	24 17 26 28 31 29 23 26 27	27 21 26 32 33 29 24 26 28
19	30 13 28 27 22 27 23 26 28	33 18 32 30 23 28 23 26 28	36 21 1 34 24 29 23 26 28	3 26 4 2 24 29 23 26 28	6 29 4 6 23 29 23 26 28	9 34 9 9 23 28 23 26 28	12 1 15 13 23 28 22 25 27	15 5 17 17 25 28 23 25 27	18 10 16 21 26 28 23 25 27	21 13 22 24 28 28 23 26 27	24 19 26 28 31 29 23 26 27	27 23 26 32 33 29 24 26 28
20	30 14 28 27 22 28 23 26 28	34 20 32 31 23 28 23 26 28	36 22 2 34 24 29 23 26 28	4 27 4 2 24 29 23 26 28	6 30 4 6 23 29 23 26 28	9 35 9 9 23 28 23 26 28	12 2 15 13 23 28 22 25 27	15 6 17 17 25 28 23 25 27	18 11 17 21 26 28 23 25 27	21 15 22 24 29 28 23 26 27	24 20 26 28 31 29 24 26 27	27 24 26 32 33 29 24 26 28
21	31 16 28 27 22 28 23 26 28	34 21 33 31 23 28 23 26 28	1 23 2 34 24 29 23 26 28	4 28 4 2 24 29 23 26 28	7 32 4 6 23 29 23 26 28	10 36 9 10 23 28 23 26 28	12 3 15 13 23 28 22 25 27	15 8 17 17 25 28 23 25 27	18 13 17 21 27 28 23 26 27	21 16 22 25 29 28 23 26 27	24 22 26 28 31 29 24 26 27	27 26 26 32 33 29 24 26 28
22	31 17 28 27 22 28 23 26 28	34 23 33 31 23 28 23 26 28	1 25 2 34 24 29 23 26 28	4 30 4 2 24 29 23 26 28	7 33 4 6 23 29 23 26 28	10 1 9 10 23 28 23 26 28	12 4 15 13 23 28 22 25 27	15 9 17 17 25 28 23 25 27	18 14 17 21 27 28 23 26 27	21 18 22 25 29 28 23 26 27	24 23 27 28 31 29 24 26 28	28 27 26 32 33 29 24 26 28
23	31 19 28 27 22 28 23 26 28	34 24 33 31 23 28 23 26 28	1 26 2 35 24 29 23 26 28	4 31 4 2 24 29 23 26 28	7 34 4 6 23 29 23 26 28	10 2 10 10 23 28 23 26 27	13 6 15 14 23 28 22 25 27	16 10 17 17 25 28 23 25 27	19 15 17 21 27 28 23 26 27	21 19 22 25 29 28 23 26 27	25 25 27 29 31 29 24 26 28	28 28 26 32 33 29 24 26 28
24	31 20 28 27 22 28 23 26 28	34 25 33 31 24 28 23 26 28	1 27 2 35 24 29 23 26 28	4 32 4 2 24 29 23 26 28	7 35 4 6 23 29 23 26 28	10 4 10 10 23 28 22 26 27	13 7 15 14 23 28 22 25 27	16 12 16 17 25 28 23 25 27	19 17 17 21 27 28 23 26 27	21 21 22 25 29 28 23 26 27	25 26 27 29 31 29 24 26 28	28 29 26 32 33 29 24 26 28
25	31 22 29 27 22 28 23 26 28	34 27 33 31 24 28 23 26 28	1 29 2 35 24 29 23 26 28	4 33 4 3 24 29 23 26 28	7 36 4 6 23 29 23 26 28	10 5 10 10 23 28 22 26 27	13 8 15 14 23 28 22 25 27	16 13 16 18 25 28 23 25 27	19 19 17 21 27 28 23 26 27	22 22 23 25 29 28 23 26 27	25 27 27 29 31 29 24 26 28	28 31 26 32 33 29 24 26 28
26	31 23 29 28 22 28 23 26 28	34 28 33 31 24 28 23 26 28	1 30 3 35 24 29 23 26 28	4 34 3 3 24 29 23 26 28	7 2 5 6 23 29 23 26 28	10 6 10 10 23 28 22 26 27	13 10 15 14 23 28 22 25 27	16 15 16 18 25 28 23 25 27	19 20 18 22 27 28 23 26 27	22 24 23 25 29 28 23 26 27	25 29 27 29 31 29 24 26 28	28 32 26 32 34 30 24 26 28
27	31 24 29 28 22 28 23 26 28	34 29 33 31 24 28 23 26 28	1 31 3 35 24 29 23 26 28	4 36 3 3 24 29 23 26 28	7 3 5 7 23 29 23 26 28	10 7 11 10 23 28 22 26 27	13 11 16 14 23 28 22 25 27	16 16 16 18 25 28 23 25 27	19 22 18 22 27 28 23 26 27	22 25 23 25 29 28 23 26 27	25 30 27 29 31 29 24 26 28	28 33 26 33 34 30 24 26 28
28	31 26 29 28 22 28 23 26 28	34 30 34 32 24 28 23 26 28	1 32 3 35 24 29 23 26 28	4 1 3 3 24 29 23 26 28	7 4 5 7 23 29 23 26 28	10 9 11 10 23 28 22 26 27	13 12 16 14 24 28 22 25 27	16 18 16 18 25 28 23 25 27	19 23 18 22 27 28 23 26 27	22 27 23 25 29 28 23 26 27	25 31 27 29 31 29 24 26 28	28 35 26 33 34 30 24 26 28
29	31 27 29 28 22 28 23 26 28	34 31 34 32 24 28 23 26 28	1 34 3 35 24 29 23 26 28	4 2 3 3 24 29 23 26 28	7 5 5 7 23 29 23 26 28	10 10 11 11 23 28 22 26 27	13 14 16 14 24 28 22 25 27	16 19 16 18 25 28 23 25 27	19 24 18 22 27 28 23 26 27	22 28 23 26 29 28 23 26 27	25 33 27 29 31 29 24 26 28	28 36 26 33 34 30 24 26 28
30	31 28 29 28 22 28 23 26 28	**1984**	1 35 3 35 24 29 23 26 28	4 3 3 3 24 29 23 26 28	7 7 5 7 23 29 23 26 28	10 11 11 11 23 28 22 26 27	13 15 16 14 24 28 22 25 27	16 21 16 18 25 28 23 25 27	19 26 18 22 27 28 23 26 27	22 29 23 26 29 28 23 26 27	25 34 27 29 32 29 24 26 28	28 1 26 33 34 30 24 26 28
31	32 29 29 28 22 28 23 26 28		2 36 3 36 24 29 23 26 28		7 8 5 7 23 29 23 26 28		13 17 16 15 24 28 22 25 27	16 22 16 18 25 28 23 25 27		22 31 24 26 29 28 23 26 27		28 2 26 33 34 30 24 26 28

	JAN	FEB	MAR	APR	MAY	JUNE	JULY	AUG	SEPT	OCT	NOV	DEC
1	29 3 26 33 34 30 24 26 28	32 8 30 36 36 30 24 26 28	35 9 35 2 2 31 24 26 28	2 13 2 2 5 32 24 26 28	5 17 2 1 7 32 24 26 28	8 23 7 3 9 32 24 26 28	10 26 13 6 11 32 24 26 28	13 31 15 9 13 32 24 26 28	16 36 15 13 15 31 24 26 28	19 3 20 17 17 31 24 26 28	22 8 25 21 19 31 24 26 28	25 11 25 24 21 32 25 26 28
2	29 5 26 33 34 30 24 26 28	32 9 31 36 36 30 24 26 28	35 10 36 2 3 31 24 26 28	2 15 2 2 5 32 24 26 28	5 19 2 1 7 32 24 26 28	8 24 7 3 9 32 24 26 28	11 28 13 6 11 32 24 26 28	13 33 15 9 13 32 24 26 28	16 1 15 13 15 31 24 26 28	19 5 20 17 17 31 24 26 28	22 9 25 21 19 31 24 26 28	25 12 25 24 21 32 25 26 28
3	29 6 26 33 34 30 24 26 28	32 10 31 1 1 30 42 26 28	35 11 36 3 3 31 24 26 28	2 16 2 2 5 32 24 26 28	5 20 2 1 7 32 24 26 28	8 26 7 3 9 32 24 26 28	11 29 13 6 11 32 24 26 28	14 34 15 10 13 32 24 26 28	17 3 15 13 15 31 24 26 28	19 6 20 17 17 31 24 26 28	23 10 25 21 19 31 24 26 28	26 14 25 24 21 32 25 26 28
4	29 7 27 33 34 30 24 26 28	32 12 31 1 1 30 24 26 28	35 13 36 3 3 31 24 26 28	2 18 2 2 5 32 24 26 28	5 22 2 1 7 32 24 26 28	8 27 7 3 9 32 34 26 28	11 31 13 6 11 32 24 26 28	14 35 15 10 13 32 24 26 28	17 4 15 13 15 31 24 26 28	20 7 20 17 17 31 24 26 28	23 12 25 21 19 31 24 26 28	26 15 25 25 21 32 25 26 28
5	29 8 27 34 34 30 24 26 28	32 13 31 1 1 30 24 26 28	35 14 36 3 3 31 24 26 28	2 19 2 2 5 32 24 26 28	5 23 2 1 7 32 24 26 28	8 28 8 3 9 32 24 26 28	11 32 13 6 11 32 24 26 28	14 1 15 10 13 32 24 26 28	17 5 15 13 15 31 24 26 28	20 8 21 17 17 31 24 26 28	23 13 25 21 19 31 24 26 28	26 16 24 25 21 32 25 26 28
6	29 10 27 34 34 30 24 26 28	32 15 31 1 1 30 24 26 28	35 16 36 3 3 31 24 26 28	2 21 2 2 5 32 24 26 28	5 25 2 1 7 32 24 26 28	8 30 8 3 9 32 24 26 28	11 33 13 6 11 32 24 26 28	14 2 15 10 13 32 24 26 28	17 6 16 14 15 31 24 26 28	20 9 21 17 17 31 24 26 28	23 14 25 21 19 31 24 26 28	26 18 24 25 21 32 25 26 28
7	29 11 27 34 34 30 24 26 28	32 16 31 1 1 31 24 26 28	35 17 1 3 3 31 24 26 28	2 22 2 2 5 32 24 26 28	5 26 3 1 7 32 24 26 28	8 31 8 4 9 32 24 26 28	11 35 14 7 11 32 24 26 28	14 3 15 10 13 32 24 26 28	17 7 16 14 15 31 24 26 28	20 11 21 17 17 31 24 26 28	23 15 25 21 19 31 24 26 28	26 19 24 25 21 32 25 26 28
8	29 12 27 34 35 30 24 26 28	32 18 32 1 1 31 24 26 28	35 19 1 3 3 31 24 26 28	2 24 2 2 5 32 24 26 28	5 28 3 1 7 32 24 26 28	8 32 8 4 9 32 24 26 28	11 36 14 7 11 32 24 26 28	14 4 14 10 13 32 24 26 28	17 9 16 14 15 31 24 26 28	20 12 21 17 17 31 24 26 28	23 17 25 21 19 31 24 26 28	26 20 24 25 21 32 25 26 28
9	29 14 27 34 35 30 24 26 28	33 19 32 1 1 31 24 26 28	35 20 1 3 3 31 24 26 28	2 25 1 2 5 32 24 26 28	5 29 3 1 7 32 24 26 28	8 34 8 4 9 32 24 26 28	11 1 14 7 11 32 24 26 28	14 5 14 10 13 32 24 26 28	17 10 16 14 15 31 24 26 28	20 13 21 18 17 31 24 26 28	23 18 25 21 19 31 24 26 28	26 22 24 25 21 32 25 26 28
10	29 15 27 34 35 30 24 26 28	33 21 32 1 1 31 24 26 28	35 22 1 3 3 31 24 26 28	3 27 1 2 5 32 24 26 28	5 30 3 1 7 32 24 26 28	8 35 9 4 10 32 24 26 28	11 2 14 7 12 32 24 26 28	14 7 14 10 14 32 24 26 28	17 11 16 14 15 31 24 26 28	20 15 21 18 17 31 24 26 28	23 20 26 22 19 31 24 26 28	26 23 24 25 21 32 25 26 28
11	30 17 27 34 35 30 24 26 28	33 22 32 1 1 31 24 26 28	36 23 1 3 3 31 24 26 28	3 28 1 1 5 32 24 26 28	6 32 3 2 8 32 24 26 28	9 36 9 4 10 32 24 26 28	11 3 14 7 12 32 24 26 28	14 8 14 11 14 32 24 26 28	17 12 16 14 16 31 24 26 28	20 16 22 18 17 31 24 26 28	23 21 26 22 19 31 24 26 28	26 25 24 25 21 32 25 26 28
12	30 18 28 34 35 30 24 26 28	33 23 32 1 1 31 24 26 28	36 24 1 3 3 31 24 26 28	3 29 1 1 5 32 24 26 28	6 33 3 2 8 32 24 26 28	9 1 9 4 10 32 24 26 28	11 5 14 7 12 32 24 26 28	14 9 14 11 14 32 24 26 28	17 13 17 14 16 31 24 26 28	20 17 22 18 18 31 24 26 28	23 23 26 22 19 31 24 26 28	26 26 24 26 21 32 25 26 28
13	30 19 28 34 35 30 24 26 28	33 25 32 1 1 31 24 26 28	36 26 1 3 3 31 24 26 28	3 31 1 1 6 32 24 26 28	6 34 3 2 8 32 24 26 28	9 3 9 4 10 32 24 26 28	12 6 14 7 12 32 24 26 28	15 10 14 11 14 32 24 26 28	18 15 17 14 16 31 24 26 28	20 19 22 18 18 31 24 26 28	24 24 26 22 20 31 24 26 28	27 28 25 26 21 32 25 26 28
14	30 21 28 35 35 30 24 26 28	33 26 33 1 1 31 24 26 28	36 27 2 3 3 31 24 26 28	3 32 1 1 6 32 24 26 28	6 35 3 2 8 32 24 26 28	9 4 10 4 10 32 24 26 28	12 7 14 7 12 32 24 26 28	15 12 14 11 14 32 24 26 28	18 16 17 15 16 31 24 26 28	21 20 22 18 18 31 24 26 28	24 26 26 22 20 31 24 26 28	27 29 25 26 21 32 25 26 28
15	30 22 28 35 35 30 24 26 28	33 27 33 2 1 31 24 26 28	36 28 2 3 3 31 24 26 28	3 33 1 1 6 32 24 26 28	6 1 4 2 8 32 24 26 28	9 5 10 4 10 32 24 26 28	12 8 14 7 12 32 24 26 28	15 13 14 11 14 32 24 26 28	18 18 17 15 16 31 24 26 28	21 22 22 18 18 31 24 26 28	24 27 26 22 20 31 24 26 28	27 31 25 26 22 32 25 26 28
16	30 24 28 35 35 30 24 26 28	33 29 33 2 1 31 24 26 28	36 30 2 3 4 31 24 26 28	3 34 1 1 6 32 24 26 28	6 2 4 2 8 32 24 26 28	9 6 10 4 10 32 24 26 28	12 9 14 8 12 32 24 26 28	15 14 14 11 14 32 24 26 28	18 19 17 15 16 31 24 26 28	21 23 22 18 18 31 24 26 28	24 29 26 22 20 32 24 26 28	27 32 25 26 22 32 25 26 28
17	30 25 28 35 35 30 24 26 28	33 30 33 2 2 31 24 26 28	36 31 2 3 4 31 24 26 28	3 36 1 1 6 32 24 26 28	6 3 4 2 8 32 24 26 28	9 7 10 5 10 32 24 26 28	12 11 15 8 12 32 24 26 28	15 16 14 11 14 32 24 26 28	18 21 17 15 16 31 24 26 28	21 25 22 19 18 31 24 26 28	24 30 26 22 20 32 24 26 28	27 34 25 26 22 32 25 26 28
18	30 26 28 35 35 30 24 26 28	33 31 33 2 2 31 24 26 28	36 32 2 3 4 31 24 26 28	3 1 1 1 6 32 24 26 28	6 4 4 2 8 32 24 26 28	9 9 10 5 10 32 24 26 28	12 12 15 8 12 32 24 26 28	15 17 14 11 14 32 24 26 28	18 22 18 15 16 31 24 26 28	21 26 23 19 18 31 24 26 28	24 31 26 23 20 32 25 26 28	27 35 25 26 22 32 25 26 28
19	30 28 28 35 35 30 24 26 28	34 33 34 2 2 31 24 26 28	36 34 2 3 4 31 24 26 28	3 2 1 1 6 32 24 26 28	6 5 4 2 8 32 24 26 28	9 10 11 5 10 32 24 26 28	12 13 15 8 12 32 24 26 28	15 19 14 11 14 32 24 26 28	18 24 18 15 16 31 24 26 28	21 28 23 19 18 31 24 26 28	24 33 26 23 20 32 25 26 28	27 36 25 26 22 32 25 26 28
20	30 29 29 35 35 30 24 26 28	34 34 34 2 2 31 24 26 28	36 35 2 3 4 31 24 26 28	3 3 1 1 6 32 24 26 28	6 6 4 2 8 32 24 26 28	9 11 11 5 10 32 24 26 28	12 15 15 8 12 32 24 26 28	15 20 14 12 14 32 24 26 28	18 25 18 15 16 31 24 26 28	21 29 23 19 18 31 24 26 28	24 34 26 23 20 32 25 26 28	27 1 25 27 22 32 25 26 28
21	31 30 29 35 36 30 24 26 28	34 35 34 2 2 31 24 26 28	1 36 2 3 4 31 24 26 28	4 4 1 1 6 32 24 26 28	6 8 5 2 8 32 24 26 28	9 12 11 5 10 32 24 26 28	12 16 15 8 12 32 24 26 28	15 21 14 12 14 31 24 26 28	18 27 18 15 16 31 24 26 28	21 30 23 19 18 31 24 26 28	24 35 26 23 20 32 25 26 28	27 3 25 27 22 32 25 26 28
22	31 32 29 35 36 30 24 26 28	34 36 34 2 2 31 24 26 28	1 1 2 3 4 31 24 26 28	4 6 1 1 6 32 24 26 28	7 9 5 2 8 32 24 26 28	10 14 11 5 10 32 24 26 28	12 17 15 8 12 32 24 26 28	15 23 14 12 14 31 24 26 28	18 28 18 15 16 31 24 26 28	21 32 23 19 18 31 24 26 28	24 36 26 23 20 32 25 26 28	28 4 25 27 22 32 25 26 28
23	31 33 29 35 36 30 24 26 28	34 2 34 2 2 31 24 26 28	1 2 2 3 4 31 24 26 28	4 7 1 1 6 32 24 26 28	7 10 5 2 8 32 24 26 28	10 15 11 5 10 32 24 26 28	13 19 15 8 12 32 24 26 28	15 24 14 12 14 31 24 26 28	18 29 19 16 16 31 24 26 28	21 33 23 19 18 31 24 26 28	25 2 26 23 20 32 25 26 28	28 5 26 27 22 32 25 26 28
24	31 34 29 36 36 30 24 26 28	34 3 34 2 2 31 24 26 28	1 4 2 3 4 31 24 26 28	4 8 1 1 6 32 24 26 28	7 11 5 2 8 32 24 26 28	10 16 12 5 10 32 24 26 28	13 20 15 8 12 32 24 26 28	16 26 14 12 14 31 24 26 28	19 31 19 16 16 31 24 26 28	22 34 23 19 18 31 24 26 28	25 3 26 23 20 32 25 26 28	28 6 26 27 22 32 25 26 28
25	31 35 29 36 36 30 24 26 28	34 4 35 2 2 31 24 26 28	1 5 2 2 4 31 24 26 28	4 9 1 1 6 32 24 26 28	7 13 5 2 8 32 24 26 28	10 18 12 5 11 32 24 26 28	13 22 15 9 12 32 24 26 28	16 27 14 12 14 31 24 26 28	19 32 19 16 16 31 24 26 28	22 36 24 20 18 31 24 26 28	25 4 26 23 20 32 25 26 28	28 7 26 27 22 32 25 26 28
26	31 1 30 36 36 30 24 26 28	34 5 35 2 2 31 24 26 28	1 6 2 2 4 31 24 26 28	4 10 1 1 6 32 24 26 28	7 14 6 3 9 32 24 26 28	10 19 12 5 11 32 24 26 28	13 23 15 9 13 32 24 26 28	16 28 14 12 15 31 24 26 28	19 33 19 16 17 31 24 26 28	22 1 24 20 18 31 24 26 28	25 5 26 24 20 32 25 26 28	28 8 26 27 22 32 25 26 28
27	31 2 30 36 36 30 24 26 28	34 6 35 2 2 31 24 26 28	1 7 2 2 4 32 24 26 28	4 12 2 1 7 32 24 26 28	7 15 6 3 9 32 24 26 28	10 21 12 6 11 32 24 26 28	13 25 15 9 13 32 24 26 28	16 30 14 12 15 31 24 26 28	19 35 19 16 17 31 24 26 28	22 2 24 20 18 31 24 26 28	25 6 25 24 20 32 25 26 28	28 10 26 27 22 32 25 26 28
28	31 3 30 36 36 30 24 26 28	34 7 35 2 2 31 24 26 28	1 8 2 2 4 32 24 26 28	4 13 2 1 7 32 24 26 28	7 17 6 3 9 32 24 26 28	10 22 12 6 11 32 24 26 28	13 26 15 9 13 32 24 26 28	16 31 14 12 15 31 24 26 28	19 36 19 16 17 31 24 26 28	22 3 24 20 19 31 24 26 28	25 8 25 24 20 32 25 26 28	28 11 26 28 22 32 25 26 28
29	31 4 30 36 36 30 24 26 28	1985	1 10 2 2 4 32 24 26 28	4 14 2 1 7 32 24 26 28	7 18 6 3 9 32 24 26 28	10 24 12 6 11 32 24 26 28	13 27 15 9 13 32 24 26 28	16 32 14 13 15 31 24 26 28	19 1 20 16 17 31 24 26 28	22 4 24 20 19 31 24 26 28	25 9 25 24 21 32 25 26 28	28 12 26 28 22 32 25 26 28
30	32 5 30 36 36 30 24 26 28		1 11 2 2 5 32 24 26 28	4 16 2 1 7 32 24 26 28	7 20 6 3 9 32 24 26 28	10 25 13 6 11 32 24 26 28	13 29 15 9 13 32 24 26 28	16 34 14 13 15 31 24 26 28	19 2 20 16 17 31 24 26 28	22 6 24 20 19 31 24 26 28	25 10 25 24 21 32 25 26 28	28 13 27 28 22 32 25 26 28
31	32 7 30 36 36 30 24 26 28		2 12 2 2 5 32 24 26 28		7 21 7 3 9 32 24 26 28		13 30 15 9 13 32 24 26 28	16 35 14 13 15 31 24 26 28		22 7 24 20 19 31 24 26 28		28 15 27 28 22 32 25 26 28

	JAN	FEB	MAR	APR	MAY	JUNE	JULY	AUG	SEPT	OCT	NOV	DEC
1	29 16 27 28 23 32 25 26 28	32 21 32 32 24 33 25 27 28	35 22 36 35 26 34 25 27 28	2 28 35 3 28 34 25 27 28	5 31 2 7 29 35 25 27 28	8 36 9 11 30 36 25 27 28	10 4 13 14 30 36 25 27 28	13 8 12 18 29 36 25 27 28	16 12 16 21 29 35 25 27 28	19 16 21 23 30 35 25 27 28	22 21 24 23 32 35 25 27 28	25 24 23 22 34 35 26 27 28
2	29 17 27 28 23 32 25 26 28	32 23 32 32 24 33 25 27 28	35 24 36 36 26 34 25 27 28	2 29 35 3 28 34 25 27 28	5 33 3 7 29 35 25 27 28	8 1 9 11 30 36 25 27 28	10 5 13 14 29 36 25 27 28	13 9 12 18 29 36 25 27 28	16 14 16 21 29 35 25 27 28	19 17 21 23 30 35 25 27 28	22 22 24 23 32 35 25 27 28	25 26 23 22 34 35 26 27 28
3	29 19 27 28 23 32 25 26 28	32 24 32 32 25 33 25 27 28	35 25 36 36 26 34 25 27 28	2 30 35 4 28 34 25 27 28	5 34 3 7 29 35 25 27 28	8 3 9 11 30 36 25 27 28	11 6 13 15 29 36 25 27 28	14 10 12 18 29 36 25 27 28	17 15 16 21 29 35 25 27 28	19 18 21 23 30 35 25 27 28	23 24 24 23 32 35 25 27 28	26 27 24 22 34 35 26 27 28
4	29 20 27 28 23 32 25 26 28	32 25 32 32 25 33 25 27 28	35 26 1 36 26 34 25 27 28	2 32 35 4 28 34 25 27 28	5 35 3 7 29 35 25 27 28	8 4 9 11 30 36 25 27 28	11 7 13 15 29 36 25 27 28	14 12 12 18 29 36 25 27 28	17 16 16 21 29 35 25 27 28	20 20 21 23 30 35 25 27 28	23 25 24 23 32 35 25 27 28	26 29 24 22 34 35 26 27 28
5	29 21 27 29 23 32 25 26 28	32 27 32 32 25 33 25 27 28	35 28 1 36 26 34 25 27 28	2 33 35 4 28 35 25 27 28	5 1 3 7 29 35 25 27 28	8 5 9 11 30 36 25 27 28	11 8 13 15 29 36 25 27 28	14 13 12 18 29 36 25 27 28	17 18 17 21 29 35 25 27 28	20 21 22 23 30 35 25 27 28	23 27 24 23 32 35 25 27 28	26 30 24 22 34 35 26 27 28
6	29 23 28 29 23 32 25 26 28	32 28 33 33 25 33 25 27 28	35 29 1 36 26 34 25 27 28	2 34 35 4 28 35 25 27 28	5 2 3 8 29 35 25 27 28	8 6 10 11 30 36 25 27 28	11 10 13 15 29 36 25 27 28	14 14 12 18 29 36 25 27 28	17 19 17 21 29 35 25 27 28	20 23 22 23 30 35 25 27 28	23 28 24 23 32 35 25 27 28	26 32 24 22 34 35 26 27 28
7	29 24 28 29 23 32 25 26 28	32 30 33 33 25 33 25 27 28	35 31 1 36 26 34 25 27 28	2 36 36 4 28 35 25 27 28	5 3 3 8 29 35 25 27 28	8 7 10 11 30 36 25 27 28	11 11 13 15 29 36 25 27 28	14 15 12 18 29 36 25 27 28	17 20 17 21 29 35 25 27 28	20 24 22 23 30 35 25 27 28	23 29 24 23 32 35 25 27 28	26 33 24 22 34 35 26 27 28
8	29 26 28 29 23 32 25 26 28	32 31 33 33 25 33 25 27 28	35 32 1 36 26 34 25 27 28	2 1 36 4 28 35 25 27 28	5 4 4 8 29 35 25 27 28	8 9 10 12 30 36 25 27 28	11 12 13 15 29 36 25 27 28	14 17 12 19 29 36 25 27 28	17 22 17 22 29 35 25 27 28	20 26 22 23 30 35 25 27 28	23 31 24 23 32 35 25 27 28	26 35 24 22 34 35 26 27 28
9	29 27 28 29 23 33 25 26 28	32 32 33 33 25 33 25 27 28	35 33 1 36 26 34 25 27 28	2 2 36 4 28 35 25 27 28	5 5 4 8 29 35 25 27 28	8 10 10 12 30 36 25 27 28	11 13 13 15 29 36 25 27 28	14 18 12 19 29 36 25 27 28	17 23 17 22 29 35 25 27 28	20 27 22 23 30 35 25 27 28	23 32 24 23 32 35 25 27 28	26 36 24 22 34 35 26 27 28
10	29 29 28 29 23 33 25 27 28	33 34 33 33 25 33 25 27 28	35 35 1 1 27 34 25 27 28	2 3 36 4 28 35 25 27 28	5 7 4 8 29 35 25 27 28	8 11 10 12 30 36 25 27 28	11 14 13 15 29 36 25 27 28	14 19 12 19 29 36 25 27 28	17 24 18 22 29 35 25 27 28	20 28 22 23 31 35 25 27 28	23 34 24 22 32 35 25 27 28	26 1 24 22 34 35 26 27 28
11	30 30 28 29 23 33 25 27 28	33 35 33 33 25 33 25 27 28	36 36 1 1 27 34 25 27 28	3 5 36 5 28 35 25 27 28	6 8 4 8 29 35 25 27 28	8 12 10 12 30 36 25 27 28	11 16 13 15 29 36 25 27 28	14 21 12 19 29 36 25 27 28	17 26 18 22 29 35 25 27 28	20 30 22 23 31 35 25 27 28	23 35 24 22 32 35 25 27 28	26 3 25 22 35 35 26 27 28
12	30 32 28 29 23 33 25 27 28	33 36 34 33 25 33 25 27 28	36 1 36 1 27 34 25 27 28	3 6 36 5 28 35 25 27 28	6 9 4 8 29 35 25 27 28	9 13 11 12 30 36 25 27 28	12 17 13 16 29 36 25 27 28	14 22 13 19 29 36 25 27 28	17 27 18 22 29 35 25 27 28	20 31 23 24 31 35 25 27 28	23 36 24 22 33 35 25 27 28	26 4 25 22 35 35 26 27 28
13	30 33 29 30 23 33 25 27 28	33 2 34 33 25 33 25 27 28	36 2 36 1 27 34 25 27 28	3 7 36 5 28 35 25 27 28	6 10 5 8 29 35 25 27 28	9 15 11 12 30 36 25 27 28	12 18 13 16 29 36 25 27 28	14 23 13 19 29 36 25 27 28	17 29 18 22 29 35 25 27 28	20 33 23 24 31 35 25 27 28	24 2 24 22 33 35 25 27 28	27 5 25 22 35 35 26 27 28
14	30 34 29 30 23 33 25 27 28	33 3 34 34 25 33 25 27 28	36 4 36 1 27 34 25 27 28	3 8 36 5 28 35 25 27 28	6 11 5 9 29 35 25 27 28	9 16 11 12 30 36 25 27 28	12 20 13 16 29 36 25 27 28	14 25 13 19 29 36 25 27 28	18 30 18 22 29 35 25 27 28	21 34 23 24 31 35 25 27 28	24 3 23 22 33 35 25 27 28	27 6 25 23 35 35 26 27 28
15	30 36 29 30 23 33 25 27 28	33 4 34 34 25 33 25 27 28	36 5 36 1 27 34 25 27 28	3 9 36 5 28 35 25 27 28	6 13 5 9 29 35 25 27 28	9 17 11 12 30 36 25 27 28	12 21 13 16 29 36 25 27 28	15 26 13 19 29 36 25 27 28	18 32 18 22 29 35 25 27 28	21 35 23 24 31 35 25 27 28	24 4 23 22 33 35 25 27 28	27 7 25 23 35 35 26 27 28
16	30 1 29 30 23 33 25 27 28	33 5 34 34 25 33 25 27 28	36 6 36 1 27 34 25 27 28	3 10 36 5 28 35 25 27 28	6 14 5 9 29 35 25 27 28	9 19 11 13 30 36 25 27 28	12 22 13 16 29 36 25 27 28	15 28 13 19 29 36 25 27 28	18 33 19 22 29 35 25 27 28	21 1 23 24 31 35 25 27 28	24 5 23 22 33 35 26 27 28	27 9 25 23 35 35 26 27 28
17	30 2 29 30 24 33 25 27 28	33 6 35 34 25 33 25 27 28	36 7 36 1 27 34 25 27 28	3 12 36 5 28 35 25 27 28	6 15 5 9 30 35 25 27 28	9 20 12 13 30 36 25 27 28	12 24 13 16 29 36 25 27 28	15 29 13 19 29 36 25 27 28	18 34 19 22 29 35 25 27 28	21 2 23 24 31 35 25 27 28	24 6 23 22 33 35 26 27 28	27 10 26 23 35 35 26 27 28
18	30 3 29 30 24 33 25 27 28	33 8 35 34 25 33 25 27 28	36 8 36 2 27 34 25 27 28	3 13 1 5 28 35 25 27 28	6 16 6 9 30 35 25 27 28	9 21 12 13 30 36 25 27 28	12 25 13 16 29 36 25 27 28	15 31 13 20 29 36 25 27 28	18 36 19 22 29 35 25 27 28	21 3 23 24 31 35 25 27 28	24 8 23 22 33 35 26 27 28	27 11 26 23 35 35 26 27 28
19	30 5 30 30 24 33 25 27 28	34 9 35 34 25 33 25 27 28	36 10 36 2 27 34 25 27 28	3 14 1 6 29 35 25 27 28	6 18 6 9 30 35 25 27 28	9 23 12 13 30 36 25 27 28	12 27 13 16 29 36 25 27 28	15 32 13 20 29 36 25 27 28	18 1 19 22 30 35 25 27 28	21 4 23 24 31 35 25 27 28	24 9 23 22 33 35 26 27 28	27 12 26 23 35 35 26 27 28
20	30 6 30 30 24 33 25 27 28	34 10 35 34 26 33 25 27 28	36 11 36 2 27 34 25 27 28	3 15 1 6 29 35 25 27 28	6 19 6 9 30 35 25 27 28	9 24 12 13 30 36 25 27 28	12 28 13 16 29 36 25 27 28	15 33 14 20 29 36 25 27 28	18 2 19 22 30 35 25 27 28	21 6 24 24 31 35 25 27 28	24 10 23 22 33 35 26 27 28	27 13 26 23 35 35 26 27 28
21	31 7 30 31 24 33 25 27 28	34 11 35 34 26 34 25 27 28	1 12 36 2 27 34 25 27 28	4 17 1 6 29 35 25 27 28	6 20 6 9 30 35 25 27 28	9 26 12 13 30 36 25 26 28	12 30 13 17 29 36 25 27 28	15 35 14 20 29 36 25 27 28	18 4 19 23 30 35 25 27 28	21 7 24 23 31 35 25 27 28	24 11 23 22 33 35 26 27 28	27 15 26 23 35 35 26 27 28
22	31 8 30 31 24 33 25 27 28	34 13 35 35 26 34 25 27 28	1 13 36 2 27 34 25 27 28	4 18 1 6 29 35 25 27 28	7 22 6 10 30 35 25 27 28	10 27 12 13 30 36 25 26 28	21 31 13 17 29 36 25 27 28	15 36 14 20 29 36 25 27 28	18 5 20 23 30 35 25 27 28	21 8 24 23 31 35 25 27 28	24 12 23 22 33 35 26 27 28	27 16 26 23 35 35 26 27 28
23	31 9 30 31 24 33 25 27 28	34 14 36 35 26 34 25 27 28	1 15 36 2 27 34 25 27 28	4 20 1 6 29 35 25 27 28	7 23 7 10 30 35 25 27 28	10 29 12 13 30 36 25 26 28	12 33 13 17 29 36 25 27 28	15 2 14 20 29 36 25 27 28	18 6 20 23 30 35 25 27 28	21 9 24 23 31 35 25 27 28	25 14 23 22 33 35 26 27 28	28 17 26 23 35 35 26 27 28
24	31 11 30 31 24 33 25 27 28	34 15 36 35 26 34 25 27 28	1 16 35 2 27 34 25 27 28	4 21 1 6 29 35 25 27 28	7 25 7 10 30 35 25 27 28	10 30 12 13 30 36 25 26 28	13 34 12 17 29 36 25 27 28	16 3 14 20 29 36 25 27 28	19 7 20 23 30 35 25 27 28	22 10 24 23 31 35 25 27 28	25 15 23 22 33 35 26 27 28	28 18 27 23 35 35 26 27 28
25	31 12 30 31 24 33 25 27 28	34 17 36 35 26 34 25 27 28	1 17 35 2 27 34 25 27 28	4 23 1 6 29 35 25 27 28	7 26 7 10 30 35 25 27 28	10 32 12 14 30 36 25 26 28	13 35 12 17 29 36 25 27 28	16 4 14 20 29 36 25 27 28	19 8 20 23 30 35 25 27 28	22 12 24 23 31 35 25 27 28	25 16 23 22 33 35 26 27 28	28 20 27 23 35 35 26 27 28
26	31 13 31 31 24 33 25 27 28	34 18 36 35 26 34 25 27 28	1 19 35 3 27 34 25 27 28	4 24 2 6 29 35 25 27 28	7 28 7 10 30 35 25 27 28	10 33 12 14 30 36 25 26 28	13 1 12 17 29 36 25 27 28	16 5 15 20 29 35 25 27 28	19 10 20 23 30 35 25 27 28	22 13 24 23 31 35 25 27 28	25 17 23 22 33 35 26 27 28	28 21 27 23 36 35 26 27 28
27	31 14 31 31 24 33 25 27 28	34 19 36 35 26 34 25 27 28	1 20 35 3 27 34 25 27 28	4 26 2 7 29 35 25 27 28	7 29 8 10 30 35 25 27 28	10 35 13 14 30 36 25 26 28	13 2 12 17 29 36 25 27 28	16 6 15 20 29 35 25 27 28	19 11 20 23 30 35 25 27 28	22 14 24 23 32 35 25 27 28	25 19 23 22 34 35 26 27 28	28 22 27 23 36 35 26 27 28
28	31 16 31 31 24 33 25 27 28	34 21 36 35 26 34 25 27 28	1 22 35 3 27 34 25 27 28	4 27 2 7 29 35 25 27 28	7 31 8 10 30 35 25 27 28	10 36 13 14 30 36 25 26 28	13 3 12 17 29 36 25 27 28	16 8 15 21 29 35 25 27 28	19 12 21 23 30 35 25 27 28	22 15 24 23 32 35 25 27 28	25 20 23 22 34 35 26 27 28	28 24 27 24 36 35 26 27 28
29	31 17 31 32 24 33 25 27 28		1 23 35 3 28 34 25 27 28	4 29 2 7 29 35 25 27 28	7 32 8 10 30 35 25 27 28	10 1 13 14 30 36 25 26 28	13 4 12 17 29 36 25 27 28	16 9 15 21 29 35 25 27 28	19 13 21 23 30 35 25 27 28	22 17 24 23 32 35 25 27 28	25 21 23 22 34 35 26 27 28	28 25 27 24 36 35 26 27 28
30	31 18 31 32 24 33 25 27 28	**1986**	1 25 35 3 28 34 25 27 28	4 30 2 7 29 35 25 27 28	7 34 8 11 30 35 25 27 28	10 2 13 14 30 36 25 26 28	13 6 12 18 29 36 25 27 28	16 10 15 21 29 35 25 27 28	19 14 21 23 30 35 25 27 28	22 18 24 23 32 35 25 27 28	25 23 23 22 34 35 26 27 28	28 27 28 24 36 35 26 27 28
31	32 20 32 32 24 33 25 27 28		1 26 35 3 28 34 25 27 28		7 35 8 11 30 36 25 27 28		13 7 12 18 29 36 25 27 28	16 11 16 21 29 35 25 27 28		22 19 24 23 32 35 25 27 28		28 28 28 24 36 35 26 27 28

	JAN	FEB	MAR	APR	MAY	JUNE	JULY	AUG	SEPT	OCT	NOV	DEC
1	29 30 28 24 36 35 26 27 28	32 35 33 27 2 36 26 27 28	34 36 34 30 4 36 27 27 28	2 5 35 34 6 1 27 27 28	5 8 4 2 8 2 27 27 28	8 12 10 5 10 3 26 27 28	10 16 11 9 12 3 26 27 28	13 20 12 13 14 3 26 27 28	16 25 17 17 16 3 26 27 28	19 29 22 20 18 3 26 27 28	22 34 22 24 20 3 26 27 28	25 2 24 28 22 3 27 27 28
2	29 31 28 24 36 35 26 27 28	32 36 33 27 2 36 26 27 28	35 1 34 30 4 1 27 27 28	2 6 35 34 6 1 27 27 28	5 9 4 2 8 2 27 27 28	8 14 10 5 10 3 26 27 28	10 17 11 9 12 3 26 27 28	13 21 12 13 14 3 26 27 28	16 26 18 17 16 3 26 27 28	19 30 22 20 18 3 26 27 28	22 36 21 24 20 3 26 27 28	25 3 24 28 22 3 27 27 28
3	29 33 28 24 36 35 26 27 28	32 2 33 27 2 36 26 27 28	35 3 34 30 4 1 27 27 28	2 7 35 34 6 1 27 27 28	5 10 4 2 8 2 27 27 28	8 15 10 6 10 3 26 27 28	11 18 11 9 12 3 26 27 28	14 23 12 13 14 3 26 27 28	16 28 18 17 16 3 26 27 28	19 32 22 21 18 3 26 27 28	23 1 21 24 20 3 26 27 28	26 5 24 28 22 3 27 27 28
4	29 34 28 24 36 35 26 27 28	32 3 33 27 2 36 26 27 28	35 4 34 31 4 1 27 27 28	2 8 35 34 6 1 27 27 28	5 12 4 2 8 2 27 27 28	8 16 10 6 10 3 26 27 28	11 19 11 9 12 3 26 27 28	14 24 12 13 14 3 26 27 28	17 29 18 17 16 3 26 27 28	20 33 22 21 18 3 26 27 28	23 2 21 25 20 3 26 27 28	26 6 25 28 22 2 27 27 28
5	29 36 28 24 36 35 26 27 28	32 4 34 27 2 36 26 27 28	35 5 34 31 4 1 27 27 28	2 10 35 34 6 1 27 27 28	5 13 5 2 8 2 27 27 28	8 17 10 6 10 3 26 27 28	11 21 11 9 12 3 26 27 28	14 26 12 13 14 3 26 27 28	17 31 18 17 16 3 26 27 28	20 35 22 21 18 3 26 27 28	23 4 21 25 20 3 26 27 28	26 7 25 28 22 2 27 27 28
6	29 1 29 24 36 35 26 27 28	32 6 34 28 2 36 26 27 28	35 6 34 31 4 1 27 27 28	2 11 35 34 7 1 27 27 28	5 14 5 2 9 2 27 27 28	8 18 10 6 11 3 26 27 28	11 22 11 10 12 3 26 27 28	14 27 12 13 14 3 26 27 28	17 32 18 17 16 3 26 27 28	20 36 22 21 18 3 26 27 28	23 5 21 25 20 3 26 27 28	26 9 25 28 22 2 27 27 28
7	29 2 29 24 36 35 26 27 28	32 7 34 28 3 36 26 27 28	35 8 34 31 4 1 27 27 28	2 12 36 35 7 1 27 27 28	5 15 5 2 9 2 27 27 28	8 20 10 6 11 3 26 27 28	11 23 11 10 13 3 26 27 28	14 28 13 13 14 3 26 27 28	17 34 18 17 16 3 26 27 28	20 2 22 21 18 3 26 27 28	23 6 21 25 20 3 26 27 28	26 10 25 29 22 2 27 27 28
8	29 3 29 25 36 35 26 27 28	32 8 34 28 3 36 26 27 28	35 9 34 31 5 1 27 27 28	2 13 36 35 7 1 27 27 28	5 16 5 2 9 2 27 27 28	8 21 11 6 11 3 26 27 28	11 25 10 10 13 3 26 27 28	14 30 13 14 15 3 26 27 28	17 35 19 17 17 3 26 27 28	20 3 22 21 18 3 26 27 28	23 8 21 25 20 3 26 27 28	26 11 25 29 22 2 27 27 28
9	29 5 29 25 1 35 26 27 28	32 9 34 28 3 36 26 27 28	35 10 34 31 5 1 27 27 28	2 14 36 35 7 1 27 27 28	5 18 5 2 9 2 26 27 28	8 22 11 6 11 3 26 27 28	11 26 10 10 13 3 26 27 28	14 31 13 14 15 3 26 27 28	17 1 19 18 17 3 26 27 28	20 4 23 21 19 3 26 27 28	23 9 21 25 21 3 26 27 28	26 12 26 29 22 2 27 27 28
10	29 6 29 25 1 35 26 27 28	33 10 34 28 3 36 26 27 28	35 11 34 31 5 1 27 27 28	2 16 36 35 7 1 27 27 28	5 19 6 3 9 2 26 27 28	8 24 11 6 11 3 26 27 28	11 28 10 10 13 3 26 27 28	14 33 13 14 15 3 26 27 28	17 2 19 18 17 3 26 27 28	20 6 23 21 19 3 26 27 28	23 10 21 25 21 3 26 27 28	26 13 26 29 23 2 27 27 28
11	30 7 29 25 1 35 26 27 28	33 11 34 28 3 36 26 27 28	35 12 34 31 5 1 27 27 28	3 17 36 35 7 1 27 27 28	5 20 6 3 9 2 26 27 28	8 25 11 6 11 3 26 27 28	11 29 10 10 13 3 26 27 28	14 34 13 14 15 3 26 27 28	17 4 19 18 17 3 26 27 28	20 7 23 22 19 3 26 27 28	23 11 21 25 21 3 26 27 28	26 15 26 29 23 2 27 27 28
12	30 8 30 25 1 35 26 27 28	33 13 35 28 3 36 26 27 28	36 14 33 32 5 1 27 27 28	3 18 36 35 7 1 27 27 28	6 22 6 3 9 2 26 27 28	9 27 11 7 11 3 26 27 28	11 31 10 10 13 3 27 27 28	14 36 13 14 15 3 26 27 28	17 5 19 18 17 3 26 27 28	20 8 23 22 19 3 26 27 28	23 13 22 26 21 3 26 27 28	26 16 26 29 23 2 27 27 28
13	30 9 30 25 1 35 26 27 28	33 14 35 28 3 36 26 27 28	36 15 33 32 5 1 27 27 28	3 19 1 35 7 1 27 27 28	6 23 6 3 9 2 26 27 28	9 28 11 7 11 3 26 27 28	12 32 10 10 13 3 26 27 28	14 1 14 14 15 3 26 27 28	17 6 19 18 17 3 26 27 28	20 9 23 22 19 3 26 27 28	24 14 22 26 21 3 26 27 28	27 17 26 29 23 2 27 27 28
14	30 11 30 25 1 35 26 27 28	33 15 35 28 3 36 26 27 28	36 16 34 32 5 1 27 27 28	3 21 1 35 7 2 27 27 28	6 24 7 3 9 2 26 27 28	9 30 11 7 11 3 26 27 28	12 34 10 11 13 3 26 27 28	15 3 14 14 15 3 26 27 28	18 7 20 18 17 3 26 27 28	21 11 23 22 19 3 26 27 28	24 15 22 26 21 3 26 27 28	27 18 26 29 23 2 27 27 28
15	30 12 30 25 1 35 26 27 28	33 16 35 29 3 36 26 27 28	36 17 34 32 5 1 27 27 28	3 22 1 36 7 2 27 27 28	6 26 7 3 9 2 26 27 28	9 31 11 7 11 3 26 27 28	12 35 10 11 13 3 26 27 28	15 4 14 14 15 3 26 27 28	18 9 20 18 17 3 26 27 28	21 12 23 22 19 3 26 27 28	24 16 22 26 21 3 27 27 28	27 19 26 30 23 2 27 27 28
16	30 13 30 25 1 36 26 27 28	33 18 35 29 3 36 26 27 28	36 19 34 32 5 1 27 27 28	3 23 1 36 7 2 27 27 28	6 27 7 3 9 2 26 27 28	9 33 11 7 11 3 26 27 28	12 36 10 11 13 3 26 27 28	15 5 14 15 15 3 26 27 28	18 10 20 18 17 3 26 27 28	21 13 23 22 19 3 26 27 28	24 17 22 26 21 3 27 27 28	27 21 26 30 23 2 27 27 28
17	30 14 30 25 1 36 26 27 28	33 1: 35 29 3 36 26 27 28	36 20 34 32 5 1 27 27 28	3 25 1 36 7 2 27 27 28	6 29 7 3 9 2 26 27 28	9 34 11 7 11 3 26 27 28	12 2 10 11 13 3 26 27 28	15 7 14 15 15 3 26 27 28	18 11 20 19 17 3 26 27 28	21 14 23 22 19 3 26 27 28	24 19 22 26 21 3 27 27 28	27 22 27 30 23 2 27 27 28
18	30 15 31 26 1 36 26 27 28	33 20 35 29 3 36 26 27 28	36 21 34 32 5 1 27 27 28	3 26 1 36 7 2 27 27 28	6 30 7 4 9 2 26 27 28	9 36 11 7 11 3 26 27 28	12 3 10 11 13 3 26 27 28	15 8 15 15 15 3 26 27 28	18 12 20 19 17 3 26 27 28	21 15 23 22 19 3 26 27 28	24 20 22 26 21 3 27 27 28	27 23 27 30 23 2 27 27 28
19	30 17 31 26 1 36 26 27 28	33 21 35 29 3 36 26 27 28	36 23 34 32 5 1 27 27 28	3 28 2 36 7 2 27 27 28	6 32 8 4 9 2 26 27 28	9 1 11 7 11 3 26 27 28	12 4 10 11 13 3 26 27 28	15 9 15 15 15 3 26 27 28	18 13 20 19 17 3 26 27 28	21 17 23 23 19 3 26 27 28	24 21 22 26 21 3 27 27 28	27 25 27 30 23 2 27 27 28
20	30 18 31 26 1 36 26 27 28	34 23 35 29 3 36 26 27 28	36 24 34 32 5 1 27 27 28	3 29 2 36 7 2 27 27 28	6 33 8 4 9 2 26 27 28	9 2 11 8 11 3 26 27 28	12 6 10 11 13 3 26 27 28	15 10 15 15 15 3 26 27 28	18 15 20 19 17 3 26 27 28	21 18 23 23 19 3 26 27 28	24 23 22 26 21 3 27 27 28	27 27 27 30 23 2 27 27 28
21	31 19 31 26 1 36 26 27 28	34 24 35 29 4 36 26 27 28	36 25 34 33 5 1 27 27 28	4 31 2 36 8 2 27 27 28	6 35 8 4 9 2 26 27 28	9 3 11 8 11 3 26 27 28	12 7 10 11 13 3 26 27 28	15 11 15 15 15 3 26 27 28	18 16 21 19 17 3 26 27 28	21 19 23 23 19 3 26 27 28	24 24 23 27 21 3 27 27 28	27 28 27 30 23 2 27 27 28
22	31 20 31 26 1 36 26 27 28	34 26 35 29 4 36 27 27 28	1 27 34 33 6 1 27 27 28	4 32 2 36 8 2 27 27 28	7 36 8 4 10 2 26 27 28	10 5 11 8 12 3 26 27 28	12 8 10 11 13 3 26 27 28	15 13 16 15 15 3 26 27 28	18 17 21 19 17 3 26 27 28	21 20 23 23 19 3 26 27 28	24 25 23 27 21 3 27 27 28	27 29 27 30 23 2 27 27 28
23	31 22 31 26 2 36 26 27 28	34 27 35 30 4 36 27 27 28	1 28 34 33 6 1 27 27 28	4 33 2 1 8 2 27 27 28	7 1 8 4 10 2 26 27 28	10 6 11 8 12 3 26 27 28	12 9 11 12 14 3 26 27 28	15 14 16 15 16 3 26 27 28	18 18 21 19 17 3 26 27 28	21 22 23 23 19 3 26 27 28	25 27 23 27 21 3 27 27 28	28 31 28 31 23 2 27 27 28
24	31 23 32 26 2 36 26 27 28	34 28 35 30 4 36 27 27 28	1 30 34 33 6 1 27 27 28	4 35 2 1 8 2 27 27 28	7 2 9 4 10 2 26 27 28	10 7 11 8 12 3 26 27 28	13 11 11 12 14 3 26 27 28	16 15 16 16 16 3 26 27 28	19 20 21 19 18 3 26 27 28	22 23 22 23 19 3 26 27 28	25 28 23 27 21 3 27 27 28	28 32 28 31 23 2 27 27 28
25	31 25 32 26 2 36 26 27 28	34 30 35 30 4 36 27 27 28	1 31 34 33 6 1 27 27 28	4 36 3 1 8 2 27 27 28	7 4 9 4 10 2 26 27 28	10 8 11 8 12 3 26 27 28	13 12 11 12 14 3 26 27 28	16 16 16 16 16 3 26 27 28	19 21 21 20 18 3 26 27 28	22 24 22 23 20 3 26 27 28	25 30 23 27 22 3 27 27 28	28 34 28 31 24 2 27 27 28
26	31 26 32 26 2 36 26 27 28	34 31 35 30 4 36 27 27 28	1 32 34 33 6 1 27 27 28	4 2 3 1 8 2 27 27 28	7 5 9 5 10 2 26 27 28	10 10 11 8 12 3 26 27 28	13 13 11 12 14 3 26 27 28	16 17 16 16 16 3 26 27 28	19 22 21 20 18 3 26 27 28	22 26 22 23 20 3 26 27 28	25 31 23 27 22 3 27 27 28	28 35 28 31 24 2 27 27 28
27	31 28 32 27 2 36 26 27 28	34 33 34 30 4 36 27 27 28	1 34 34 33 6 1 27 27 28	4 3 3 1 8 2 27 27 28	7 6 9 5 10 2 26 27 28	10 11 11 8 12 3 26 27 28	13 14 11 12 14 3 26 27 28	16 19 16 16 16 3 26 27 28	19 23 21 20 18 3 26 27 28	22 27 22 24 20 3 26 27 28	25 33 23 27 22 3 27 27 28	28 36 28 31 24 2 27 27 28
28	31 29 32 27 2 36 26 27 28	34 34 34 30 4 36 27 27 28	1 35 34 33 6 1 27 27 28	4 4 3 1 8 2 27 27 28	7 8 9 5 10 3 26 27 28	10 12 11 9 12 3 26 27 28	13 15 11 12 14 3 26 27 28	16 20 17 16 16 3 26 27 28	19 25 21 20 18 3 26 27 28	22 29 22 24 20 3 26 27 28	25 34 24 27 22 3 27 27 28	28 2 28 31 24 2 27 27 28
29	31 31 32 27 2 36 26 27 28		1 1 35 34 6 1 27 27 28	4 5 3 1 8 2 27 27 28	7 9 9 5 10 3 26 27 28	10 13 11 9 12 3 26 27 28	13 16 11 12 14 3 26 27 28	16 21 17 16 16 3 26 27 28	19 26 22 20 18 3 26 27 28	22 30 22 24 20 3 26 27 28	25 35 24 28 22 3 27 27 28	28 3 29 31 24 2 27 27 28
30	31 32 33 27 2 36 26 27 28		1 2 35 34 6 1 27 27 28	4 7 4 1 8 2 27 27 28	7 10 9 5 10 3 26 27 28	10 14 11 9 12 3 26 27 28	13 18 11 12 14 3 26 27 28	16 22 17 16 16 3 26 27 28	19 28 22 20 18 3 26 27 28	22 31 22 24 20 3 26 27 28	25 1 24 28 22 3 27 27 28	28 4 29 31 24 2 27 27 28
31	32 34 33 27 2 36 26 27 28	1987	1 3 35 34 6 1 27 27 28		7 11 10 5 10 3 26 27 28		13 19 11 13 14 3 26 27 28	16 24 17 16 16 3 26 27 28		22 32 22 24 20 3 26 27 28		28 6 29 32 24 2 27 27 28

	JAN	FEB	MAR	APR	MAY	JUNE
1	28 7 29 32 24 3 27 27 28	32 12 33 35 26 3 27 27 28	35 14 32 3 28 3 28 28 28	2 18 36 6 30 4 28 28 29	5 21 6 9 32 5 28 28 29	8 26 9 9 34 5 28 27 28
2	29 8 29 32 24 3 27 27 28	32 13 33 36 26 3 27 27 28	35 15 32 3 28 3 28 28 28	2 19 36 6 30 4 28 28 29	5 23 6 9 32 5 28 28 29	8 28 9 9 34 5 28 27 28
3	29 9 29 32 24 3 27 27 28	32 14 33 36 26 3 27 27 28	35 16 32 3 28 3 28 28 28	2 21 36 6 30 4 28 28 29	5 24 6 9 32 5 28 28 29	8 29 9 9 34 5 28 27 28
4	29 11 29 32 24 3 27 27 28	32 15 33 36 26 3 27 27 28	35 17 32 3 28 3 28 28 28	2 22 36 7 30 4 28 28 29	5 25 6 9 32 5 28 28 29	8 31 9 9 34 6 28 27 28
5	29 12 30 32 24 3 27 27 28	32 16 33 36 26 3 27 27 28	35 18 32 3 28 3 28 28 28	2 23 1 7 30 4 28 28 29	5 27 7 9 32 5 28 28 29	8 32 9 9 34 6 28 27 28
6	29 13 30 32 24 3 27 27 28	32 18 33 36 26 3 27 27 28	35 20 32 3 28 3 28 28 28	2 24 1 7 30 4 28 28 29	5 28 7 9 32 5 28 28 29	8 33 9 9 34 6 28 27 28
7	29 14 30 32 24 3 27 27 28	32 19 33 36 26 3 27 27 28	35 21 32 4 28 3 28 28 28	2 26 1 7 31 4 28 28 29	5 29 7 9 33 5 28 28 29	8 35 9 9 34 6 28 27 28
8	29 15 30 33 24 3 27 27 28	32 20 33 36 27 3 27 27 28	35 22 33 4 28 3 28 28 28	2 27 1 7 31 4 28 28 29	5 31 7 9 33 5 28 28 29	8 36 9 9 35 6 28 27 28
9	29 17 30 33 25 3 27 27 28	32 21 33 36 27 3 27 27 28	35 23 33 4 29 4 28 28 28	2 28 1 7 31 4 28 28 29	5 32 7 9 33 5 28 28 28	8 2 9 9 35 6 28 27 28
10	29 18 30 33 25 3 27 27 28	33 22 33 1 27 3 27 27 28	35 25 33 4 29 4 28 28 28	3 30 1 7 31 4 28 28 29	5 34 7 9 33 5 28 28 28	8 3 9 9 35 6 28 27 28
11	29 19 31 33 25 3 27 27 28	33 24 33 1 27 3 27 27 28	36 26 33 4 29 4 28 28 28	3 31 2 7 31 4 28 28 29	6 35 8 9 33 5 28 28 28	9 4 9 9 35 6 27 27 28
12	30 20 31 33 25 3 27 27 28	33 25 33 1 27 3 27 27 28	36 27 33 4 29 4 28 28 28	3 33 2 7 31 4 28 28 29	6 1 8 9 33 5 28 28 28	9 6 9 9 35 6 27 27 28
13	30 22 31 33 25 3 27 27 28	33 26 32 1 27 3 27 27 28	36 29 33 4 29 4 28 28 28	3 34 2 7 31 4 28 28 29	6 2 8 9 33 5 28 28 28	9 7 9 9 35 6 27 27 28
14	30 23 31 33 25 3 27 27 28	33 28 32 1 27 3 28 27 28	36 30 33 4 29 4 28 28 28	3 36 2 7 31 4 28 28 29	6 3 8 9 33 5 28 28 28	9 8 9 9 35 6 27 27 28
15	30 24 31 33 25 3 27 27 28	33 29 32 1 27 3 28 28 28	36 32 33 4 29 4 28 28 28	3 1 2 8 31 4 28 28 29	6 5 8 9 33 5 28 28 28	9 10 9 9 35 6 27 27 28
16	30 26 31 34 25 3 27 27 28	33 31 32 1 27 3 28 28 28	36 33 33 5 29 4 28 28 29	3 2 3 8 31 4 28 28 29	6 6 8 9 33 5 28 28 28	9 11 9 9 35 6 27 27 28
17	30 27 32 34 25 3 27 27 28	33 32 32 1 27 3 28 28 28	36 35 34 5 29 4 28 28 29	3 4 3 8 31 4 28 28 29	6 7 8 9 33 5 28 28 28	9 12 9 8 35 6 27 27 28
18	30 28 32 34 25 3 27 27 28	33 34 32 1 27 3 28 28 28	36 36 34 5 29 4 28 28 29	3 5 3 8 31 4 28 28 29	6 9 8 10 33 5 28 28 28	9 13 8 8 35 6 27 27 28
19	30 30 32 34 25 3 27 27 28	33 35 32 2 27 3 28 28 28	36 2 34 5 29 4 28 28 29	3 7 3 8 31 4 28 28 29	6 10 9 10 33 5 28 28 28	9 15 8 8 35 6 27 27 28
20	30 32 32 34 25 3 27 27 28	34 1 32 2 27 3 28 28 28	36 3 34 5 29 4 28 28 29	4 8 3 8 31 4 28 28 29	6 11 9 10 33 5 28 28 28	9 16 8 8 35 6 27 27 28
21	31 33 32 34 25 3 27 27 28	34 2 32 2 27 3 28 28 28	1 4 34 5 29 4 28 28 29	4 9 4 8 31 4 28 28 29	7 13 9 10 33 5 28 28 28	9 17 8 8 35 6 27 27 28
22	31 35 32 34 25 3 27 27 28	34 4 32 2 27 3 28 28 28	1 6 34 5 29 4 28 28 29	4 11 4 8 32 5 28 28 29	7 14 9 10 33 5 28 28 28	10 18 8 8 35 6 27 27 28
23	31 36 33 34 25 3 27 27 28	34 5 32 2 28 3 28 28 28	1 7 34 5 29 4 28 28 29	4 12 4 8 32 5 28 28 29	7 15 9 10 34 5 28 28 28	10 19 8 8 35 6 27 27 28
24	31 1 33 35 26 3 27 27 28	34 6 32 2 28 3 28 28 28	1 8 35 5 30 4 28 28 29	4 13 4 8 32 5 28 28 29	7 16 9 10 34 5 28 28 28	10 21 8 8 35 6 27 27 28
25	31 3 33 35 26 3 27 27 28	34 8 32 2 28 3 28 28 28	1 10 35 6 30 4 28 28 29	4 14 5 8 32 5 28 28 29	7 17 9 10 34 5 28 28 28	10 22 8 8 36 6 27 27 28
26	31 4 33 35 26 3 27 27 28	34 9 32 2 28 3 28 28 28	1 11 35 6 30 4 28 28 29	4 15 5 8 32 5 28 28 29	7 19 9 10 34 5 28 27 28	10 23 8 8 36 6 27 27 28
27	31 5 33 35 26 3 27 27 28	34 10 32 3 28 3 28 28 28	1 12 35 6 30 4 28 28 29	4 17 5 9 32 5 28 28 29	7 20 9 10 34 5 28 27 28	10 24 8 8 36 6 27 27 28
28	31 7 33 35 26 3 27 27 28	34 11 32 3 28 3 28 28 28	1 13 35 6 30 4 28 28 29	4 18 5 9 32 5 28 28 29	7 21 9 9 34 5 28 27 28	10 26 8 8 36 6 27 27 28
29	31 8 33 35 26 3 27 27 28	34 12 32 3 28 3 28 28 28	1 15 35 6 30 4 28 28 29	4 19 5 9 32 5 28 28 29	7 22 9 9 34 5 28 27 28	10 27 8 8 36 6 27 27 28
30	31 9 33 35 26 3 27 27 28	**1988**	1 16 35 6 30 4 28 28 29	4 20 6 9 32 5 28 28 29	7 24 9 9 34 5 28 27 28	10 29 8 8 36 6 27 27 28
31	32 10 33 35 26 3 27 27 28		2 17 35 6 30 4 28 28 29		7 25 9 9 34 5 28 27 28	

	JULY	AUG	SEPT	OCT	NOV	DEC
1	10 30 8 8 36 6 27 27 28	13 35 13 9 1 7 27 27 28	16 5 19 12 2 7 27 27 28	19 8 21 15 1 7 27 27 28	22 13 21 19 36 7 27 27 28	25 16 25 22 1 6 28 27 28
2	11 32 9 8 36 6 27 27 28	13 1 13 9 1 7 27 27 28	16 6 19 12 2 7 27 27 28	19 10 21 15 1 7 27 27 28	22 14 21 19 1 7 27 27 28	26 17 26 23 1 6 28 27 28
3	11 33 9 8 36 6 27 27 28	14 2 14 9 1 7 27 27 28	17 7 19 12 2 7 27 27 28	20 11 21 15 1 7 27 27 28	23 15 21 19 1 7 27 27 28	26 18 26 23 1 6 28 28 28
4	11 34 9 8 36 6 27 27 28	14 4 14 9 1 7 27 27 28	17 9 19 12 2 7 27 27 28	20 12 21 15 1 7 27 27 28	23 16 21 19 1 7 27 27 28	26 20 26 23 1 6 28 28 28
5	11 36 9 8 36 6 27 27 28	14 5 14 9 1 7 27 27 28	17 10 19 12 2 7 27 27 28	20 13 21 16 1 7 27 27 28	23 18 21 19 1 7 27 27 28	26 21 26 23 1 6 28 28 28
6	11 1 9 8 36 6 27 27 28	14 6 14 9 1 7 27 27 28	17 11 19 12 2 7 27 27 28	20 14 21 16 1 7 27 27 28	23 19 21 19 1 7 27 27 28	26 22 26 23 1 6 28 28 28
7	11 3 9 8 36 6 27 27 28	14 8 14 10 1 7 27 27 28	17 12 19 12 2 7 27 27 28	20 16 21 16 1 7 27 27 28	23 20 22 19 1 7 27 27 28	26 23 26 23 1 6 28 28 28
8	11 4 9 8 36 6 27 27 28	14 9 15 10 1 7 27 27 28	17 14 20 13 2 7 27 27 28	20 17 21 16 1 7 27 27 28	23 21 22 20 1 7 27 27 28	26 25 26 23 1 6 28 28 28
9	11 5 9 8 36 6 27 27 28	14 10 15 10 1 7 27 27 28	17 15 20 13 2 7 27 27 28	20 18 21 16 1 7 27 27 28	23 22 22 20 1 7 27 27 28	26 26 27 23 1 6 28 28 28
10	11 7 9 8 36 6 27 27 28	14 11 15 10 1 7 27 27 28	17 16 20 13 2 7 27 27 28	20 19 20 16 1 7 27 27 28	23 24 22 20 1 7 27 27 28	26 27 27 24 1 6 28 28 28
11	11 8 9 8 36 6 27 27 28	14 13 15 10 1 7 27 27 28	17 17 20 13 1 7 27 27 28	20 20 20 16 1 7 27 27 28	23 25 22 20 1 7 27 27 28	26 29 27 24 2 6 28 28 28
12	11 9 9 8 36 6 27 27 28	14 14 15 10 2 7 27 27 28	17 18 20 13 1 7 27 2 28	20 22 20 16 1 7 27 27 28	23 26 22 20 1 7 27 27 28	27 30 27 24 2 6 28 28 28
13	12 11 10 8 36 6 27 27 28	15 15 16 10 2 7 27 27 28	18 19 20 13 1 7 27 27 28	20 23 20 16 1 7 27 27 28	24 28 23 20 1 7 28 27 28	27 31 27 24 2 6 28 28 28
14	12 12 10 8 1 6 27 27 28	15 16 16 10 2 7 27 27 28	18 21 20 13 1 7 27 27 28	21 24 20 17 1 7 27 27 28	24 29 23 20 1 7 28 27 28	27 33 27 24 2 6 28 28 28
15	12 13 10 8 1 6 27 27 28	15 17 16 10 2 7 27 27 28	18 22 20 13 1 7 27 27 28	21 25 20 17 1 7 27 27 28	24 30 23 20 1 7 28 27 28	27 34 28 24 2 6 28 28 28
16	12 14 10 8 1 6 27 27 28	15 19 16 10 2 7 27 27 28	18 23 20 13 1 7 27 27 28	21 27 20 17 1 7 27 27 28	24 32 23 21 1 7 28 27 28	27 36 28 24 2 6 28 28 28
17	12 15 10 8 1 6 27 27 28	15 20 16 10 2 7 27 27 28	18 24 21 14 1 7 27 27 28	21 28 20 17 1 7 27 27 28	24 33 23 21 1 7 28 27 28	27 1 28 24 2 6 28 28 28
18	12 17 10 8 1 6 27 27 28	15 21 16 10 2 7 27 27 28	18 26 21 14 1 7 27 27 28	21 29 20 17 1 7 27 27 28	24 35 23 21 1 7 28 27 28	27 2 28 25 2 6 28 28 28
19	12 18 11 8 1 6 27 27 28	15 22 17 11 2 7 27 27 28	18 27 21 14 1 7 27 27 28	21 31 20 17 1 7 27 27 28	24 36 23 21 1 7 28 27 28	27 4 28 25 2 6 28 28 28
20	12 19 11 8 1 6 27 27 28	15 23 17 11 2 7 27 27 28	18 28 21 14 1 7 27 27 28	21 32 20 17 1 7 27 27 28	24 1 24 21 1 7 28 27 28	27 5 28 25 2 6 28 28 28
21	12 20 11 8 1 6 27 27 28	15 25 17 11 2 7 27 27 28	18 30 21 14 1 7 27 27 28	21 34 20 17 1 7 27 27 28	24 3 24 21 1 7 28 27 28	27 7 29 25 2 6 28 28 28
22	12 21 11 8 1 7 27 27 28	15 26 17 11 2 7 27 27 28	18 31 21 14 1 7 27 27 28	21 35 20 18 1 7 27 27 28	24 4 24 21 1 7 28 27 28	28 8 29 25 2 6 28 28 28
23	13 23 11 8 1 7 27 27 28	16 27 17 11 2 7 27 27 28	19 33 21 14 1 7 27 27 28	21 36 20 18 1 7 27 27 28	25 6 24 21 1 7 28 27 28	28 9 29 25 2 6 28 28 28
24	13 24 11 9 1 7 27 27 28	16 29 17 11 2 7 27 27 28	19 34 21 14 1 7 27 27 28	22 2 20 18 36 7 27 27 28	25 7 24 22 1 7 28 27 28	28 11 29 25 2 6 28 28 28
25	13 25 12 9 1 7 27 27 28	16 30 18 11 2 7 27 27 28	19 36 21 14 1 7 27 27 28	22 3 20 18 36 7 27 27 28	25 9 24 22 1 7 28 27 28	28 12 29 25 2 6 28 28 28
26	13 27 12 9 1 7 27 27 28	16 32 18 11 2 7 27 27 28	19 1 21 14 1 7 27 27 28	22 5 20 18 36 7 27 27 28	25 10 25 22 1 7 28 27 28	28 13 29 26 2 6 28 28 28
27	13 28 12 9 1 7 27 27 28	16 33 18 11 2 7 27 27 28	19 3 21 14 1 7 27 27 28	22 6 20 18 36 7 27 27 28	25 11 25 22 1 7 28 27 28	28 14 29 26 2 6 28 28 28
28	13 29 12 9 1 7 27 27 28	16 35 18 11 2 7 27 27 28	19 4 21 14 1 7 27 27 28	22 8 20 18 36 7 27 27 28	25 12 25 22 1 7 28 27 28	28 16 30 26 2 6 28 28 28
29	13 31 13 9 1 7 27 27 28	16 36 18 12 2 7 27 27 28	19 6 21 14 1 7 27 27 28	22 9 20 18 36 7 27 27 28	25 14 25 22 1 7 28 27 28	28 17 30 26 2 6 28 28 28
30	13 32 13 9 1 7 27 27 28	16 2 18 12 2 7 27 27 28	19 7 21 14 1 7 27 27 28	22 10 20 19 36 7 27 27 28	25 15 25 22 1 7 28 27 28	28 18 30 26 2 6 28 28 28
31	13 34 13 9 1 7 27 27 28	16 3 19 12 2 7 27 27 28		22 12 21 19 36 7 27 27 28		28 19 30 26 2 6 28 28 28

	JAN	FEB	MAR	APR	MAY	JUNE	JULY	AUG	SEPT	OCT	NOV	DEC
1	29 20 30 26 3 6 28 28 28	32 25 30 30 4 6 28 28 29	35 26 32 34 6 6 29 28 29	2 31 1 2 8 7 29 28 29	5 34 7 5 10 7 29 28 29	8 4 6 9 12 8 29 28 29	10 8 9 13 13 9 29 28 29	13 13 15 16 15 10 28 28 29	16 17 19 20 17 10 28 28 28	19 20 18 24 19 10 28 28 28	22 25 22 27 21 11 28 28 29	25 28 26 30 23 10 29 28 29
2	29 22 30 26 3 6 28 28 28	32 26 30 30 4 6 28 28 29	35 27 32 34 6 6 29 28 29	2 32 1 2 8 7 29 28 29	5 36 7 5 10 7 29 28 29	8 5 6 9 12 8 29 28 29	11 9 9 13 13 9 29 28 29	13 14 15 17 15 10 28 28 29	16 18 19 20 17 10 28 28 28	19 22 18 24 19 10 28 28 28	22 26 22 27 21 11 28 28 29	25 30 27 30 23 10 29 28 29
3	29 23 31 27 3 6 28 28 29	32 28 30 30 4 6 28 28 29	35 28 32 34 6 6 29 28 29	2 33 2 2 8 7 29 28 29	5 1 7 5 10 7 29 28 29	8 7 6 9 12 8 29 28 29	11 10 9 13 14 9 29 28 29	14 15 15 17 15 10 28 28 29	17 20 19 20 17 10 28 28 28	19 23 18 24 19 10 28 28 28	23 27 22 27 21 11 28 28 29	26 31 27 30 23 10 29 28 29
4	29 24 31 27 3 6 28 28 29	32 29 30 31 4 6 28 28 29	35 30 33 34 6 6 29 28 29	2 35 2 2 8 7 29 28 29	5 3 7 6 10 8 29 28 29	8 8 6 9 12 8 29 28 29	11 12 9 13 14 9 29 28 29	14 16 15 17 16 10 28 28 29	17 21 19 21 17 10 28 28 28	20 24 18 24 19 10 28 28 28	23 29 22 27 21 11 28 28 29	26 32 27 30 24 10 29 28 29
5	29 25 31 27 3 6 28 28 29	32 30 30 31 4 6 28 28 29	35 31 33 34 6 6 29 28 29	2 36 2 2 8 7 29 28 29	5 4 7 6 10 8 29 28 29	8 9 6 10 12 8 29 28 29	11 13 9 13 14 9 29 28 29	14 18 15 17 16 10 28 28 29	17 22 19 21 18 10 28 28 28	20 25 18 24 20 10 28 28 28	23 30 22 27 22 11 28 28 29	26 33 27 30 24 10 29 28 29
6	29 27 31 27 3 6 28 28 29	32 32 30 31 4 6 28 28 29	35 33 33 34 6 6 29 28 29	2 2 2 2 8 7 29 28 29	5 6 7 6 10 8 29 28 29	8 11 6 10 12 8 29 28 29	11 14 10 13 14 9 29 28 29	14 19 16 17 16 10 28 28 29	17 23 19 21 18 10 28 28 28	20 26 18 24 20 11 28 28 28	23 31 23 28 22 11 28 28 29	26 35 27 30 24 10 29 28 29
7	29 28 31 27 3 6 28 28 29	32 33 30 31 5 6 28 28 29	35 34 33 34 6 6 29 28 29	2 3 2 2 8 7 29 28 29	5 7 7 6 10 8 29 28 29	8 12 6 10 12 8 29 28 29	11 16 10 13 14 9 29 28 29	14 20 16 17 16 10 28 28 29	17 24 19 21 18 10 28 28 28	20 28 18 24 20 11 28 28 28	23 32 23 28 22 11 28 28 29	26 36 27 30 24 10 29 28 29
8	29 30 31 27 3 6 28 28 29	32 35 30 31 5 6 28 28 29	35 36 33 35 6 6 29 28 29	2 5 3 2 8 7 29 28 29	5 9 7 6 10 8 29 28 29	8 13 6 10 12 8 29 28 29	11 17 10 14 14 9 29 28 29	14 21 16 17 16 10 28 28 29	17 26 19 21 18 10 28 28 28	20 29 18 24 20 11 28 28 28	23 34 23 28 22 11 28 28 29	26 2 28 30 24 10 29 28 29
9	29 31 31 27 3 6 28 28 29	33 36 30 31 5 6 28 28 29	35 1 33 35 6 6 29 28 29	2 6 3 3 8 7 29 28 29	5 10 7 6 10 8 29 28 29	8 15 6 10 12 8 29 28 29	11 18 10 14 14 9 29 28 29	14 22 16 17 16 10 28 28 29	17 27 20 21 18 10 28 28 28	20 30 18 25 20 11 28 28 28	23 35 23 28 22 11 28 28 29	26 3 28 30 24 10 29 28 29
10	29 32 31 27 3 6 28 28 29	33 2 30 31 5 6 29 28 29	35 3 33 35 6 6 29 28 29	3 8 3 3 8 7 29 28 29	5 11 7 6 10 8 29 28 29	8 16 6 10 12 8 29 28 29	11 19 10 14 14 9 29 28 29	14 24 16 18 16 10 28 28 29	17 28 20 21 18 10 28 28 28	20 32 18 25 20 11 28 28 28	23 1 23 28 22 11 29 28 29	26 5 28 30 24 10 29 28 29
11	30 34 31 28 3 6 28 28 29	33 3 30 31 5 6 29 28 29	36 4 34 35 6 6 29 28 29	3 9 3 3 8 7 29 28 29	6 13 7 6 10 8 29 28 29	9 17 6 10 12 8 29 28 29	11 20 11 14 14 9 28 28 29	14 25 16 18 16 10 28 28 29	17 29 20 21 18 10 28 28 28	20 33 18 25 20 11 28 28 28	23 2 23 28 22 11 29 28 29	26 6 28 31 24 10 20 28 29
12	30 35 32 28 3 6 28 28 29	33 5 30 32 5 6 29 28 29	36 6 34 35 7 7 29 28 29	3 11 4 3 8 7 29 28 29	6 14 7 7 10 8 29 28 29	9 18 6 10 12 8 29 28 29	11 22 11 14 14 9 28 28 29	14 26 17 18 16 10 28 28 29	17 31 20 21 18 10 28 28 28	20 34 19 25 20 11 28 28 28	23 4 24 28 22 11 29 28 29	26 8 28 31 24 10 29 28 29
13	30 1 32 28 3 6 28 28 29	33 6 30 32 5 6 29 28 29	36 7 34 35 7 7 29 28 29	3 12 4 3 9 7 29 28 29	6 15 7 7 10 8 29 28 29	9 20 7 11 12 8 29 28 29	12 23 11 14 14 9 28 28 29	15 27 17 18 16 10 28 28 29	18 32 20 22 18 10 28 28 28	20 36 19 25 20 11 28 28 28	24 5 24 28 22 11 29 28 29	27 9 28 31 24 10 29 28 29
14	30 2 32 28 3 6 28 28 29	33 7 30 32 5 6 29 28 29	36 8 34 35 7 7 29 28 29	3 13 4 3 9 7 29 28 29	6 16 7 7 10 8 29 28 29	9 21 7 11 12 8 29 28 29	12 24 11 14 14 9 28 28 29	15 29 17 18 16 10 28 28 28	18 34 20 22 18 10 28 28 28	21 1 19 25 20 11 28 28 28	24 7 24 28 22 11 29 28 29	27 10 28 31 24 10 29 28 29
15	30 4 32 28 3 6 28 28 29	33 9 31 32 5 6 29 28 29	36 10 34 35 7 7 29 28 29	3 14 4 3 9 7 29 28 29	6 18 7 7 10 8 29 28 29	9 22 7 11 12 8 29 28 29	12 25 11 14 14 9 28 28 29	15 30 17 18 16 10 28 28 28	18 35 20 22 18 10 28 28 28	21 3 19 25 20 11 28 28 28	24 8 24 28 22 11 29 28 29	27 12 29 31 24 10 29 28 29
16	30 5 32 28 3 6 28 28 29	33 10 31 32 5 6 29 28 29	36 11 34 36 7 7 29 28 29	3 16 4 3 9 7 29 28 29	6 19 7 7 11 8 29 28 29	9 23 7 11 12 9 29 28 29	12 26 12 15 14 9 28 28 29	15 31 17 18 16 10 28 28 28	18 1 19 22 18 10 28 28 28	21 4 19 25 20 11 28 28 28	24 10 24 29 22 11 29 28 29	27 13 29 31 24 10 29 28 29
17	30 6 32 28 3 6 28 28 29	33 11 31 32 5 6 29 28 29	36 12 35 36 7 7 29 28 29	3 17 5 4 9 7 29 28 29	6 20 7 7 11 8 29 28 29	9 24 7 11 13 9 29 28 29	12 28 12 15 14 9 28 28 29	15 33 17 18 16 10 28 28 28	18 2 19 22 18 10 28 28 28	21 6 19 25 20 11 28 28 28	24 11 24 29 22 11 29 28 29	27 15 29 31 24 10 29 28 29
18	30 8 32 28 3 6 28 28 29	33 12 31 32 5 6 29 28 29	36 13 35 36 7 7 29 28 29	3 18 5 4 9 7 29 28 29	6 21 7 7 11 8 25 28 29	9 26 7 11 13 9 29 28 29	12 29 12 15 14 9 28 28 29	15 34 17 18 16 10 28 28 28	18 4 19 22 18 10 28 28 28	21 7 20 26 20 11 28 28 28	24 12 24 29 22 11 29 28 29	27 16 29 31 24 10 29 28 29
19	30 9 32 29 3 6 28 28 29	34 14 31 32 5 6 29 28 29	36 15 35 36 7 7 29 28 29	3 19 5 4 9 7 29 28 29	6 22 7 7 11 8 29 28 29	9 27 7 11 13 9 29 28 29	12 30 12 15 15 9 28 28 29	15 36 18 19 16 10 28 28 28	18 5 19 22 18 10 28 28 28	21 9 20 26 20 11 28 28 28	24 13 25 29 22 11 29 28 29	27 17 29 31 25 10 29 28 29
20	30 10 32 29 4 6 28 28 29	34 15 31 33 5 6 29 28 29	36 16 35 36 7 7 29 28 29	3 20 5 4 9 7 29 28 29	6 24 7 8 11 8 29 28 29	9 28 7 11 13 9 29 28 29	12 32 12 15 15 9 28 28 29	15 1 18 19 17 10 28 28 28	18 6 19 22 19 10 28 28 28	21 10 20 26 20 11 28 28 28	24 15 25 29 23 11 29 28 29	27 18 29 31 25 10 29 28 29
21	31 12 31 29 4 6 28 28 29	34 16 31 33 5 6 29 28 29	1 17 35 36 7 7 29 28 29	4 21 5 4 9 7 29 28 29	6 25 7 8 11 8 29 28 29	9 30 7 11 13 9 29 28 29	12 33 13 15 15 9 28 28 29	15 3 18 19 17 10 28 28 28	18 8 19 22 19 10 28 28 28	21 12 20 26 21 11 28 28 28	24 16 25 29 23 11 29 28 29	27 20 29 31 25 10 29 28 29
22	31 13 31 29 4 6 28 28 29	34 17 31 33 5 6 29 28 29	1 18 35 36 7 7 29 28 29	4 23 5 4 9 7 29 28 29	7 26 7 8 11 8 29 28 29	10 31 7 12 13 9 29 28 29	12 35 13 15 15 9 28 28 29	15 4 18 19 17 10 28 28 28	18 9 19 23 19 10 28 28 28	21 13 20 26 21 11 28 28 28	24 17 25 29 23 10 29 28 29	28 21 29 31 25 10 29 28 29
23	31 14 31 29 4 6 28 28 29	34 18 31 33 6 6 29 28 29	1 19 36 36 7 7 29 28 29	4 24 6 4 9 7 29 28 29	7 27 7 8 11 8 29 28 29	10 32 7 12 13 9 29 28 29	13 36 13 15 15 9 28 28 29	15 5 18 19 17 10 28 28 28	18 11 19 23 19 10 28 28 28	21 14 20 26 21 11 28 28 28	25 19 25 29 23 10 29 28 29	28 22 30 31 25 10 29 28 29
24	31 15 31 29 4 6 28 28 29	34 20 31 33 6 6 29 28 29	1 21 36 1 7 7 29 28 29	4 25 6 4 9 7 29 28 29	7 29 7 8 11 8 29 28 29	10 34 8 12 13 9 29 28 29	13 2 13 15 15 9 28 28 29	16 7 18 19 17 10 28 28 28	19 12 19 23 19 10 28 28 28	22 15 20 26 21 11 28 28 28	25 20 25 29 23 10 29 28 29	28 23 30 31 25 10 29 28 29
25	31 16 31 29 4 6 28 28 29	34 21 32 33 6 6 29 28 29	1 22 36 1 7 7 29 28 29	4 26 6 4 9 7 29 28 29	7 30 7 8 11 8 29 28 29	10 35 8 12 13 9 29 28 29	13 3 13 16 15 9 28 28 29	16 8 18 19 17 10 28 28 28	19 13 19 23 19 10 28 28 28	22 17 21 26 21 11 28 28 28	25 21 26 29 23 10 29 28 29	28 24 30 31 25 10 29 28 29
26	31 18 31 29 4 6 28 28 29	34 22 32 33 6 6 29 28 29	1 23 36 1 7 7 29 28 29	4 28 6 5 9 7 29 28 29	7 31 7 8 11 8 29 28 29	10 36 8 12 13 9 29 28 29	13 4 14 16 15 9 28 28 29	16 10 18 19 17 10 28 28 28	19 14 19 23 19 10 28 28 28	22 18 21 26 21 11 28 28 28	25 22 26 29 23 10 29 28 29	28 25 30 31 25 10 29 28 29
27	31 19 31 30 4 6 28 28 29	34 23 32 33 6 6 29 28 29	1 24 36 1 7 7 29 28 29	4 29 6 5 9 7 29 28 29	7 33 7 8 11 8 29 28 29	10 2 8 12 13 9 29 28 29	13 6 14 16 15 9 28 28 29	16 11 19 20 17 10 28 28 28	19 16 18 23 19 10 28 28 28	22 19 21 27 21 11 28 28 28	25 23 26 30 23 10 29 28 29	28 27 30 31 25 10 29 28 29
28	31 20 31 30 4 6 28 28 29	34 24 32 34 6 6 29 28 29	1 25 36 1 8 7 29 28 29	4 30 6 5 9 7 29 28 29	7 34 7 9 11 8 29 28 29	10 3 8 12 13 9 29 28 29	13 7 14 16 15 9 28 28 29	16 12 19 20 17 10 28 28 28	19 17 18 23 19 10 28 28 28	22 20 21 27 21 11 28 28 28	25 25 26 30 23 10 29 28 29	28 28 30 31 25 10 29 28 29
29	31 21 31 30 4 6 28 28 29	1989	1 27 1 1 8 7 29 28 29	4 32 6 5 9 8 29 28 29	7 35 6 9 11 8 29 28 29	10 5 8 12 13 9 29 28 29	13 9 14 16 15 9 28 28 29	16 13 19 20 17 10 28 28 28	19 18 18 23 19 10 28 28 28	22 21 21 27 21 11 28 28 29	25 26 26 30 23 10 29 28 29	28 29 30 31 25 10 29 28 29
30	32 22 30 30 4 6 28 28 29		1 28 1 1 8 7 29 28 29	4 33 7 5 10 7 29 28 29	7 1 6 9 11 8 29 28 29	10 6 8 13 13 9 29 28 29	13 10 14 16 15 9 28 28 29	16 15 19 20 17 10 28 28 28	19 19 18 24 19 10 28 28 28	22 23 21 27 21 11 28 28 29	25 27 26 30 23 10 29 28 29	28 31 30 31 25 10 29 28 29
31	32 24 30 30 4 6 28 28 29		2 29 1 1 8 7 29 28 29		7 2 6 9 11 8 29 28 29		13 11 15 16 15 10 28 28 29	16 16 19 20 17 10 28 28 28		22 24 22 27 21 11 28 28 29		28 32 30 31 25 10 29 28 29

	JAN	FEB	MAR	APR	MAY	JUNE	JULY	AUG	SEPT	OCT	NOV	DEC
1	29 33 30 31 25 10 29 28 29	32 2 29 30 28 10 29 28 29	35 3 33 30 30 10 30 28 29	2 9 3 33 32 10 30 28 29	5 12 5 36 34 10 30 28 29	8 17 5 4 1 11 30 28 29	10 21 10 7 3 11 30 28 29	13 25 16 11 5 12 30 28 29	16 29 18 15 10 13 29 28 29	19 33 18 18 8 13 29 28 29	22 2 23 22 8 14 30 28 29	25 5 27 26 7 14 30 28 29
2	29 35 30 31 26 10 29 28 29	32 4 29 30 28 10 29 28 29	35 5 33 30 30 10 30 28 29	2 10 3 33 32 10 30 28 29	5 14 5 36 34 10 30 28 29	8 19 5 4 1 11 30 28 29	10 22 10 7 3 11 30 28 29	13 26 16 11 5 12 30 28 29	16 31 18 15 10 13 29 28 29	19 34 18 19 8 13 29 28 29	22 3 23 22 8 14 30 28 29	25 7 27 26 7 14 30 28 29
3	29 36 30 31 26 10 29 28 29	32 5 29 30 28 10 29 28 29	35 6 33 30 30 10 30 28 29	2 12 3 33 32 10 30 28 29	5 15 5 36 34 10 30 28 29	8 20 5 4 1 11 30 28 29	11 23 11 7 3 11 30 28 29	14 27 16 11 5 12 30 28 29	17 32 18 15 10 13 29 28 29	19 35 18 19 8 13 29 28 29	23 5 23 23 8 14 30 28 29	26 9 28 26 7 14 30 28 29
4	29 1 30 31 26 10 29 28 29	32 7 29 30 28 10 29 28 29	35 8 34 31 30 10 30 28 29	2 13 3 33 32 10 30 28 29	5 16 5 36 34 10 30 28 29	8 21 5 4 1 11 30 28 29	11 24 11 8 3 11 30 28 29	14 29 16 11 5 12 30 28 29	17 33 17 15 10 13 29 28 29	20 1 18 19 8 13 29 28 29	23 6 23 23 8 14 30 28 29	26 10 28 26 7 14 30 28 29
5	29 3 30 31 26 10 29 28 29	32 8 30 30 28 10 29 28 29	35 9 34 31 30 10 30 28 29	2 14 4 33 32 10 30 28 29	5 18 5 1 35 10 30 28 29	8 22 6 4 1 11 30 28 29	11 25 11 8 3 12 30 28 29	14 30 16 11 5 12 30 28 29	17 35 17 15 10 13 29 28 29	20 2 18 19 8 13 29 28 29	23 8 24 23 8 14 30 28 29	26 12 28 27 7 14 30 28 29
6	29 4 30 31 26 10 29 28 29	32 9 30 30 28 10 29 28 29	35 10 34 31 30 10 30 28 29	2 15 4 33 32 10 30 28 29	5 19 5 1 35 10 30 28 29	8 23 6 4 1 11 30 28 29	11 27 11 8 3 12 30 28 29	14 31 16 12 5 12 30 28 29	17 36 17 15 10 13 29 28 29	20 4 19 19 8 13 29 28 29	23 9 24 23 8 14 30 28 29	26 13 28 27 7 14 30 28 29
7	29 6 30 31 26 10 29 28 29	32 11 30 30 28 10 29 28 29	35 12 34 31 30 10 30 28 29	2 17 4 34 32 10 30 28 29	5 20 5 1 35 10 30 28 29	8 24 6 4 1 11 30 28 29	11 28 11 8 3 12 30 28 29	14 32 17 12 5 12 30 28 29	17 1 17 15 10 13 29 28 29	20 5 19 19 8 13 29 28 29	23 11 24 23 8 14 30 28 29	26 14 28 27 7 14 30 28 29
8	29 7 29 31 26 10 29 28 29	32 12 30 30 28 10 30 28 29	35 13 34 31 30 10 30 28 29	2 18 4 34 33 10 30 28 29	5 21 5 1 35 10 30 28 29	8 26 6 4 1 11 30 28 29	11 29 12 8 3 12 30 28 29	14 34 17 12 5 12 30 28 29	17 3 17 16 10 13 29 28 29	20 7 19 19 8 13 29 28 29	23 12 24 23 8 14 30 28 29	26 16 28 27 7 14 30 28 29
9	29 8 29 31 26 10 29 28 29	32 14 30 30 28 10 30 28 29	35 14 34 31 30 10 30 28 29	2 19 4 34 33 10 30 28 29	5 22 5 1 35 10 30 28 29	8 27 6 5 1 11 30 28 29	11 30 12 8 3 12 30 28 29	14 35 17 12 5 12 30 28 29	17 4 17 16 10 13 29 28 29	20 8 19 19 8 13 29 28 29	23 13 24 23 8 14 30 28 29	26 17 28 27 7 14 30 28 29
10	29 10 29 31 26 10 29 28 29	33 15 30 30 28 10 30 28 29	35 16 35 31 30 10 30 28 29	2 20 4 34 33 10 30 28 29	5 24 4 1 35 10 30 28 29	8 28 6 5 1 11 30 28 29	11 31 12 8 3 12 30 28 29	14 36 17 12 5 12 30 28 29	17 6 17 16 10 13 29 28 29	20 10 19 20 8 13 29 28 29	23 15 24 23 8 14 30 28 29	26 18 28 27 7 14 30 28 29
11	30 11 29 31 26 10 29 28 29	33 16 30 30 28 10 30 28 29	36 17 35 31 30 10 30 28 29	3 22 4 34 33 10 30 28 29	6 25 4 1 35 10 30 28 29	8 29 6 5 1 11 30 28 29	11 33 12 9 3 12 30 28 29	14 2 17 12 5 12 30 28 29	17 7 17 16 10 13 29 28 29	20 11 19 20 8 13 29 28 29	23 16 25 24 8 14 30 28 29	26 20 28 27 7 14 30 28 29
12	30 13 29 31 26 10 29 28 29	33 17 30 30 28 10 30 28 29	36 18 35 31 31 10 30 28 29	3 23 5 34 33 10 30 28 29	6 26 4 1 35 10 30 28 29	9 31 6 5 1 11 30 28 29	11 34 13 9 3 12 30 28 29	14 3 17 12 5 12 30 28 29	17 9 17 16 10 13 29 28 29	20 12 20 20 8 13 29 28 29	23 17 25 24 8 14 30 28 29	26 21 28 27 7 14 30 28 29
13	30 14 29 31 26 10 29 28 29	33 19 31 30 29 10 30 28 29	36 19 35 31 31 10 30 28 29	3 24 5 34 33 10 30 28 29	6 27 4 2 35 10 30 28 29	9 32 7 5 1 11 30 28 29	12 35 13 9 4 12 30 28 29	15 5 17 12 5 12 30 28 29	17 10 17 16 10 13 29 28 29	20 14 20 20 8 14 29 28 29	24 19 25 24 8 14 30 28 29	27 22 28 28 7 14 30 28 29
14	30 15 29 31 26 10 29 28 29	33 20 31 30 29 10 30 28 29	36 21 35 31 31 10 30 28 29	3 25 5 34 33 10 30 28 29	6 28 4 2 35 10 30 28 29	9 33 7 5 1 11 30 28 29	12 1 13 9 4 12 30 28 29	15 6 17 13 6 12 29 28 29	18 11 17 16 10 13 29 28 29	21 15 20 20 8 14 29 28 29	24 20 25 24 8 14 30 28 29	27 23 28 28 7 14 30 28 29
15	30 17 29 31 26 10 29 28 29	33 21 31 30 29 10 30 28 29	36 22 36 31 31 10 30 28 29	3 26 5 34 33 10 30 28 29	6 30 4 2 35 10 30 28 29	9 34 7 5 2 11 30 28 29	12 2 13 9 4 12 30 28 29	15 7 17 13 6 12 29 28 29	18 13 17 16 10 13 29 28 29	21 16 20 20 8 14 29 28 29	24 21 25 24 8 14 30 28 29	27 24 29 28 6 14 30 28 29
16	30 18 29 31 27 10 29 28 29	33 22 31 30 29 10 30 28 29	36 23 36 31 31 10 30 28 29	3 27 5 35 33 10 30 28 29	6 31 4 2 35 10 30 28 29	9 36 7 5 2 11 30 28 29	12 4 13 9 4 12 30 28 29	15 9 17 13 6 12 29 28 29	18 14 16 17 10 13 29 28 29	21 18 20 20 8 14 29 28 29	24 22 25 24 7 14 30 28 29	27 26 28 28 6 14 30 28 29
17	30 19 29 30 27 10 29 28 29	33 23 31 30 29 10 30 28 29	36 24 36 32 31 10 30 28 29	3 29 5 35 33 10 30 28 29	6 32 4 2 35 10 30 28 29	9 1 7 6 2 11 30 28 29	12 5 13 9 4 12 30 28 29	15 10 18 13 6 12 29 28 29	18 15 16 17 10 13 29 28 29	21 19 20 20 8 14 29 28 29	24 24 25 24 7 14 30 28 29	27 27 28 28 6 14 30 28 29
18	30 20 29 30 27 10 29 28 29	33 25 31 30 29 10 30 28 29	36 25 36 32 31 10 30 28 29	3 30 5 35 33 10 30 28 29	6 33 4 2 36 11 30 28 29	9 3 8 6 2 11 30 28 29	12 6 14 9 4 12 30 28 29	15 12 18 13 6 12 29 28 29	18 17 16 17 10 13 29 28 29	21 20 21 21 8 14 29 28 29	24 25 26 24 7 14 30 28 29	27 28 28 28 6 14 30 28 29
19	30 21 28 30 27 10 29 28 29	34 26 31 30 29 10 30 28 29	36 27 36 32 31 10 30 28 29	3 31 5 35 33 10 30 28 29	6 35 4 2 36 11 30 28 29	9 4 8 6 2 11 30 28 29	12 8 14 9 4 12 30 28 29	15 13 18 13 6 13 29 28 29	18 18 16 17 10 13 29 28 29	21 21 21 21 8 14 29 28 29	24 26 26 25 7 14 30 28 29	27 29 28 28 6 14 30 28 29
20	30 23 28 30 27 10 29 28 29	34 27 32 30 29 10 30 28 29	36 28 1 32 31 10 30 28 29	3 32 5 35 33 10 30 28 29	6 36 4 2 36 11 30 28 29	9 5 8 6 2 11 30 28 29	12 9 14 9 4 12 30 28 29	15 15 18 13 6 13 29 28 29	18 19 17 17 10 13 29 28 29	21 23 21 21 8 14 29 28 29	24 27 26 25 7 14 30 28 29	27 30 28 28 6 14 30 28 29
21	31 24 28 30 27 10 29 28 29	34 28 32 30 29 10 30 28 29	1 29 1 32 31 10 30 28 29	4 34 5 35 34 10 30 28 29	6 2 4 2 36 11 30 28 29	9 7 8 6 2 11 30 28 29	12 11 14 10 4 12 30 28 29	15 16 18 13 6 13 29 28 29	18 21 17 17 10 13 29 28 29	21 24 21 21 8 14 29 28 29	24 28 26 25 7 14 30 28 29	27 32 28 29 6 14 30 28 29
22	31 25 28 30 27 10 29 28 29	34 30 32 30 29 10 30 28 29	1 30 1 32 31 10 30 28 29	4 35 5 35 34 10 30 28 29	7 3 4 3 36 11 30 28 29	10 8 8 6 2 11 30 28 29	12 12 14 10 4 12 30 28 29	15 17 18 13 6 13 29 28 29	18 22 17 17 10 13 29 28 29	21 25 21 21 8 14 29 28 29	24 29 26 25 7 14 30 28 29	27 33 28 29 6 14 30 28 29
23	31 26 29 30 27 10 29 28 29	34 31 32 30 29 10 30 28 29	1 32 1 32 31 10 30 28 29	4 1 5 35 34 10 30 28 29	7 5 4 3 36 11 30 28 29	10 10 8 6 2 11 30 28 29	12 14 14 10 4 12 30 28 29	15 18 18 14 6 13 29 28 29	18 23 17 17 10 13 29 28 29	21 26 21 21 8 14 29 28 29	25 31 26 25 7 14 30 28 29	28 34 28 29 6 14 30 28 29
24	31 28 29 30 27 10 29 28 29	34 32 32 30 29 10 30 28 29	1 33 1 32 31 10 30 28 29	4 2 5 35 34 10 30 28 29	7 6 4 3 36 11 30 28 29	10 11 9 6 2 11 30 28 29	13 15 15 10 4 12 30 28 29	16 20 18 14 6 13 29 28 29	19 24 17 18 10 13 29 28 29	22 27 22 21 8 14 29 28 29	25 32 26 25 7 14 30 28 29	28 35 28 29 6 14 30 28 29
25	31 29 29 30 27 10 29 28 29	34 34 32 30 29 10 30 28 29	1 34 2 32 31 10 30 28 29	4 4 5 35 34 10 30 28 29	7 8 5 3 36 11 30 28 29	10 13 9 6 2 11 30 28 29	13 16 15 10 4 12 30 28 29	16 21 18 14 6 13 29 28 29	19 25 17 18 11 13 29 28 29	22 29 22 22 8 14 29 28 29	25 33 27 25 7 14 30 28 29	28 1 28 29 6 14 30 28 29
26	31 30 29 30 27 10 29 28 29	34 35 33 30 29 10 30 28 29	1 36 2 32 32 10 30 28 29	4 5 5 36 34 10 30 28 29	7 9 5 3 36 11 30 28 29	10 14 9 7 2 11 30 28 29	13 18 15 10 4 12 30 28 29	16 22 18 14 6 13 29 28 29	19 27 17 18 11 13 29 28 29	22 30 22 22 8 14 29 28 29	25 34 27 25 7 14 30 28 29	28 2 27 29 6 14 30 28 29
27	31 31 29 30 27 10 29 28 29	34 36 33 30 30 10 30 28 29	1 1 2 32 32 10 30 28 29	4 7 5 36 34 10 30 28 29	7 11 5 3 36 11 30 28 29	10 16 9 7 2 11 30 28 29	13 19 15 10 4 12 30 28 29	16 23 18 14 6 13 29 28 29	19 28 17 18 11 13 29 28 29	22 31 22 22 8 14 29 28 29	25 36 27 26 7 14 30 28 29	28 3 27 29 6 14 30 28 29
28	31 33 29 30 27 10 29 28 29	34 2 33 30 30 10 30 28 29	1 3 2 33 32 10 30 28 29	4 8 5 36 34 10 30 28 29	7 12 5 3 36 11 30 28 29	10 17 10 7 2 11 30 28 29	13 20 15 10 5 12 30 28 29	16 25 18 14 6 13 29 28 29	19 29 17 18 11 13 29 28 29	22 32 22 22 8 14 29 28 29	25 1 27 26 7 14 30 28 29	28 5 27 29 6 14 30 28 29
29	31 34 29 30 27 10 29 28 29		1 4 2 33 32 10 30 28 29	4 10 5 36 34 10 30 28 29	7 13 5 3 36 11 30 28 29	10 18 10 7 3 11 30 28 29	13 21 15 11 5 12 30 28 29	16 26 18 14 6 13 29 28 29	19 30 17 18 11 13 29 28 29	22 34 22 22 8 14 29 28 29	25 2 27 26 7 14 30 28 29	28 6 27 30 6 14 30 28 29
30	31 36 29 30 28 10 29 28 29	1990	1 6 3 33 32 10 30 28 29	4 11 5 36 34 10 30 28 29	7 15 5 3 36 11 30 28 29	10 19 10 7 3 11 30 28 29	13 23 16 11 5 12 30 28 29	16 27 18 14 6 13 29 28 29	19 31 18 18 11 13 29 28 29	22 35 23 23 8 14 29 28 29	25 4 27 26 7 14 30 28 29	28 8 27 30 6 14 30 28 29
31	32 1 29 30 28 10 29 28 29		2 7 3 33 32 10 30 28 29		7 16 5 4 36 11 30 28 29		13 24 16 11 5 12 30 28 29	16 28 18 15 6 13 29 28 29		22 36 23 23 8 14 29 28 29		28 9 27 30 6 14 30 28 29

	JAN	FEB	MAR	APR	MAY	JUNE	JULY	AUG	SEPT	OCT	NOV	DEC
1	29 11 27 30 6 14 30 28 29	32 16 30 34 7 13 30 29 29	34 17 34 1 8 13 31 29 29	2 22 3 5 9 13 31 29 29	5 25 2 9 11 13 31 29 29	8 29 6 12 13 13 31 29 29	10 33 12 15 15 14 31 29 29	13 1 16 16 17 15 31 29 29	16 6 15 15 18 15 31 28 29	19 10 19 15 20 16 31 28 29	22 16 24 18 23 16 31 29 29	25 19 27 21 25 17 31 29 29
2	29 12 27 30 6 14 30 28 29	32 17 30 34 7 13 30 29 29	35 18 35 1 8 13 31 29 29	2 23 3 5 9 13 31 29 29	5 26 2 9 11 13 31 29 29	8 31 6 12 13 13 31 29 29	10 34 12 15 15 14 31 29 29	13 3 16 16 17 15 31 29 29	16 8 15 15 19 15 31 28 29	19 12 19 15 21 16 31 28 29	22 17 24 18 23 16 31 29 29	25 21 27 21 25 17 31 29 29
3	29 14 27 30 6 14 30 28 29	32 19 30 34 7 13 30 29 29	35 19 35 2 8 13 31 29 29	2 24 3 5 9 13 31 29 29	5 27 2 9 11 13 31 29 29	8 32 6 12 13 13 31 29 29	11 35 12 15 15 14 31 29 29	14 4 16 16 17 15 31 29 29	17 9 15 15 19 15 31 28 29	19 13 19 15 21 16 31 28 29	23 18 24 18 23 16 31 29 29	26 22 27 21 25 17 31 29 29
4	29 15 27 30 6 14 30 28 29	32 20 30 34 7 13 30 29 29	35 21 35 2 8 13 31 29 29	2 25 3 5 10 13 31 29 29	5 28 2 9 11 13 31 29 29	8 33 6 12 13 13 31 29 29	11 36 12 15 15 14 31 29 29	14 5 16 16 17 15 31 29 29	17 10 15 15 19 15 31 28 29	20 14 20 15 21 16 31 28 29	23 20 24 18 23 16 31 29 29	26 23 27 21 25 17 31 29 29
5	29 17 27 30 6 14 30 28 29	32 21 30 34 7 13 30 29 29	35 22 35 2 8 13 31 29 29	2 26 3 6 10 13 31 29 29	5 30 2 9 11 13 31 29 29	8 34 6 12 13 13 31 29 29	11 2 13 15 15 14 31 29 29	14 7 16 16 17 15 31 29 29	17 12 15 15 19 15 31 28 29	20 16 20 15 21 16 31 28 29	23 21 25 18 23 17 31 29 29	26 24 27 21 25 17 31 29 29
6	29 18 27 31 6 14 30 29 29	32 23 31 34 7 13 30 29 29	35 23 35 2 8 13 31 29 29	2 28 3 6 10 13 31 29 29	5 31 3 9 11 13 31 29 29	8 35 7 12 13 13 31 29 29	11 3 13 15 15 14 31 29 29	14 8 16 16 17 15 31 29 29	17 13 15 15 19 15 31 28 29	20 17 20 15 21 16 31 28 29	23 22 25 18 23 17 31 29 29	26 26 26 21 25 17 31 29 29
7	29 19 27 31 6 14 30 29 29	32 24 31 35 7 13 31 29 29	35 25 36 2 8 13 31 29 29	2 29 3 6 10 13 31 29 29	5 32 3 9 11 13 31 29 29	8 1 7 13 13 13 31 29 29	11 4 13 15 15 14 31 29 29	14 10 16 16 17 15 31 29 29	17 15 15 15 19 15 31 28 29	20 19 20 16 21 16 31 28 29	23 24 25 18 23 17 31 29 29	26 27 26 22 25 17 31 29 29
8	29 20 27 31 6 14 30 29 29	32 25 31 35 7 13 31 29 29	35 26 36 2 8 13 31 29 29	2 30 3 6 10 13 31 29 29	5 33 3 9 11 13 31 29 29	8 2 7 13 13 14 31 29 29	11 6 13 15 15 14 31 29 29	14 11 16 16 17 15 31 29 29	17 16 15 15 19 15 31 28 29	20 20 20 16 21 16 31 28 29	23 25 25 18 23 17 31 29 29	26 28 26 22 25 17 31 29 29
9	29 22 27 31 6 14 30 29 29	32 26 31 35 7 13 31 29 29	35 27 36 2 8 13 31 29 29	2 31 3 6 10 13 31 29 29	5 35 3 9 11 13 31 29 29	8 3 7 13 13 14 31 29 29	11 7 13 15 15 14 31 29 29	14 13 16 16 17 15 31 29 29	17 18 15 15 19 15 31 28 29	20 21 20 16 21 16 31 29 29	23 26 25 18 23 17 31 29 29	26 29 26 22 25 17 31 29 29
10	29 23 27 31 6 14 30 29 29	33 27 31 35 7 13 31 29 29	35 28 36 2 8 13 31 29 29	2 32 3 6 10 13 31 29 29	5 36 3 10 12 13 31 29 29	8 5 7 13 13 14 31 29 29	11 9 13 15 15 14 31 29 29	14 14 16 16 17 15 31 29 29	17 19 15 15 19 15 31 28 29	20 23 21 16 21 16 31 29 29	23 27 25 19 23 17 31 29 29	26 30 26 22 25 17 31 29 29
11	30 24 27 31 6 14 30 29 29	33 28 31 35 7 13 31 29 29	36 29 36 3 8 13 31 29 29	3 34 3 6 10 13 31 29 29	5 1 3 10 12 13 31 29 29	8 6 8 13 13 14 31 29 29	11 10 14 15 15 14 31 29 29	14 16 16 16 17 15 31 29 29	17 21 16 15 19 15 31 28 29	20 24 21 16 21 16 31 29 29	23 28 25 19 23 17 31 29 29	26 32 26 22 25 17 31 29 29
12	30 25 27 31 6 14 30 29 29	33 30 31 35 7 13 31 29 29	36 30 1 3 8 13 31 29 29	3 35 3 6 10 13 31 29 29	6 3 3 10 12 13 31 29 29	9 7 8 13 13 14 31 29 29	11 12 14 16 15 14 31 29 29	14 17 16 16 17 15 31 29 29	17 22 16 15 19 16 31 28 29	20 25 21 16 21 16 31 29 29	23 30 26 19 23 17 31 29 29	26 33 26 22 25 17 31 29 29
13	30 26 27 31 6 14 30 29 29	33 31 32 35 7 13 31 29 29	36 32 1 3 8 13 31 29 29	3 36 3 6 10 13 31 29 29	6 4 3 10 12 13 31 29 29	9 9 8 13 14 14 31 29 29	12 13 14 16 15 14 31 29 29	14 18 16 16 17 15 31 29 29	17 23 16 15 19 16 31 28 29	20 26 21 16 21 16 31 29 29	24 31 26 19 23 17 31 29 29	27 34 26 22 25 17 31 29 29
14	30 28 27 32 6 14 30 29 29	33 32 32 35 7 13 31 29 29	36 33 1 3 8 13 31 29 29	3 2 3 7 10 13 31 29 29	6 6 3 10 12 13 31 29 29	9 11 8 13 14 14 31 29 29	12 15 14 16 15 14 31 29 29	15 20 16 16 17 15 31 29 29	18 24 16 15 19 16 31 28 29	21 28 21 16 21 16 31 29 29	24 32 26 19 23 17 31 29 29	27 35 25 22 26 17 31 29 29
15	30 29 28 32 6 14 30 29 29	33 33 32 36 7 13 31 29 29	36 34 1 3 9 13 31 29 29	3 3 3 7 10 13 31 29 29	6 7 3 10 12 13 31 29 29	9 12 9 13 14 14 31 29 29	12 16 14 16 15 14 31 29 29	15 21 16 16 17 15 31 29 29	18 26 16 15 19 16 31 28 29	21 29 21 16 21 16 31 29 29	24 33 26 19 24 17 31 29 29	27 36 25 23 26 17 31 29 29
16	30 30 28 32 6 14 30 29 29	33 35 32 36 7 13 31 29 29	36 36 1 3 9 13 31 29 29	3 5 3 7 10 13 31 29 29	6 8 3 10 12 13 31 29 29	9 14 9 13 14 14 31 29 29	12 18 14 16 16 14 31 29 29	15 22 16 16 17 15 31 29 29	18 27 16 15 19 16 31 28 29	21 30 22 16 21 16 31 29 29	24 34 26 19 24 17 31 29 29	27 2 25 23 26 17 31 29 29
17	30 31 28 32 6 14 30 29 29	33 36 32 36 7 13 31 29 29	36 1 1 3 9 13 31 29 29	3 6 3 7 10 13 31 29 29	6 10 4 10 12 13 31 29 29	9 15 9 14 14 14 31 29 25	12 19 14 16 16 14 31 29 29	15 24 16 16 18 15 31 29 29	18 28 16 15 20 16 31 28 29	21 31 22 16 22 16 31 29 29	24 36 26 19 24 17 31 29 29	27 3 25 23 26 17 31 29 29
18	30 32 28 32 6 14 30 29 29	33 1 32 36 7 13 31 29 29	36 2 2 3 9 13 31 29 29	3 8 3 7 10 13 31 29 29	6 11 4 10 12 13 31 29 29	9 17 9 14 14 14 31 29 29	12 20 15 16 16 14 31 29 29	15 25 16 16 18 15 31 29 29	18 29 17 15 20 16 31 28 29	21 32 22 16 22 16 31 29 29	24 1 26 19 24 17 31 29 29	27 4 25 23 26 17 31 29 29
19	30 34 28 32 6 13 30 29 29	33 3 33 36 7 13 31 29 29	36 4 2 4 9 13 31 29 29	3 9 3 7 10 13 31 29 29	6 13 4 11 12 13 31 29 29	9 18 9 14 14 14 31 29 29	12 22 15 16 16 14 31 29 29	15 26 16 16 18 15 31 29 29	18 30 17 15 20 16 31 28 29	21 34 22 16 22 16 31 29 29	24 2 26 20 24 17 31 29 29	27 6 25 23 26 17 31 29 29
20	30 35 28 32 6 13 30 29 29	34 4 33 36 7 13 31 29 29	36 5 2 4 9 13 31 29 29	3 10 3 7 10 13 31 29 29	6 14 4 11 12 13 31 29 29	9 19 10 14 14 14 31 29 29	12 23 15 16 16 14 31 29 29	15 27 15 16 18 15 31 29 29	18 32 17 15 20 16 31 28 29	21 35 22 17 22 16 31 29 29	24 4 26 20 24 17 31 29 29	27 7 25 23 26 17 31 29 29
21	31 36 28 32 6 13 30 29 29	34 5 33 36 8 13 31 29 29	36 7 2 4 9 13 31 29 29	4 12 3 7 10 13 31 29 29	6 16 4 11 12 13 31 29 29	9 21 10 14 14 14 31 29 29	12 24 15 16 16 14 31 29 29	15 28 15 16 18 15 31 29 29	18 33 17 15 20 16 31 28 29	21 36 22 17 22 16 31 29 29	24 5 27 20 24 17 31 29 29	27 9 25 23 26 17 31 29 29
22	31 2 28 33 7 13 30 29 29	34 7 33 36 8 13 31 29 29	1 8 2 4 9 13 31 29 29	4 13 2 8 11 13 31 29 29	7 17 4 11 12 13 31 29 29	10 22 10 14 14 14 31 29 29	12 25 15 16 16 14 31 29 29	15 30 15 15 18 15 31 29 29	18 34 17 15 20 16 31 28 29	21 1 23 17 22 16 31 29 29	24 6 27 20 24 17 31 29 29	27 10 25 23 26 17 31 29 29
23	31 3 29 33 7 13 30 29 29	34 8 33 1 8 13 31 29 29	1 9 2 4 9 13 31 29 29	4 15 2 8 11 13 31 29 29	7 18 4 11 12 13 31 29 29	10 23 10 14 14 14 31 29 29	12 26 15 16 16 14 31 29 29	15 31 15 15 18 15 31 29 29	18 35 18 15 20 16 31 28 29	21 3 23 17 22 16 31 29 29	25 8 27 20 24 17 31 29 29	28 12 25 23 26 17 31 29 29
24	31 4 29 33 7 13 30 29 29	34 10 33 1 8 13 31 29 29	1 11 3 4 9 13 31 29 29	4 16 2 8 11 13 31 29 29	7 20 4 11 12 13 31 29 29	10 24 11 14 14 14 31 29 29	13 28 15 16 16 14 31 29 29	16 32 15 15 18 15 31 29 29	19 1 18 15 20 16 31 28 29	22 4 23 17 22 16 31 29 29	25 9 27 20 24 17 31 29 29	28 13 26 24 26 17 31 29 29
25	31 6 29 33 7 13 30 29 29	34 11 34 1 8 13 31 29 29	1 12 3 4 9 13 31 29 29	4 17 2 8 11 13 31 29 29	7 21 5 11 12 13 31 29 29	10 25 11 14 14 14 31 29 29	13 29 15 16 16 14 31 29 29	16 33 15 15 18 15 31 29 29	19 2 18 15 20 16 31 28 29	22 6 23 17 22 16 31 29 29	25 11 27 20 24 17 31 29 29	28 15 26 24 26 17 31 29 29
26	31 7 29 33 7 13 30 29 29	34 13 34 1 8 13 31 29 29	1 14 3 4 9 13 31 29 29	4 19 2 8 11 13 31 29 29	7 22 5 11 12 13 31 29 29	10 27 11 14 14 14 31 29 29	13 30 15 16 16 14 31 29 29	16 34 15 15 18 15 31 29 29	19 3 18 15 20 16 31 28 29	22 7 23 17 22 16 31 29 29	25 12 27 20 24 17 31 29 29	28 16 26 24 26 17 31 29 29
27	31 9 29 33 7 13 30 29 29	34 14 34 1 8 13 31 29 29	1 15 3 4 9 13 31 29 29	4 20 2 8 11 13 31 29 29	7 23 5 11 13 13 31 29 29	10 28 11 14 14 14 31 29 29	13 31 16 16 16 14 31 29 29	16 36 15 15 18 15 31 29 29	19 5 18 15 20 16 31 28 29	22 8 23 17 22 16 31 29 29	25 14 27 20 24 17 31 29 29	28 18 26 24 27 17 31 29 29
28	31 10 29 33 7 13 30 29 29	34 15 34 1 8 13 31 29 29	1 16 3 5 9 13 31 29 29	4 21 2 8 11 13 31 29 29	7 25 5 12 13 13 31 29 29	10 29 11 15 14 14 31 29 29	13 32 16 16 16 14 31 29 29	16 1 15 15 18 15 31 29 29	19 6 18 15 20 16 31 28 29	22 10 23 17 22 16 31 29 29	25 15 27 21 24 17 31 29 29	28 19 26 24 27 17 31 29 29
29	31 12 29 33 7 13 30 29 29		1 18 3 5 9 13 31 29 29	4 22 2 8 11 13 31 29 29	7 26 5 12 13 13 31 29 29	10 30 12 15 14 14 31 29 29	13 34 16 16 16 15 31 29 29	16 2 15 15 18 15 31 29 29	19 7 19 15 20 16 31 28 29	22 11 24 17 22 16 31 29 29	25 17 27 21 24 17 31 29 29	28 20 26 24 27 17 31 29 29
30	31 13 29 34 7 13 30 29 29	1991	1 19 3 5 9 13 31 29 29	4 24 2 8 11 13 31 29 29	7 27 5 12 13 13 31 29 29	10 31 12 15 15 14 31 29 29	13 35 16 16 16 15 31 29 29	16 4 15 15 18 15 31 29 29	19 9 19 15 20 16 31 28 29	22 13 24 17 22 16 31 29 29	25 18 27 21 25 17 31 29 29	28 22 26 24 27 17 31 29 29
31	32 15 30 34 7 13 30 29 29		1 20 3 5 9 13 31 29 29		7 28 6 12 13 13 31 29 29		13 36 16 16 16 15 31 29 29	16 5 15 15 18 15 31 28 29		22 14 24 18 22 16 31 29 29		28 23 26 24 27 17 31 29 29

	JAN	FEB	MAR	APR	MAY	JUNE	JULY	AUG	SEPT	OCT	NOV	DEC
1	28 24 26 25 27 17 31 29 29	32 29 31 28 29 17 31 29 29	35 31 36 32 31 16 32 29 29	2 35 1 36 34 16 32 29 29	5 2 2 3 36 16 32 29 29	8 7 8 7 2 16 32 29 29	10 11 13 11 5 16 32 29 29	13 17 14 15 7 17 32 29 29	16 22 15 19 9 17 32 29 29	19 25 20 22 11 18 32 29 29	22 30 25 26 12 19 32 29 29	25 33 24 30 12 19 32 29 29
2	29 25 26 25 27 17 31 29 29	32 30 31 28 29 17 31 29 29	35 32 36 32 31 16 32 29 29	2 36 1 36 34 16 32 29 29	5 4 2 4 36 16 32 29 29	8 9 8 7 3 16 32 29 29	11 13 13 11 5 16 32 29 29	13 18 14 15 7 17 32 29 29	16 23 15 19 9 17 32 29 29	19 27 21 22 11 18 32 29 29	22 31 25 26 12 19 32 29 29	26 34 24 30 12 19 32 29 29
3	29 26 27 25 27 17 31 29 29	32 31 31 29 29 17 31 29 29	35 33 36 32 32 16 32 29 29	2 2 1 36 34 16 32 29 29	5 5 2 4 36 16 32 29 29	8 10 8 7 3 16 32 29 29	11 14 13 11 5 17 32 29 29	14 19 14 15 7 17 32 29 29	17 24 15 19 9 17 32 29 29	20 28 21 22 11 18 32 29 29	23 32 25 26 12 19 32 29 29	26 35 24 30 12 20 32 29 29
4	29 28 27 25 27 17 31 29 29	32 32 31 29 29 17 31 29 29	35 34 1 32 32 16 32 29 29	2 3 36 36 34 16 32 29 29	5 6 3 4 36 16 32 29 29	8 12 8 8 3 16 32 29 29	11 16 13 11 5 17 32 29 29	14 21 13 15 7 17 32 29 29	17 26 16 19 9 17 32 29 29	20 29 21 23 11 18 32 29 29	23 33 25 26 12 19 32 29 29	26 1 24 30 12 20 32 29 29
5	29 29 27 25 27 17 31 29 29	32 33 32 29 29 17 31 29 29	35 35 1 32 32 16 32 29 29	2 4 36 36 34 16 32 29 29	5 8 3 4 36 16 32 29 29	8 13 8 8 3 16 32 29 29	11 17 13 11 5 17 32 29 29	14 22 13 15 7 17 32 29 29	17 27 16 19 9 17 32 29 29	20 30 21 23 11 18 32 29 29	23 35 25 26 12 19 32 29 29	26 2 24 30 12 20 32 29 29
6	29 30 27 25 27 17 31 29 29	32 35 32 29 30 17 32 29 29	35 1 1 33 32 16 32 29 29	2 6 36 36 34 16 32 29 29	5 9 3 4 1 16 32 29 29	8 15 9 8 3 16 32 29 29	11 18 14 12 5 17 32 29 29	14 24 13 15 7 17 32 29 29	17 28 16 19 9 17 32 29 29	20 31 21 23 11 18 32 29 29	23 36 25 27 12 19 32 29 29	26 3 24 30 12 20 32 29 29
7	29 31 27 25 27 17 31 29 29	32 36 32 29 30 17 32 29 29	35 2 1 33 32 16 32 29 29	2 7 36 36 34 16 32 29 29	5 11 3 4 1 16 32 29 29	8 16 9 8 3 16 32 29 29	11 20 14 12 5 17 32 29 29	14 25 13 15 7 17 32 29 29	17 29 16 19 9 17 32 29 29	20 33 21 23 11 18 32 29 29	23 1 25 27 12 19 32 29 29	26 4 24 30 12 20 32 29 29
8	29 32 27 25 27 17 31 29 29	32 1 32 29 30 17 32 29 29	35 3 1 33 32 16 32 29 29	2 8 36 1 34 16 32 29 29	5 12 3 4 1 16 32 29 29	8 17 9 8 3 16 32 29 29	11 21 14 12 5 17 32 29 29	14 26 13 16 7 17 32 29 29	17 31 16 19 9 17 32 29 29	20 34 22 23 11 18 32 29 29	23 2 25 27 12 19 32 29 29	26 6 24 30 12 20 32 29 29
9	29 34 27 26 27 17 31 29 29	32 2 32 29 30 17 32 29 29	35 5 1 33 32 16 32 29 29	2 10 36 1 34 16 32 29 29	5 13 3 4 1 16 32 29 29	8 19 9 8 3 16 32 29 29	11 23 14 12 5 17 32 29 29	14 27 13 16 7 17 32 29 29	17 32 17 20 9 17 32 29 29	20 35 22 23 11 18 32 29 29	23 4 25 27 12 19 32 29 29	26 7 24 31 12 20 32 29 29
10	29 35 27 26 28 17 31 29 29	33 4 32 29 30 17 32 29 29	35 6 1 33 32 16 32 29 29	3 11 36 1 35 16 32 29 29	5 15 3 5 1 16 32 29 29	8 20 10 8 3 16 32 29 29	11 24 14 12 5 17 32 29 29	14 29 13 16 7 17 32 29 29	17 33 17 20 9 17 32 29 29	20 36 22 23 11 18 32 29 29	23 5 25 27 12 19 32 29 29	26 8 24 31 12 20 32 29 29
11	30 36 28 26 28 17 31 29 29	33 5 33 30 30 17 32 29 29	36 7 1 33 32 16 32 29 29	3 12 36 1 35 16 32 29 29	6 16 3 5 1 16 32 29 29	9 22 10 8 3 16 32 29 29	11 25 14 12 5 17 32 29 29	14 30 13 16 8 17 32 29 29	17 34 17 20 9 17 32 29 29	20 1 22 23 11 19 32 29 29	23 6 25 27 12 19 32 29 29	26 10 24 31 12 20 32 29 29
12	30 1 28 26 28 17 31 29 29	33 6 33 30 30 17 32 29 29	36 9 1 33 32 16 32 29 29	3 14 36 1 35 16 32 29 29	6 18 4 5 1 16 32 29 29	9 23 10 9 3 16 32 29 29	11 26 14 12 5 17 32 29 29	14 31 13 16 8 17 32 29 29	17 35 17 20 9 17 32 29 29	20 3 22 24 11 19 32 29 29	23 7 25 27 12 19 32 29 29	27 11 24 31 12 20 32 29 29
13	30 3 28 26 28 17 31 29 29	33 8 33 30 30 17 32 29 29	36 10 2 33 32 16 32 29 29	3 15 36 1 35 16 32 29 29	6 19 4 5 1 16 32 29 29	9 24 10 9 3 16 32 29 29	12 28 14 12 6 17 32 29 29	15 32 13 16 8 17 32 29 29	18 1 17 20 9 17 32 29 29	20 4 22 24 11 19 32 29 29	24 9 25 27 12 19 32 29 29	27 13 25 31 12 20 32 29 29
14	30 4 28 26 28 17 31 29 29	33 9 33 30 30 17 32 29 29	36 11 2 34 32 16 32 29 29	3 17 36 1 35 16 32 29 29	6 21 4 5 1 16 32 29 29	9 25 10 9 3 16 32 29 29	12 29 14 13 6 17 32 29 29	15 33 13 16 8 17 32 29 29	18 2 18 20 10 17 32 29 29	21 5 22 24 11 19 32 29 29	24 10 25 28 12 19 32 29 29	27 14 25 31 12 20 32 29 29
15	30 5 28 26 28 17 31 29 29	33 10 33 30 30 17 32 29 29	36 13 2 34 32 16 32 29 29	3 18 1 1 35 16 32 29 29	6 22 4 5 1 16 32 29 29	9 27 11 9 4 16 32 29 29	12 30 14 13 6 17 32 29 29	15 34 13 16 8 17 32 29 29	18 3 18 20 10 17 32 29 29	21 6 23 24 11 19 32 29 29	24 12 25 28 12 19 32 29 29	27 15 25 31 12 20 32 29 29
16	30 7 28 26 28 17 31 29 29	33 12 33 30 30 17 32 29 29	36 14 2 34 33 16 32 29 29	3 20 1 2 35 16 32 29 29	6 23 4 5 1 16 32 29 29	9 28 11 9 4 16 32 29 29	12 31 14 13 6 17 32 29 29	15 36 13 17 8 17 32 29 29	18 4 18 20 10 17 32 29 29	21 8 23 24 11 19 32 29 29	24 13 25 28 12 19 32 29 29	27 17 25 31 12 20 32 29 29
17	30 8 29 26 28 17 31 29 29	33 13 33 30 30 17 32 29 29	36 16 2 34 33 16 32 29 29	3 21 1 2 35 16 32 29 29	6 25 5 5 1 16 32 29 29	9 29 11 9 4 16 32 29 29	12 32 14 13 6 17 32 29 29	15 1 13 17 8 17 32 29 29	18 6 18 21 10 17 32 29 29	21 9 23 24 11 19 32 29 29	24 14 25 28 12 19 32 29 29	27 18 25 31 12 20 32 29 29
18	30 10 29 27 28 17 31 29 29	33 15 33 30 30 17 32 29 29	36 17 2 34 33 16 32 29 29	3 22 1 2 35 16 32 29 29	6 26 5 6 1 16 32 29 29	9 30 11 9 4 16 32 29 29	12 34 14 13 6 17 32 29 29	15 2 13 17 8 17 32 29 29	18 7 18 21 10 17 32 29 29	21 10 23 24 11 19 32 29 29	24 16 25 28 12 19 32 29 29	27 20 25 32 12 20 32 29 29
19	30 11 29 27 28 17 31 29 29	33 16 34 31 31 17 32 29 29	36 19 2 34 33 16 32 29 29	3 24 1 2 35 16 32 29 29	6 27 5 6 2 16 32 29 29	9 32 11 9 4 16 32 29 29	12 35 14 13 6 17 32 29 29	15 3 13 17 8 17 32 29 29	18 8 18 21 10 17 32 29 29	21 12 23 24 11 19 32 29 29	24 17 25 28 12 19 32 29 29	27 21 25 32 12 20 32 29 29
20	30 13 29 27 28 17 31 29 29	34 18 34 31 31 17 32 29 29	36 20 2 34 33 16 32 29 29	4 25 1 2 35 16 32 29 29	6 28 5 6 2 16 32 29 29	9 33 11 10 4 16 32 29 29	12 36 14 13 6 17 32 29 29	15 5 13 17 8 17 32 29 29	18 9 19 21 10 17 32 29 29	21 13 23 25 11 19 32 29 29	24 19 25 28 12 19 32 29 29	27 22 25 32 12 20 32 29 29
21	31 14 29 27 28 17 31 29 29	34 19 34 31 31 17 32 29 29	1 22 2 34 33 16 32 29 29	4 26 1 2 35 16 32 29 29	7 30 5 6 2 16 32 29 29	9 34 12 10 4 16 32 29 29	12 1 14 13 6 17 32 29 29	15 6 13 17 8 17 32 29 29	18 11 19 21 10 17 32 29 29	21 15 23 25 11 19 32 29 29	24 20 25 28 12 19 32 29 29	27 24 26 32 12 20 32 29 29
22	31 16 29 27 28 17 31 29 29	34 21 35 31 31 17 32 29 29	1 23 1 34 33 16 32 29 29	4 28 1 2 35 16 32 29 29	7 31 5 6 2 16 32 29 29	10 35 12 10 4 16 32 29 29	12 3 14 13 6 17 32 29 29	15 7 14 17 8 17 32 29 29	18 12 19 21 10 17 32 29 29	21 16 24 25 11 19 32 29 29	24 21 24 29 12 19 32 29 29	28 25 26 32 12 20 32 29 29
23	31 17 29 27 29 17 31 29 29	34 22 35 31 31 17 32 29 29	1 24 1 35 33 16 32 29 29	4 29 1 2 36 16 32 29 29	7 32 6 6 2 16 32 29 29	10 36 12 10 4 16 32 29 29	13 4 14 14 6 17 32 29 29	16 8 14 17 8 17 32 29 29	19 13 19 21 10 17 32 29 29	21 18 24 25 11 19 32 29 29	25 23 24 29 12 19 32 29 29	28 26 26 32 12 20 32 29 29
24	31 19 30 27 29 17 31 29 29	34 23 35 31 31 17 32 29 29	1 25 1 35 33 16 32 29 29	4 30 1 3 36 16 32 29 29	7 33 6 6 2 16 32 29 29	10 2 12 10 4 16 32 29 29	13 5 14 14 6 17 32 29 29	16 10 14 18 8 17 32 29 29	19 15 19 21 10 17 32 29 29	22 19 24 25 12 19 32 29 29	25 24 24 29 12 19 32 29 29	28 28 26 32 12 20 32 29 29
25	31 20 30 27 29 17 31 29 29	34 25 35 31 31 17 32 29 29	1 27 1 35 33 16 32 29 29	4 31 1 3 36 16 32 29 29	7 34 6 6 2 16 32 29 29	10 3 12 10 4 16 32 29 29	13 6 14 14 6 17 32 29 29	16 12 14 18 8 18 32 29 29	19 17 20 21 10 17 32 29 29	22 21 24 25 12 19 32 29 29	25 26 24 29 12 19 32 29 29	28 29 26 32 12 20 32 29 29
26	31 21 30 28 29 17 31 29 29	34 26 35 31 31 17 32 29 29	1 28 1 35 33 16 32 29 29	4 32 1 3 36 16 32 29 29	7 35 6 6 2 16 32 29 29	10 4 12 10 4 16 32 29 29	13 8 14 14 6 17 32 29 29	16 13 14 18 8 18 32 29 29	19 18 20 22 10 17 32 29 29	22 22 24 25 12 19 32 29 29	25 27 24 29 12 19 32 29 29	28 30 26 32 12 20 32 29 29
27	31 23 30 28 29 17 31 29 29	34 27 35 32 31 16 32 29 29	1 29 1 35 33 16 32 29 29	4 33 2 3 36 16 32 29 29	7 1 7 7 2 16 32 29 29	10 5 12 10 4 16 32 29 29	13 9 14 14 7 17 32 29 29	16 14 14 18 9 18 32 29 29	19 20 20 22 10 17 32 29 29	22 23 24 25 12 19 32 29 29	25 28 24 29 12 19 32 29 29	28 31 27 33 12 20 32 29 29
28	31 24 30 28 29 17 31 29 29	34 28 36 32 31 16 32 29 29	1 30 1 35 33 16 32 29 29	4 35 2 3 36 16 32 29 29	7 2 7 7 2 16 32 29 29	10 7 13 11 4 16 32 29 29	13 10 14 14 7 17 32 29 29	16 16 14 18 9 18 32 29 29	19 21 20 22 10 17 32 29 29	22 25 24 26 12 19 32 29 29	25 29 24 29 12 19 32 29 29	28 33 27 33 12 20 32 29 29
29	31 25 30 28 29 17 31 29 29	34 29 36 32 31 16 32 29 29	1 31 1 35 34 16 32 29 29	4 36 2 3 36 16 32 29 29	7 3 7 7 2 16 32 29 29	10 8 13 11 5 16 32 29 29	13 12 14 14 7 17 32 29 29	16 17 15 18 9 18 32 29 29	19 23 20 22 10 17 32 29 29	22 26 24 26 12 19 32 29 29	25 31 24 29 12 19 32 29 29	28 34 27 33 12 20 32 29 29
30	31 26 31 28 29 17 31 29 29	**1992**	1 33 1 35 34 16 32 29 29	4 1 2 3 36 16 32 29 29	7 5 7 7 2 16 32 29 29	10 10 13 11 5 16 32 29 29	13 13 14 14 7 17 32 29 29	16 19 15 18 9 18 32 29 29	19 24 20 22 10 17 32 29 29	22 27 25 26 12 19 32 29 29	25 32 24 29 12 19 32 29 29	28 35 27 33 12 20 32 29 29
31	32 27 31 28 29 17 31 29 29		2 34 1 36 34 16 32 29 29		7 6 7 7 2 16 32 29 29		13 15 14 15 7 17 32 29 29	16 20 15 18 9 18 32 29 29		22 29 25 26 12 19 32 29 29		28 36 27 33 12 20 32 29 29

	JAN	FEB	MAR	APR	MAY	JUNE	JULY	AUG	SEPT	OCT	NOV	DEC
1	29 1 27 33 12 19 32 29 29	32 6 32 36 11 20 32 29 29	35 7 36 2 10 20 33 29 29	2 12 35 2 11 19 33 30 30	5 15 3 1 13 19 33 30 30	8 21 9 3 14 19 34 30 30	10 25 12 6 16 19 33 30 30	13 30 12 9 18 19 33 29 29	16 34 17 13 20 20 33 29 29	19 2 21 17 22 21 33 29 29	22 6 23 20 24 21 33 29 29	25 9 24 24 26 22 33 29 29
2	29 3 27 33 12 19 32 29 29	32 7 32 36 10 20 33 29 29	35 8 36 2 10 20 33 29 29	2 13 35 2 11 19 33 30 30	5 17 3 1 13 19 33 30 30	8 22 9 3 14 19 34 30 30	11 26 12 6 16 19 33 30 30	13 31 12 10 18 19 33 29 29	16 35 17 13 20 20 33 29 29	19 3 22 17 22 21 33 29 29	22 7 23 21 24 21 33 29 29	25 11 24 24 26 22 33 29 29
3	29 4 28 33 11 19 32 29 29	32 9 33 1 10 20 33 29 29	35 9 36 2 11 20 33 29 29	2 15 35 2 11 19 33 30 30	5 18 3 1 13 19 33 30 30	8 24 10 3 14 19 34 30 30	11 27 12 6 16 19 33 30 30	14 32 12 10 18 20 33 29 29	17 1 17 13 20 20 33 29 29	19 4 22 17 22 21 33 29 29	22 8 23 21 24 21 33 29 29	26 12 24 25 26 22 33 30 29
4	29 5 28 34 11 19 32 29 29	32 10 33 1 10 20 33 29 29	35 11 36 2 11 20 33 29 29	2 16 35 2 11 19 33 30 30	5 20 4 1 13 19 33 30 30	8 25 10 3 14 19 34 30 30	11 29 12 6 16 19 33 30 29	14 33 12 10 18 20 33 29 29	17 2 17 13 20 20 33 29 29	20 5 22 17 22 21 33 29 29	23 10 23 21 24 21 33 29 29	26 13 24 25 26 22 33 30 29
5	29 6 28 34 11 19 32 29 29	32 11 33 1 10 20 33 29 29	35 12 36 2 11 20 33 29 29	2 17 35 1 11 19 33 30 30	5 21 4 1 13 19 33 30 30	8 27 10 3 14 19 34 30 30	11 30 12 6 16 19 33 30 29	14 35 12 10 18 20 33 29 29	17 3 17 13 20 20 33 29 29	20 6 22 17 22 21 33 29 29	23 11 23 21 24 21 33 29 29	26 15 24 25 26 22 33 30 29
6	29 8 28 34 11 19 32 29 29	32 13 33 1 10 20 33 29 29	35 14 36 2 11 20 33 29 29	2 19 35 1 12 19 33 30 30	5 23 4 1 13 19 33 30 30	8 28 10 3 15 19 34 30 30	11 31 12 6 16 19 33 30 29	14 36 12 10 18 20 33 29 29	17 4 18 14 20 20 33 29 29	20 7 22 17 22 21 33 29 29	23 12 23 21 24 21 33 29 29	26 16 24 25 26 22 33 30 29
7	29 9 28 34 11 19 32 29 29	32 14 33 1 10 20 33 29 29	35 15 36 2 11 20 33 29 29	2 21 35 1 12 19 33 30 30	5 24 4 1 13 19 33 30 30	8 29 10 4 15 19 34 30 30	11 33 12 7 16 19 33 30 29	14 1 12 10 18 20 33 29 29	17 5 18 14 20 20 33 29 29	20 9 22 17 22 21 33 29 29	23 14 23 21 24 21 33 29 29	26 17 24 25 27 22 33 30 29
8	29 11 28 34 11 19 32 29 29	32 16 34 1 10 20 33 29 29	35 17 35 2 11 20 33 29 29	2 22 36 1 12 19 33 30 30	5 26 4 1 13 19 33 30 30	8 30 10 4 15 19 34 30 30	11 34 12 7 16 19 33 30 29	14 2 12 10 18 20 33 29 29	17 7 18 14 20 20 33 29 29	20 10 22 18 22 21 33 29 29	23 15 23 21 24 21 33 29 29	26 19 25 25 27 22 33 30 29
9	29 12 28 34 11 19 32 29 29	33 17 34 1 10 20 33 29 29	35 18 35 2 11 20 33 29 29	2 23 36 1 12 19 33 30 30	5 27 5 1 13 19 33 30 30	8 32 11 4 15 19 34 30 30	11 35 12 7 16 19 33 30 29	14 3 12 10 18 20 33 29 29	17 8 18 14 20 20 33 29 29	20 11 23 18 22 21 33 29 29	23 16 23 21 24 21 33 29 29	26 20 25 25 27 22 33 30 29
10	29 13 29 34 11 19 32 29 29	33 19 34 1 10 20 33 29 29	35 20 35 2 11 20 33 29 29	3 25 36 1 12 19 33 30 30	5 28 5 1 13 19 33 30 30	8 33 11 4 15 19 34 30 30	11 36 12 7 16 19 33 30 29	14 5 12 10 18 20 33 29 29	17 9 18 14 20 20 33 29 29	20 13 23 18 22 21 33 29 29	23 18 22 22 25 21 33 29 29	26 22 25 25 27 22 33 30 29
11	30 15 29 34 11 19 32 29 29	33 20 34 1 10 20 33 30 29	36 21 35 3 11 20 33 29 29	3 26 36 1 12 19 33 30 30	6 30 5 1 13 19 33 30 30	9 34 11 4 15 19 34 30 30	11 1 12 7 17 19 33 30 29	14 6 13 11 18 20 33 29 29	17 10 18 14 20 20 33 29 29	20 14 23 18 22 21 33 29 29	23 19 22 22 25 22 33 29 29	26 23 25 26 27 22 33 30 29
12	30 16 29 34 11 19 32 29 29	33 22 34 1 10 20 33 30 29	36 23 35 3 11 20 33 29 29	3 28 36 1 12 19 33 30 30	6 31 5 2 13 19 33 30 30	9 35 11 4 15 19 34 30 30	11 3 12 7 17 19 33 30 29	14 7 13 11 18 20 33 29 29	17 12 19 14 20 20 33 29 29	20 15 23 18 23 21 33 29 29	23 21 22 22 25 22 33 29 29	26 25 25 26 27 22 33 30 29
13	30 18 29 35 11 19 32 29 29	33 23 34 1 10 20 33 30 29	36 24 35 2 11 20 33 29 29	3 29 36 1 12 19 33 30 30	6 32 5 2 13 19 33 30 30	9 1 11 4 15 19 34 30 30	12 4 12 7 17 19 33 30 29	15 8 13 11 19 20 33 29 29	18 13 19 14 21 20 33 29 29	20 17 23 18 23 21 33 29 29	24 22 22 22 25 22 33 29 29	27 26 25 26 27 22 33 30 29
14	30 19 29 35 11 19 32 29 29	33 24 35 1 10 20 33 30 29	36 25 35 2 11 20 33 29 29	3 30 36 1 12 19 33 30 30	6 33 6 2 13 19 33 30 30	9 2 11 4 15 19 34 30 30	12 5 12 7 17 19 33 30 29	15 10 13 11 19 20 33 29 29	18 15 19 15 21 20 33 29 29	21 18 23 18 23 21 33 29 29	24 24 22 22 25 22 33 29 29	27 27 26 26 27 22 33 30 29
15	30 21 29 35 11 19 32 29 29	33 26 35 2 10 20 33 30 29	36 27 35 2 11 20 33 29 29	3 31 36 1 12 19 33 30 30	6 35 6 2 13 19 33 30 30	9 3 11 4 15 19 34 30 30	12 6 12 7 17 19 33 30 29	15 11 13 11 19 20 33 29 29	18 16 19 15 21 20 33 29 29	21 20 23 18 23 21 33 29 29	24 25 22 22 25 22 33 29 29	27 29 26 26 27 22 33 30 29
16	30 22 30 35 11 19 32 29 29	33 27 35 2 10 20 33 30 30	36 28 35 2 11 20 33 29 29	3 33 1 1 12 19 33 30 30	6 36 6 2 13 19 33 30 30	9 4 11 4 15 19 34 30 30	12 7 12 8 17 19 33 30 29	15 12 13 11 19 20 33 29 29	18 18 19 15 21 20 33 29 29	21 21 23 18 23 21 33 29 29	24 27 22 22 25 22 33 29 29	27 30 26 26 27 22 33 30 29
17	30 24 30 35 11 19 32 29 29	33 28 35 2 10 20 33 30 30	36 30 35 2 11 20 33 29 29	3 34 1 1 12 19 33 30 30	6 1 6 2 13 19 33 30 30	9 5 12 5 15 19 34 30 30	12 9 12 8 17 19 33 30 29	15 14 14 11 19 20 33 29 29	18 19 19 15 21 20 33 29 29	21 23 23 18 23 21 33 29 29	24 28 22 22 25 22 33 29 29	27 32 26 26 27 22 33 30 29
18	30 25 30 35 11 19 32 29 29	33 30 35 2 10 20 33 30 30	36 31 35 2 11 20 33 29 29	3 35 1 1 12 19 33 30 30	6 2 6 2 14 19 33 30 30	9 7 12 5 15 19 34 30 30	12 10 12 8 17 19 33 29 29	15 15 14 11 19 20 33 29 29	18 21 20 15 21 20 33 29 29	21 24 23 19 23 21 33 29 29	24 29 22 23 25 22 33 29 29	27 33 26 26 27 22 33 30 29
19	30 26 30 35 11 19 32 29 29	34 31 35 2 10 20 33 30 30	36 32 35 2 11 20 33 29 29	3 36 1 1 12 19 33 30 30	6 3 7 2 14 19 33 30 30	9 8 12 5 15 19 34 30 30	12 12 12 8 17 19 33 29 29	15 17 14 11 19 20 33 29 29	18 22 20 15 21 20 33 29 29	21 26 23 19 23 21 33 29 29	24 31 22 23 25 22 33 29 29	27 34 26 27 27 22 33 30 29
20	30 27 30 35 11 19 32 29 29	34 32 35 2 10 20 33 30 30	36 33 35 2 11 29 33 29 29	3 1 1 1 12 19 33 30 30	6 5 7 2 14 19 33 30 30	9 9 12 5 15 19 34 30 30	12 13 11 8 17 19 33 29 29	15 18 14 12 19 20 33 29 29	18 24 20 15 21 20 33 29 29	21 27 24 19 23 21 33 29 29	24 32 22 23 25 22 33 29 29	27 35 26 27 27 22 33 30 30
21	31 29 30 35 11 19 32 29 29	34 33 36 2 10 20 33 30 30	1 34 35 2 11 20 33 29 29	4 2 1 1 12 19 33 30 30	6 6 7 2 14 19 33 30 30	9 11 12 5 15 19 34 30 30	12 14 11 8 17 19 33 29 29	15 20 14 12 19 20 33 29 29	18 25 20 15 21 20 33 29 29	21 29 24 19 23 21 33 29 29	24 33 22 23 25 22 33 29 29	27 36 27 27 28 22 33 30 30
22	31 30 31 35 11 19 32 29 29	34 34 36 2 10 20 33 30 30	1 35 35 2 11 20 33 29 29	4 4 1 1 12 19 33 30 30	7 7 7 2 14 19 34 30 30	10 12 12 5 15 19 34 30 30	12 16 11 8 17 19 33 29 29	15 21 15 12 19 20 33 29 29	18 26 20 16 21 20 33 29 29	21 30 24 19 23 21 33 29 29	24 34 23 23 25 22 33 29 29	28 2 27 27 28 22 33 30 30
23	31 31 31 36 11 19 32 29 29	34 36 36 2 10 20 33 30 30	1 36 35 2 11 20 33 29 29	4 5 2 1 12 19 33 30 30	7 8 8 2 14 19 34 30 30	10 13 12 5 15 19 34 30 30	13 17 11 8 17 19 33 29 29	15 23 15 12 19 20 33 29 29	18 28 20 16 21 20 33 29 29	21 31 24 19 23 21 33 29 29	25 36 23 23 25 22 33 29 29	28 3 27 27 28 22 33 30 30
24	31 32 31 36 11 19 32 29 29	34 1 36 2 10 20 33 30 30	1 2 35 2 11 20 33 29 29	4 6 2 1 12 19 33 30 30	7 10 8 2 14 19 34 30 30	10 15 12 5 16 19 34 30 30	13 19 11 8 17 19 33 29 29	16 24 15 12 19 20 33 29 29	19 29 20 16 21 20 33 29 29	22 32 24 19 23 21 33 29 29	25 1 23 23 26 22 33 29 29	28 4 27 27 28 22 33 30 30
25	31 33 31 36 11 19 32 29 29	34 2 36 2 10 20 33 30 30	1 3 35 2 11 20 33 29 29	4 7 2 1 12 19 33 30 30	7 11 8 2 14 19 34 30 30	10 16 12 5 16 19 34 30 30	13 20 11 9 17 19 33 29 29	16 25 15 12 19 20 33 29 29	19 30 21 16 21 21 33 29 29	22 34 24 20 23 21 33 29 29	25 2 23 23 26 22 33 29 29	28 5 27 27 28 22 33 30 30
26	31 35 31 36 11 19 32 29 29	34 3 36 2 10 20 33 30 30	1 4 35 2 11 20 33 29 29	4 9 2 1 12 19 33 30 30	7 12 8 3 14 19 34 30 30	10 18 12 5 16 19 34 30 30	13 22 11 9 17 19 33 29 29	16 27 15 12 19 20 33 29 29	19 32 21 16 21 21 33 29 29	22 35 24 20 23 21 33 29 29	25 3 23 24 26 22 33 29 29	28 6 27 27 28 22 33 30 30
27	31 36 31 36 11 19 32 29 29	34 4 36 2 10 20 33 30 30	1 5 35 2 11 20 33 29 29	4 10 2 1 12 19 33 30 30	7 14 8 3 14 19 34 30 30	10 19 12 6 16 19 34 30 30	13 23 11 9 18 19 33 29 29	16 28 16 12 19 20 33 29 29	19 33 21 16 21 21 33 29 29	22 36 24 20 24 21 33 29 29	25 4 23 24 26 22 33 29 29	28 8 28 28 28 22 33 30 30
28	31 1 32 36 11 19 32 29 29	34 6 36 2 10 20 33 30 30	1 6 35 2 11 20 33 29 29	4 11 2 1 13 19 33 30 30	7 15 9 3 14 19 34 30 30	10 21 12 6 16 19 34 30 30	13 24 11 9 18 19 33 29 29	16 29 16 13 20 20 33 29 29	19 34 21 16 22 21 33 29 29	22 1 24 20 24 21 33 29 29	25 6 23 24 26 22 33 29 29	28 9 28 28 28 22 33 30 30
29	31 2 32 36 11 19 32 29 29		1 8 35 2 11 19 33 29 29	4 13 3 1 13 19 33 30 30	7 17 9 3 14 19 34 30 30	10 22 12 6 16 19 33 30 30	13 26 11 9 18 19 33 29 29	16 31 16 13 20 20 33 29 29	19 35 21 16 22 21 33 29 29	22 2 24 20 24 21 33 29 29	25 7 23 24 26 22 33 29 29	28 10 28 28 28 22 33 30 30
30	32 3 32 36 11 19 32 29 29		1 9 35 2 11 19 33 29 29	4 14 3 1 13 19 33 30 30	7 18 9 3 14 19 34 30 30	10 23 12 6 16 19 34 30 30	13 27 11 9 18 19 33 29 29	16 32 16 13 20 20 33 29 29	19 36 21 17 22 21 33 29 29	22 3 24 20 24 21 33 29 29	25 8 23 24 26 22 33 29 29	28 12 28 28 28 22 33 30 30
31	32 5 32 36 11 19 32 29 29	1993	2 10 35 2 11 19 33 29 29		7 19 9 3 14 19 34 30 30		13 28 11 9 18 19 33 29 29	16 33 16 13 20 20 33 29 29		22 4 24 20 24 21 33 29 29		28 13 28 28 28 22 33 30 30

	JAN	FEB	MAR	APR	MAY	JUNE	JULY	AUG	SEPT	OCT	NOV	DEC
1	29 14 28 28 28 22 33 30 30	32 20 33 32 31 23 34 30 30	35 21 33 36 33 23 34 30 30	2 26 35 3 35 23 34 30 30	5 30 5 7 2 22 35 30 30	8 34 10 11 4 22 35 30 30	10 2 10 14 6 22 35 30 30	13 6 12 18 8 22 35 30 30	16 10 18 21 10 22 34 30 30	19 14 22 23 12 23 34 30 30	22 19 21 23 14 24 34 30 30	25 23 25 22 15 24 34 30 30
2	29 16 29 28 28 22 33 30 30	32 21 34 32 31 23 34 30 30	35 22 33 36 33 23 34 30 30	2 27 35 4 36 23 34 30 30	5 31 5 7 2 22 35 30 30	8 36 10 11 4 22 35 30 30	10 3 10 14 6 22 35 30 30	13 7 12 18 9 22 35 30 30	16 12 18 21 11 22 34 30 30	19 15 22 23 12 23 34 30 30	22 20 21 23 14 24 34 30 30	25 24 25 22 15 24 34 30 30
3	29 17 29 28 29 23 33 30 30	32 22 34 32 31 23 34 30 30	35 24 33 36 33 23 34 30 30	2 29 35 4 36 23 34 30 30	5 32 5 7 2 22 35 30 30	8 1 10 11 4 22 35 30 30	11 4 9 15 6 22 35 30 30	14 8 12 18 9 22 35 30 30	17 13 18 21 11 23 34 30 30	19 17 22 23 12 23 34 30 30	23 22 21 23 14 24 34 30 30	26 26 25 22 15 24 34 30 30
4	29 19 29 29 29 23 33 30 30	32 24 34 32 31 23 34 30 30	35 25 33 36 33 23 34 30 30	2 30 36 4 36 23 34 30 30	5 33 5 7 2 22 35 30 30	8 2 10 11 4 22 35 30 30	11 5 9 15 7 22 35 30 30	14 10 13 18 9 22 35 30 30	17 14 18 21 11 23 34 30 30	20 18 22 23 12 23 34 30 30	23 23 21 22 14 24 34 30 30	26 27 25 22 15 24 34 30 30
5	29 20 29 29 29 23 33 30 30	32 25 34 33 31 23 34 30 30	35 26 33 36 33 23 34 30 30	2 31 36 4 36 23 34 30 30	5 35 5 8 2 22 35 30 30	8 3 10 11 4 22 35 30 30	11 6 9 15 7 22 35 30 30	14 11 13 18 9 22 35 30 30	17 16 19 21 11 23 34 30 30	20 19 22 23 13 23 34 30 30	23 25 21 22 14 24 34 30 30	26 29 25 22 15 24 34 30 30
6	29 21 29 29 29 23 33 30 30	32 27 34 33 31 23 34 30 30	35 28 33 36 33 23 34 30 30	2 33 36 4 36 23 34 30 30	5 36 6 8 2 22 35 30 30	8 4 10 11 4 22 35 30 30	11 7 9 15 7 22 35 30 30	14 12 13 18 9 22 35 30 30	17 17 19 21 11 23 34 30 30	20 21 22 23 13 23 34 30 30	23 26 21 22 14 24 34 30 30	26 30 25 22 15 24 34 30 30
7	29 23 29 29 29 23 33 30 30	32 28 34 33 31 23 34 30 30	35 29 33 36 33 23 34 30 30	2 34 36 4 36 23 34 30 30	5 1 6 8 2 22 35 30 30	8 6 10 12 4 22 35 30 30	11 9 9 15 7 22 35 30 30	14 13 13 18 9 22 35 30 30	17 19 19 21 11 23 34 30 30	20 22 22 23 13 23 34 30 30	23 28 21 22 14 24 34 30 30	26 31 26 22 15 24 34 30 30
8	29 24 30 29 29 23 33 30 30	32 29 34 33 31 23 34 30 30	35 30 33 36 34 23 34 30 30	2 35 36 4 36 23 34 30 30	5 2 6 8 2 22 35 30 30	8 7 10 12 5 22 35 30 30	11 10 9 15 7 22 35 30 30	14 15 13 19 9 22 35 30 30	17 20 19 22 11 23 34 30 30	20 24 22 23 13 23 34 30 30	23 29 21 22 14 24 34 30 30	26 33 26 22 15 24 34 30 30
9	29 26 30 29 29 23 33 30 30	33 31 34 33 31 23 34 30 30	35 32 33 1 34 23 34 30 30	2 36 36 4 36 23 34 30 30	5 3 6 8 2 22 35 30 30	8 8 10 12 5 22 35 30 30	11 11 9 15 7 22 35 30 30	14 16 14 19 9 22 35 30 30	17 21 19 22 11 23 34 30 30	20 25 22 23 13 23 34 30 30	23 31 21 22 14 24 34 30 30	26 34 26 22 15 24 34 30 30
10	29 27 30 29 29 23 33 30 30	33 32 34 33 32 23 34 30 30	35 33 33 1 34 23 34 30 30	2 1 1 5 36 23 34 30 30	5 5 7 8 2 22 35 30 30	8 9 10 12 5 22 35 30 30	11 13 9 15 7 22 35 30 30	14 18 14 19 9 22 35 30 30	17 23 19 22 11 23 34 30 30	20 27 22 23 13 23 34 30 30	23 32 21 22 14 24 34 30 30	26 35 26 22 15 25 34 30 30
11	30 28 30 29 29 23 33 30 30	33 33 34 33 32 23 34 30 30	36 34 33 1 34 23 34 30 30	3 3 1 5 36 23 34 30 30	6 6 7 8 3 22 35 30 30	8 10 10 12 5 22 35 30 30	11 14 10 15 7 22 35 30 30	14 19 14 19 9 22 35 30 30	17 24 20 22 11 23 34 30 30	20 28 22 23 13 23 34 30 30	23 33 22 22 14 24 34 30 30	26 1 26 22 15 25 34 30 30
12	30 30 30 30 29 23 33 30 30	33 34 34 33 32 23 34 30 30	36 35 33 1 34 23 34 30 30	3 4 1 5 36 23 34 30 30	6 7 7 8 3 22 35 30 30	9 12 10 12 5 22 35 30 30	11 15 10 16 7 22 35 30 30	14 20 14 19 9 22 35 30 30	17 26 20 22 11 23 34 30 30	20 30 22 23 13 23 34 30 30	23 35 22 22 14 24 34 30 30	26 2 26 22 15 25 34 30 30
13	30 31 30 30 29 23 33 30 30	33 36 34 34 32 23 34 30 30	36 1 33 1 34 23 34 30 30	3 5 1 5 36 23 34 30 30	6 8 7 9 3 22 35 30 30	9 13 10 12 5 22 35 30 30	12 17 10 16 7 22 35 30 30	15 22 15 19 9 22 35 30 30	17 27 20 22 11 23 34 30 30	20 31 22 23 13 23 34 31 30	24 36 22 22 14 24 34 30 30	27 3 27 22 16 25 34 30 30
14	30 32 30 30 29 23 33 30 30	33 1 34 34 32 23 34 30 30	36 2 33 1 34 23 34 30 30	3 6 1 5 36 23 34 30 30	6 9 7 9 3 22 35 30 30	9 14 10 12 5 22 35 30 30	12 18 10 16 7 22 35 30 30	15 23 15 19 9 22 35 30 30	18 29 20 22 11 23 34 30 30	21 32 22 23 13 23 34 30 30	24 1 22 22 15 24 34 30 30	27 4 27 22 16 25 34 30 30
15	30 34 31 30 29 23 33 30 30	33 2 34 34 32 23 34 30 30	36 3 33 1 34 23 34 30 30	3 7 1 5 1 23 34 30 30	6 11 7 9 3 22 35 30 30	9 16 10 12 5 22 35 30 30	12 19 10 16 7 22 35 30 30	15 25 15 19 9 22 35 30 30	18 30 20 22 11 23 34 30 30	21 34 22 23 13 23 34 30 30	24 2 22 22 15 24 34 30 30	27 5 27 23 16 25 34 30 30
16	30 35 31 30 30 23 33 30 30	33 3 34 34 32 23 34 30 30	36 4 33 1 34 23 34 30 30	3 9 2 5 1 23 34 30 30	6 12 8 9 3 22 35 30 30	9 17 10 13 5 22 35 30 30	12 21 10 16 7 22 35 30 30	15 26 15 19 9 22 35 30 30	18 31 20 22 11 23 34 30 30	21 35 22 23 13 23 34 30 30	24 3 22 22 15 24 34 30 30	27 7 27 23 16 25 34 30 30
17	30 36 31 30 30 23 33 30 30	33 4 34 34 32 23 34 30 30	36 5 33 2 34 23 34 30 30	3 10 2 5 1 23 34 30 30	6 13 8 9 3 22 35 30 30	9 18 10 13 5 22 35 30 30	12 22 10 16 7 22 35 30 30	15 27 15 19 10 22 35 30 30	18 33 20 22 11 23 34 30 30	21 36 22 23 13 23 34 30 30	24 5 22 22 15 24 34 30 30	27 8 27 23 16 25 34 30 30
18	30 1 31 30 30 23 33 30 30	33 6 34 34 32 23 34 30 30	36 6 33 2 34 23 34 30 30	3 11 2 5 1 23 34 30 30	6 15 8 9 3 22 35 30 30	9 20 10 13 5 22 35 30 30	12 24 10 16 7 22 35 30 30	15 29 15 20 10 22 35 30 30	18 34 20 22 12 23 34 30 30	21 1 22 23 13 23 34 30 30	24 6 23 22 15 24 34 30 30	27 9 27 23 16 25 34 30 30
19	30 2 31 30 30 23 33 30 30	34 7 34 34 32 23 34 30 30	36 8 34 2 34 23 34 30 30	3 12 2 6 1 23 34 30 30	6 16 8 9 3 22 35 30 30	9 21 10 13 5 22 35 30 30	12 25 10 16 8 22 35 30 30	15 30 16 20 10 22 35 30 30	18 35 21 22 12 23 34 30 30	21 2 22 23 13 23 34 30 30	24 7 23 22 15 24 34 30 30	27 10 27 23 16 25 34 30 30
20	30 4 32 31 30 23 33 30 30	34 8 34 34 32 23 34 30 30	36 9 34 2 34 23 34 30 30	3 14 2 6 1 23 34 30 30	6 17 8 9 3 22 35 30 30	9 23 10 13 5 22 35 30 30	12 26 10 16 8 22 35 30 30	15 32 16 20 10 22 34 30 30	18 36 21 22 12 23 34 30 30	21 4 21 23 13 23 34 30 30	24 8 23 22 15 24 34 30 30	27 11 28 23 16 25 34 30 30
21	31 5 32 31 30 23 33 30 30	34 9 34 35 32 23 34 30 30	1 10 34 2 35 23 34 30 30	4 15 3 6 1 23 34 30 30	6 19 9 9 3 22 35 30 30	9 24 10 13 6 22 35 30 30	12 28 10 17 8 22 35 30 30	15 33 16 20 10 22 34 30 30	18 2 21 22 12 23 34 30 30	21 5 21 23 13 23 34 30 30	24 9 23 22 15 24 34 30 30	27 13 28 23 16 25 34 30 30
22	31 6 32 31 30 23 33 30 30	34 11 33 35 32 23 34 30 30	1 11 34 2 35 23 34 30 30	4 16 3 6 1 23 34 30 30	7 20 9 10 3 22 35 30 30	10 26 10 13 6 22 35 30 30	12 29 10 17 8 22 35 30 30	15 34 16 20 10 22 34 30 30	18 3 21 23 12 23 34 30 30	21 6 21 23 13 23 34 30 30	24 10 23 22 15 24 34 30 30	27 14 28 23 16 25 34 30 30
23	31 7 32 31 30 23 33 30 30	34 12 33 35 33 23 34 30 30	1 13 34 2 35 23 34 30 30	4 18 3 6 1 23 34 30 30	7 22 9 10 3 22 35 30 30	10 27 10 13 6 22 35 30 30	12 31 11 17 8 22 35 30 30	15 36 16 20 10 22 34 30 30	18 4 21 23 12 23 34 30 30	21 7 21 23 13 23 34 30 30	25 12 23 22 15 24 34 30 30	.8 15 28 23 16 25 34 30 30
24	31 8 32 31 30 23 33 30 30	34 13 33 35 33 23 34 30 30	1 14 34 2 35 23 34 30 30	4 19 3 6 1 23 34 30 30	7 23 9 10 4 22 35 30 30	10 28 10 14 6 22 35 30 30	13 32 11 17 8 22 35 30 30	16 1 17 20 10 22 34 30 30	19 5 21 23 12 23 34 30 30	22 8 21 23 13 23 34 30 30	25 13 24 22 15 24 34 30 30	28 16 28 23 16 25 34 30 30
25	31 10 32 31 30 23 33 30 30	34 15 33 35 33 23 34 30 30	1 15 34 3 35 23 34 30 30	4 21 3 6 1 23 34 30 30	7 25 9 10 4 22 35 30 30	10 30 10 14 6 22 35 30 30	13 33 11 17 8 22 35 30 30	16 2 17 20 10 22 34 30 30	19 6 21 23 12 23 34 30 30	22 10 21 23 14 23 34 30 30	25 14 24 22 15 24 34 30 30	28 18 28 23 16 25 34 30 30
26	31 11 33 31 30 23 33 30 30	34 16 33 35 33 23 34 30 30	1 16 34 3 35 23 34 30 30	4 22 4 6 1 23 34 30 30	7 26 9 10 4 22 35 30 30	10 31 10 14 6 22 35 30 30	13 35 11 17 8 22 35 30 30	16 3 17 20 10 22 34 30 30	19 8 21 23 12 23 34 30 30	22 11 21 23 14 23 34 30 30	25 15 24 22 15 24 34 30 30	28 19 29 23 16 25 34 30 30
27	31 12 33 31 30 23 33 30 30	34 18 33 35 33 23 34 30 30	1 18 34 3 35 23 34 30 30	4 24 4 7 1 23 34 30 30	7 28 9 10 4 22 35 30 30	10 33 10 14 6 22 35 30 30	13 36 11 17 8 22 35 30 30	16 4 17 20 10 22 34 30 30	19 9 21 23 12 23 34 30 30	22 12 21 23 14 23 34 30 30	25 17 24 22 15 24 34 30 30	28 21 29 23 16 25 34 30 30
28	31 14 33 32 30 23 33 30 30	34 19 33 35 33 23 34 30 30	1 20 35 3 35 23 34 30 30	4 25 4 7 2 23 34 30 30	7 29 9 10 4 22 35 30 30	10 34 10 14 6 22 35 30 30	13 1 11 17 8 22 35 30 30	16 6 17 21 10 22 34 30 30	19 10 22 23 12 23 34 30 30	22 13 21 23 14 23 34 30 30	25 18 24 22 15 24 34 30 30	28 22 29 24 16 25 34 30 30
29	31 15 33 32 31 23 34 30 30		1 21 35 3 35 23 34 30 30	4 27 4 7 2 22 35 30 30	7 30 10 10 4 22 35 30 30	10 35 10 14 6 22 35 30 30	13 2 12 17 8 22 35 30 30	16 7 17 21 10 22 34 30 30	19 11 22 23 12 23 34 30 30	22 15 21 23 14 23 34 30 30	25 20 24 22 15 24 34 30 30	28 23 29 24 16 25 34 30 30
30	31 17 33 32 31 23 34 30 30		1 23 35 3 35 23 34 30 30	4 28 4 7 2 22 35 30 30	7 32 10 11 4 22 35 30 30	10 36 10 14 6 22 35 30 30	13 4 12 18 8 22 35 30 30	16 8 18 21 10 22 34 30 30	19 12 22 23 12 23 34 30 30	22 16 21 23 14 23 34 30 30	25 21 24 22 15 24 34 30 30	28 25 29 24 16 25 34 30 30
31	32 18 33 32 31 23 34 30 30	1994	2 24 35 3 35 23 34 30 30		7 33 10 11 4 22 35 30 30		13 5 12 18 8 22 35 30 30	16 9 18 21 10 22 34 30 30		22 17 21 23 14 23 34 30 30		28 26 29 24 16 25 34 30 30

	JAN	FEB	MAR	APR	MAY	JUNE	JULY	AUG	SEPT	OCT	NOV	DEC
1	29 28 30 24 16 25 34 30 30	32 33 32 27 15 26 35 30 30	34 34 32 30 14 26 35 30 30	2 3 36 34 14 26 35 30 30	5 6 6 2 15 26 36 31 30	8 10 8 5 16 26 36 31 30	10 14 8 9 17 25 36 30 30	13 18 14 13 19 25 36 30 30	16 24 19 17 21 25 36 30 30	19 27 20 20 23 26 36 30 30	22 33 21 24 25 26 35 30 30	25 36 26 28 28 27 35 30 30
2	29 29 30 24 16 25 34 30 30	32 34 32 27 15 26 35 30 30	35 35 32 30 14 26 35 30 30	2 4 36 34 14 26 35 31 30	5 7 6 2 15 26 36 31 30	8 12 8 5 16 26 36 31 30	10 15 8 9 17 25 36 30 30	13 20 14 13 19 25 36 30 30	16 25 19 17 21 25 36 30 30	19 29 20 20 23 26 36 30 30	22 34 21 24 25 26 35 30 30	25 2 26 28 28 27 35 30 30
3	29 31 30 24 16 25 34 30 30	32 36 32 27 15 26 35 30 30	35 1 32 31 14 26 35 30 30	2 5 1 34 14 26 35 31 30	5 8 7 2 15 26 36 31 30	8 13 8 6 16 26 36 31 30	11 16 8 9 17 25 36 30 30	14 21 14 13 19 25 36 30 30	17 26 19 17 21 25 36 30 30	19 30 20 21 23 26 35 30 30	23 35 21 24 25 26 35 30 30	26 3 26 28 28 27 35 30 30
4	29 32 30 24 16 25 34 30 30	32 1 32 27 15 26 35 30 30	35 2 32 31 14 26 35 30 30	2 6 1 34 14 26 35 31 30	5 9 7 2 15 26 36 31 30	8 14 8 6 16 26 36 31 30	11 17 9 9 18 25 36 30 30	14 22 14 13 19 25 36 30 30	17 28 19 17 21 25 36 30 30	20 32 20 21 23 26 35 30 30	23 1 21 25 26 26 35 30 30	26 4 26 28 28 27 35 30 30
5	29 34 30 24 16 25 34 30 30	32 2 32 28 15 26 35 30 30	35 3 32 31 14 26 35 30 30	2 7 1 35 14 26 35 31 30	5 11 7 2 15 26 36 31 30	8 15 8 6 16 26 36 31 30	11 19 9 9 18 25 36 30 30	14 24 15 13 19 25 36 30 30	17 29 19 17 21 25 36 30 30	20 33 20 21 23 26 35 30 30	23 2 22 25 26 26 35 30 30	26 5 26 28 28 27 35 30 30
6	29 35 30 24 16 25 34 30 30	32 3 32 28 15 26 35 30 30	35 4 32 31 14 26 35 30 30	2 9 1 35 14 26 35 31 30	5 12 7 2 15 26 36 31 30	8 16 8 6 16 25 36 31 30	11 20 9 10 18 25 36 30 30	14 25 15 13 19 25 36 30 30	17 31 19 17 21 25 36 30 30	20 34 20 21 23 26 35 30 30	23 3 22 25 26 26 35 30 30	26 7 27 29 28 27 35 30 30
7	29 36 31 24 16 25 34 30 30	32 5 32 28 15 26 35 30 30	35 5 32 31 14 26 35 30 30	2 10 1 35 14 26 35 31 30	5 13 7 2 15 26 36 31 30	8 18 8 6 16 25 36 31 30	11 21 9 10 18 25 36 30 30	14 27 15 14 20 25 36 30 30	17 32 20 17 21 25 36 30 30	20 36 19 21 24 26 35 30 30	23 5 22 25 26 26 35 30 30	26 8 27 29 28 27 35 30 30
8	29 1 31 25 16 25 34 30 30	32 6 31 28 15 26 35 30 30	35 7 33 31 14 26 35 30 30	2 11 2 35 14 26 35 31 30	5 14 7 2 15 26 36 31 30	8 19 8 6 16 25 36 31 30	11 23 9 10 18 25 36 30 30	14 28 15 14 20 25 36 30 30	17 33 20 17 22 25 36 30 30	20 1 19 21 24 26 35 30 30	23 6 22 25 26 26 35 30 30	26 9 27 29 28 27 35 30 30
9	29 3 31 25 16 25 34 30 30	32 7 31 28 15 26 35 30 30	35 8 33 31 14 26 35 30 30	2 12 2 35 14 26 35 31 30	5 16 7 3 15 26 36 31 30	8 20 8 6 16 25 36 30 30	11 24 9 10 18 25 36 30 30	14 30 15 14 20 25 36 30 30	17 35 20 18 22 25 36 30 30	20 2 19 21 24 26 35 30 30	23 7 22 25 26 26 35 30 30	26 10 27 29 28 27 35 30 30
10	29 4 31 25 16 25 34 30 30	33 8 31 28 15 26 35 30 30	35 9 33 31 14 26 35 30 30	2 13 2 35 14 26 35 31 30	5 17 8 3 15 26 36 31 30	8 22 8 6 16 25 36 30 30	11 26 9 10 18 25 36 30 30	14 31 15 14 20 25 36 30 30	17 36 20 18 22 25 36 30 30	20 4 19 21 24 26 35 30 30	23 8 22 25 26 26 35 30 30	26 11 27 29 28 27 35 30 30
11	30 5 31 25 16 25 34 30 30	33 9 31 28 15 26 35 30 30	35 10 33 31 14 26 35 30 30	3 15 2 35 14 26 35 31 30	5 18 8 3 15 26 36 31 30	8 23 8 7 16 25 36 30 30	11 27 10 10 18 25 36 30 30	14 33 16 14 20 25 36 30 30	17 2 20 18 22 25 36 30 30	20 5 19 22 24 26 35 30 30	23 9 23 26 26 26 35 30 30	26 13 27 29 28 27 35 30 30
12	30 6 31 25 16 25 34 30 30	33 11 31 28 15 26 35 30 30	36 11 33 32 14 26 35 30 30	3 16 2 35 14 26 35 31 30	6 20 8 3 15 26 36 31 30	9 25 8 7 16 25 36 30 30	11 29 10 10 18 25 36 30 30	14 34 16 14 20 25 36 30 30	17 3 20 18 22 25 36 30 30	20 6 19 22 24 26 35 30 30	23 11 23 26 26 26 35 30 30	26 14 27 29 28 27 35 30 30
13	30 7 31 25 16 25 34 30 30	33 12 31 28 15 26 35 30 30	36 13 33 32 14 26 35 30 30	3 17 3 35 14 26 35 31 30	6 21 8 3 15 26 36 31 30	9 26 8 7 16 25 36 30 30	12 30 10 10 18 25 36 30 30	14 35 16 14 20 25 36 30 30	17 4 20 18 22 25 36 30 30	20 7 19 22 24 26 35 30 30	24 12 23 26 26 26 35 30 30	27 15 28 29 28 27 35 30 30
14	30 9 32 25 16 25 34 30 30	33 13 31 29 15 26 35 30 30	36 14 33 32 14 26 35 30 30	3 19 3 36 14 26 35 31 30	6 23 8 3 15 26 36 31 30	9 28 8 7 16 25 36 30 30	12 32 10 11 18 25 36 30 30	15 1 16 14 20 25 36 30 30	18 5 20 18 22 25 36 30 30	21 9 19 22 24 26 35 30 30	24 13 23 26 26 26 35 30 30	27 16 28 30 29 27 35 30 30
15	30 10 32 25 16 25 34 30 30	33 14 31 29 15 26 35 30 30	36 15 34 32 14 26 35 30 30	3 20 3 36 14 26 35 31 30	6 24 8 3 15 26 36 31 30	9 29 8 7 16 25 36 30 30	12 33 10 11 18 25 36 30 30	15 2 16 15 20 25 36 30 30	18 7 20 18 22 25 36 30 30	21 10 19 22 24 26 35 30 30	24 14 23 26 26 26 35 30 30	27 17 28 30 29 27 35 30 30
16	30 11 32 25 16 25 34 30 30	33 16 31 29 15 26 35 30 30	36 17 34 32 14 26 35 30 30	3 22 3 36 14 26 35 31 30	6 26 8 3 15 26 36 31 30	9 31 7 7 17 25 36 30 30	12 35 10 11 18 25 36 30 30	15 3 17 15 20 25 36 30 30	18 8 20 18 22 25 36 30 30	21 11 19 22 24 26 35 30 30	24 15 23 26 26 26 35 30 30	27 19 28 30 29 27 35 30 30
17	30 12 32 25 16 25 34 30 30	33 17 31 29 15 26 35 30 30	36 18 34 32 14 26 35 30 30	3 23 3 36 14 26 35 31 30	6 27 8 4 15 26 36 31 30	9 32 7 7 17 25 36 30 30	12 36 11 11 18 25 36 30 30	15 5 17 15 20 25 36 30 30	18 9 20 19 22 25 36 30 30	21 12 19 22 24 26 35 30 30	24 17 24 26 26 26 35 30 30	27 20 28 30 29 27 35 30 30
18	30 14 32 26 16 25 34 30 30	33 18 31 29 15 26 35 30 30	36 19 34 32 14 26 35 30 30	3 25 4 36 14 26 36 31 30	6 29 8 4 15 26 36 31 30	9 34 7 7 17 25 36 30 30	12 1 11 11 18 25 36 30 30	15 6 17 15 20 25 36 30 30	18 10 20 19 22 25 36 30 30	21 13 19 22 24 26 35 30 30	24 18 24 26 27 26 35 30 30	27 21 28 30 29 27 35 30 30
19	30 15 32 26 16 25 34 30 30	33 20 31 29 15 26 35 30 30	36 21 34 32 14 26 35 30 30	3 26 4 36 14 26 36 31 30	6 30 8 4 15 26 36 31 30	9 35 7 8 17 25 36 30 30	12 3 11 11 18 25 36 30 30	15 7 17 15 20 25 36 30 30	18 11 20 19 22 25 36 30 30	21 15 19 23 24 26 35 30 30	24 19 24 26 27 26 35 30 30	27 23 29 30 29 27 35 30 30
20	30 16 32 26 16 25 34 30 30	34 21 31 29 14 26 35 30 30	36 22 34 33 14 26 35 30 30	3 28 4 36 14 26 36 31 30	6 31 8 4 15 26 36 31 30	9 36 8 8 17 25 36 30 30	12 4 11 11 18 25 36 30 30	15 8 17 15 20 25 36 30 30	18 13 20 19 22 25 36 30 30	21 16 19 23 24 26 35 30 30	24 21 24 27 27 27 35 30 30	27 24 29 30 29 27 35 30 30
21	31 17 32 26 16 25 34 30 30	34 23 31 29 14 26 35 30 30	36 24 34 33 14 26 35 30 30	4 29 4 36 14 26 36 31 30	6 33 8 4 15 26 36 31 30	9 2 8 8 17 25 36 30 30	12 5 11 11 18 25 36 30 30	15 9 17 15 20 25 36 30 30	18 14 21 19 22 25 36 30 30	21 17 19 23 25 26 35 30 30	24 22 24 27 27 27 35 30 30	27 26 29 30 29 27 35 30 30
22	31 19 33 26 16 25 34 30 30	34 24 31 29 14 26 35 30 30	1 25 35 33 14 26 35 30 30	4 30 4 36 14 26 36 31 30	7 34 8 4 15 26 36 31 30	10 3 8 8 17 25 36 30 30	12 6 12 12 19 25 36 30 30	15 11 17 15 20 25 36 30 30	18 15 21 19 22 25 36 30 30	21 18 20 23 25 26 35 30 30	24 24 24 27 27 27 35 30 30	27 27 29 31 29 27 35 30 30
23	31 20 33 26 15 25 35 30 30	34 25 31 30 14 26 35 30 30	1 27 35 33 14 26 35 30 30	4 32 5 1 14 26 36 31 30	7 35 8 4 15 26 36 31 30	10 4 8 8 17 25 36 30 30	12 7 12 12 19 25 36 30 30	15 12 18 15 21 25 36 30 30	18 16 21 19 23 25 36 30 30	21 20 20 23 25 26 35 30 30	25 25 25 27 27 27 35 30 30	28 29 29 31 29 27 35 30 30
24	31 22 33 26 15 25 35 30 30	34 27 31 30 14 26 35 30 30	1 28 35 33 14 26 35 30 30	4 33 5 1 14 26 36 31 30	7 1 8 4 15 26 36 31 30	10 5 8 8 17 25 36 30 30	13 9 12 12 19 25 36 30 30	16 13 18 16 21 25 36 30 30	19 18 21 19 23 25 36 30 30	22 21 20 23 25 26 35 30 30	25 27 25 27 27 27 35 30 30	28 30 29 31 29 27 35 30 30
25	31 23 33 26 15 25 35 30 30	34 28 31 30 14 26 35 30 30	1 29 35 33 14 26 35 30 30	4 34 5 1 14 26 36 31 30	7 2 8 4 15 26 36 31 30	10 6 8 8 17 25 36 30 30	13 10 12 12 19 25 36 30 30	16 14 18 16 21 25 36 30 30	19 19 20 20 23 25 36 30 30	22 23 20 23 25 26 35 30 30	25 28 25 27 27 27 35 30 30	28 32 29 31 29 27 35 30 30
26	31 24 33 26 15 25 35 30 30	34 30 32 30 14 26 35 30 30	1 31 35 33 14 26 35 30 30	4 36 5 1 14 26 36 31 30	7 3 8 5 16 26 36 31 30	10 8 8 8 17 25 36 30 30	13 11 13 12 19 25 36 30 30	16 16 18 16 21 25 36 30 30	19 20 20 20 23 25 36 30 30	22 24 20 23 25 26 35 30 30	25 30 25 27 27 27 35 30 30	28 33 30 31 29 27 35 30 30
27	31 26 33 27 15 25 35 30 30	34 31 32 30 14 26 35 30 30	1 32 35 33 14 26 35 30 30	4 1 5 1 14 26 36 31 30	7 4 8 5 16 26 36 31 30	10 9 8 8 17 25 36 30 30	13 12 13 12 19 25 36 30 30	16 17 18 16 21 25 36 30 30	19 22 20 20 23 25 36 30 30	22 26 20 24 25 26 35 30 30	25 31 25 27 27 27 35 30 30	28 35 30 31 30 27 35 30 30
28	31 27 33 27 15 25 35 30 30	34 33 32 30 14 26 35 30 30	1 33 36 33 14 26 35 30 30	4 2 6 1 14 26 36 31 30	7 6 8 5 16 26 36 31 30	10 10 8 9 17 25 36 30 30	13 13 13 12 19 25 36 30 30	16 18 18 16 21 25 36 30 30	19 23 20 20 23 26 36 30 30	22 27 20 24 25 26 35 30 30	25 32 25 28 27 27 35 30 30	28 36 30 31 30 27 35 30 30
29	31 29 33 27 15 25 35 30 30		1 35 36 34 14 26 35 30 30	4 4 6 1 14 26 36 31 30	7 7 8 5 16 26 36 31 30	10 11 8 9 17 25 36 30 30	13 15 13 12 19 25 36 30 30	16 19 18 16 21 25 36 30 30	19 25 20 20 23 26 36 30 30	22 29 20 24 25 26 35 30 30	25 34 25 28 27 27 35 30 30	28 1 30 31 30 27 35 30 30
30	31 30 32 27 15 26 35 30 30	1995	1 36 36 34 14 26 35 30 30	4 5 6 1 14 26 36 31 30	7 8 8 5 16 26 36 31 30	10 12 8 9 17 25 36 30 30	13 16 13 13 19 25 36 30 30	16 21 19 16 21 25 36 30 30	19 26 20 20 23 26 36 30 30	22 30 21 24 25 26 35 30 30	25 35 26 28 27 27 35 30 30	28 3 30 32 30 27 35 30 30
31	32 32 32 27 15 26 35 30 30		1 1 36 34 14 26 35 30 30		7 9 8 5 16 26 36 31 30		13 17 14 13 19 25 36 30 30	16 22 19 16 21 25 36 30 30		22 31 21 24 25 26 35 30 30		28 4 30 32 30 27 35 30 30

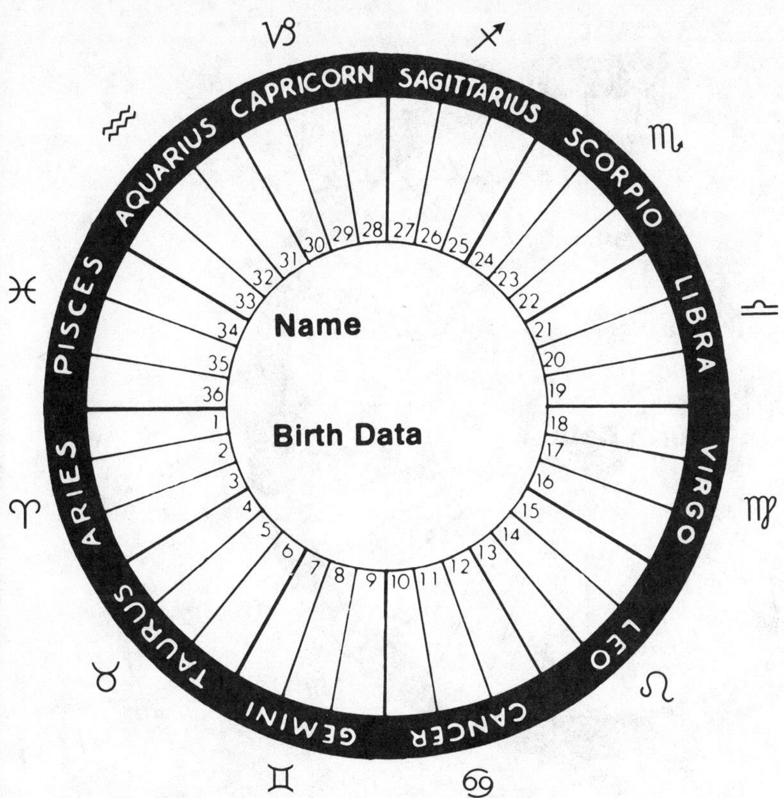

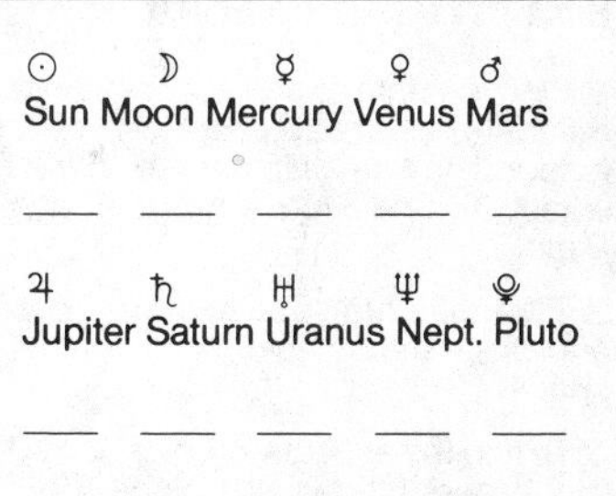

HOW TO USE THIS FORM

1. Find the date and year of birth in the tables and write the numbers in the exact order that you find them under the corresponding blanks in the box to the right of the horoscope wheel. To find Pluto's position, use the special table for Pluto.

2. Find the corresponding numbered space on the wheel and place the symbol for the planet, Sun or Moon in that space.

3. To find the aspects, use the Aspect Finder wheel. Cut out the Aspect Finder and place it on the large horoscope wheel.

a) Note the planets which appear in the same space. These are in conjunction aspect.

b) Point the arrow to the space occupied by the Sun. Note which planets form aspects indicated on the Aspect finder.

c) Follow the same procedure with the Moon and each of the planets.

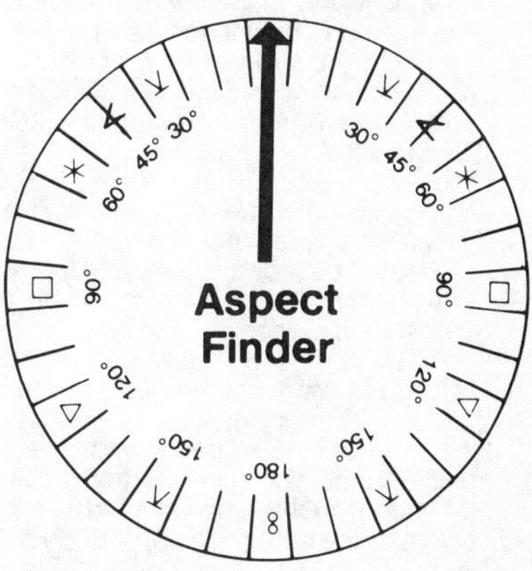

Note: The tables indicate planetary placements within each *decanate* of a sign of the zodiac. Each sign contains 30 degrees. A decanate is ⅓, or ten degrees, of a sign. (e.g. 0-9° Aries is indicated in Space #1 on the horoscope wheel, 10-19° Aries is Space #2, etc.).

The results of this procedure will give you a *roughly* calculated chart, not a precise one such as you can obtain through a professional astrological service. Once you have the chart calculated based upon the precise time, date and place of birth, you may even find the Sun, Moon or planets in different signs! We use this form as a *simplified* method to calculate the birth chart and introduce you to an easy way to find aspects!

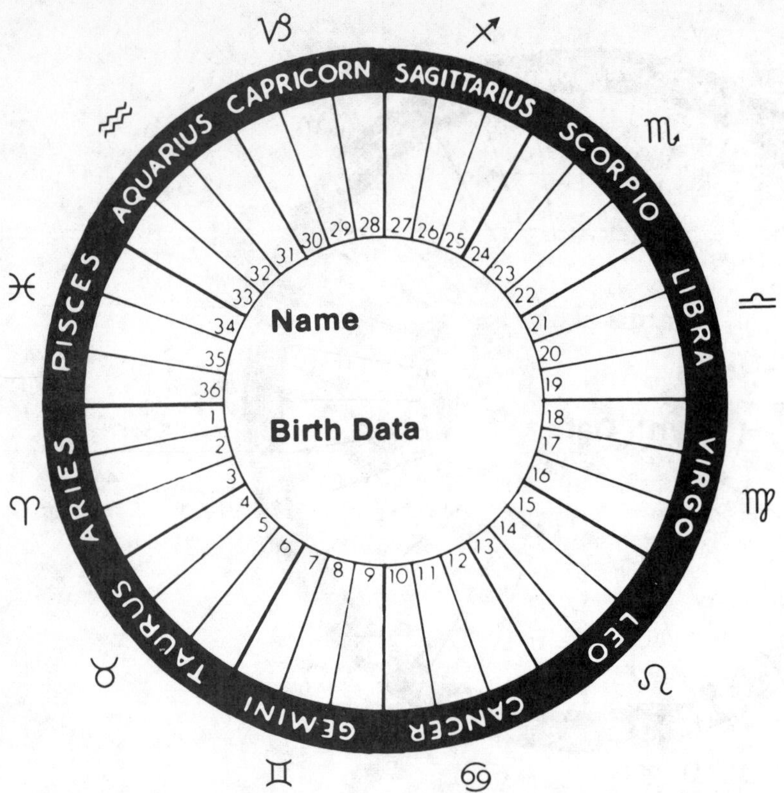

HOW TO USE THIS FORM

1. Find the date and year of birth in the tables and write the numbers in the exact order that you find them under the corresponding blanks in the box to the right of the horoscope wheel. To find Pluto's position, use the special table for Pluto.

2. Find the corresponding numbered space on the wheel and place the symbol for the planet, Sun or Moon in that space.

3. To find the aspects, use the Aspect Finder wheel. Cut out the Aspect Finder and place it on the large horoscope wheel.

a) Note the planets which appear in the same space. These are in conjunction aspect.

b) Point the arrow to the space occupied by the Sun. Note which planets form aspects indicated on the Aspect finder.

c) Follow the same procedure with the Moon and each of the planets.

Note: The tables indicate planetary placements within each *decanate* of a sign of the zodiac. Each sign contains 30 degrees. A decanate is ⅓, or ten degrees, of a sign. (e.g. 0-9° Aries is indicated in Space #1 on the horoscope wheel, 10-19° Aries is Space #2, etc.).

The results of this procedure will give you a *roughly* calculated chart, not a precise one such as you can obtain through a professional astrological service. Once you have the chart calculated based upon the precise time, date and place of birth, you may even find the Sun, Moon or planets in different signs! We use this form as a *simplified* method to calculate the birth chart and introduce you to an easy way to find aspects!

☉ Sun	☽ Moon	☿ Mercury	♀ Venus	♂ Mars
___	___	___	___	___
♃ Jupiter	♄ Saturn	♅ Uranus	♆ Nept.	♇ Pluto
___	___	___	___	___

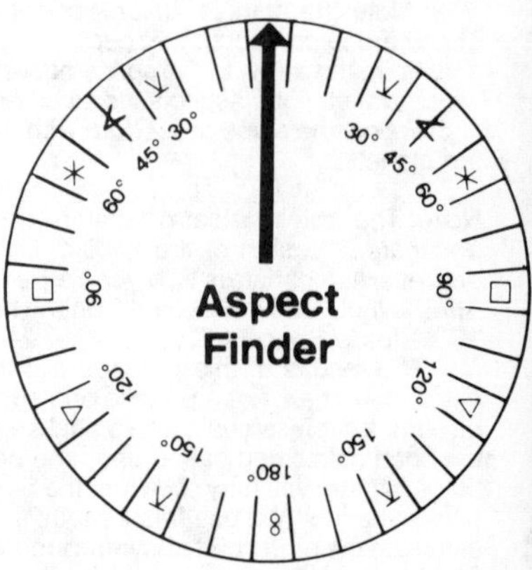

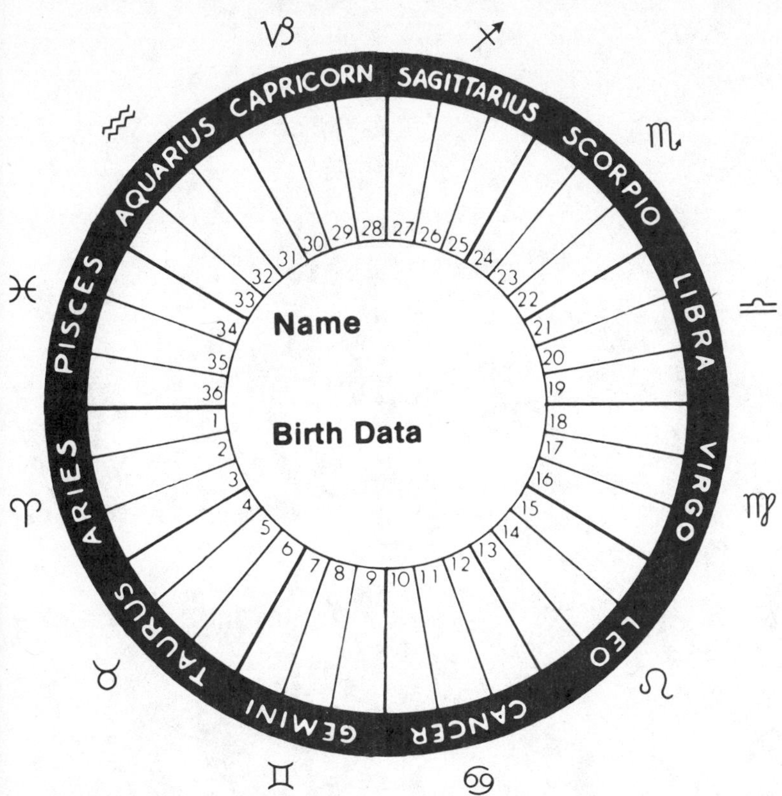

☉ Sun	☽ Moon	☿ Mercury	♀ Venus	♂ Mars
____	____	____	____	____
♃ Jupiter	♄ Saturn	♅ Uranus	♆ Nept.	♇ Pluto
____	____	____	____	____

HOW TO USE THIS FORM

1. Find the date and year of birth in the tables and write the numbers in the exact order that you find them under the corresponding blanks in the box to the right of the horoscope wheel. To find Pluto's position, use the special table for Pluto.

2. Find the corresponding numbered space on the wheel and place the symbol for the planet, Sun or Moon in that space.

3. To find the aspects, use the Aspect Finder wheel. Cut out the Aspect Finder and place it on the large horoscope wheel.

a) Note the planets which appear in the same space. These are in conjunction aspect.

b) Point the arrow to the space occupied by the Sun. Note which planets form aspects indicated on the Aspect finder.

c) Follow the same procedure with the Moon and each of the planets.

Note: The tables indicate planetary placements within each *decanate* of a sign of the zodiac. Each sign contains 30 degrees. A decanate is ⅓, or ten degrees, of a sign. (e.g. 0-9° Aries is indicated in Space #1 on the horoscope wheel, 10-19° Aries is Space #2, etc.).

The results of this procedure will give you a *roughly* calculated chart, not a precise one such as you can obtain through a professional astrological service. Once you have the chart calculated based upon the precise time, date and place of birth, you may even find the Sun, Moon or planets in different signs! We use this form as a *simplified* method to calculate the birth chart and introduce you to an easy way to find aspects!

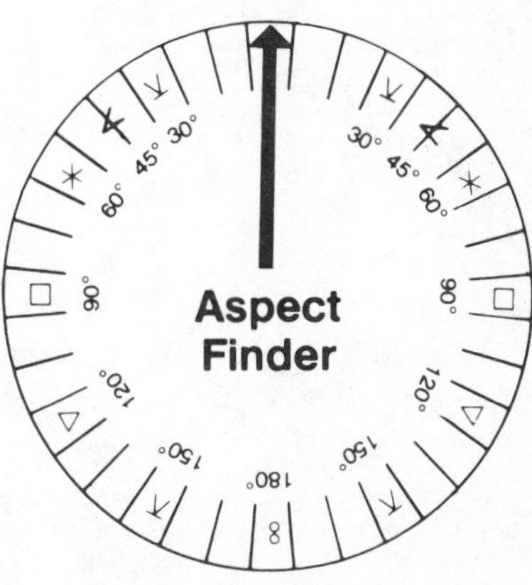

Bibliography

Arroyo, Stephen, *Astrology, Karma and Transformation.* Davis, CA.: CRCS, 1978.

Arroyo, Stephen, *Astrology, Psychology and the Four Elements.* Davis, CA.: CRCS, 1975.

Cunningham, Donna, *An Astrological Guide to Self-Awareness.* Reno, Nevada: CRCS Publications, 1978.

Greene, Liz, *The Astrology of Fate.* York Beach, Maine: Samuel Weiser Inc., 1984.

Greene, Liz, *Saturn.* New York: Samuel Weiser, Inc., 1976.

Hand, Robert, *Planets in Youth.* Rockport, Mass.: Para Research, 1977.

Hand, Robert, *Horoscope Symbols.* Rockport, Mass.: Para Research, 1981.

Hebel, Doris, *Chart Interpretation.* New York: Astrology 77, 1977.

Hickey, Isabel, *Astrology, a Cosmic Science.* Watertown, Mass.: Altieri Press, 1970.

Lewi, Grant, *Heaven Knows What.* St. Paul, Minn.: Llewellyn Publications, 1969.

Oken, Alan, *As Above, So Below.* New York: Bantam Books, 1973.

Pearce, Joseph Chilton, *Magical Child.*

Rodden, Lois, *American Book of Charts.* San Diego, Ca.: Astro Computing Services, 1980.

Rudhyar, Dane, *The Astrological Houses.* Garden City, N.Y.: Doubleday and Co., 1972.

Rudhyar, Dane, *Astrological Signs—The Pulse of Life.* Garden City, N.Y.: Doubleday and Co., 1963.

Sakoian, F. and Acker, L., *Astrologer's Handbook.* New York: Harper and Row, 1976.

Sargent, Lois Haines, *How to Handle Your Human Relations.* Washington, D.C.: American Federation of Astrologers, 1970.

Tyl, Noel, *The Horoscope as Identity.* St. Paul, Minn.: Llewellyn Publications, 1974.

STAY IN TOUCH

On the following pages you will find listed, with their current prices, some of the books and tapes now available on related subjects. Your book dealer stocks most of these, and will stock new titles in the Llewellyn series as they become available. We urge your patronage.

However, to obtain our full catalog, to keep informed of new titles as they are released and to benefit from informative articles and helpful news, you are invited to write for our bi-monthly news magazine/catalog. A sample copy is free, and it will continue coming to you at no cost as long as you are an active mail customer. Or you may keep it coming for a full year with a donation of just $2.00 in U.S.A. ($7.00 for Canada & Mexico, $20.00 overseas, first class mail). Many bookstores also have *The Llewellyn New Times* available to their customers. Ask for it.

Stay in touch! In *The Llewellyn New Times'* pages you will find news and reviews of new books, tapes and services, announcements of meetings and seminars, articles helpful to our readers, news of authors, advertising of products and services, special money-making opportunities, and much more.

The Llewellyn New Times
P.O. Box 64383-Dept. 740, St. Paul, MN 55164-0383, U.S.A.

• • •

TO ORDER BOOKS AND TAPES

If your book dealer does not have the books and tapes described on the following pages readily available, you may order them direct from the publisher by sending full price in U.S. funds, plus $1.00 for handling and 50¢ each book or item for postage within the United States; outside USA surface mail add $1.00 extra per item. Outside USA air mail add $7.00 per item.

FOR GROUP STUDY AND PURCHASE

Because there is a great deal of interest in group discussion and study of the subject matter of this book, we feel that we should encourage the adoption and use of this particular book by such groups by offering a special "quantity" price to group leaders or "agents".

Our Special Quality Price for a minimum order of five copies of OPTIMUM CHILD is $29.85 Cash-With-Order. This price includes postage and handling within the United States. Minnesota residents must add 6% sales tax. For additional quantities, please order in multiples of five. For Canadian and foreign orders, add postage and handling charges as above. Credit Card (VISA, MasterCard, American Express, Diners' Club) Orders are accepted. Charge Card Orders only may be phoned free ($15.00 minimum order) within the U.S.A. by dialing 1-800-THE MOON (in Canada call: 1-800-FOR-SELF). Customer Service calls dial 1-612-291-1970 and ask for "Kae." Mail Orders to:

LLEWELLYN PUBLICATIONS
P.O. Box 64383-Dept. 740 / St. Paul, MN 55164-0383, U.S.A.

PLUTO: The Evolutionary Journey of the Soul
by Jeff Green

If you have ever asked "Why am I here?" or "What are my lessons?" then this book will help you to objectively learn the answers from an astrological point of view. Green shows you how the planet Pluto relates to the evolutionary and karmic lessons in this life and how past lives can be understood through the position of Pluto in your chart.

Beyond presenting key principles and ideas about the nature of the evolutionary journey of the Soul, this book supplies practical, concise and specific astrological methods and techniques that pinpoint the answers to the above questions. If you are a professional counselor or astrologer, this book is indispensable to your practice. The reader who studies this material carefully and applies it to his or her own chart will discover an objective vehicle to uncover the essence of his or her own state of being. The understanding that this promotes can help you cooperate with, instead of resist, the evolutionary and karmic lessons in your life.

Green describes the position of Pluto through all of the signs and houses, explains the aspects and transits of Pluto, discusses Pluto in aspect to the Moon's Nodes, and gives sample charts and readings. It is the most complete look at this "new" planet ever.

0-87542-296-9, 6 x 9, 360 pages, Charts, softcover $12.95

CHIRON
by Barbara Hand Clow

This new astrology book is about the most recently discovered planet, Chiron. This little-known planet was first sighted in 1977. It has an eccentric orbit, on a 50-51 year cycle between Saturn and Uranus. It brought farsightedness into astrology because Chiron is the *bridge to the outer planets*, Neptune and Pluto, from the inner ones.

This is the most important astrological book yet about Chiron! *Chiron* presents exciting new insights on astrology. *Chiron* reveals *how* the New Age Initiation will affect each one of us. Chiron is an Initiator, an Alchemist, a Healer, and a Spiritual Guide.

For those who are astrologers, *Chiron* has more information than any other book about this planet.

- Learn *why* Chiron rules Virgo and the Sixth House.
- Have the necessary information about Chiron in each house, in each sign, and how the aspects affect each person's chart.

The influences of Chiron are an important new factor in understanding capabilities and potentials which we all have. Chiron rules: Healing with the hands, Healing with crystals, Initiation and Alchemy and Alteration of the body by Mind and Spirit. Chiron also rules Cartomancy and the Tarot reader. As such it is an especially vital resource for everyone who uses the Tarot.

0-87542-094-X, 6 x 9, 300 pages, charts, softcover $9.95

Llewellyn's Personal Astrological Services

CHILD GUIDANCE

Give us the full birth data for a child, and a professional astrologer will tell you where that child's talents lie and the ways of encouraging positive and discouaging negative behavior. Here is real help for dealing with unruly children and helping them to reach their true potential.

APS03-118 **$60.00**

SIMPLE NATAL CHART

This is a *computer calculated chart print-out* that we guarantee to be accurate when you give us your correct birth data. It includes no *interpretation* of the chart. It will automatically be set up with the Placidus house system and the Tropical zodiac (the standard Western system) unless you ask for another.

APS03-119 **$5.00**

DETAILED NATAL CHART

Besides getting your chart as above, you will also receive a full and detailed analysis of your natal horoscope as interpreted by a professional astrologer. The astrologer will also focus on one special area of your life, whatever you request. Include a separate letter stating where you would like more information. Give full birth data as below.

APS03-102 **$65.00**

Llewellyn's Computerized Charts

PERSONALITY PROFILE HOROSCOPE

This reading is divided into ten parts to give you a complete look at how the planets affect you, including:

- **General characteristics and life patterns.**
- **Emotional needs, feelings, and habits**
- **Abilities to express oneself**
- **Enthusiasm, abundance, and good fortune**
- **Imagination, the psychic and mysteries**

This is an excellent way to become acquainted with astrology and to learn more about yourself or someone else. All you need to know is the birth date and time along with the place of birth.

APS03-503 **$10.00**

COMPATIBILITY PROFILE

Find out if he (or she) is right for you! Astrologically, each person is represented by a chart of the planets and houses at the moment of birth. By comparing and contrasting the interrelationship of two separate charts, the computer can reveal the many ways and levels on which two people relate. Every relationship contains points of harmony and points of discord. Through understanding, it is possible to encourage the positive and keep the relationship growing. Be sure to give full birth data for both people when you order.

APS03-504 **$20.00**

When ordering any astrological service, be sure to give exact birth time, date, year, and location (including county). If 2 people are involved, give data for both.

HEAVEN KNOWS WHAT
by Grant Lewi

Heaven Knows What contains everything you need to cast and interpret complete natal charts without learning any symbols, without confusion from tricky calculations, without previous experience or training.

How does the system work? Simply look up the positions of the planets in the tables at the back of the book. Plot these positions on the handy tear-out horoscope blanks. Use the aspect wheel provided to determine the planetary aspects and then read the relevant paragraphs describing their influence.

It's easy, fast, and amazingly accurate! Grant Lewi interprets the influence of the Sun and Moon positions at birth, and describes the effects of every possible planetary aspect in language designed for the modern reader. The tables have been updated so that you can cast a chart for any birth from 1890 through 1999.

Heaven Knows What forms an excellent astrological background for the beginner, yet Lewi's interpretations are so relevant that even long-practicing astrologers gain new psychological insight into the characteristics of the signs and the meanings of the aspects.

0-87542-444-9, 300 pages, softcover. $9.95

ARCHETYPES OF THE ZODIAC
Kathleen Burt

This is the most comprehensive look at all of the signs and myths connected with them ever published! Jungian writings, along with those of Alice Bailey and others, help you realize the myth of your sign and what the archetypes are that you are resonating with. Each sign is discussed fully in this huge volume, along with the 30-year cycles of the Sun progressions. In some cases there are several myths connected with a sign—and some will surprise you! Find out where you fit in, use it when counseling and dealing with clients, learn more about astrology through the archetypes involved and find out more about the philosophy surrounding astrology. This book is the best source for all of this vital information. The author is scholarly and the book is not only well written, but also easy to understand and apply.

0-87542-088-5, 6 x 9, fully illus., 350 + pages, softcover
(forthcoming)

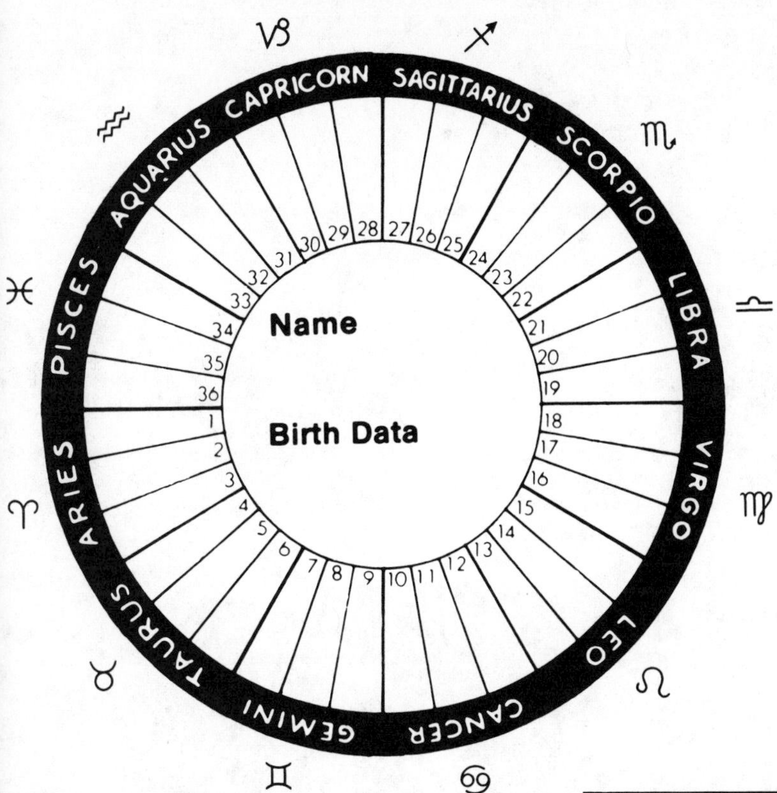

HOW TO USE THIS FORM

1. Find the date and year of birth in the tables and write the numbers in the exact order that you find them under the corresponding blanks in the box to the right of the horoscope wheel. To find Pluto's position, use the special table for Pluto.

2. Find the corresponding numbered space on the wheel and place the symbol for the planet, Sun or Moon in that space.

3. To find the aspects, use the Aspect Finder wheel. Cut out the Aspect Finder and place it on the large horoscope wheel.

a) Note the planets which appear in the same space. These are in conjunction aspect.

b) Point the arrow to the space occupied by the Sun. Note which planets form aspects indicated on the Aspect finder.

c) Follow the same procedure with the Moon and each of the planets.

Note: The tables indicate planetary placements within each *decanate* of a sign of the zodiac. Each sign contains 30 degrees. A decanate is ⅓, or ten degrees, of a sign. (e.g. 0-9° Aries is indicated in Space #1 on the horoscope wheel, 10-19° Aries is Space #2, etc.).

The results of this procedure will give you a *roughly* calculated chart, not a precise one such as you can obtain through a professional astrological service. Once you have the chart calculated based upon the precise time, date and place of birth, you may even find the Sun, Moon or planets in different signs! We use this form as a *simplified* method to calculate the birth chart and introduce you to an easy way to find aspects!

☉ Sun	☽ Moon	☿ Mercury	♀ Venus	♂ Mars
___	___	___	___	___
♃ **Jupiter**	♄ **Saturn**	♅ **Uranus**	♆ **Nept.**	♇ **Pluto**
___	___	___	___	___

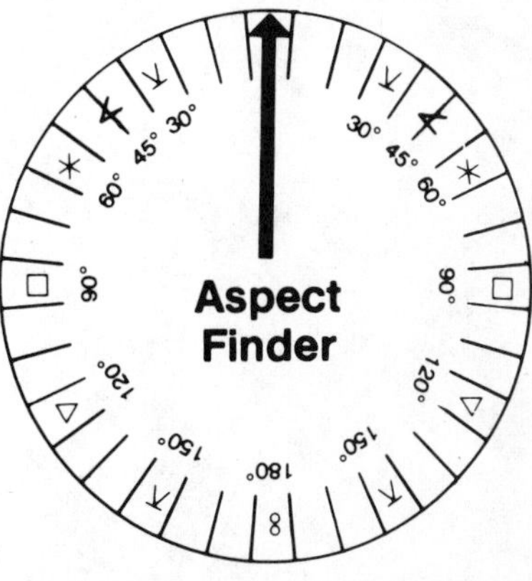

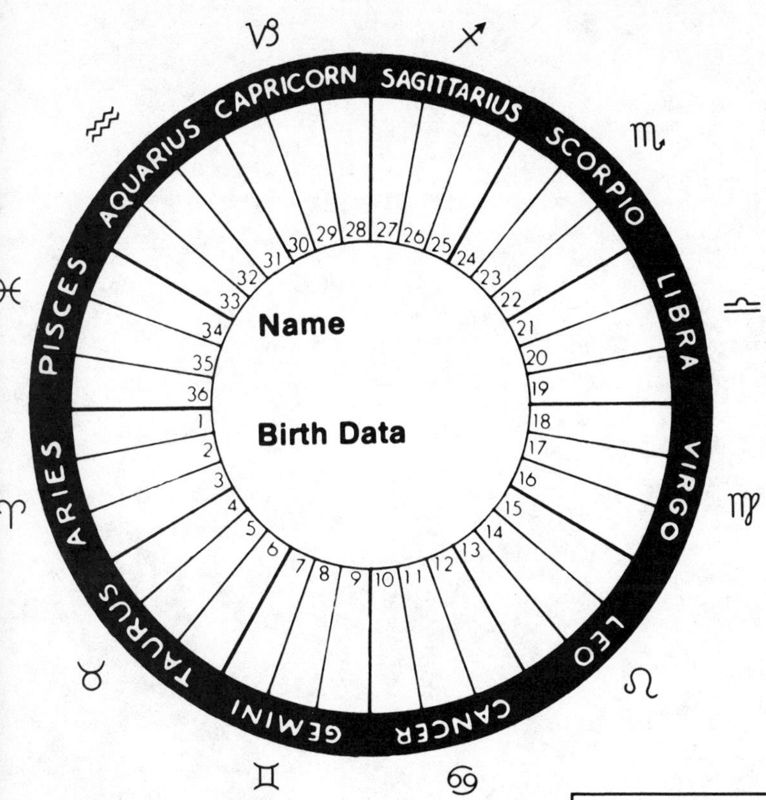

HOW TO USE THIS FORM

1. Find the date and year of birth in the tables and write the numbers in the exact order that you find them under the corresponding blanks in the box to the right of the horoscope wheel. To find Pluto's position, use the special table for Pluto.

2. Find the corresponding numbered space on the wheel and place the symbol for the planet, Sun or Moon in that space.

3. To find the aspects, use the Aspect Finder wheel. Cut out the Aspect Finder and place it on the large horoscope wheel.

a) Note the planets which appear in the same space. These are in conjunction aspect.

b) Point the arrow to the space occupied by the Sun. Note which planets form aspects indicated on the Aspect finder.

c) Follow the same procedure with the Moon and each of the planets.

Note: The tables indicate planetary placements within each *decanate* of a sign of the zodiac. Each sign contains 30 degrees. A decanate is ⅓, or ten degrees, of a sign. (e.g. 0-9° Aries is indicated in Space #1 on the horoscope wheel, 10-19° Aries is Space #2, etc.).

The results of this procedure will give you a *roughly* calculated chart, not a precise one such as you can obtain through a professional astrological service. Once you have the chart calculated based upon the precise time, date and place of birth, you may even find the Sun, Moon or planets in different signs! We use this form as a *simplified* method to calculate the birth chart and introduce you to an easy way to find aspects!

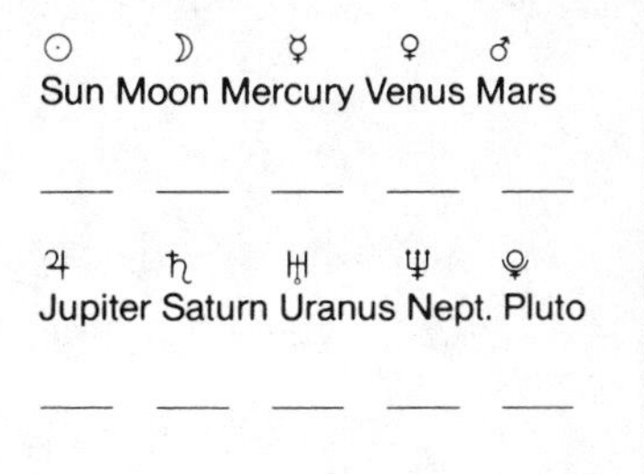

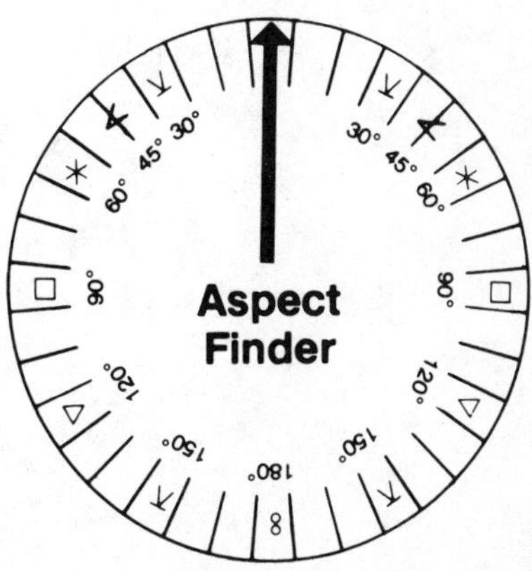

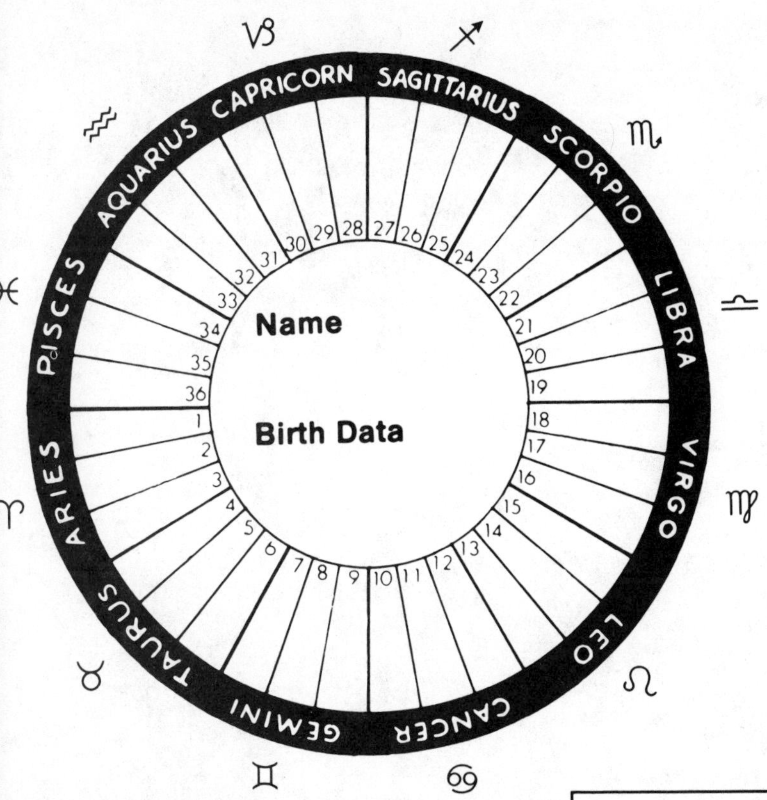

☉ Sun	☽ Moon	☿ Mercury	♀ Venus	♂ Mars
____	____	____	____	____
♃ Jupiter	♄ Saturn	♅ Uranus	♆ Nept.	♇ Pluto
____	____	____	____	____

HOW TO USE THIS FORM

1. Find the date and year of birth in the tables and write the numbers in the exact order that you find them under the corresponding blanks in the box to the right of the horoscope wheel. To find Pluto's position, use the special table for Pluto.

2. Find the corresponding numbered space on the wheel and place the symbol for the planet, Sun or Moon in that space.

3. To find the aspects, use the Aspect Finder wheel. Cut out the Aspect Finder and place it on the large horoscope wheel.

a) Note the planets which appear in the same space. These are in conjunction aspect.

b) Point the arrow to the space occupied by the Sun. Note which planets form aspects indicated on the Aspect finder.

c) Follow the same procedure with the Moon and each of the planets.

Note: The tables indicate planetary placements within each *decanate* of a sign of the zodiac. Each sign contains 30 degrees. A decanate is ⅓, or ten degrees, of a sign. (e.g. 0-9° Aries is indicated in Space #1 on the horoscope wheel, 10-19° Aries is Space #2, etc.).

The results of this procedure will give you a *roughly* calculated chart, not a precise one such as you can obtain through a professional astrological service. Once you have the chart calculated based upon the precise time, date and place of birth, you may even find the Sun, Moon or planets in different signs! We use this form as a *simplified* method to calculate the birth chart and introduce you to an easy way to find aspects!

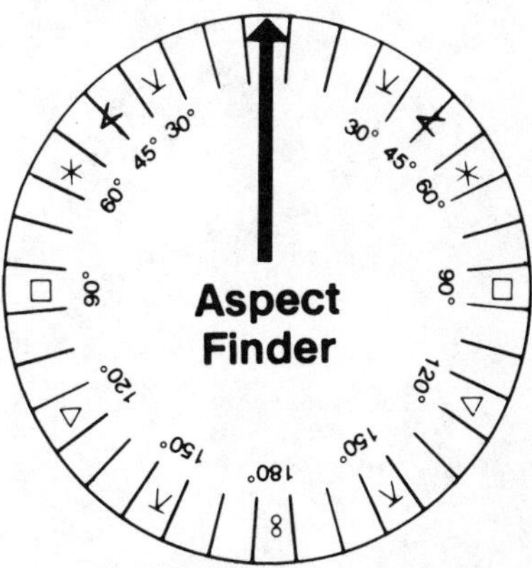